Senate Select Committee on Intelligence

Committee Study of Central Intelligence Agency's Detention and Interrogation Program

Forward by Senate Select Committee on Intelligence Chairman Diane Feinstein

Findings and Conclusions

Executive Summary

Volume 2 of 2

This edition published in 2014 by eStar Books, LLC.
Cover Art by eStar Publishing
www.estarbooks.com
ISBN 1505508657

Editors Note:

Due to the length of this report it was decided to make it into two volumes. This also allows for the inclusion of Additional Views that were also published by the Senate Select Committee on Intelligence in Volume 2. Volume 1 contains pages 1 through 300. Volume 2 contains pages 301 through 525 (the end of the report) and the Senate Select Committee Additional Views documents.

Amelia St. John

Dec 2014

understanding of the cyber messages and also in finding new cyber leads. Exploitation of computers and other information obtained in raids before and during the case also contributed significantly, as did surveillance. However, none of these tools are stand-alones. Good old fashioned hard targeting and analysis of these maddeningly vague and disparate and incomplete threads of information was the glue that put it all together."[1550]

(TS// ███████████ //NF) On September 10, 2004, the Interagency Intelligence Committee on Terrorism (IICT) disseminated a report entitled, "Homeland: Reappraising al-Qa'ida's Election Threat," which states:

> "We do not know the projected timeframe for any attacks Issa was planning to execute in the UK, but it is unlikely he would have been ready to strike in the near term. Upon returning to the UK in mid-2004, Issa attempted to gather materials to build explosives for future attacks in the UK... [U.K.] authorities have been unable to locate any explosives precursors, and it is possible he had not yet acquired the necessary materials at the time of his detention. The detainee [Abu Talha al-Pakistani] also noted that some of Issa's operatives required further training—most likely in explosives—and that [Issa] intended to send an associate to Pakistan for three months to receive instruction from senior al-Qa'ida explosives experts."[1551]

The assessment adds, "Issa appears to have been in an early phase of operational planning at the time of his capture."[1552]

(TS// ███████████ //NF) In November 2004, ████ authorities informed the CIA that "it was largely through the investigation of Nisar Jalal's associates that [the U.K.] was able to identify Dhiren Barot as being [identifiable] with Issa al-Hindi."[1553]

(TS// ███████████ //NF) A December 14, 2004, FBI Intelligence Assessment entitled, "The Gas Limos Project: An al-Qa'ida Urban Attack Plan Assessment," evaluated "the feasibility and lethality of this plot" based on "documents captured during raids" against "al-Qa'ida operatives in Pakistan and the United Kingdom in July and August 2004, and on custodial interviews conducted in the weeks following these raids." The FBI concluded that "the main plot presented in the Gas Limos Project is unlikely to be as successful as described." The report continued: "We assess that the Gas Limos Project, while ambitious and creative, is far-fetched."[1554]

[1550] "Capture of Al-Qa'ida Operative Abu Issa al-Hindi (aka Dhiren Barot, aka Abu Issa al-Britani)" multiple iterations of talking points, including the revised version cited, found in an email from: [REDACTED]; to: [REDACTED], with multiple ccs; subject: "IMMEDIATE: al-Hindi TPs for ADCI Tuesday Briefing of Kerry/Edwards"; date: August 30, 2004, at 02:51 PM.

[1551] Disseminated intelligence product by the IICT entitled, "Homeland: Reappraising al-Qa'ida's "Election Threat," dated September 10, 2004.

[1552] Disseminated intelligence product by the IICT entitled, "Homeland: Reappraising al-Qa'ida's "Election Threat," dated September 10, 2004.

[1553] [REDACTED] 29759 ██████████

[1554] FBI Intelligence Assessment, "The Gas Limos Project: An al-Qa'ida Urban Attack Plan Assessment," dated December 14, 2004.

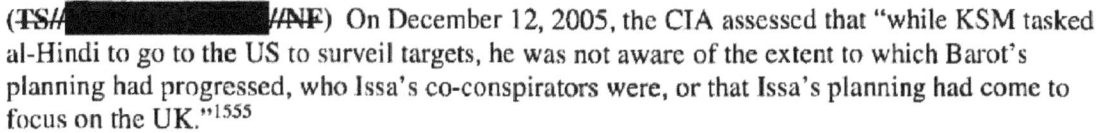
(TS/ ████████ //NF) On December 12, 2005, the CIA assessed that "while KSM tasked al-Hindi to go to the US to surveil targets, he was not aware of the extent to which Barot's planning had progressed, who Issa's co-conspirators were, or that Issa's planning had come to focus on the UK."[1555]

(TS/ ████████ //NF) On November 7, 2006, Dhiren Barot was sentenced to life imprisonment in the United Kingdom. On May 16, 2007, Dhiren Barot's sentence was reduced to 30 years after a British Court of Appeal found that expert assessments describing the plot as "amateurish," "defective," and unlikely to succeed were not provided to the sentencing judge.[1556]

5. The Identification, Capture, and Arrest of Iyman Faris

(TS/ ████████ //NF) *Summary:* The CIA represented that its enhanced interrogation techniques were effective and produced critical, otherwise unavailable intelligence, which thwarted plots and saved lives. Over a period of years, the CIA provided the "identification," "arrest," "capture," "investigation," and "prosecution" of Iyman Faris as evidence for the effectiveness of the CIA's enhanced interrogation techniques. These representations were inaccurate. Iyman Faris was identified, investigated, and linked directly to al-Qa'ida prior to any mention of Iyman Faris by KSM or any other CIA detainee. When approached by law enforcement, Iyman Faris voluntarily provided information and made self-incriminating statements. On May 1, 2003, Iyman Faris pled guilty to terrorism-related charges and admitted "to casing a New York City bridge for al Qaeda, and researching and providing information to al Qaeda regarding the tools necessary for possible attacks on U.S. targets."

(TS/ ████████ //NF) *Further Details:* Iyman Faris was an Ohio-based truck driver tasked by KSM with procuring "tools and devices needed to collapse suspension bridges," as well as tools that could be used to derail trains.[1557] Faris had met KSM through his self-described "best friend," Maqsood Khan,[1558] who was a Pakistan-based al-Qa'ida facilitator and Majid Khan's uncle.[1559]

(TS/ ████████ //NF) The identification and arrest of Iyman Faris is one of the eight most frequently cited examples provided by the CIA as evidence for the effectiveness of the CIA's enhanced interrogation techniques. Over a period of years, CIA documents prepared for and provided to senior policymakers, intelligence officials, and the Department of Justice represent the identification, capture, and/or arrest of Iyman Faris as an example of how "[k]ey intelligence

---

[1555] Email from: [REDACTED]; to: [REDACTED] and others; subject: "Re: need answer: request for any info deemed operationally sensitive be passed to brits concerning Dhiren Barot (aka Issa al-Hindi)"; date: December 12, 2005, at 6:08:01 PM, in preparation of a document entitled, "Addendum in Respect of Disclosure - Al Hindi.pdf."
[1556] *See* Royal Courts of Justice Appeal, Barot v R [2007], EWCA Crim 1119 (16 May 2007). The expert assessments determined that the plotting involved "a professional-looking attempt from amateurs who did not really know what they were doing." *See also* June 15, 2007, *Bloomberg* news article entitled, "Terrorist Gang Jailed for Helping London and New York Bomb Plot."
[1557] WHDC ████ (242226Z MAR 03) (includes information acquired by the FBI on March 20, 2003)
[1558] ALEC ████ (261745Z MAR 03)
[1559] ALEC ████ (180200Z MAR 03). *See also* ████████ .

collected from HVD interrogations *after* applying interrogation techniques" had "enabled CIA to disrupt terrorist plots" and "capture additional terrorists."[1560] The CIA further represented that the intelligence acquired from the CIA's enhanced interrogation techniques was "otherwise unavailable" and "saved lives."[1561]

[1560] Italics included in CIA Memorandum to the Office of Legal Counsel, entitled, "Effectiveness of the CIA Counterterrorist Interrogation Techniques," from March 2, 2005.

[1561] From 2003 through 2009, the CIA's representations regarding the effectiveness of the CIA's enhanced interrogation techniques provided a specific set of examples of terrorist plots "disrupted" and terrorists captured that the CIA attributed to information obtained from the use of its enhanced interrogation techniques. CIA representations further asserted that the intelligence obtained from the use of the CIA's enhanced interrogation techniques was unique, otherwise unavailable, and resulted in "saved lives." Among other CIA representations, *see*: (1) CIA representations in the Department of Justice Office of Legal Counsel Memorandum, dated May 30, 2005, which relied on a series of highly specific CIA representations on the type of intelligence acquired from the use of the CIA's enhanced interrogation techniques to assess their legality. The CIA representations referenced by the OLC include that the use of the CIA's enhanced interrogation techniques was "necessary" to obtain "critical," "vital," and "otherwise unavailable actionable intelligence" that was "essential" for the U.S. government to "detect and disrupt" terrorist threats. The OLC memorandum further states that "[the CIA] ha[s] informed [the OLC] that the CIA believes that this program is largely responsible for preventing a subsequent attack within the United States." (*See* Memorandum for John A. Rizzo, Senior Deputy General Counsel, Central Intelligence Agency, from Steven G. Bradbury, Principal Deputy Assistant Attorney General, Office of Legal Counsel, May 30, 2005, Re: Application of United States Obligations Under Article 16 of the Convention Against Torture to Certain Techniques that May Be Used in the Interrogation of High Value al Qaeda Detainees.) (2) CIA representations in the Department of Justice Office of Legal Counsel Memorandum dated July 20, 2007, which also relied on CIA representations on the type of intelligence acquired from the use of the CIA's enhanced interrogation techniques. Citing CIA documents and the President's September 6, 2006, speech describing the CIA's interrogation program (which was based on CIA-provided information), the OLC memorandum states: "The CIA interrogation program—and, in particular, its use of enhanced interrogation techniques—is intended to serve this paramount interest [security of the Nation] by producing substantial quantities of otherwise unavailable intelligence. ...As the President explained [on September 6, 2006], 'by giving us information about terrorist plans we could not get anywhere else, the program has saved innocent lives.'" (*See* Memorandum for John A. Rizzo, Acting General Counsel, Central Intelligence Agency, from Steven G. Bradbury, Principal Deputy Assistant Attorney General, Office of Legal Counsel, July 20, 2007, Re: Application of the War Crimes Act, the Detainee Treatment Act, and Common Article 3 of the Geneva Conventions to Certain Techniques that May Be Used by the CIA in the Interrogation of High Value al Qaeda Detainees.) (3) CIA briefings for members of the National Security Council in July and September 2003 represented that "the use of Enhanced Techniques of one kind or another had produced significant intelligence information that had, in the view of CIA professionals, saved lives," and warned policymakers that "[t]ermination of this program will result in loss of life, possibly extensive." (*See* August 5, 2003 Memorandum for the Record from Scott Muller, Subject: Review of Interrogation Program on 29 July 2003; Briefing slides, CIA Interrogation Program, July 29, 2003; September 4, 2003, CIA Memorandum for the Record, Subject: Member Briefing; and September 26, 2003, Memorandum for the Record from Muller, Subject: CIA Interrogation Program.) (4) The CIA's response to the Office of Inspector General draft Special Review of the CIA program, which asserts: "Information [the CIA] received... as a result of the lawful use of enhanced interrogation techniques ('EITs') has almost certainly saved countless American lives inside the United States and abroad. The evidence points clearly to the fact that without the use of such techniques, we and our allies would [have] suffered major terrorist attacks involving hundreds, if not thousands, of casualties." (*See* Memorandum for: Inspector General; from: James Pavitt, Deputy Director for Operations; subject: re (S) Comments to Draft IG Special Review, "Counterterrorism Detention and Interrogation Program" 2003-7123-IG; date: February 27, 2004; attachment: February 24, 2004, Memorandum re Successes of CIA's Counterterrorism Detention and Interrogation Activities.) (5) CIA briefing documents for CIA Director Leon Panetta in February 2009, which state that the "CIA assesses that the RDI program worked and the [enhanced interrogation] techniques were effective in producing foreign intelligence," and that "[m]ost, if not all, of the timely intelligence acquired from detainees in this program would not have been discovered or reported by other means." (*See* CIA briefing documents for Leon Panetta, entitled, "Tab 9: DCIA Briefing on RDI Program-18FEB.2009" and graphic attachment, "Key Intelligence and Reporting Derived from Abu Zubaydah and Khalid

(TS/ ██████████ /NF) For example, in a July 2003 CIA briefing for White House officials on the CIA interrogation program, the CIA represented that "[m]ajor threats were countered and attacks averted," and that "[t]ermination of this [CIA] program will result in loss of life, possibly extensive." The CIA further represented that "the use of the [CIA's enhanced interrogation] techniques has produced significant results" and "saved lives."[1562] Under the heading, "RESULTS: MAJOR THREAT INFO," a briefing slides states:

> "KSM: Al-Qa'ida Chief of Operations… - *Identification* of Iyman Faris"[1563]

(TS/ ██████████ /NF) Similarly, on February 27, 2004, DDO James Pavitt responded to the CIA Inspector General's draft Special Review and included a representation related to Iyman Faris. Pavitt stated that the Inspector General's Special Review should have come to the "conclusion that our efforts have thwarted attacks and saved lives," and that "EITs (including the water board) have been indispensable to our successes."[1564] Pavitt provided materials to the OIG that stated:

> "Specifically, as a result of the lawful use of EITs, KSM identified a truck driver who is now serving time in the United States for his support to al-Qa'ida."[1565]

The final CIA Inspector General Special Review, "Counterterrorism Detention and Interrogation Program," published in May 2004, states:

Shaykh Muhammad (KSM)," including "DCIA Briefing on RDI Program" agenda, CIA document "EITs and Effectiveness," with associated documents, "Key Intelligence Impacts Chart: Attachment (AZ and KSM)," "Background on Key Intelligence Impacts Chart: Attachment," and "supporting references," to include "Background on Key Captures and Plots Disrupted.") (6) CIA document faxed to the Senate Select Committee on Intelligence on March 18, 2009, entitled, "SWIGERT and DUNBAR," located in Committee databases at DTS #2009-1258, which provides a list of "some of the key captures and disrupted plots" that the CIA had attributed to the use of the CIA's enhanced interrogation techniques, and stating: "CIA assesses that most, if not all, of the timely intelligence acquired from detainees in this program would not have been discovered or reported by any other means." *See* Volume II for additional CIA representations asserting that the CIA's enhanced interrogation techniques enabled the CIA to obtain unique, otherwise unavailable intelligence that "saved lives."

[1562] CIA memorandum for the Record, "Review of Interrogation Program on 29 July 2003," prepared by CIA General Counsel Scott Muller, dated August 5, 2003; briefing slides entitled, "*CIA Interrogation Program,*" dated July 29, 2003, presented to senior White House officials.

[1563] Italics added. CIA memorandum for the Record, "Review of Interrogation Program on 29 July 2003," prepared by CIA General Counsel Scott Muller, dated August 5, 2003; briefing slides entitled, "*CIA Interrogation Program,*" dated July 29, 2003, presented to senior White House officials.

[1564] Memorandum to the Inspector General from James Pavitt, CIA's Deputy Director for Operations, dated February 27, 2004, with the subject line, "Comments to Draft IG Special Review, 'Counterterrorism Detention and Interrogation Program' (2003-7123-IG)," Attachment, "Successes of CIA's Counterterrorism Detention and Interrogation Activities," dated February 24, 2004.

[1565] Memorandum to the Inspector General from James Pavitt, CIA's Deputy Director for Operations, dated February 27, 2004, with the subject line, "Comments to Draft IG Special Review, 'Counterterrorism Detention and Interrogation Program' (2003-7123-IG)," Attachment, "Successes of CIA's Counterterrorism Detention and Interrogation Activities," dated February 24, 2004.

"Khalid Shaykh Muhammad's information also *led to the investigation and prosecution of Iyman Faris*, the truck driver arrested in early 2003 in Ohio."[1566]

This passage in the CIA Inspector General Special Review was declassified and publicly released on August 24, 2009.[1567]

(TS// ~~████████~~ //NF) Likewise, information prepared by the CIA for CIA Director Leon Panetta in February 2009 on the effectiveness of the CIA's enhanced interrogation techniques states that the "CIA assesses... the techniques were effective in producing foreign intelligence," and that "most, if not all, of the timely intelligence acquired from detainees in this program would not have been discovered or reported by other means." The document provides examples of "some of the key captures, disrupted plots, and intelligence gained from HVDs interrogated," including the "*arrest* of Iyman Faris."[1568] In March 2009, the CIA provided a three-page document to the chairman of the Committee stating, "CIA assesses that most, if not all, of the timely intelligence acquired from detainees in this program would not have been discovered or reported by any other means," before listing "Iyman Faris" as one of the "key captures" resulting from the CIA interrogation program.[1569]

(TS// ~~████████~~ //NF) The CIA provided similar inaccurate representations regarding the identification and capture of Iyman Faris in nine of the 20 documents and briefings provided to policymakers and the Department of Justice between July 2003 and March 2009.[1570]

[1566] Italics added. CIA Office of Inspector General, Special Review – Counterterrorism Detention and Interrogation Program, (2003-7123-IG), May 2004.

[1567] The relevant sections of the Special Review were also cited in the OLC's May 30, 2005, memorandum, which stated that "we understand that interrogations have led to specific, actionable intelligence," and that "[w]e understand that the use of enhanced techniques in the interrogations of KSM, Zubaydah and others... has yielded critical information." (*see* memorandum for John A. Rizzo, Senior Deputy General Counsel, Central Intelligence Agency, from Steven G. Bradbury, Principal Deputy Assistant Attorney General, Office of Legal Counsel, May 30, 2005, Re: Application of United States Obligations Under Article 16 of the Convention Against Torture to Certain Techniques that May be Used in the Interrogation of High Value Al Qaeda Detainees, p. 9 (DTS #2009-1810, Tab 11), citing *Special Review* at 86, 90-91). Like the Special Review, the OLC memorandum has been declassified with redactions.

[1568] Italics added. CIA briefing documents for Leon Panetta, entitled, "Tab 9: DCIA Briefing on RDI Program-18FEB.2009" and graphic attachment, "Key Intelligence and Reporting Derived from Abu Zubaydah and Khalid Shaykh Muhammad (KSM)." The documents include "DCIA Briefing on RDI Program" agenda, CIA document "EITs and Effectiveness," with associated documents, "Key Intelligence Impacts Chart: Attachment (AZ and KSM)," "Background on Key Intelligence Impacts Chart: Attachment," and "supporting references," to include "Background on Key Captures and Plots Disrupted."

[1569] CIA document faxed to the Senate Select Committee on Intelligence on March 18, 2009, at 3:46 PM, entitled, "[SWIGERT and DUNBAR]" (DTS #2009-1258).

[1570] *See* list of CIA prepared briefings and memoranda from 2003 through 2009 with representations on the effectiveness of the CIA's enhanced interrogation techniques referenced in this summary and described in detail in Volume II.

(TS// ████████ //NF) A review of CIA operational cables and other records found that the CIA's Detention and Interrogation Program and the CIA's enhanced interrogation techniques played no role in the identification and capture of Iyman Faris.[1571]

(TS// ████████ //NF) CIA records indicate that Iyman Faris was known to the U.S. Intelligence Community prior to the attacks of September 11, 2001. On March ██, 2001, the FBI opened an international terrorism investigation targeting Iyman Faris.[1572] According to CIA records, the "predication of the [FBI] Faris investigation was information provided by [foreign] authorities that [revealed] Faris' telephone number had been called by Islamic extremists operating in France, Belgium, Turkey and Canada," including "millennium bomber" Ahmad Ressam.[1573] Ressam, currently serving a 65-year U.S. prison term, was arrested on December 14, 1999, en route to Los Angeles International Airport with explosives in the trunk of his car. According to CIA records, as "a result of a post 9/11 lead," the FBI interviewed Iyman Faris shortly after the attacks of September 11, 2001.[1574] On November ██, 2001, the FBI closed its investigation of Iyman Faris for unknown reasons.[1575]

(TS// ████████ //NF) On March 5, 2003, Majid Khan was taken into Pakistani custody.[1576] That same day, FISA coverage of Majid Khan's residence in Maryland indicated that Majid Khan's ████████████ made a suspicious phone call to an individual at a residence associated with Iyman Faris.[1577] The call included discussion of Majid Khan's possible arrest and potential FBI surveillance of ████████, who asked the individual in Ohio if he had been approached and questioned.[1578] ████████ warned the Ohio-based individual not to contact anyone using his phone.[1579] That same day, ████████ informed FBI special agents that the other party to the intercepted conversation was Iyman Faris.[1580] By March 6, 2003, the FBI had officially reopened its international terrorism investigation of Iyman Faris.[1581]

[1571] The CIA's June 2013 Response acknowledges that "we incorrectly stated or implied that KSM's information led to the investigation of Faris." Elsewhere, the CIA's June 2013 Response states that "[CIA] imprecisely characterized KSM's information as having 'led' to the investigation of Iyman Faris, rather than more accurately characterizing it as a key contribution to the investigation." As described in more detail in Volume II, the CIA and FBI had significant information on Iyman Faris prior to any reporting from KSM. The CIA's June 2013 Response also states that the CIA's inaccurate statements that KSM's reporting "led" to the investigation of Iyman Faris were only made "[i]n a few cases," and "[i]n a small number of... representations." As described in the full Committee Study, the CIA repeatedly represented that KSM's reporting "led" to the investigation of Iyman Faris, and was responsible for the "identification" and "capture" of Iyman Faris.

[1572] Information provided by the FBI to the Committee on November, 30, 2010. Records do not provide an explanation for the closing of the investigation.

[1573] WHDC ████ (102129Z MAR 03). See also ALEC ████ (180200Z MAR 03).

[1574] ALEC ████ (261725Z MAR 03)

[1575] Information provided to the Committee by the FBI on November, 30, 2010.

[1576] ████████ 13658 (050318Z MAR 03). See the section on the capture of Majid Khan in this summary and in Volume II.

[1577] ALEC ████ (060353Z MAR 03)

[1578] ALEC ████ (060353Z MAR 03)

[1579] ALEC ████ (060353Z MAR 03)

[1580] FBI information relayed in ALEC ████ ████ ██.

[1581] FBI information confirmed for the Committee on November, 30, 2010.

(TS// ██████████ //NF) While U.S. law enforcement investigations of Iyman Faris moved forward, Majid Khan, in foreign government custody, was being questioned by foreign government interrogators. According to CIA records, the interrogators were using rapport-building techniques, confronting Khan with inconsistencies in his story and obtaining information on Majid Khan's al-Qa'ida connections.[1582] On March 11, 2003, Majid Khan identified a photo of Iyman Faris.[1583] Majid Khan stated that he knew Faris as "Abdul Raof," and claimed Faris was a 35-year-old truck driver of Pakistani origin who was a "business partner of his father."[1584] In addition to describing business deals Iyman Faris was involved in with Khan's family, Majid Khan stated that Faris spoke Urdu and excellent English and had a "colorful personality."[1585] The next day, while still in foreign government custody, Majid Khan stated that Iyman Faris was "an Islamic extremist."[1586] According to CIA cables, on March 14, 2003, Majid Khan provided "more damning information" on Iyman Faris, specifically that Faris was a "mujahudden during the Afghan/Soviet period" and was a close associate of his uncle, Maqsood Khan. Maqsood was a known al-Qa'ida associate whom Majid Khan had already admitted was in contact with senior al-Qa'ida members. Majid Khan told foreign government interrogators that it was Maqsood who provided the money for Majid Khan's al-Qa'ida-related travels.[1587] Majid Khan further stated that "after the KSM arrest became public knowledge," Iyman Faris contacted Majid Khan's family and requested the family pass a message to Maqsood Khan regarding the status of KSM.[1588] This information on Iyman Faris was acquired prior to— and independently of—any reporting from the CIA's Detention and Interrogation Program.[1589]

(TS// ██████████ //NF) On March 10, 2003, in response to a requirements cable from CIA Headquarters reporting that al-Qa'ida was targeting U.S. suspension bridges,[1590] KSM stated that any such plans were "theoretical" and only "on paper." He also stated that no one was currently pursuing such a plot.[1591] KSM repeated this assertion on March 16, 2003,[1592] noting that, while UBL officially endorsed attacks against suspension bridges in the United States, he "had no planned targets in the US which were pending attack and that after 9/11 the US had become too hard a target."[1593] On neither occasion did KSM reference Iyman Faris.

[1582] ██████ 13678 (070724Z MAR 03). The cable states: "a [foreign government officer] talked quietly to [Majid Khan] alone for about ten minutes before the interview began and was able to establish an excellent level of rapport. The first hour and [a] half of the interview was a review of bio-data and information previously [reported]. When [foreign government interrogators] started putting pressure on [Majid Khan] by pulling apart his story about his 'honeymoon' in Bangkok and his attempt to rent an apartment, safehouse, for his cousin [Mansoor Maqsood, aka Iqbal, aka Talha, aka Moeen, aka Habib], at 1400, [Majid Khan] slumped in his chair and said he would reveal everything to officers...."

[1583] ██████ 13758 ██████████ ; FBI information later relayed in ALEC ██████ ██████ ; and information provided to the Committee by the FBI on November, 30, 2010. *See* FBI case file ██████

[1584] ██████ 13758 ██████████
[1585] 13758
[1586] 13765
[1587] 13785 ██████ ; ██████ 13713 ██████
[1588] 13785
[1589] For additional information, *see* intelligence chronology in Volume II.
[1590] ALEC ██████ (071757Z MAR 03)
[1591] 10752 (102320Z MAR 03); DIRECTOR ██████ (122101Z MAR 03). *See also* ██████ .
[1592] 10858 (170747Z MAR 03)
[1593] 10858 (170747Z MAR 03)

(TS// ██████████████ //NF) On March 15, 2003, deputy chief of ALEC Station, ██████████ ██████, who was reading the intelligence from the foreign government interrogations of Majid Khan, requested a photograph of Majid Khan and additional information to use with KSM.[1594] In response, CIA Headquarters sent the detention site photographs of Majid Khan's family and associates, including Iyman Faris.[1595]

(TS// ██████████████ //NF) On March 17, 2003, eleven days after the FBI officially reopened its investigation of Iyman Faris, KSM was shown photographs of both Iyman Faris and Majid Khan.[1596] According to CIA cables, KSM was also asked detailed questions based on email communications, which a cable stated served as "an effective means to convey to [KSM] the impression that the USG already possessed considerable information and that the information would be used to check the accuracy of his statements."[1597] In this context, KSM identified the photograph of Iyman Faris as a "truck driver" and a relative of Majid Khan. KSM claimed that he could not remember the truck driver's name. KSM described the "truck driver" as a "colorful character who liked to drink and have girlfriends and was very interested in business."[1598] The next day, March 18, 2003, KSM stated that in February 2002 he tasked the "truck driver" to procure specialized machine tools that would be useful to al-Qa'ida to loosen the nuts and bolts of suspension bridges in the United States. According to KSM, in March 2002, the "truck driver" asked Mansour Khan [son of Maqsood Khan][1599] to inform KSM that he (the "truck driver") could not find such tools. KSM stated that he made no further requests of the "truck driver."[1600]

(TS// ██████████████ //NF) According to a CIA cable, on the evening of March 20, 2003, the FBI informed the CIA that "Ohio police had been following [Iyman] Faris for 'some time,' and had stopped him and questioned him about his relationship to Shoukat Ali Khan [Majid Khan's

---

[1594] Memorandum for: ███████████, [REDACTED]; from: [REDACTED],OFFICE: ██████/[DETENTION SITE BLUE]; subject: Baltimore boy and KSM; date: 15 March 2003, at 07:08:32 PM.

[1595] Email from: ██████████; to: [REDACTED]; cc: [REDACTED]; subject: Re: Baltimore boy and KSM; date: March 15, 2003, at 2:32 PM; ALEC ████ (152212Z MAR 03).

[1596] Having read reporting from the interrogations of Majid Khan, one of KSM's debriefers at the CIA's DETENTION SITE BLUE, deputy chief of ALEC Station, ██████████ requested the photographs to "use with Ksm [sic] et al." (See Memorandum for ████████████, [REDACTED]; from [REDACTED],OFFICE: ██████/[DETENTION SITE BLUE]; subject: Baltimore boy and KSM; date: 15 March 2003, at 07:08:32 PM.) The photographs were sent to DETENTION SITE BLUE shortly thereafter. See ALEC ████ (152212Z MAR 03).

[1597] ██████ 10865 (171648Z MAR 03), disseminated as ████████████; ██████ 10866 (171832Z MAR 03); ██████ 10870 (172017Z MAR 03)

[1598] ██████ 10866 (171832Z MAR 03). KSM explained that Majid Khan was married to Maqsood Khan's niece, and that "another Maqsood Khan relative was a truck driver in Ohio." KSM stated that he had met him "on at least one occasion" at the home of Maqsood Khan in Karachi in approximately 1999 or 2000. This information was also sent on March 18, 2003, in ALEC ████ (180200Z MAR 03). See also ████████████.

[1599] ALEC ████ (261745Z MAR 03)

[1600] ██████ 10886 (182219Z MAR 03); ALEC ████ (180200Z MAR 03). In assessing the session for CIA Headquarters, personnel at DETENTION SITE BLUE wrote that "KSM will selectively lie, provide partial truths, and misdirect when he believes he will not be found out and held accountable." On the other hand, they wrote that "KSM appears more inclined to make accurate disclosures when he believes people, emails, or other source material are available to the USG for checking his responses." See ██████ 10884 (182140Z MAR 03).

father] of Baltimore."[1601] According to a CIA officer, "[w]hen the FBI approached Faris he talked voluntarily."[1602] Records indicate that Faris "initially claimed to know Shoukat Ali Khan though the gas station business" and agreed to take a polygraph examination. According to FBI records, prior to the polygraph, Faris admitted to being associated with KSM and provided details on his relationships with al-Qa'ida members in Pakistan.[1603] Specifically, Iyman Faris told FBI and Ohio police that he had met KSM twice and had been "tasked with procuring items." Faris detailed how KSM had a plan "to cut the suspension cables on the Brooklyn Bridge to cause its collapse using gas cutters."[1604] Faris maintained that he "thought that the task to take down the bridge was impossible"[1605] and did not take further action.[1606]

[1601] See WHDC ████ (242226Z MAR 03), which discusses information obtained by FBI officials on March 20, 2003; and FBI case file ███████████.

[1602] CIA Office of Inspector General interview of ███████████, Chief of the ███ Branch of the UBL Group at CTC, by ███████████, Office of the Inspector General, July 30, 2003. The interview report states: "CIA initiated the lead (not from detainees) to an individual believed to live in Baltimore – Majid Khan. He was believed to be in contact with a nephew of [KSM]. The FBI initiated trash coverage (using their special authorities to tap e-mail) on the Baltimore residence where Khan had lived and family members still lived. Meanwhile, using ███████ ███████ FISA coverage ███████████ the Agency, with the help of [a foreign government], located [Majid] Khan. The Baltimore house placed a call to Ohio (to Iyman Faris) which became another FBI lead. When the FBI approached Faris he talked voluntarily."

[1603] See FBI case file ███████████; WHDC ████ (211522Z MAR 03) and WHDC ████ (242226Z MAR 03). Faris described Maqsood Khan as "the 'right foot' of Usama bin Ladin (UBL)."

[1604] See WHDC ████ (242226Z MAR 03); and WHDC ████ (211522Z MAR 03) (discusses information obtained by FBI officials on March 20, 2003).

[1605] ALEC ████ (261745Z MAR 03). A senior CIA counterterrorism official, who had previously served as chief of the Bin Ladin Unit, commented on the intelligence obtained from Iyman Faris on the Brooklyn Bridge plotting, stating: "i guess we have to take these guys at their word, but if these are the types of attacks ksm was planning, [KSM] was more of a nuisnace [sic] than a threat and you have to wonder how he ever thought of anything as imaginative as the 11 sept attacks. i wonder if he had two tracks going: ops like 11 sept and a whole other series half-baked, secular palestinian-style ops like those majid khan, faris, and the other yahoos are talking about. perhaps he believe [sic] if we caught the yahoos, we would relax a bit and they would be better able to hit us with an effective attack? the other alternative, is that ksm himself is a yahoo. strange stuff." (See email from: ███████████; to: ███████████, ███████████, ███████████, ███████████, ███████████, [REDACTED]; subject: attacks in conus; date: March 25, 2003, at 6:19:18 AM, referencing cable WHDC ████ (242226Z MAR 03), with the subject line, "EYES ONLY: Majid Khan: Imminent al-Qa'ida Plots to Attack NYC and WDC Targets Aborted by KSM Capture.") In a separate email, the senior official wrote: "again, odd. ksm wants to get 'machine tools' to loosen the bolts on bridges so they collapse? did he think no one would see or hear these yahoos trying to unscrew the bridge? that everyone would drive by and just ignore the effort to unbolt a roadway? and what about opsec: 'yup, we were just going to recruit a few of the neighbors to help knock down the brooklyn bridge.'" See email from: ███████████; to: ███████████, ███████████, ███████████, ███████████; date: March 25, 2003, at 6:35:18 AM.

[1606] ALEC ████ (261745Z MAR 03). During this period, the CIA was receiving updates from the FBI debriefings of Iyman Faris. See TRRS-03-03-0610, referenced in ███████ 10984 (242351Z MAR 03). On March 20, 2003, KSM confirmed that he had tasked "the truck driver...to procure machine tools that would be useful to al-Qa'ida in its plan to loosen the nuts and bolts of suspension bridges," but stated he had "never divulged specific targeting information to the truck driver." (See ███████████ 10910 (202108Z MAR 03).) A CIA cable from March 24, 2003, noted that KSM's CIA interrogators were "reviewing latest ███████ readout on Majid Khan debriefs [who was in foreign government custody] and FBI [intelligence reports] from debriefings of the truck driver Faris Iyman [sic]," and that the CIA team was therefore "focused entirely on sorting out the information on Majid's claim...as well as truck driver details on the threat." (See ███████ 10984 (242351Z MAR 03).) According to another cable, KSM indicated that while the original plan was to sever the cables, he determined that it would be easier to acquire machine tools that would allow the operatives to "loosen the large nuts and bolts of the bridges." (See ███████████ 10985 (242351Z MAR 03).) The disseminated intelligence report from this interrogation added that KSM stated his

(**TS//**█████████**//NF**) Over several weeks Iyman Faris continued to voluntarily cooperate with law enforcement officials and engaged in efforts to assist in the capture of Maqsood Khan.[1607] Faris provided additional details on his activities related to the Khan family, KSM, his meeting with UBL, and two extremists in the United States who had discussed wanting "to kill Americans in a Columbus area shopping mall with a Kalashnikov automatic rifle."[1608] On April 22, 2003, "Faris had accepted a plea agreement"[1609] and continued to cooperate, including by sending email messages to al-Qa'ida members in Pakistan for the purposes of intelligence collection.[1610] On May 1, 2003, Faris was transported from Quantico, Virginia, where he was voluntarily residing and working with the FBI, to a federal court in Alexandria, Virginia, where he pled guilty to material support to terrorism charges.[1611] He was subsequently sentenced to 20 years in prison.[1612]

(**TS//**█████████**//NF**) On April 3, 2003, the Interagency Intelligence Committee on Terrorism (IICT) assessed that the use of tools to loosen the bolts of suspension bridges were "methods that appear to be unrealistic."[1613]

6. The Identification, Capture, and Arrest of Sajid Badat

(**TS//**█████████**//NF**) *Summary:* The CIA represented that its enhanced interrogation techniques were effective and produced critical, otherwise unavailable intelligence, which thwarted plots and saved lives. Over a period of years, the CIA provided the identification, discovery, capture, and arrest of Sajid Badat as evidence for the effectiveness of the CIA's enhanced interrogation techniques. These representations were inaccurate. U.K. domestic investigative efforts, reporting from foreign intelligence services, international law enforcement efforts, and U.S. military reporting resulted in the identification and arrest of Sajid Badat.

---

last communication with Iyman Faris was shortly before his capture on March 1, 2003, and that he (KSM) was "severely disappointed to learn that Iyman had not yet been successful in his mission to purchase the necessary materials." (*See* DIRECTOR ████ (25111Z MAR 03).) Later, on April 10, 2003, a CIA cable stated that KSM told CIA interrogators that al-Qa'ida members had "cased" the Brooklyn Bridge and that KSM had discussed attacking suspension bridges with other senior al-Qa'ida operatives. *See* HEADQUARTERS ████ (100928Z APR 03).

[1607] *See* FBI case file ██████, ALEC ████ (261725Z MAR 03), and Department of Justice release dated October 28, 2003, entitled, "Iyman Faris Sentenced for Providing Material Support to Al Qaeda." During these interviews Iyman Faris provided detailed information on a variety of matters, including his ongoing relationship with Maqsood Khan; the aliases he used in Pakistan ("Mohmed Rauf" and "Gura"); how he became acquainted with KSM and al-Qa'ida; as well as his interaction with the Majid Khan family. Iyman Faris further provided information on his initial meeting with UBL and how he helped Maqsood Khan obtain supplies "for usage by Usama Bin Ladin" when he was in Pakistan.

[1608] ALEC ████ (022304Z APR 03); ALEC ████ (030128Z APR 03); ALEC ████ (022304Z APR 03); WHDC ████ (011857Z APR 03). *See also* ALEC ████ (261725Z MAR 03); ALEC ████ (010200Z APR 03); ALEC ████ (261933Z MAR 03).

[1609] WHDC ████ (232240Z APR 03)

[1610] *See* Department of Justice comments in "The Triple Life of a Qaeda Man," *Time Magazine,* June 22, 2003.

[1611] *See* FBI case file ██████████.

[1612] *See* Department of Justice release dated October 28, 2003, entitled, "Iyman Faris Sentenced for Providing Material Support to Al Qaeda."

[1613] "Khalid Shaykh Muhammad's Threat Reporting – Precious Truths, Surrounded by a Bodyguard of Lies," IICT, April 3, 2003.

(TS// ████████ //NF) *Further Details:* Sajid Badat[1614] was selected by al-Qa'ida leaders, including Abu Hafs al-Masri and Sayf al-'Adl, to carry out an attack against a Western airliner with Richard Reid using a shoe bomb explosive device in December 2001.[1615] Sajid Badat returned to the United Kingdom in late 2001 and sent a message to his al-Qa'ida handler, Ammar al-Baluchi, stating that he was withdrawing from the operation.[1616] On December 22, 2001,

---

[1614] Note on CIA records related to U.K.-based "Issas": Two United Kingdom-based al-Qa'ida associates, Dhiren Barot and Sajid Badat, were known by the same common aliases, Issa, Abu Issa, Abu Issa al-Britani ("[of] Britain") and/or Issa al-Pakistani. Both individuals were British Indians who had been independently in contact with senior al-Qa'ida leaders in Pakistan. Reporting indicated that the Issas were located in the United Kingdom and engaged in terrorist targeting of the U.K. The investigation into their true identities was a U.K.-led operation. As a result, the CIA sometimes had limited insight into U.K.-based activities to identify and locate the Issas. Senior CIA personnel expressed frustration that the U.K. was not sharing all known information on its investigations, writing in August 2003 that "[the FBI is] clearly working closely with the [U.K. service] on these matters and [the CIA is] at the mercy" of what it is told. In June 2003, the CIA informed the FBI that the CIA had "no electronic record of receiving any transcripts or summaries from your agency's interviews with [Richard] Reid, and would appreciate dissemination of summaries of questioning for the purposes of [CIA] analysis." Until the arrest of one of the Issas, Sajid Badat, on November 27, 2003, the U.S. Intelligence Community and U.K. authorities often confused the two al-Qa'ida associates. As a result, the quality and clarity of detainee reporting on the Issas (including reporting from detainees in the custody of the CIA, U.S. military, Department of Justice, and foreign services) varied. CIA personnel ████████ reported in September 2003 that there were "two (or three) Abu Issas" in intelligence reporting and that because of their similarities, it was often "unclear which Issa the detainees [were] referring to at different stages." Once detained in the United Kingdom in November 2003, Sajid Badat (one of the Issas) cooperated with U.K. authorities and provided information about the other "Issa." Badat stated that "people often asked [Badat] about [the other] Issa, as they were both British Indians." According to Sajid Badat, "anyone who had been involved with jihad in Britain since the mid-90s" would know Issa al-Hindi (aka Dhiren Barot), to include Babar Ahmed, Moazzem Begg, Richard Reid, Zacarias Moussaoui, and KSM. The other Issa, Dhiren Barot, arrested on August 3, 2004, was found to have been especially well-known among the U.K.-based extremist community, having written a popular book in 1999 expounding the virtues of jihad in Kashmir under the alias, "Esa al-Hindi." CIA records include a reference to the book and a description of its author ("a brother from England who was a Hindu and became a Muslim...[who] got training in Afghanistan...") as early as December 1999 (disseminated by the CIA on 12/31/99 in ████████. The ████████ [foreign partner] would later report that Dhiren Barot "frequently" appeared "in reporting of terrorist training" and had "involvement in Jihad in occupied Kashmir, Pakistan, Afghanistan, and Malaysia, throughout the 1990s." The Committee Study is based on more than six million pages of material related to the CIA's Detention and Interrogation Program provided by the CIA. Access was not provided to intelligence databases of the CIA or any other U.S. or foreign intelligence or law enforcement agency. Insomuch as intelligence from these sources is included, it was, unless noted otherwise, found within the CIA's Detention and Interrogation Program material produced for this Study. It is likely that significant intelligence unrelated to the CIA's Detention and Interrogation Program on Sajid Badat and Dhiren Barot exists in U.S. intelligence and law enforcement records and databases. *See* intelligence chronology in Volume II, including: ALEC ████████ (112157Z JUN 03); ████████ 19907 (231744Z APR 04); ████████ 99093 (020931Z SEP 03); ALEC ████████ (212117Z AUG 03); CIA WASHINGTON DC ████████ (162127Z JUN 03); and a series of emails between ████████ and ████████ (with multiple ccs) on August 22, 2003, at 9:24:43 AM.

[1615] Among other documents, *see* ████████ 19760 (251532Z JUN 02); ████████ 80508 (081717Z AUG 02); CIA ████████ (311736Z OCT 02), ████████; and ████████ 99093 (020931Z SEP 03). The CIA's June 2013 Response states that "KSM's reporting also clearly distinguished between, and thereby focused investigations of, two al-Qa'ida operatives known as Issa al-Britani." As detailed in the KSM detainee review in Volume III, KSM did discuss the two operatives, but he did not identify either by name (or, in the case of Dhiren Barot, by his more common *kunya*, Issa al-Hindi), and provided no actionable intelligence that contributed to the eventual identification of, or locational information for, either individual.

[1616] Among other documents, *see* CIA Headquarters document, entitled, "OPERATIONAL DEVELOPMENTS AGAINST GLOBAL SUNNI EXTREMIST TERRORISM," dated, "14 January 2002 1630 Hours"; CIA Headquarters document, entitled, "OPERATIONAL DEVELOPMENTS AGAINST GLOBAL SUNNI

Richard Reid attempted to detonate a shoe bomb on a flight from Paris, France, to Miami, Florida. The plane was diverted to Boston, Massachusetts, and Reid was taken into custody.[1617]

(TS// ██████████ //NF) The discovery, identification, capture, and arrest of Sajid Badat, "the shoe bomber," is one of the eight most frequently cited examples provided by the CIA as evidence for the effectiveness of the CIA's enhanced interrogation techniques. Over a period of years, CIA documents prepared for and provided to senior policymakers, intelligence officials, and the Department of Justice represent the discovery, identification, capture, and/or arrest of Sajid Badat as an example of how "[k]ey intelligence collected from HVD interrogations *after* applying interrogation techniques" had "enabled CIA to disrupt terrorist plots" and "capture additional terrorists."[1618] In at least one CIA document prepared for the president, the CIA specifically highlighted the waterboard interrogation technique in enabling the CIA to learn "that Sajid Badat was the operative slated to launch a simultaneous shoe bomb attack with Richard Reid in 2001."[1619] The CIA further represented that the intelligence acquired from the CIA's enhanced interrogation techniques was "otherwise unavailable" and "saved lives."[1620]

EXTREMIST TERRORISM," dated, "22 January 2002 1630 Hours"; ALEC ██████ (142334Z MAY 03); and ████████ 13120 ████████.

[1617] *See* intelligence chronology in Volume II and multiple open source reports, as well as Department of Justice materials, including *United States v. Richard Reid* Indictment, U.S. District Court, District of Massachusetts, January 16, 2002. According to a CIA operational update, in early December 2001, a unilateral CIA source reported that a known extremist "indicated there would be an attack on either an American or British airliner, originating in France, Germany, or Britain, with the use of explosives concealed in shoes." According to CIA records, an unclassified notice distributed to airlines concerning information from the CIA source in early December 2001 "is credited with having alerted flight crew personnel and their having reacted so swiftly to Reid's actions" aboard Flight 63. *See* intelligence chronology in Volume II, including CIA Headquarters document, entitled, "OPERATIONAL DEVELOPMENTS AGAINST GLOBAL SUNNI EXTREMIST TERRORISM," dated, "9 April 2002 1630 Hours."

[1618] Italics included in CIA Memorandum to the Office of Legal Counsel, entitled, "Effectiveness of the CIA Counterterrorist Interrogation Techniques," from March 2, 2005.

[1619] *See* document entitled, "DCIA Talking Points: Waterboard 06 November 2007," dated November 6, 2007, with the notation the document was "sent to DCIA Nov. 6 in preparation for POTUS meeting."

[1620] From 2003 through 2009, the CIA's representations regarding the effectiveness of the CIA's enhanced interrogation techniques provided a specific set of examples of terrorist plots "disrupted" and terrorists captured that the CIA attributed to information obtained from the use of its enhanced interrogation techniques. CIA representations further asserted that the intelligence obtained from the use of the CIA's enhanced interrogation techniques was unique, otherwise unavailable, and resulted in "saved lives." Among other CIA representations, *see*: (1) CIA representations in the Department of Justice Office of Legal Counsel Memorandum, dated May 30, 2005, which relied on a series of highly specific CIA representations on the type of intelligence acquired from the use of the CIA's enhanced interrogation techniques to assess their legality. The CIA representations referenced by the OLC include that the use of the CIA's enhanced interrogation techniques was "necessary" to obtain "critical," "vital," and "otherwise unavailable actionable intelligence" that was "essential" for the U.S. government to "detect and disrupt" terrorist threats. The OLC memorandum further states that "[the CIA] ha[s] informed [the OLC] that the CIA believes that this program is largely responsible for preventing a subsequent attack within the United States." (*See* Memorandum for John A. Rizzo, Senior Deputy General Counsel, Central Intelligence Agency, from Steven G. Bradbury, Principal Deputy Assistant Attorney General, Office of Legal Counsel, May 30, 2005, Re: Application of United States Obligations Under Article 16 of the Convention Against Torture to Certain Techniques that May Be Used in the Interrogation of High Value al Qaeda Detainees.) (2) CIA representations in the Department of Justice Office of Legal Counsel Memorandum dated July 20, 2007, which also relied on CIA representations on the type of intelligence acquired from the use of the CIA's enhanced interrogation techniques. Citing CIA documents and the President's September 6, 2006, speech describing the CIA's interrogation program (which was based on CIA-provided information), the OLC memorandum states: "The CIA interrogation program—

(TS//████████//NF) As an example, on October 26, 2007, the CIA faxed a document to the Senate Appropriations Committee appealing a proposed elimination of funding for the CIA's Rendition and Detention Program. The CIA appeal states that "[m]ost, if not all, of the intelligence acquired from high-value detainees in this program would likely not have been discovered or reported in any other way." Representing the success of the CIA interrogation program, the document states:

> "Detainees have... permitted discovery of terrorist cells, key individuals and the interdiction of numerous plots, including... the *discovery* of an

---

and, in particular, its use of enhanced interrogation techniques—is intended to serve this paramount interest [security of the Nation] by producing substantial quantities of otherwise unavailable intelligence. ...As the President explained [on September 6, 2006], 'by giving us information about terrorist plans we could not get anywhere else, the program has saved innocent lives.'" (*See* Memorandum for John A. Rizzo, Acting General Counsel, Central Intelligence Agency, from Steven G. Bradbury, Principal Deputy Assistant Attorney General, Office of Legal Counsel, July 20, 2007, Re: Application of the War Crimes Act, the Detainee Treatment Act, and Common Article 3 of the Geneva Conventions to Certain Techniques that May Be Used by the CIA in the Interrogation of High Value al Qaeda Detainees.) (3) CIA briefings for members of the National Security Council in July and September 2003 represented that "the use of Enhanced Techniques of one kind or another had produced significant intelligence information that had, in the view of CIA professionals, saved lives," and warned policymakers that "[t]ermination of this program will result in loss of life, possibly extensive." (*See* August 5, 2003 Memorandum for the Record from Scott Muller, Subject: Review of Interrogation Program on 29 July 2003; Briefing slides, CIA Interrogation Program, July 29, 2003; September 4, 2003, CIA Memorandum for the Record, Subject: Member Briefing; and September 26, 2003, Memorandum for the Record from Muller, Subject: CIA Interrogation Program.) (4) The CIA's response to the Office of Inspector General draft Special Review of the CIA program, which asserts: "Information [the CIA] received... as a result of the lawful use of enhanced interrogation techniques ('EITs') has almost certainly saved countless American lives inside the United States and abroad. The evidence points clearly to the fact that without the use of such techniques, we and our allies would [have] suffered major terrorist attacks involving hundreds, if not thousands, of casualties." (*See* Memorandum for: Inspector General; from: James Pavitt, Deputy Director for Operations; subject: re (S) Comments to Draft IG Special Review, "Counterterrorism Detention and Interrogation Program" 2003-7123-IG; date: February 27, 2004; attachment: February 24, 2004, Memorandum re Successes of CIA's Counterterrorism Detention and Interrogation Activities.) (5) CIA briefing documents for CIA Director Leon Panetta in February 2009, which state that the "CIA assesses that the RDI program worked and the [enhanced interrogation] techniques were effective in producing foreign intelligence," and that "[m]ost, if not all, of the timely intelligence acquired from detainees in this program would not have been discovered or reported by other means." (*See* CIA briefing documents for Leon Panetta, entitled, "Tab 9: DCIA Briefing on RDI Program-18FEB.2009" and graphic attachment, "Key Intelligence and Reporting Derived from Abu Zubaydah and Khalid Shaykh Muhammad (KSM)," including "DCIA Briefing on RDI Program" agenda, CIA document "EITs and Effectiveness," with associated documents, "Key Intelligence Impacts Chart: Attachment (AZ and KSM)," "Background on Key Intelligence Impacts Chart: Attachment," and "supporting references," to include "Background on Key Captures and Plots Disrupted.") (6) CIA document faxed to the Senate Select Committee on Intelligence on March 18, 2009, entitled, "[SWIGERT] and [DUNBAR]," located in Committee databases at DTS #2009-1258, which provides a list of "some of the key captures and disrupted plots" that the CIA had attributed to the use of the CIA's enhanced interrogation techniques, and stating: "CIA assesses that most, if not all, of the timely intelligence acquired from detainees in this program would not have been discovered or reported by any other means." *See* Volume II for additional CIA representations asserting that the CIA's enhanced interrogation techniques enabled the CIA to obtain unique, otherwise unavailable intelligence that "saved lives."

operative who was preparing another attack[1621] like that attempted by 'shoe bomber' Richard Reid."[1622]

(~~TS//~~█████████~~//NF~~) Similarly, in early March 2005, the CIA compiled talking points on the effectiveness of the CIA's enhanced interrogation techniques for use in a meeting with the National Security Council. The document states, "[t]he Central Intelligence Agency can advise you that this program works and the techniques are effective in producing foreign intelligence." The document states that "*after* applying interrogation techniques," the CIA "learned from KSM and Ammar that Sajid Badat was the operative slated to launch a simultaneous shoe bomb attack with Richard Reid in December 2001."[1623] A month later, on April 15, 2005, the CIA faxed an eight-page document to the Department of Justice's Office of Legal Counsel entitled, "Briefing Notes on the Value of Detainee Reporting" which contained similar information.[1624] The Office of Legal Counsel used the information to support its May 30, 2005, legal opinion on whether certain "enhanced interrogation techniques" were consistent with United States obligations under Article 16 of the United Nations Convention Against Torture and Other Cruel, Inhumane or Degrading Treatment or Punishment.[1625] The CIA-provided document states:

> *"Identifying the 'other' shoe bomber.* Leads provided by KSM in November 2003 led directly to the arrest of shoe bomber Richard Reid's one-time partner Sajid Badat in the UK. KSM had volunteered the existence of Badat—whom

---

[1621] As detailed in the intelligence chronology in Volume II, there is no evidence to support the CIA assertion in October 2007 that Sajid Badat was "preparing another attack like that attempted by 'shoe bomber' Richard Reid." A body of intelligence collected after the December 22, 2001, attempted shoe bomb attack by Richard Reid indicated that the proposed partner "backed out of the operation." This information was corroborated by signals intelligence. Once detained on November 27, 2003, Sajid Badat cooperated with U.K. authorities and described how he withdrew from the operation. *See,* among other CIA records, CIA Headquarters document, entitled, "OPERATIONAL DEVELOPMENTS AGAINST GLOBAL SUNNI EXTREMIST TERRORISM," dated "14 January 2002 1630 Hours."

[1622] Italics added. CIA fax from CIA employee [REDACTED] to U.S. Senate Committee on Appropriations, Subcommittee on Defense, with fax cover sheet entitled, "Talking points," sent on October 26, 2007, at 5:39:48 PM; document faxed entitled, "Talking Points Appeal of the $█ Million reduction in CIA/CTC's Rendition and Detention Program." As detailed in the intelligence chronology in Volume II, there is no evidence that Sajid Badat was "preparing another attack like that attempted by 'shoe bomber' Richard Reid." All intelligence collected after the December 22, 2001, attempted shoe bomb attack by Richard Reid indicated that his proposed partner "backed out of the operation." *See,* for example, CIA Headquarters document, entitled, "OPERATIONAL DEVELOPMENTS AGAINST GLOBAL SUNNI EXTREMIST TERRORISM," dated, "14 January 2002 1630 Hours."

[1623] Italics in original. CIA Talking Points entitled, "Talking Points for 10 March 2005 DCI Meeting PC: Effectiveness of the High-Value Detainee Interrogation (HVDI) Techniques."

[1624] CIA "Briefing Notes on the Value of Detainee Reporting" faxed from the CIA to the Department of Justice on April 15, 2005, at 10:47AM. *See also* a CIA document dated December 20, 2005, and entitled, "Examples of Detainee Reporting Used by Our CT Partners to Thwart Terrorists, 2003-2005," which includes four columns: "Detainees," "What They Told Us," "Actions Taken By Our CT Partners," and "Results." Under the heading of KSM and Ammar al-Baluchi, the document states: "What They Told Us..." "Provided lead information to Issa al-Britani, a.k.a. Sajid Badat in the United Kingdom, November 2003. KSM said Badat was an operative slated to launch a shoe-bomb attack simultaneously with Richard Reid in December 2001. Ammar al-Baluchi provided additional information on Badat...Results...Disrupted a shoe-bomb attack."

[1625] For additional information, *see* Volume I and Volume II.

he knew as 'Issa al-Pakistani'[1626]—as the operative who was slated to launch a simultaneous shoe bomb attack with Richard Reid in December 2001."[1627]

(TS// ████████████ //NF) The CIA provided similar inaccurate representations regarding the purported role of KSM and Ammar al-Baluchi[1628] in the discovery, identification, capture, and arrest of Sajid Badat in 16 of the 20 documents provided to policymakers and the Department of Justice between July 2003 and March 2009.[1629] However, in an additional case, a March 4, 2005, CIA briefing for Vice President Cheney, the CIA credited Abu Zubaydah with identifying Sajid Badat,[1630] despite a lack of any reporting on Sajid Badat from Abu Zubaydah.[1631]

[1626] There are no records of KSM identifying Sajid Badat as "Issa al-Pakistani." CIA records indicate that KSM stated he did not know Richard Reid's partner's true name, but referred to him only as "Abu Issa al-Britani" (described in CIA cables as "Abu Issa the Britain" [sic]), or as "Issa Richard." *See* intelligence chronology in Volume II, including ALEC ███████ (112157Z JUN 03).

[1627] CIA "Briefing Notes on the Value of Detainee Reporting" faxed from the CIA to the Department of Justice on April 15, 2005, at 10:47AM. As detailed in Volume II, there are no CIA records of KSM providing any reporting in November 2003 contributing to Sajid Badat's arrest.

[1628] CIA Briefing for Obama National Security Team- "Renditions, Detentions, and Interrogations (RDI)," including "Tab 7," named "RDG Copy- Briefing on RDI Program 09 Jan. 2009": "...[L]eads provided by KSM and Ammar al-Baluchi in November 2003 led directly to the arrest in the United Kingdom of Sajid Badat the operative who was slated to launch a simultaneous shoe-bomb attack with Richard Reid in December 2001." Ammar al-Baluchi, while still in foreign government custody, and prior to being transferred to CIA custody and subjected to the CIA's enhanced interrogation techniques, stated that he had contacted "Abu Issa" on behalf of KSM, but the CIA believed that Ammar al-Baluchi was providing inaccurate information. (*See* ALEC 206234 ██████████). ██████ [foreign partner] authorities later indicated that they believed that Ammar al-Baluchi was providing accurate reporting on Abu Issa. (*See* ██████ 10054 ██████████ Later, in CIA custody, Ammar al-Baluchi described Issa's connection to the Richard Reid plot. The CIA credited confronting Ammar al-Baluchi with emails as "key in gaining Ammar's admissions." (*See* ALEC ██████████ .) As detailed in Volume II, Ammar al-Baluchi, like KSM, was unable, or unwilling, to identify Sajid Badat by name.

[1629] *See* list of CIA prepared briefings and memoranda from 2003 through 2009 with representations on the effectiveness of the CIA's enhanced interrogation techniques referenced in this summary and described in detail in Volume II.

[1630] CIA briefing for Vice President Cheney, dated March 4, 2005, entitled, "Briefing for Vice President Cheney: CIA Detention and Interrogation Program." The briefing document states: "Shoe Bomber: Sajid Badat, an operative slated to launch a simultaneous shoe bomb attack with Richard Reid in December 2001, identified and captured. Source: Abu Zubaydah." There are no CIA records to support this statement. On August 17, 2003, Abu Zubaydah was shown a picture of Sajid Badat that a CIA officer stated "looks an awful lot like the sketches" from a detainee in foreign government custody. Abu Zubaydah stated he did not recognize the person in the photo. On August 22, 2003, sketches of Badat were shown to Abu Zubaydah, who did not recognize the individual depicted. *See* email from: ████████ ; to: ████████ (multiple ccs); subject: "Re: Meeting with ██████ "; date: August 17, 2003, at 1:04 PM; ██████ 12679 (181124Z AUG 03); ██████ 12713 (231932Z AUG 03).

[1631] The CIA also credited Abu Zubaydah, who was captured in March 2002, with identifying Richard Reid, who was arrested in December 2001. This inaccurate information was presented to select National Security Council principals, Secretary of State Powell and Secretary of Defense Rumsfeld, and Assistant Attorney General Jack Goldsmith. *See* CIA briefing slides entitled, "*CIA Interrogation Program,*" dated July 29, 2003, presented to senior White House officials (Memorandum for the Record; subject: CIA Interrogation Program; September 27, 2003 (OGC-FO-2003-50088); Slides, CIA Interrogation Program, 16 September 2003). The Memorandum for the Record drafted by John Bellinger refers to a "detailed handout" provided by the CIA. *See* John B. Bellinger III, Senior Associate Counsel to the President and Legal Advisor, National Security Council; Memorandum for the Record; subject: Briefing of Secretaries Powell and Rumsfeld regarding Interrogation of High-Value Detainees; date: September 30, 2003. *See also* Scott W. Muller; Memorandum for the Record; Interrogation briefing for Jack Goldsmith; date: 16 October 2003 (OGC-FO-2003-50097).

(TS// ███████████ //NF) Contrary to CIA representations, a review of CIA operational cables and other documents found that the CIA's enhanced interrogation techniques did not result in otherwise unavailable intelligence leading to the discovery, identification, capture, or arrest of Sajid Badat. According to CIA records and the U.K.'s own investigative summary,[1632] the investigation of Sajid Badat was a United Kingdom-led operation, and the intelligence that alerted security officials to: (1) a U.K.-based "Issa" (aka, Sajid Badat); (2) a potential second "shoe bomber" related to Richard Reid;[1633] (3) a suspected U.K. terrorist named "Sajid Badat";[1634] (4) Sajid Badat's connection to Richard Reid; (5) Sajid Badat's physical description; (6) Sajid Badat's location; and (7) the initial identification of a U.K. surveillance photo of Sajid Badat, the "shoe bomber,"[1635] was unrelated to information acquired from CIA detainees during or after the use of the CIA's enhanced interrogation techniques. CIA records indicate that the information that led to Sajid Badat's arrest and U.K. criminal prosecution was also not derived from the CIA's Detention and Interrogation Program.[1636]

(TS// ███████████ //NF) Prior to any reporting from CIA detainees, and as early as January 14, 2002, the FBI informed the CIA that Richard Reid "had an unidentified partner who allegedly backed out of the operation at the last minute."[1637] This information was later

---

[1632] ███████ 13165 ███████

[1633] The CIA's June 2013 Response maintains that "KSM was the first to tell [the CIA] there was a second shoe bomber and that he remained at large." The Committee found this statement to be incongruent with CIA records. There were multiple reports that Richard Reid had an unidentified partner prior to the provision of any information from KSM (captured on March 1, 2003). The CIA's June 2013 Response addresses only one of two documented efforts by the FBI in January 2002 to inform the CIA that Richard Reid had "an unidentified partner who allegedly backed out of the operation at the last minute." The CIA's June 2013 Response acknowledges that this FBI information was provided to senior CIA leadership in writing, but states that, on one of the two days the information was provided, "the Reid investigation came on page 10 of 15 pages of updates that day," and that the information did not "exist in any searchable CIA data repositories." The CIA's June 2013 Response also does not address the CIA's own source reporting on "another operative" who existed alongside Richard Reid. In April 2002, a reliable CIA source—who had warned of the Richard Reid shoe-bomb attack weeks before it occurred—reported that, in addition to Richard Reid, "another operative existed." The source stated that, instead of an airliner departing from Paris, as had Richard Reid's flight, "this attack would occur against an airliner originating from Heathrow International Airport in London." Once captured, Sajid Badat would confirm this reporting. Despite acknowledging evidence to the contrary, and without further explanation, the CIA stated in meetings with the Committee in 2013 that the CIA stands by its representations that "KSM was the first to tell [the CIA] there was a second shoe bomber and that he remained at large."

[1634] See Volume II, including FBI WASHINGTON DC ███████ (160429Z JUL 02). The CIA's June 2013 Response acknowledges that there was intelligence reporting that Sajid Badat was involved in terrorist activities and "targeting American interests," but defends its past assertions highlighting the effectiveness of the CIA's enhanced interrogation techniques in obtaining otherwise unavailable intelligence by asserting that, at the time of this reporting, there "was nothing at the time on Badat to lead [the CIA] to prioritize him over others."

[1635] The CIA's June 2013 Response states: "KSM was the first person to provide—in March 2003, after having undergone enhanced interrogation techniques in CIA custody—a detailed and authoritative narrative of al-Qa'ida development of and plans to use shoe bombs operationally." The CIA's June 2013 Response does not acknowledge intelligence acquired by the Intelligence Community on these matters prior to any reporting from KSM and does not address the significant amount of fabricated reporting KSM provided. See Volume II for additional information.

[1636] See Volume II for additional information.

[1637] The FBI information was provided to the CIA. See CIA Headquarters document, entitled, "OPERATIONAL DEVELOPMENTS AGAINST GLOBAL SUNNI EXTREMIST TERRORISM," dated, "14 January 2002 1630 Hours." The CIA's June 2013 Response acknowledges the existence of this CIA document and that the information in the document was "compiled... for counterterrorism seniors at CIA." The CIA's June 2013 Response nonetheless states that "[t]here is no reference to this possibility [of a possible second operative] in official communications

corroborated by a credible CIA source prior to any reporting from the CIA's Detention and Interrogation Program.[1638] In July 2002, a foreign government reported that pre-paid phone cards recovered by the FBI from Richard Reid upon his arrest were used by an individual named Sajid Badat to call a known terrorist, Nizar Trabelsi.[1639] FBI interviews of Trabelsi—officially relayed to the CIA in July 2002—reported that "L. Badad Sajid" was "involved in operations targeting American interests."[1640] The CIA highlighted in a July 2002 cable that this information matched previous reporting from a European government that identified a "Saajid Badat," of Gloucester, United Kingdom, with a date of birth of March 28, 1979, as a person suspected of being involved in terrorist activity.[1641] Additional analysis of the phone card connecting Badat and Reid—as well as other intelligence—placed Sajid Badat and Richard Reid together in Belgium in September 2001.[1642]

(TS// ███████████ //NF) According to ███████████ , Sajid Badat was linked to other well-known extremists in the United Kingdom who were already under investigation. Specifically, Badat was known to ███████████ as "a member of Babar Ahmad's group," and was a "particularly close associate of Mirza Beg." ███ reporting also determined that Badat had attended a jihad training camp in Afghanistan."[1643]

(TS// ███████████ //NF) Concurrent with the emergence of information linking Sajid Badat to Richard Reid, there was an ongoing international effort to identify one or more U.K.-based al-Qa'ida operatives known as "Issa."[1644] As early as June 2002, CIA records indicate that an

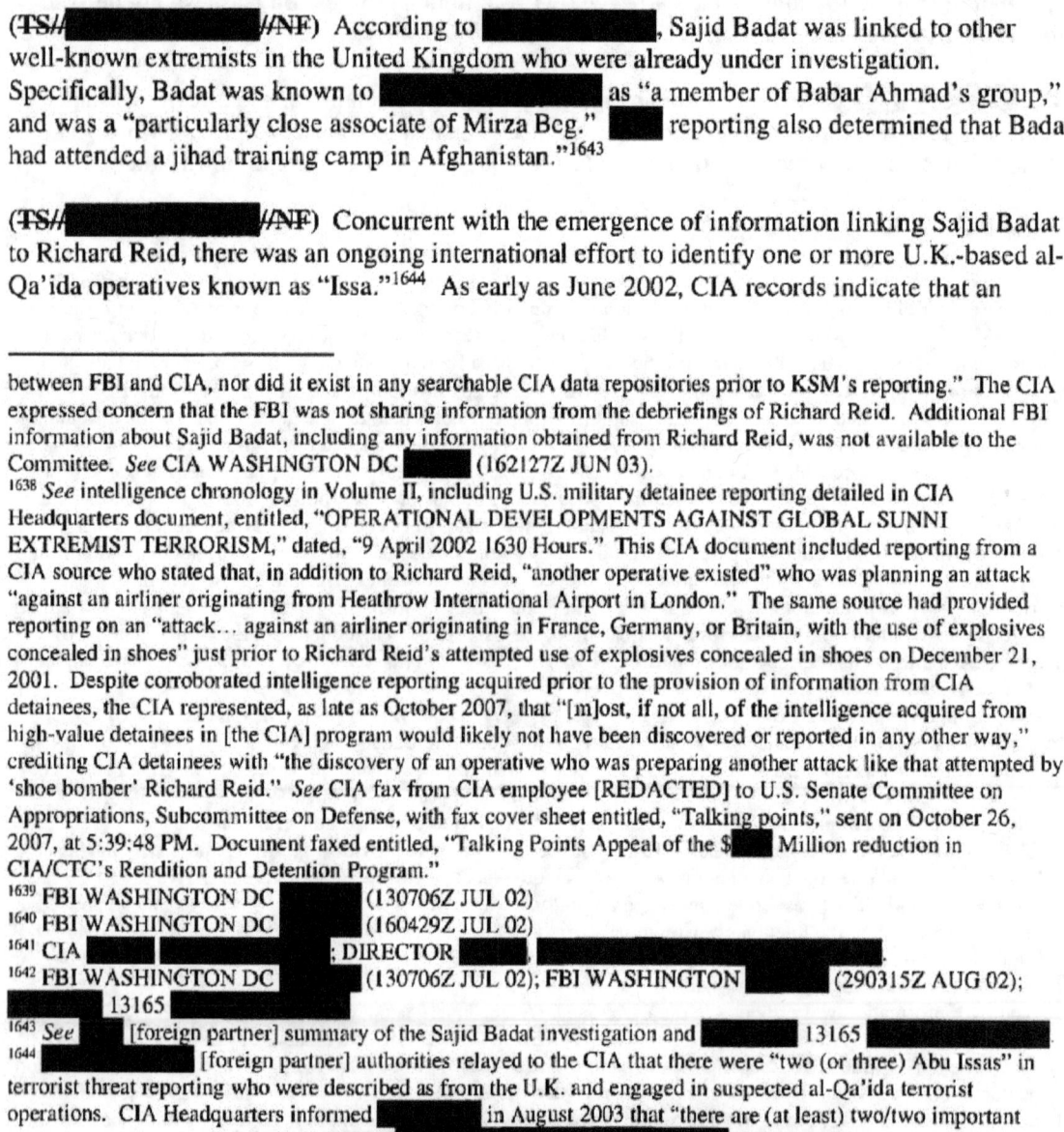

between FBI and CIA, nor did it exist in any searchable CIA data repositories prior to KSM's reporting." The CIA expressed concern that the FBI was not sharing information from the debriefings of Richard Reid. Additional FBI information about Sajid Badat, including any information obtained from Richard Reid, was not available to the Committee. *See* CIA WASHINGTON DC ███ (162127Z JUN 03).

[1638] *See* intelligence chronology in Volume II, including U.S. military detainee reporting detailed in CIA Headquarters document, entitled, "OPERATIONAL DEVELOPMENTS AGAINST GLOBAL SUNNI EXTREMIST TERRORISM," dated, "9 April 2002 1630 Hours." This CIA document included reporting from a CIA source who stated that, in addition to Richard Reid, "another operative existed" who was planning an attack "against an airliner originating from Heathrow International Airport in London." The same source had provided reporting on an "attack… against an airliner originating in France, Germany, or Britain, with the use of explosives concealed in shoes" just prior to Richard Reid's attempted use of explosives concealed in shoes on December 21, 2001. Despite corroborated intelligence reporting acquired prior to the provision of information from CIA detainees, the CIA represented, as late as October 2007, that "[m]ost, if not all, of the intelligence acquired from high-value detainees in [the CIA] program would likely not have been discovered or reported in any other way," crediting CIA detainees with "the discovery of an operative who was preparing another attack like that attempted by 'shoe bomber' Richard Reid." *See* CIA fax from CIA employee [REDACTED] to U.S. Senate Committee on Appropriations, Subcommittee on Defense, with fax cover sheet entitled, "Talking points," sent on October 26, 2007, at 5:39:48 PM. Document faxed entitled, "Talking Points Appeal of the $ ██ Million reduction in CIA/CTC's Rendition and Detention Program."

[1639] FBI WASHINGTON DC ████ (130706Z JUL 02)
[1640] FBI WASHINGTON DC ████ (160429Z JUL 02)
[1641] CIA ██████ : DIRECTOR ██████ .
[1642] FBI WASHINGTON DC ████ (130706Z JUL 02); FBI WASHINGTON ███ (290315Z AUG 02); ████████ 13165 ████
[1643] *See* ███ [foreign partner] summary of the Sajid Badat investigation and ████ 13165 ██████
[1644] ███████ [foreign partner] authorities relayed to the CIA that there were "two (or three) Abu Issas" in terrorist threat reporting who were described as from the U.K. and engaged in suspected al-Qa'ida terrorist operations. CIA Headquarters informed ██████ in August 2003 that "there are (at least) two/two important

individual in the custody of a foreign government, Abu Zubair al-Ha'ili, repeatedly referenced an "Abu Issa al-Pakistani" as a British-born Pakistani associated with Richard Reid and engaged in plotting in the United Kingdom at the behest of KSM.[1645] This information was corroborative of other intelligence reporting.[1646] In May 2003, this detainee met with CIA officers to produce several sketches that were described as having "achieved a 95% likeness" of this individual.[1647] On August 17, 2003, CIA officers noted that a photograph of Sajid Badat provided by ███████ ████████ [a foreign partner] looked "an awful lot like the sketches" of the Richard Reid associate made with the assistance of the detainee in foreign government custody.[1648]

(TS// ████████████ //NF) CIA Headquarters requested that the photograph be shown to CIA detainees. According to CIA records, on August 18, 2003, "KSM viewed the picture for a while, but said he did not recognize the person in the photo." When KSM was asked if Issa's name could be Sajid Badat, "KSM shrugged and said that the Badat name was not the name he recalled." Pressed further, KSM stated, "he was confident that the name Sajid Badat was not Issa's name."[1649] On August 22, 2003, emails among CIA officers stated that "CTC believes that Abu Issa's true name is Sajid Badat... KSM says that Badat is not Abu Issa—but he might be lying."[1650] On August 23, 2003, the detailed sketches derived from interviews of the detainee in

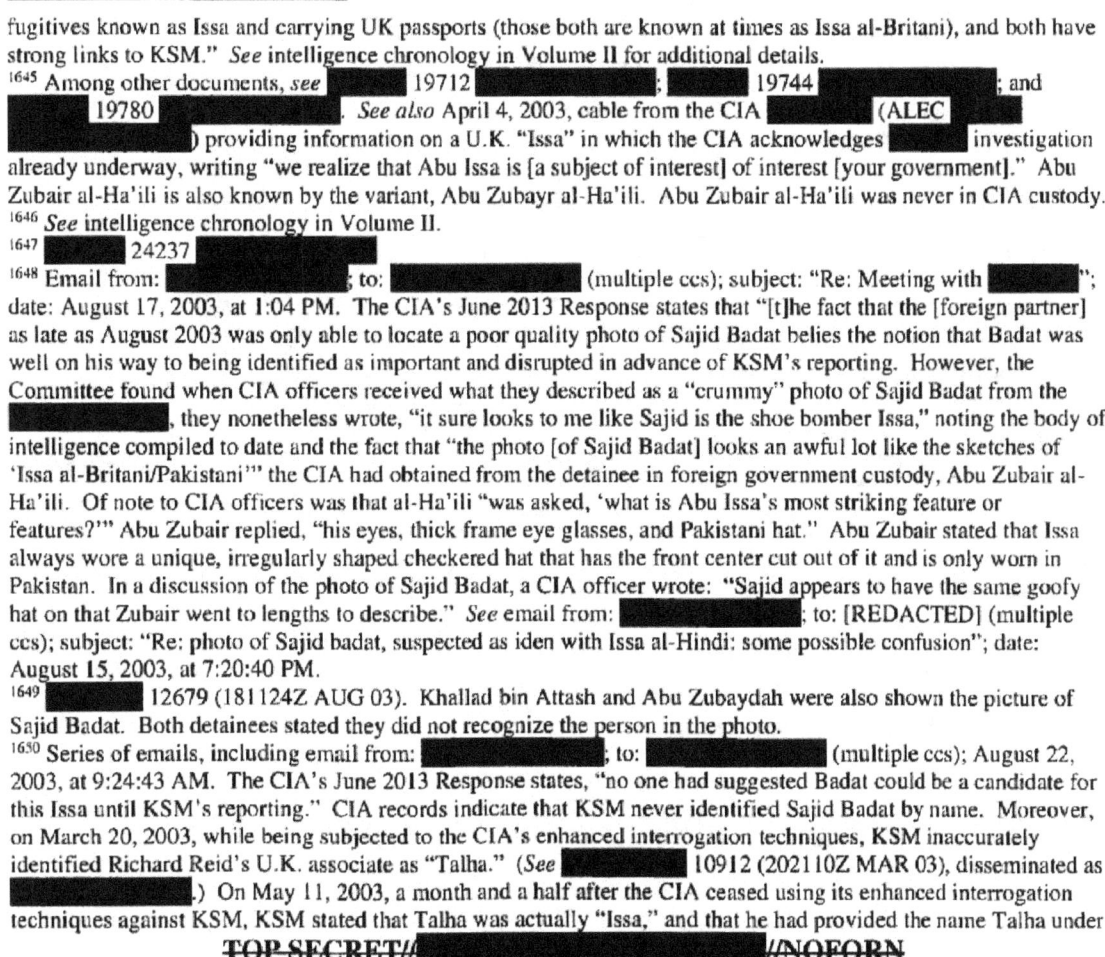

fugitives known as Issa and carrying UK passports (those both are known at times as Issa al-Britani), and both have strong links to KSM." *See* intelligence chronology in Volume II for additional details.
[1645] Among other documents, *see* ██████ 19712 ██████ ; ██████ 19744 ██████ ; and ██████ 19780 ██████ . *See also* April 4, 2003, cable from the CIA ██████ (ALEC ██████) providing information on a U.K. "Issa" in which the CIA acknowledges ██████ investigation already underway, writing "we realize that Abu Issa is [a subject of interest] of interest [your government]." Abu Zubair al-Ha'ili is also known by the variant, Abu Zubayr al-Ha'ili. Abu Zubair al-Ha'ili was never in CIA custody.
[1646] *See* intelligence chronology in Volume II.
[1647] ██████ 24237 ██████
[1648] Email from: ██████ ; to: ██████ (multiple ccs); subject: "Re: Meeting with ██████ "; date: August 17, 2003, at 1:04 PM. The CIA's June 2013 Response states that "[t]he fact that the [foreign partner] as late as August 2003 was only able to locate a poor quality photo of Sajid Badat belies the notion that Badat was well on his way to being identified as important and disrupted in advance of KSM's reporting. However, the Committee found when CIA officers received what they described as a "crummy" photo of Sajid Badat from the ██████ , they nonetheless wrote, "it sure looks to me like Sajid is the shoe bomber Issa," noting the body of intelligence compiled to date and the fact that "the photo [of Sajid Badat] looks an awful lot like the sketches of 'Issa al-Britani/Pakistani'" the CIA had obtained from the detainee in foreign government custody, Abu Zubair al-Ha'ili. Of note to CIA officers was that al-Ha'ili "was asked, 'what is Abu Issa's most striking feature or features?'" Abu Zubair replied, "his eyes, thick frame eye glasses, and Pakistani hat." Abu Zubair stated that Issa always wore a unique, irregularly shaped checkered hat that has the front center cut out of it and is only worn in Pakistan. In a discussion of the photo of Sajid Badat, a CIA officer wrote: "Sajid appears to have the same goofy hat on that Zubair went to lengths to describe." *See* email from: ██████ ; to: [REDACTED] (multiple ccs); subject: "Re: photo of Sajid badat, suspected as iden with Issa al-Hindi: some possible confusion"; date: August 15, 2003, at 7:20:40 PM.
[1649] ██████ 12679 (181124Z AUG 03). Khallad bin Attash and Abu Zubaydah were also shown the picture of Sajid Badat. Both detainees stated they did not recognize the person in the photo.
[1650] Series of emails, including email from: ██████ ; to: ██████ (multiple ccs); August 22, 2003, at 9:24:43 AM. The CIA's June 2013 Response states, "no one had suggested Badat could be a candidate for this Issa until KSM's reporting." CIA records indicate that KSM never identified Sajid Badat by name. Moreover, on March 20, 2003, while being subjected to the CIA's enhanced interrogation techniques, KSM inaccurately identified Richard Reid's U.K. associate as "Talha." (*See* ██████ 10912 (202110Z MAR 03), disseminated as ██████ .) On May 11, 2003, a month and a half after the CIA ceased using its enhanced interrogation techniques against KSM, KSM stated that Talha was actually "Issa," and that he had provided the name Talha under

foreign custody, Abu Zubair al-Ha'ili—the sketches CIA officers stated so closely resembled the ███ [foreign partner]-provided photos of Sajid Badat—were shown to KSM. KSM stated he did not recognize the individual in the sketches.[1651]

(TS// ██████████ //NF) Meanwhile, on August 21, 2003, a CIA cable noted that the ███ [foreign partner] had informed the CIA that joint interviews by the FBI and ███ [foreign partner] authorities of an individual in FBI custody, James Ujaama, led investigators in the U.K. to a home "formerly occupied by both Mirza [Beg] and Sajid [Badat]."[1652] The ███ [foreign partner] authorities relayed to the CIA that "at least one of these men was known by the alias Issa," and that the subjects were related to a separate ongoing terrorism investigation.[1653] On September 2, 2003, ███ [foreign partner] authorities informed the CIA that "secret and reliable" reporting indicated that Sajid Badat is the Richard Reid associate and shoe bomber. According to the ███ [foreign partner] report, ████████ [foreign partner information] linked Badat to a larger ██████ network in the United Kingdom, which was part of the larger aforementioned ███ [foreign partner] investigation.[1654]

(TS// ██████████ //NF) On September 9, 2003, a detainee in U.S. military custody at Guantanamo Bay, Cuba, identified a photograph of Sajid Badat to a visiting U.K. official as Abu Issa the "shoe bomber."[1655] The next day, KSM identified a photograph of Sajid Badat as "Issa al-Britani, aka Issa Richard"—the associate of Richard Reid. Other detainees in U.S. military custody subsequently identified the same photograph of Sajid Badat as "Abu Issa" the "shoebomber."[1656]

---

pressure and had now remembered the right name – Issa – after he had time to think about the question. *See* ███████ 11584 (111753Z MAY 03); DIRECTOR ███████ (121729Z MAY 03).
[1651] ███████ 12713 (231932Z AUG 03)
[1652] Ujaama had pled guilty to terrorism-related charges on April 14, 2003, and had agreed to continue cooperating with FBI officials on terrorism investigations. Earnest James Ujaama entered a guilty plea to a charge of conspiracy to provide goods and services to the Taliban on April 14, 2003. *See* U.S. Department of Justice press release dated April 14, 2003, and entitled, "Earnest James Ujaama Pleads Guilty to Conspiracy to Supply Goods and Services to the Taliban, Agrees to Cooperate with Terrorism Investigations."
[1653] ALEC ███████ (212117Z AUG 03). CIA records state that sometime prior to August 21, 2003, the FBI had entered Sajid Badat, with the correct identifying information, into ████████████ databases.
[1654] ████ 99093 (████████)
[1655] DIRECTOR ███████ ███ SEP 03)/ ████████████ . [REDACTED]. *See also* CIA ███ ███ DEC 03), which includes a "Comment" that "during a 9 September 2003 interview of [Feroze Ali] Abassi at Guantanamo Bay, Abbasi identified Badat as a participant in the 'information gathering course' at al-Faruq" terrorist training camp, about which Abassi had previously provided detailed information.
[1656] *See* ███████ 12806 (101910Z SEP 03) and ████████ 54986 (300927Z OCT 03). The CIA's June 2013 Response acknowledges that a U.S. military detainee first identified Sajid Badat, but argues that CIA representations on the effectiveness of the CIA's enhanced interrogation techniques in producing otherwise unavailable intelligence in this case were nonetheless accurate. The CIA's June 2013 Response states that KSM "did provide unique intelligence," and that "KSM's identification of Badat [in the ███ photo] was more important than others who also recognized the photograph—including one who identified the photo a day before KSM did—because only KSM at the time had characterized this Issa as a partner to Reid and as a would-be shoe bomber." As detailed in this summary and in greater detail in Volume II, the CIA's 2013 Response is incongruent with internal CIA records. After the arrest of Sajid Badat, U.K. authorities described their investigation of Sajid Badat ████████████ ████████████ . The United Kingdom highlighted information from a ████████ [specific U.K. intelligence collection on Sajid Badat] not further identified in CIA records. The U.K. record of investigation makes no reference to KSM's photo identification, but rather states: "reporting on 9 September 2003 confirmed that a U.S. military detainee had positively identified Saajid Badat as Abu Issa. We assess that Sajid Badat is identical with both

(~~TS/~~ ████████ ~~//NF~~) After conducting extensive surveillance of Sajid Badat, U.K. authorities arrested Badat on November 27, 2003.[1657] Badat immediately cooperated with U.K. investigators and confirmed he withdrew from a shoe bomb operation with Richard Reid in December 2001.[1658] On November 28, 2003, the United Kingdom provided a detailed account to the CIA on how investigative efforts in the United Kingdom led to the identification of Sajid Badat, noting that "key aspects" of reporting acquired from CIA, U.S. military, and foreign government detainees matched those of a "████████████" [specific U.K. intelligence collection on Sajid Badat]. The "████████████" [specific U.K. intelligence collection on Sajid Badat] was not previously referenced in U.K. investigative updates to the CIA.[1659]

(~~TS/~~ ████████ ~~//NF~~) After pleading guilty in a U.K. court on February 28, 2005, to terrorism-related charges, Sajid Badat was sentenced to 13 years in prison. ████████████ ██ Sajid "Badat was voluntarily cooperative throughout much of his pre-sentencing incarceration."[1660] On November 13, 2009, Sajid Badat's 13-year prison sentence was reduced to 11 years. In March 2010, approximately five years after his sentencing, Sajid Badat was released under an agreement whereby Badat became a cooperating witness for U.S. and U.K. authorities.[1661] The legal agreement came to light when Sajid Badat testified against Adis Medunjanin, a U.S. terrorism suspect on trial in New York, via a video-link from the United Kingdom in April 2012.[1662]

7. The Thwarting of the Heathrow Airport and Canary Wharf Plotting

---

Sajid and Abu Issa the shoebomber." *See* ████████ 13165 ████████NOV 03); DIRECTOR ████ (████SEP 03)████████████; [REDACTED]; CIA ████ (████DEC 03). *See also* the intelligence chronology in Volume II.

[1657] ALEC ████████████████; ████████ 13120 ████████████

[1658] ████ 13120 ████████████████

[1659] ████ 13165 ████████NOV 03). The ████ [foreign partner] report highlights how the "[a named foreign government] reported that on the 13 September 2001 Nizar [Trabelsi] was arrested for his alleged involvement in planning a terrorist attack against the American Embassy in Paris" and how Trabelsi was connected to a phone card "recovered from Richard Colvin Reid" but found to have been used by Sajid Badat. The report references a larger U.K. investigation, stating that Badat was found to be "a member of Babar Ahmad's group" and to have "attended a jihad training camp in Afghanistan." The ████ [foreign partner] report closes by stating: "Further reporting on 9 September 2003 confirmed that a U.S. military detainee had positively identified Saajid Badat as Abu Issa. We assess that Sajid Badat is identical with both Sajid and Abu Issa the shoebomber."

[1660] Email from: ████████████; to: [REDACTED], with multiple ccs; subject: "Re: Profile on Saajid Badat for coord by 6pm, 19 October 2005; date: October 19, 2005, at 3:14:29 PM.

[1661] *See* open source reporting, including "Secret Life of Shoe Bomb Saajid Badat Funded By The Taxpayer," U.K. *Telegraph,* dated April 23, 2012; "US court hears Bin Ladin testimony from UK bomb plotter," *BBC News,* dated April 24, 2012; "Operative Details Al Qaeda Plans to Hit Planes in Wake of 9/11," *CNN,* dated April 25, 2012; and "'Convention' of Convicted Terrorists at NY Trial," *NPR News,* dated April 24, 2012.

[1662] *See* open source reporting, including "Secret Life of Shoe Bomb Saajid Badat Funded By The Taxpayer," U.K. *Telegraph,* dated April 23, 2012; "US court hears Bin Ladin testimony from UK bomb plotter," *BBC News,* dated April 24, 2012; "Operative Details Al Qaeda Plans to Hit Planes in Wake of 9/11," *CNN,* dated April 25, 2012; "'Convention' of Convicted Terrorists at NY Trial," *NPR News,* dated April 24, 2012; and "Man Convicted of a Terrorist Plot to Bomb Subways Is Sent to Prison for Life," *New York Times,* dated November 16, 2012.

(TS// ██████████ //NF) *Summary:* The CIA represented that its enhanced interrogation techniques were effective and produced critical, otherwise unavailable intelligence, which thwarted plots and saved lives. Over a period of years, the CIA provided the identification and thwarting of the Heathrow Airport Plot as evidence for the effectiveness of the CIA's enhanced interrogation techniques. These representations were inaccurate. A review of records indicates that the Heathrow Airport and Canary Wharf plotting had not progressed beyond the initial planning stages when the operation was fully disrupted with the detentions of Ramzi bin al-Shibh, KSM, Ammar-al-Baluchi, and Khallad bin Attash. None of these individuals were captured as a result of reporting obtained during or after the use of the CIA's enhanced interrogation techniques against CIA detainees.

(TS// ██████████ //NF) *Further Details:* After the September 11, 2001, attacks against the United States, KSM sought to target the United Kingdom using hijacked aircraft and surmised that Heathrow Airport and a building in Canary Wharf, a major business district in London, were powerful economic symbols.[1663] The initial plan was for al-Qa'ida operatives to hijack multiple airplanes departing Heathrow Airport, turn them around, and crash them into the airport itself. Security was assessed to be too tight at Heathrow Airport and the plan was altered to focus on aircrafts departing from mainly Eastern European airports to conduct attacks against Heathrow Airport. Al-Qa'ida was unable to locate pilots to conduct these attacks.[1664] Once KSM was detained in Pakistan on March 1, 2003, responsibility for the planning was passed to Ammar al-Baluchi and Khallad bin Attash, who were at the time focused on carrying out attacks against Western interests in Karachi, Pakistan.[1665]

(TS// ██████████ //NF) The thwarting of the Heathrow Airport and Canary Wharf plotting is one of the eight most frequently cited examples provided by the CIA as evidence for the effectiveness of the CIA's enhanced interrogation techniques. Over a period of years, CIA documents prepared for and provided to senior policymakers, intelligence officials, and the Department of Justice represent the Heathrow Airport and Canary Wharf plotting as an example of how "[k]ey intelligence collected from HVD interrogations *after* applying interrogation techniques" had "enabled CIA to disrupt terrorist plots" and "capture additional terrorists."[1666] The CIA further represented that the intelligence acquired from the CIA's enhanced interrogation techniques was "otherwise unavailable" and "saved lives."[1667]

[1663] While the CIA refers to "Canary Wharf" as a potential target of KSM's plotting, intelligence records suggest the actual target was likely "One Canada Square," the tallest building in the United Kingdom at the time of the plotting, which is located in Canary Wharf, a major business district in London.

[1664] *See* detailed intelligence chronology in Volume II.

[1665] *See* the Karachi Plots section in this summary, as well as additional details in Volume II.

[1666] Italics included in CIA Memorandum to the Office of Legal Counsel, entitled, "Effectiveness of the CIA Counterterrorist Interrogation Techniques," from March 2, 2005.

[1667] From 2003 through 2009, the CIA's representations regarding the effectiveness of the CIA's enhanced interrogation techniques provided a specific set of examples of terrorist plots "disrupted" and terrorists captured that the CIA attributed to information obtained from the use of its enhanced interrogation techniques. CIA representations further asserted that the intelligence obtained from the use of the CIA's enhanced interrogation techniques was unique, otherwise unavailable, and resulted in "saved lives." Among other CIA representations, *see:* (1) CIA representations in the Department of Justice Office of Legal Counsel Memorandum, dated May 30, 2005, which relied on a series of highly specific CIA representations on the type of intelligence acquired from the use of the CIA's enhanced interrogation techniques to assess their legality. The CIA representations referenced by the OLC include that the use of the CIA's enhanced interrogation techniques was "necessary" to obtain "critical,"

(~~TS//~~ ████████ ~~//NF~~) For example, on December 23, 2005, CIA Director Porter Goss explained in a letter to National Security Advisor Stephen Hadley, Homeland Security Advisor Frances Townsend, and Director of National Intelligence John Negroponte, that he was

---

"vital," and "otherwise unavailable actionable intelligence" that was "essential" for the U.S. government to "detect and disrupt" terrorist threats. The OLC memorandum further states that "[the CIA] ha[s] informed [the OLC] that the CIA believes that this program is largely responsible for preventing a subsequent attack within the United States." (*See* Memorandum for John A. Rizzo, Senior Deputy General Counsel, Central Intelligence Agency, from Steven G. Bradbury, Principal Deputy Assistant Attorney General, Office of Legal Counsel, May 30, 2005, Re: Application of United States Obligations Under Article 16 of the Convention Against Torture to Certain Techniques that May Be Used in the Interrogation of High Value al Qaeda Detainees.) (2) CIA representations in the Department of Justice Office of Legal Counsel Memorandum dated July 20, 2007, which also relied on CIA representations on the type of intelligence acquired from the use of the CIA's enhanced interrogation techniques. Citing CIA documents and the President's September 6, 2006, speech describing the CIA's interrogation program (which was based on CIA-provided information), the OLC memorandum states: "The CIA interrogation program— and, in particular, its use of enhanced interrogation techniques—is intended to serve this paramount interest [security of the nation] by producing substantial quantities of otherwise unavailable intelligence. ...As the President explained [on September 6, 2006], 'by giving us information about terrorist plans we could not get anywhere else, the program has saved innocent lives.'" (*See* Memorandum for John A. Rizzo, Acting General Counsel, Central Intelligence Agency, from Steven G. Bradbury, Principal Deputy Assistant Attorney General, Office of Legal Counsel, July 20, 2007, Re: Application of the War Crimes Act, the Detainee Treatment Act, and Common Article 3 of the Geneva Conventions to Certain Techniques that May Be Used by the CIA in the Interrogation of High Value al Qaeda Detainees.) (3) CIA briefings for members of the National Security Council in July and September 2003 represented that "the use of Enhanced Techniques of one kind or another had produced significant intelligence information that had, in the view of CIA professionals, saved lives," and warned policymakers that "[t]ermination of this program will result in loss of life, possibly extensive." (*See* August 5, 2003 Memorandum for the Record from Scott Muller, Subject: Review of Interrogation Program on 29 July 2003; Briefing slides, CIA Interrogation Program, July 29, 2003; September 4, 2003, CIA Memorandum for the Record, Subject: Member Briefing; and September 26, 2003, Memorandum for the Record from Muller, Subject: CIA Interrogation Program.) (4) The CIA's response to the Office of Inspector General draft Special Review of the CIA program, which asserts: "Information [the CIA] received... as a result of the lawful use of enhanced interrogation techniques ('EITs') has almost certainly saved countless American lives inside the United States and abroad. The evidence points clearly to the fact that without the use of such techniques, we and our allies would [have] suffered major terrorist attacks involving hundreds, if not thousands, of casualties." (*See* Memorandum for: Inspector General; from: James Pavitt, Deputy Director for Operations; subject: re (S) Comments to Draft IG Special Review, "Counterterrorism Detention and Interrogation Program" 2003-7123-IG; date: February 27, 2004; attachment: February 24, 2004, Memorandum re Successes of CIA's Counterterrorism Detention and Interrogation Activities.) (5) CIA briefing documents for CIA Director Leon Panetta in February 2009, which state that the "CIA assesses that the RDI program worked and the [enhanced interrogation] techniques were effective in producing foreign intelligence," and that "[m]ost, if not all, of the timely intelligence acquired from detainees in this program would not have been discovered or reported by other means." (*See* CIA briefing documents for Leon Panetta, entitled, "Tab 9: DCIA Briefing on RDI Program-18FEB.2009" and graphic attachment, "Key Intelligence and Reporting Derived from Abu Zubaydah and Khalid Shaykh Muhammad (KSM)," including "DCIA Briefing on RDI Program" agenda, CIA document "EITs and Effectiveness," with associated documents, "Key Intelligence Impacts Chart: Attachment (AZ and KSM)," "Background on Key Intelligence Impacts Chart: Attachment," and "supporting references," to include "Background on Key Captures and Plots Disrupted.") (6) CIA document faxed to the Senate Select Committee on Intelligence on March 18, 2009, entitled, "SWIGERT and DUNBAR," located in Committee databases at DTS #2009-1258, which provides a list of "some of the key captures and disrupted plots" that the CIA had attributed to the use of the CIA's enhanced interrogation techniques, and stating: "CIA assesses that most, if not all, of the timely intelligence acquired from detainees in this program would not have been discovered or reported by any other means." *See* Volume II for additional CIA representations asserting that the CIA's enhanced interrogation techniques enabled the CIA to obtain unique, otherwise unavailable intelligence that "saved lives."

suspending the use of the CIA's enhanced interrogation techniques because of the passage of the Detainee Treatment Act (the "McCain amendment"). The letter stated:

> "...only 29 [CIA detainees] have undergone an interrogation that used one or more of the 13 [CIA enhanced interrogation] techniques.[1668] These interrogations produced intelligence that allowed the U.S., and its partners, to disrupt attacks such as 911-style attacks planned for the U.S. West Coast and *for Heathrow airport*. I can inform you with confidence that this program has allowed the U.S. to *save hundreds, if not thousands, of lives*."[1669]

(TS// ███████████ //NF) Similarly, the CIA informed the CIA inspector general on February 27, 2004, that:

> "As a result of the lawful use of EITs, *KSM also provided information on an al-Qa'ida plot for suicide airplane attacks outside of the United States that would have killed thousands of people in the United Kingdom.* ...Of note, even after KSM reported that al-Qa'ida was planning to target Heathrow, he at first repeatedly denied there was any other target than the airport. *Only after the repeated lawful use of EITs did he stop lying and admit that the sketch of a beam labeled Canary Wharf in his notebook was in fact an illustration that KSM the engineer drew himself in order to show another AQ operative that the beams in the Wharf* - like those in the World Trade Center would likely melt and collapse the building, killing all inside.... We are still debriefing detainees and following up on leads to destroy this cell, but *at a minimum the lawful use of EIT's on KSM provided us with critical information that alerted us to these threats*...."[1670]

(TS// ███████████ //NF) The CIA provided similar inaccurate representations regarding the Heathrow and Canary Wharf Plotting in 20 of the 20 documents provided to policymakers and the Department of Justice between July 2003 and March 2009.[1671]

(TS// ███████████ //NF) A review of CIA operational cables and other documents found that contrary to CIA representations, information acquired during or after the use of the CIA's

---

[1668] This information was incorrect. CIA records indicate that by December 23, 2005, at least 38 CIA detainees had been subjected to the CIA's enhanced interrogation techniques.

[1669] Italics added. "Impact of the Loss of the Detainee Program to CT Operations and Analysis," prepared to support a letter from CIA Director Goss to Stephen J. Hadley, Assistant to the President/National Security Advisor, Frances F. Townsend, Assistant to the President/Homeland Security Advisor, and Ambassador John D. Negroponte, dated December 23, 2005.

[1670] Italics added. CIA memorandum to the CIA Inspector General from James Pavitt, CIA's Deputy Director for Operations, dated February 27, 2004, with the subject line, "Comments to Draft IG Special Review, 'Counterterrorism Detention and Interrogation Program' (2003-7123-IG)," Attachment, "Successes of CIA's Counterterrorism Detention and Interrogation Activities," dated February 24, 2004.

[1671] *See* list of CIA prepared briefings and memoranda from 2003 through 2009 with representations on the effectiveness of the CIA's enhanced interrogation techniques referenced in this summary and described in detail in Volume II.

enhanced interrogation techniques played no role in "alert[ing]" the CIA to the threat to—or "disrupt[ing]" the plotting against—Heathrow Airport and Canary Wharf.[1672]

(TS// ███████████ //NF) Prior to the detention and interrogation of the CIA detainees credited by the CIA with providing information on the plot, the CIA and other intelligence agencies were already "alerted" to al-Qa'ida's efforts to target Heathrow Airport. Specifically, the CIA knew that: (1) KSM and al-Qa'ida were targeting "a national symbol in the United Kingdom" and that this symbol was the "Heathrow airport";[1673] (2) the attack plan called for hijacking commercial aircraft and crashing them directly into Heathrow airport;[1674] (3) no pilots had been identified by al-Qa'ida and the planned attack was not imminent;[1675] (4) KSM, Ammar

---

[1672] As described in this Study, the CIA consistently represented from 2003 through 2009 that the use of the CIA's enhanced interrogation techniques resulted in "disrupted plots," listed the "Heathrow Plot" as disrupted "as a result of the EITs," and informed policymakers that the information acquired to disrupt the plotting could not have been obtained from other intelligence sources or methods available to the U.S. government. In at least one CIA representation to White House officials that highlighted the Heathrow plotting, the CIA represented that "the use of the [CIA's enhanced interrogation] techniques has produced significant results," and warned policymakers that "[t]ermination of this [CIA] program will result in loss of life, possibly extensive." The CIA's June 2013 Response states: "CIA disagrees with the *Study's* assessment that [the CIA] incorrectly represented that information derived from interrogating detainees helped disrupt al-Qa'ida's targeting of Heathrow Airport and Canary Wharf in London, including in President Bush's 2006 speech on the Program. Detainee reporting, including some which was acquired after enhanced interrogation techniques were applied, played a critical role in uncovering the plot, understanding it, detaining many of the key players, and ultimately allowing us to conclude it had been disrupted. It is a complex story, however, and we should have been clearer in delineating the roles played by different partners." As described in this summary, past CIA representations concerning the Heathrow Airport plotting and intelligence acquired "as a result of" the CIA's enhanced interrogation techniques were inaccurate. (*See,* among other records, the September 6, 2006, speech by President Bush, based on CIA information and vetted by the CIA, which describes the CIA's use of "an alternative set" of interrogation procedures and stating: "These are some of the plots that have been stopped because of the information of this vital program. Terrorists held in CIA custody...have helped stop a plot to hijack passenger planes and fly them into Heathrow or Canary Wharf in London.") Contrary to the CIA's June 2013 assertion, CIA records indicate that information related to the use of the CIA's enhanced interrogation techniques played *no* role in "detaining many of the key players" and played *no* role in "uncovering the [Heathrow] plot." CIA records indicate the Heathrow Airport plotting had not progressed beyond the initial planning stages when the operation was fully disrupted with the detention of Ramzi bin al-Shibh (detained on September 11, 2002), KSM (detained on March 1, 2003), Ammar-al-Baluchi (detained on April 29, 2003), and Khallad bin Attash (detained on April 29, 2003). The CIA's June 2013 Response states that "[b]y all accounts, KSM's arrest was the action that most disrupted the [Heathrow] plot." As detailed in this summary and in greater detail in Volume II, the capture of these detainees—including KSM—was unrelated to any reporting from CIA detainees. CIA records further indicate that details on al-Qa'ida's targeting of Heathrow Airport were acquired prior to any reporting from CIA detainees. For example, prior to receiving any information from CIA detainees, the CIA acquired detailed information about al-Qa'ida's targeting of Heathrow Airport, to include, but not limited to, the al-Qa'ida senior leaders involved, the method of the planned attack, the status of the operation, and the *kunyas* of two potential unwitting operatives in the United Kingdom. Finally, the CIA's June 2013 Response claims that its past CIA representations were accurate and that CIA "detainee reporting, including some which was acquired after enhanced interrogation techniques were applied, played a critical role" in providing information, "ultimately allowing [CIA] to conclude it had been disrupted." Prior to June 2013, the CIA had never represented that the use of the CIA's enhanced interrogation techniques produced information "allowing [CIA] to conclude [the Heathrow Plot] had been disrupted." Rather, as detailed in this summary and more fully in Volume II, the CIA represented that the information acquired "as a result of EITs" produced unique, otherwise unavailable "actionable intelligence" that "saved lives" and disrupted the plotting itself. As detailed, these representations were inaccurate.

[1673] DIRECTOR ███ (172132Z OCT 02)
[1674] DIRECTOR ███ (172132Z OCT 02)
[1675] DIRECTOR ███ (172132Z OCT 02)

al-Baluchi, and Ramzi bin al-Shibh were involved in or knowledgeable about the plotting;[1676] (5) al-Qa'ida was seeking to recruit numerous operatives, but potentially already had two operatives in place in the United Kingdom named "Abu Yusif" and "Abu Adel," although the two operatives were unwitting of the plot;[1677] and (6) KSM was seeking Saudi and British passport holders over the age of 30 for the attack.[1678]

(TS// ███████████ //NF) A review of records indicates that the Heathrow Airport plotting had not progressed beyond the initial planning stages when the operation was fully disrupted with the detentions of Ramzi bin al-Shibh (detained on September 11, 2002),[1679] KSM (detained on March 1, 2003),[1680] Ammar-al-Baluchi (detained on April 29, 2003), and Khallad bin Attash (detained on April 29, 2003,).[1681] There are no CIA records to indicate that any of the individuals were captured as a result of CIA detainee reporting. A draft National Terrorism Bulletin from March 2006 states: "the [Heathrow Airport] operation was disrupted mid-cycle, around the spring of 2003, when several of the key plotters, including KSM, were detained."[1682] Foreign government intelligence analysis came to the same conclusion.[1683]

(TS// ███████████ //NF) While each of these four detainees provided information on the plotting during their detentions, none of this information played any role in the disruption of the plot. A wide body of intelligence reporting indicated that no operatives were informed of the

---

[1676] [REDACTED] 20901 (301117Z SEP 02). *See also* ██████████, CIA ████████████████

[1677] CIA ████ ████████. In October 2002, months prior to KSM's capture, Ramzi bin al-Shibh (RBS), who had not yet been rendered to CIA custody and therefore not yet subjected to the CIA's enhanced interrogation techniques, identified Abu Yusef and Abu Adil as potential U.K.-based Heathrow operatives. RBS described how the two English-speaking "al-Qa'ida suicide operatives" were dispatched to the United Kingdom by KSM. RBS provided a detailed description of the two potential operatives, as well as their travel. (*See* CIA ████ ████ ██████) KSM was captured on March 1, 2003. The CIA's June 2013 Response nonetheless asserts that "KSM also was responsible for helping us identify two potential operatives—known only as Abu Yusef and Abu Adil— whom al-Qa'ida had deployed to the United Kingdom by early 2002 and whom KSM wanted to tap for a role in a future Heathrow operation." U.K. investigative efforts led to the identification of Abu Yusef, who then identified Abu Adil—who was already an investigative target of the U.K. government. In February 2004, the CIA reported that no CIA detainee was able to identify a photograph of Abu Yusif. *See* ALEC ████ (262236Z FEB 04).

[1678] DIRECTOR ████ (172132Z OCT 02)

[1679] *See* section of this summary and Volume II on the "Capture of Ramzi bin al-Shibh." The CIA's June 2013 Response states that "the information provided by Abu Zubaydah played a key role in the capture of Ramzi Bin al-Shibh." As described in the "Capture of Ramzi bin al-Shibh" in this summary and in greater detail in Volume II, Ramzi bin al-Shibh was not captured as a result of information acquired during or after the use of the CIA's enhanced interrogation techniques against Abu Zubaydah.

[1680] *See* section of this summary and Volume II on the Capture of Khalid Shaykh Mohammad (KSM). The CIA's June 2013 Response acknowledges that "[b]y all accounts, KSM's arrest was the action that most disrupted the [Heathrow] plot." The CIA's June 2013 Response asserts, however, that "[Abu] Zubaydah's reporting also contributed to KSM's arrest." As described in the "Capture of KSM" in this summary and in more detail in Volume II, the capture of KSM was not attributable to any information obtained from the CIA's Detention and Interrogation Program.

[1681] As described in the section of this summary related to the "Karachi Plot(s)" and in more detail in Volume II, information from CIA detainees played no role in the arrests of Ammar al-Baluchi or Khallad bin Attash.

[1682] *See* series of emails dated March 22, 2006, with the subject line, "RE:Abu Adel NTB Coord: Please Respond by 14:00 Today (3/22). *See also* series of emails dated March 22, 2006, with the subject line, "RE:Abu Adel NTB Coord: Please Respond by 14:00 Today (3/22).

[1683] DIRECTOR ████ ████

plot, no pilots were ever identified by al-Qa'ida for the attacks, and only schedules of potential flights were collected for review.[1684]

(~~TS//~~ █████████ ~~//NF~~) CIA detainee records indicate that reporting from CIA detainees on aspects of the Heathrow plotting was often unreliable and not believed by CIA officers. For example, KSM retracted information he provided while being subjected to the CIA's enhanced interrogation techniques, including information linking Jaffar al-Tayyar to the Heathrow Plot.[1685] On May 20, 2003, nearly two months after the CIA ceased using its enhanced interrogation techniques against KSM, a CIA analyst wrote that KSM had provided three different stories related to the Heathrow plotting, writing to CIA colleagues: "Bottom Line: KSM knows more about this plot than he's letting on."[1686] By late June 2004, KSM had retracted much of the varied reporting he had provided on the Heathrow plotting, most importantly the information KSM provided on tasking potential operatives to obtain flight training.[1687] KSM stated that during March 2003—when he was being subjected to the CIA's enhanced interrogation techniques—"he may have given false information," and that, in many cases, the information he provided was "just speculation."[1688] The value of other CIA detainee reporting was also questioned by CIA officers.[1689] In July 2003, a cable from the CIA's ALEC Station stated that "HQS/ALEC remains concerned with what we believe to be paltry information coming from detainees about operations in the U.K."[1690]

(~~TS//~~ █████████ ~~//NF~~) In addition, KSM withheld information linking Abu Talha al-Pakistani to the Heathrow plotting. According to CIA interrogation records, KSM discussed Canary Wharf the first time he was shown his notebook, in which the words "Canary Wharf" were written.[1691] KSM stated, however, that he had drawn the sketch for Ammar al-Baluchi. In

---

[1684] Among other documents, *see* DIRECTOR █████ (172132Z OCT 02).
[1685] *See* CIA WASHINGTON DC █████ (122310Z MAR 03); █████ 10883 (182127Z MAR 03); █████ 10828 (151310Z MAR 03); █████ 11717 (201722Z MAY 03); █████ 10778 (121549Z MAR 03).
[1686] *See* email from: [REDACTED]; to: █████; cc: █████, █████; subject: "KSM on Heathrow"; date: May 20, 2003, at 03:44 PM.
[1687] █████ 22939 (031541Z JUL 04)
[1688] █████ 22939 (031541Z JUL 04)
[1689] In March 2003, after Ramzi bin al-Shibh had been rendered to CIA custody and subjected to the CIA's enhanced interrogation techniques, CIA officers wrote that they did "not believe [Ramzi] bin al-Shibh" was "being completely honest" about potential Heathrow operatives. (*See* ALEC █████████.) A June 2003 CIA cable states that "KSM, Ammar, and Khallad remain loathe to reveal details of the Heathrow plot," and that the CIA believed the detainees were withholding information that could lead to the capture of Abu Talha al-Pakistani, noting specifically that the CIA detainees had "so far clung to such information" and "deflected questions." By this time KSM, Ammar al-Baluchi and Khallad bin Attash had all been rendered to CIA custody and subjected to the CIA's enhanced interrogation techniques. See ALEC █████ (172242Z JUN 03) and Volume III for additional information.
[1690] ALEC █████ (161821Z JUL 03)
[1691] █████ 10787 (130716Z MAR 03). As described, the CIA represented that KSM "first repeatedly denied there was any other target than the airport," and "[o]nly after the repeated lawful use of EITs did [KSM] stop lying and admit that the sketch of a beam labeled Canary Wharf in his notebook was in fact an illustration that KSM the engineer drew himself in order to show another AQ operative that the beams in the Wharf – like those in the World Trade Center would likely melt and collapse the building, killing all inside" (*See* CIA memorandum to the CIA Inspector General from James Pavitt, CIA's Deputy Director for Operations, dated February 27, 2004, with the subject line, "Comments to Draft IG Special Review, 'Counterterrorism Detention and Interrogation Program' (2003-7123-IG)," Attachment, "Successes of CIA's Counterterrorism Detention and Interrogation Activities," dated

June 2003, after being confronted with contradictory reporting from Ammar al-Baluchi, KSM admitted that he had actually shown the sketch to "Talha," whom KSM had not previously mentioned.[1692]

8. The Capture of Hambali

(TS// ███████████ //NF) *Summary:* The CIA represented that its enhanced interrogation techniques were effective and produced critical, otherwise unavailable intelligence, which thwarted plots and saved lives. Over a period of years, the CIA provided the capture of Hambali as evidence for the effectiveness of the CIA's enhanced interrogation techniques. Specifically, the CIA consistently represented that, as a result of the CIA's enhanced interrogation techniques, KSM provided the "*first*" information on a money transfer by Majid Khan that eventually led to Hambali's capture. These CIA representations were inaccurate. Majid Khan, who was in foreign government custody, provided this information prior to any reporting from KSM. CIA records indicate that the intelligence that led to Hambali's capture in Thailand was based on signals intelligence, a CIA source, and Thai investigative activities.

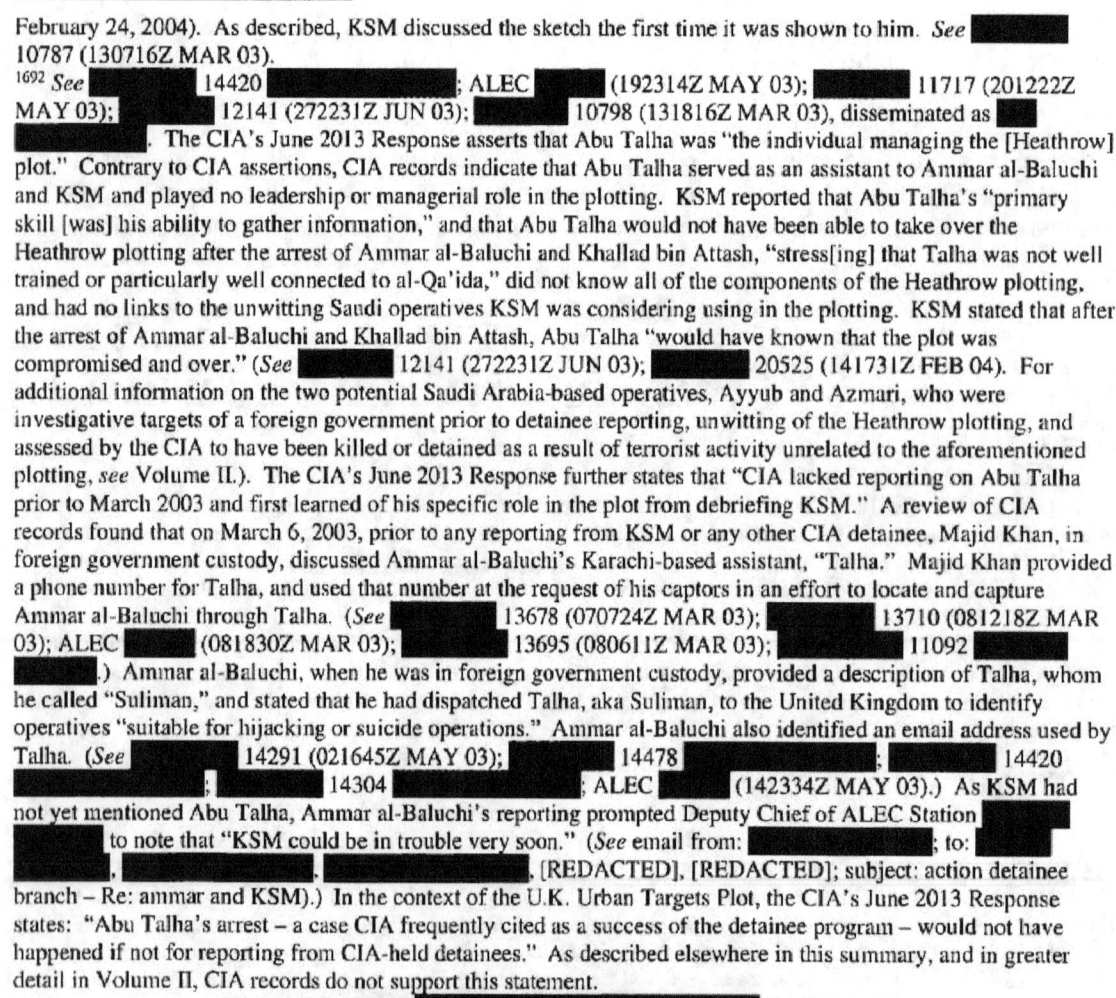

February 24, 2004). As described, KSM discussed the sketch the first time it was shown to him. *See* ███████████
10787 (130716Z MAR 03).

[1692] *See* ████ 14420 ████████ ; ALEC ████ (192314Z MAY 03); ████ 11717 (201222Z MAY 03); ████ 12141 (272231Z JUN 03); ████ 10798 (131816Z MAR 03), disseminated as ████ . The CIA's June 2013 Response asserts that Abu Talha was "the individual managing the [Heathrow] plot." Contrary to CIA assertions, CIA records indicate that Abu Talha served as an assistant to Ammar al-Baluchi and KSM and played no leadership or managerial role in the plotting. KSM reported that Abu Talha's "primary skill [was] his ability to gather information," and that Abu Talha would not have been able to take over the Heathrow plotting after the arrest of Ammar al-Baluchi and Khallad bin Attash, "stress[ing] that Talha was not well trained or particularly well connected to al-Qa'ida," did not know all of the components of the Heathrow plotting, and had no links to the unwitting Saudi operatives KSM was considering using in the plotting. KSM stated that after the arrest of Ammar al-Baluchi and Khallad bin Attash, Abu Talha "would have known that the plot was compromised and over." (*See* ████ 12141 (272231Z JUN 03); ████ 20525 (141731Z FEB 04). For additional information on the two potential Saudi Arabia-based operatives, Ayyub and Azmari, who were investigative targets of a foreign government prior to detainee reporting, unwitting of the Heathrow plotting, and assessed by the CIA to have been killed or detained as a result of terrorist activity unrelated to the aforementioned plotting, *see* Volume II.). The CIA's June 2013 Response further states that "CIA lacked reporting on Abu Talha prior to March 2003 and first learned of his specific role in the plot from debriefing KSM." A review of CIA records found that on March 6, 2003, prior to any reporting from KSM or any other CIA detainee, Majid Khan, in foreign government custody, discussed Ammar al-Baluchi's Karachi-based assistant, "Talha." Majid Khan provided a phone number for Talha, and used that number at the request of his captors in an effort to locate and capture Ammar al-Baluchi through Talha. (*See* ████ 13678 (070724Z MAR 03); ████ 13710 (081218Z MAR 03); ALEC ████ (081830Z MAR 03); ████ 13695 (080611Z MAR 03); ████ 11092 ████ .) Ammar al-Baluchi, when he was in foreign government custody, provided a description of Talha, whom he called "Suliman," and stated that he had dispatched Talha, aka Suliman, to the United Kingdom to identify operatives "suitable for hijacking or suicide operations." Ammar al-Baluchi also identified an email address used by Talha. (*See* ████ 14291 (021645Z MAY 03); ████ 14478 ; ████ 14420 ████████ ; ████ 14304 ████ ; ALEC ████ (142334Z MAY 03).) As KSM had not yet mentioned Abu Talha, Ammar al-Baluchi's reporting prompted Deputy Chief of ALEC Station ████ to note that "KSM could be in trouble very soon." (*See* email from: ████ ; to: ████ , ████ , ████ , [REDACTED], [REDACTED]; subject: action detainee branch – Re: ammar and KSM.) In the context of the U.K. Urban Targets Plot, the CIA's June 2013 Response states: "Abu Talha's arrest – a case CIA frequently cited as a success of the detainee program – would not have happened if not for reporting from CIA-held detainees." As described elsewhere in this summary, and in greater detail in Volume II, CIA records do not support this statement.

(TS// ███████ //NF) *Further Details:* Riduan bin Isomuddin, aka Hambali, was a senior member of Jemaah Islamiyah (JI), a Southeast Asia-based terrorist group, and served as an interface between the JI and al-Qa'ida. Hambali was linked to terrorist activity prior to the September 11, 2001, attacks. Shortly after those attacks, Hambali was described as the CIA's "number one target" in Southeast Asia.[1693] When the October 12, 2002, terrorist attacks occurred on the Indonesian island of Bali, killing more than 200 individuals, Hambali was immediately suspected of being the "mastermind" of the attacks and was further described as "one of the world's most wanted terrorists."[1694]

(TS// ███████ //NF) The capture of Hambali is one of the eight most frequently cited examples provided by the CIA as evidence for the effectiveness of the CIA's enhanced interrogation techniques. Over a period of years, CIA documents prepared for and provided to senior policymakers, intelligence officials, and the Department of Justice represent the capture of Hambali as an example of how "[k]ey intelligence collected from HVD interrogations *after* applying interrogation techniques" had "enabled CIA to disrupt terrorist plots" and "capture additional terrorists."[1695] The CIA further represented that the intelligence acquired from the CIA's enhanced interrogation techniques was "otherwise unavailable" and "saved lives."[1696]

[1693] DIRECTOR ███ (241921Z MAR 02)

[1694] Among other news sources, *see* "The Secret Mastermind Behind the Bali Horror," *The Observer*, 19 October 2002.

[1695] Italics included in CIA Memorandum to the Office of Legal Counsel, entitled, "Effectiveness of the CIA Counterterrorist Interrogation Techniques," from March 2, 2005.

[1696] From 2003 through 2009, the CIA's representations regarding the effectiveness of the CIA's enhanced interrogation techniques provided a specific set of examples of terrorist plots "disrupted" and terrorists captured that the CIA attributed to information obtained from the use of its enhanced interrogation techniques. CIA representations further asserted that the intelligence obtained from the use of the CIA's enhanced interrogation techniques was unique, otherwise unavailable, and resulted in "saved lives." Among other CIA representations, *see*: (1) CIA representations in the Department of Justice Office of Legal Counsel Memorandum, dated May 30, 2005, which relied on a series of highly specific CIA representations on the type of intelligence acquired from the use of the CIA's enhanced interrogation techniques to assess their legality. The CIA representations referenced by the OLC include that the use of the CIA's enhanced interrogation techniques was "necessary" to obtain "critical," "vital," and "otherwise unavailable actionable intelligence" that was "essential" for the U.S. government to "detect and disrupt" terrorist threats. The OLC memorandum further states that "[the CIA] ha[s] informed [the OLC] that the CIA believes that this program is largely responsible for preventing a subsequent attack within the United States." (*See* Memorandum for John A. Rizzo, Senior Deputy General Counsel, Central Intelligence Agency, from Steven G. Bradbury, Principal Deputy Assistant Attorney General, Office of Legal Counsel, May 30, 2005, Re: Application of United States Obligations Under Article 16 of the Convention Against Torture to Certain Techniques that May Be Used in the Interrogation of High Value al Qaeda Detainees.) (2) CIA representations in the Department of Justice Office of Legal Counsel Memorandum dated July 20, 2007, which also relied on CIA representations on the type of intelligence acquired from the use of the CIA's enhanced interrogation techniques. Citing CIA documents and the President's September 6, 2006, speech describing the CIA's interrogation program (which was based on CIA-provided information), the OLC memorandum states: "The CIA interrogation program— and, in particular, its use of enhanced interrogation techniques—is intended to serve this paramount interest [security of the Nation] by producing substantial quantities of otherwise unavailable intelligence. ...As the President explained [on September 6, 2006], 'by giving us information about terrorist plans we could not get anywhere else, the program has saved innocent lives.'" (*See* Memorandum for John A. Rizzo, Acting General Counsel, Central Intelligence Agency, from Steven G. Bradbury, Principal Deputy Assistant Attorney General, Office of Legal Counsel, July 20, 2007, Re: Application of the War Crimes Act, the Detainee Treatment Act, and Common Article 3 of the Geneva Conventions to Certain Techniques that May Be Used by the CIA in the Interrogation of High Value

(TS// ██████████ //NF) As an example, in a briefing prepared for the president's chief of staff, Josh Bolten, on May 2, 2006, the CIA represented that the "[u]se of the DOJ-authorized *enhanced interrogation techniques*, as part of a comprehensive interrogation approach, has enabled us to disrupt terrorist plots, capture additional terrorists, and collect a high volume of critical intelligence on al-Qa'ida."[1697] The briefing document represents that "[a]ssessing the effectiveness of individual interrogation techniques is difficult," but provides 11 specific examples of "Key Intelligence Collected from HVD Interrogations," including:

> "Hambali's Capture: During KSM's interrogation we acquired information
> that led to the capture of Hambali in August 2003 and to the partial
> dismantling of the Jemaah Islamiyah leadership in SE Asia. *KSM first told us*
> about Majid Khan's role in delivering $50,000 to Hambali operatives for an
> attack KSM believed was imminent. *We then confronted Khan with KSM's*
> *admission* and [signals intelligence] confirming the money transfer and Khan's
> travel to Bangkok. Khan admitted he delivered the money to an operative
> named 'Zubair,' whom we subsequently identified and captured. Zubair's
> capture led to the identification and subsequent capture of an operative named

---

al Qaeda Detainees.) (3) CIA briefings for members of the National Security Council in July and September 2003 represented that "the use of Enhanced Techniques of one kind or another had produced significant intelligence information that had, in the view of CIA professionals, saved lives," and warned policymakers that "[t]ermination of this program will result in loss of life, possibly extensive." (*See* August 5, 2003 Memorandum for the Record from Scott Muller, Subject: Review of Interrogation Program on 29 July 2003; Briefing slides, CIA Interrogation Program, July 29, 2003; September 4, 2003, CIA Memorandum for the Record, Subject: Member Briefing; and September 26, 2003, Memorandum for the Record from Muller, Subject: CIA Interrogation Program.) (4) The CIA's response to the Office of Inspector General draft Special Review of the CIA program, which asserts: "Information [the CIA] received... as a result of the lawful use of enhanced interrogation techniques ('EITs') has almost certainly saved countless American lives inside the United States and abroad. The evidence points clearly to the fact that without the use of such techniques, we and our allies would [have] suffered major terrorist attacks involving hundreds, if not thousands, of casualties." (*See* Memorandum for: Inspector General; from: James Pavitt, Deputy Director for Operations; subject: re (S) Comments to Draft IG Special Review, "Counterterrorism Detention and Interrogation Program" 2003-7123-IG; date: February 27, 2004; attachment: February 24, 2004, Memorandum re Successes of CIA's Counterterrorism Detention and Interrogation Activities.) (5) CIA briefing documents for CIA Director Leon Panetta in February 2009, which state that the "CIA assesses that the RDI program worked and the [enhanced interrogation] techniques were effective in producing foreign intelligence," and that "[m]ost, if not all, of the timely intelligence acquired from detainees in this program would not have been discovered or reported by other means." (*See* CIA briefing documents for Leon Panetta, entitled, "Tab 9: DCIA Briefing on RDI Program-18FEB.2009" and graphic attachment, "Key Intelligence and Reporting Derived from Abu Zubaydah and Khalid Shaykh Muhammad (KSM)," including "DCIA Briefing on RDI Program" agenda, CIA document "EITs and Effectiveness," with associated documents, "Key Intelligence Impacts Chart: Attachment (AZ and KSM)," "Background on Key Intelligence Impacts Chart: Attachment," and "supporting references," to include "Background on Key Captures and Plots Disrupted.") (6) CIA document faxed to the Senate Select Committee on Intelligence on March 18, 2009, entitled, "[SWIGERT] and [DUNBAR]," located in Committee databases at DTS #2009-1258, which provides a list of "some of the key captures and disrupted plots" that the CIA had attributed to the use of the CIA's enhanced interrogation techniques, and stating: "CIA assesses that most, if not all, of the timely intelligence acquired from detainees in this program would not have been discovered or reported by any other means." *See* Volume II for additional CIA representations asserting that the CIA's enhanced interrogation techniques enabled the CIA to obtain unique, otherwise unavailable intelligence that "saved lives."

[1697] *See* May 2, 2006, Briefing for the Chief of Staff to the President: Briefing for Chief of Staff to the President Josh Bolten: CIA Rendition, Detention and Interrogation Programs.

Lilie who was providing forged passports to Hambali. Lilie identified the house in Bangkok where Hambali was hiding."[1698]

(TS// ███████████ //NF) Similarly, on July 13, 2004, the CIA disseminated an Intelligence Assessment entitled, "Khalid Shaykh Muhammad: Preeminent Source on Al-Qa'ida."[1699] On April 22, 2005, the paper, as well as other materials on CIA detainee reporting, was faxed from ██████████ CTC Legal, to the Office of Legal Counsel at the Department of Justice, to support the OLC's legal review of the CIA's enhanced interrogation techniques.[1700] The document states:

> "...information that KSM provided on Majid Khan in the spring of 2003 was the *crucial first link* in the chain that led us to the capture of prominent JI leader and al-Qa'ida associate Hambali in August 2003, and more than a dozen Southeast Asian operatives slated for attacks against the US homeland. KSM told us about [Majid] Khan's role in delivering $50,000 in December 2002 to operatives associated with Hambali. ...[Majid] Khan—who had been detained in Pakistan in early 2003—was confronted with KSM's information about the money and acknowledged that he delivered the money to an operative named 'Zubair.' ...Based on that information, Zubair was captured in June 2003.[1701]

On August 24, 2009, this document was declassified with redactions and publicly released with the inaccurate information unredacted.[1702]

(TS// ███████████ //NF) The CIA provided similar inaccurate representations regarding the capture of Hambali in 18 of the 20 documents provided to policymakers and the Department of

---

[1698] Italics added. *See* May 2, 2006, Briefing for Chief of Staff to the President Josh Bolten: CIA Rendition, Detention and Interrogation Programs. The CIA's June 2013 Response maintains that the chronology in this passage and similar representations are correct. The CIA's June 2013 Response describes the following as "standard language" and the CIA's "typical representation" of Hambali's capture: "KSM provided information about an al-Qa'ida operative, Majid Khan, who he was aware had recently been captured. KSM—possibly believing the detained operatives was 'talking' admitted to having tasked Majid with delivering a large sum of money to individuals working for another senior al-Qa'ida associate. In an example of how information from one detainee can be used in debriefing another detainee in a 'building block' process, *Khan—confronted with KSM's information about the money—acknowledged that he delivered the money to an operative named Zubair and provided Zubair's physical description and contact number*" (italics added). The CIA's June 2013 Response states that this chronology is "accurate." As detailed in this summary, and in greater detail in Volume II, this June 2013 CIA representation is inaccurate. Majid Khan—who was in foreign government custody—first provided information on the money exchange and Zubair, prior to any reporting from KSM.
[1699] CIA, "Khalid Shaykh Muhammad: Preeminent Source On Al-Qa'ida," was authored by [REDACTED], CTC/UBLD/AQPO/AQLB.
[1700] CIA fax to the Department of Justice, entitled, "██, Materials on KSM and Abu Zubaydah. ██," dated 22 April 2005. For background on the intelligence product, *see* DTS #2004-3375.
[1701] Italics added. CIA Directorate of Intelligence, "Khalid Shaykh Muhammad: Preeminent Source on Al-Qa'ida," dated July 13, 2004, faxed to the Department of Justice, April 22, 2005, entitled, "██, Materials on KSM and Abu Zubaydah. ██." This report was widely disseminated in the Intelligence Community and provided to the Senate Select Committee on Intelligence on July 15, 2004.
[1702] *See* www.washingtonpost.com/wp-srv/nation/documents/Khalid_Shayhk_Mohammad.pdf.

Justice between July 2003 and March 2009.[1703] In these representations, the CIA consistently asserted that *"after applying"* the CIA's enhanced interrogation techniques, KSM provided *"the crucial first link"* that led to the capture of Hambali.[1704]

(TS//████████████//NF) A review of CIA operational cables and other records found that information obtained from KSM during and after the use of the CIA's enhanced interrogation techniques played no role in the capture of Hambali. A review of CIA records further found that prior to reporting from CIA detainees subjected to the CIA's enhanced interrogation techniques, the CIA had intelligence on: (1) Hambali's role in the Jemaah Islamiyah; (2) funding by al-Qa'ida and KSM of Hambali's terrorist activities; (3) the operative to whom Majid Khan delivered the money, Zubair, and Zubair's links to terrorism, Jemaah Islamiyah, and Hambali; and (4) Majid Khan's $50,000 money transfer from al-Qa'ida to Zubair in December 2002. CIA records indicate that the intelligence that led to Hambali's capture was based on signals intelligence, a CIA source, and Thai investigative activities in Thailand.[1705]

(TS//████████████//NF) Prior to his capture, Hambali was known to have played a supporting role in the KSM and Ramzi Yousef "Bojinka Plot," an effort in early 1995 to place explosives on 12 United States-flagged aircraft and destroy them mid-flight.[1706] By the end of 2001, Hambali was suspected of playing a supporting role in the September 11, 2001, terrorist attacks, as well as helping to enroll Zacarias Moussaoui in flight school.[1707] By early 2002, a body of intelligence reporting unrelated to the CIA's Detention and Interrogation Program indicated that KSM was providing Hambali with funding to conduct terrorist operations in Southeast Asia.[1708] In March 2002, Hambali was described as the CIA's "number one target" in

---

[1703] *See* list of CIA prepared briefings and memoranda from 2003 through 2009 with representations on the effectiveness of the CIA's enhanced interrogation techniques referenced in this summary and described in detail in Volume II.

[1704] Among other documents, *see* CIA Directorate of Intelligence, "Khalid Shaykh Muhammad: Preeminent Source on Al-Qa'ida," dated July 13, 2004, faxed to the Department of Justice, April 22, 2005, fax entitled, "████, Materials on KSM and Abu Zubaydah. ████." This Intelligence Assessment was widely disseminated in the Intelligence Community and provided to the Senate Select Committee on Intelligence on July 15, 2004. On March 31, 2009, former Vice President Cheney requested the declassification of this Intelligence Assessment, which was publicly released with redactions on August 24, 2009. *See also* CIA Memorandum for Steve Bradbury at Office of Legal Counsel, Department of Justice, dated March 2, 2005, from ████████, ████ Legal Group, DCI Counterterrorist Center, subject "Effectiveness of the CIA Counterterrorist Interrogation Techniques" and Classified Statement for the Record, Senate Select Committee on Intelligence, provided by General Michael V. Hayden, Director, Central Intelligence Agency, 12 April 2007 (DTS #2007-1563).

[1705] *See* intelligence chronology in Volume II for detailed information.

[1706] *See* United States Court of Appeals, August Term, 2001, *U.S. v Ramzi Ahmed Yousef*, and DIRECTOR ████ (████ JAN 02). *See also* ████████ CIA ████ ████ MAR 02).

[1707] December 15, 2001, CIA Briefing Document, "DCI Highlights." *See also* ALEC ████ (262150Z APR 02) and email from: REDACTED; to: REDACTED, ████, ████, ████, and others; subject: "Debriefing results of Omani al-Qa'ida cell leader yields further connections between possibly Khalid Shaykh Muhammed and the East Asia al-Qa'ida network"; date: April 16, 2002, at 9:56:34 AM. *See also* 9/11 Commission Report.

[1708] *See* intelligence chronology in Volume II, including ALEC ████ (262150Z APR 02). *See also* email from: [REDACTED]; to [REDACTED], ████, ████, ████, and others; subject: "Debriefing results of Omani al-Qa'ida cell leader yields further connections between possibly Khalid Shaykh Muhammed and the East Asia al-Qa'ida network"; date: April 16, 2002, at 9:56:34 AM.

Southeast Asia.[1709] That same month, the FBI provided information to the CIA stating that foreign government detainee reporting indicated that KSM reimbursed terrorism-related expenditures made by Hambali for the JI.[1710] By June of 2002, the CIA had entered into discussions with representatives of the ████ government regarding their willingness to accept custody of Hambali once he was captured.[1711] On September 25, 2002, the CIA reported that an individual in FBI custody since May 2002, Mohammed Mansour Jabarah, reported that in November 2001, he collected $50,000 from KSM for a Hambali-directed terrorist operation targeting U.S. interests, as well as at least one other $10,000 payment.[1712] On the same day, September 25, 2002, a CIA cable stated that Masran bin Arshad, while in the custody of a foreign government, had detailed his connections to Abu Ahmad al-Kuwaiti and KSM.[1713] According to bin Arshad, after KSM's "Second Wave" plotting was "abandoned" in late 2001, bin Arshad was tasked by KSM to meet with Abu Ahmad al-Kuwaiti in Pakistan and to deliver $50,000 to Hambali for terrorist operations. Bin Arshad stated he was unable to deliver the money.[1714] When the October 12, 2002, terrorist attacks occurred on the Indonesian island of Bali, killing more than 200 individuals, Hambali was immediately suspected of being the "mastermind" of the attacks and was further described as "one of the world's most wanted terrorists."[1715] Open source information in October 2002 identified the funding for the Bali bombings as flowing through Hambali from al-Qa'ida leadership in Pakistan. Through November 2002, news reports highlighted links between senior al-Qa'ida leadership—including KSM—and JI in the context of the Bali bombings. Hambali continued to be identified as a potential mastermind of the bombing and likely residing in Thailand. These same reports identified a Malaysian named "Zubair" as one of three individuals sought by security officials for the Hambali-linked Bali bombings.[1716]

(**TS//**████████████//**NF**) In early January 2003, coverage of a known al-Qa'ida email account uncovered communications between that account and the account of a former Baltimore, Maryland, resident, Majid Khan. The communications indicated that Majid Khan traveled to Bangkok, Thailand, in December 2002 for terrorist support activities and was in contact there

---

[1709] DIRECTOR ████ (241921Z MAR 02)
[1710] ALEC ████ (22150Z APR 02)
[1711] ALEC ████ (041957Z JUN 02)
[1712] ████████████████. *See also* "Terror Informant for FBI Allegedly Targeted Agents," *Washington Post*, dated January 19, 2008, and Department of Justice documents on Mohammed Mansour Jabarah, including Jabarah's "Sentencing Memorandum."
[1713] *See* section of this summary and Volume II on the "Information on the Facilitator That Led to the UBL Operation" for additional information on Abu Ahmad al-Kuwaiti. Masran bin Arshad was in the custody of the government of ████ at this time.
[1714] DIRECTOR ████ (251938Z SEP 02); ████ 65903 ████ AUG 02); CIA ████ AUG 02); ████ 65903 (████ AUG 02); ████ 65902 (████ AUG 02)
[1715] Among other open sources, *see* "The Secret Mastermind Behind the Bali Horror," *The Observer*, 19 October 2002.
[1716] Among other open source reporting, *see* "The Sadness of Bali is the Sadness of the World," *The Strait Times*, dated November 16, 2002; "Jemaah Islamiyah Still Capable of Major Terrorist Attacks," Philippine *Headline News*, dated November 27, 2002; "Police Arrest 13 Linked to Bali Bombers, Uncovers Plot to Blow Up Bank," *AFP*, dated November 26, 2002; "Bali Friends Have Arabia Link," *New York Post*, dated December 2, 2002; "Finger Is Pointed At Bomber," *AFP-Hong Kong*, dated November 26, 2002; and "Mastermind of Bali Bomb Arrested," *The Strait Times*, dated November 22, 2002.

with a "Zubair."[1717] By this time, the CIA had significant information—prior to KSM's capture—indicating that a "Zubair" played a central supporting role in the JI, was affiliated with al-Qa'ida figures like KSM, had expertise in ████████████ in Southeast Asia, and was suspected of playing a role in Hambali's October 12, 2002, Bali bombings.[1718] This information was derived from traditional intelligence collection, open source reporting, and FBI debriefings of Abu Zubaydah (prior to Abu Zubaydah being subjected to the CIA's enhanced interrogation techniques).[1719] On March 4, 2003, the day before Majid Khan's capture, the FBI requested additional information from the CIA on the "Zubair" referenced in Majid Khan's emails.[1720]

(TS// ███████████████ //NF) On March 6, 2003, the day after Majid Khan was captured in Pakistan, and while being questioned by foreign government interrogators using rapport-building techniques,[1721] Majid Khan described how he traveled to Bangkok in December 2002 and

---

[1717] ALEC ██████ (170117Z JAN 03). At this time open source reporting also placed Hambali in Thailand. *See*, for example, "FBI Report Pointed to Bali Bombing," *The Age*, dated January 23, 2003; "Thailand's Denial of Threat Fails to Convince," *AFP*, dated November 15, 2002; "We'll Hit You: Pre-Bali Alert," *Herald (Australia)*, dated November 16, 2002; "JI Terror Group Still Major Threat Despite Arrests," *Agence France Presse (AFP)*, dated November 26, 2002; "Indonesia Arrests a Top Suspect in Southeast Asia Terror Network," *New York Times*, dated December 4, 2002; and "Inside the Bali Plot: A TIME Inquiry Unearths the Roots of the Bombings and Shows How the Masterminds Remain at Large," *Time Magazine*, dated December 9, 2002.

[1718] The CIA's June 2013 Response acknowledges that the CIA "had some other information linking Zubair to al-Qa'ida's Southeast Asia network," but states "that it was KSM's information that caused us to focus on [Zubair] as an inroad to Hambali." The CIA's June 2013 Response further asserts: "KSM provided information on an al-Qa'ida operative named Zubair, we shared this information with Thai authorities, they detained Zubair, and he gave actionable intelligence information that helped us identify Hambali's location." This statement in the CIA's June 2013 Response is inaccurate. On October 25, 2013, the CIA acknowledged the inaccuracy. Confirming information in the Committee Study, the CIA stated that an additional review of CIA records by the CIA found that "No, KSM did not name Zubair in his debriefings."

[1719] In May 2002, prior to the application of the CIA's enhanced interrogation techniques, Abu Zubaydah identified "Zubair" as a Malaysian national who was associated with KSM and who could be used by KSM to conduct attacks in Thailand. According to Abu Zubaydah, Zubair also "assisted Abu Zubaydah in obtaining passports from a printer facility in either Thailand or Malaysia." (*See* DIRECTOR ██████ (271937Z MAY 02) ██████.) In June 2002, Abu Zubaydah told an FBI interrogator that he sent a Canadian who sought to "help defend Muslims" in Indonesia to a Malaysian named Abu Zubair. (*See* ██████ 10475 (141605Z JUN 02).) In July 2002, a U.S. military detainee stated that "Zubair" was a member of the Jemaah Islamiyah and was connected to Jemaah Islamiyah senior leaders. (*See* ██████ 11691 (141712Z JUL 02). For other intelligence identifying "Zubair" as one of several individuals suspected of being connected to the October 2002 Bali bombings, *see* ██████ 95612 (290615Z OCT 02); DIRECTOR ██████ (202057Z OCT 02); and DIRECTOR ████████████.) Open source news reports highlighted links between senior al-Qa'ida leadership—including KSM—and Jemaah Islamiyah in the context of the Bali bombings. Hambali continued to be identified as a potential mastermind of the bombing—and likely residing in Thailand. These same reports identified a Malaysian named "Zubair" as one of three individuals sought by security officials for Hambali's Bali bombings. Among other open source reporting, *see* "The Secret Mastermind Behind the Bali Horror," *The Observer*, 19 October 2002; "The Sadness of Bali is the Sadness of the World," *The Strait Times*, dated November 16, 2002; "Jemaah Islamiyah Still Capable of Major Terrorist Attacks," *Philippine Headline News*, dated November 27, 2002; "Police Arrest 13 Linked to Bali Bombers, Uncovers Plot to Blow Up Bank," *AFP*, dated November 26, 2002; "Bali Friends Have Arabia Link," *New York Post*, dated December 2, 2002; "Finger Is Pointed At Bomber," *AFP-Hong Kong*, dated November 26, 2002; "Inside the Bali Plot: A TIME Inquiry Unearths the Roots of the Bombings and Shows How the Masterminds Remain at Large," *Time Magazine*, dated December 9, 2002; and "Mastermind of Bali Bomb Arrested," *The Strait Times*, dated November 22, 2002. *See* intelligence chronology in Volume II for additional detailed information.

[1720] *See* ██████ 89601 (042006Z MAR 03).

[1721] ██████ 13678 (070724Z MAR 03). According to CIA records, "a [foreign government officer] talked quietly to [Majid Khan] alone for about ten minutes before the interview began and was able to establish an

provided $50,000 USD to "Zubair" at the behest of al-Qa'ida. Khan also stated that he updated KSM's nephew, Ammar al-Baluchi, via email about the money exchange. Majid Khan's physical description of Zubair matched previous intelligence reporting already collected on Zubair.[1722] On March 10, 2003, the CIA ███████████ requested that information about Majid Khan's travel to Thailand and his delivery of money to "Zubair" be shared with Thai authorities, along with the physical description of "Zubair" and a phone number for Zubair provided by Majid Khan. CIA ███████████ proposed that it inform the Thais that "[w]e are very concerned that the money mentioned may be funding terrorist activities, as well as the individuals in question," and that ███████ request the Thai government "provide any details regarding these individuals and phone numbers."[1723]

(~~TS//~~███████~~//NF~~) On March 11, 2003, after being confronted with information that confirmed KSM's financial support to Hambali, KSM admitted to providing Hambali with $50,000 to conduct a terrorist attack "in approximately November 2002." KSM made no reference to Majid Khan or Zubair.[1724] On March 17, 2003, after being confronted with Majid Khan's reporting and a photograph of Majid Khan, KSM confirmed that Majid Khan—whom he stated he knew only as "Yusif"—was involved in the money transfer to Hambali.[1725] KSM denied knowing Zubair—who would be the critical link to Hambali's capture—or any other Hambali representative in Thailand.[1726]

(~~TS//~~███████~~//NF~~) By May 2003, the CIA had learned that a source the CIA had been developing █████████████████, received a call from a phone number associated with Zubair. When the source was contacted by the CIA, he described a Malaysian man ███████████████████████████████.[1727] CIA officers

---

excellent level of rapport. The first hour and [a] half of the interview was a review of bio-data and information previously [reported]. When [foreign government interrogators] started putting pressure on [Majid Khan] by pulling apart his story about his 'honeymoon' in Bangkok and his attempt to rent an apartment, safehouse, for his cousin [Mansoor Maqsood, aka Iqbal, aka Talha, aka Moeen, aka Habib], at 1400, [Majid Khan] slumped in his chair and said he would reveal everything to officers...."

[1722] ███████ 13678 (070724Z MAR 03). Records indicate that this information was also disseminated in FBI channels. See ALEC ████████. For previous intelligence on Zubair's physical description, see ███████ 11715 ███████. See also DIRECTOR ███████. See intelligence chronology in Volume II for detailed information.

[1723] ███████ 81553 (101010Z MAR 03). The request was approved by CIA Headquarters on March 12, 2003 (DIRECTOR ███ (March 12, 2003)).

[1724] ███████ 10755 (111455Z MAR 03). See also DIRECTOR ███████ (112152Z MAR 03). ALEC Station had sent interrogators at the CIA's DETENTION SITE BLUE at least two "requirements" cables with information to use in the interrogation of KSM specifically about Hambali and KSM's money transfers to Hambali. See ALEC ███████ (072345Z MAR 03); ALEC ███████ (090015Z MAR 03). KSM was rendered to CIA custody on March █, 2003, and immediately subjected to the CIA's enhanced interrogation techniques through March 25, 2003.

[1725] KSM was told the CIA had "stacks and stacks of emails," and that CIA officers were going to do a "test of his honesty" by asking him a series of questions. See ███████ 10865 (171648Z MAR 03).

[1726] The CIA's June 2013 Response states: "KSM provided information on an al-Qa'ida operative named Zubair, we shared this information with Thai authorities, they detained Zubair, and he gave actionable intelligence information that helped us identify Hambali's location." This statement in the CIA's June 2013 Response is inaccurate. In a document submitted to the Committee on October 25, 2013, the CIA acknowledged the inaccuracy. Confirming information in the Committee Study, the CIA stated that an additional review of CIA records by the CIA found that, "No, KSM did not name Zubair in his debriefings." See DTS #2013-3152.

[1727] ███████ 84783 ███████; ███████ 84837 ███████

suspected this individual was the "Zubair" associated with Hambali and Majid Khan.[1728] ██
██████ later, the source alerted the CIA that the person suspected of being Zubair would be
██████████████. When Zubair arrived at ████████████████████████, he was
photographed and followed by Thai authorities.[1729] A detainee in foreign government custody
confirmed the individual in the surveillance photo was Zubair.[1730] On June 8, 2003, Zubair was
detained by the government of Thailand.[1731] While still in Thai custody, Zubair was questioned
about his efforts to obtain fraudulent ████ documents, as well as his phone contact with ██████
████████████████████ [Business Q].[1732] Zubair admitted to seeking illegal
documents on behalf of Hambali, as well as using ████████ [Business Q]
████.[1733] Signals intelligence had alerted the CIA that a phone number associated with
Zubair had been in frequent contact with ████████ [Business Q].[1734] After being transferred
to CIA custody and rendered to the CIA's COBALT detention site, Zubair was immediately
subjected to the CIA's enhanced interrogation techniques.[1735] Days later, Zubair was asked
about his efforts to obtain illegal ████ documents for Hambali, at which point he again
acknowledged using ████████████ [Business Q]
██.[1736] When Thai authorities unilaterally approached a "contact" at ██████████ [Business

---

[1728] ████ 84257 ████████. See also ████ 84783 ████████ and ████ 84837

[1729] ████ 84783 ████████; ████ 84837 ████████

[1730] ████ 31768 ████████. The detainee was in the custody of the government of ████████.

[1731] ████ 84854

[1732] ████ 84854 ████; ████ 84876 ████████; ████ 87617
████; ████ 84908 ████. The Committee has used "Business Q" to refer to a specific
company.

[1733] ████ 84854 ████; ████ 84876 ████████; ████ 87617
████ 84908

[1734] ████ 84908 ████████. It is unclear what specific actions the CIA or local authorities engaged in
as a result of the information Zubair provided on ████████ [Business Q] while in foreign government custody.
CIA records indicate that Thai authorities were engaged in their own unilateral efforts to track and identify leads
related to Hambali and Zubair. A June 28, 2003, CIA cable states that local authorities were investigating Zubair's
links to various ████████ [businesses]. Later, in July 2003, the CIA learned that Thai authorities had
approached a "contact" who worked at ████████ [Business Q]. ████████████
████████████. The CIA's June 2013 Response acknowledges that prior to being transferred to CIA
custody, "[d]uring [foreign government] debriefings, Zubair reported on the ████████████
and corroborated reporting on ████████ [Business Q] ████████. This information
when combined with reporting from other sources to form a complete picture of Hambali's status was critical in
helping identify Hambali's general location and led to his arrest on 11 August by Thai [authorities]." A review of
CIA records found that the reporting referenced was obtained prior to Zubair's rendition to CIA custody.

[1735] ████████ 40568 ████████████

[1736] ████ 84876 ████; ████ 84908 ████████
40915 ████; 41017 ████ ██ ████████

████████████████████████████████████. In response to this
information, ████████ wrote, "Wow..this is just great... you guys are soooo closing in on Hmabali [sic]."
(See email from: ████████; to: ████████, and others; subject: "wohoo---hilite for EA team
pls....aliases for Hambali"; date: June ██, 2003, at 9:51:30 AM.) As noted, CIA records indicate that Thai
authorities were unilaterally following investigative leads related to Hambali and Zubair. It is unknown what
specific investigative steps were taken by Thai authorities (or by the CIA) between early June 2003 and July 16,

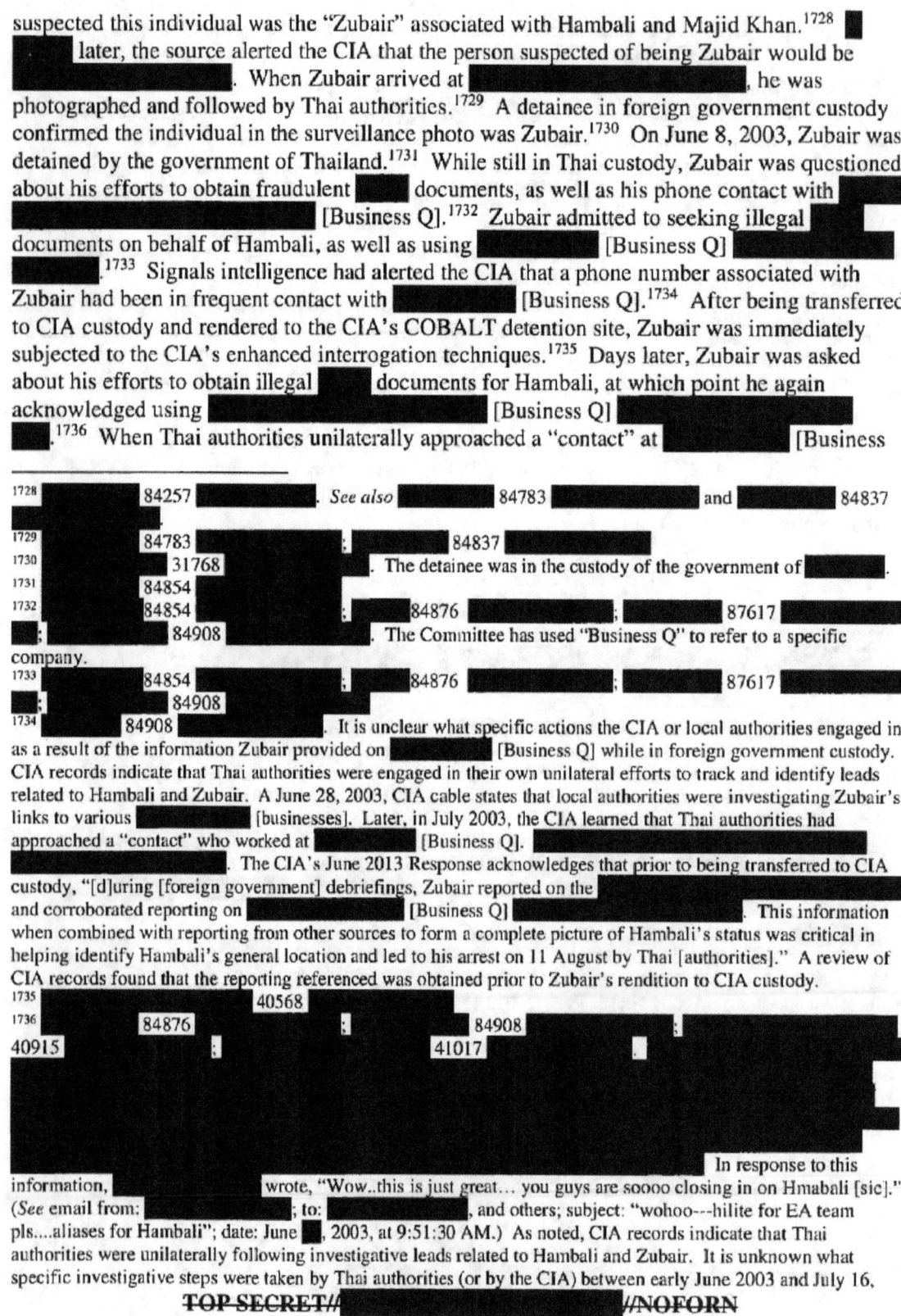

Q], they obtained ██
████.[1737] An operation targeting ████████████████████ was developed that focused
on surveillance of ████████ [Business Q]. As a result of this surveillance, and the
cooperation of ████████████, Hambali associate Amer was arrested on August 11, 2003.[1738]
Amer was immediately cooperative and assisted in an operation that led to the arrest of Lillie,
aka Bashir bin Lap, that same day.[1739] Lillie was found to have a key fob in his possession
imprinted with an address of an apartment building in Ayutthaya, Thailand. In response to
questioning, "within minutes of capture," Lillie admitted that the address on the key fob was the
address where Hambali was located. Fewer than four hours later, an operation successfully led
to Hambali's capture at the address found on the key fob.[1740]

(TS// ████████████ //NF) On November 28, 2005, the chief of the CTC's Southeast Asia
Branch explained how Hambali was captured in an interview with the CIA's Oral History
Program, stating:

> "Frankly, we stumbled onto Hambali. We stumbled onto the [the source]
> ...picking up the phone and calling his case officer to say there's ████████
> ████████ [related to Zubair]. ...we really stumbled over it. It wasn't police
> work, it wasn't good targeting, it was we stumbled over it and it yielded up
> Hambali. What I tell my people is you work really, really hard to be in a
> position to get lucky."[1741]

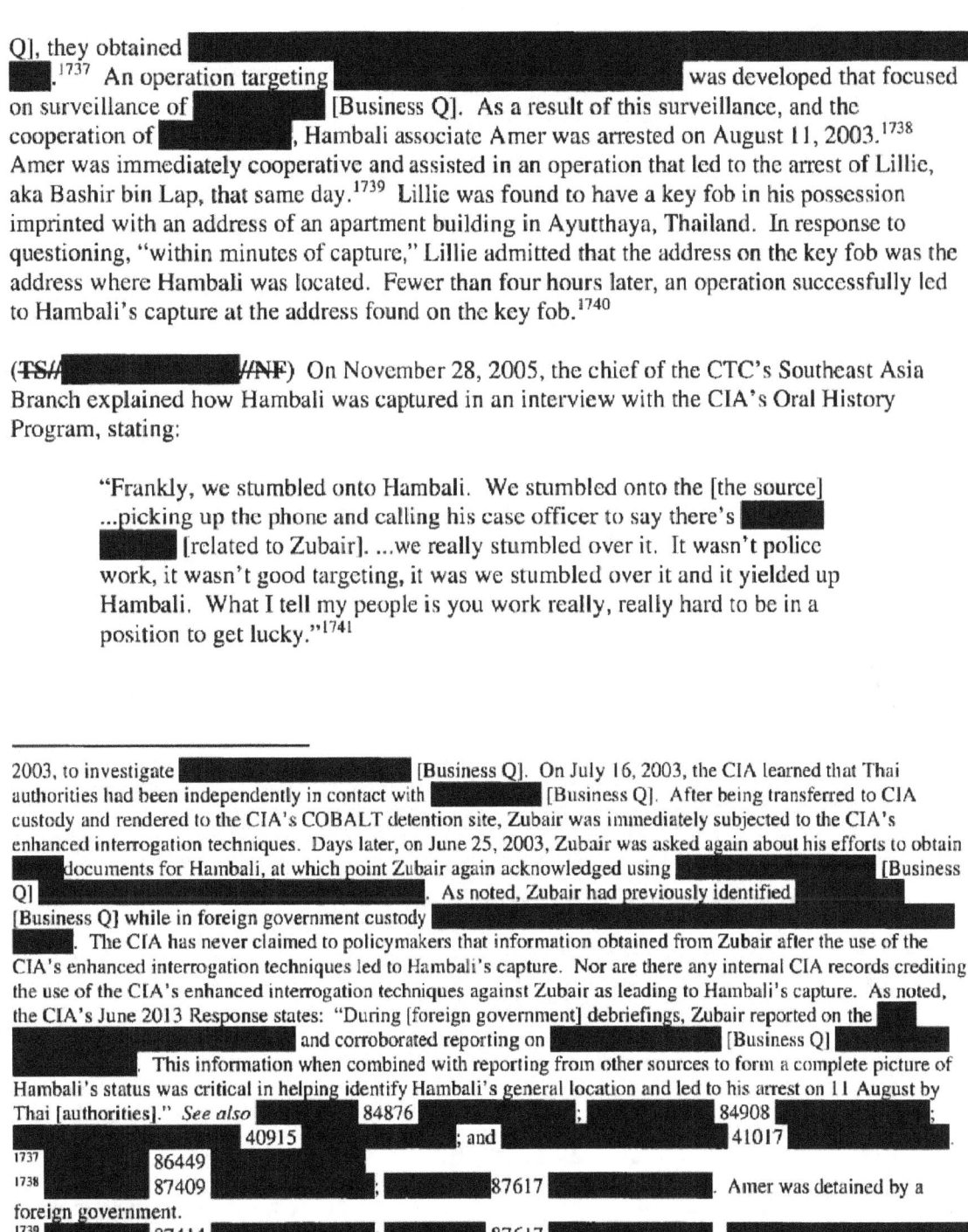

2003, to investigate ████████████████ [Business Q]. On July 16, 2003, the CIA learned that Thai
authorities had been independently in contact with ████████ [Business Q]. After being transferred to CIA
custody and rendered to the CIA's COBALT detention site, Zubair was immediately subjected to the CIA's
enhanced interrogation techniques. Days later, on June 25, 2003, Zubair was asked again about his efforts to obtain
████ documents for Hambali, at which point Zubair again acknowledged using ████████████ [Business
Q] ████████████████████. As noted, Zubair had previously identified ████████
[Business Q] while in foreign government custody ████████████████████████
████. The CIA has never claimed to policymakers that information obtained from Zubair after the use of the
CIA's enhanced interrogation techniques led to Hambali's capture. Nor are there any internal CIA records crediting
the use of the CIA's enhanced interrogation techniques against Zubair as leading to Hambali's capture. As noted,
the CIA's June 2013 Response states: "During [foreign government] debriefings, Zubair reported on the ████
████████████ and corroborated reporting on ████████ [Business Q] ████████
████. This information when combined with reporting from other sources to form a complete picture of
Hambali's status was critical in helping identify Hambali's general location and led to his arrest on 11 August by
Thai [authorities]." *See also* ████████ 84876 ████; ████ 84908 ████;
████████ 40915 ████; and ████ 41017 ████.
[1737] ████ 86449 ████
[1738] ████ 87409 ████; ████ 87617 ████████. Amer was detained by a
foreign government.
[1739] ████ 87414 ████; ████ 87617 ████
██
[1740] *See* ████ 9515 ████; ████ 87617 ████; ████ 87414
████; and ████████ "Hambali Capture." Lillie was later rendered to CIA custody.
[1741] Lillie had not yet been rendered to CIA custody. CIA Oral History Program Documenting Hambali capture,
interview of [REDACTED], interviewed by [REDACTED], on November 28, 2005.

(~~TS//~~~~~~~~~~~~~~~//NF~~) Hambali was rendered to CIA custody on August ▮, 2003, and almost immediately subjected to the CIA's enhanced interrogation techniques.[1742] On September 4, 2006, he was transferred to U.S. military custody.[1743]

    G. CIA Secondary Effectiveness Representations—Less Frequently Cited Disrupted Plots, Captures, and Intelligence that the CIA Has Provided As Evidence for the Effectiveness of the CIA's Enhanced Interrogation Techniques

(~~TS//~~~~~~~~~~~~~//NF~~) In addition to the eight most frequently cited "thwarted" plots and terrorists captured, the Committee examined 12 other less frequently cited intelligence successes that the CIA has attributed to the effectiveness of its enhanced interrogation techniques.[1744] These representations are listed below:

	Additional Intelligence the CIA Has Attributed to the Effectiveness of the CIA's Enhanced Interrogation Techniques
1	The Identification of Khalid Shaykh Mohammad (KSM) as the Mastermind of the September 11, 2001, Attacks
2	The Identification of KSM's "Mukhtar" Alias
3	The Capture of Ramzi bin al-Shibh
4	The Capture of KSM
5	The Capture of Majid Khan
6	The Thwarting of the Camp Lemonier Plotting
7	The Assertion That Enhanced Interrogation Techniques Help Validate Sources
8	The Identification and Arrests of Uzhair and Saifullah Paracha
9	Critical Intelligence Alerting the CIA to Jaffar al-Tayyar
10	The Identification and Arrest of Saleh al-Marri
11	The Collection of Critical Tactical Intelligence on Shkai, Pakistan
12	Information on the Facilitator That Led to the UBL Operation

---

[1742] ▮▮▮▮▮▮▮▮ 1241 ▮▮▮▮▮▮

[1743] ▮▮▮▮ 1242 (050744Z SEP 06); ▮▮▮▮▮▮▮ 2215 (051248Z SEP 06)

[1744] The CIA's June 2013 Response states: "our review showed that the *Study* failed to include examples of important information acquired from detainees that CIA cited more frequently and prominently in its representations than several of the cases the authors chose to include." This is inaccurate. The CIA's June 2013 Response provided three examples: the "Gulf shipping plot" (which is addressed in the full Committee Study and in this summary in the context of the interrogation of Abd al-Rahim al-Nashiri), "learning important information about al-Qa'ida's anthrax plotting and the role of Yazid Sufaat" (which is addressed in the full Committee Study and in this summary in the context of the interrogation of KSM), and "the detention of Abu Talha al-Pakistani" (which is addressed in the full Committee Study and in this summary in the section on the "Thwarting of the United Kingdom Urban Targets Plot and the Capture of Dhiren Barot, aka Issa al-Hindi.").

1. *The Identification of Khalid Shaykh Mohammad (KSM) as the Mastermind of the September 11, 2001, Attacks*

(TS// ██████████ //NF) The CIA represented that CIA detainee Abu Zubaydah provided "important" and "vital" information by identifying Khalid Shaykh Mohammed (KSM) as the mastermind behind the attacks of September 11, 2001.[1745] CIA Director Hayden told the Committee on April 12, 2007, that:

> "…it was Abu Zubaydah, early in his detention, who identified KSM as the mastermind of 9/11. Until that time, KSM did not even appear in our chart of key al-Qa'ida members and associates."[1746]

(TS// ██████████ //NF) On at least two prominent occasions, the CIA represented, inaccurately, that Abu Zubaydah provided this information after the use of the CIA's enhanced interrogation techniques. On May 30, 2005, the Office of Legal Counsel wrote in a now-declassified memorandum:

> "Interrogations of [Abu] Zubaydah—again, once enhanced interrogation techniques were employed—furnished detailed information regarding al Qaeda's 'organization structure, key operatives, and modus operandi' and identified KSM as the mastermind of the September 11 attacks."[1747]

[1745] For example, in the September 6, 2006, speech validated by the CIA, President George W. Bush stated that: "[Abu] Zubaydah disclosed Khalid Sheikh Mohammed, or KSM, was the mastermind behind the 9/11 attacks and used the alias Mukhtar. This was a vital piece of the puzzle that helped our intelligence community pursue KSM." *See also* CIA document dated July 16, 2006, entitled, "DRAFT Potential Public Briefing of CIA's High-Value Terrorist Interrogations Program," and "CIA Validation of Remarks on Detainee Policy" drafts supporting the September 6, 2006, speech by President George W. Bush. *See also* unclassified Office of the Director of National Intelligence release, entitled, "Summary of the High Value Terrorist Detainee Program," as well as CIA classified Statement for the Record, Senate Select Committee on Intelligence, provided by General Michael V. Hayden, Director, Central Intelligence Agency, 12 April 2007 (DTS #2007-1563).

[1746] CIA classified Statement for the Record, Senate Select Committee on Intelligence, provided by General Michael V. Hayden, Director, Central Intelligence Agency, 12 April 2007; and accompanying Senate Select Committee on Intelligence hearing transcript for April 12, 2007, entitled, "Hearing on Central Intelligence Agency Detention and Interrogation Program." (*See* DTS #2007-1563 and DTS #2007-3158.) This testimony contradicted statements made in 2002 to the Joint Inquiry by ██████████, in which she indicated that an operative arrested in February 2002 in ████, prior to the capture of Abu Zubaydah, provided "proof… that KSM was a senior al-Qa'ida terrorist planner." (*See* interview by the Joint Inquiry of ██████████, ██████████, [REDACTED], ██████████, [REDACTED]; subject: Khalid Shaykh Mohammad (KSM); date: 12 August 2002 (DTS #2002-4630).)

[1747] Memorandum for John A. Rizzo, Senior Deputy General Counsel, Central Intelligence Agency, from Steven G. Bradbury, Principal Deputy Assistant Attorney General, Office of Legal Counsel, May 30, 2005, Re: Application of United States Obligations Under Article 16 of the Convention Against Torture to Certain Techniques that May be Used in the Interrogation of High Value Al Qaeda Detainees.

(TS//█████████//NF) The OLC memorandum cited a document provided by the CIA to support the statement.[1748] The OLC memorandum further stated that the CIA's enhanced interrogation techniques provide the U.S. government with "otherwise unavailable actionable intelligence," that "ordinary interrogation techniques had little effect on…Zubaydah," and that the CIA had "reviewed and confirmed the accuracy of [the OLC's] description of the interrogation program, including its purposes, methods, limitations, and results."[1749]

(TS//█████████//NF) In November 2007, the CIA prepared a set of documents and talking points for the CIA director to use in a briefing with the president on the effectiveness of the CIA's waterboard interrogation technique. The documents prepared assert that Abu Zubaydah identified KSM as the "mastermind" of the September 11, 2001, attacks after the use of the CIA's enhanced interrogation techniques.[1750]

(TS//█████████//NF) While Abu Zubaydah did provide information on KSM's role in the September 11, 2001, attacks, this information was corroborative of information already in CIA databases and was obtained prior to the use of the CIA's enhanced interrogation techniques. There is no evidence to support the statement that Abu Zubaydah's information—obtained by FBI interrogators prior to the use of the CIA's enhanced interrogation techniques and while Abu Zubaydah was hospitalized—was uniquely important in the identification of KSM as the "mastermind" of the 9/11 attacks.

(U) The following describes information available to the CIA prior to the capture of Abu Zubaydah:

- (U) Both the Congressional Joint Inquiry Into the Intelligence Community Activities Before and After the Terrorist Attacks of September 11, 2001, and the CIA Office of the Inspector General Report on CIA Accountability With Respect to the 9/11 Attacks include lengthy chronologies of the Intelligence Community's interest in KSM prior to the attacks of September 11, 2001. The timelines begin in 1995, when the United States determined that KSM was linked to the 1993 bombing of the World Trade Center, leading to the determination by the National Security Council's Policy Coordination

---

[1748] See CIA Briefing Notes on the Value of Detainee Reporting, faxed to the OLC in April 2005. The "Briefing Notes" state: "Within months of his arrest, Abu Zubaydah provided details about al-Qa'ida's organization structure, key operatives, and modus operandi. It also was Abu Zubaydah, early in his detention, who identified KSM as the mastermind of 9/11." As described in detail in Volume II, this CIA document did not specifically reference the CIA's enhanced interrogation techniques; however, it was provided to the OLC to support the OLC's legal analysis of the CIA's enhanced interrogation techniques. The document included most of the same examples the CIA had previously provided as examples of the effectiveness of the CIA's enhanced interrogation techniques. There are no records to indicate that the CIA, in reviewing draft versions of the OLC memorandum, sought to correct the inaccurate OLC statements.

[1749] Memorandum for John A. Rizzo, Senior Deputy General Counsel, Central Intelligence Agency, from Steven G. Bradbury, Principal Deputy Assistant Attorney General, Office of Legal Counsel, May 30, 2005, Re: Application of United States Obligations Under Article 16 of the Convention Against Torture to Certain Techniques that May be Used in the Interrogation of High Value Al Qaeda Detainees.

[1750] "DCIA Talking Points: Waterboard 06 November 2007," and supporting materials, dated November 6, 2007, with the notation the document was "sent to DCIA Nov. 6 in preparation for POTUS meeting."

Group that KSM was a top priority target for the United States.[1751] The Congressional Joint Inquiry further noted that information obtained prior to the September 11, 2001, attacks "led the CIA to see KSM as part of Bin Ladin's organization."[1752] There was also CIA reporting in 1998 that KSM was "very close" to UBL.[1753] On June 12, 2001, it was reported that "Khaled" was actively recruiting people to travel outside Afghanistan, including to the United States where colleagues were reportedly already in the country to meet them, to carry out terrorist-related activities for UBL. According to the 9/11 Commission Report, the CIA presumed this "Khaled" was KSM.[1754]

- (~~TS//~~█████████~~//NF~~) On September 12, 2001, a foreign government source, described as a member of al-Qa'ida, stated "the 11 September attacks had been masterminded from Kabul by three people," to include "Shaykh Khalid," who was related to Ramzi Yousef.[1755]

- (~~TS//~~█████████~~//NF~~) Also on September 12, 2001, a CIA officer familiar with KSM wrote a cable stating that "[o]ne of the individuals who has the capability to organize the kind of strikes we saw in the World Trade Center and the Pentagon is Khalid Shaykh Mohammad."[1756]

- (~~TS//~~█████████~~//NF~~) On September 15, 2001, a CIA officer wrote to a number of senior CTC officers, "I would say the percentages are pretty high that Khalid Sheikh Mohammad is involved [in the September 11, 2001, attacks]."[1757]

- (~~TS//~~█████████~~//NF~~) On October 16, 2001, an email from a CTC officer who had been tracking KSM since 1997, stated that although more proof was needed, "I believe KSM may have been the mastermind behind the 9-11 attacks."[1758]

[1751] Joint Inquiry Into the Intelligence Community Activities Before and After the Terrorist Attacks of September 11, 2001, Report of the Senate Select Committee on Intelligence and the House Permanent Select Committee on Intelligence, December 2002, pp. 325 – 331 (DTS #2002-5162); CIA Office of the Inspector General Report on CIA Accountability With Respect to the 9/11 Attacks, June 2005, pp. xi, 100-126 (DTS #2005-3477).

[1752] Joint Inquiry Into the Intelligence Community Activities Before and After the Terrorist Attacks of September 11, 2001, Report of the Senate Select Committee on Intelligence and the House Permanent Select Committee on Intelligence, December 2002, p. 329 (DTS #2002-5162).

[1753] DIRECTOR ████ (████SEP 98), disseminated as ████████, Office of the Inspector General Report on CIA Central Intelligence Agency Accountability Regarding Findings and Conclusions of the Report of the Joint Inquiry Into Intelligence Community Activities Before and After the Terrorist Attacks of September 11, 2001 (DTS #2005-3477), pp. 105-107.

[1754] The 9/11 Commission Report; Final Report of the National Commission on Terrorist Attacks Upon the United States, p. 277.

[1755] ████ 64626 (131842Z SEP 01); ████ 64627 (131843Z SEP 01)

[1756] CIA Office of the Inspector General Report on CIA Accountability With Respect to the 9/11 Attacks, June 2005, p. 113 (DTS #2005-3477).

[1757] Email from: ████; to: ████; cc: ████, ████, [REDACTED], ████, [REDACTED]; subject: Re: RAMZI LEADS...; date: September 15, 2001, at 5:04:38 AM.

[1758] CIA CTC internal email from: [REDACTED]; to multiple [REDACTED]; date: October 16, 2001, at 09:34:48 AM.

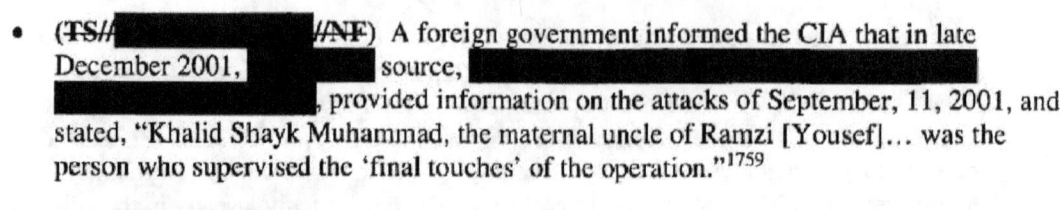

- (TS// ███████ //NF) A foreign government informed the CIA that in late December 2001, ███████ source, ████████████, provided information on the attacks of September, 11, 2001, and stated, "Khalid Shayk Muhammad, the maternal uncle of Ramzi [Yousef]... was the person who supervised the 'final touches' of the operation."[1759]

- (TS// ███████ //NF) Other reporting prior to the capture of Abu Zubaydah stated that KSM was: "one of the individuals considered the potential mastermind";[1760] "one of the top candidates for having been involved in the planning for the 11 September attacks" and one of "the masterminds";[1761] and "one of the leading candidates to have been a hands-on planner in the 9/11 attacks."[1762]

2. *The Identification of KSM's "Mukhtar" Alias*

(TS// ███████ //NF) The CIA represented that CIA detainee Abu Zubaydah provided "important" and "vital" information by identifying Khalid Shaykh Mohammed's (KSM) alias, "Mukhtar."[1763] In at least one instance in November 2007, in a set of documents and talking points for the CIA director to use in a briefing with the president on the effectiveness of the CIA's waterboard interrogation technique, the CIA asserted that Abu Zubaydah identified KSM as "Mukhtar" after the use of the CIA's enhanced interrogation techniques.[1764]

(TS// ███████ //NF) While Abu Zubaydah did provide information on KSM's alias, this information was provided by Abu Zubaydah to FBI interrogators prior to the initiation of the CIA's enhanced interrogation techniques—and while Abu Zubaydah was still in the intensive care unit of a ███████ hospital recovering from a gunshot wound incurred during his capture. Further, the information was corroborative of information already in CIA databases.[1765] Prior to the information provided by Abu Zubaydah, the CIA had intelligence, including a cable from August 28, 2001, indicating that KSM was now being called "Mukhtar."[1766]

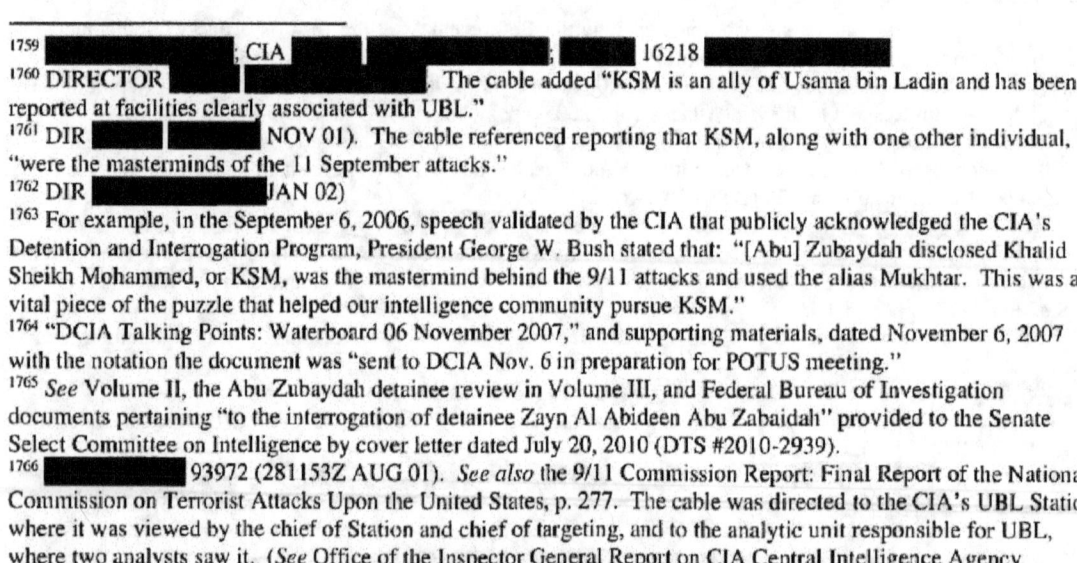

[1759] ███████ , CIA ███████ ; ███████ 16218 ███████
[1760] DIRECTOR ███████ . The cable added "KSM is an ally of Usama bin Ladin and has been reported at facilities clearly associated with UBL."
[1761] DIR ███████ NOV 01). The cable referenced reporting that KSM, along with one other individual, "were the masterminds of the 11 September attacks."
[1762] DIR ███████ JAN 02)
[1763] For example, in the September 6, 2006, speech validated by the CIA that publicly acknowledged the CIA's Detention and Interrogation Program, President George W. Bush stated that: "[Abu] Zubaydah disclosed Khalid Sheikh Mohammed, or KSM, was the mastermind behind the 9/11 attacks and used the alias Mukhtar. This was a vital piece of the puzzle that helped our intelligence community pursue KSM."
[1764] "DCIA Talking Points: Waterboard 06 November 2007," and supporting materials, dated November 6, 2007 with the notation the document was "sent to DCIA Nov. 6 in preparation for POTUS meeting."
[1765] See Volume II, the Abu Zubaydah detainee review in Volume III, and Federal Bureau of Investigation documents pertaining "to the interrogation of detainee Zayn Al Abideen Abu Zabaidah" provided to the Senate Select Committee on Intelligence by cover letter dated July 20, 2010 (DTS #2010-2939).
[1766] ███████ 93972 (281153Z AUG 01). See also the 9/11 Commission Report: Final Report of the National Commission on Terrorist Attacks Upon the United States, p. 277. The cable was directed to the CIA's UBL Station, where it was viewed by the chief of Station and chief of targeting, and to the analytic unit responsible for UBL, where two analysts saw it. (See Office of the Inspector General Report on CIA Central Intelligence Agency Accountability Regarding Findings and Conclusions of the Report of the Joint Inquiry Into Intelligence Community

3. *The Capture of Ramzi bin al-Shibh*

(TS/ ████████████ //NF) The CIA has represented that information acquired from CIA detainee Abu Zubaydah, as a result of the CIA's enhanced interrogation techniques, led to the capture of Ramzi bin al-Shibh. This CIA representation was included in President Bush's September 6, 2006, speech on the CIA's Detention and Interrogation Program. The speech, which was based on CIA information and vetted by the CIA, stated that the intelligence provided by CIA detainees "cannot be found any other place," and that the nation's "security depends on getting this kind of information."[1767] The speech included the following:

> "Zubaydah *was questioned using these procedures* [the CIA's enhanced interrogation techniques], and soon he began to provide information on key al-Qa'ida operatives, including information that helped us find and capture more of those responsible for the attacks on September the 11th.[1768] For example, Zubaydah *identified* one of KSM's accomplices in the 9/11 attacks, a terrorist named Ramzi bin al-Shibh. *The information Zubaydah provided helped lead to the capture of bin al-Shibh.* And together these two terrorists provided information that helped in the planning and execution of the operation that captured Khalid Sheikh Mohammed."[1769]

(TS/ ████████████ //NF) While the speech provided no additional detail on the capture of bin al-Shibh, an internal email among senior CIA personnel provided additional background for

---

Activities Before and After the Terrorist Attacks of September 11, 2001 (DTS #2005-3477), p. 112.) The CIA's June 2013 Response states that "[w]e continue to assess that Abu Zubaydah's information was a critical piece of intelligence." The CIA's June 2013 Response acknowledges the August 28, 2001, cable identifying KSM as "Mukhtar," but states that CIA officers "overlooked" and "simply missed" the cable.

[1767] *See* President George W. Bush, Speech on Terrorism and the CIA's Detention and Interrogation Program, September 6, 2006; and CIA Validation of Remarks on Detainee Policy, Wednesday, September 6, 2006, Draft #3 (validating speech received on August 29, 2006); email from: [REDACTED]; to: █████████████, █████ ███████; cc: [REDACTED], [REDACTED], [REDACTED], [REDACTED], [REDACTED], [REDACTED], [REDACTED], [REDACTED], [REDACTED], [REDACTED], [REDACTED], [REDACTED], ████████, [REDACTED]; subject: "Speechwriter's Questions on Monday"; date: September 5, 2006, at 10:30:32 AM.

[1768] Italics added. As described in this summary and in the Abu Zubaydah detainee review in Volume III, this statement was inaccurate. Abu Zubaydah provided information on al-Qa'ida activities, plans, capabilities, and relationships, in addition to information on its leadership structure, including personalities, decision-making processes, training, and tactics prior to, during, and after the utilization of the CIA's enhanced interrogation techniques. Abu Zubaydah's inability to provide information on the next attack in the United States and operatives in the United States was the basis for CIA representations that Abu Zubaydah was "uncooperative" and the CIA's determination that Abu Zubaydah required the use of the CIA's enhanced interrogation techniques to become "compliant" and reveal the information the CIA believed he was withholding—the names of operatives in the United States or information to stop the next terrorist attack. At no point during or after the use of the CIA's enhanced interrogation techniques did Abu Zubaydah provide this type of information.

[1769] Italics added. *See* President George W. Bush, Speech on Terrorism and the CIA's Detention and Interrogation Program, September 6, 2006; and CIA Validation of Remarks on Detainee Policy, Wednesday, September 6, 2006, Draft #3 (validating speech received on August 29, 2006); email from: [REDACTED]; to: ████████████, ████ ██████; cc: [REDACTED], [REDACTED], [REDACTED], [REDACTED], [REDACTED], [REDACTED], [REDACTED], [REDACTED], [REDACTED], [REDACTED], [REDACTED], [REDACTED], ████████, [REDACTED]; subject: "Speechwriter's Questions on Monday"; date: September 5, 2006, at 10:30:32 AM.

why the CIA included "the capture of Ramzi bin al-Shibh" in the president's speech as an example of the effectiveness of the CIA's enhanced interrogation techniques. After the speech, the chief of the ████████ Department in CTC, ████████████, sent an email to the chief of CTC, ████████████, ████████ CTC Legal, ████████████, and two officers in the CIA Office of Public Affairs, among others. The email addressed press speculation that the intelligence successes attributed to CIA detainees and the CIA's enhanced interrogation techniques in the president's speech were not accurate. Defending the accuracy of the speech, the chief of the ████████ Department in CTC wrote: "The NY Times has posted a story predictably poking holes in the President's speech." Regarding the CIA assertion that Abu Zubaydah provided information after the use of the CIA's enhanced interrogation techniques that led to the capture of Ramzi bin al-Shibh, the chief explained:

> "...we knew Ramzi bin al-Shibh was involved in 9/11 before AZ was captured; however, AZ gave us information on his recent activities that –when added into other information—helped us track him. Again, on this point, we were very careful and the speech is accurate in what it says about bin al-Shibh."[1770]

(~~TS//~~ ████████ ~~//NF~~) In addition, on February 17, 2007, the deputy chief of the ████ ████ Department in CTC, ████████████, testified to the Senate Select Committee on Intelligence that Abu Zubaydah "led us to Ramzi bin al-Shibh, who in kind of [sic] started the chain of events" that led to the capture of KSM.[1771]

[1770] *See* email from: ████████████; to: ████████████, ████████████, Mark Mansfield, Paul Gimigliano, and others; subject: "Questions about Abu Zubaydah's Identification of KSM as 'Mukhtar'"; date: September 7, 2006. A September 7, 2006, article (published September 8, 2006) in the *New York Times*, by Mark Mazzetti, entitled, "Questions Raised About Bush's Primary Claims of Secret Detention System" included comments by CIA officials defending the assertions in the President's speech: "Mr. Bush described the interrogation techniques used on the C.I.A. prisoners as having been 'safe, lawful and effective,' and he asserted that torture had not been used. ...Mr. Bush also said it was the interrogation of Mr. Zubaydah that identified Mr. bin al-Shibh as an accomplice in the Sept. 11 attacks. American officials had identified Mr. bin al-Shibh's role in the attacks months before Mr. Zubaydah's capture. A December 2001 federal grand jury indictment of Zacarias Moussaoui, the so-called 20th hijacker, said that Mr. Moussaoui had received money from Mr. bin al-Shibh and that Mr. bin al-Shibh had shared an apartment with Mohamed Atta, the ringleader of the plot. A C.I.A. spokesman said Thursday [September 7, 2006] that the agency had vetted the president's speech and stood by its accuracy. ...[CIA] spokesman, Paul Gimigliano, said in a statement... 'Abu Zubaydah not only identified Ramzi Bin al-Shibh as a 9/11 accomplice — something that had been done before — he provided information that helped lead to his capture." For additional news accounts on this subject, *see* former CIA Director Michael Hayden's interview with the *New York Times* in 2009, in which former Director Hayden "disputed an article in the *New York Times* on Saturday [4/18/2009] that said Abu Zubaydah had revealed nothing new after being waterboarded, saying that he believed that after unspecified 'techniques' were used, Abu Zubaydah revealed information that led to the capture of another terrorist, Ramzi Binalshibh." *See* "Waterboarding Used 266 Times on 2 Suspects," *New York Times*, dated April 20, 2009.

[1771] CIA Testimony of ████████████, Transcript, Senate Select Committee on Intelligence, February 14, 2007 (DTS #2007-1337). *See also* Memorandum to the Inspector General from James Pavitt, CIA's Deputy Director for Operations, dated February 27, 2004, with the subject line, "Comments to Draft IG Special Review, 'Counterterrorism Detention and Interrogation Program' (2003-7123-IG)," Attachment, "Successes of CIA's Counterterrorism Detention and Interrogation Activities," dated February 24, 2004. Pavitt states: "Abu Zubaydah - a master al-Qa'ida facilitator – was similarly arrogant and uncooperative before the lawful use of EITs. ...His information is *singularly unique* and valuable from an intelligence point of view, but it also has produced concrete results that have helped saved lives. His knowledge of al-Qa'ida lower-level facilitators, modus operandi and

(TS// ███████ //NF) A review of CIA records found no connection between Abu Zubaydah's reporting on Ramzi bin al-Shibh and Ramzi bin al-Shibh's capture. CIA records indicate that Ramzi bin al-Shibh was captured unexpectedly—on September 11, 2002, when Pakistani authorities, ███████████████, were conducting raids targeting Hassan Ghul in Pakistan.[1772]

(TS// ███████ //NF) While CIA records indicate that Abu Zubaydah provided information on Ramzi bin al-Shibh, there is no indication in CIA records that Abu Zubaydah provided information on bin al-Shibh's whereabouts. Further, while Abu Zubaydah provided information on bin al-Shibh while being subjected to the CIA's enhanced interrogation techniques, he provided similar information to FBI special agents prior to the initiation of the CIA's enhanced interrogation techniques.[1773] Prior to the application of the CIA's enhanced interrogation techniques, during interrogation sessions on May 19, 2003, and May 20, 2003, Abu Zubaydah reviewed photographs of individuals known by his interrogators to be associated with

---

safehouses, which he shared with us *as a result of the use of EITs*, for example, played a *key role* in the ultimate capture of Ramzi Bin al-Shibh" (italics added).

[1772] Among other records, *see* CIA ██████ (██████ SEP 02) █████████; CIA ██████ (██████ SEP 02) ██████████; ALEC ██████ (111551Z SEP 02).

[1773] *See* additional information below, as well as the Abu Zubaydah detainee review in Volume III, and Federal Bureau of Investigation documents pertaining "to the interrogation of detainee Zayn Al Abideen Abu Zabaidah" provided to the Senate Select Committee on Intelligence by cover letter dated July 20, 2010 (DTS# 2010-2939). The CIA's June 2013 Response includes the following: "...the Study states that Abu Zubaydah 'provided similar information to FBI interrogators prior to the initiation of the CIA's enhanced interrogation techniques.' This is incorrect. Abu Zubaydah's unique information concerning his contact with Hassan Gul was collected on 20 August 2002, after he had been subjected to enhanced interrogation techniques." This assertion in the CIA's June 2013 Response contains several errors: First, as described, the statement in the December 13, 2012, Committee Study pertains to Abu Zubaydah's reporting on Ramzi bin al-Shibh, not Hassan Ghul. As detailed in this summary and in other areas of the full Committee Study, while Abu Zubaydah provided information on Ramzi bin al-Shibh after the use of the CIA's enhanced interrogation techniques, he provided similar information on bin al-Shibh to FBI interrogators prior to the use and approval of the CIA's enhanced interrogation techniques. Second, as detailed in the full Committee Study, Abu Zubaydah provided considerable information on Hassan Ghul prior to the use of the CIA's enhanced interrogation techniques. (Some of this reporting has been declassified; for example, *see* the 9/11 Commission Report, specifically the Staff Report, "9/11 and Terrorist Travel," which highlights reporting by Abu Zubaydah on Hassan Ghul that was disseminated by the CIA on June 20, 2002.) Third, in referencing information that Abu Zubaydah provided on Hassan Ghul on August 20, 2002, the CIA's June 2013 Response asserts that this was "unique information." The CIA's June 2013 Response states: "Abu Zubaydah stated that if he personally needed to reach Hassan Gul, he would contact ███████████████████ [a well-known associate of Hassan Ghul]. We provided this information to Pakistani authorities, who then interviewed [the well-known associate] and ███████████████ [a specific family member of the well-known associate]—which ultimately led them to an apartment linked to Gul." The CIA's June 2013 Response adds that the "unique information concerning his contact with Hassan Gul was collected on 20 August 2002, after [Abu Zubaydah] had been subjected to enhanced interrogation techniques." CIA records indicate, however, that the information described in the CIA's Response was not unique. Pakistani authorities had raided the home and interviewed ██ ██████ [the same well-known associate] more than a month earlier on July █, 2002, based on similar reporting from a cooperating detainee in foreign government custody. The CIA had specific and detailed knowledge of this raid and the resulting interview of ███████████ [the well-known associate]. Pakistani authorities remained in contact with ███████████ [the well-known associate], the primary person interviewed, who was cooperative and sent ██████ to help Pakistani authorities identify a possible al-Qa'ida safe house—which the CIA noted was "extremely close to (if not an exact match)" for a safe house the FBI connected KSM to weeks earlier on June 18, 2002.

the bombing of the *USS Cole*, as well as the September 11, 2001, attacks. Abu Zubaydah identified a picture of Ramzi bin al-Shibh as "al-Shiba" and "noted that he is always with" KSM.[1774] Another record of this interrogation stated that showing Abu Zubaydah the photos:

> "was done to gauge his willingness to cooperate and provide details about people, the last times he saw them, where they were going, etc. He appeared to be very cooperative, provided details on people that we expected him to know, the collective groups when they departed Afghanistan, where he thinks they may now be, etc."[1775]

(TS// ████████████ //NF) Shortly thereafter, on June 2, 2002, an FBI special agent showed Abu Zubaydah the FBI "PENTTBOM photobook"[1776] which contained photographs numbered 1-35. A cable states that Abu Zubaydah was volunteering information and was "forthcoming and respond[ing] directly to questioning." Abu Zubaydah, who was not asked any "preparatory questions regarding these photographs," identified photograph #31, known to the interrogators as Ramzi bin al-Shibh, as a man he knew as al-Shiba, and stated al-Shiba was with KSM in Qandahar circa December 2001. Abu Zubaydah stated that al-Shiba spoke Arabic like a Yemeni and noted that al-Shiba was in the media after the September 11, 2001, attacks.[1777]

(TS// ████████████ //NF) In early June 2002, Abu Zubaydah's interrogators recommended that Abu Zubaydah spend several weeks in isolation while the interrogation team members traveled ████ "as a means of keeping [Abu Zubaydah] off-balance and to allow the team needed time off for a break and to attend to personal matters ████ ," as well as to discuss "the endgame" of Abu Zubaydah ████ with officers from CIA Headquarters.[1778] As a result, on June 18, 2002, Abu Zubaydah was placed in isolation.[1779] Abu Zubaydah spent the remainder of June 2002 and all of July 2002, 47 days in total, in solitary detention without being asked any questions. During this period, Abu Zubaydah's interrogators ████████████ . The FBI special agents never returned to the detention site.[1780]

(TS// ████████████ //NF) When CIA officers next interrogated Abu Zubaydah, on August 4, 2002, they immediately used the CIA's enhanced interrogation techniques on Abu Zubaydah, including the waterboard.[1781] On August 21, 2002, while Abu Zubaydah was still being subjected to the CIA's enhanced interrogation techniques, a CIA cable noted that Abu Zubaydah

---

[1774] DIRECTOR ████ (271905Z MAY 02) ████████ . *See* the Abu Zubaydah detainee review in Volume III for additional details.

[1775] Federal Bureau of Investigation documents pertaining "to the interrogation of detainee Zayn Al Abideen Abu Zabaidah" and provided to the Senate Select Committee on Intelligence by cover letter dated July 20, 2010 (DTS #2010-2939).

[1776] Federal Bureau of Investigation documents pertaining "to the interrogation of detainee Zayn Al Abideen Abu Zabaidah" and provided to the Senate Select Committee on Intelligence by cover letter dated July 20, 2010 (DTS #2010-2939).

[1777] ████ 10428 (071058Z JUN 02)

[1778] ████ 10424 (070814Z JUN 02)

[1779] ████ 10487 (181656Z JUN 02)

[1780] *See* Abu Zubaydah detainee review in Volume III for additional details.

[1781] ████ 10644 (201235Z AUG 02) and email from: [REDACTED]; to: ████████ and [REDACTED]; subject: "Re: So it begins."; date: August 4, 2002, at 09:45:09 AM.

was shown several photographs and "immediately recognized the photograph of Ramzi bin al-Shibh."[1782] Abu Zubaydah described bin al-Shibh as having "very dark, almost African looking" skin and noted that he first met bin al-Shibh after the 9/11 attacks in Kandahar, but added that he "did not have in-depth conversations with him."[1783] A cable stated that, after being shown the photograph of bin al-Shibh, Abu Zubaydah told interrogators that he was told bin al-Shibh stayed at the same safe house that KSM "had established for the pilots and others destined to be involved in the 9/11 attacks."[1784] An accompanying intelligence cable stated that Abu Zubaydah informed interrogators that he did not know—and did not ask—whether bin al-Shibh had been involved in the attacks of September 11, 2001, but did state that he believed that bin al-Shibh was "one of the operatives working for Mukhtar aka Khalid Shaykh Mohammad."[1785]

(~~TS//~~██████████~~//NF~~) The information Abu Zubaydah provided while being subjected to the CIA's enhanced interrogation techniques was described by CIA interrogators as "significant new details."[1786] However, the information provided by Abu Zubaydah was similar to information Abu Zubaydah provided prior to the application of the CIA's enhanced interrogation techniques, or was otherwise already known to the CIA. CIA records indicate that as early as September 15, 2001, Ramzi bin al-Shibh was identified as an associate of the September 11, 2001, hijackers who attempted to obtain flight training in Florida.[1787] A July 27, 2002, cable from the CIA's ALEC Station provided "background information" on bin al-Shibh and stated that he was "suspected of being the original '20th hijacker,' whose participation in the 11 September attacks was thwarted by his inability to obtain a visa to enter the United States."[1788] Ramzi bin al-Shibh was also identified as "a member of the Hamburg cell that included hijacker Mohammed Atta,"[1789] and bin al-Shibh was featured in one of "five suicide testimonial videos found in December 2001 at the residence of former UBL [Usama bin Ladin] lieutenant Mohammad Atef in Afghanistan."[1790]

(~~TS//~~██████████~~//NF~~) None of the above information resulted in Ramzi bin al-Shibh's capture. As detailed below, Ramzi bin al-Shibh was captured unexpectedly during raids in Pakistan on September 11, 2002, targeting Hassan Ghul.[1791]

(~~TS//~~██████████~~//NF~~) Prior to Abu Zubaydah's capture, the CIA considered Hassan Ghul a "First Priority Raid Target," based on reporting that:

[1782] ███████ 10654 (211318Z AUG 02); ███████ 10656 (211349Z AUG 02)
[1783] ███████ 10654 (211318Z AUG 02); ███████ 10656 (211349Z AUG 02)
[1784] ███████ 10654 (211318Z AUG 02); ███████ 10656 (211349Z AUG 02)
[1785] DIRECTOR ███ (261338Z AUG 02)
[1786] ███████ 10654 (211318Z AUG 02); ███████ 10656 (211349Z AUG 02)
[1787] ALEC ███ (222334Z SEP 01); ███ 92557 (15SEP01)
[1788] ALEC ███ (270132Z JUL 02)
[1789] ALEC ███ (270132Z JUL 02). *See also* ███ 97470 (281317Z MAR 02) ("In November 1998, [Muhammad] Atta, [Ramzi] Binalshibh, and [Said] Bahaji moved into the 54 Marienstrasse apartment in Hamburg that became the hub of the Hamburg cell.").
[1790] ALEC ███ (270132Z JUL 02). *See also* ███ 62533 ████████ (information from a foreign government concerning the al-Qa'ida suicide operatives portrayed on videotapes found in Afghanistan).
[1791] ALEC ███ (292345Z AUG 02); ALEC ███ (111551Z SEP 02)

"Ghul has been a major support player within the al-Qa'ida network and has assisted al-Qa'ida and Mujahadin operatives by facilitating their travel. He is a senior aide to Abu Zubaydah who was heavily involved in fund raising for a terrorist operation in spring 2001."[1792]

(TS// ██████████ //NF) Additional reporting noted that Hassan Ghul's phone number had been linked to a terrorist operative who "was ready to conduct a 'surgical operation' at any time,"[1793] while other reporting indicated that Hassan Ghul was working on a "program" believed to be related to terrorist activity.[1794]

(TS// ██████████ //NF) According to CIA cables, once captured, and prior to the initiation of the CIA's enhanced interrogation techniques, Abu Zubaydah confirmed that Hassan Ghul was a high-level al-Qa'ida facilitator who had contact with senior al-Qa'ida members, including Hamza Rabi'a and Abu Musab al-Zarqawi.[1795] Abu Zubaydah also corroborated intelligence in CIA databases that Ghul was involved in al-Qa'ida fundraising efforts.[1796] During this same period, the CIA continued to receive additional intelligence on Ghul from foreign governments, including that Ghul was responsible for facilitating the movement of Saudi fighters through Pakistan.[1797] As noted, on June 18, 2002, Abu Zubaydah was placed in isolation and was not asked any questions for 47 days.[1798]

(TS// ██████████ //NF) In early July 2002, Pakistani authorities and the CIA were continuing their efforts to locate and capture Hassan Ghul. A detainee in Pakistani custody, ████████, ██████████████████████████████, was providing detailed information to Pakistani authorities on Hassan Ghul.[1799] ████████ [the detainee in Pakistani custody] had been arrested with ██████████ in ██████████, on May ██, 2002, during ██████████ government raids on multiple residences thought to be associated with al-Qa'ida.[1800] During interviews with Pakistani authorities concerning how to locate and capture Hassan Ghul, ██████████ [the detainee in Pakistani custody] identified ██████████ [a well-known associate of Hassan Ghul] and the location of the [well-known associate's] home.[1801]

(TS// ██████████ //NF) On July █, 2002, seeking to capture Hassan Ghul, Pakistani authorities ██████████ raided the home of ██████████████████████ ████████ [the well-known associate of Hassan Ghul]. When the raid occurred, present at the home

---

[1792] ALEC ████ (241447Z MAR 02)
[1793] ALEC ████ (261712Z MAR 02)
[1794] ████████ 17369 (131519Z APR 02)
[1795] ████████ 10091 (210959Z APR 02); ████████ 10102 (230707Z APR 02); ████████ 10144 (271949Z APR 02); ████████ 10271 (151654Z MAY 02); ████████ 1295 (████ JAN 04); ████████ 1308 (████████ JAN 04)
[1796] ████████ 10091 (210959Z APR 02); ████████ 10102 (230707Z APR 02); ████████ 10144 (271949Z APR 02); ████████ 10271 (151654Z MAY 02); ALEC ████ (241447Z MAR 02)
[1797] DIRECTOR ████ (102312Z MAY 02)
[1798] ████████ 10487 (181656Z JUN 02)
[1799] ████████ 11746
[1800] ████████ 11336 ████ MAY 02)
[1801] ████████ 11746

was ████████████████ [the well-known associate], ████████████████
████████████ [and family members of the well-known associate]. A ████████ providing
details on the raid states that "████ [the well-known associate] was interviewed on the spot
and was fully cooperative with [Pakistani authorities]." ████████████ [the well-known
associate] stated that he had not seen Hassan Ghul or ████████████████████
since June 3, 2002, but that he believed they were still in Karachi. According to ████ [the
well-known associate], he had already informed Pakistani authorities that Hassan Ghul was an
al-Qa'ida member. According to a cable ████████████████ [the well-known associate]
stated that, as a result of his reporting on Ghul to Pakistani officials, he received "a death threat
from Hassan Ghul," causing Ghul to "cease coming to the ████████ [the well-known
associate's] house."[1802]

(TS// ████████ //NF) CIA records indicate that Pakistani authorities continued to
interview the ████████ [the well-known associate] in an effort to acquire information and
capture Hassan Ghul. A CIA cable dated July █, 2002, states that the Pakistani government "is
keying on any information which could get █ closer to bagging [Hassan] Ghul," specifically
"through ongoing interviews of ████████████████████████████████ [the
well-known associate of Hassan Ghul]." According to the cable, during one of the interviews,
████ [the well-known associate] told Pakistani authorities about an address where Hassan
Ghul used to reside circa December 2001. ████ [the well-known associate] sent ████ with
the Pakistani officers to identify the home.[1803] The CIA officers wrote that the location "is
extremely close to (if not an exact match)" to a location where KSM once resided, according to a
June 18, 2002, report from the FBI.[1804] The identified home was raided, but found empty. The
CIA wrote "█ are hitting the right places [safe houses], albeit at the wrong time. Our efforts
have got us closer than ever to at least Hassan Ghul."[1805] During the meetings between the
Pakistani authorities and ████████ [the well-known associate], ████████ [the
well-known associate] provided the Pakistani authorities with a copy of a ████ "reportedly
belonging to Hassan Ghul" ████████████████████." In the same cable, the
CIA reported that ████ [the well-known associate] had "approached the police for assistance
in retrieving ████," who was ████████ [a specific family member of the well-
known associate].[1806]

(TS// ████████ //NF) On July █, 2002, CTC officers at CIA Headquarters wrote that they
were reading the cables from the CIA ████████, noting they were "particularly interested
in the interview of raid target ████████ [the well-known associate of Hassan Ghul],
who admitted ████████████████████ to his knowledge of Ghul's
involvement in al-Qa'ida activities." The cable stated:

> "[r]ecognize that ████ [the well-known associate] claims his contact with
> Ghul stopped approximately one month ago, when he reported Ghul to the
> Pakistani authorities. However, given ████████████ [his close

[1802] ████ 11746 ████████
[1803] 11755
[1804] 11755 ████. Referenced cable is ALEC ████ (181900Z JUN 02).
[1805] 11755
[1806] See references to prior acquisition of passport in ████ 12151 (301107Z AUG 02).

association] to one of our high interest targets, request ████████ initiate technical surveillance of ██████ [the well-known associate's] telephone... to determine if they may yield any information on Ghul's current whereabouts."[1807]

CIA records do not indicate if "technical surveillance" of ████████████ [the well-known associate's] telephone was conducted.[1808]

(TS// ████████ //NF) According to CIA records, once captured, and prior to the initiation of the CIA's enhanced interrogation techniques, Abu Zubaydah confirmed that Hassan Ghul was a high-level al-Qa'ida facilitator who had contact with senior al-Qa'ida members, including Hamza Rabi'a and Abu Musab al-Zarqawi. Abu Zubaydah also corroborated intelligence in CIA databases that Ghul was involved in al-Qa'ida fundraising efforts.[1809] As noted, on June 18, 2002, Abu Zubaydah was placed in isolation and therefore was not questioned on the July 2002 raids on ████████████████ [the well-known associate's] home or the information acquired from the interviews of ████████████ [the well-known associate] conducted by Pakistani authorities.[1810] On August 4, 2002, after Abu Zubaydah spent 47 days in isolation, CIA interrogators entered his cell and immediately began subjecting Abu Zubaydah to the CIA's enhanced interrogation techniques, including the waterboard.[1811] As he had before the use of the CIA's enhanced interrogation techniques, when asked questions, Abu Zubaydah continued to provide intelligence, including on Hassan Ghul. On August 20, 2002—while still being subjected to the CIA's enhanced interrogation techniques—Abu Zubaydah was asked specifically how he would find Hassan Ghul. There are no records indicating that Abu Zubaydah had previously been asked this question. In response, Abu Zubaydah provided corroborative reporting: that Hassan Ghul could possibly be located through ████████████ ██████ [the well-known associate of Hassan Ghul].[1812] There are no CIA records indicating that Abu Zubaydah provided information on the location of ████████ [the well-known

---

[1807] ALEC ████ ████

[1808] As noted throughout this Study, CIA produced more than six million pages of material, including records detailing the interrogation of CIA detainees, as well as the disseminated intelligence derived from the interrogation of CIA detainees. The CIA did not provide—nor was it requested to provide—intelligence records that were unrelated to the CIA's Detention and Interrogation Program. In other words, this Study was completed without direct access to reporting from CIA HUMINT assets, foreign liaison assets, electronic intercepts, military detainee debriefings, law enforcement-derived information, and other methods of intelligence collection. Insomuch as this material is included in the analysis herein, it was provided by the CIA within the context of documents directly related to the CIA Detention and Interrogation Program. As such, there is likely significant intelligence related to the terrorist plots, terrorists captured, and other intelligence matters examined in this Study that is within the databases of the U.S. Intelligence Community, but which has not been identified or reviewed by the Committee for this Study.

[1809] ██████ 10091 (210959Z APR 02); ██████ 10102 (230707Z APR 02); ████ 10144 (271949Z APR 02); ██████ 10271 (151654Z MAY 02); ALEC ████ (241447Z MAR 02)

[1810] ██████ 10487 (181656Z JUN 02)

[1811] ██████ 10644 (201235Z AUG 02) and email from: [REDACTED]; to: ████████ and [REDACTED]; subject: "Re: So it begins."; date: August 4, 2002, at 09:45:09 AM.

[1812] ALEC ████ (292345Z AUG 02)

associate's] home, which, as noted, had been raided weeks earlier, on July █, 2002, and was already known to the CIA and Pakistani authorities.[1813]

(TS//███████████//NF) Nine days after Abu Zubaydah referenced ███████████ [the well-known associate of Hassan Ghul], on August 29, 2002, CIA Headquarters asked ███████████ to request that Pakistani authorities "reinterview █████ [the well-known associate] for additional intelligence on Hassan Ghul."[1814] The next day, August 30, 2002, ███████████ informed CIA Headquarters that Pakistani authorities were "in contact with the ███████████ [the well-known associate]," but that █████ would nonetheless ask the Pakistani authorities to question ███████████ [the well-known associate] again about Hassan Ghul's location.[1815] On August 31, 2002, █████ relayed that Pakistani authorities and █████ believed it was possible that ███████████ [the well-known associate] was not being fully truthful in his interviews with Pakistani authorities.[1816] On September 3, 2002, █████ reported that Pakistani authorities had re-interviewed ███████████ [the well-known associate] an unknown number of times, and that the Pakistani authorities noted that at times ███████████ [the well-known associate] contradicted himself.[1817] Approximately one week later, on September 9, 2002, Pakistani authorities returned again to ███████████ [the well-known associate's] home and interviewed ███████████ [a specific family member of the well-known associate], who had recently returned to ███████████ [the well-known associate's home].[1818]

[1813] ███████████ 11746 ███████████ The CIA's June 2013 Response highlights the following statement in the December 13, 2012, Committee Study: "It is possible that the sourcing for CIA claims that 'as a result of the use of EITs' Abu Zubaydah provided information that 'played a key role in the ultimate capture of Ramzi Bin al-Shibh,' are related to Abu Zubaydah's information indicating that Hassan Ghul could be located through ███████████ [the well-known associate]." The CIA's June 2013 Response states: "It is true that Abu Zubaydah provided no information specifically on Bin al-Shibh's whereabouts, but as the Study explicitly acknowledges, he did provide information on another al-Qa'ida facilitator that prompted Pakistani action that netted Bin al-Shibh." The Committee could find no CIA records of the CIA ever making this claim externally, or internally within the CIA, prior to the CIA's June 2013 Response. Rather, as described, the CIA claimed both before and after the President's September 2006 speech that Abu Zubaydah provided information related to bin al-Shibh that resulted in bin al-Shibh's capture. In an email from ███████████ to ███████████ and ███████████, dated September 7, 2006, █████ states: "...AZ gave us information on his recent activities that –when added into other information—helped us track him." The CIA's June 2013 Response asserts that the information Abu Zubaydah provided—that Hassan Ghul could possibly be located through ███████████ [a well-known associate of Hassan Ghul]—was "unique information" and that bin al-Shibh's "capture would not have occurred" "without Abu Zubaydah's information," which was collected "after he had been subjected to the enhanced interrogation techniques." As detailed in this summary, and in greater detail in Volume II, the statement provided by Abu Zubayah was not unique, but corroborative of information already collected and acted upon by government authorities.

[1814] ALEC ███████ (292345Z AUG 02)

[1815] ███████ 12148 (300601Z AUG 02)

[1816] ███████ 12151 (301107Z AUG 02)

[1817] ███████ 12207 (050524Z SEP 02)

[1818] While it is unclear from CIA records how Pakistani authorities learned ███████████ [the specific family member of the well-known associate] had returned home, ███████████ [the well-known associate] had sought the help of Pakistani authorities in retrieving ███████████ [the specific family member of the well-known associate]. Further, the CIA in early July 2002 had requested "technical surveillance" of ███████████ [the well-known associate's] telephone, and CIA records indicate that Pakistani authorities were maintaining regular contact with ███████████ [the well-known associate] after the initial July 2002 raid.

(TS// ██████████ //NF) In interviews with Pakistani authorities, ██████████ [the specific family member of the well-known associate] was cooperative and told the Pakistani authorities where Hassan Ghul's last apartment was located.[1819] Based on the information provided on Ghul's apartment, Pakistani authorities conducted a raid, but found the apartment empty.[1820]

(TS// ██████████ //NF) Pakistani authorities then located and interviewed ██████████ ██████████ [a third individual at the apartment complex]. From the interview [of the third individual], Pakistani authorities learned that while Hassan Ghul had vacated the apartment, he was scheduled to return to the complex ██████████ ██████████. Based on this information, Pakistani authorities placed the complex under surveillance and waited for Hassan Ghul to return.[1821] On September 10, 2002, Pakistani authorities arrested two individuals believed to be Hassan Ghul and his driver outside of the apartment complex.[1822] A CIA cable noted that "Ghul had returned to the apartment to ██████████, however, he got more than he bargained for."[1823] Another CIA cable stated:

> "Interestingly, he denies being Hassan Ghul – claiming Hassan Ghul is
> someone else. While ██████████ are fairly certain we do in fact have
> Hassan Ghul in custody, we would like to make every effort to verify."[1824]

(TS// ██████████ //NF) By September 11, 2002, it was determined that an individual named Muhammad Ahmad Ghulam Rabbani, aka Abu Badr, and his driver were arrested, not Hassan Ghul.[1825] Abu Badr's driver, Muhammad Madni, was immediately cooperative and told the arresting officers that Abu Badr was a "major al-Qa'ida [facilitator]." He then proceeded to provide Pakistani authorities with information about al-Qa'ida-affiliated residences and safe houses in Karachi.[1826]

(TS// ██████████ //NF) Based on the information provided by Muhammad Madni, Pakistani authorities ██████████ conducted ██████████ raids in Karachi over the next two days.[1827] Raids of the initial sites resulted in the recovery of "a number of modified electrical switch type mechanisms, modified circuit and 'game' boards and other miscellaneous wires with alligator clips and battery attachments."[1828] On September 11, 2002, additional raids resulted in

---

[1819] ██ 12249 (091259Z SEP 02)
[1820] ██ 12249 (091259Z SEP 02)
[1821] ██ 12249 (091259Z SEP 02)
[1822] ██ 12251 (██ SEP 02); CIA ██ (██ SEP 02) ██████████
[1823] ██ 12251 (██ SEP 02); CIA ██ (██ SEP 02) ██████████
[1824] ██ 12254 (100510Z SEP 02)
[1825] ██ 33363 (111226Z SEP 02)
[1826] ██ 12251 (██ SEP 02); CIA ██ (██ SEP 02) ██████████
[1827] ALEC ██ (111551Z SEP 02). The CIA's June 2013 Response states that Muhammad Ahmad Ghulam Rabbani, aka Abu Badr, provided the information on the "safe houses in Karachi." This is inaccurate. Multiple CIA records state this information was provided by Abu Badr's driver, Muhammad Madni, who was cooperating with Pakistani authorities and providing information for the raids.
[1828] ALEC ██ (101749Z SEP 02)

the arrest of 11 individuals, including Ramzi bin al-Shibh.[1829] According to CIA records, bin al-Shibh initially identified himself as 'Umar Muhammad 'Abdullah ba-'Amr, aka "Abu 'Ubyadah," but the CIA noted:

> "This individual strongly resembled pictures of Ramzi bin al-Shibh. When asked if he was videotaped in al-Qa'ida videos, he answered yes."[1830]

(TS// ████████ //NF) Shortly thereafter the CIA confirmed Ramzi bin al-Shibh was the individual in Pakistani custody.[1831]

(TS// ████████ //NF) Hassan Ghul was ultimately captured by foreign authorities in the Iraqi Kurdistan Region, on January ██, 2004.[1832] Hassan Ghul's capture was unrelated to any reporting from the CIA's Detention and Interrogation Program.[1833]

4. The Capture of Khalid Shaykh Mohammad (KSM)

(TS// ████████ //NF) On September 6, 2006, President Bush delivered a speech based on information provided by the CIA, and vetted by the CIA, that included the following statement:

> "Zubaydah *was questioned using these procedures* [the CIA's enhanced interrogation techniques], and soon he began to provide information on key al-Qa'ida operatives, including information that helped us find and capture more of those responsible for the attacks on September the 11th. For example, Zubaydah identified one of KSM's accomplices in the 9/11 attacks, a terrorist named Ramzi bin al-Shibh. The information Zubaydah provided helped lead to the capture of bin al-Shibh. *And together these two terrorists provided information that helped in the planning and execution of the operation that captured Khalid Sheikh Mohammed.*"[1834]

[1829] ALEC ████ (111551Z SEP 02).
[1830] CIA ████ (████ SEP 02)
[1831] ALEC ████ (130206Z SEP 02). The CIA's June 2013 Response does not dispute the narrative described by the Committee, and states the "[CIA] should have more clearly explained the contribution [Abu Zubaydah's] reporting made to this operation."
[1832] ████ 21753 ████
[1833] On January ██, 2004, Hassan Ghul was transferred to U.S. military custody. On January ██, 2004, Hassan Ghul was transferred to CIA custody. On August ██, 2006, Ghul was rendered to ████. On May ██, 2007, he was released ████ Hassan Ghul ████. *See* ████ 21815 ████; ████ 1642 ████ JAN 04); ████ 2441 ████; HEADQUARTERS ████; ████ 1635 ████; ████ 1712 ████; HEADQUARTERS ████; ████ 1775; ████ 173426 ████; and Committee Notification from the CIA dated ████ (DTS #2012-3802).
[1834] Italics added. President George W. Bush, Speech on the CIA's Terrorist Detention Program, (September 6, 2006). *See also* CIA officer ████████'s February 14, 2007, testimony to the Senate Select Committee on Intelligence in which she stated that Abu Zubaydah "really pointed us towards Khalid Shaykh Mohammad and how to find him," adding "[h]e led us to Ramzi bin al-Shibh, who in kind of [sic] started the chain of events." *See* transcript, Senate Select Committee on Intelligence, February 14, 2007 (DTS #2007-1337).

(TS// ███████████ //NF) Contrary to CIA representations, there are no CIA records to support the assertion that Abu Zubaydah, Ramzi bin al-Shibh, or any other CIA detainee played any role in the "the planning and execution of the operation that captured Khalid Sheikh Mohammed." CIA records clearly describe how the capture of KSM was attributable to a unilateral CIA asset ("ASSET X"[1835]) who gained access to KSM through ███████████, with whom the CIA asset had prior independent connections. ASSET X's possible access to KSM through ███████ was apparent to the CIA as early as the fall of 2001, prior to his formal recruitment. The CIA had multiple opportunities to exploit ASSET X's access to KSM's ████████ ███████ in 2001, and in 2002, after he was recruited, but did not. In February-March 2003, ASSET X led the CIA directly to KSM. The contemporaneous documentary record of this narrative is supported by numerous after-action interviews conducted by the CIA's Oral History Program. As the CIA officer who "handled" ASSET X and who was directly involved in the capture of KSM stated, "[t]he op[eration] was a HUMINT op pretty much from start to finish."[1836]

(TS// ███████████ //NF) Within days after the attacks of September 11, 2001, CTC officers suspected KSM of playing a key role in the September 11, 2001, terrorist attacks.[1837] Shortly thereafter, CTC officers also noted the "striking similarities" between the September 11, 2001, attacks, and the 1993 World Trade Center bombing by KSM's nephew, Ramzi Yousef, ████████ ██████████████████████████████.[1838] On September 26, 2001, the CIA's ALEC Station issued a cable on KSM and Ramzi Yousef that described extensive derogatory information on ███████████████████████████████████████ ████████████████████.[1839] The CIA officer who drafted the September 26, 2001,

---

[1835] CIA records provided to the Committee identify the pseudonym created by the CIA for the asset. The Study lists the asset as "ASSET X" to further protect his identity.

[1836] TD INTERVIEW, CIA ORAL HISTORY PROGRAM, SEPTEMBER 14, 2004], Presentation to the CTC ████████████ 14 September 2004 by ███████████. See also Interview of [REDACTED], by [REDACTED], 14 October 2004, CIA Oral History Program; Interview of [REDACTED], by [REDACTED], 14 September 2004, CIA Oral History Program; Interview of [REDACTED], by [REDACTED], 3 December 2004, CIA Oral History Program; Interview of [REDACTED], by [REDACTED], 30 November 2004, CIA Oral History Program; Interview of ████████, by [REDACTED], 25 October 2004, CIA Oral History Program; Interview of [REDACTED], by [REDACTED]; 24 November & 15 December 2004, CIA Oral History Program.

[1837] See, for example, the September 15, 2001, email from a CIA officer to ████████████ of ALEC Station, in which the officer wrote, "I would say the percentages are pretty high that Khalid Sheikh Mohammad is involved [in the September 11, 2001, attacks]." See email from: ███████████; to: ███████████; cc: ████████████, █████████, [REDACTED], ███████████, [REDACTED]; subject: Re: RAMZI LEADS...; date: September 15, 2001, at 5:04:38 AM). See also DIRECTOR ██████ (132018Z SEP 01), disseminated as ██████████.

[1838] ALEC ██████ (231718Z SEP 01). Ramzi Yousef is serving a life sentence in the United States.

[1839] A CIA source from 1995 reported that "all members of ██████████████████████ are acting together on behalf of a larger and well organized group." ███████ the source said, "are true terrorists and villains." (See WHDC ████████ OCT 95).) Reporting from 1998 indicated that "Sheikh Khalid" (KSM), along with ██████████, had "switched their allegiance" and were "part of the bin Ladin organization in Afghanistan." (See DIRECTOR ████████ SEP 98), disseminated as ██████████).) CIA cables describe ███ ██ [specific intelligence collected on KSM's ███████]. See ██████ 484112 ██████ JUL 99); WHDC ████████ OCT 95); ████████ 89173 ████ JUN 95); ██████ 90757 ██████ JUL 95); CIA █ ████ APR 95); ████████

cable wrote in an email that ████████████████████ were "associated with terrorists," and that ████████████████ "probably is a close associate of KSM."[1840] In a separate email, the CIA officer wrote that, "at a minimum, we should go after" ███. Both emails were sent to CIA officers who, a few days later, would consider ASSET X, a potential CIA source whose access to KSM through ████████ was readily apparent.[1841]

(~~TS//~~ ████████ ~~NF~~) ASSET X came to the CIA's attention in the spring of 2001 ███. ████████████████. However, CIA officers did not meet with ASSET X until after the September 11, 2001, attacks.[1842] On September 28, 2001, ALEC Station sent a cable ████████████████████████████, noting that "[g]iven the events of 11 September... [w]e are very interested in exploring whatever information [ASSET X] may have with regard to terrorist plans by [UBL]."[1843] The CIA held its first meeting with ASSET X on ████████, 2001, at which time ASSET X indicated that he knew ████████████████.[1844] The cable describing the first meeting states that "[ASSET X's] knowledge ████████████ appears to check out and demonstrates some degree of access/knowledge ████████████."[1845] On ████████, 2001, the cable describing the first meeting with ASSET X was forwarded by the drafter of the September 26, 2001, cable on the derogatory information concerning ████████████ to a number of CTC officers in an email with the subject line: "Re: [ASSET X] Information Re

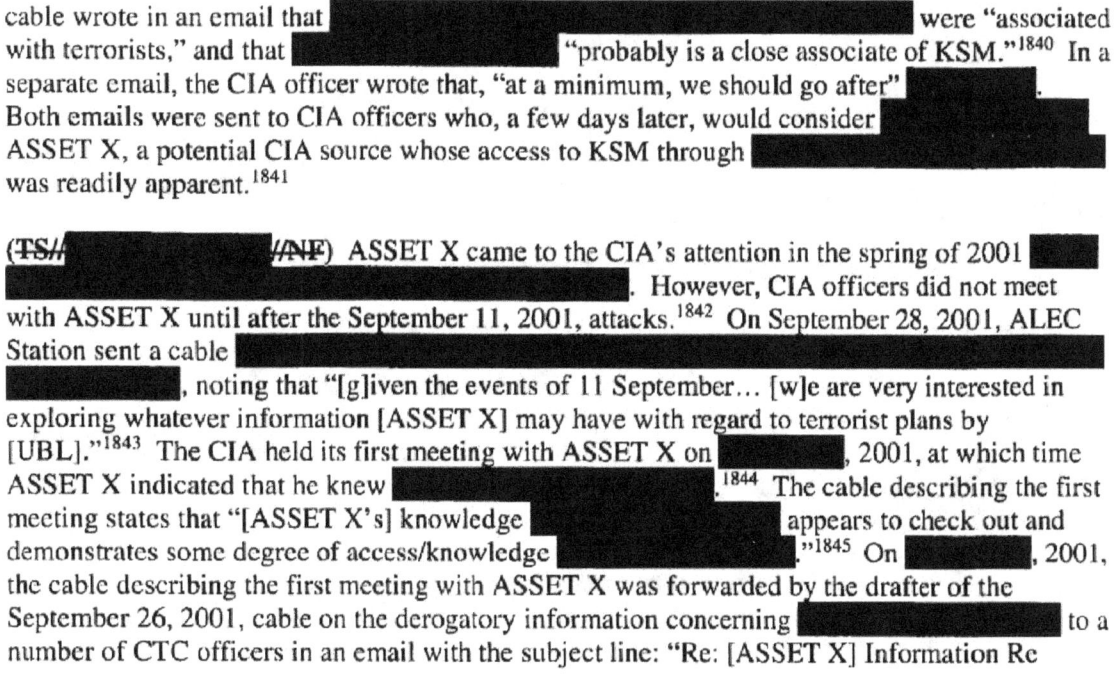

_____

████████ 91147 ████ AUG 95); DIRECTOR ████████ FEB 96), disseminated as ████
██████; ████ 69789 ████ FEB 95); ████ 85526 ████ FEB 95); ALEC ████
█ SEP 01); ████ 70158 ████ MAR 95); ████ 88666 ████ JUN 95); DIRECTOR
████ JUL 00); ALEC ████████ APR 99).

[1840] Email from: ████████; to: ████████, ████████,
[REDACTED]; subject: the yousef cohorts ████; date: September 25, 2001, at 6:58:17 PM.

[1841] Email from: ████████; to: ████████; cc: ████████, ████████; subject:
Re: ████████; date: October 4, 2001, at 12:52:46 PM. The CIA's June 2013 Response states that the Study "claims it was [ASSET X], not detainees, who first identified KSM's ████ for us." This is inaccurate. The Committee Study does not claim it was ASSET X who first identified KSM's ████ for the CIA. The Committee Study details how the CIA had extensive information on KSM's ████ as early as 1995; and how in ████ 2001, prior to CIA detainee reporting, ASSET X highlighted how KSM's ████████ to locating and capturing KSM.

[1842] The subject of the cable from the CIA ████████, was "possible lead to UBL target." (See
████ 73245 ████ [spring] 01). See also ████ 41495 ████; Interview of [REDACTED], by [REDACTED], 14 October 2004, CIA Oral History Program.) In ████ [spring] 2001, ASSET X would further indicate, ████████████. See WDC
████ ████; Interview of [REDACTED], by [REDACTED], 14 September 2004, CIA Oral History Program.

[1843] ALEC ████ (282144Z SEP 01)

[1844] ████ 66193 ████████. ASSET X identified ████████. The CIA cable also describes ASSET X's ████████
████ 66177 ████ ; ████ 66193 ████ ; ████ 66178 ████
. See also ████ 41495 ████; DIRECTOR ████ ; ████ 37701

[1845] ████ 66193 ████

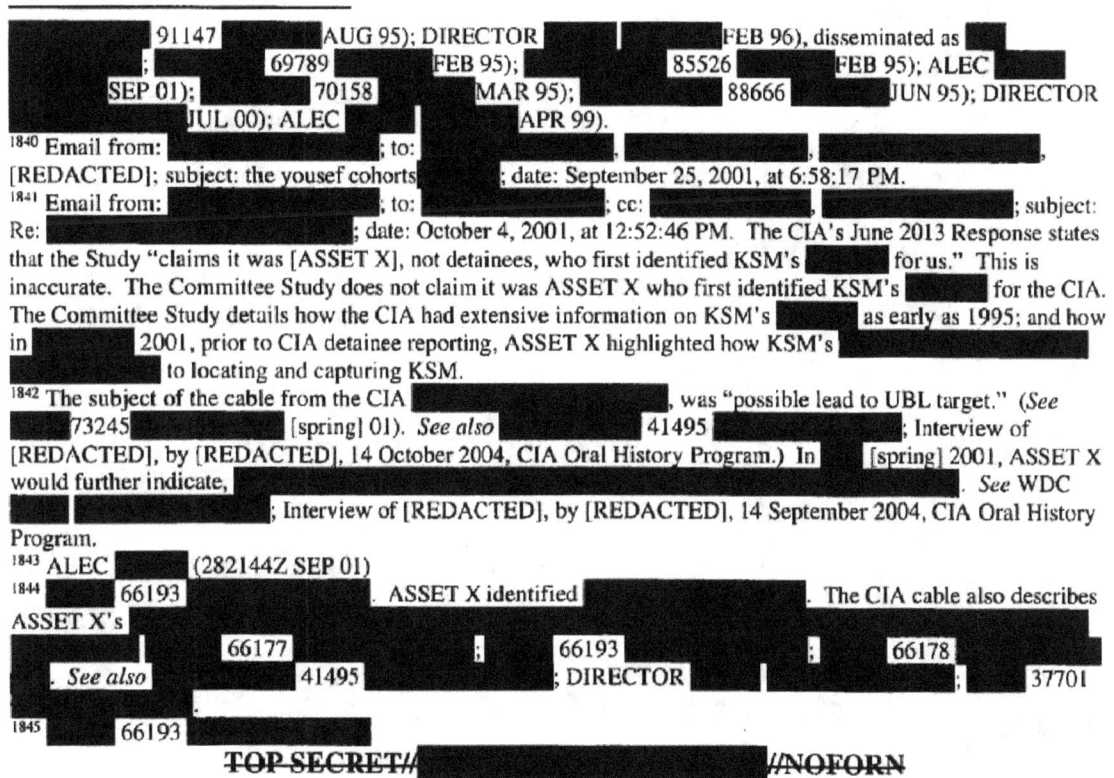

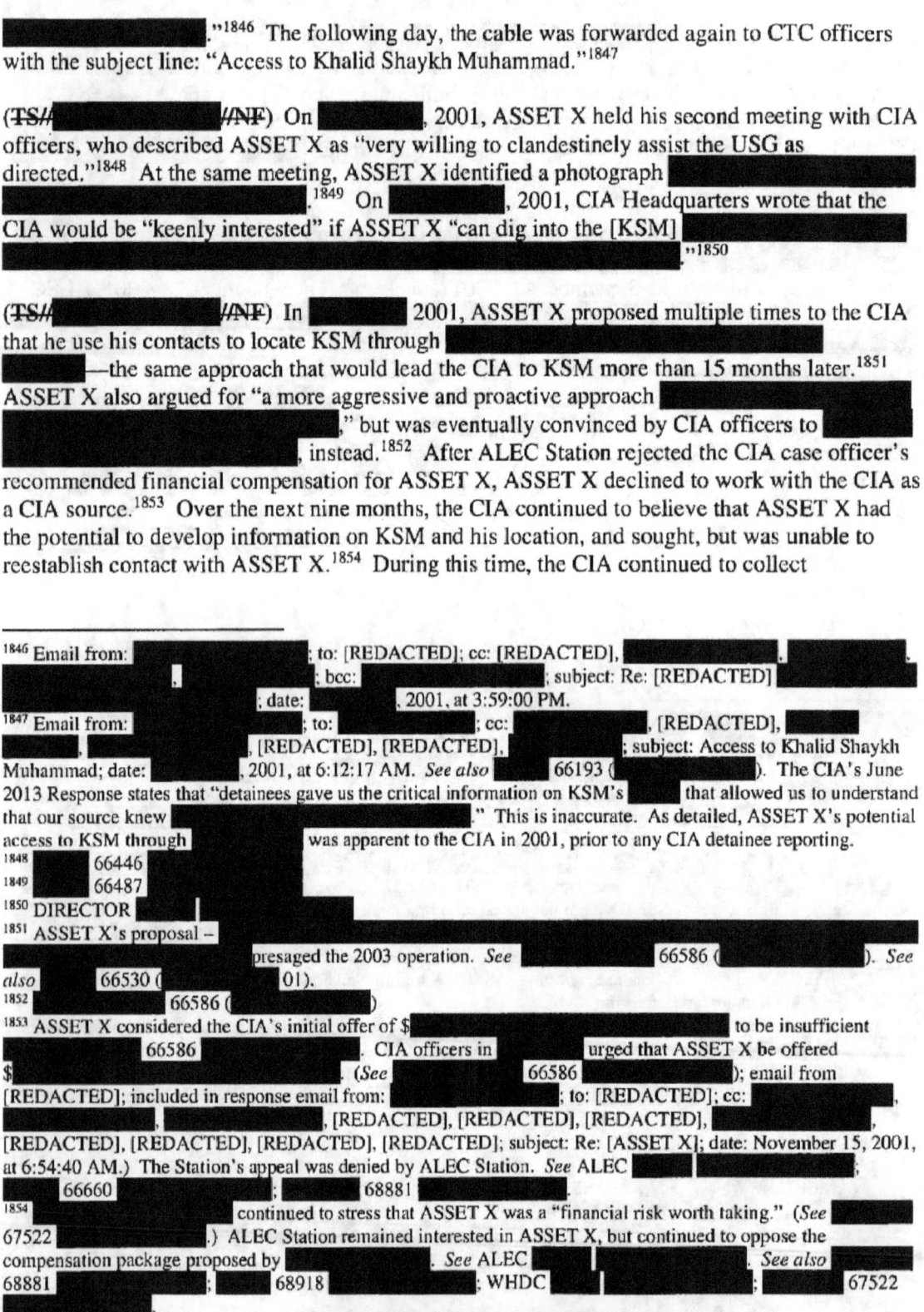

████████ ."[1846] The following day, the cable was forwarded again to CTC officers with the subject line: "Access to Khalid Shaykh Muhammad."[1847]

(TS// ████████ //NF) On ████████, 2001, ASSET X held his second meeting with CIA officers, who described ASSET X as "very willing to clandestinely assist the USG as directed."[1848] At the same meeting, ASSET X identified a photograph ████████ ████████ .[1849] On ████████, 2001, CIA Headquarters wrote that the CIA would be "keenly interested" if ASSET X "can dig into the [KSM] ████████ ████████ ."[1850]

(TS// ████████ //NF) In ████████ 2001, ASSET X proposed multiple times to the CIA that he use his contacts to locate KSM through ████████ ████████ —the same approach that would lead the CIA to KSM more than 15 months later.[1851] ASSET X also argued for "a more aggressive and proactive approach ████████ ████████ ," but was eventually convinced by CIA officers to ████████ ████████, instead.[1852] After ALEC Station rejected the CIA case officer's recommended financial compensation for ASSET X, ASSET X declined to work with the CIA as a CIA source.[1853] Over the next nine months, the CIA continued to believe that ASSET X had the potential to develop information on KSM and his location, and sought, but was unable to reestablish contact with ASSET X.[1854] During this time, the CIA continued to collect

---

[1846] Email from: ████████ ; to: [REDACTED]; cc: [REDACTED], ████████ ; bcc: ████████ ; subject: Re: [REDACTED] ; date: ████████, 2001, at 3:59:00 PM.
[1847] Email from: ████████ ; to: ████████ ; cc: ████████, [REDACTED], ████████, [REDACTED], [REDACTED], ████████ ; subject: Access to Khalid Shaykh Muhammad; date: ████████, 2001, at 6:12:17 AM. See also ████████ 66193 (████████). The CIA's June 2013 Response states that "detainees gave us the critical information on KSM's ████████ that allowed us to understand that our source knew ████████ ." This is inaccurate. As detailed, ASSET X's potential access to KSM through ████████ was apparent to the CIA in 2001, prior to any CIA detainee reporting.
[1848] ████████ 66446 ████████
[1849] ████████ 66487 ████████
[1850] DIRECTOR ████████
[1851] ASSET X's proposal – ████████ presaged the 2003 operation. See ████████ 66586 (████████). See also ████████ 66530 (████████ 01).
[1852] ████████ 66586 (████████)
[1853] ASSET X considered the CIA's initial offer of $████████ to be insufficient ████████ 66586 ████████ . CIA officers in ████████ urged that ASSET X be offered $████████ . (See ████████ 66586 (████████); email from [REDACTED]; included in response email from: ████████ ; to: [REDACTED]; cc: ████████, ████████, [REDACTED], [REDACTED], [REDACTED], [REDACTED], [REDACTED], [REDACTED], [REDACTED]; subject: Re: [ASSET X]; date: November 15, 2001, at 6:54:40 AM.) The Station's appeal was denied by ALEC Station. See ALEC ████████ ████████ 66660 ████████ ; ████████ 68881 ████████ .
[1854] ████████ continued to stress that ASSET X was a "financial risk worth taking." (See ████████ 67522 ████████.) ALEC Station remained interested in ASSET X, but continued to oppose the compensation package proposed by ████████ . See ALEC ████████ . See also ████████ 68881 ████████ ; ████████ 68918 ████████ ; WHDC ████████ ; ████████ 67522

intelligence on KSM's ███████,[1855] and sought other opportunities to gain access to KSM through ██████.[1856] In July 2002, a detainee in foreign government custody provided extensive information on KSM's ████ and confirmed that KSM was "very close" to ███████ who "should know how to contact KSM."[1857]

(TS// ███████ //NF) When the CIA finally located and met again with ASSET X on ██████, 2002, ASSET X stated that "he could ███████ within a few weeks," and was "willing to travel ███████ to locate ███████."[1858] ASSET X was recruited as a source by the CIA, but, despite his offer to track KSM's ███████, ASSET X was dispatched by the CIA to ███████

[1859]

[1860]

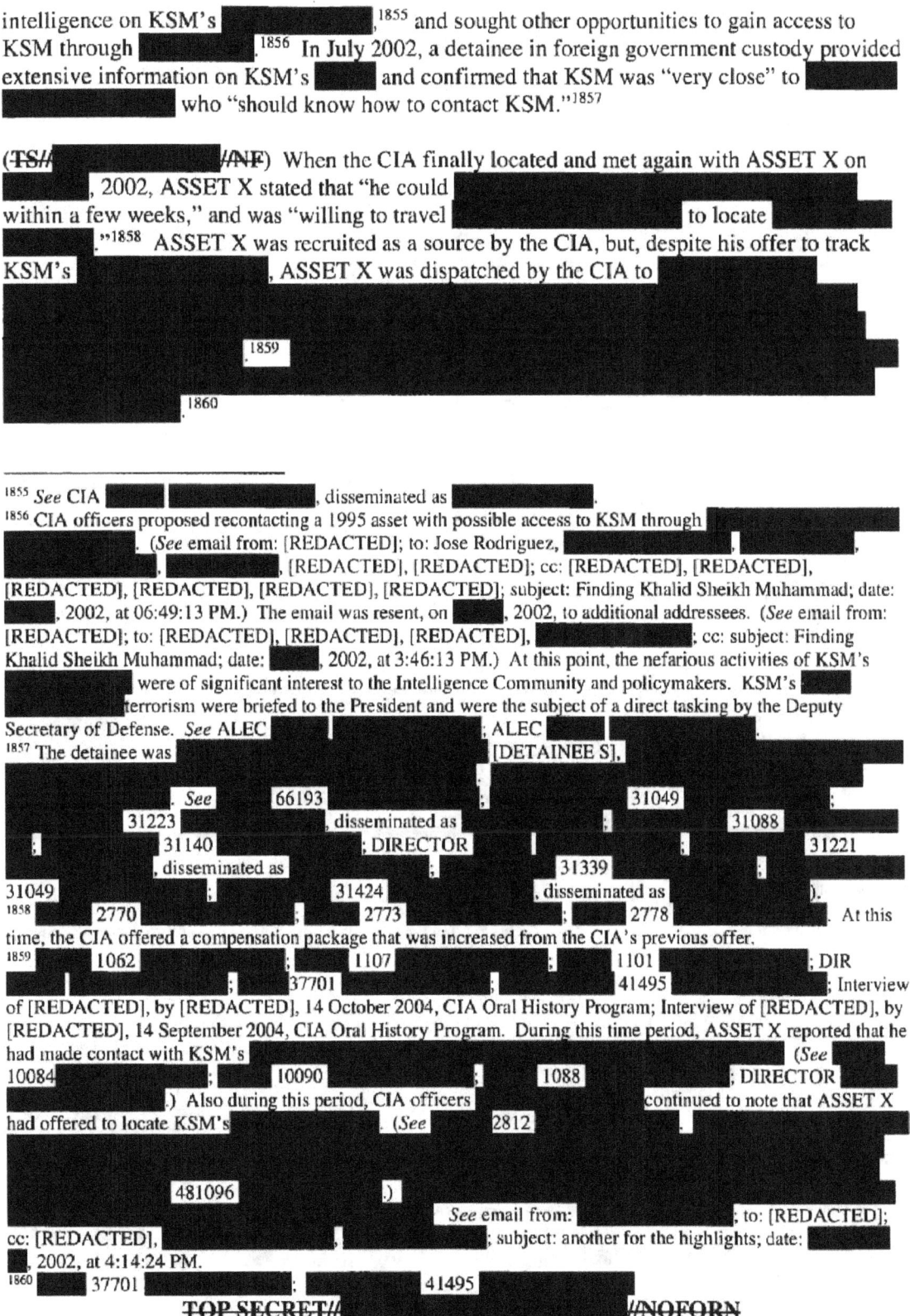

[1855] *See* CIA ████████████, disseminated as ████████.

[1856] CIA officers proposed recontacting a 1995 asset with possible access to KSM through ███████. (*See* email from: [REDACTED]; to: Jose Rodriguez, ███████, ███████, [REDACTED], [REDACTED]; cc: [REDACTED], [REDACTED], [REDACTED], [REDACTED], [REDACTED], [REDACTED]; subject: Finding Khalid Sheikh Muhammad; date: ████, 2002, at 06:49:13 PM.) The email was resent, on ████, 2002, to additional addressees. (*See* email from: [REDACTED]; to: [REDACTED], [REDACTED], [REDACTED], ███████; cc: subject: Finding Khalid Sheikh Muhammad; date: ████, 2002, at 3:46:13 PM.) At this point, the nefarious activities of KSM's ███████ were of significant interest to the Intelligence Community and policymakers. KSM's ████ ███████ terrorism were briefed to the President and were the subject of a direct tasking by the Deputy Secretary of Defense. *See* ALEC ███████; ALEC ███████.

[1857] The detainee was ███████ [DETAINEE S], ███████. *See* 66193 ███████ 31049 ███████; 31223 disseminated as ███████; 31088 ███████; 31140 ; DIRECTOR ; 31221 ███████, disseminated as ███████; 31339 ███████; 31049 ; 31424 , disseminated as).

[1858] 2770 ; 2773 ; 2778 ███████. At this time, the CIA offered a compensation package that was increased from the CIA's previous offer.

[1859] 1062 ; 1107 ; 1101 ; DIR ███████; 37701 ; 41495 ; Interview of [REDACTED], by [REDACTED], 14 October 2004, CIA Oral History Program; Interview of [REDACTED], by [REDACTED], 14 September 2004, CIA Oral History Program. During this time period, ASSET X reported that he had made contact with KSM's ███████ (*See* 10084 ; 10090 ; 1088 ; DIRECTOR ███████.) Also during this period, CIA officers ███████ continued to note that ASSET X had offered to locate KSM's ███████ (*See* 2812 ███████ 481096 ███████) ███████ *See* email from: ███████; to: [REDACTED]; cc: [REDACTED], ███████; subject: another for the highlights; date: ████, 2002, at 4:14:24 PM.

[1860] ████ 37701 ███████; 41495 ███████

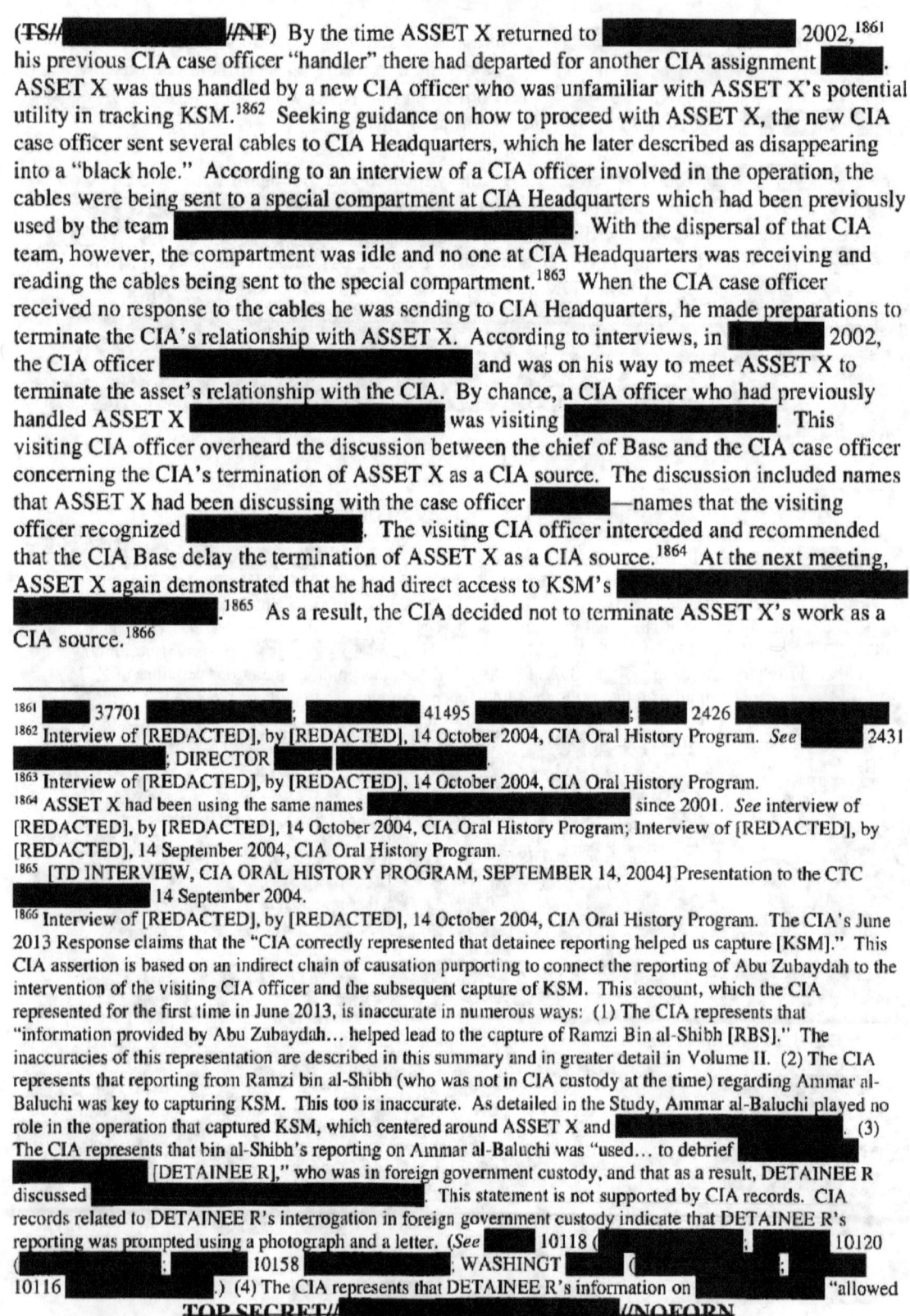

(TS//███████████//NF) By the time ASSET X returned to ████████████ 2002,[1861] his previous CIA case officer "handler" there had departed for another CIA assignment ████. ASSET X was thus handled by a new CIA officer who was unfamiliar with ASSET X's potential utility in tracking KSM.[1862] Seeking guidance on how to proceed with ASSET X, the new CIA case officer sent several cables to CIA Headquarters, which he later described as disappearing into a "black hole." According to an interview of a CIA officer involved in the operation, the cables were being sent to a special compartment at CIA Headquarters which had been previously used by the team ████████████████████████████. With the dispersal of that CIA team, however, the compartment was idle and no one at CIA Headquarters was receiving and reading the cables being sent to the special compartment.[1863] When the CIA case officer received no response to the cables he was sending to CIA Headquarters, he made preparations to terminate the CIA's relationship with ASSET X. According to interviews, in █████ 2002, the CIA officer ████████████████████ and was on his way to meet ASSET X to terminate the asset's relationship with the CIA. By chance, a CIA officer who had previously handled ASSET X ███████████████ was visiting ████████████. This visiting CIA officer overheard the discussion between the chief of Base and the CIA case officer concerning the CIA's termination of ASSET X as a CIA source. The discussion included names that ASSET X had been discussing with the case officer █████—names that the visiting officer recognized ████████████. The visiting CIA officer interceded and recommended that the CIA Base delay the termination of ASSET X as a CIA source.[1864] At the next meeting, ASSET X again demonstrated that he had direct access to KSM's ████████████████████ ████████████.[1865] As a result, the CIA decided not to terminate ASSET X's work as a CIA source.[1866]

[1861] ████ 37701 ████████████; ████ 41495 ████████████; ████ 2426 ████████████
[1862] Interview of [REDACTED], by [REDACTED], 14 October 2004, CIA Oral History Program. See ████ 2431 ████████████████; DIRECTOR ████ ████████.
[1863] Interview of [REDACTED], by [REDACTED], 14 October 2004, CIA Oral History Program.
[1864] ASSET X had been using the same names ████████████████████ since 2001. See interview of [REDACTED], by [REDACTED], 14 October 2004, CIA Oral History Program; Interview of [REDACTED], by [REDACTED], 14 September 2004, CIA Oral History Program.
[1865] [TD INTERVIEW, CIA ORAL HISTORY PROGRAM, SEPTEMBER 14, 2004] Presentation to the CTC ████████████ 14 September 2004.
[1866] Interview of [REDACTED], by [REDACTED], 14 October 2004, CIA Oral History Program. The CIA's June 2013 Response claims that the "CIA correctly represented that detainee reporting helped us capture [KSM]." This CIA assertion is based on an indirect chain of causation purporting to connect the reporting of Abu Zubaydah to the intervention of the visiting CIA officer and the subsequent capture of KSM. This account, which the CIA represented for the first time in June 2013, is inaccurate in numerous ways: (1) The CIA represents that "information provided by Abu Zubaydah... helped lead to the capture of Ramzi Bin al-Shibh [RBS]." The inaccuracies of this representation are described in this summary and in greater detail in Volume II. (2) The CIA represents that reporting from Ramzi bin al-Shibh (who was not in CIA custody at the time) regarding Ammar al-Baluchi was key to capturing KSM. This too is inaccurate. As detailed in the Study, Ammar al-Baluchi played no role in the operation that captured KSM, which centered around ASSET X and ████████████████████. (3) The CIA represents that bin al-Shibh's reporting on Ammar al-Baluchi was "used... to debrief ████████████████ [DETAINEE R]," who was in foreign government custody, and that as a result, DETAINEE R discussed ████████████████████. This statement is not supported by CIA records. CIA records related to DETAINEE R's interrogation in foreign government custody indicate that DETAINEE R's reporting was prompted using a photograph and a letter. (See ████ 10118 (████████; ████ 10120 (████████; ████ 10158 ████████████, WASHINGT██ (████████; ████ 10116 ████████.) (4) The CIA represents that DETAINEE R's information on ████████ "allowed

(TS// ████████ //NF) Shortly thereafter, in ████ 2003, ASSET X traveled on his own volition, and without prior discussion with the CIA, to ████████████████, and ████ a face-to-face meeting with KSM. When ASSET X later informed CIA officers about his trip, direct access to KSM

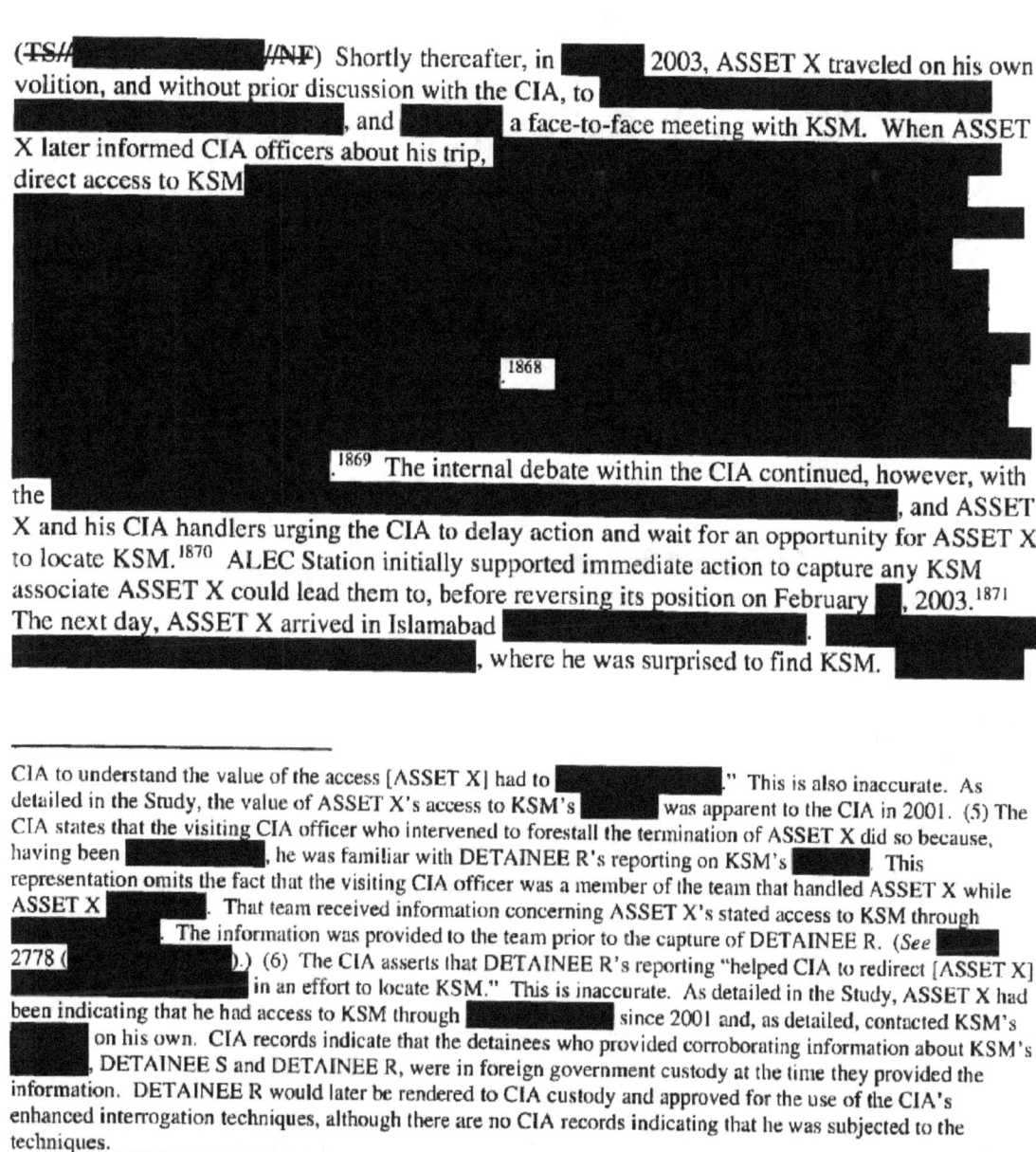

.¹⁸⁶⁹ The internal debate within the CIA continued, however, with the ██████████████████████████, and ASSET X and his CIA handlers urging the CIA to delay action and wait for an opportunity for ASSET X to locate KSM.[1870] ALEC Station initially supported immediate action to capture any KSM associate ASSET X could lead them to, before reversing its position on February ██, 2003.[1871] The next day, ASSET X arrived in Islamabad ██████████████████, where he was surprised to find KSM.

CIA to understand the value of the access [ASSET X] had to ████████." This is also inaccurate. As detailed in the Study, the value of ASSET X's access to KSM's ████ was apparent to the CIA in 2001. (5) The CIA states that the visiting CIA officer who intervened to forestall the termination of ASSET X did so because, having been ████████, he was familiar with DETAINEE R's reporting on KSM's ████. This representation omits the fact that the visiting CIA officer was a member of the team that handled ASSET X while ASSET X ████. That team received information concerning ASSET X's stated access to KSM through ████. The information was provided to the team prior to the capture of DETAINEE R. (See ████ 2778 (████).) (6) The CIA asserts that DETAINEE R's reporting "helped CIA to redirect [ASSET X] ████ in an effort to locate KSM." This is inaccurate. As detailed in the Study, ASSET X had been indicating that he had access to KSM through ████ since 2001 and, as detailed, contacted KSM's ████ on his own. CIA records indicate that the detainees who provided corroborating information about KSM's ████, DETAINEE S and DETAINEE R, were in foreign government custody at the time they provided the information. DETAINEE R would later be rendered to CIA custody and approved for the use of the CIA's enhanced interrogation techniques, although there are no CIA records indicating that he was subjected to the techniques.

[1867] DIR ████████; Interview of [REDACTED], by [REDACTED], 14 October 2004, CIA Oral History Program; ████████;

[1868] Interview of [REDACTED], by [REDACTED], 14 October 2004, CIA Oral History Program; Interview of [REDACTED], by [REDACTED], 3 December 2004, CIA Oral History Program.

[1869] Interview of [REDACTED], by [REDACTED], 14 October 2004, CIA Oral History Program.

[1870] Interview of [REDACTED], by [REDACTED], 14 October 2004, CIA Oral History Program; Interview of [REDACTED], by [REDACTED], 14 September 2004, CIA Oral History Program; Interview of [REDACTED], by [REDACTED]; 24 November & 15 December 2004, CIA Oral History Program; Interview of [REDACTED], by [REDACTED], 30 November 2004. See ████████ 41034 ████████.

[1871] Interview of [REDACTED], by [REDACTED], 3 December 2004, CIA Oral History Program; DIRECTOR ████████.

████████, ASSET X ██████████████ sent a text message to his CIA handler stating: "I M W KSM."[1872]

(TS// ██████ //NF) ██ [1873] ████████████████████████████████████ [1874] ████████████████████, ASSET X contacted the CIA and conveyed what had just occurred.[1875]

(TS// ██████ //NF) ████████████████████████████ [1876] In an interview with the CIA's Oral History Program, the CIA case officer described what happened:

> "We went around, you know, ████████████████████. [ASSET X] turns around to me and says, look I don't know, I guess I'm nervous, ████████████████. I said, 'Look brother there are twenty five million frigging reasons why you need to find ████████.' That's what the reward was. He looks at me and says, 'I understand. I understand.'"[1877]

(TS// ██████████ //NF) Shortly thereafter, ASSET X found ████████ and, in the early morning hours of March 1, 2003, Pakistani authorities conducted a raid and captured KSM.[1878] On March █, 2003, KSM was rendered to CIA custody.[1879]

[1872] Interview of [REDACTED], by [REDACTED], 14 October 2004, CIA Oral History Program.
[1873] Interview of [REDACTED], by [REDACTED], 14 October 2004, CIA Oral History Program; Interview of [REDACTED], by [REDACTED], 3 December 2004, CIA Oral History Program; ████████████ 41490 ████████████); Interview of ████████, by [REDACTED], 25 October 2004, CIA Oral History Program; Interview of [REDACTED], by [REDACTED], 14 September 2004, CIA Oral History Program.
[1874] Interview of [REDACTED], by [REDACTED], 14 October 2004, CIA Oral History Program; Interview of [REDACTED], by [REDACTED], 3 December 2004, CIA Oral History Program; ████████████ 41490 (████████████).
[1875] Interview of [REDACTED], by [REDACTED], 14 October 2004, CIA Oral History Program; Interview of [REDACTED], by [REDACTED], 3 December 2004, CIA Oral History Program; ████████████ 41490 (████████████).
[1876] ████████ 41490 (████████████).
[1877] Interview of [REDACTED], by [REDACTED], 14 September 2004, CIA Oral History Program.
[1878] ████████ 41351 ████████; ████████ 41490 ████████████; ALEC ████████████ 41490 ████████████).
[1879] See ████████ 10983 (242321Z MAR 03); ████████ 10972 (241122Z MAR 03); and the KSM detainee review in Volume III.

5. *The Capture of Majid Khan*

(TS// ███████ //NF) The CIA represented that intelligence derived from the use of the CIA's enhanced interrogation techniques against CIA detainee KSM led to the capture of Majid Khan. These representations were inaccurate.

(TS// ███████ //NF) In multiple interviews with the CIA Office of Inspector General, CIA officers stated that "information from KSM led to the capture of [Majid] Kahn [sic]," and that "KSM gave us Majid Khan."[1880] The deputy chief of ALEC Station and former KSM debriefer ██████████ represented that KSM "provided information that helped lead to the arrest of... Majid Khan, an operative who could get into the U.S. easily."[1881] The draft OIG Special Review repeated the representations of ██████ and others, stating that KSM "provided information that helped lead to the arrests of terrorists including... Majid Khan, an operative who could enter the United States easily and was tasked to research attacks against U.S. water reservoirs."[1882] On February 27, 2004, DDO James Pavitt submitted the CIA's formal response to the draft Inspector General Special Review. Pavitt's submission represented that Majid Khan was in custody "because of the information we were able lawfully to obtain from KSM."[1883] The final, and now declassified, CIA Inspector General Special Review states that KSM "provided information that helped lead to the arrests of terrorists including... Majid Khan, an operative who could enter the United States easily and was tasked to research attacks...."[1884] In its analysis of the legality of the CIA's enhanced interrogation techniques, the OLC relied on passages of the Inspector General's Special Review that included this inaccurate representation.[1885]

(TS// ███████ //NF) On July 29, 2003, CIA leadership met with select members of the National Security Council to obtain reaffirmation of the CIA interrogation program. The CIA stated that "detainees subject[ed] to the use of Enhanced Techniques of one kind or another had produced significant intelligence information that had, in the view of CIA professionals, saved

---

[1880] Interview of John E. McLaughlin, by [REDACTED] and [REDACTED], Office of the Inspector General, September 5, 2003; ██████████, Memorandum for the Record; subject: Meeting with Deputy Chief, Counterterrorist Center Al-Qa'ida Department; date: 28 July 2003; Interview of ██████████, by ████ ████, Office of the Inspector General, August 18, 2003.

[1881] ██████████, Memorandum for the Record; subject: Meeting with Deputy Chief, Counterterrorist Center ALEC Station; date: 17 July 2003.

[1882] CIA Inspector General, Special Review, Counterterrorism Detention and Interrogation Program (2003-7123-IG), January 2004.

[1883] Memorandum for: Inspector General; from: James Pavitt, Deputy Director for Operations; subject: re (S) Comments to Draft IG Special Review, "Counterterrorism Detention and Interrogation Program" (2003-7123-IG); date: February 27, 2004; attachment: February 24, 2004, Memorandum re Successes of CIA's Counterterrorism Detention and Interrogation Activities.

[1884] CIA Office of Inspector General, Special Review – Counterterrorism Detention and Interrogation Program, (2003-7123-IG), May 2004.

[1885] Memorandum for John A. Rizzo, Senior Deputy General Counsel, Central Intelligence Agency, from Steven G. Bradbury, Principal Deputy Assistant Attorney General, Office of Legal Counsel, May 30, 2005, Re: Application of United States Obligations Under Article 16 of the Convention Against Torture to Certain Techniques that May be Used in the Interrogation of High Value Al Qaeda Detainees, pp. 10-11, citing CIA Office of Inspector General, Special Review, pp. 85-91.

lives."[1886] Briefing slides provided by the CIA stated that "major threat" information was acquired, providing the "Identification of... the Majid Khan Family" by KSM as an example.[1887] The same slides were used, at least in part, for subsequent briefings.[1888] On September 16, 2003, a briefing was conducted for Secretary of State Colin Powell and Secretary of Defense Donald Rumsfeld, the content of which was described as "virtually identical" to the July 29, 2003, briefing.[1889] The slides were also used in an October 7, 2003, briefing for Assistant Attorney General Jack Goldsmith.[1890]

(TS// ███████ //NF) CIA records indicate that Majid Khan was identified and located prior to any reporting from KSM. There is no indication in CIA records that reporting from KSM—or any other CIA detainee—played any role in the identification and capture of Majid Khan.[1891]

(TS// ███████ //NF) On January 10, 2003, the FBI's Baltimore Field Office opened a full field international terrorism investigation on the email account "BobDesi(@)hotmail.com." According to FBI investigative records, the investigation was "predicated upon information received through the Central Intelligence Agency (CIA) concerning" a known al-Qa'ida email account that was already "under FISA coverage ███████."[1892] Six days later, on January 16, 2003, open source research related to the "BobDesi" email account "revealed a personal website

---

[1886] CIA Memorandum for the Record, "Review of Interrogation Program on 29 July 2003," prepared by CIA General Counsel Scott Muller, dated August 5, 2003; briefing slides entitled, "*CIA Interrogation Program,*" dated July 29, 2003, presented to senior White House officials.

[1887] *See* briefing slides entitled, "*CIA Interrogation Program,*" dated July 29, 2003, presented to senior White House officials. Those attending the meeting included Vice President Richard Cheney, National Security Advisor Condoleezza Rice, White House Counsel Alberto Gonzales, Attorney General John Ashcroft, Acting Assistant Attorney General Patrick Philbin, and counsel to the National Security Council, John Bellinger.

[1888] The CIA's June 2003 Response states that "CIA mistakenly provided incorrect information to the Inspector General (IG) that led to a one-time misrepresentation of this case in the IG's 2004 *Special Review.*" The CIA's June 2013 Response adds that, "[t]his mistake was not, as it is characterized in the 'Findings and Conclusions' section of the *Study,* a 'repeatedly represented' or 'frequently cited' example of the effectiveness of CIA's enhanced interrogation program." The CIA's June 2013 assertion that this was a "one-time misrepresentation" is inaccurate. As described, the inaccurate information was provided numerous times to the Inspector General, in multiple interviews and in the CIA's official response to the draft Special Review. Afterwards, the CIA relied on the section of the Special Review that included the inaccurate information on the capture of Majid Khan in obtaining legal approval for the use of the CIA's enhanced interrogation techniques from the Department of Justice. This information was also provided by the CIA to the CIA's Blue Ribbon Panel for their review of the CIA's Detention and Interrogation Program. The CIA also included the inaccurate representation about the identification of Majid Khan and his family to the National Security Council principals on multiple occasions. Further, as noted, the inaccurate information in the CIA OIG Special Review was declassified and has been used in multiple open source articles and books, often as an example of the effectiveness of the CIA program.

[1889] Memorandum for the Record; subject: CIA Interrogation Program; September 27, 2003 (OGC-FO-2003-50088). Slides, CIA Interrogation Program, 16 September 2003. John B. Bellinger III, Senior Associate Counsel to the President and Legal Advisor, National Security Council; Memorandum for the Record; subject: Briefing of Secretaries Powell and Rumsfeld regarding Interrogation of High-Value Detainees; date: September 30, 2003.

[1890] Scott W. Muller; Memorandum for the Record; Interrogation briefing for Jack Goldsmith; date: 16 October 2003 (OGC-FO-2003-50097).

[1891] For additional details, *see* Volumes II and Volume III.

[1892] *See* FBI 302 on FBI case file ███████████████████, and ███████ 88793 ███████
███.

for the user, Majid Khan."[1893] In February 2003, ███████ was tracking Majid Khan's Internet activity and was confident he was located at his brother's house in Karachi, Pakistan.[1894] On March 4, 2003, ALEC Station noted that activity on an al-Qa'ida email account—associated with Khallad bin Attash—that was in contact with Majid Khan, had been dormant. ALEC Station recommended that ████████████████████████████ move to capture Majid Khan in the hope that Majid Khan could lead CIA officers to Khallad bin Attash.[1895] The following morning, March 5, 2003, officers from Pakistan ███████████ carried out a raid on Majid Khan's brother's house, detaining Majid Khan.[1896]

(TS// ███████████ //NF) On March 15, 2003, Deputy Chief of ALEC Station ████████ sent an email to CIA Headquarters noting that she had read the reporting from Majid Khan's foreign government interrogations and was requesting photographs of Majid Khan and his associates to use in the KSM interrogations.[1897] CIA Headquarters provided the photographs the same day.[1898] On March 17, 2003, KSM was shown the photograph of Majid Khan and discussed the person he stated he knew as "Yusif," for the first time.[1899]

6. *The Thwarting of the Camp Lemonier Plotting*

(TS// ███████████ //NF) The CIA represented that intelligence derived from the use of the CIA's enhanced interrogation techniques thwarted plotting against the U.S. military base, Camp Lemonier, in Djibouti. These representations were inaccurate.

(U) In the September 6, 2006, speech, acknowledging the CIA's Detention and Interrogation Program, which was based on CIA-provided information and vetted by the CIA, President George W. Bush stated:

> "This is intelligence that cannot be found any other place. And our security depends on getting this kind of information."

The speech continued:

> "These are some of the plots that have been stopped because of information from this vital program. Terrorists held in CIA custody have also provided

---

[1893] ALEC ████████ (160141Z JAN 03)
[1894] ████████ 13571 (260330Z FEB 03)
[1895] ALEC ████████ (040329Z MAR 03)
[1896] ████████ 13658 (050318Z MAR 03); ████████ 13659 (050459Z MAR 03); DIRECTOR ████████ (050459Z MAR 03).
[1897] Memorandum for: ████████, [REDACTED]; from: [REDACTED],OFFICE: ████████/DETENTION SITE BLUE]; subject: Baltimore boy and KSM; date: 15 March 2003, at 07:08:32 PM.
[1898] ALEC Station sent DETENTION SITE BLUE photographs for use with KSM and other detainees. They included Majid Khan, Muhammad Khan, Sohail Munir, Iyman Faris, Majid Khan's cousin (Mansour), Fayyaz Kamran, Aydinbelge, Khalid Jamil, and Aafia Siddiqui. *See* ALEC ████████ (152212Z MAR 03).
[1899] ████████ 10865 (171648Z MAR 03); ████████ 10886 (182219Z MAR 03); ████████ 10870 (172017Z MAR 03)

information that helped stop the planned strike on U.S. Marines at Camp Lemonier in Djibouti."[1900]

(TS// ███████ //NF) An Office of the Director of National Intelligence public release accompanying the September 6, 2006, speech, states that "the CIA designed a new interrogation program that would be safe, effective, and legal." The document asserts: "In early 2004, *shortly after his capture*, al-Qa'ida facilitator Gouled Hassan Dourad *revealed* that in mid-2003 al-Qa'ida East Africa cell leader Abu Talha al-Sudani sent him from Mogadishu to Djibouti to case the US Marine base Camp Lemonier, as part of a plot to send suicide bombers with a truck bomb."[1901]

(TS// ███████ //NF) Similarly, in a prepared briefing for the chairman of the House Defense Appropriations Subcommittee, John Murtha, on October 30, 2007, the CIA represented that the CIA could not conduct its detention operations at Guantanamo Bay, Cuba, because "interrogations conducted on US military installations must comply with the Army Field Manual." The CIA presentation stated that the CIA program was "critical to [the CIA's] ability

---

[1900] *See* "CIA Validation of Remarks on Detainee Policy," drafts supporting the September 6, 2006, speech by President George W. Bush acknowledging and describing the CIA's Detention and Interrogation Program, as well as an unclassified Office of the Director of National Intelligence release, entitled, "Summary of the High Value Terrorist Detainee Program." In October 2007 CIA officers discussed a section of the President's speech, which was based on CIA information and vetted by the CIA, related to Camp Lemonier. Addressing the section of the speech that states, "[t]errorists held in CIA custody have also provided information that helped stop the planned strike on U.S. Marines at Camp Lemonier in Djibouti," a senior CIA officer highlighted that the plotting had not been stopped, but in fact was ongoing. The officer wrote: "I have attached the cable from Guleed that was used to source the Sept '06 speech as well as a later cable from a different detainee affirming that as of mid-2004, AQ members in Somalia were still intent on attacking Camp Lemonier... As of 2004, the second detainee indicates that AQ was still working on attacking the base." The CIA officer explained that the "reasoning behind validation of the language in the speech—and remember, we can argue about whether or not 'planning' consistitutes [sic] a 'plot' and about whether anything is ever disrupted—was that the detainee reporting increased our awareness of attack plotting against the base, leading to heightened security." (*See* email from: ███████, to: ███████; subject: "More on Camp Lemonier"; date: October 22, 2007, at 5:33 PM). The President's reference to Camp Lemonier in the context of "this vital program" came immediately after the passage of the speech referencing the use of the CIA's enhanced interrogation techniques against KSM and immediately before statements about the thwarting of the Karachi and Heathrow Airport plots, both of which have been explicitly attributed by the CIA to the use of the CIA's enhanced interrogation techniques. The disruption of the Camp Lemonier plotting was also referenced as an intelligence success in the context of the March 2008 presidential veto of legislation that would have effectively banned the CIA's enhanced interrogation techniques. *See* "Text: Bush on Veto of Intelligence Bill," *The New York Times,* dated March 8, 2008, which states, the "main reason this program has been effective is that it allows the CIA to use specialized interrogation procedures... limiting the CIA's interrogation methods to those in the Army field manual would be dangerous...."

[1901] Italics added. Unclassified Office of the Director of National Intelligence release, entitled, "Summary of the High Value Terrorist Detainee Program." CIA records indicate that the CIA had intelligence that al-Qa'ida affiliated individuals were targeting Camp Lemonier with an "explosives-laden truck" in early 2003. The CIA sought to detain Gouled because of the intelligence already collected, indicating that in 2003—at the likely behest of Abu Talha al-Sudani—Gouled was conducting casings of Camp Lemonier. Once captured, and prior to being transferred to CIA custody, Gouled confirmed that he cased Camp Lemonier for a potential terrorist attack. Despite the use of the term "revealed" in the 2006 document, the CIA's June 2013 Response states: "We did not represent that we initially learned of the plot from detainees, or that it was disrupted based solely on information from detainees in CIA custody." The CIA's June 2013 Response further states that the CIA "agree[s] with the *Study* that [the CIA] had threat reporting against Camp Lemonier prior to the March 2004 detention and rendition" of Guleed Hassan Dourad.

to protect the American homeland and US forces and citizens abroad from terrorist attack," that "[m]ost, if not all, of the intelligence acquired from high-value detainees in this [CIA] program would likely not have been discovered or reported in any other way," that the CIA program "is in no way comparable to the detainee programs run by our military," and that the CIA used information derived from the program "to disrupt terrorist plots—**including against our military.**"[1902] The CIA presentation then stated:

> "[A CIA detainee] informed us[1903] of an operation underway to attack the U.S. military at Camp Lemonier in Djibouti. We believe our understanding of this plot helped us to prevent the attack."[1904]

(TS// ███████████ //NF) A review of CIA records found that: (1) the detainee to whom the CIA's representations refer—Guleed (variant, Gouled) Hassan Dourad—was not subjected to the CIA's enhanced interrogation techniques; (2) the CIA was aware of and reported on the terrorist threat to Camp Lemonier prior to receiving any information from CIA detainees;[1905] (3) Guleed provided corroborative reporting on the threat prior to being transferred to CIA custody; and (4) contrary to CIA representations, the plotting did not "stop" because of information acquired from CIA detainee Guleed in 2004, but rather, continued well into 2007.[1906]

[1902] Emphasis in original. *See* CIA Talking Points dated October 30, 2007, entitled, "DCIA Meeting with Chairman Murtha re Rendition and Detention Programs" and attachments.

[1903] The CIA's June 2013 Response states: "We did not represent that we initially learned of the plot from detainees, or that it was disrupted based solely on information from detainees in CIA custody." The CIA's October 30, 2007, talking points for the chairman of the House Defense Appropriations Subcommittee, John Murtha, make no reference to the CIA receiving intelligence on the Camp Lemonier plotting from other intelligence sources prior to CIA detainee reporting. Nor do the talking points indicate that the CIA detainee initially provided information on the plotting prior to being transferred to CIA custody. In addition, as described, an Office of the Director of National Intelligence public release on the CIA's Detention and Interrogaton Program from September 6, 2006, states that "the CIA designed a new interrogation program that would be safe, effective, and legal;" and that "al-Qa'ida facilitator Gouled Hassan Dourad revealed" that he had been sent to "case the US Marine base Camp Lemonier."

[1904] *See* CIA Talking Points dated October 30, 2007, entitled, "DCIA Meeting with Chairman Murtha re Rendition and Detention Programs" and attachments. The talking points further state that the "Presidentially-mandated detention program is critical to our ability to protect the American homeland and US forces and citizens abroad from terrorist attack." The attachment to the document, labeled "points from CTC," further asserts that while CIA rendition activities "did yield intelligence, it did not do so in a timely, efficient, and thorough way, raising unacceptable risks," and that the CIA "experience has shown that exclusive control by CIA, in a Agency designed, built, and managed facility, allows us complete oversight and control over all aspects of detention, to include conditions of confinement, approved interrogation activities, humane standards, medical treatment, detainee engagement, security, hygiene, and infrastructure." The document references a U.S. House of Representatives Appropriations bill providing a reduction in funding for the Covert Action CT Program and states: "Had the mark been directed against the rendition and detention programs specifically, the CIA would have recommended a Presidential veto. In its appeal, CIA detailed the impact of a $██ million cut to the CA CT Program. The Agency also made it clear that it would continue the rendition and detention program because of the high value of these activities."

[1905] *See* aforementioned CIA representations that: (1) "This is intelligence that cannot be found any other place. And our security depends on getting this kind of information." and (2) "Most, if not all, of the intelligence acquired from high-value detainees in this [CIA] program would likely not have been discovered or reported in any other way." As noted, the CIA's June 2013 Response states that the CIA "agree[s] with the *Study* that [the CIA] had threat reporting against Camp Lemonier prior to the March 2004 detention and rendition" of Guleed.

[1906] *See* intelligence chronology in Volume II for additional information.

(TS// ███████████ //NF) On March 4, 2004, Guleed was captured in Djibouti based on information obtained from a foreign government and a CIA source.[1907] Prior to entering CIA custody, Guleed was confronted with information acquired from signals intelligence, and he confirmed that he cased Camp Lemonier for a potential terrorist attack.[1908] CIA sought to render Guleed to CIA custody in order to question Guleed about senior al-Qa'ida East Africa members Abu Talha al-Sudani and Saleh ali Saleh Nabhan. A CIA cable states:

> "Guleed represents the closest we have come to an individual with first hand, face-to-face knowledge of Abu Talha [al-Sudani] and Nabhan, and our hope is that Guleed will provide key intelligence necessary for the capture of these senior al-Qa'ida members."[1909]

(TS// ███████████ //NF) Prior to Guleed's rendition to CIA custody, he provided detailed information on his casing of Camp Lemonier to CIA officers.[1910] On March ██, 2004, Guleed was rendered to CIA custody.[1911] There are no records to indicate that Guleed was subjected to the CIA's enhanced interrogation techniques, nor are there any CIA records to indicate that Guleed provided the information that was the basis for his rendition to CIA custody—information leading to the capture of Abu Talha al-Sudani or Saleh ali Saleh Nabhan.

(TS// ███████████ //NF) While in CIA custody, Guleed continued to provide information on his targeting of Camp Lemonier. Guleed stated that Abu Talha al-Sudani had not yet picked the operatives for the attack against Camp Lemonier,[1912] that the attack was "on hold while they-

---

[1907] HEADQUAR ████████████; ████ 1313 (041624Z MAR 04); HEADQUAR ████ (041935Z MAR 04). See also ████████ 15623.
[1908] ████ 93364 (January 8, 2008)
[1909] HEADQUAR ████████; ████ 93364 (January 8, 2008).
[1910] ████ 1329 ████████. The CIA's June 2013 Response states: "In March 2004, ████████████████ ████████, based [on] information from a clandestine source-detained and rendered to CIA custody the primary facilitator for al-Qa'ida's Camp Lemonier plot, Guleed Hassan Ahmed, who had cased the Camp on behalf of al-Qa'ida. Guleed provided details about the plot and al-Qa'ida's Somali support network, which drove CIA's targeting efforts." As described in this summary and in greater detail in Volume II, Guleed confirmed intelligence reporting already collected on his casing of Camp Lemonier prior to being rendered to CIA custody. See reference to material on recorded interrogations of Guleed Hassan Dourad in the cable, ████ 93364 (January 8, 2008).
[1911] ████ 1543 ████
[1912] ████ 1573 (160217Z MAR 04), later reissued as CIA ████ (021549Z APR 04)/ ████████, and used to support the president's speech on September 6, 2006.

raised the necessary funds via the bank robbery operation,"[1913] and that "he [Guleed] was not informed of the operational plan."[1914]

(TS// ███████████ //NF) Neither the detention of Guleed, nor the information he provided, thwarted terrorist plotting against Camp Lemonier; and CIA records indicate that attack planning against Camp Lemonier continued well after Guleed's capture in March 2004, to include a time period beyond the president's September 6, 2006, speech. In March 2005, the CIA sought approval to render an associate of Guleed whom the CIA stated was "planning terrorist attacks on U.S. targets in East Africa, particularly against Camp Lemonier in Djibouti."[1915] In October 2005, a cable stated, "a body of reporting indicates that East Africa al-Qa'ida network operatives are currently planning attacks on U.S. interests in the region, particularly... the U.S. military base Camp Lemonier in Djibouti."[1916] In April 2007, the continued terrorist threat reporting against Camp Lemonier resulted in a request for the Camp to further "alter their security practices."[1917]

(TS// ███████████ //NF) In October 2007, in light of the ongoing threat reporting related to Camp Lemonier, CIA officer ████████████ attempted to explain the CIA-validated statement in the president's September 6, 2006, speech that "[t]errorists held in CIA custody" "helped stop the planned strike on U.S. Marines at Camp Lemonier in Djibouti."[1918] ████████████,

---

[1913] ███████████. The CIA's June 2013 Response links the "disrupt[ion]" of the Camp Lemonier plotting to the CIA's Detention and Interrogation Program via the arrest of KSM, stating: "According to Khalid Shaykh Muhammad (KSM), his arrest in March 2003 (which we note in Example 12 resulted in part from information provided by Ramzi Bin al-Shibh) prevented him from transferring 30,000 euros from al-Qa'ida in Pakistan to al-Qa'ida in East Africa leaders, some of whom were plotting the Camp Lemonier attack. Funding shortages were cited repeatedly by detainees and in ███████████ [technical collection] as a reason for the Camp Lemonier plot's delays." Prior to the CIA's June 2013 Response, there were no CIA records attributing the delay or disruption of the plotting to the capture or detention of KSM. While a body of intelligence reporting indicated that funding shortages contributed to delays in the targeting of Camp Lemonier, no CIA intelligence records were identified that cite any deficit of expected funds resulting from KSM's capture. As detailed in this Study, KSM was captured on March 1, 2003. Intelligence reporting indicates that Abu Talha al-Sudani sent Guleed to case the security at Camp Lemonier more than six months later, in September 2003. In early March 2004, the CIA reported that ███████████ [technical collection] revealed that "Abu Talha and Guleed were working together in search of funding necessary to carry out planned operations." In late March 2004, after Guleed's detention, several associates were detained after an attack on a German aid delegation, which was suspected of being an attempt to kidnap individuals for ransom. A cable reporting this information stated that ███████████ [technical collection] "indicated Abu Talha continues to press forward on plans to target Western interests in Djibouti." Several days later, CIA officers surmised that the kidnapping attempt was likely an attempt "by Abu Talha to raise the operational funds for his plan to attack Camp Lemonier." (See intelligence chronology in Volume II, including reporting referenced in HEADQUARTERS ████ (101756Z MAR 04) and connected to ███████████; ALEC ████ (222122Z MAR 04); and ALEC ████ (292353Z MAR 04).) As detailed in the section of this summary and Volume II on the Capture of Khalid Shaykh Mohammad (KSM), the capture of KSM did not result from information provided by Ramzi bin al-Shibh.

[1914] ███████████

[1915] Draft cable in an email from: ███████████; to: ███████████ and ███████████; subject: "██████ DDO Approval to render Somali Jihadist and al-Qa'ida facilitator Ahmed Abdi Aw Mohammad to [CIA] control"; date: May 11, 2005, at 5:42:50 PM.

[1916] HEADQUARTERS ████ (252044Z OCT 05)

[1917] ███████████ 10555 (101434Z APR 07)

[1918] See "CIA Validation of Remarks on Detainee Policy," drafts supporting the September 6, 2006, speech by President George W. Bush acknowledging and describing the CIA's Detention and Interrogation Program, as well as who was involved in vetting of the speech, wrote to a CIA colleague tracking the ongoing threats to Camp Lemonier that:

> "The reasoning behind [the CIA] validation of the language in the speech--and remember, we can argue about whether or not 'planning' consistitutes [sic] a 'plot' and about whether anything is ever disrupted--was that the detainee reporting increased our awareness of attack plotting against the base, leading to heightened security."[1919]

(TS// ███████████ //NF) A review of CIA records, however, found no indication that CIA detainee reporting from Guleed, or any other CIA detainee, alerted the CIA or the U.S. military to increased terrorist targeting of Camp Lemonier. To the contrary, CIA records indicate that the CIA was in possession of substantial threat reporting demonstrating that Camp Lemonier in Djibouti was being targeted by al-Qa'ida and al-Qa'ida affiliated extremists prior to the detention of Guleed on March 4, 2004.[1920] For example, on January 28, 2003, a foreign government report disseminated by the CIA stated that al-Qa'ida operatives were planning "to ram an explosives-laden truck into a military base, probably Camp Lemonier."[1921] On March 10, 2003, a "Terrorist Advisory" was issued, which stated that "U.S. forces stationed at Camp Lemonier in Djibouti... could be targeted."[1922] Similar reporting continued through 2003, and by the end of the year, the CIA had ████ coverage[1923] indicating that Guleed and other identified operatives were being

---

an unclassified Office of the Director of National Intelligence release, entitled, "Summary of the High Value Terrorist Detainee Program."

[1919] *See* email from: ███████████ ; to ███████ and others; subject: "More on Camp Lemonier"; October 22, 2007, at 5:33 PM. In a reply email, a CIA officer wrote that Guleed's statement was only "that the plan was suspended while Abu Talha tried to acquire the necessary funds," and continued, "I don't want anyone to walk away from this thinking that the POTUS speech from 2006 is the only language/view we are allowed to hold, especially since most or all of us were not involved in the original coordination" of the President's September 6, 2006, speech. *See* email from: ███████ ; to [REDACTED] and [REDACTED]; cc: ███████████ ; subject: "Camp Lemonier"; date: October 24, 2007, at 1:22:44 PM.

[1920] ███████ 1313 (041624Z MAR 04)

[1921] *See* January 28, 2003, CIA Presidential Daily Brief, entitled, "Al-Qa'ida Planning Attack in Djibouti." The CIA's June 2013 Response states that the CIA "agree[s] with the *Study* that [the CIA] had threat reporting against Camp Lemonier prior to the March 2004 detention and rendition" of Guleed, but argues that the threat reporting provided to the President on January 28, 2003, had "no relation to [al-Sudani's] plot," and was "later recalled after being revealed to be a fabrication." The CIA did not provide a date for the recall. The reporting, which indicated al-Qa'ida operatives were planning "to ram an explosives-laden truck into a military base, probably Camp Lemonier," would later be corroborated by other intelligence reporting, including by Guleed in his description of al-Sudani's plotting. *See* intelligence chronology in Volume II.

[1922] CIA WASHINGTON DC ███ (110056Z MAR 03). *See also* ███████ 17366 (121355Z MAR 03). The CIA's June 2013 Response asserts that the March 2003 reporting was "an analytical assessment that Djibouti was a potential target given its US Military presence," was "not based on specific intelligence," and was analysis related to "a different al-Qa'ida cell." The CIA's June 2013 Response also disputes the relevance of the May 2003 reporting that al-Qa'ida affiliates were "waiting for the right time to carry out large-scale attacks, possibly involving suicide bombers, against a U.S. military base or U.S. naval ship in or near Djibouti." The CIA's June 2013 Response states that this threat reporting "was later found to be unrelated." Notwithstanding these assertions, the CIA's June 2013 Response states that the CIA "agree[s] with the *Study* that [the CIA] had threat reporting against Camp Lemonier prior to the March 2004 detention and rendition" of Guleed.

[1923] ALEC ███████ (021825Z OCT 03)

directed by Abu Talha al-Sudani to target Camp Lemonier.[1924] By the end of December 2003, Djiboutian authorities confirmed that Guleed had cased Camp Lemonier and that Guleed appeared to have "formulate[d] a complete targeting package, which included an escape route."[1925] It was this reporting that led ███████ to capture Guleed on March 4, 2004.[1926]

7. *The Assertion that CIA Detainees Subjected to Enhanced Interrogation Techniques Help Validate CIA Sources*

(TS// ███████████ //NF) In addition to CIA claims that information produced during or after the use of CIA's enhanced interrogation techniques led to the disruption of terrorist plots and the capture of specific terrorists, the CIA also represented that its enhanced interrogation techniques were necessary to validate CIA sources. The claim was based on one CIA detainee—Janat Gul—contradicting the reporting of one CIA asset.

(TS// ███████████ //NF) The CIA repeatedly represented to policymakers that information acquired after the use of the CIA's enhanced interrogation techniques helped to "validate" CIA sources. For example, CIA Director Michael Hayden provided testimony to the Committee on April 12, 2007, that:

> "Detainee information is a key tool for validating clandestine sources. In fact, in one case, the detainee's information proved to be the accurate story, and the clandestine source was confronted and subsequently admitted to embellishing or fabricating some or all [of] the details in his report."[1927]

(TS// ███████████ //NF) Similarly, in January 2009, the CIA compiled a detailed briefing book for a planned three-hour briefing of the CIA's Detention and Interrogation Program for President-elect Obama's national security staff. Included in the materials was a document that stated, "[k]ey intelligence [was] collected from HVD interrogations *after* applying [the CIA's enhanced] interrogation techniques." After this statement, the CIA provided examples, including that the "most significant reporting" acquired from CIA detainee Janat Gul after applying the CIA's enhanced interrogation techniques was information that helped the CIA "validate a CIA asset."[1928] The document states:

[1924] Referenced in HEADQUAR ████ (101756Z MAR 04) and connected to ███████████ . *See also* ███████████

[1925] CIA WASHINGTON DC ████ (302034Z DEC 03) / SERIAL: ███████

[1926] ████ 1313 (041624Z MAR 04)

[1927] CIA classified Statement for the Record, Senate Select Committee on Intelligence, provided by General Michael V. Hayden, Director, Central Intelligence Agency, 12 April 2007; and accompanying Senate Select Committee on Intelligence hearing transcript for April 12, 2007, entitled, "Hearing on Central Intelligence Agency Detention and Interrogation Program" (DTS #2007-1563). *See also* CIA Intelligence Assessment, "Detainee Reporting Pivotal for the War Against Al-Qa'ida," June 2005, which CIA records indicate was provided to White House officials on June 1, 2005, and was broadly disseminated on June 3, 2005, as an Intelligence Assessment. On March 31, 2009, former Vice President Cheney requested the declassification of this Intelligence Assessment, which was publicly released with redactions on August 24, 2009.

[1928] Italics in original. CIA Briefing for Obama National Security Team - "Renditions, Detentions, and Interrogations (RDI)" including "Tab 7," named "RDG Copy- Briefing on RDI Program 09 Jan. 2009." Referenced materials attached to cover memorandum with the title, "D/CIA Conference Room Seating Visit by President-elect Barrack [sic] Obama National Security Team Tuesday, 13 January 2009; 8:30 – 11:30 a.m." Expected participants

"Pakistan-based facilitator *Janat Gul's most significant reporting* helped us validate a CIA asset who was providing information about the 2004 pre-election threat. The asset claimed that Gul had arranged a meeting between himself and al-Qa'ida's chief of finance, Shaykh Sa'id, a claim that Gul vehemently denied. Gul's reporting was later matched with information obtained from Sharif al-Masri and Abu Talha al-Pakistani, captured after Gul. With this reporting in hand, CIA ████████ the asset, who subsequently admitted to fabricating his reporting about the meeting."[1929]

(TS// ████████ //NF) The CIA representation that the CIA's enhanced interrogation techniques produced information that allowed the CIA to identify the reporting of a CIA asset as fabricated lacked critical contextual information. The CIA representations did not describe how the CIA asset's reporting was already doubted by CIA officers prior to the use of the CIA's enhanced interrogation techniques against Gul. Nor did the CIA representations acknowledge that the asset's fabricated reporting was the reason that Janat Gul was subjected to the techniques in the first place. The CIA concluded that Janat Gul was not a high-level al-Qa'ida figure and did not possess threat information, but this conclusion was not included in CIA representations.

(TS// ████████ //NF) In March 2004, the CIA received reporting from a CIA asset, "ASSET Y,"[1930] that Janat Gul was planning with senior al-Qa'ida leaders to conduct attacks inside the United States. The attacks were reportedly planned to occur prior to the U.S. elections in November 2004.[1931] ASSET Y, who cited Janat Gul as the source of the information, stated that Gul was going to facilitate a meeting between Abu Faraj al-Libi and ASSET Y in support of the operation.[1932] As noted, CIA officers expressed doubts about ASSET Y's reporting at the

---

included, "Senator Boren, Mr. McDonough, Mr. Brennan, General Jones, Mr. Craig, Mr. Lippert, Mr. Smith, Senator Hagel," as well as several CIA officials, including Director Hayden, ████████, John Rizzo, [REDACTED], and ██CTC Legal ████████. The briefing book includes the document "Briefing Notes on the Value of Detainee Reporting," dated 15 May 2006, which provided the same intelligence claims found in the document of the same name, but dated April 15, 2005. The "Briefing Notes" document was provided to the Department of Justice in April 2005, in the context of the Department's analysis of the CIA's enhanced interrogation techniques.

[1929] Italics added. CIA Briefing for Obama National Security Team - "Renditions, Detentions, and Interrogations (RDI)" including "Tab 7," named "RDG Copy- Briefing on RDI Program 09 Jan. 2009." Referenced materials attached to cover memorandum with the title, "D/CIA Conference Room Seating Visit by President-elect Barrack [sic] Obama National Security Team Tuesday, 13 January 2009; 8:30 – 11:30 a.m." Expected participants included, "Senator Boren, Mr. McDonough, Mr. Brennan, General Jones, Mr. Craig, Mr. Lippert, Mr. Smith, Senator Hagel," as well as several CIA officials, including Director Hayden, ████████, John Rizzo, [REDACTED], and ██CTC Legal ████████. The briefing book includes the document "Briefing Notes on the Value of Detainee Reporting," dated 15 May 2006, which provided the same intelligence claims found in the document of the same name, but dated April 15, 2005. The "Briefing Notes" document was provided to the Department of Justice in April 2005, in the context of the Department's analysis of the CIA's enhanced interrogation techniques.

[1930] CIA records provided to the Committee identify the pseudonym created by the CIA for the asset. The Study lists the asset as "ASSET Y" to further protect his identity.

[1931] WASHINGTON ████ ██ 04); ████ 19045 ████ MAR 04)

[1932] ████ 19045 ████ MAR 04); ████ 3633 ████ 04)

time it was received.[1933] A senior CIA officer, ███████████, who formerly served as chief of the Bin Ladin Unit, raised questions about the reliability of the asset's reporting on March ██, 2004, stating that the reporting was "vague" and "worthless in terms of actionable intelligence," and that al-Qa'ida "loses nothing" by disclosing the information. He further stated that, given an al-Qa'ida statement emphasizing a lack of desire to strike before the U.S. election, and al-Qa'ida's knowledge that "threat reporting causes panic in Washington" and "leaks soon after it is received," the report "would be an easy way [for al-Qa'ida] to test" ASSET Y.[1934] ALEC Station officer ███████████ expressed similar doubts about the source's reporting in response to the email.[1935]

(TS// ███████████ //NF) Less than three months later, Janat Gul was captured in ██████ on June ██, 2004.[1936] On June ██, 2004, CIA's ███████████ proposed that Gul be rendered to CIA custody, citing ASSET Y's reporting.[1937] During this period, however, the use of the CIA's enhanced interrogation techniques had been suspended by the CIA director.[1938] On June 29, 2004, a draft memorandum from DCI Tenet to National Security Adviser Rice sought special approval from the National Security Council Principals Committee to use the CIA's enhanced interrogation techniques against Janat Gul to learn more about the threat reporting from ASSET Y.[1939] The memorandum referenced ASSET Y's reporting and stated that if the CIA could use the techniques, "the Agency would be in an optimum position to obtain from Gul critical intelligence necessary to save American lives by disrupting the pre-election plot, locating senior al-Qa'ida leaders still at large, and learning how Usama Bin Laden communicates with his operatives." The memorandum further stated that "[g]iven the magnitude of the danger posed by

[1933] Email from: ███████████; to: ███████████, ███████████, [REDACTED], ███████████, ███████████; subject: could AQ be testing [ASSET Y] and [Source Name REDACTED]?; date: March ██, 2004, at 06:55 AM.
[1934] Email from: ███████████; to: ███████████, ███████████, [REDACTED], ███████████, ███████████; subject: could AQ be testing [ASSET Y] and [Source Name REDACTED]?; date: March ██, 2004, at 06:55 AM. The email references a March 17, 2004, al-Qa'ida statement. Speaking of a second source providing threat reporting, ███████████ noted that "i [sic] have always been concerned that [the asset] ███████████."
[1935] Email from: ███████████; to ███████████; cc: ███████████, ███████████, [REDACTED], ███████████; subject: Re: could AQ be testing [ASSET Y] and [Source Name REDACTED]?; date: March ██, 2004, at 7:52:32 AM.
[1936] ███████████ 3121 ███████████; ███████████ 3111 ███████████
[1937] See ███████████ 3633 (███████████ 04), which states "Gul is the source of [ASSET Y's] pre-election threat information. This information forms a substantial part of the USG's current pre-election threat assessment. Station believes that if Gul has pre-election threat information, we must exploit him using our best resources. Those resources do not exist in ██████. Station has interrogated many al-Qa'ida members in ██████ and while we have been successful at times, our best information is obtained when the detainee is interrogated in a CIA controlled facility ([DETENTION SITE COBALT] or blacksite)."
[1938] Memorandum for Deputy Director for Operations from Director of Central Intelligence, June 4, 2004, subject, "Suspension of Use of Interrogation Techniques." Memorandum for the National Security Advisor from DCI George Tenet, June 4, 2004, re Review of CIA Interrogation Program.
[1939] Draft memorandum from George Tenet to National Security Advisor re Counterterrorist Interrogation Techniques, attached to email from: ███████████; to: John Moseman, [REDACTED], [REDACTED], Stanley Moskowitz, Scott Muller, John Rizzo, ███████████ and ███████████; subject: Draft Documents for Friday's NSC Meeting; date: June 29, 2004.

the pre-election plot, and [Janat] Gul's almost certain knowledge of any intelligence about that plot, I request the fastest possible resolution of the above issues."[1940]

(TS// ███████████ //NF) On July 2, 2004, the day that CIA Headquarters approved the rendition of Janat Gul to CIA custody,[1941] the CIA represented to select members of the National Security Council that Janat Gul was one of the "most senior radical Islamic facilitators in Pakistan," and noted that he was "assessed by a key source on [the] pre-election plot to be involved in or [to] have information on the plot."[1942] On July 15, 2004, based on the reporting of ASSET Y, the CIA represented to the chairman and vice chairman of the Committee that Janat Gul was associated with a pre-election plot to conduct an attack in the United States.[1943] On July 20, 2004, select National Security Council principals met again, and according to CIA records, agreed that, "[g]iven the current threat and risk of delay, CIA was authorized and directed to utilize the techniques with Janat Gul as necessary."[1944] On July 22, 2004, Attorney General Ashcroft approved the use of the CIA's enhanced interrogation techniques against Janat Gul based on ASSET Y's reporting.[1945]

[1940] Draft memorandum from George Tenet to National Security Advisor re Counterterrorist Interrogation Techniques, attached to email from: ███████████; to: John Moseman, [REDACTED], [REDACTED], Stanley Moskowitz, Scott Muller, John Rizzo, ███████████ and ███████████; subject: Draft Documents for Friday's NSC Meeting; date: June 29, 2004.

[1941] DIRECTOR ██████ (022300Z JUL 04)

[1942] The CIA briefing slides further asserted that ████ debriefings of Janat Gul by ██████ [foreign government] ██████ officials were "not working." (See CIA briefing slides, CIA Request for Guidance Regarding Interrogation of Janat Gul, July 2, 2004). National Security Advisor Rice later stated in a letter to the CIA Director that "CIA briefers informed us that Gul likely has information about preelection terrorist attacks against the United States as a result of Gul's close ties to individuals involved in these alleged plots." See July 6, 2004, Memorandum from Condoleezza Rice, Assistant to the President for National Security Affairs, to the Honorable George Tenet, Director of Central Intelligence, re Janat Gul.

[1943] According to handwritten notes of the briefing, CIA briefers described Janat Gul as "senior AQ" and a "key facilitator" with "proximity" to a suspected pre-election plot. Committee records indicate that CIA briefers told the chairman and vice chairman that, given the pre-election threat, it was "incumbent" on the CIA to "review [the] need for EITs," following the suspension of "EITs." (See Handwritten notes of Andrew Johnson (DTS #2009-2077); CIA notes (DTS #2009-2024 pp. 92-95); CIA notes (DTS #2009-2024, pp. 110-121).) ███████████ CTC Legal ██████ later wrote that the "only reason" for the chairman and vice chairman briefing on Janat Gul was the "potential gain for us" as "the vehicle for briefing the committees on our need for renewed legal and policy support for the CT detention and interrogation program." See email from: ███████████; to: [REDACTED]; subject: Re: Priority: congressional notification on Janat Gul; date: July 29, 2004.

[1944] July 29, 2004, Memorandum for the Record from CIA General Counsel Scott Muller re Principals Meeting relating to Janat Gul on 20 July 2004.

[1945] Letter from Attorney General Ashcroft to Acting DCI McLaughlin, July 22, 2004 (DTS #2009-1810, Tab 4). Attorney General Ashcroft, who attended the July 2, 2004, meeting, had opined earlier on the use of the CIA's enhanced interrogation techniques against Janat Gul. See letter from Assistant Attorney General Ashcroft to General Counsel Muller, July 7, 2004 (DTS #2009-1810, Tab 3); July 2, 2004, CIA Memorandum re Meeting with National Security Advisor Rice in the White House Situation Room, Friday 2 July re Interrogations and Detainee Janat Gul; July 6, 2004, Memorandum from Condoleezza Rice, Assistant to the President for National Security Affairs to George Tenet, Director of Central Intelligence re Janat Gul; Memorandum from ███████████, to Jose Rodriguez, John P. Mudd, ███████████, ███████████, [REDACTED], re standard interrogation techniques – DOJ limits, July 2, 2004.

(TS// ███████ //NF) Janat Gul was rendered to CIA custody on July ██, 2004.[1946] On August 2, 2004, Janat Gul denied knowledge of any imminent threats against the United States homeland. Gul's denial was deemed a "strong resistance posture" by CIA detention site personnel.[1947] Janat Gul was then subjected to the CIA's enhanced interrogation techniques from August 3, 2004, to August 10, 2004, and then again from August 21, 2004, to August 25, 2004.[1948]

(TS// ███████ //NF) On August 19, 2004, CIA personnel wrote that the interrogation "team does not believe [Gul] is withholding imminent threat information."[1949] On August 25, 2004, CIA interrogators sent a cable to CIA Headquarters stating that Janat Gul "may not possess all that [the CIA] believes him to know." The interrogators added that the interrogation "team maintains a degree of caution in some areas, as many issues linking [Gul] to al-Qaida are derived from single source reporting," a reference to the CIA source, ASSET Y.[1950]

(TS// ███████ //NF) That same day, August 25, 2004, the CIA's associate general counsel provided a letter to the DOJ seeking approval to use additional CIA enhanced interrogation techniques against Janat Gul: dietary manipulation, nudity, water dousing, and the abdominal slap. The letter asserted that Janat Gul had information concerning "imminent threats to the United States" and "information that might assist in locating senior al-Qa'ida operatives whose removal from the battlefield could severely disrupt planned terrorist attacks against the United States." The letter stated:

> "In addition, CIA understands that before his capture, Gul had been working to facilitate a direct meeting between the ██████ CIA ██████ source reporting on the pre-election threat [ASSET Y] and Abu Faraj himself; Gul had arranged a previous meeting between [ASSET Y] and al-Qa'ida finance chief Shaykh Sa'id at which elements of the pre-election threat were discussed."[1951]

(TS// ███████ //NF) The letter from the CIA's associate general counsel asserted that Janat Gul's "resistance increases when questioned about matters that may connect him to al-Qa'ida or evidence he has direct knowledge of operational terrorist activities."[1952] The letter stated that the CIA sought approval to add four enhanced interrogation techniques to Janat Gul's

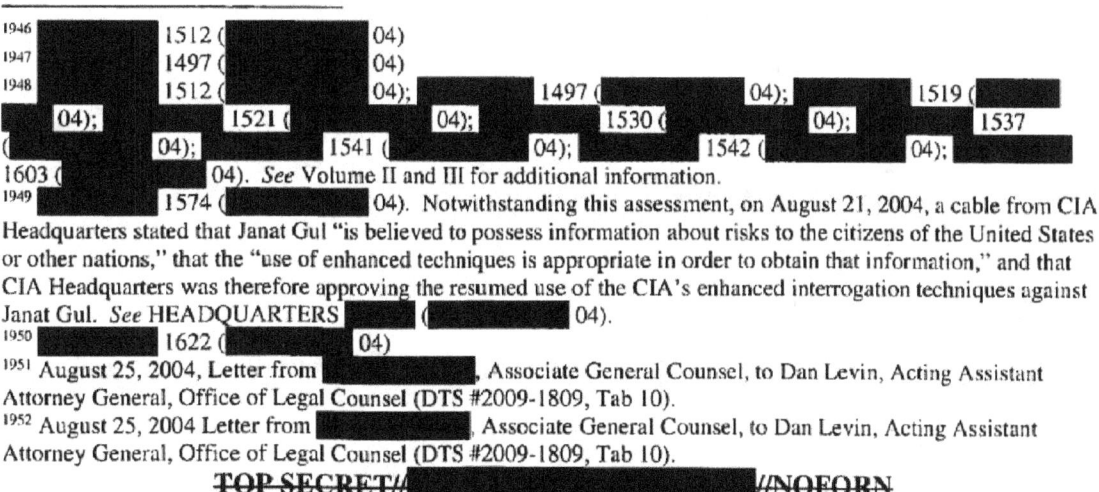

[1946] ██████ 1512 (███████ 04)
[1947] ██████ 1497 (██████ 04)
[1948] ██████ 1512 (███████ 04); ████ 1497 (██████████ 04); ██████ 1519 (██████
████ 04); ██████ 1521 (██████ 04); ████ 1530 (████████ 04); ██████ 1537
██████ 04); ██████ 1541 (██████ 04); ████ 1542 (██████ 04);
1603 (████████ 04). *See* Volume II and III for additional information.
[1949] ████████ 1574 (████████ 04). Notwithstanding this assessment, on August 21, 2004, a cable from CIA Headquarters stated that Janat Gul "is believed to possess information about risks to the citizens of the United States or other nations," that the "use of enhanced techniques is appropriate in order to obtain that information," and that CIA Headquarters was therefore approving the resumed use of the CIA's enhanced interrogation techniques against Janat Gul. *See* HEADQUARTERS ██████ (██████ 04).
[1950] ██████ 1622 (████████ 04)
[1951] August 25, 2004, Letter from ████████, Associate General Counsel, to Dan Levin, Acting Assistant Attorney General, Office of Legal Counsel (DTS #2009-1809, Tab 10).
[1952] August 25, 2004 Letter from ████████, Associate General Counsel, to Dan Levin, Acting Assistant Attorney General, Office of Legal Counsel (DTS #2009-1809, Tab 10).

interrogation plan "in order to reduce markedly Gul's strong resistance posture and provide an opportunity for the interrogation team to obtain his cooperation."[1953] On August 26, 2004, Acting Assistant Attorney General Dan Levin informed CIA Acting General Counsel Rizzo that the use of the four additional enhanced interrogation techniques did not violate any U.S. statutes, the U.S. Constitution, or U.S. treaty obligations. Levin's letter stated that "[w]e understand that [Janat] Gul is a high-value al Qaeda operative who is believed to possess information concerning an imminent terrorist threat to the United States."[1954]

(TS// ███████████ //NF) On August 27, 2004, Gul's CIA interrogators reported that "in terms of overt indications of resistance, [Gul's] overall resistance is currently judged to be minimal."[1955] Nonetheless, on August 31, 2004, the CIA interrogators asked CIA Headquarters to approve an extension of all CIA enhanced interrogation techniques against Janat Gul.[1956] The CIA's associate general counsel objected, writing:

> "In the end, its [sic] going to be an operational call. I just want to be sure that the record is clear that we're not acting precipitously and are taking into consideration everything we're learning about this guy. We open ourselves up to possible criminal liability if we misuse the interrogation techniques. I reflect again on the cable or cables from the interrogation team that opines that physical EITs (facial slap, walling, etc.) do not work on him. I would strongly encourage, then, HQS not to approval [sic] the use of physical interrogation techniques because if they don't work, then our motives are questionable. If our motives might be questioned, then we get ourselves in trouble."[1957]

(TS// ███████████ //NF) Despite these concerns, on September 3, 2004, CIA Headquarters released a cable extending approval for sleep deprivation for 30 days. CIA records indicate, however, that Gul was not subjected to sleep deprivation, or any other enhanced interrogation technique, following this approval.[1958]

(TS// ███████████ //NF) On September 7, 2004, more than a month after Janat Gul was rendered to CIA custody, a CIA officer who had observed the interrogations of Gul prepared a memorandum for the leadership of the CIA's Renditions, Detentions, and Interrogations Group, stating:

> "The definition of an HVD has probably become blurred over the past year as [CIA] began to render a higher number of MVDs [medium value detainees], but [Janat Gul] would not be considered an HVD when compared to Abu

---

[1953] August 25, 2004 Letter from ███████████ , Associate General Counsel, to Dan Levin, Acting Assistant Attorney General, Office of Legal Counsel (DTS #2009-1809, Tab 10).

[1954] Letter to John Rizzo, Acting General Counsel, CIA; from Daniel Levin, Acting Assistant Attorney General, August 26, 2004 (DTS #2009-1810, Tab 6).

[1955] ███████ 1631 (271859Z AUG 04)

[1956] ███████ 1650 (311620Z AUG 04)

[1957] See email from: ███████████ ; to: ███████████ , ███████████ , ███████████ , ███████████ , [REDACTED], and [REDACTED]; subject: "Req to extend authorization to use EITs"; date; September 1, 2004.

[1958] HEADQUARTERS ███████ (032155Z SEP 04)

Zubaydah, KSM, and similar level HVDs. [Janat Gul] should likewise not be considered an operational planner or even an operator. It is very likely that [Janat Gul] came into contact with operational information, but we lack credible information that ties him to pre-election threat information or direct operational planning against the United States, at home or abroad. Likewise, we lack any substantive information that connects [Janat Gul] to UBL, Zawahiri, and Abu Faraj Al-Libi."[1959]

(TS// █████████ //NF) On September 16, 2004, CIA detention site personnel wrote that Janat Gul's reporting directly contradicted information from ASSET Y from March 2004, and stated that, "[m]uch of our derogatory information on [Gul] came from [ASSET Y] reporting, as did much of our pre-election threat information."[1960]

(TS// █████████ //NF) On September 17, 2004, following the reports about the discrepancies between the comments made by Janat Gul and ASSET Y, as well as similar denials from Sharif al-Masri, who was in foreign government custody, the CIA undertook a counterintelligence review of ASSET Y to assess the validity of ASSET Y's reporting.[1961]

(TS// █████████ //NF) On October █, 2004, and October █, 2004, CIA officers provided a ████████ assessment of ASSET Y. That ████████ assessment indicated that ASSET Y was deceptive in response to questions regarding his alleged meeting with a senior al-Qa'ida official, Shaykh Sa'id, at which ASSET Y claimed to have learned about the pre-election threat. ASSET Y then admitted to having fabricated the information about the meeting.[1962]

(TS// █████████ //NF) Despite the recantation of reporting from ASSET Y, officers from the CIA's ALEC Station continued to assess that Janat Gul "was one of the highest-ranking facilitators in Pakistan with long-standing access to senior leaders in al-Qa'ida" and other groups.[1963] This assessment was not shared by CIA personnel involved in Gul's interrogation. On November 10, 2004, the CIA's chief of Base at DETENTION SITE BLACK, the CIA detention site hosting Gul, wrote that the words used by ALEC Station to describe Janat Gul:

[1959] Rather than a "high value detainee," the memo characterized Janat Gul as a "senior facilitator." The CIA officer concluded that Gul was likely "not directly included in operational planning and operations." *See* September 7, 2004, CIA Document EYES ONLY – ████████, written by ████████.

[1960] ████████ 1706 (161749Z SEP 04). The CIA's June 2013 Response states that "Janat Gul's claim that [ASSET Y] never met the al-Qa'ida finance chief—who [ASSET Y] said told him about the pre-election threat—was vital to CIA's assessment and handling of the case. CIA officers assessed Gul was cooperating during his interrogations by that time, leading CIA to ████████ [ASSET Y] on the meeting and the plot, which he ultimately recanted." As described earlier, CIA records indicate that Janat Gul denied knowledge of any imminent threats against the United States homeland, which had been reported by ASSET Y, prior to the use of the use of the CIA's enhanced interrogation techniques against Gul. At the time, Gul's denial was deemed a "strong resistance posture" by the CIA. *See* ████████ 1497 (████████ 04).

[1961] HEADQUARTERS ████████ (████████ 04); ████████ 4267 (████████ 04)

[1962] ████████ 1411 (████████ 04). The cable states: "After ████████ deception ████████ on the question of meeting Sa'id, [ASSET Y] quickly confessed to [the CIA officer] that he had fabricated his meeting and blamed pressure from his handling [CIA] officer to produce leads as the catalyst for his lies." ASSET Y continued to assert that he discussed the pre-election threat with Janat Gul, who, as noted, had denied to CIA interrogators that he had any knowledge of imminent threats to the United States.

[1963] ALEC ████████ (092126Z NOV 04)

"...fly in the face of what is now a rather long history of debriefings which, I would assert, paint a very different picture of him. While [Janat Gul] was certainly a facilitator, describing him as 'highest-ranking' gives him a stature which is undeserved, overblown and misleading. Stating that he had 'long standing access to senior leaders in al-Qa'ida' is simply wrong.... To put it simply, [Janat Gul] is not the man we thought he was. While he no doubt had associations and interactions with people of interest, [Janat Gul] is not the pivotal figure our pre-detention descriptions of him suggest. We do a disservice to ourselves, the mission and even [Janat Gul] by allowing misperceptions of this man to persist."[1964]

(TS// ████████ //NF) On November 22, 2004, a CIA officer noted the discrepancy between the CIA's description of Janat Gul as a "potential source of intelligence information regarding an attack by al-Qa'ida" in a draft OLC memorandum and the current assessment of Janat Gul.[1965] In an email, the CIA officer indicated that he had spoken to the CIA's associate general counsel, ██████████, who had informed him that "the state of our knowledge about Gul had evolved since he was captured." The email noted that, "[a]t first, we believed he had attack information of a more imminent nature," but "[n]ow it appears that he does not have such information." The email indicated that ███████ would talk to personnel at OLC about the issue to "[amend] the draft opinion to reflect the state of our knowledge."[1966] The OLC memorandum was not updated.

(TS// ████████ //NF) On December 19, 2004, CIA detention site personnel wrote again that Janat Gul was "not/not the man [CIA Headquarters] made him out to be," and that "[h]e is a very simple man who, no doubt, did a capable job as a facilitator but he is not the link to senior AQ leaders that [CIA Headquarters] said he was/is."[1967]

[1964] Email from: [REDACTED]; to: ████████, ████████, ████████, ████████; subject: re ALEC ████; date: November 10, 2004.
[1965] See email from: ████████; to: ████████; subject: re Gul and ████ Report; date: November 22, 2004, at 8:25 AM.
[1966] See email from: ████████; to: ████████; subject: re Gul and ████ Report; date: November 22, 2004, at 8:25 AM.
[1967] CIA "Comments on Detainees," December 19, 2004, notes from DETENTION SITE BLACK. In April 2005, the chief of Base where Janat Gul was held emailed that "[Janat Gul] was never the person we thought he was. He is not the senior Al-Qa'ida facilitator that he has been labeled. He's a rather poorly educated village man with a very simple outlook on life. He's also quite lazy and it's the combination of his background and lack of initiative that got him in trouble. He was looking to make some easy money for little work and he was easily persuaded to move people and run errands for folks on our target list. While he openly admits that he helped move people, it's pretty well established that the vast majority of his work involved seeking medical care and providing housing for family members of Tahir Jan's Uzbek organization. There simply is no 'smoking gun' that we can refer to that would justify our continued holding of [Janat Gul] at a site such as [DETENTION SITE BLACK]. It should be noted, however, that [Janat Gul] has made what I think is great progress. He fingered [ASSET Y] as a fabricator and has been generally responsive to requirements though, it must be said, he never had access to most of the information we seek from him." See email from: [REDACTED] (COB DETENTION SITE BLACK); to: ████████ ████████; cc: ████████, ████████, ████████; subject: re ████████; date: April 30, 2005.

(TS// ██████████ //NF) On April 6, 2005, as the OLC approached completion of its analysis of the legality of the CIA's enhanced interrogation techniques, the OLC asked the CIA about the interrogation of Gul using the CIA's enhanced interrogation techniques, specifically, "what [the CIA] got from Janat Gul, was it valuable, [and] did it help anything...."[1968] The CIA did not immediately respond to this request and the CIA's Associate General Counsel ████ ████ noted that OLC personnel had "taken to calling [him] daily" for information.[1969] On April 14, 2005, a CIA officer emailed ████████ talking points stating that:

> "Pakistan-based facilitator Janat Gul's most significant reporting helped us validate a CIA asset who was providing information about the 2004 pre-election threat. The asset claimed that Gul had arranged a meeting between himself and al-Qa'ida's chief of finance, Shaykh Sa'id, a claim that Gul vehemently denied.
>
> Gul's reporting was later matched with information obtained from Sharif al-Masri and Abu Talha, captured after Gul. With this reporting in hand, CIA ████████ the asset, who subsequently admitted to fabricating his reporting about the meeting."[1970]

(TS// ██████████████ //NF) On May 10, 2005, the OLC issued a formal memorandum that included a discussion of the legality of the use of the CIA's enhanced interrogation techniques against Janat Gul.[1971] Citing information provided in the CIA's August 25, 2004, letter, the OLC memorandum stated:

> "You asked for our advice concerning these interrogation techniques in connection with their use on a specific high value al Qaeda detainee named Janat Gul. You informed us that the CIA believed Gul had information about al Qaeda's plans to launch an attack within the United States. According to CIA's information, Gul had extensive connections to various al Qaeda leaders, members of the Taliban, and the al-Zarqawi network, and had arranged meetings between an associate and al Qaeda's finance chief to discuss such an attack. ...Our conclusions depend on these assessments."[1972]

[1968] Email from: ████████; to: ████████, ████████, ████████, ████████, and [REDACTED]; subject: questions from OLC for Art 16 opinion; date: April 6, 2005.

[1969] Email from: ████████; to: ████████, ████████, ████████, ████████, and [REDACTED]; subject: questions from OLC for Art 16 opinion; date: April 12, 2005; email from: ████████; to: ████████, ████████, ████████, ████████, and [REDACTED]; subject: Re: questions from OLC for Art 16 opinion; date: April 14, 2005.

[1970] Email from: ████████; to: ████████, ████████, ████████, ████████, and ████████; subject: response to no. 5 request from ████████: OTA's Detainee Reporting Brief; date: April 14, 2005.

[1971] Memorandum for John A. Rizzo, Senior Deputy General Counsel, Central Intelligence Agency, from Steven G. Bradbury, Principal Deputy Assistant Attorney General, Office of Legal Counsel, May 10, 2005, Re: Application of 18 U.S.C. §§ 2340-2340A to Certain Techniques That May Be Used in the Interrogation of a High Value al Qaeda Detainee.

[1972] Memorandum for John A. Rizzo, Senior Deputy General Counsel, Central Intelligence Agency, from Steven G. Bradbury, Principal Deputy Assistant Attorney General, Office of Legal Counsel, May 10, 2005, Re: Application of

(TS// ███████████ //NF) On May 30, 2005, the OLC issued a memorandum concluding that the use of the CIA's enhanced interrogation techniques against CIA detainees did not violate Article 16 of the Convention Against Torture.[1973] In the memorandum, Principal Deputy Assistant Attorney General Steven G. Bradbury used the example of Janat Gul as a detainee who was "representative of the high value detainees on whom enhanced techniques have been, or might be, used."[1974]

(TS// ███████████ //NF) Citing information from the CIA's August 25, 2004, letter, Bradbury wrote:

> "the CIA believed [that Janat Gul] had actionable intelligence concerning the pre-election threat to the United States... Gul had extensive connections to various al Qaeda leaders, members of the Taliban, and the al-Zarqawi network, and intelligence indicated that 'Gul had arranged a... meeting between [a ███████ source] and al-Qa'ida finance chief Shaykh Sa'id at which elements of the pre-election threat were discussed.'"[1975]

(TS// ███████████ //NF) As noted, the CIA had represented that the use of the CIA's enhanced interrogation techniques was necessary for Janat Gul to provide information on an imminent threat to the United States, the pre-election threat. As further noted, Gul did not provide this information and records indicate that the threat was based on fabricated CIA source reporting. When the OLC requested the results of using the CIA's enhanced interrogation techniques against Janat Gul, the CIA represented that "Gul has provided information that has helped the CIA with validating one of its key assets reporting on the pre-election threat." This information was included in the May 30, 2005, OLC memorandum, which also stated that Gul's information "contradicted the asset's contention that Gul met with Shaykh Sa'id," and that, "[a]rmed with Gul's assertions, the CIA ███████ the asset, who then admitted that he had lied about the meeting."[1976] There are no indications in the memorandum that the CIA informed

18 U.S.C. §§ 2340-2340A to Certain Techniques That May Be Used in the Interrogation of a High Value al Qaeda Detainee.

[1973] Memorandum for John A. Rizzo, Senior Deputy General Counsel, Central Intelligence Agency, from Steven G. Bradbury, Principal Deputy Assistant Attorney General, Office of Legal Counsel, May 30, 2005, Re: Application of United States Obligations Under Article 16 of the Convention Against Torture to Certain Techniques that May be Used in the Interrogation of High Value Al Qaeda Detainees.

[1974] Memorandum for John A. Rizzo, Senior Deputy General Counsel, Central Intelligence Agency, from Steven G. Bradbury, Principal Deputy Assistant Attorney General, Office of Legal Counsel, May 30, 2005, Re: Application of United States Obligations Under Article 16 of the Convention Against Torture to Certain Techniques that May be Used in the Interrogation of High Value Al Qaeda Detainees.

[1975] Memorandum for John A. Rizzo, Senior Deputy General Counsel, Central Intelligence Agency, from Steven G. Bradbury, Principal Deputy Assistant Attorney General, Office of Legal Counsel, May 30, 2005, Re: Application of United States Obligations Under Article 16 of the Convention Against Torture to Certain Techniques that May Be Used in the Interrogation of High Value al Qaeda Detainees (brackets in the original). The OLC memorandum also cited an "Undated CIA Memo, 'Janat Gul' ('Janat Gul Memo'). The OLC also relied on CIA representations that Janat Gul's interrogations "greatly increased the CIA's understanding of our enemy and its plans."

[1976] Memorandum for John A. Rizzo, Senior Deputy General Counsel, Central Intelligence Agency, from Steven G. Bradbury, Principal Deputy Assistant Attorney General, Office of Legal Counsel, May 30, 2005, Re: Application of

the OLC that CIA officers had concluded that Gul had no information about the pre-election threat and had determined that Gul was "not the man we thought he was."[1977] As noted, after the May 30, 2005, OLC memorandum, the CIA continued to represent that the use of the CIA's enhanced interrogation techniques allowed the CIA to validate sources.[1978]

8. *The Identification and Arrests of Uzhair and Saifullah Paracha*

(TS// ██████████ //NF) The CIA represented that information obtained through the use of the CIA's enhanced interrogation techniques produced otherwise unavailable intelligence that led to the identification and/or arrest of Uzhair Paracha and his father Saifullah Paracha (aka, Sayf al-Rahman Paracha). These CIA representations include inaccurate information and omit significant material information—specifically a body of intelligence reporting acquired prior to CIA detainee reporting that linked the Parachas to al-Qa'ida-related activities.

(TS// ██████████ //NF) CIA representations also credit the use of the CIA's enhanced interrogation techniques with the identification of a plot to smuggle explosives into the United States involving the Parachas.[1979] CIA records indicate that the plotting was denied by the supposed participants, and that at least one senior CIA counterterrorism official questioned the plausibility of the explosives smuggling plot given the relative ease of acquiring explosive material in the United States.[1980]

(TS// ██████████ //NF) The CIA provided information to the CIA Office of Inspector General that "EITs (including the water board) have been indispensable to our successes," and stated that the CIA OIG Special Review should have come to the "conclusion that our efforts have thwarted attacks and saved lives."[1981] The CIA further represented to the OIG that KSM

United States Obligations Under Article 16 of the Convention Against Torture to Certain Techniques that May Be Used in the Interrogation of High Value al Qaeda Detainees.

[1977] The OLC relied on CIA representations that Janat Gul had information, but that he withheld it. In describing the interrogation process, the OLC stated that Janat Gul's resistance increased as questioning moved to his "'knowledge of operational terrorist activities.'" The OLC also wrote that "Gul apparently feigned memory problems (which CIA psychologists ruled out through intelligence and memory tests) in order to avoid answering questions." The OLC further conveyed that the "CIA believes that Janat Gul continues to downplay his knowledge." *See* Memorandum for John A. Rizzo, Senior Deputy General Counsel, Central Intelligence Agency, from Steven G. Bradbury, Principal Deputy Assistant Attorney General, Office of Legal Counsel, May 30, 2005, Re: Application of United States Obligations Under Article 16 of the Convention Against Torture to Certain Techniques that May Be Used in the Interrogation of High Value al Qaeda Detainees.

[1978] As described elsewhere, on April 21, 2009, a CIA spokesperson confirmed the accuracy of the information in the OLC memorandum in response to the partial declassification of this memorandum and others.

[1979] Among other documents, *see* Memorandum for: Inspector General; from: James Pavitt, Deputy Director for Operations; subject: re (S) Comments to Draft IG Special Review, "Counterterrorism Detention and Interrogation Program" (2003-7123-IG); date: February 27, 2004; attachment: February 24, 2004, Memorandum re Successes of CIA's Counterterrorism Detention and Interrogation Activities.

[1980] *See* details in the intelligence chronology in Volume II.

[1981] CIA memorandum to the CIA Inspector General from James Pavitt, CIA's Deputy Director for Operations, dated February 27, 2004, with the subject line, "Comments to Draft IG Special Review, 'Counterterrorism Detention and Interrogation Program' (2003-7123-IG)," Attachment, "Successes of CIA's Counterterrorism Detention and Interrogation Activities," dated February 24, 2004.

"provided information that helped lead to the arrest of… Uzair Paracha, a smuggler,"[1982] and that "as a result of the lawful use of EITs":

> "KSM identified a mechanism for al-Qa'ida to smuggle explosives into the US via a Pakistani businessman and textile merchant who shipped his material to the US. The businessman had agreed to use this method to help al-Qa'ida smuggle in explosives for follow-on attacks to 9/11."[1983]

(~~TS//~~ ████████ ~~//NF~~) Similarly, on July 29, 2003, the CIA made a presentation to a select group of National Security Council principals, including Vice President Cheney, seeking policy reaffirmation of the CIA interrogation program. The CIA briefing materials state that "the use of the [CIA interrogation] techniques has produced significant results," and warned that "[t]ermination of this [CIA] program will result in loss of life, possibly extensive." The CIA conveyed that "[m]ajor threats were countered and attacks averted," and under a briefing slide entitled "RESULTS: MAJOR THREAT INFO," represented that information obtained from KSM after the use of the CIA's enhanced interrogation techniques led to the "identification" of Saifullah Paracha.[1984]

(~~TS//~~ ████████ ~~//NF~~) A widely disseminated CIA Intelligence Assessment, entitled "Detainee Reporting Pivotal for the War Against Al-Qa'ida," that was described in internal CIA emails as being "put together using past assessments" and initially intended for the White House only, with "marching orders" to "throw everything in it,"[1985] states:

> "Since 11 September 2001, detainee reporting has become a crucial pillar of US counterterrorism efforts, aiding… operations to capture additional terrorists, helping to thwart terrorist plots… *KSM's revelation in March 2003*

[1982] ██████████, Memorandum for the Record; subject: Meeting with Deputy Chief, Counterterrorist Center ALEC Station; date: 17 July 2003. These representations were included in the final, and now declassified Special Review of the Inspector General, which states that KSM "provided information that helped lead to the arrests of terrorists including Sayfullah Paracha and his son Uzair, businessmen whom Khalid Shaykh Muhammad planned to use to smuggle explosives in New York." (*See* CIA Inspector General Special Review, Counterterrorism Detention and Interrogation Activities (September 2001 – October 2003) (2003-7123-IG), 7 May 2004). The statements in the Special Review regarding the purported effectiveness of the program, including the reference to the Parachas, were cited by the Office of Legal Counsel in its analysis of the CIA's enhanced interrogation techniques. *See* Memorandum for John A. Rizzo, Senior Deputy General Counsel, Central Intelligence Agency, from Steven G. Bradbury, Principal Deputy Assistant Attorney General, Office of Legal Counsel, May 30, 2005, Re: Application of United States Obligations Under Article 16 of the Convention Against Torture to Certain Techniques that May Be Used in the Interrogation of High Value al Qaeda Detainees, pp. 10-11, citing IG Special Review, pp. 85-91.
[1983] Email from: ██████████; to: ██████████; cc: ████████, [REDACTED], [REDACTED], ████████; subject: re Addition on KSM/AZ and measures; date: February 9, 2004. Memorandum for: Inspector General; from: James Pavitt, Deputy Director for Operations; subject: re (S) Comments to Draft IG Special Review, "Counterterrorism Detention and Interrogation Program" (2003-7123-IG); date: February 27, 2004; attachment: February 24, 2004, Memorandum re Successes of CIA's Counterterrorism Detention and Interrogation Activities.
[1984] CIA memorandum for the Record, "Review of Interrogation Program on 29 July 2003," prepared by CIA General Counsel Scott Muller, dated August 5, 2003; briefing slides entitled, "*CIA Interrogation Program,*" dated July 29, 2003, presented to senior White House officials.
[1985] *See* email from: [REDACTED]; to: multiple addresses; subject: "Draft of IA on 'Detainee Reporting Pivotal to the War on Terrorism'"; date: May 16, 2005, at 2:08 PM.

that he was plotting with Sayf al-Rahman Paracha—who also used the name Saifullah al-Rahman Paracha—to smuggle explosives into the United States for a planned attack in New York prompted the FBI to investigate Paracha's business ties in the United States."[1986]

(TS//████████████//NF) CIA representations related to the "identification" of the Parachas and/or the arrest of Uzair Paracha—as well as the identification of an explosives smuggling plot—omit significant information acquired by the Intelligence Community prior to any reporting from CIA detainees. Specifically, prior to KSM's reporting, the Intelligence Community had already collected and acted upon significant information related to the Paracha family's connections to al-Qa'ida and international terrorism:

- Information on Saifullah Paracha was found in documents seized during a March 28, 2002, raid against al-Qa'ida targets associated with Hassan Ghul, which resulted in the capture of Abu Zubaydah. The documents identified "Saifullah Piracha" (the spelling found in the document seized during the raid) and phone numbers, which would be associated with his Karachi-based business, International Merchandise Pvt Ltd, as early as April 2002. An address associated with the business was also identified.[1987]

- The name "Saifullah Piracha" was provided to Pakistani officials by the CIA in December 2002. The CIA wrote: "Information below leads us to believe that the following individual and phone numbers may have a connection to al-Qa'ida and international terrorism.... We request your assistance in investigating this individual to determine if he is involved in terrorist activity." The request included three phone numbers found in the documents seized on March 28, 2002, one of which was associated with Saifullah Paracha's Karachi-based company, International Merchandise Pvt Ltd.[1988]

- In April 2002, the FBI opened an investigation on another ████████████████, at a New York-based business associated with Saifullah Paracha. During the course of the investigation, the FBI interviewed an employer at a New York address and acquired additional information on the business and the Parachas. ██████████ business card, identifying him as an employee of International Merchandise Limited, was found among documents seized during the April 2002 Karachi raid.[1989]

[1986] Italics added. CIA Intelligence Assessment, "Detainee Reporting Pivotal for the War Against Al-Qa'ida," June 2005, which CIA records indicate was provided to White House officials on June 1, 2005. The Intelligence Assessment at the SECRET//NOFORN classification level was more broadly disseminated on June 3, 2005. On March 31, 2009, former Vice President Cheney requested the declassification of this Intelligence Assessment, which was publicly released with redactions on August 24, 2009.

[1987] DIRECTOR ██████ (221835Z APR 02); ALEC ████ (222235Z DEC 02); DIRECTOR ██████ (221835Z APR 02)

[1988] ALEC ██████ (222235Z DEC 02)

[1989] FBI WASHINGTON DC (271623Z MAR 03); ALEC ██████ (191630Z MAY 03) (cables explaining previous FBI investigative action on Paracha). On March 28, 2003, the FBI would return to the same employer and the same address, leading to the apprehension of Uzhair Paracha, who would voluntarily provide significant reporting to the FBI.

- Months later, financial documents seized during the September 11, 2002, raids that resulted in the capture of Ramzi bin al-Shibh identified an email address attributed to International Merchandise Pvt Ltd., with the same contact—Saifullah A. Paracha—as well as the same address and phone number as the business identified after the March 2002 raid.[1990]

- Based on the information obtained during the September 2002 raids, the CIA informed the FBI, the NSA, and the Department of Treasury that they suspected "Saifullah Paracha" was engaged in terrorist financing activities, specifically for al-Qa'ida. The cable included detailed information on Saifullah Paracha and International Merchandise Pvt Ltd in Karachi, and noted the CIA's ongoing interest in, and analysis of, the information.[1991]

- FBI investigative activity of terrorism subject Iyman Faris found that Faris was linked to Paracha Imports via his Ohio-based housemates.[1992]

- Majid Khan, who was in foreign government custody, provided reporting that "Uzhair" ran the New York branch of his father's Karachi-based import-export business. According to the reporting, Uzhair was assisting Majid Khan and Ammar al-Baluchi in their efforts to resettle Majid Khan in the United States for terrorism-related purposes. Khan provided a detailed physical description of both Uzhair and his father.[1993]

(TS// ████████████ //NF) KSM was captured on March 1, 2003. On March █, 2003, KSM was rendered to CIA custody and immediately subjected to the CIA's enhanced interrogation techniques.[1994] A CIA interrogation report from March 24, 2003, states that during the afternoon, KSM continued to be subjected to the CIA's enhanced interrogation techniques, including the waterboard, for failing to provide information on operations in the United States and for having "lied about poison and biological warfare programs."[1995] That evening, KSM's interrogators received reports on information being provided by Majid Khan,[1996] who was in foreign government custody and being interviewed by FBI special agents and foreign government officers. The information included details on a U.S.-based individual associated with al-Qa'ida named Uzhair. According to Khan, this Uzhair ran the New York branch of his

---

[1990] CIA ████████ (040123Z DEC 02)/ ████████████████ . See also ████████████ .
[1991] CIA ████████ (040123Z DEC 02)/ ████████████████ . See also ████████████ and ALEC ████████ (222235Z DEC 02).
[1992] See FBI investigative file ████████████████████
[1993] ████████ 13890 ████████ . The cable describing Majid Khan's foreign government interrogation also included Khan's reporting on how Ammar al-Baluchi intended to have Uzhair use Majid Khan's credit card to create the appearance that Majid Khan was already in the United States. As described in the full Committee Study, the cable further detailed Khan's two meetings with Uzhair and his father, and a subsequent phone call with Uzhair (following Uzhair's return to the United States), all of which were facilitated by Ammar al-Baluchi.
[1994] See ████████ 10983 (242321Z MAR 03); ████████ 10972 (241122Z MAR 03); and the KSM detainee review in Volume III.
[1995] ████████ 10983 (242321Z MAR 03); ████████ 10972 (241122Z MAR 03)
[1996] Majid Khan was detained in Pakistani on March 5, 2003. See ████████ 13658 (050318Z MAR 03); ████████ 13659 (050459Z MAR 03); DIRECTOR ████████ (050459Z MAR 03).

father's Karachi-based import-export business.[1997] CIA cables describe KSM as being "boxed in" by reporting from Majid Khan[1998] before providing the following information on the Parachas and a smuggling plot:

- KSM corroborated reporting from Majid Khan that Ammar al-Baluchi and Majid Khan approached Uzhair Paracha for assistance in resettling Majid Khan in the United States.[1999]

- KSM stated that he was close to Uzhair's father, Sayf al-Rahman Paracha, who provided assistance through his business and by helping to find safe houses in Karachi.[2000]

- KSM claimed that Ammar al-Baluchi and Majid Khan approached Sayf al-Rahman Paracha with a plan to use Sayf al-Rahman Paracha's textile business to smuggle explosives into the United States. KSM stated that Paracha agreed to this plan and was arranging the details with Ammar al-Baluchi and Majid Khan at the time of his (KSM's) capture.[2001] A later CIA cable provided additional background, stating: "KSM did not volunteer [the explosives plot] information on Paracha. He provided this reporting only when confronted with details on his role and other information on the plot, which had been provided by detainee Majid Khan," who was in foreign government custody.[2002]

(TS// ████████ //NF) According to CIA records, on March 28, 2003, at a FBI field office, Uzhair Paracha provided significant information to interviewing FBI special agents on his father's links to al-Qa'ida and his own efforts to assist Majid Khan's reentry to the United States. Uzhair denied knowing anything about an explosives smuggling plot.[2003]

(TS// ████████ //NF) On April 29, 2003, Ammar al-Baluchi was detained by Pakistani authorities as a result of reporting unrelated to the CIA's Detention and Interrogation Program. Records indicate Ammar al-Baluchi provided significant information prior to being transferred to CIA custody.[2004] On May █, 2003, Ammar al-Baluchi was rendered to CIA custody and

---

[1997] ████████ 13890 ████████ ; ████████ 10984 (242351Z MAR 03)

[1998] ████████ 10983 (242321Z MAR 03). The CIA's June 2013 Response asserts that "[r]eporting from interrogations of KSM was directly and uniquely responsible for the arrests of Saifullah Paracha and his son Uzhair Paracha." The CIA Response also asserts that Majid Khan's reporting "was disseminated just _after_ KSM provided the information that allowed us to identify Paracha" (emphasis in the original). This is inaccurate. The cable describing KSM's interrogation specifically references the cable describing Majid Khan's detailed reporting from interrogations in foreign government custody and how KSM was "boxed in" by the information provide by Majid Khan.

[1999] ████████ 10984 (242351Z MAR 03), disseminated as ████████

[2000] ████████ 10984 (242351Z MAR 03), disseminated as ████████

[2001] ████████ 10984 (242351Z MAR 03), disseminated as ████████

[2002] ALEC ████████ (052230Z MAY 03)

[2003] ALEC ████████ (012248Z APR 03)

[2004] _See_ section of this summary on the Karachi Plots, including ████████ 14291 (021645Z MAY 03) and ALEC ████████ (142334Z MAY 03). A CIA cable describes a CIA officers meeting with the foreign government officer who used rapport-building techniques to acquire information from Ammar al-Baluchi. The officer stated that Ammar al-Baluchi was "more chatty" than Khallad bin Attash (who was also in foreign government custody at the time), and that Ammar "acknowledged plans to attack U.S. Consulate officials at the airport, the Consul General's Residence and the Consulate itself." _See_ ████████ 19647 ████████ 04).

immediately subjected to the CIA's enhanced interrogation techniques.[2005] The CIA stopped using the CIA's enhanced interrogation techniques on Ammar al-Baluchi on May 20, 2003.[2006] A June 18, 2003, cable states that Ammar al-Baluchi denied that he and Sayf al-Rahman Paracha agreed to smuggle explosives into the United States. Ammar al-Baluchi stated he only asked Sayf al-Rahman Paracha questions and made inquiries about how explosives shipping could be done. Ammar al-Baluchi maintained that he did not take any action based on the discussion.[2007]

(TS// ██████████ //NF) On July 5, 2003, Saifullah Paracha was detained in ██████, in an operation orchestrated by the FBI.[2008] Shortly thereafter, Saifullah Paracha was rendered to U.S. military custody at Bagram Air Force Base.[2009] At Bagram, Saifullah Paracha was questioned by an FBI special agent.[2010] A CIA cable from July 17, 2003, relays that Saifullah Paracha stated that Ammar al-Baluchi had asked if he knew a forwarding agent who could ship garments and "materials" to Europe, which Saifullah Paracha inferred were either explosives or chemicals. Paracha stated he had no information to provide to Ammar al-Baluchi on this topic and that no further action was taken on the matter.[2011]

(TS// ██████████ //NF) With regards to the explosives smuggling reporting, a senior CIA counterterrorism official commented:

> "again, another ksm op worthy of the lamentable knuckleheads... why
> 'smuggle' in explosives when you can get them here? neither fertilizer for
> bombs or regular explosives are that hard to come by. ramzi yousef came to

---

[2005] Ammar al-Baluchi was detained in Pakistan on April 29, 2003, and transferred to CIA custody on May ██, 2003. *See* ██████ 14259 ██████; ██████ 45028 ██████; ██████ 14282 ██████; ██████ 38402 ██████; [REDACTED] 38325 ██████; [REDACTED] 38389 ██████.

[2006] For additional details, *see* detainee review for Ammar al-Baluchi in Volume III.

[2007] DIRECTOR ██████ (181929Z JUN 03), disseminated as ██████; ██████ 39239 (301600Z MAY 03)

[2008] Email from: ██████, to: ██████, [REDACTED]; subject: For coordination - DCI Highlight on Paracha; date: July 7, 2003, at 11:10 AM; email from: ██████; to: ██████; cc: [REDACTED]; subject: Re: For coordination - DCI Highlight on Paracha; date: July 7, 2003, at 11:18:39 AM.

██████ (*See* interview of ██████, by ██████, Office of the Inspector General, August 5, 2003). The CIA originally sought to take direct custody of Saifullah Paracha. On May 6, 2003, CTC's chief of operations, ██████, sent an email to ██████ CTC Legal, ██████, and CTC attorney ██████, with a proposal for the CIA to detain Saifullah Paracha and interrogate him using the CIA's enhanced interrogation techniques, writing: "we MUST have paracha arrested without delay and transferred to cia custody for interrogation using enhanced measures. i understand that paracha's us person status makes this difficult, but this is dynamite and we have to move forward with alacrity. what do you need to do that? what do we need to do that?" *See* CIA document for: ██████, ██████; from: ██████; date: 6 May 2003. According to CIA records noted above, Saifullah Paracha's eventual capture and rendition to U.S. military custody was complicated by ██████. According to emails within CTC Legal, Paracha was "██████."

[2009] ██████ 86058 ██████

[2010] Email from: ██████, to: ██████, [REDACTED]; subject: For coordination - DCI Highlight on Paracha; date: July 7, 2003, at 11:10 AM; email from: ██████; to: ██████; cc: [REDACTED]; subject: Re: For coordination - DCI Highlight on Paracha; date: July 7, 2003, at 11:18:39 AM.

[2011] ██████ 13588 (171505Z JUL 03)

conus with a suitcase and hundred bucks and got everything he needed right here. this may be true, but it just seems damn odd to me."[2012]

9. Critical Intelligence Alerting the CIA to Jaffar al-Tayyar

(TS// ███████████ //NF) The CIA made repeated claims that the use of the CIA's enhanced interrogation techniques resulted in "key intelligence" from Abu Zubaydah and KSM on an operative named Jaffar al-Tayyar,[2013] later identified as Adnan el-Shukrijumah.[2014] These CIA representations frequently asserted that information obtained from KSM after the use of the CIA's enhanced interrogation techniques resulted in an FBI investigation that prompted al-Tayyar to flee the United States. These representations were inaccurate. KSM was captured on March 1, 2003. Jaffar al-Tayyar departed the United States in May 2001.[2015]

(TS// ███████████ //NF) CIA representations also omitted key contextual facts, including that: (1) the Intelligence Community was interested in the Florida-based Adnan el-Shukrijumah prior to the detention of the CIA's first detainee;[2016] (2) CIA detainee Abu Zubaydah provided a description and information on a KSM associate named Jaffar al-Tayyar to FBI special agents in

---

[2012] Email from: ███████████ ; to: ███████████ , ███████████ , ███████ ███████ ; subject: see highlight: again, another ksm op worthy of the lamentable; date: March 25, 2003, at 6:29:08 AM.

[2013] Also known as (aka) Adnan Gulshair Muhammad el-Shukrijumah, Jafaar al-Tayyar, and Abu Jafar al-Tayer. Spelling used throughout the Committee Study reflects, to the extent possible, the spelling found within intelligence records.

[2014] CIA Memorandum for Steve Bradbury at Office of Legal Counsel, Department of Justice, dated March 2, 2005, from ███████████ , ███████ Legal Group, DCI Counterterrorist Center, subject "Effectiveness of the CIA Counterterrorist Interrogation Techniques." *See also* CIA classified Statement for the Record, Senate Select Committee on Intelligence, provided by General Michael V. Hayden, Director, Central Intelligence Agency, 12 April 2007 (DTS #2007-1563). *See also* CIA Intelligence Assessment, "Detainee Reporting Pivotal for the War Against Al-Qa'ida," June 2005, which CIA records indicate was provided to White House officials on June 1, 2005. The Intelligence Assessment at the SECRET//NOFORN level was more broadly disseminated on June 3, 2005. On March 31, 2009, former Vice President Cheney requested the declassification of this Intelligence Assessment, which was publicly released with redactions on August 24, 2009. *See also* CIA graphic attachment to several CIA briefings on the CIA's enhanced interrogation techniques, entitled, "Key Intelligence and Reporting Derived from Abu Zubaydah and Khalid Shaykh Muhammad (KSM)." *See also* CIA briefing documents for Leon Panetta entitled, "Tab 9: DCIA Briefing on RDI Program- 18FEB.2009."

[2015] The CIA's June 2013 Response states that "there were cases in which we either made a factual error or used imprecise language, but these mistakes were not central to our representations and none invalidates our assessment that detainee reporting provided key intelligence on this important terrorist." As one of two examples, the CIA's June 2013 Response acknowledges that the "[CIA] incorrectly stated al-Tayyar fled the United States in response to the FBI investigation, although he had in fact already departed the United States by this time." The Committee found that this inaccurate statement was central to the CIA's representations. The CIA asserted that "Ja'far al-Tayyar" fled the United States because of KSM's reporting after the use of the CIA's enhanced interrogation techniques in the context of representations that the use of the techniques "has been a key reason why al-Qa'ida has failed to launch a spectacular attack in the West."

[2016] ALEC ██████ (210218Z MAR 03). Extensive open source records include "Broward Man Sought as Terror Suspect," *Miami Herald*, dated March 21, 2003; "Pursuit of al-Qaeda keeps coming back to Fla.," *USA Today*, dated June 15, 2003; and "A Hunt for 'The Pilot,'" *U.S. News and World Report*, dated March 30, 2003. For context, *see also* United States District Court Southern District Florida, Case No. 02-60096, *United States of America v. Imran Mandhai and Shueyb Mossa Jokhan*, filed May 16, 2002.

May 2002, prior to being subjected to the CIA's enhanced interrogation techniques;[2017] (3) CIA personnel distrusted KSM's reporting on Jaffar al-Tayyar—stating that KSM fabricated information and had inserted al-Tayyar "into practically every story, each time with a different role";[2018] (4) other CIA detainee reporting differed from KSM's reporting in significant ways;[2019] and (5) CIA records indicate that KSM did not identify al-Tayyar's true name and that it was Jose Padilla—in military custody and being questioned by the FBI—who provided al-Tayyar's true name as Adnan el-Shukrijumah.[2020] Finally, the CIA attributed to KSM the characterization of al-Tayyar as the "next Mohammed Atta," despite clarifications from KSM to the contrary.[2021]

(TS// ██████████████ //NF) For example, in a March 2, 2005, CIA memorandum with the subject line, "Effectiveness of the CIA Counterterrorist Interrogation Techniques," the CIA responded to a request from the Office of Legal Counsel "for the intelligence the Agency obtained from detainees who, before their interrogations, were not providing any information of intelligence [value]." Under a section entitled, "Results," the CIA stated:

> "CIA's use of DOJ-approved enhanced interrogation techniques, as part of a comprehensive interrogation approach, has enabled CIA to disrupt terrorist plots, capture additional terrorists, and collect a high volume of critical intelligence on al-Qa'ida. We believe that intelligence acquired from these interrogations has been a key reason why al-Qa'ida has failed to launch a spectacular attack in the West since 11 September 2001. Key intelligence

---

[2017] *See* Abu Zubaydah detainee review in Volume III and ██████████████ .
[2018] ██████████ 10884 (182140Z MAR 03); email from: ██████████████ ; to [REDACTED]; cc: [REDACTED]; subject: Re: Reissue/Correction: CT: Comments on Khalid Shaykh Muhammad on imminent threats to U.S. targets in Thailand, Indonesia, and the Philipines; date: March 12, 2003, at 9:36:57 AM; ██████████████ 42247 (210357Z JUL 03); email from: ██████████████ ; to: [REDACTED], ██████████████ , ██████████████ , [REDACTED], [REDACTED]; cc: [REDACTED], [REDACTED], [REDACTED], [REDACTED], [REDACTED], [REDACTED], [REDACTED]; subject: RATHER PROFOUND IMPLICATIONS... Ammar al-Baluchi's Comments on Jaffar al-Tayyar--If Ammar is Correct, then KSM Appears to Have a Focused Us on Jaffar in a Extended Deception Scheme--and His Deception Capabilities are Not Broken Down; date: 07/21/03 11:24 AM.
[2019] Email from: ██████████████ ; to [REDACTED]; cc: [REDACTED]; subject: Re: REISSUE/CORRECTION: CT: CT: Comments on Khalid Shaykh Muhammad on imminent threats to U.S. targets in Thailand, Indonesia, and the Philipines; date: March 12, 2003, at 9:36:57 AM; National Counterterrorism Center, REFLECTIONS, "Ja'far al-Tayyar: An Unlikely Al-Qa'ida Operational Threat," 22 December 2005; ██████████████ 42247 (210357Z JUL 03); email from: ██████████████ ; to: [REDACTED], ██████████████ , ██████████████ , [REDACTED], [REDACTED]; cc: [REDACTED], [REDACTED], [REDACTED], [REDACTED], [REDACTED], [REDACTED], [REDACTED]; subject: RATHER PROFOUND IMPLICATIONS... Ammar al-Baluchi's Comments on Jaffar al-Tayyar--If Ammar is Correct, then KSM Appears to Have a Focused Us on Jaffar in a Extended Deception Scheme--and His Deception Capabilities are Not Broken Down; date: 07/21/03 11:24 AM.
[2020] CIA "Briefing Notes on the Value of Detainee Reporting" faxed from the CIA to the Department of Justice on April 15, 2005, at 10:47AM. For KSM's inability to identify name, *see* ██████████ 10741 (100917Z MAR 03); ██████████ 10740 (092308Z MAR 03), disseminated as ██████████████ .
[2021] ██████████ 10787 (130716Z MAR 03); ██████████ 10863 (171028Z MAR 03). For example, November 6, 2006, talking points prepared for a briefing with the President stated that "KSM described Tayyar as the next Muhammad Atta." *See* CIA document entitled, "DCIA Talking Points: Waterboard 06 November 2007," dated November 6, 2007, with the notation the document was "sent to DCIA Nov. 6 in preparation for POTUS meeting."

collected from HVD interrogations *after* applying interrogation techniques:"[2022]

(TS// ████████ //NF) The CIA then listed "Jafaar al-Tayyar" as one of 11 examples, stating:

> "Jafaar al-Tayyar: Tayyar is an al-Qa'ida operative who was conducting casing in the US for KSM prior to 9/11, according to KSM and other HVDs. KSM confirmed that he recruited Tayyar—who is still at large—to conduct a major operation against US interests. KSM described Tayyar as the next Muhammad Atta. Tayyar's family is in Florida and we have identified many of his extremist contacts. Acting on this information, the FBI quickly publicized Tayyar's true name and aggressively followed up with his family and friends in the United States, causing Tayyar to flee the United States. ████████████ and we are actively pursuing his capture. ████████
> ████████[2023]

(TS// ████████ //NF) In January 2009, the CIA compiled a detailed briefing book—and CIA Director Hayden produced his own prepared remarks—for a three-hour briefing on the CIA's Detention and Interrogation Program for President-elect Obama's national security staff.[2024] Included in the materials was a document entitled, "Key Impacts," which states:

> "**Results**: CIA's use of DOJ-approved enhanced interrogation techniques, as part of a comprehensive interrogation approach, has enabled CIA to disrupt terrorist plots, capture additional terrorists, and collect a high volume of critical intelligence on al-Qa'ida. We believe that intelligence acquired from these interrogations has been a key reason why al-Qa'ida has failed to launch a spectacular attack in the West since 11 September 2001. Key intelligence collected from HVD interrogations *after* applying interrogation techniques:[2025]

[2022] Emphasis in original document. CIA Memorandum for Steve Bradbury at Office of Legal Counsel, Department of Justice, dated March 2, 2005, from ████████, ████ Legal Group, DCI Counterterrorist Center, subject "Effectiveness of the CIA Counterterrorist Interrogation Techniques."

[2023] CIA Memorandum for Steve Bradbury at Office of Legal Counsel, Department of Justice, dated March 2, 2005, from ████████, ████ Legal Group, DCI Counterterrorist Center, subject "Effectiveness of the CIA Counterterrorist Interrogation Techniques."

[2024] CIA Briefing for Obama National Security Team - "Renditions, Detentions, and Interrogations (RDI)" including "Tab 7," named "RDG Copy- Briefing on RDI Program 09 Jan. 2009." Referenced materials attached to cover memorandum with the title, "D/CIA Conference Room Seating Visit by President-elect Barrack [sic] Obama National Security Team Tuesday, 13 January 2009; 8:30 – 11:30 a.m." The briefing book includes the previously mentioned "Briefing Notes on the Value of Detainee Reporting" dated 15 May 2006, which provided the same intelligence claims found in the document of the same name, but dated April 15, 2005. Expected participants included "Senator Boren, Mr. McDonough, Mr. Brennan, General Jones, Mr. Craig, Mr. Lippert, Mr. Smith, Senator Hagel," as well as several CIA officials, including Director Hayden, ████████, John Rizzo, [REDACTED], and ████████ Legal, ████████.

[2025] Emphasis in original.

... Jafaar al-Tayyar: Tayyar is an al-Qa'ida operative who was conducting casing in the US for KSM prior to 9/11, according to KSM and other HVDs. KSM confirmed that he recruited Tayyar—who is still at large—to conduct a major operation against US interests. KSM described Tayyar as the next Muhammad Atta. Tayyar's family is in Florida and we have identified many of his extremist contacts. Acting on this information, the FBI quickly publicized Tayyar's true name and aggressively followed up with his family and friends in the United States, causing Tayyar to flee the United States.[2026] ██████████ and we are actively pursuing his capture. ██████████

██████████ [2027]

(TS// ██████████ //NF) Prior to receiving information from the CIA's Detention and Interrogation Program, the U.S. Intelligence Community was interested in Adnan el-Shukrijumah. According to CIA and open source records, the FBI interviewed the parents of Adnan el-Shukrijumah several times between September 2001 and October 2002 concerning their son and his suspected contact with a known extremist. The family provided no significant information on their son, except to alert the FBI that he had departed the United States circa May 2001.[2028]

(TS// ██████████ //NF) CIA representations that Jaffar al-Tayyar fled the United States in 2003 in response to an investigation prompted by reporting from KSM were incongruent with CIA records at the time of the representations, which indicated that al-Tayyar had already relocated to Pakistan. In March 2003, when Jose Padilla identified Jaffar al-Tayyar as Adnan al-Shukrijumah, he stated that he had last seen al-Tayyar at a KSM safehouse in Karachi, Pakistan, in March 2002.[2029] Other reporting indicated al-Tayyar's presence in Pakistan in 2002 and 2003, as well. For example, KSM consistently reported that al-Tayyar was not in the United States and noted during a 2004 interrogation that al-Tayyar "would not return to the United States because

---

[2026] The CIA's June 2013 Response states that "[i]n some of the *early* representations, we incorrectly stated al-Tayyar fled the United States in response to the FBI investigation, although he had in fact already departed the United States by this time" (italics added). As noted, this representation was made by the CIA as late as January 2009, to President-elect Obama's national security team.

[2027] Emphases in original. CIA Briefing for Obama National Security Team - "Renditions, Detentions, and Interrogations (RDI)" including "Tab 7," named "RDG Copy- Briefing on RDI Program 09 Jan. 2009." Referenced materials attached to cover memorandum with the title, "D/CIA Conference Room Seating Visit by President-elect Barrack [sic] Obama National Security Team Tuesday, 13 January 2009; 8:30 – 11:30 a.m." The briefing book includes the previously mentioned "Briefing Notes on the Value of Detainee Reporting" dated 15 May 2006, which provided the same intelligence claims in the document of the same name, but dated April 15, 2005. *See* "RDI Key Impacts."

[2028] ALEC ██████ (210218Z MAR 03). Extensive open source records include "Pursuit of al-Qaeda keeps coming back to Fla.," *USA Today*, dated June 15, 2003; "Broward Man Sought as Terror Suspect," *Miami Herald*, dated March 21, 2003; and "A Hunt for 'The Pilot,'" *U.S. News and World Report*, dated March 30, 2003. The FBI confirmed for the Committee that Adnan el-Shukrijumah departed the United States in May 2001. *See* DTS #2013-0391.

[2029] Email from: ██████████ ; to: ██████████ , [REDACTED]; cc: ██████████ , ██████████ ██████ ; subject: Padilla Breaks; date: May 1, 2003, at 08:51 AM; CIA "Briefing Notes on the Value of Detainee Reporting" faxed from the CIA to the Department of Justice on April 15, 2005, at 10:47AM; ALEC ██████ (210218Z MAR 03).

his name was known to U.S. authorities."[2030] Further, ████████████████████
████████████ [2031]

(~~TS//~~████████~~//NF~~) On May 20, 2002, prior to the initiation of the CIA's enhanced interrogation techniques—and while being questioned by FBI special agents—CIA detainee Abu Zubaydah provided information on "Abu Jafar al-Tayer" in the context of discussing associates of KSM. Abu Zubaydah provided a detailed description of "Abu Jafar al-Tayer" and stated that he was an English speaker who had studied in the United States. Abu Zubaydah stated that he first met "Abu Jafar al-Tayer" in Birmal, Afghanistan, circa January 2002, and that "Abu Jafar al-Tayer" was at that time seeking to travel to Pakistan. Abu Zubaydah repeated that "Abu Jafar al-Tayer" spoke "very good English" and was "short and stocky with black hair and dark skin."[2032] Abu Zubaydah did not provide significant additional information on Abu Jaffar al-Tayyar after the CIA used its enhanced interrogation techniques against him in August 2002.[2033]

(~~TS//~~████████~~//NF~~) On September 11, 2002, Ramzi bin al-Shibh was captured in Karachi, Pakistan.[2034] During the capture operation, a letter referencing Jaffar al-Tayyar was seized. According to a translation of the letter, it stated "tell an unidentified pilot named Ja'far that he should be ready for travel."[2035] Shortly after his capture, bin al-Shibh was rendered to foreign government custody.[2036] In November 2002, while still in foreign government custody, bin al-Shibh was questioned on "Ja'far the Pilot" and provided a physical description of "Ja'far."[2037]

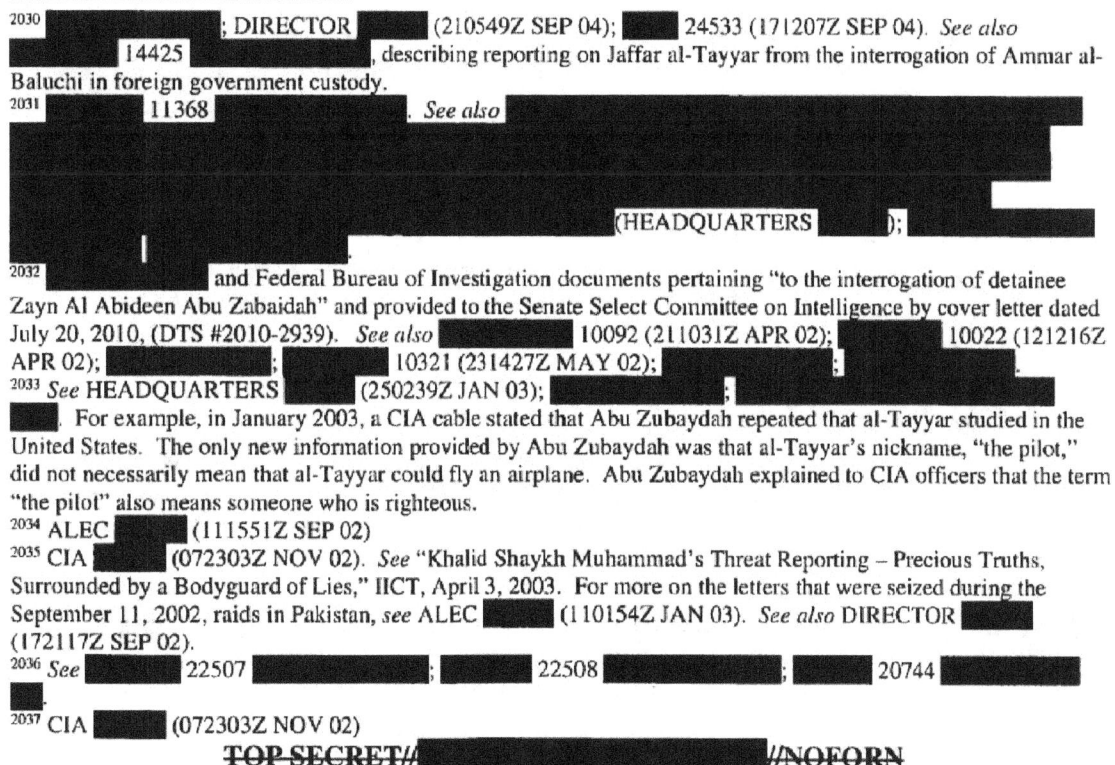

[2030] ████████; DIRECTOR ████ (210549Z SEP 04); ████ 24533 (171207Z SEP 04). *See also* ████████ 14425 ████████, describing reporting on Jaffar al-Tayyar from the interrogation of Ammar al-Baluchi in foreign government custody.

[2031] ████ 11368 ████. *See also* ██ (HEADQUARTERS ████);
████████████████

[2032] ████████ and Federal Bureau of Investigation documents pertaining "to the interrogation of detainee Zayn Al Abideen Abu Zabaidah" and provided to the Senate Select Committee on Intelligence by cover letter dated July 20, 2010, (DTS #2010-2939). *See also* ████ 10092 (211031Z APR 02); ████ 10022 (121216Z APR 02); ████; ████ 10321 (231427Z MAY 02); ████;

[2033] *See* HEADQUARTERS ████ (250239Z JAN 03); ████;
████. For example, in January 2003, a CIA cable stated that Abu Zubaydah repeated that al-Tayyar studied in the United States. The only new information provided by Abu Zubaydah was that al-Tayyar's nickname, "the pilot," did not necessarily mean that al-Tayyar could fly an airplane. Abu Zubaydah explained to CIA officers that the term "the pilot" also means someone who is righteous.

[2034] ALEC ████ (111551Z SEP 02)

[2035] CIA ████ (072303Z NOV 02). *See* "Khalid Shaykh Muhammad's Threat Reporting – Precious Truths, Surrounded by a Bodyguard of Lies," IICT, April 3, 2003. For more on the letters that were seized during the September 11, 2002, raids in Pakistan, *see* ALEC ████ (110154Z JAN 03). *See also* DIRECTOR ████ (172117Z SEP 02).

[2036] *See* ████ 22507 ████████; ████ 22508 ████████; ████ 20744 ████████
████.

[2037] CIA ████ (072303Z NOV 02) ████████

(TS// ██████████ //NF) On March 1, 2003, KSM was captured. A notebook associated with KSM retrieved during the capture operation included the name "Jafar al-TAYYAR."[2038] After his capture, KSM was rendered to CIA custody, and immediately subjected to the CIA's enhanced interrogation techniques.[2039]

(TS// ██████████ //NF) On March 7, 2003, CIA Headquarters sent information on Jaffar al-Tayyar to the CIA's DETENTION SITE BLUE, where KSM was located, for use in the interrogation of KSM.[2040] The documents included the following:

- a "targeting study" on Jaffar al-Tayyar completed by the CIA in January 2003;[2041]
- a letter from KSM to bin al-Shibh referencing "Jafar the Pilot" and indicating that "Jafar" "ought to prepare himself" to smuggle himself from Mexico into an unspecified country;
- a letter from Jaffar al-Tayyar to Ramzi bin al-Shibh asking for clarification of KSM's letter; and
- additional background and reporting information on Jaffar al-Tayyar.[2042]

(TS// ██████████ //NF) The requirements cable from CIA Headquarters to the detention site included numerous specific questions, relying on the information already known about Jaffar al-Tayyar.[2043]

(TS// ██████████ //NF) According to CIA records, on March 9, 2003—while KSM was being interrogated using the CIA's enhanced interrogation techniques, but before he was subjected to the waterboard interrogation technique—the CIA interrogation team used two letters referencing al-Tayyar as the "interrogation vehicle" to elicit information from KSM on Jaffar al-Tayyar.[2044] CIA cables state that KSM did not provide—and claimed not to know—Jaffar al-Tayyar's true name. However, KSM stated that Jaffar al-Tayyar's father lived in Florida and was named "Shukri Sherdil."[2045] This information was not accurate. Open source reporting indicates that Jaffar al-Tayyar's father's true name was "Gulshair El Shukrijumah.[2046]

[2038] April 3, 2003, Intelligence Community Terrorist Threat Assessment regarding KSM threat reporting, entitled "Khalid Shaykh Muhammad's Threat Reporting—Precious Truths, Surrounded by a Bodyguard of Lies."
[2039] See KSM detainee review in Volume III.
[2040] ALEC ███ (072215Z MAR 03)
[2041] ALEC ███ (110209Z JAN 03)
[2042] ALEC ███ (072215Z MAR 03)
[2043] ALEC ███ (072215Z MAR 03). For more on the letters that were seized during the September 11, 2002, raids in Pakistan, and Abu Zubaydah's reporting, see ALEC ███ (110154Z JAN 03); DIRECTOR ███ (172117Z SEP 02); ███ 10092 (211031Z APR 02); ███ 10022 (121216Z APR 02); ███ ; ███ 10321 (231427Z MAY 02); ███ ; ███ ; Federal Bureau of Investigation documents pertaining "to the interrogation of detainee Zayn Al Abideen Abu Zabaidah" and provided to the Senate Select Committee on Intelligence by cover letter dated July 20, 2010 (DTS #2010-2939).
[2044] ███ 10741 (100917Z MAR 03)
[2045] ███ 10741 (100917Z MAR 03); ███ 10740 (092308Z MAR 03), disseminated as ███
[2046] Among other open source news reports, see "Father denies son linked to terror." St. Petersburg Times, published March 22, 2003.

(TS// ███████ //NF) Over the course of the next two weeks, during the period when KSM was being subjected to the CIA's enhanced interrogation techniques—including the waterboard—KSM referred to Jaffar al-Tayyar as being engaged in multiple terrorist operations. As a result, the CIA's detention site began describing Jaffar as the "all-purpose" al-Tayyar whom KSM had "woven… into practically every story, each time with a different role."[2047] CIA records confirm that KSM made numerous statements about Jaffar al-Tayyar's terrorist plotting that were deemed not to be credible by CIA personnel,[2048] including, but not limited to, statements that:

- al-Tayyar was engaged in terrorist plotting with Jose Padilla;[2049]
- al-Tayyar was engaged in terrorist plots against Heathrow Airport;[2050]
- al-Tayyar was involved in terrorist plotting with Majid Khan;[2051] and
- al-Tayyar was engaged in an assassination plot against former President Jimmy Carter.[2052]

(TS// ███████ //NF) On March 12, 2003, when KSM was confronted with a page in his notebook about al-Tayyar, KSM stated that he "considered al-Tayyar to be the 'next 'emir' for an attack against the US, in the same role that Muhammad Atta had for 11 September."[2053] On March 16, 2003, KSM stated that the only comparison between Atta and al-Tayyar was their education and experience in the West.[2054]

(TS// ███████ //NF) An email exchange the afternoon of March 18, 2003, between CIA personnel expressed the views of interrogators and officers at CIA Headquarters with regard to KSM and Jaffar al-Tayyar. The email from KSM debriefer ███████████ stated:

> "we've finally gotten [KSM] to admit that al-Tayyar is meant for a plan in the US, but I'm still not sure he's fessing up as to what Jafar's role/plan really is. Today he's working with Majid Khan, yesterday the London crowd, the day

[2047] ████ 10884 (182140Z MAR 03)
[2048] ████████ 42247 (210357Z JUL 03); email from: ██████████; to: [REDACTED], ████████████████, ████████████, [REDACTED], [REDACTED]; cc: [REDACTED], [REDACTED], [REDACTED], [REDACTED], [REDACTED], [REDACTED], [REDACTED]; subject: RATHER PROFOUND IMPLICATIONS... Ammar al-Baluchi's Comments on Jaffar al-Tayyar--If Ammar is Correct, then KSM Appears to Have a Focused Us on Jaffar in a Extended Deception Scheme--and His Deception Capabilities are Not Broken Down; date: 07/21/03, at 11:24 AM. *See also* CIA ██████ (072303Z NOV 02) and "Khalid Shaykh Muhammad's Threat Reporting – Precious Truths, Surrounded by a Bodyguard of Lies," IICT, April 3, 2003.
[2049] ██████ 10741 (100917Z MAR 03); ██████ 11377 (231943Z APR 03), disseminated as ██████████
[2050] ██████ 10778 (121549Z MAR 03), disseminated as ██████████ ; ██████ 10883 (182127Z MAR 03), disseminated as ██████████ ; ██████ 11717 (201722Z MAY 03), disseminated as ██████████
[2051] ██████ 10894 (191513Z MAR 03); ██████ 10902 (201037Z MAR 03)
[2052] ██████ 10959 (231205Z MAR 03); ██████ 10950 (222127Z MAR 03)
[2053] ██████ 10787 (130716Z MAR 03)
[2054] ██████ 10863 (171028Z MAR 03). It is unclear if KSM made the comparison in the first instance, or if the March 13, 2003, cable provided an inaccurate account of KSM's statements. The CIA's June 2013 Response states that "KSM did not call al-Tayyar 'the next Muhammad Atta.'" The CIA's June 2013 Response characterizes the inaccuracy as "an imprecise paraphrase of KSM."

before Padilla – you get the point. Anyway, I'm still worried he might be misdirecting us on Jafar."[2055]

(TS// ████████ //NF) An officer from CIA Headquarters responded, "I agree...KSM is yanking our chain about Jafar... really trying hard to throw us off course... suggesting whatever Jafar really is up to must be baaaad [sic]." The officer noted that "[a]nother big hole is Jafar's true name," and relayed that KSM's use of "another Abu name... Abu Arif... doesn't get us far."[2056] When KSM was confronted with the reporting he had provided on Jaffar al-Tayyar, KSM claimed that he had been forced to lie about al-Tayyar because of the pressure he was under from his CIA interrogators, who had been subjecting KSM to the CIA's enhanced interrogation techniques since his rendition to CIA custody.[2057]

(TS// ████████ //NF) Additional CIA records from this period indicate that, while KSM claimed not to know Jaffar al-Tayyar's true name, KSM suggested that Jose Padilla, then in U.S. military custody, would know his name. According to CIA records, the "FBI began participating in the military debriefings [of Jose Padilla] in March 2003, after KSM reported Padilla might know the true name of a US-bound al-Qa'ida operative known at the time only as Jaffar al-Tayyar. Padilla confirmed Jaffar al-Tayyar's true name as Adnan El Shukrijumah."[2058]

(TS// ████████ //NF) In March 2003, a senior CTC officer noted differences between KSM's reporting and reporting from Ramzi bin al-Shibh.[2059] In April 2003, an Intelligence Community assessment concluded, based on comments from other detainees—including those not in CIA custody—that "[i]t seemed obvious that KSM was lying with regard to Jaffar al-Tayyar."[2060] In July 2003, after Ammar al-Baluchi stated that Jaffar al-Tayyar was not suited to be an operative and was "not doing much of anything," the deputy chairman of the Community Counterterrorism Board warned:

> "If [KSM] has pulled off focusing us on a person who is actually no threat, it would mean that our interrogation techniques have not/not broken down his resistance to any appreciable extent – and that we will have to doubt even more strongly anything he says."[2061]

[2055] Note for: [REDACTED]; from: [REDACTED], OFFICE: [DETENTION SITE BLUE]; Subject: JAFAR REQUEST; date: March 18, 2003, at 08:16:07 PM.

[2056] Email from: [REDACTED]; to: [REDACTED]; subject: Re: JAFAR REQUEST; date: March 18, 2003, at 03:49:33 PM.

[2057] ████ 10902 (201037Z MAR 03); ████ 10959 (231205Z MAR 03); ████ 10950 (222127Z MAR 03); ████ 11377 (231943Z APR 03), disseminated as ████

[2058] CIA "Briefing Notes on the Value of Detainee Reporting" faxed from the CIA to the Department of Justice on April 15, 2005, at 10:47AM. On March 21, 2003, CIA records state that a photograph of Gulshair El Shukrijumah's son was obtained from the FBI and shown to KSM, Ramzi bin al-Shibh, and Abu Zubaydah, who all identified the photograph as that of al-Tayyar. See ALEC ████ (210218Z MAR 03).

[2059] Email from: ████; to [REDACTED]; cc: [REDACTED]; subject: Re: REISSUE/CORRECTION: CT: COMMENTS OF KHALID SHAYKH MUHAMMAD ON IMMINENT THREATS TO U.S. TARGETS IN THAILAND, INDONESIA, AND THE PHILIPPINES; date: March 12, 2003, at 9:36:57 AM.

[2060] "Khalid Shaykh Muhammad's Threat Reporting – Precious Truths, Surrounded by a Bodyguard of Lies," IICT, April 3, 2003.

[2061] ████ 42247 (210357Z JUL 03); email from: ████; to: [REDACTED], ████, [REDACTED],

(TS// ███████████ //NF) In December 2005, an NCTC Red Team report, entitled "Ja'far al-Tayyar: An Unlikely Al-Qa'ida Operational Threat," highlighted the possibility that the information provided by KSM on al-Tayyar's capabilities and terrorist plotting was simply "deception." The report described a large body of other detainee reporting—from Abu Faraj al-Libi, Abu Talha al-Pakistani, 'Abd al-Rahim Ghulam Rabbani, and Ammar al-Baluchi—consisting of largely dismissive statements about Jaffar al-Tayyar's capabilities and role in al-Qa'ida.[2062]

10. The Identification and Arrest of Saleh al-Marri

(TS// ███████████ //NF) The CIA represented to the CIA Office of Inspector General that "as a result of the lawful use of EITs,"[2063] KSM "provided information that helped lead to the arrests of terrorists including... Saleh Almari, a sleeper operative in New York."[2064] This information was included in the final version of the OIG's May 2004 Special Review under the heading, "Effectiveness."[2065] This CIA representation is inaccurate. KSM was captured on March 1, 2003.[2066] Saleh al-Marri was arrested in December 2001.[2067]

(TS// ███████████ //NF) The inaccurate statements about al-Marri to the OIG began with the July 16, 2003, OIG interview of Deputy Chief of ALEC Station ██████████,[2068] and

---

[REDACTED]; cc: [REDACTED], [REDACTED], [REDACTED], [REDACTED], [REDACTED], [REDACTED], [REDACTED]; subject: RATHER PROFOUND IMPLICATIONS; subject: RATHER PROFOUND IMPLICATIONS... Ammar al-Baluchi's Comments on Jaffar al-Tayyar--If Ammar is Correct, then KSM Appears to Have a Focused Us on Jaffar in a Extended Deception Scheme--and His Deception Capabilities are Not Broken Down; date: 07/21/03, at 11:24 AM.

[2062] National Counterterrorism Center, REFLECTIONS, "Ja'far al-Tayyar: An Unlikely Al-Qa'ida Operational Threat," 22 December 2005. While NCTC's "mainline analytic group" disagreed with the Red Team's analytical conclusions, records do not indicate that the Red Team's account of the contrary detainee reporting was challenged. Draft MEMORANDUM FOR THE DIRECTOR OF NATIONAL INTELLIGENCE from the Office of the Director of National Intelligence General Counsel; SUBJECT: ███████████████████████████

[2063] See CIA memorandum to the CIA Inspector General from James Pavitt, CIA's Deputy Director for Operations, dated February 27, 2004, with the subject line, "Comments to Draft IG Special Review, 'Counterterrorism Detention and Interrogation Program' (2003-7123-IG)," Attachment, "Successes of CIA's Counterterrorism Detention and Interrogation Activities," dated February 24, 2004.

[2064] ██████████, Memorandum for the Record; subject: Meeting with Deputy Chief, Counterterrorist Center ALEC Station; date: 17 July 2003; and CIA Office of Inspector General, Special Review – Counterterrorism Detention and Interrogation Program, (2003-7123-IG), May 2004.

[2065] CIA Office of Inspector General, Special Review – Counterterrorism Detention and Interrogation Program, (2003-7123-IG), May 2004.

[2066] ██████ 41351 ██████████.

[2067] Information on ALI SALEH M K AL-MARRI, provided by the FBI to the Committee, March 26, 2002 (DTS #2002-1819).

[2068] On July 16, 2003, ██████ informed the OIG that KSM's information "helped lead to the arrest of" al-Marri. (See ██████████, Memorandum for the Record; subject: Meeting with Deputy Chief, Counterterrorist Center ALEC Station; date: 17 July 2003). Two days later, ██████ wrote an email with information intended for CIA leadership that stated, accurately, that al-Marri "had been detained on a material witness warrant based on information linking him to the 911 financier Hasawi." (See email from: ██████████████ to: ██████████████, [REDACTED], ██████████, [REDACTED], [REDACTED], ██████████, ██████████, subject: value of detainees; date: July 18, 2003, at 2:30:09 PM).

were repeated in DDO Pavitt's formal response to the draft OIG Special Review.[2069] The inaccurate statements were then included in the final May 2004 Special Review.[2070] The "Effectiveness" section of the Special Review was used repeatedly as evidence for the effectiveness of the CIA's enhanced interrogation techniques, including in CIA representations to the Department of Justice. The passage in the OIG Special Review that includes the inaccurate CIA representation that KSM provided information helping to lead to the arrest of al-Marri was referenced in the May 30, 2005, OLC memorandum analyzing the legality of the CIA's enhanced interrogation techniques.[2071] The portion of the Special Review discussing al-Marri has been declassified, as has the OLC memorandum.[2072]

(TS// ████████ //NF) The CIA also represented, in Pavitt's formal response to the OIG, that prior to reporting from KSM, the CIA possessed "no concrete information" on al-Marri.[2073]

[2069] The January 2004 draft OIG Special Review included the inaccurate information provided by ████, that KSM "provided information that helped lead to the arrests of terrorists including... Saleh Almery, a sleeper operative in New York." (See CIA Inspector General, Special Review, Counterterrorism Detention and Interrogation Program (2003-7123-IG) January 2004). CTC's response to the draft Special Review was likewise prepared by ████, who wrote: "KSM also identified a photograph of a suspicious student in New York whom the FBI suspected of some involvement with al-Qa'ida, but against whom we had no concrete information." After describing KSM's reporting, ████ wrote, "[t]his student is now being held on a material witness warrant." (See email from: ████; to: ████; cc: ████, [REDACTED], [REDACTED], ████; subject: re Addition on KSM/AZ and measures; date: February 9, 2004.) DDO Pavitt's formal response to the OIG draft Special Review included this representation, adding that the information was provided "as a result of the lawful use of EITs." Pavitt's memo to the OIG did not acknowledge that the "student now being held on a material witness warrant" had been arrested more than a year prior to the capture of KSM. Nor did it correct the inaccurate information in the OIG's draft Special Review that KSM's information "helped lead to the arrest" of al-Marri. See memorandum for Inspector General from James Pavitt, Deputy Director for Operations; subject: re (S) Comments to Draft IG Special Review, "Counterterrorism Detention and Interrogation Program" (2003-7123-IG); date: February 27, 2004; attachment: February 24, 2004, Memorandum re Successes of CIA's Counterterrorism Detention and Interrogation Activities.

[2070] CIA Office of Inspector General, Special Review – Counterterrorism Detention and Interrogation Program, (2003-7123-IG), May 2004.

[2071] In its May 30, 2005, memorandum, the OLC wrote, "we understand that interrogations have led to specific, actionable intelligence," and "[w]e understand that the use of enhanced techniques in the interrogations of KSM, Zubaydah and others... has yielded critical information" (Memorandum for John A. Rizzo, Senior Deputy General Counsel, Central Intelligence Agency, from Steven G. Bradbury, Principal Deputy Assistant Attorney General, Office of Legal Counsel, May 30, 2005, Re: Application of United States Obligations Under Article 16 of the Convention Against Torture to Certain Techniques that May be Used in the Interrogation of High Value Al Qaeda Detainees (DTS #2009-1810, Tab 11), citing IG Special Review at 86, 90-91.

[2072] The CIA's June 2013 Response states: "CIA mistakenly provided incorrect information to the Inspector General (IG) that led to a one-time misrepresentation of this case in the IG's 2004 Special Review." The CIA's June 2013 Response states that "[t]his mistake was not, as it is characterized in the 'Findings and Conclusions' section of the Study, a 'repeatedly represented' or 'frequently cited' example of the effectiveness of CIA's interrogation program." The Committee found that, in addition to the multiple representations to the CIA OIG, the inaccurate information in the final OIG Special Review was, as noted above, provided by the CIA to the Department of Justice to support the Department's analysis of the lawfulness of the CIA's enhanced interrogation techniques. The OIG Special Review was also relied upon by the Blue Ribbon Panel evaluating the effectiveness of the CIA's enhanced interrogation techniques, and later was cited in multiple open source articles and books, often in the context of the "effectiveness" of the CIA program.

[2073] Email from: ████; to: ████; cc: ████, [REDACTED], [REDACTED], ████; subject: re Addition on KSM/AZ and measures; date: February 9, 2004. Memorandum for: Inspector General; from: James Pavitt, Deputy Director for Operations; subject: re (S) Comments to Draft IG Special Review, "Counterterrorism Detention and Interrogation Program" (2003-7123-IG); date: February 27, 2004;

This representation is incongruent with CIA records. CIA records indicate that prior to the CIA's detention of KSM, the CIA possessed significant information on al-Marri, who was arrested after making attempts to contact a telephone number associated with al-Qa'ida member and suspected 9/11 facilitator, Mustafa al-Hawsawi.[2074] CIA records indicate that al-Marri had suspicious information on his computer upon his arrest,[2075] that al-Marri's brother had travelled to Afghanistan in 2001 to join in jihad against the United States,[2076] and that al-Marri was directly associated with KSM, as well as with al-Hawsawi.[2077]

(TS//████████//NF) The FBI also had extensive records on al-Marri. On March 26, 2002, a year before any reporting from KSM, the FBI provided the Committee with biographical and derogatory information on al-Marri, including al-Marri's links to Mustafa al-Hawsawi, suspicious information found on al-Marri's computer, and al-Marri's connections to other extremists.[2078]

11. The Collection of Critical Tactical Intelligence on Shkai, Pakistan

(TS//████████//NF) In the context of the effectiveness of the CIA's enhanced interrogation techniques, the CIA represented to policymakers over several years that "key intelligence" was obtained from the use of the CIA's enhanced interrogation techniques that revealed Shkai, Pakistan, to be "a major al-Qa'ida hub in the tribal areas," and resulted in "tactical intelligence ████████████████████████████ in Shkai, Pakistan."[2079] These CIA

---

attachment: February 24, 2004, Memorandum re Successes of CIA's Counterterrorism Detention and Interrogation Activities.

[2074] ALEC ████ (292319Z APR 03)

[2075] The laptop contained files and Internet bookmarks associated with suspicious chemicals and chemical distributors, as well as computer programs typically used by hackers. *See* WASHINGTON ████ (122314Z MAR 03); ALEC ████ (292319Z APR 03).

[2076] CIA WASHINGTON DC ████ (260018Z MAR 03)

[2077] Prior to the capture of KSM, Abd al-Rahim Ghulam Rabbani told the FBI that al-Marri had called KSM and had been seen with KSM at an al-Qa'ida guesthouse. In addition, email accounts found on a computer seized during the raid that captured KSM revealed links to accounts associated with al-Marri. *See* ALEC ████ (292319Z APR 03); WASHINGTON ████ (122314Z MAR 03); ALEC ████ (031759Z MAR 03); ALEC ████ (052341Z MAR 03).

[2078] The FBI information included that al-Marri's brother "traveled to Afghanistan in 1997-1998 to train in Bin – Laden camps." It also indicated that al-Marri's computer revealed bookmarks to websites associated with religious extremism and various criminal activities, as well as hacking tools (*See* FBI document on Ali Saleh MK Al-Marri, provided to the Committee, March 26, 2002 (DTS #2002-1819)). Despite the extensive derogatory information on al-Marri in the possession of both the CIA and FBI, the CIA's June 2013 Response repeats previous CIA representations that prior to KSM's reporting, the CIA had "no concrete information" on al-Marri. The CIA's June 2013 Response also states that the previously obtained information was "fragmentary," and that while the CIA and FBI were aware of al-Marri's links to al-Qa'ida and "strongly suspected him of having a nefarious objective," "both agencies... lacked detailed reporting to confirm these suspicions...."

[2079] Among other documents, *see*: (1) CIA memorandum to "National Security Advisor," from "Director of Central Intelligence," Subject: "Effectiveness of the CIA Counterterrorist Interrogation Techniques," included in email from: ████████ ; to: ████████ , ████████ , and ████████ ; subject: "paper on value of interrogation techniques"; date: December 6, 2004, at 5:06:38 PM. The email references the attached "information paper to Dr. Rice explaining the value of the interrogation techniques," (2) CIA Memorandum for Steve Bradbury at Office of Legal Counsel, Department of Justice, dated March 2, 2005, from ████████ , ████ Legal Group, DCI Counterterrorist Center, subject "Effectiveness of the CIA Counterterrorist Interrogation Techniques," (3) CIA Talking Points entitled, "Talking Points for 10 March 2005 DCI Meeting PC: Effectiveness of

representations were based on the CIA's experience with one CIA detainee, Hassan Ghul. While CIA records indicate that Hassan Ghul did provide information on Shkai, Pakistan, a review of CIA records found that: (1) the vast majority of this information, including the identities, activities, and locations of senior al-Qa'ida operatives in Shkai, was provided prior to Hassan Ghul being subjected to the CIA's enhanced interrogation techniques; (2) CIA's ███████ ████████ assessed that Ghul's reporting prior to the use of the CIA's enhanced interrogation techniques contained sufficient detail to press the Pakistani ████████████████████; and (3) the CIA assessed that the information provided by Ghul corroborated earlier reporting that the Shkai valley of Pakistan served as al-Qa'ida's command and control center after the group's 2001 exodus from Afghanistan.[2080]

(TS// ███████████ //NF) As an example of one of the CIA's representations on Shkai, Pakistan, and the effectiveness of the CIA's enhanced interrogation techniques, on March 2, 2005, the CIA responded to a request from the OLC "for the intelligence the Agency obtained from detainees who, before their interrogations, were not providing any information of intelligence [value]." The resulting CIA memorandum, with the subject line "Effectiveness of the CIA Counterterrorist Interrogation Techniques," included the following under the heading, "Results":

> "CIA's use of DOJ-approved enhanced interrogation techniques, as part of a comprehensive interrogation approach, has enabled CIA to disrupt terrorist plots, capture additional terrorists, and collect a high volume of critical intelligence on al-Qa'ida. We believe that intelligence acquired from these interrogations has been a key reason why al-Qa'ida has failed to launch a spectacular attack in the West since 11 September 2001. Key intelligence collected from HVD interrogations *after* applying interrogation techniques:"[2081]

(TS// ███████████ //NF) The CIA then listed "Shkai, Pakistan" as an example, stating:

> "Shkai, Pakistan: The interrogation of Hassan Ghul provided detailed tactical intelligence showing that Shkai, Pakistan was a major Al-Qa'ida hub in the tribal areas. Through use of ████████████████ during the Ghul

---

the High-Value Detainee Interrogation (HVDI) Techniques," (4) CIA briefing document dated May 2, 2006, entitled, "BRIEFING FOR CHIEF OF STAFF TO THE PRESIDENT 2 May 2006 Briefing for Chief of Staff to the President Josh Bolten: CIA Rendition, Detention and Interrogation Programs," (5) CIA classified Statement for the Record, Senate Select Committee on Intelligence, provided by General Michael V. Hayden, Director, Central Intelligence Agency, 12 April 2007 (DTS #2007-1563), and accompanying Senate Select Committee on Intelligence hearing transcript for April 12, 2007, entitled, "Hearing on Central Intelligence Agency Detention and Interrogation Program" (DTS #2007-3158), and (6) CIA Briefing for Obama National Security Team - "Renditions, Detentions, and Interrogations (RDI)" including "Tab 7," named "RDG Copy- Briefing on RDI Program 09 Jan. 2009, " prepared "13 January 2009."

[2080] Email from: [REDACTED]; to: [REDACTED]; subject: Re: Detainee Profile on Hassan Ghul for coord; date: December 30, 2005, at 8:14:04 AM.

[2081] Italics in original document. CIA Memorandum for Steve Bradbury at Office of Legal Counsel, Department of Justice, dated March 2, 2005, from ████████, ████ Legal Group, DCI Counterterrorist Center, subject "Effectiveness of the CIA Counterterrorist Interrogation Techniques."

interrogation, we mapped out and pinpointed the residences of key AQ leaders in Shkai. This intelligence was provided ███████████████████████ ."[2082]

(TS// ███████████ //NF) The CIA representation that the use of the CIA's enhanced interrogation techniques produced otherwise unavailable tactical intelligence related to Shkai, Pakistan, was provided to senior policymakers and the Department of Justice between 2004 and 2009.[2083]

(TS// ███████████ //NF) Hassan Ghul was captured on January ██, 2004, by foreign authorities in the Iraqi Kurdistan Region.[2084] Ghul was reportedly first interrogated by ██ ██,[2085] then transferred to U.S. military custody and questioned, and then rendered to CIA custody on January ██, 2004.[2086] Hassan Ghul spent two days at DETENTION SITE COBALT before being transferred to the CIA's DETENTION SITE BLACK on January ██, 2004. Prior to his capture, the CIA assessed that Ghul possessed substantial knowledge of al-Qa'ida facilities and procedures in Wana and Shkai, Pakistan.[2087]

(TS// ███████████ //NF) During Hassan Ghul's two days at DETENTION SITE COBALT, CIA interrogators did not use the CIA's enhanced interrogation techniques on Ghul. Instead, CIA cables state that upon his arrival at the CIA detention site, Hassan Ghul was "examined, and

---

[2082] CIA Memorandum for Steve Bradbury at Office of Legal Counsel, Department of Justice, dated March 2, 2005, from ███████, ████ Legal Group, DCI Counterterrorist Center, subject "Effectiveness of the CIA Counterterrorist Interrogation Techniques." In its June 2013 Response, the CIA states: "We never represented that Shkai was previously unknown to us or that Gul only told us about it after he was subjected to enhanced interrogation techniques. We said that after these techniques were used, Gul provided 'detailed tactical intelligence.' That intelligence differed significantly in granularity and operational utility from what he provided before enhanced techniques." As described in this summary, CIA representations about intelligence on Shkai were used as evidence of the necessity and effectiveness of the CIA's enhanced interrogation techniques. The CIA did not inform policymakers or the Department of Justice about the extensive information provided by Hassan Ghul on Shkai prior to the use of the CIA's enhanced interrogation techniques.

[2083] See, for example, CIA memorandum to "National Security Advisor," from "Director of Central Intelligence," Subject: "Effectiveness of the CIA Counterterrorist Interrogation Techniques," included in email from: ████ ████████; to: ████████, ████████, and ████████; subject: "paper on value of interrogation techniques"; date: December 6, 2004, at 5:06:38 PM; CIA Memorandum for Steve Bradbury at Office of Legal Counsel, Department of Justice, dated March 2, 2005, from ████████, ████ Legal Group, DCI Counterterrorist Center, subject "Effectiveness of the CIA Counterterrorist Interrogation Techniques."

[2084] ████████ 21753 ████████; HEADQUARTERS ████ ████ JAN 04)

[2085] On April 16, 2013, the Council on Foreign Relations hosted a forum in relation to the screening of the film, "Manhunt." The forum included former CIA officer Nada Bakos, who states in the film that Hassan Ghul provided critical information on Abu Ahmed al-Kuwaiti's connection to UBL to Kurdish officials prior to entering CIA custody. When asked about the interrogation techniques used by the Kurds, Bakos stated: "...honestly, Hassan Ghul...when he was being debriefed by the Kurdish government, he literally was sitting there having tea. He was in a safe house. He wasn't locked up in a cell. He wasn't handcuffed to anything. He was—he was having a free flowing conversation. And there's—you know, there's articles in Kurdish papers about sort of their interpretation of the story and how forthcoming he was." See www.cfr.org/counterterrorism/film-screening-manhunt/p30560.

[2086] ████████ 21815 ████████, ████████ 21753 ████████; HEADQUARTERS ████████ JAN 04); ████████ 1642 ████ JAN 04); DIRECTOR ████████ JAN 04)

[2087] ████ 1308 (████ JAN 04); ████ 1299 (████ JAN 04); ████████ 1308 (████ JAN 04); ████ 1313 (████ JAN 04); ████ 1320 (████ FEB 04)

placed in a cell, given adequate clothing, bedding, water and a waste bucket."[2088] During this two-day period (January ██, 2004, and January ██, 2004),[2089] Ghul provided information for at least 21 intelligence reports.[2090] As detailed below, Ghul's reporting on Shkai, Pakistan, and al-Qa'ida operatives who resided in or visited Shkai, was included in at least 16 of these intelligence reports.[2091] The reports included information on the locations, movements, and operational security and training of senior al-Qa'ida leaders living in Shkai, Pakistan, as well as the visits of leaders and operatives to the area. The information provided by Ghul included details on various groups operating in Shkai, Pakistan, and conflicts among the groups. Hassan Ghul also identified and decoded phone numbers and email addresses contained in a notebook seized with him, some of which were associated with Shkai-based operatives.[2092]

(TS// ███████████████ //NF) Hassan Ghul described the origins of al-Qa'ida's presence in Shkai, including how Abd al-Hadi al-Iraqi became the original group's military commander and its al-Qa'ida representative.[2093] He discussed tensions between al-Hadi and others in Shkai, the

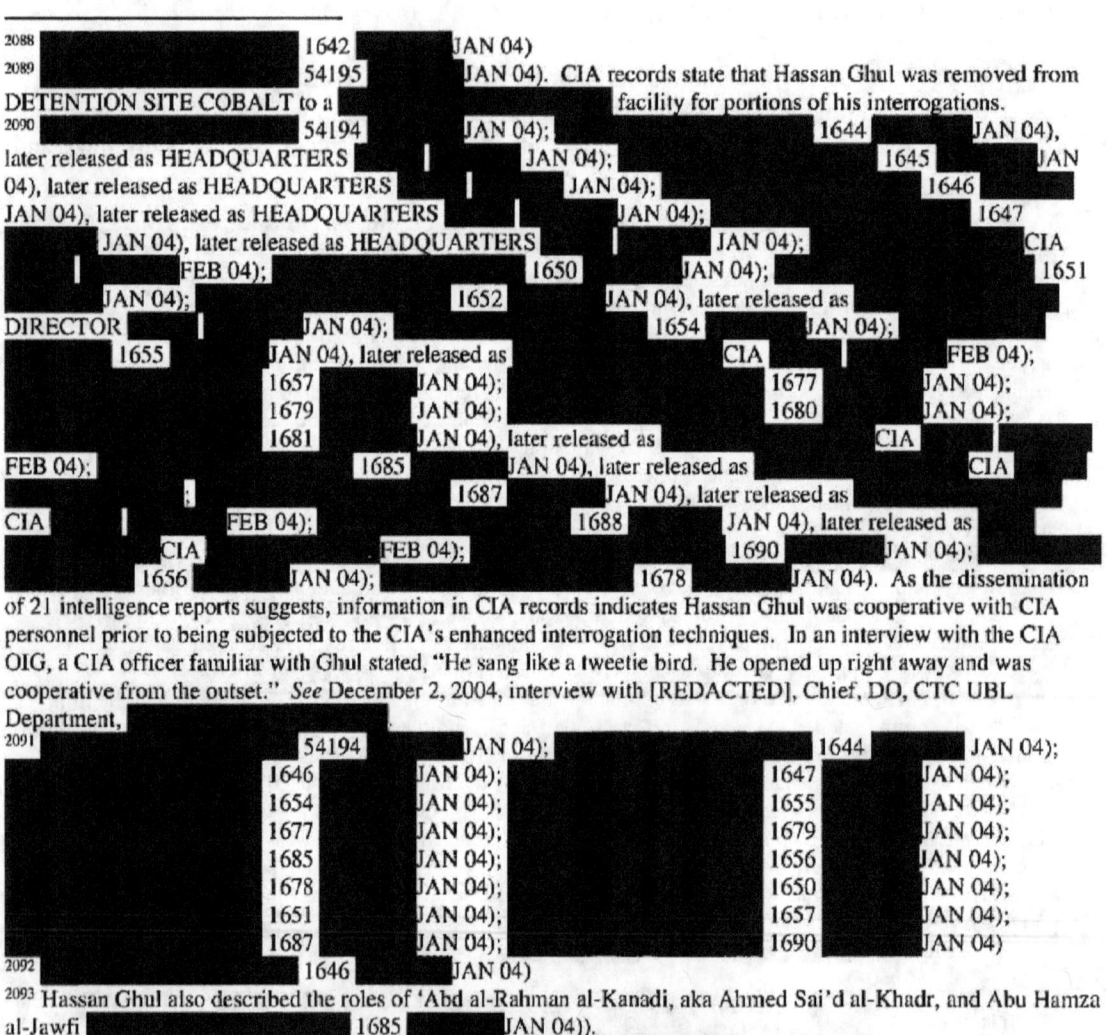

[2088] ████████████████ 1642 █████ JAN 04)
[2089] ████████████████ 54195 █████ JAN 04). CIA records state that Hassan Ghul was removed from DETENTION SITE COBALT to a ████████████████ facility for portions of his interrogations.
[2090] ████████████ 54194 ████ JAN 04); ████████ 1644 ████ JAN 04), later released as HEADQUARTERS ████ █ JAN 04); ████ 1645 ████ JAN 04), later released as HEADQUARTERS ████ █ JAN 04); ████ 1646 ████ JAN 04, later released as HEADQUARTERS ████ █ JAN 04); ████ 1647 ████ JAN 04), later released as HEADQUARTERS ████ █ JAN 04); ████ CIA ████ FEB 04); ████ 1650 ████ JAN 04); ████ 1651 ████ JAN 04); ████ 1652 ████ JAN 04), later released as DIRECTOR █ JAN 04); ████ 1654 ████ JAN 04); ████ 1655 ████ JAN 04), later released as ████ CIA ████ FEB 04); ████ 1657 ████ JAN 04); ████ 1677 ████ JAN 04); ████ 1679 ████ JAN 04); ████ 1680 ████ JAN 04); ████ 1681 ████ JAN 04), later released as ████ CIA ████ FEB 04); ████ 1685 ████ JAN 04), later released as ████ CIA ████ █ JAN 04), later released as ████ 1687 ████ JAN 04), later released as ████ CIA █ FEB 04); ████ 1688 ████ JAN 04), later released as ████ CIA ████ FEB 04); ████ 1690 ████ JAN 04); ████ 1656 ████ JAN 04); ████ 1678 ████ JAN 04). As the dissemination of 21 intelligence reports suggests, information in CIA records indicates Hassan Ghul was cooperative with CIA personnel prior to being subjected to the CIA's enhanced interrogation techniques. In an interview with the CIA OIG, a CIA officer familiar with Ghul stated, "He sang like a tweetie bird. He opened up right away and was cooperative from the outset." See December 2, 2004, interview with [REDACTED], Chief, DO, CTC UBL Department, ████████████
[2091] ████████████ 54194 ████ JAN 04); ████ 1644 ████ JAN 04); 1646 JAN 04); 1647 JAN 04); 1654 JAN 04); 1655 JAN 04); 1677 JAN 04); 1679 JAN 04); 1685 JAN 04); 1656 JAN 04); 1678 JAN 04); 1650 JAN 04); 1651 JAN 04); 1657 JAN 04); 1687 JAN 04); 1690 JAN 04)
[2092] ████████████ 1646 ████ JAN 04)
[2093] Hassan Ghul also described the roles of 'Abd al-Rahman al-Kanadi, aka Ahmed Sai'd al-Khadr, and Abu Hamza al-Jawfi ████████████ 1685 ████ JAN 04)).

mediating role of Abu Faraj al-Libi, and the role of Khalid Habib.[2094] Hassan Ghul explained how he moved to Shkai due to concerns about Abu Musa'b al-Baluchi's contacts with ████████ ████████, how he traveled to Shkai to make contact with Abd al-Hadi al-Iraqi, and how Abu Faraj mediated between Ghul and Hamza Rabi'a.[2095] Ghul stated that he last saw Abu Faraj in the summer of 2003, when Ghul was seeking Abu Faraj's assistance in moving money from Saudi Arabia to deliver to al-Hadi for support of their community in Shkai.[2096]

(TS// ████████████ //NF) According to Hassan Ghul, Abd al-Hadi al-Iraqi moved periodically among various houses within the village, including that of Abu Hussein and ████ ████████, whom he described as "senior media people for al-Qa'ida."[2097] Elaborating on al-Hadi's location, Hassan Ghul described the importance of both a *madrassa* and a guesthouse in Shkai known as the "bachelor house," where unaccompanied men stayed. Ghul stated that he last saw al-Hadi in December 2003 when al-Hadi came to the "bachelor house" to visit with other Arabs.[2098] Ghul also identified other permanent and transient residents of the "bachelor house."[2099] He stated that al-Hadi, who he believed was seeking another safehouse in Shkai at which to hold meetings, had approximately 40 to 50 men under his command. Hassan Ghul also identified a phone number used to contact al-Hadi.[2100]

[2094] ████████████████ 1685 ████ JAN 04)
[2095] ████████████████ 1677 ████ JAN 04)
[2096] Hassan Gul stated that Abu Faraj was with his associate, Mansur Khan, aka Hassan. (*See* ████████ ████ 1654 ████████ JAN 04).) Hassan Ghul's reporting on Abd al-Hadi al-Iraqi and Abu Faraj al-Libi included discussion of Abu Ahmed al-Kuwaiti's links to UBL. According to Ghul, during his time in Shkai in 2003, al-Hadi would periodically receive brief handwritten messages from UBL via Abu Faraj, which he would share with their group. Ghul stated that this did not necessarily mean that Abu Faraj knew the location of UBL, but rather that he had a window into UBL's courier network. It was at this point that Hassan Ghul described the role of Abu Ahmed al-Kuwaiti and his connections to UBL. *See* ████████████ 1647 ████ JAN 04).
[2097] ████ 1654 ████ JAN 04). Hassan Ghul stated ██ " *See* ████████ 1679 ████ JAN 04).
[2098] Hassan Ghul stated that al-Hadi, who did not travel with a security detail, visited the *madrassa* every few days, but less frequently of late due to the deteriorating security condition in Waziristan for Arabs. Ghul stated that when he last saw al-Hadi, he was accompanied by an Afghan assistant named Sidri, aka S'aid al-Rahman. He also identified Osaid al-Yemeni as an individual who assisted al-Hadi. *See* ████████████ 1654 ████ JAN 04).
[2099] Hassan Ghul identified Yusif al-Baluchi, Mu'awiyya al-Baluchi, a Kurd named Qassam al-Surri, Usama al-Filistini, and Khatal al-Uzbeki as living in the "bachelor house." *See* ████████████ 1654 ████ JAN 04). The CIA's June 2013 Response states: "After being subjected to enhanced techniques, [Hassan Ghul] provided more granular information." According to the CIA Response, it was in this context that Hassan Ghul identified the "bachelor house," where he had met al-Hadi, and where "several unmarried men associated with al-Qa'ida" lived, including ████████████. A review of CIA records found that Hassan Ghul provided this information prior to the use of the CIA's enhanced interrogation techniques.
[2100] Hassan Ghul identified a phone number in his phone book that he said had been provided to him by Hamza al-Jawfi to pass messages to al-Hadi in emergencies. The phone number was under the name Baba Jan, aka Ida Khan. Ghul also identified a number for Major, aka Ridwan, aka Bilal, who, he said, brought equipment to Pakistan. *See* ████████████ 1654 ████████ JAN 04); ████████ 1646 ████ JAN 04)).

(TS// ██████████ //NF) According to Hassan Ghul, as of December 2003, approximately 60 Arab males and between 150 and 200 Turkic/Uzbek males were living in Shkai, along with a "significant population" of Baluchis who assisted the Arabs and Uzbeks.[2101] Ghul described al-Qa'ida training, including an electronics course taught in the fall of 2003 by Abu Bakr al-Suri at the house of Hamza Rabi'a where, he believed, individuals were being trained for an ongoing operation.[2102] Ghul discerned from the training and Rabi'a's statements that al-Qa'ida operatives in Shkai were involved in an assassination attempt against Pakistani President Pervez Musharraf.[2103] Ghul stated Hamza Rabi'a was also likely planning operations into Afghanistan, but had no specifics.[2104]

(TS// ██████████ //NF) Hassan Ghul elaborated on numerous other al-Qa'ida operatives he said resided in or visited Shkai, Pakistan, including Shaikh Sa'id al-Masri,[2105] Sharif al-Masri,[2106]

[2101] ██████████ 1655 ██████ JAN 04)

[2102] Hassan Ghul stated that Abu Jandal and another Saudi of African descent took part in the electronics course. (See ██████████ 1654 ██████ JAN 04); ██████████ 1655 ██████ JAN 04).) As described in a separate cable, Ghul stated that he had seen 10-15 Pakistanis training with Rabi'a and Abu Bakr al-Suri, whom he described as an al-Qa'ida explosives expert, in early to mid-October 2003. (See ██████████ ██████ 1656 ██████ JAN 04).) The CIA's June 2013 Response states that Hassan Ghul reported that Hamza Rabi'a "was using facilities in Shkai to train operatives for attacks outside Pakistan," without noting Ghul's reporting, prior to the use of the CIA's enhanced interrogation techniques, on Rabi'a's training of operatives.

[2103] Ghul explained that he was in Shkai following a previous assassination attempt, in early December 2003, when there was "frequent talk among the brothers" about who might have been responsible. When Ghul asked around, "there was a lot of talk" that Rabi'a was involved in planning a subsequent operation. Rabi'a's statement that there would be an unspecified operation soon, combined with the training conducted by Rabi'a and al-Suri, led Ghul to believe that the second assassination attempt was conducted by al-Qa'ida. See ██████████ 1656 ██████ JAN 04).

[2104] Hassan Ghul stated that it was unlikely that Abd al-Hadi al-Iraqi had any planned operations, although al-Hadi would likely assist if there were any. See ██████████ 1654 ██████ JAN 04).

[2105] Hassan Ghul stated that Shaikh Sa'id al-Masri, aka Mustafa Ahmad (Abu al-Yazid), came to Shkai around November 2003 and currently resided there. Ghul stated that Shaikh Sa'id's son, Abdullah, travelled between Shkai and a location in the greater Dera Ismail Khan area, where the rest of Shaikh Sa'id's family lived. See ██████████ ██████ 1679 ██████ JAN 04).

[2106] Hassan Ghul stated that Sharif al-Masri, who came to Shkai around October/November 2003 for a brief visit, was handling operations in Qandahar while living just outside Quetta. Ghul identified two of Sharif al-Masri's assistants. See ██████████ 1679 ██████ JAN 04).

Abu Maryam,[2107] Janat Gul,[2108] Khalil Deek,[2109] Abu Talha al-Pakistani,[2110] Firas,[2111] and others.[2112]

(TS//██████████//NF) Finally, Hassan Ghul described his interactions with Abu Mus'ab al-Zarqawi, which also related to al-Qa'ida figures in Shkai, in particular Abd al-Hadi al-Iraqi.[2113] Ghul described al-Zarqawi's request to al-Hadi for money, explosive experts, and electronic experts, and provided details of his own trip to Iraq on behalf of al-Hadi.[2114] Hassan

---

[2107] Hassan Ghul was asked about Tariq Mahmoud, whom he thought might be Abu Maryam, a British citizen of Pakistani descent whom Ghul met in Pakistan. According to Ghul, Maryam had been inside Afghanistan and had participated in training in Shkai, but was apprehended in Islamabad. (*See* ████████ 1679 ████ JAN 04).) Ghul identified a phone number for Abu Maryam. *See* ████████ 1646 ████ JAN 04).

[2108] Hassan Ghul stated that he last saw Janat Gul in December 2003 in Shkai, when Janat Gul was delivering three Arabs who had come from Iran. Janat Gul came to the "bachelor house" accompanied by Khatal. Ghul also described a discussion from September/October 2003 at Hamza al-Jawfi's house in Shkai with al-Hadi and Abu 'Abd al-Rahman BM in which Janat Gul claimed to know Russians who could provide anti-aircraft missiles. Gul asked for money, but al-Hadi was reluctant to make the commitment and did not want to work with Gul. According to Hassan Ghul, Janat Gul left and subsequent conversations revealed that Janat Gul likely made the story up. Hassan Ghul provided a phone number for Janat Gul. *See* ████████ 1679 ████ JAN 04); ████████ 1646 ████ JAN 04).

[2109] Hassan Ghul also discussed Abu Bilal al-Suri, aka, Shafiq, who was the father-in-law of Khalil Deek, aka Joseph Jacob Adams, aka Abu 'Abd al-Rahman BM, aka Abu Ayad al-Filistini. While Ghul did not know where Abu Bilal was located, he had recently seen Abu Bilal's son preparing a residence in Shkai. *See* ████████ 1679 ████ JAN 04).

[2110] Hassan Ghul stated that he knew Talha al-Pakistani, aka Suleiman, peripherally, through KSM and Ammar al-Baluchi. Ghul last saw Talha in Shkai around October/November 2003 at the residence of Hamza Rabi'a with a group that was undertaking unspecified training. Ghul stated that he was not sure if Talha was a participant or simply an observer. *See* ████████ 1679 ████ JAN 04).

[2111] Hassan Ghul was shown photos of individuals apprehended by ████████ on █ October 2003 ████████ and identified one as a Yemeni named Firas, "a well-trained fighter and experienced killer, who was known to be an excellent shot." Ghul reported that, when he first arrived in Shkai, Firas was living there. Prior to hearing about Firas' arrest, Ghul's understanding was that Firas was in Angorada with Khalid Habib, which Ghul characterized as the "front line." The other photo identified by Ghul was that of an Algerian named Abu Maryam, whom helped "hide out" in Shkai. *See* ████████ 1678 ████ JAN 04).

[2112] For Hassan Ghul's reporting on Abu Umama, aka Abu Ibrahim al-Masri, *see* ████████ 1687 ████ JAN 04).

[2113] ████████ 1644 ████ JAN 04; ████████ 54194 ████ JAN 04); DIRECTOR ████ JAN 04), disseminated as ████████ ; ████████ 54195 ████ JAN 04)

[2114] Hassan Ghul stated that in the late summer of 2003, al-Zarqawi made the request through Luay Muhammad Hajj Bakr al-Saqa (aka Abu Hamza al-Suri, aka Abu Muhammad al-Turki, aka Ala' al-Din), but that al-Hadi had not wanted to assist. According to Ghul, al-Hadi had previously sent Abdullah al-Kurdi to Iraq, but al-Kurdi did not want to engage in any activities and was rumored to be "soft." This led al-Hadi to send Ghul to Iraq to speak with al-Zarqawi regarding the possibility of select al-Qa'ida members traveling to Iraq to fight. According to the cable, "Ghul claimed that the Arabs in Waziristan were tired, and wanted change," and that Ghul "was tasked to both discuss this issue with Zarqawi, and to recon the route." (*See* ████████ 1644 ████ JAN 04).) Ghul also describe the roles of Yusif al-Baluchi, Mu'awiyya al-Baluchi, and Wasim aka Ammar aka Little Ammar aka Ammar Choto, in facilitating Ghul's trip out of Pakistan, as well as his exact route. Ghul identified Yusif's phone number in his notebook and described how Yusif had come to Shkai to gain al-Hadi's approval for a plan to kidnap Iranian VIPs to gain the release of senior al-Qa'ida Management Council members in Iranian custody. (*See* ████████ 1690 ████ JAN 04).)

Ghul identified four email addresses for contacting al-Zarqawi directly,[2115] and described a phone code he would use to communicate with al-Zarqawi.[2116] Ghul also described his conversations with al-Zarqawi, interpreted the notes he had taken of the last of his conversations with al-Zarqawi, identified operatives whom al-Zarqawi and al-Hadi agreed to send to Iraq,[2117] and discussed strategic differences between al-Zarqawi and al-Hadi related to Iraq.[2118]

(TS// ███████████████ //NF) On January █, 2004, after two days at DETENTION SITE COBALT, during which Hassan Ghul provided the aforementioned information about al-Qa'ida activities in Shkai and other matters, Ghul was transferred to the CIA's DETENTION SITE BLACK.[2119] Ghul was immediately, and for the first time, subjected to the CIA's enhanced interrogation techniques. He was "shaved and barbered, stripped, and placed in the standing position."[2120] According to a CIA cable, Hassan Ghul provided no new information during this period and was immediately placed in standing sleep deprivation with his hands above his head, with plans to lower his hands after two hours.[2121] In their request to use the CIA's enhanced interrogation techniques on Ghul, CIA detention site personnel wrote:

> "The interrogation team believes, based on [Hassan Ghul's] reaction to the
> initial contact, that his al-Qa'ida briefings and his earlier experiences with U.S.
> military interrogators have convinced him there are limits to the physical
> contact interrogators can have with him. The interrogation team believes the
> approval and employment of enhanced measures should sufficiently shift

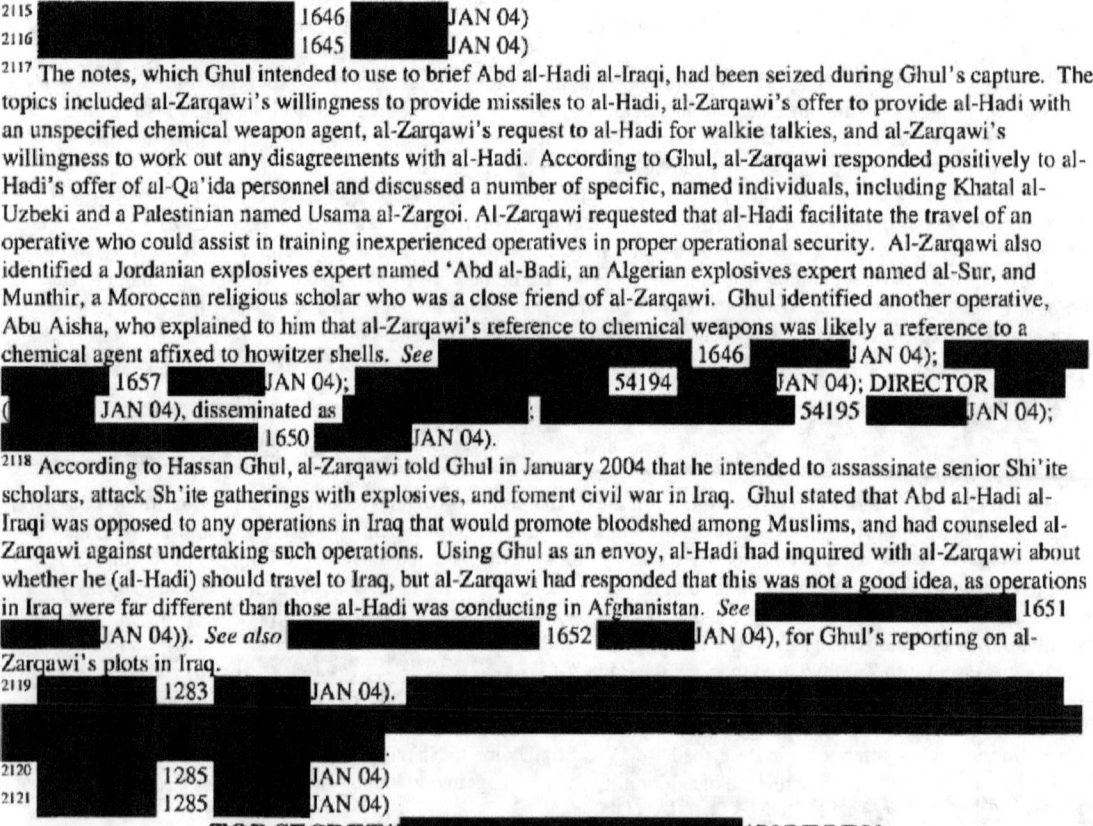

[2115] ████████████████ 1646 ████ JAN 04)
[2116] ████████████████ 1645 ████ JAN 04)
[2117] The notes, which Ghul intended to use to brief Abd al-Hadi al-Iraqi, had been seized during Ghul's capture. The topics included al-Zarqawi's willingness to provide missiles to al-Hadi, al-Zarqawi's offer to provide al-Hadi with an unspecified chemical weapon agent, al-Zarqawi's request to al-Hadi for walkie talkies, and al-Zarqawi's willingness to work out any disagreements with al-Hadi. According to Ghul, al-Zarqawi responded positively to al-Hadi's offer of al-Qa'ida personnel and discussed a number of specific, named individuals, including Khatal al-Uzbeki and a Palestinian named Usama al-Zargoi. Al-Zarqawi requested that al-Hadi facilitate the travel of an operative who could assist in training inexperienced operatives in proper operational security. Al-Zarqawi also identified a Jordanian explosives expert named 'Abd al-Badi, an Algerian explosives expert named al-Sur, and Munthir, a Moroccan religious scholar who was a close friend of al-Zarqawi. Ghul identified another operative, Abu Aisha, who explained to him that al-Zarqawi's reference to chemical weapons was likely a reference to a chemical agent affixed to howitzer shells. See ████████████████ 1646 ████ JAN 04); ████████████ 1657 ████ JAN 04); ████████ 54194 ████ JAN 04); DIRECTOR ██████ (██████ JAN 04), disseminated as ██████ ; ████ 54195 ████ JAN 04); ████████ 1650 ██████ JAN 04).
[2118] According to Hassan Ghul, al-Zarqawi told Ghul in January 2004 that he intended to assassinate senior Shi'ite scholars, attack Sh'ite gatherings with explosives, and foment civil war in Iraq. Ghul stated that Abd al-Hadi al-Iraqi was opposed to any operations in Iraq that would promote bloodshed among Muslims, and had counseled al-Zarqawi against undertaking such operations. Using Ghul as an envoy, al-Hadi had inquired with al-Zarqawi about whether he (al-Hadi) should travel to Iraq, but al-Zarqawi had responded that this was not a good idea, as operations in Iraq were far different than those al-Hadi was conducting in Afghanistan. See ████████████ 1651 ████████ JAN 04)). See also ████████████ 1652 ████ JAN 04), for Ghul's reporting on al-Zarqawi's plots in Iraq.
[2119] ████████ 1283 ████ JAN 04). ███████████████████████████
██
[2120] ████████ 1285 ████ JAN 04)
[2121] ████████ 1285 ████ JAN 04) ████████████████

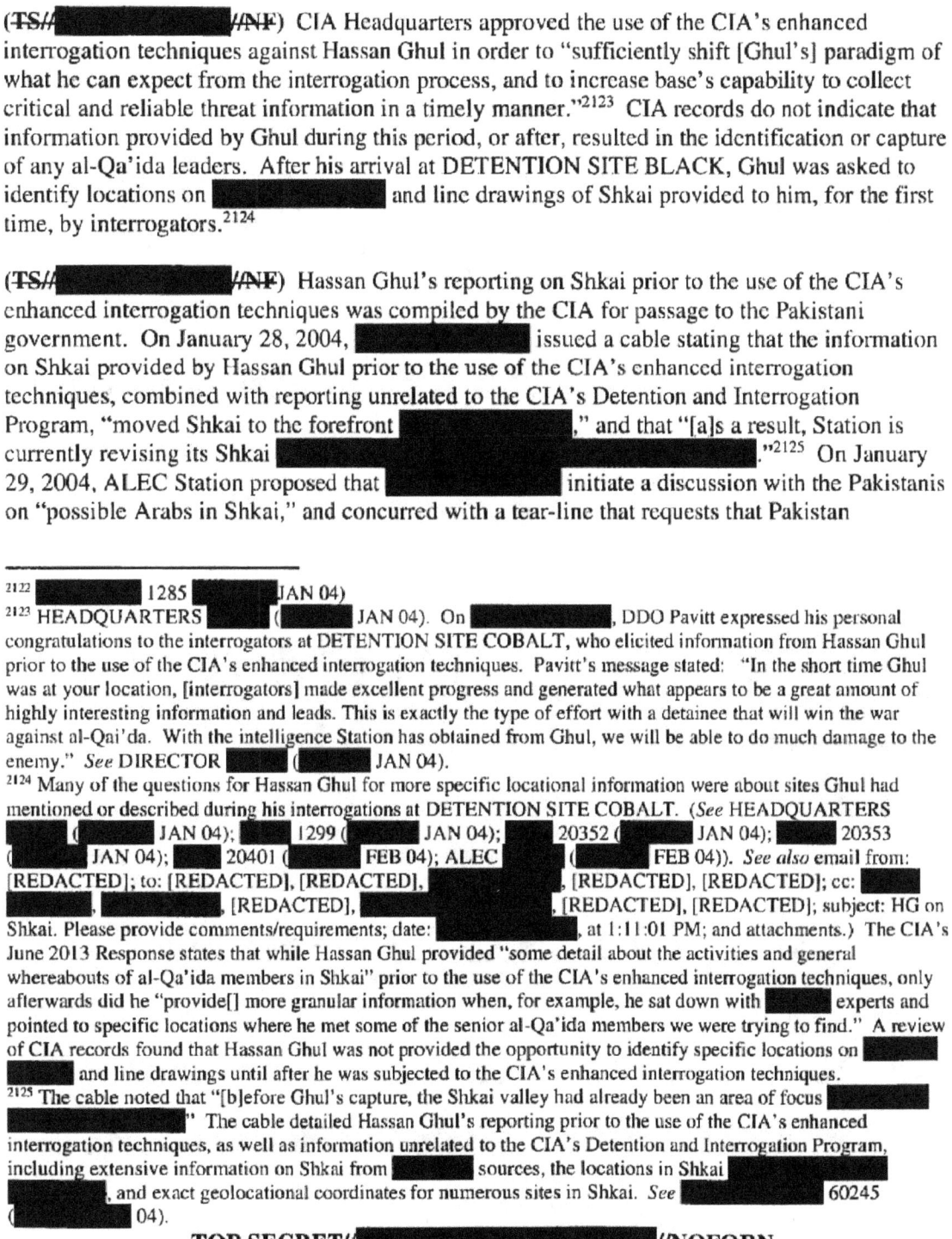

[Hassan Ghul's] paradigm of what he expects to happen. The lack of these increasd [sic] measures may limit the team's capability to collect critical and reliable information in a timely manner."[2122]

(TS// ███████ //NF) CIA Headquarters approved the use of the CIA's enhanced interrogation techniques against Hassan Ghul in order to "sufficiently shift [Ghul's] paradigm of what he can expect from the interrogation process, and to increase base's capability to collect critical and reliable threat information in a timely manner."[2123] CIA records do not indicate that information provided by Ghul during this period, or after, resulted in the identification or capture of any al-Qa'ida leaders. After his arrival at DETENTION SITE BLACK, Ghul was asked to identify locations on ███████ and line drawings of Shkai provided to him, for the first time, by interrogators.[2124]

(TS// ███████ //NF) Hassan Ghul's reporting on Shkai prior to the use of the CIA's enhanced interrogation techniques was compiled by the CIA for passage to the Pakistani government. On January 28, 2004, ███████ issued a cable stating that the information on Shkai provided by Hassan Ghul prior to the use of the CIA's enhanced interrogation techniques, combined with reporting unrelated to the CIA's Detention and Interrogation Program, "moved Shkai to the forefront ███████," and that "[a]s a result, Station is currently revising its Shkai ███████."[2125] On January 29, 2004, ALEC Station proposed that ███████ initiate a discussion with the Pakistanis on "possible Arabs in Shkai," and concurred with a tear-line that requests that Pakistan

---

[2122] ███████ 1285 ███████ JAN 04)
[2123] HEADQUARTERS ███████ (███████ JAN 04). On ███████, DDO Pavitt expressed his personal congratulations to the interrogators at DETENTION SITE COBALT, who elicited information from Hassan Ghul prior to the use of the CIA's enhanced interrogation techniques. Pavitt's message stated: "In the short time Ghul was at your location, [interrogators] made excellent progress and generated what appears to be a great amount of highly interesting information and leads. This is exactly the type of effort with a detainee that will win the war against al-Qai'da. With the intelligence Station has obtained from Ghul, we will be able to do much damage to the enemy." See DIRECTOR ███████ (███████ JAN 04).
[2124] Many of the questions for Hassan Ghul for more specific locational information were about sites Ghul had mentioned or described during his interrogations at DETENTION SITE COBALT. (See HEADQUARTERS ███████ (███████ JAN 04); ███████ 1299 (███████ JAN 04); ███████ 20352 (███████ JAN 04); ███████ 20353 (███████ JAN 04); ███████ 20401 (███████ FEB 04); ALEC ███████ (███████ FEB 04)). See also email from: [REDACTED]; to: [REDACTED], [REDACTED], ███████, [REDACTED], [REDACTED]; cc: ███████, ███████ [REDACTED], ███████, [REDACTED], [REDACTED]; subject: HG on Shkai. Please provide comments/requirements; date: ███████, at 1:11:01 PM; and attachments.) The CIA's June 2013 Response states that while Hassan Ghul provided "some detail about the activities and general whereabouts of al-Qa'ida members in Shkai" prior to the use of the CIA's enhanced interrogation techniques, only afterwards did he "provide[] more granular information when, for example, he sat down with ███████ experts and pointed to specific locations where he met some of the senior al-Qa'ida members we were trying to find." A review of CIA records found that Hassan Ghul was not provided the opportunity to identify specific locations on ███████ ███████ and line drawings until after he was subjected to the CIA's enhanced interrogation techniques.
[2125] The cable noted that "[b]efore Ghul's capture, the Shkai valley had already been an area of focus ███████" The cable detailed Hassan Ghul's reporting prior to the use of the CIA's enhanced interrogation techniques, as well as information unrelated to the CIA's Detention and Interrogation Program, including extensive information on Shkai from ███████ sources, the locations in Shkai ███████ ███████, and exact geolocational coordinates for numerous sites in Shkai. See ███████ 60245 (███████ 04).

"undertake to verify" the presence of "a large number of Arabs" in Shkai "as soon as possible."[2126]

(TS// ████████████ //NF) On January 31, 2004, CIA's ████████████ drafted a cable with an extensive "tear-line" for Pakistan, much of it related to Shkai. The cable from ████████ ████ referenced nine cables describing Hassan Ghul's reporting prior to the use of the CIA's enhanced interrogation techniques,[2127] and no cables describing Ghul's reporting after the use of the techniques.[2128] The cable from ████████████ then stated that "Station sees the type of information coming from [Hassan Ghul's] interrogations as perfect fodder for pressing [Pakistan] into action against ████ associates of Hassan Ghul in Pakistan, ████████████ , and other terrorist ████ in Pakistan ████████████ ." The tear-line for Pakistan included extensive information provided by Hassan Ghul prior to the use of the CIA's enhanced interrogation techniques.[2129] On February 3, 2004, CIA Headquarters requested that the tear-line be passed to the Pakistanis, but deferred to ████████████ on the portions dealing with Shkai.[2130] As CIA's ████████████ informed CIA Headquarters on February 9, 2004, it intended to hold the information on Shkai until the DCI's visit to Pakistan the following day. As Station noted, "this tearline will prove critical ████████████ ████████ ."[2131] In the meantime and afterwards, additional tear-lines were prepared for the Pakistanis that were based primarily on reporting from Hassan Ghul prior to the use of the CIA's enhanced interrogation techniques, combined with Ghul's subsequent reporting, and information from sources unrelated to the CIA's Detention and Interrogation Program.[2132]

[2126] ALEC ████ (290157Z JAN 04)
[2127] ████████ 1681 ████ JAN 04); ████████ 1680 ████ JAN 04);
████ 1679 ████ JAN 04); ████████ 1678 ████ JAN 04);
████ 1677 ████ JAN 04); ████████ 1656 ████ JAN 04);
████ 1654 ████ JAN 04); ████████ 1647 ████ JAN 04),
████ 1644 ████ JAN 04).
[2128] ████ 2714 (311146Z JAN 04)
[2129] ████████ 2714 (311146Z JAN 04). The CIA's June 2013 Response states that "CIA continues to assess that the information derived from Hassan Gul after the commencement of enhanced techniques provided new and unique insight into al-Qa'ida's presence and operations in Shkai, Pakistan." The CIA's June 2013 Response also defends past CIA representations that "after these techniques were used, Gul provided 'detailed tactical intelligence,'" that "differed significantly in granularity and operational ████ from what he provided before enhanced techniques." The CIA's Response then states that "[a]s a result of his information, we were able to make a persuasive case ████████████████████████ ." A review of CIA records found that the CIA had previously determined that the information provided by Hassan Ghul prior to the use of the CIA's enhanced interrogation techniques was the "perfect fodder for pressing [Pakistan] into action."
[2130] HEADQUAR ████ (032357Z FEB 04)
[2131] ████ 2742 (090403Z FEB 04)
[2132] ████ 60796 (051600Z FEB 04); ALEC ████ (████ FEB 04); DIRECTOR ████ (FEB 04). The CIA's June 2013 Response states that "[s]enior US officials during the winter and spring of 2004 presented the Agency's analysis of Gul's debriefings and other intelligence about Shkai ████████████ ████████████████████ ." As support, the CIA Response cites two cables that relied heavily on information provided by Hassan Ghul prior to the use of the CIA's enhanced interrogation techniques, as well as information from unrelated sources. (See ALEC ████ (████ FEB 04); DIRECTOR ████ (████ FEB 04)).

(TS// ███████ //NF) In July 2004, the CIA assessed ████████████████ that "al-Qa'ida operatives ██████████████████████ are continuing with their activities and waiting for the situation to normalize in the tribal areas." In particular, "[a]l-Qa'ida's senior operatives who were in Shkai before the military's offensive remained in South Waziristan as of mid-June [2004]."[2133] Later, in December 2005, a CIA detainee profile of Hassan Ghul assessed that the information provided by Ghul confirmed earlier reporting in CIA's possession that the Shkai valley of Pakistan served as al-Qa'ida's command and control center after the group's 2001 exodus from Afghanistan.[2134] Hassan Ghul was ██████████ ██████████, and later released.[2135]

█████[2136]

12. Information on the Facilitator that Led to the UBL Operation

(TS// ██████████ //NF) Shortly after the raid on the Usama bin Ladin (UBL) compound on May 1, 2011, which resulted in UBL's death, CIA officials described the role of reporting from the CIA's Detention and Interrogation Program in the operation—and in some cases connected the reporting to the use of the CIA's enhanced interrogation techniques.[2137] The vast majority of

---

[2133] Directorate of Intelligence, *Al-Qa'ida's Waziristan Sanctuary Disrupted but Still Viable*, 21 July 2004 (DTS #2004-3240).

[2134] Email from: [REDACTED]; to: [REDACTED]; subject: Re: Detainee Profile on Hassan Ghul for coord; date: December 30, 2005, at 8:14:04 AM.

[2135] ████ 2441 ████████; HEADQUARTERS ████ ████████; ████ 1635 ████████; ████ 1712 ████████; HEADQUARTERS ██████; ████ 1775 ████; 173426 █████.

[2136] Congressional Notification (DTS #2012-3802).

[2137] In addition to classified representations to the Committee, shortly after the operation targeting UBL on May 1, 2011, there were media reports indicating that the CIA's Detention and Interrogation Program had produced "*the lead information*" that led to Abu Ahmad al-Kuwaiti, the UBL compound, and/or the overall operation that led to UBL's death. In an interview with *Time Magazine*, published May 4, 2011, Jose Rodriguez, the former CIA chief of CTC, stated that: "Information provided by KSM and Abu Faraj al-Libbi about bin Laden's courier was *the lead information* that eventually led to the location of [bin Laden's] compound and the operation that led to his death." *See* "Ex-CIA Counterterror Chief: 'Enhanced Interrogation' Led U.S. to bin Laden." *Time Magazine*, May 4, 2011 (italics added). Former CIA Director Michael Hayden stated that: "What we got, the *original lead information*— and frankly it was incomplete identity information on the couriers—*began with information from CIA detainees at the black sites.*" In another interview, Hayden stated: "…the lead information I referred to a few minutes ago did come from CIA detainees, *against whom enhanced interrogation techniques* have been used" (italics added). *See* Transcript from *Scott Hennen Show*, dated May 3, 2011, with former CIA Director Michael Hayden; and interview with Fareed Zakaria, *Fareed Zakaria GPS*, CNN, May 8, 2011. *See also* "The Waterboarding Trail to bin Laden," by Michael Mukasey, *Wall Street Journal*, May 6, 2011. Former Attorney General Mukasey wrote: "Consider how the intelligence that led to bin Laden came to hand. It began with a disclosure from Khalid Sheikh Mohammed (KSM), who broke like a dam under the pressure of harsh interrogation techniques that included waterboarding. He loosed a torrent of information—including eventually the nickname of a trusted courier of bin Laden." The CIA's June 2013 Response confirms information in the Committee Study, stating: "Even after undergoing enhanced techniques, KSM lied about Abu Ahmad, and Abu Faraj denied knowing him." The CIA's September 2012 "Lessons from the Hunt for Bin Ladin," (DTS #2012-3826) compiled by the CIA's Center for the Study of Intelligence, indicates that the CIA sought to publicly attribute the UBL operation to detainee reporting months prior to the execution of the operation. Under the heading, "The Public Roll-Out," the "Lessons from the Hunt for Bin Ladin" document explains that the CIA's Office of Public Affairs was "formally brought into the [UBL] operation in late March 2011." The document states that the "material OPA prepared for release" was intended to "describe the

the documents, statements, and testimony highlighting information obtained from the use of the CIA's enhanced interrogation techniques, or from CIA detainees more generally, was inaccurate and incongruent with CIA records.

(TS// ███████████ //NF) CIA records indicate that: (1) the CIA had extensive reporting on Abu Ahmad al-Kuwaiti (variant Abu Ahmed al-Kuwaiti),[2138] the UBL facilitator whose identification and tracking led to the identification of UBL's compound and the operation that resulted in UBL's death, prior to and independent of information from CIA detainees; (2) the most accurate information on Abu Ahmad al-Kuwaiti obtained from a CIA detainee was provided by a CIA detainee who had not yet been subjected to the CIA's enhanced interrogation techniques; and (3) CIA detainees who were subjected to the CIA's enhanced interrogation techniques withheld and fabricated information about Abu Ahmad al-Kuwaiti.

(TS// ███████████ //NF) Within days of the raid on UBL's compound, CIA officials represented that CIA detainees provided the "tipoff"[2139] information on Abu Ahmad al-Kuwaiti.[2140] A review of CIA records found that the initial intelligence obtained, as well as the

---

hunt and the operation," among other matters. The document details how, prior to the operation, "agreed-upon language" was developed for three "vital points," the first of which was "the critical nature of detainee reporting in identifying Bin Ladin's courier."

[2138] CIA documents and cables use various spellings, most frequently "Abu Ahmed al-Kuwaiti" and "Abu Ahmad al-Kuwaiti." To the extent possible, the Study uses the spelling referenced in the CIA document being discussed.

[2139] Testimony from the CIA to the Senate Select Committee on Intelligence and the Senate Armed Services Committee on May 4, 2011. In testimony, CIA Director Leon Panetta referenced CIA "interviews" with 12 CIA detainees, and stated that "I want to be able to get back to you with specifics...But clearly the tipoff on the couriers came from those interviews." The CIA's June 2013 Response states: "CIA has never represented that information acquired through its interrogations of detainees was either the first or the only information that we had on Abu Ahmad." Former CIA Director Michael Hayden provided similar public statements. *See* transcript of Scott Hennen talk-radio show, dated May 3, 2011. Hayden: "What we got, the *original lead information*—and frankly it was incomplete identity information on the couriers—*began with information from CIA detainees at the black sites.* And let me just leave it at that" (italics added).

[2140] *See* CIA letter to the Senate Select Committee on Intelligence dated May 5, 2011, which includes a document entitled, "Background Detainee Information on Abu Ahmad al-Kuwaiti," with an accompanying six-page chart entitled, "Detainee Reporting on Abu Ahmad al-Kuwaiti" (DTS #2011-2004).

information the CIA identified as the most critical—or the most valuable—on Abu Ahmad al-Kuwaiti,[2141] was not related to the use of the CIA's enhanced interrogation techniques.[2142]

(TS// ███████████ //NF) The CIA did not receive any information from CIA detainees on Abu Ahmad al-Kuwaiti until 2003. Nonetheless, by the end of 2002, the CIA was actively targeting Abu Ahmad al-Kuwaiti and had collected significant reporting on Abu Ahmad al-Kuwaiti—to include reporting on Abu Ahmad al-Kuwaiti's close links to UBL. CIA records indicate that prior to receiving any information from CIA detainees, the CIA had collected:

- *Reporting on Abu Ahmad al-Kuwaiti's Telephonic Activity:* A phone number associated with Abu Ahmad al-Kuwaiti was under U.S. government intelligence collection as early as January 1, 2002.[2143] In March 2002, this phone number would be found in Abu Zubaydah's address book under the heading "Abu Ahmad K."[2144] In April 2002, the same phone number was found to be in contact with UBL family members.[2145] In June 2002, a person using the identified phone number and believed at the time to be "al-Kuwaiti" called a number

---

[2141] The CIA's June 2013 Response states that the December 13, 2012, Committee Study "incorrectly characterizes the intelligence we had on Abu Ahmad before acquiring information on him from detainees in CIA custody as 'critical.'" This is incorrect. The Committee uses the CIA's own definition of what information was important and critical, as conveyed to the Committee by the CIA. In documents and testimony to the Committee, the CIA highlighted specific information on Abu Ahmad al-Kuwaiti that the CIA viewed as especially valuable or critical to the identification and tracking of Abu Ahmad al-Kuwaiti. For example, in May 4, 2011, CIA testimony, a CIA officer explained how "a couple of early detainees" "identi[fied]" Abu Ahmed al-Kuwaiti as someone close to UBL. The CIA officer stated: "I think the clearest way to think about this is, in 2002 a couple of early detainees, Abu Zubaydah and an individual, Riyadh the Facilitator, talked about the activities of an Abu Ahmed al-Kuwaiti. At this point we don't have his true name. And they identify him as somebody involved with AQ and facilitation and some potential ties to bin Ladin." As detailed in this summary, CIA records confirm that Riyadh the Facilitator provided information in 2002 closely linking al-Kuwaiti to UBL, but these records confirm that this information was acquired prior to Riyadh the Facilitator being rendered to CIA custody (the transfer occurred more than a year later, in January 2004). Abu Zubaydah provided no information on Abu Ahmad al-Kuwaiti in 2002. According to CIA records, Abu Zubaydah was not asked about Abu Ahmad al-Kuwaiti until July 7, 2003, when he denied knowing the name. As an additional example, see CIA documents and charts provided to the Committee (DTS #2011-2004) and described in this summary, in which the CIA ascribes value to specific intelligence acquired on al-Kuwaiti.

[2142] In other words, the information the CIA cited was acquired from a detainee *not* in CIA custody, obtained from a CIA detainee who was not subjected to the CIA's enhanced interrogation techniques, obtained from a CIA detainee prior to the use of the CIA's enhanced interrogation techniques, or acquired from a source unrelated to detainee reporting. As described, the information contained herein is based on a review of CIA Detention and Interrogation Program records. Although the CIA has produced more than six million pages of material associated with CIA detainees and the CIA's Detention and Interrogation Program, the Committee did not have direct access to other, more traditional intelligence records, to include reporting from CIA HUMINT assets, foreign government assets, electronic intercepts, military detainee debriefings, law enforcement derived information, and other methods of collection. Based on the information found in the CIA detainee-related documents, it is likely there is significant intelligence on "Abu Ahmad al-Kuwaiti" acquired from a variety of intelligence collection platforms that the Committee did not have access to for this review.

[2143] CIA record ("Call Details Incoming and Outgoing") relating to calling activity for ██████ phone number #███████. A CIA document provided to the Committee on October 25, 2013, (DTS #2013-3152), states that the CIA was collecting on Abu Ahmad al-Kuwaiti's phone (#███████) as early as November 2001, and that it was collection from this time that was used to make voice comparisons to later collection targeting Abu Ahmad al-Kuwaiti.

[2144] CIA ██████ (032031Z APR 02)

[2145] CIA ██████ (102158Z APR 02)

associated with KSM.[2146] All of this information was acquired in 2002, prior to any reporting on Abu Ahmad al-Kuwaiti from CIA detainees.

- *Reporting on Abu Ahmad al-Kuwaiti's Email Communications:* In July 2002, the CIA had obtained an email address believed to be associated with Abu Ahmad al-Kuwaiti.[2147] As early as August 24, 2002, the CIA was collecting and tracking al-Kuwaiti's email activity. A cable from that day states that an email account associated with KSM "intermediary Abu Ahmed al-Kuwaiti" remained active in Karachi.[2148] On September 17, 2002, the CIA received reporting on al-Kuwaiti's email address from a detainee in the custody of a foreign government. The detainee reported that al-Kuwaiti shared an email address with Ammar al-Baluchi, and that al-Kuwaiti was "coordinating martyrdom operations."[2149] When KSM was captured on March 1, 2003, an email address associated with al-Kuwaiti was found on a laptop believed to be used by KSM.[2150] All of this information was acquired prior to any reporting on Abu Ahmad al-Kuwaiti from CIA detainees.

- *A Body of Intelligence Reporting on Abu Ahmad al-Kuwaiti's Involvement in Operational Attack Planning with KSM—Including Targeting of the United States:* On June 10, 2002, the CIA received reporting from a detainee in the custody of a foreign government indicating that Abu Ahmad al-Kuwaiti was engaged in operational attack planning with KSM.[2151] On June 25, 2002, the CIA received reporting from another detainee in the custody of a foreign government corroborating information that al-Kuwaiti was close with KSM, as well as reporting that al-Kuwaiti worked on "secret operations" with KSM prior to the September 11, 2001, terrorist attacks.[2152] By August 9, 2002, the CIA had received reporting from a third detainee in the custody of a foreign government indicating that Abu Ahmad al-Kuwaiti was supporting KSM's operational attack planning targeting the United States.[2153] By October 20, 2002, the CIA had received reporting from a fourth detainee in the custody of a foreign government indicating that a known terrorist—Hassan Ghul—"received funding and instructions primarily from Abu Ahmad, a close associate of KSM."[2154] All of this

---

[2146] Included in several cables and repeated in ALEC ███████ ███████ JUL 02).
[2147] ███████████ 31049 (███████ 2002). The CIA's June 2013 Response downplays the importance of the email address and phone numbers collected on Abu Ahmad al-Kuwaiti, stating that the accounts were later discontinued by Abu Ahmad al-Kuwaiti and were "never linked" to bin Ladin's known locations. However, on October 25, 2013, the CIA (DTS #2013-3152) acknowledged that the "voice cuts" from Abu Ahmad al-Kuwaiti were acquired during this period (2001-2002) from the (███) phone number cited in the Committee Study. According to CIA records, in February 2009 and September 2009, the voice samples collected from the Abu Ahmad al-Kuwaiti (███) phone number (under collection in 2002) were compared to voice samples collected against ███████████████████████, which led the Intelligence Community to assess that ███████, who was geo-located to a specific area of Pakistan, was likely Abu Ahmad al-Kuwaiti. In August 2010, Abu Ahmad ███████ ████████████████████ and tracked to the UBL compound. *See* intelligence chronology in Volume II for additional details.
[2148] ALEC ███████ (240057Z AUG 02)
[2149] [REDACTED] 64883 (171346Z SEP 02). This information was repeated in ALEC ███████ (302244Z SEP 02).
[2150] ALEC ███████ (102238Z MAR 03)
[2151] ███████ 19448 (101509Z JUN 02)
[2152] DIRECTOR ███████ (251833Z JUN 02)
[2153] [REDACTED] 65902 (080950Z AUG 02); ALEC ███████ (092204Z AUG 02)
[2154] DIRECTOR ███████ (202147Z OCT 02)

information was acquired in 2002, prior to any reporting on Abu Ahmad al-Kuwaiti from CIA detainees.

- *Significant Corroborative Reporting on Abu Ahmad al-Kuwaiti's Age, Physical Description, and Family—Including Information the CIA Would Later Cite As Pivotal:* In September 2001, the CIA received reporting on al-Kuwaiti's family that the CIA would later cite as pivotal in identifying al-Kuwaiti's true name.[2155] From January 2002 through October 2002, the CIA received significant corroborative reporting on al-Kuwaiti's age, physical appearance, and family from detainees held in the custody of foreign governments and the U.S. military.[2156] All of this information was acquired prior to any reporting on Abu Ahmad al-Kuwaiti from CIA detainees.

- *Multiple Reports on Abu Ahmad al-Kuwaiti's Close Association with UBL and His Frequent Travel to See UBL:*[2157] As early as April 2002, CIA had signals intelligence linking a phone number associated with al-Kuwaiti with UBL's family, specifically al-Qa'ida member Sa'ad Bin Ladin.[2158] On June 5, 2002, the CIA received reporting from a detainee in the custody of a foreign government indicating that "Abu Ahmad" was one of three al-Qa'ida associated individuals—to include Sa'ad bin Ladin and KSM—who visited him. The detainee—Ridha al-Najjar—was a former UBL caretaker.[2159] On June 25, 2002, the CIA received reporting from another detainee in the custody of a foreign government—Riyadh the Facilitator— suggesting al-Kuwaiti may have served as a courier for UBL. Riyadh the Facilitator

---

[2155] *See* intelligence chronology in Volume II, specifically ██████████, dated 17 September 2001, [REDACTED] 60077 (09/17/2001). *See also* foreign government reporting from September 27, 2002, describing information from a detainee who was *not* in CIA custody (CIA ███ (271730Z SEP 02)). That reporting is also highlighted in a CIA document, entitled, "Background Detainee Information on Abu Ahmad al-Kuwaiti," dated May 4, 2011 (DTS #2011-2004). The document highlights that "Detainee Abdallah Falah al-Dusari provided what he thought was a partial true name for Abu Ahmad—Habib al-Rahman—whom [CIA] ultimately identified as one of Abu Ahmad's deceased brothers. However, this partial true name for his brother eventually helped [CIA] map out Abu Ahmad's entire family, including the true name of Abu Ahmad himself." The CIA document did not identify that Abdallah Falah al-Dusari was *not* a CIA detainee. In June 2002, the CIA also obtained another alias for Abu Ahmad al-Kuwaiti—"Hamad al-Kuwaiti"—that included a component of his true name. This information was provided by a foreign government and was unrelated to the CIA's Detention and Interrogation Program. *See* DIRECTOR ███ (251833Z JUN 02).

[2156] *See* intelligence chronology in Volume II, including ██████ 63211 (30 JAN 2002); DIRECTOR ██████ (251833Z JUN 02); ██████████ July 25, 2002; DIRECTOR ██████ (221240Z AUG 02); CIA ██████ (271730Z SEP 02); DIRECTOR ██████ (171819Z OCT 02); ██████████.

[2157] In testimony on May 4, 2011, the CIA informed the Committee that "From the beginning, CIA focused on the inner circle around bin Ladin, the people that were around him, as a way to try and go after bin Laden." *See* DTS #2011-2049.

[2158] CIA ████ (102158Z APR 02). Sa'ad bin Ladin was a known senior al-Qa'ida member and had been associated with individuals engaged in operational planning targeting the United States. *See,* for example, ALEC ████ (062040Z MAR 02) for his association with KSM operative Masran bin Arshad, who was involved in KSM's "Second Wave" plotting. Phone number(s) associated with Sa'ad bin Ladin were under intelligence collection and resulted in the identification of other al-Qa'ida targets. *See* ██████ 293363 (051121Z JUN 02) and ██████ 285184, as well as ██████ 20306 (241945Z JAN 04). ██████

[2159] ██ [REDACTED] 11515, June 5, 2002. As detailed in this summary and in Volume III, Ridha al-Najjar was later rendered to CIA custody and subjected to the CIA's enhanced interrogation techniques.

highlighted that al-Kuwaiti was "actively working in secret locations in Karachi, but traveled frequently" to "meet with Usama bin Ladin."[2160] Months earlier the CIA disseminated signals intelligence indicating that Abu Ahmad al-Kuwaiti and Riyadh the Facilitator were in phone contact with each other.[2161] In August 2002, another detainee in the custody of a foreign government with known links to al-Kuwaiti[2162]—Abu Zubair al-Ha'ili—reported that al-Kuwaiti "was one of a few close associates of Usama bin Ladin."[2163] All of this information was acquired in 2002, prior to any reporting on Abu Ahmad al-Kuwaiti from CIA detainees.[2164]

(TS// ███████████ //NF) Within a day of the UBL operation, the CIA began providing classified briefings to Congress on the overall operation and the intelligence that led to the raid and UBL's death.[2165] On May 2, 2011, CIA officials, including CIA Deputy Director Michael Morell, briefed the Committee. A second briefing occurred on May 4, 2011, when CIA Director Leon Panetta and other CIA officials briefed both the Senate Select Committee on Intelligence and the Senate Armed Services Committee. Both of these briefings indicated that CIA detainee information—and the CIA's enhanced interrogation techniques—played a substantial role in developing intelligence that led to the UBL operation. The testimony contained significant inaccurate information.

(TS// ███████████ //NF) For example, in the May 2, 2011, briefing, the CIA informed the Senate Select Committee on Intelligence that:

> "However, there remained one primary line of investigation that was proving the most difficult to run to ground, and that was the case of a courier named Abu Ahmed al-Kuwaiti. Abu Ahmed had totally dropped off our radar in about the 2002-2003 time frame *after several detainees in our custody* had highlighted him as a key facilitator for bin Ladin."[2166]

[2160] *See* intelligence chronology in Volume II, including DIRECTOR ████ (251833Z JUN 02). Riyadh the Facilitator was eventually rendered into the CIA's Detention and Interrogation Program in January 2004. CIA records indicate he was not subjected to the CIA's enhanced interrogation techniques. The referenced information was provided while Riyadh the Facilitator was in foreign government custody.

[2161] CIA ████ (102158Z APR 02)

[2162] DIRECTOR ████ (251833Z JUN 02)

[2163] DIRECTOR ████ (221240Z AUG 02). Abu Zubair al-Ha'ili never entered the CIA's Detention and Interrogation Program.

[2164] The CIA's June 2013 Response ignores or minimizes the extensive reporting on Abu Ahmad al-Kuwaiti listed in the text of this summary (as well as additional reporting on Abu Ahmad al-Kuwaiti in the intelligence chronology in Volume II), describing this intelligence as "insufficient to distinguish Abu Ahmad from many other Bin Ladin associates" before crediting CIA detainees with providing "additional information" that "put [the previously collected reporting] into context." While the Committee could find no internal CIA records to support the assertion in the CIA's June 2013 Response, as detailed, the most detailed and accurate intelligence collected from a CIA detainee on Abu Ahmad al-Kuwaiti and his unique links to UBL was from Hassan Ghul, and was acquired prior to the use of the CIA's enhanced interrogation techniques against Ghul.

[2165] A series of public statements by members of Congress linking the CIA's Detention and Interrogation Program and the UBL operation appeared in the media during the time of the congressional briefings. The statements reflect the inaccurate briefings provided by the CIA.

[2166] Italics added. CIA testimony of the Senate Select Committee on Intelligence briefing on May 2, 2011 (DTS #2011-1941).

(TS// ██████████ //NF) The information above is not fully congruent with CIA records. As described, the CIA was targeting Abu Ahmad al-Kuwaiti prior to any reporting from CIA detainees. Al-Kuwaiti was identified as early as 2002 as an al-Qa'ida member engaged in operational planning who "traveled frequently" to see UBL.[2167] No CIA detainee provided reporting on Abu Ahmad al-Kuwaiti in 2002. While CIA detainees eventually did provide some information on Abu Ahmad al-Kuwaiti beginning in the spring of 2003, the majority of the accurate intelligence acquired on Abu Ahmad al-Kuwaiti was collected outside of the CIA's Detention and Interrogation Program, either from detainees not in CIA custody, or from other intelligence sources and methods unrelated to detainees, to include human sources and foreign partners.[2168] The most accurate CIA detainee-related intelligence was obtained in early 2004, from a CIA detainee who had not yet been subjected to the CIA's enhanced interrogation techniques.[2169] That detainee—Hassan Ghul—listed Abu Ahmed al-Kuwaiti as one of three individuals likely to be with UBL,[2170] stated that "it was well known that [UBL] was always with Abu Ahmed [al-Kuwaiti],"[2171] and described al-Kuwaiti as UBL's "closest assistant,"[2172] who "likely handled all of UBL's needs."[2173] The detainee further relayed that he believed "UBL's security apparatus would be minimal, and that the group likely lived in a house with a family somewhere in Pakistan."[2174]

(TS// ██████████ //NF) In the May 4, 2011, briefing, CIA Director Leon Panetta provided the following statement to the Senate Select Committee on Intelligence and the Senate Armed Services Committee (which mirrored similar statements by a "senior administration official" in a White House Press Briefing from May 2, 2011)[2175]:

> "*The detainees* in the post-9/11 period flagged for us that there were individuals that provided direct support to bin Ladin... *and one of those identified was a courier who had the nickname Abu Ahmad al-Kuwaiti. That was back in 2002.*"[2176]

[2167] *See* intelligence chronology in Volume II.

[2168] *See* intelligence chronology in Volume II, including ALEC ██████ (240057Z AUG 02); CIA record ("Call Details Incoming and Outgoing") relating to calling activity for ██████ phone number # ██████; [REDACTED] 65902 (080950Z AUG 02); ALEC ██████ (092204Z AUG 02); ██████, dated 17 September 2001; [REDACTED] 60077 (09/17/2001); DIRECTOR ██████ (221240Z AUG 02); and DIRECTOR ██████ (251833Z JUN 02).

[2169] *See* HEADQUARTERS ██████ ██████ JAN 04) and intelligence chronology in Volume II for additional details.

[2170] ██████ 1679 ██████ JAN 04)

[2171] HEADQUARTERS ██████ ██████ JAN 04)

[2172] ██████ 1679 ██████ JAN 04)

[2173] HEADQUARTERS ██████ JAN 04)

[2174] HEADQUARTERS ██████ JAN 04). UBL was eventually located in a home with a family in Pakistan with minimal security.

[2175] *See* May 2, 2011, 12:03AM, White House "Press Briefing by Senior Administration Officials on the Killing of Osama bin Laden." The transcript, posted on the White House website (www.whitehouse.gov/the-press-office/2011/5/02/press-briefing-senior-administration-officials-killing-osama-bin-laden).

[2176] Italics added. Testimony of CIA Director Panetta, transcript of the May 4, 2011, briefing of the Senate Select Committee on Intelligence and the Senate Armed Services Committee (DTS #2011-2049).

(TS// ██████████ //NF) As previously detailed, no CIA detainees provided information on Abu Ahmad al-Kuwaiti in 2002. As such, for the statement to be accurate, it can only be a reference to detainees in foreign government custody who provided information in 2002.[2177] As noted, prior to any reporting from CIA detainees, the CIA was targeting Abu Ahmad al-Kuwaiti—to include al-Kuwaiti's phone number and email address.[2178] Further, prior to 2003, the CIA possessed a body of intelligence reporting linking Abu Ahmad al-Kuwaiti to KSM and UBL and to operational targeting of the United States, as well as reporting that Abu Ahmad al-Kuwaiti was "one of a few close associates of Usama bin Ladin"[2179] and "traveled frequently" to "meet with Usama bin Ladin."[2180]

(TS// ██████████ //NF) In the same May 4, 2011, briefing, a CIA officer elaborated on the previously provided statements and provided additional detail on how "a couple of early detainees" "identi[fied]" Abu Ahmad al-Kuwaiti as someone close to UBL:

> "I think the clearest way to think about this is, in 2002 *a couple of early detainees, Abu Zubaydah and an individual, Riyadh the Facilitator, talked about the activities of an Abu Ahmed al-Kuwaiti.* At this point we don't have his true name. *And they identify him as somebody involved with AQ and facilitation and some potential ties to bin Ladin.*"[2181]

(TS// ██████████ //NF) This testimony is inaccurate. There are no CIA records of Abu Zubaydah discussing Abu Ahmad al-Kuwaiti in 2002.[2182] The first reference to Abu Zubaydah

---

[2177] As described in this summary, the CIA provided documents to the Committee indicating that individuals detained in 2002 provided "Tier One" information—linking "Abu Ahmad to Bin Ladin." The document did not state when the information was provided, or when the detainee entered CIA custody. Internal CIA records indicate that no CIA detainee provided information on Abu Ahmad al-Kuwaiti in 2002. *See* CIA six-page chart entitled, "Detainee Reporting on Abu Ahmad al-Kuwaiti," which lists 12 detainees in "CIA Custody" (DTS #2011-2004).
[2178] CIA record ("Call Details Incoming and Outgoing") relating to calling activity for ██████ phone number # ██████ ; ALEC ██████ (240057Z AUG 02).
[2179] *See* intelligence chronology in Volume II, including [REDACTED] 65902 (080950Z AUG 02); ALEC ██████ (092204Z AUG 02); DIRECTOR ██████ (221240Z AUG 02); and DIRECTOR ██████ (251833Z JUN 02).
[2180] *See* intelligence chronology in Volume II, including DIRECTOR ██████ (251833Z JUN 02).
[2181] Italics added. CIA testimony from CIA officer [REDACTED] and transcript of the Senate Select Committee on Intelligence and the Senate Armed Services Committee briefing on May 4, 2011. (*See* DTS #2011-2049.) As discussed in this summary and in greater detail in Volume II, the CIA provided additional information to the Committee on May 5, 2011, that listed Riyadh the Facilitator as a detainee in "CIA custody," who was "detained February 2002," and provided the referenced information. The CIA document omitted that Riyadh the Facilitator was not in CIA custody when he provided the referenced information in June 2002. Riyadh the Facilitator was not rendered to CIA custody until January 2004. *See* Volume III and DTS #2011-2004.
[2182] The CIA's June 2013 Response does not address the Committee Study finding that Abu Zubaydah did not provide reporting on Abu Ahmad al-Kuwaiti in 2002. However, on October 25, 2013, the CIA responded in writing that the December 13, 2012, Committee Study was correct, and confirmed that the "first report from Abu Zubaydah discussing Abu Ahmad al-Kuwaiti was in 2003." (*See* DTS #2013-3152.) As described in the intelligence chronology in Volume II, on June 13, 2002, the CIA's ALEC Station sent a cable requesting that Abu Zubaydah be questioned regarding his knowledge of Abu Ahmad al-Kuwaiti, whom the CIA believed was then in Pakistan. Despite this request, CIA records indicate that Abu Zubaydah was not asked about Abu Ahmad al-Kuwaiti at this time. (*See* ALEC ██████ (130117Z JUN 02).) Days later, on June 18, 2002, Abu Zubaydah was placed in isolation, without any questioning or contact. On August 4, 2002, the CIA resumed contact and immediately began using the CIA's enhanced interrogation techniques against Abu Zubaydah, including the waterboard. CIA records indicate that Abu Zubaydah was not asked about Abu Ahmad al-Kuwaiti until July 7, 2003, when he denied

providing information related to al-Kuwaiti is on July 7, 2003, when Abu Zubaydah denied knowing the name.[2183] CIA records indicate that the information in 2002 that the CIA has represented as the initial lead information on Abu Ahmad al-Kuwaiti was not obtained from the CIA's Detention and Interrogation Program, but was collected by the CIA from other intelligence sources, including from detainees in foreign government custody. Riyadh the Facilitator provided substantial information on Abu Ahmad al-Kuwaiti in 2002, including information suggesting al-Kuwaiti may have served as a courier, as al-Kuwaiti reportedly "traveled frequently" to see UBL.[2184] Consistent with the testimony, CIA records indicate that the information provided by Riyadh the Facilitator was important information; however, Riyadh the Facilitator was not in CIA custody in 2002, but was in the custody of a foreign government.[2185] Riyadh the Facilitator was not transferred to CIA custody until January ▌, 2004.[2186] As noted, in 2002, the CIA received additional reporting from another detainee in the custody of a foreign government, Abu Zubair al-Ha'ili, that "Ahmad al-Kuwaiti" was "one of a few close associates of Usama bin Ladin."[2187]

(TS// ██████████ //NF) At the May 4, 2011, briefing, a Senator asked, "I guess what we're trying to get at here, or certainly I am, was any of this information obtained through [enhanced] interrogation measures?" A CIA officer replied:

> "Senator, *these individuals were in our program* and *were subject to some form of enhanced interrogation.* Because of the time involved and the relationship to the information and the fact that I'm not a specialist on that program, I would ask that you allow us to come back to you with some detail."[2188]

(TS// ██████████ //NF) The information above is not fully congruent with CIA records. As is detailed in the intelligence chronology in Volume II, the vast majority of the intelligence

---

knowing the name. (*See* ██████ 12236 (072032Z JUL 03).) As is detailed in the intelligence chronology in Volume II, on April 3, 2002, the CIA sent a cable stating that on page 8 of a 27-page address book found with Abu Zubaydah, there was the name "Abu Ahmad K." with a phone number that was found to be already under U.S. intelligence collection. *See* CIA ██████ (032031Z APR 02).

[2183] ██████ 12236 (072032Z JUL 03)

[2184] DIRECTOR ██████ (251833Z JUN 02)

[2185] Riyadh the Facilitator, aka Sharqawi Ali Abdu al-Hajj, was captured on February 7, 2002. (*See* ██ 10480 (██████ FEB 02).) Al-Hajj was transferred to ██████ custody on February ▌, 2002. (*See* 18265 (██████ FEB 02).) On January ▌, 2004, al-Hajj was rendered to CIA custody. (*See* ██████ ██ 1591 ██████ JAN 04).) Al-Hajj was transferred to U.S. military custody on May ▌, 2004. *See* ██████ 2335 ██████.

[2186] ██████ 1591 ██████ JAN 04). Documents provided to the Committee on "detainee reporting" related to the UBL operation (incorrectly) indicate that Riyadh the Facilitator was in CIA custody. *See* May 5, 2011, six-page CIA chart entitled, "Detainee Reporting on Abu Ahmad al-Kuwaiti"(DTS #2011-2004).

[2187] DIRECTOR ██████ (221240Z AUG 02). Abu Zubair al-Ha'ili never entered the CIA's Detention and Interrogation Program.

[2188] Italics added. CIA testimony from CIA officer [REDACTED] and transcript of the Senate Select Committee on Intelligence and the Senate Armed Services Committee briefing on May 4, 2011 (DTS #2011-2049). The CIA subsequently provided the Committee with a letter dated May 5, 2011, which included a document entitled, "Background Detainee Information on Abu Ahmad al-Kuwaiti," with an accompanying six-page chart entitled, "Detainee Reporting on Abu Ahmad al-Kuwaiti" (DTS #2011-2004). *See also* a similar, but less detailed CIA document entitled, "Detainee Reporting on Abu Ahmad al-Kuwaiti's Historic Links to Usama Bin Laden."

acquired on Abu Ahmad al-Kuwaiti was originally acquired from sources unrelated to the CIA's Detention and Interrogation Program, and the most accurate information acquired from a CIA detainee was provided prior to the CIA subjecting the detainee to the CIA's enhanced interrogation techniques.[2189] As detailed in CIA records, and acknowledged by the CIA in testimony, information from CIA detainees subjected to the CIA's enhanced interrogation techniques—to include CIA detainees who had clear links to Abu Ahmad al-Kuwaiti based on a large body of intelligence reporting—provided fabricated, inconsistent, and generally unreliable information on Abu Ahmad al-Kuwaiti throughout their detention.[2190]

[2189] On May 5, 2004, the CIA provided several documents to the Committee, including a chart entitled, "Detainee Reporting on Abu Ahmad al-Kuwaiti," described in this summary. For additional details, *see* intelligence chronology in Volume II.

[2190] Below are specific details on the reporting of Abu Zubaydah, KSM, Khallad bin Attash, Ammar al-Baluchi, and Abu Faraj al-Libi related to Abu Ahmad al-Kuwaiti: 1) Abu Zubaydah was captured on March 28, 2002, with a 27-page address book that included a phone number for "Abu Ahmad K," which matched a ███████ mobile phone number that was already under intelligence collection by the U.S. Intelligence Community. (As early as July 2002, the CIA associated the phone number with al-Kuwaiti.) As detailed in the Study, Abu Zubaydah provided significant intelligence, primarily to FBI special agents, from the time of his capture on March 28, 2002, through June 18, 2002, when he was placed in isolation for 47 days. On June 13, 2002, less than a week before he was placed in isolation, CIA Headquarters requested that interrogators ask Abu Zubaydah about his knowledge of Abu Ahmad al-Kuwaiti, who was believed to be in Pakistan, according to the request from CIA Headquarters. There are no CIA records indicating that the interrogators asked Abu Zubaydah about al-Kuwaiti. Instead, as described, Abu Zubaydah was placed in isolation beginning on June 18, 2002, with the FBI and CIA interrogators departing the detention site. The FBI did not return. On August 4, 2002, CIA interrogators reestablished contact with Abu Zubaydah and immediately began to subject Abu Zubaydah to the non-stop use of the CIA's enhanced interrogation techniques for 17 days, which included at least 83 applications of the CIA's waterboard interrogation technique. According to CIA records, Abu Zubaydah was not asked about Abu Ahmad al-Kuwaiti until July 7, 2003, when he denied knowing the name. On April 27, 2004, Abu Zubaydah again stated that he did not recognize the name "Abu Ahmed al-Kuwaiti." In August 2005, Abu Zubaydah speculated on an individual the CIA stated might be "identifiable with Abu Ahmad al-Kuwaiti, aka Abu Ahmad al-Pakistani," but Abu Zubaydah stated the person in question was not close with UBL. 2) KSM was captured on March 1, 2003, during a raid in Pakistan. An email address associated with Abu Ahmad al-Kuwaiti was found on a laptop that was assessed to be associated with KSM. Once rendered to CIA custody on March █, 2003, KSM was immediately subjected to the CIA's enhanced interrogation techniques, which continued through March 25, 2003, and included at least 183 applications of the CIA's waterboard interrogation technique. On March 5, 2003, KSM provided information concerning a senior al-Qa'ida member named "Abu Khalid," whom KSM later called "Abu Ahmad al-Baluchi." The information KSM provided could not be corroborated by other intelligence collected by the CIA, and KSM provided no further information on the individual. On May 5, 2003, KSM provided his first information on an individual named "Abu Ahmed al-Kuwaiti" when he was confronted with reporting from a detainee not in CIA custody, Masran bin Arshad. KSM confirmed bin Arshad's reporting regarding Abu Ahmad al-Kuwaiti, specifically that bin Arshad was originally tasked by KSM to get money from Abu Ahmad al-Kuwaiti in Pakistan. KSM further relayed that Abu Ahmad al-Kuwaiti worked with Hassan Ghul helping to move families from Afghanistan to Pakistan. On May 22, 2003, KSM was specifically asked about a UBL courier named Abu Ahmed. KSM again described a courier for UBL whose name was Abu Ahmed al-Baluchi, but noted that this Abu Ahmed was more interested in earning money than in serving al-Qa'ida. According to KSM, Abu Ahmed was working with Hassan Ghul in April or May 2002, but speculated that Abu Ahmed was in Iran as of early March 2003. In July 2003, KSM stated that Abu Ahmad al-Kuwaiti worked with Abu Zubaydah's group prior to September 2001 and later with Abu Sulayman al-Jaza'iri. In September 2003, KSM was confronted with reporting from another detainee in foreign government custody on Abu Ahmad al-Kuwaiti. KSM confirmed that he had told Hambali to work with Abu Ahmad al-Kuwaiti as he transited Pakistan, but KSM downplayed al-Kuwaiti's importance, claiming to have contacted Abu Ahmad al-Kuwaiti only three to four times when he was in Peshawar and stating that Abu Ahmad worked "primarily with lower level members" and appeared to have a higher status than he actually had in al-Qa'ida because KSM relied on al-Kuwaiti for travel facilitation. In January 2004, based on statements made by Hassan Ghul—provided prior to the use of the CIA's enhanced interrogation techniques—that it was "well known" that UBL was always with al-Kuwaiti, CIA Headquarters asked CIA interrogators to reengage KSM on the relationship between al-Kuwaiti and UBL, noting the "serious disconnect" between Ghul's reporting linking UBL and Abu Ahmad al-Kuwaiti and KSM's "pithy" description of al-Kuwaiti. CIA Headquarters wrote that unlike Hassan Ghul, KSM had made "no reference to a link between Abu Ahmed and al-Qa'ida's two top leaders" and that KSM "has some explaining to do about Abu Ahmed and his support to UBL and Zawahiri." On May 31, 2004, KSM claimed that al-Kuwaiti was "not very senior, nor was he wanted," noting that al-Kuwaiti could move about freely, and might be in Peshawar. In August 2005, KSM stated that Abu Ahmad al-Kuwaiti was not a courier and that he had never heard of Abu Ahmad transporting letters for UBL. Instead, KSM claimed that al-Kuwaiti was focused on family after he married in 2002. 3) Khallad bin Attash was arrested with Ammar al-Baluchi in a unilateral operation by Pakistani authorities resulting from criminal leads on April 29, 2003. On May ██, 2003, he was rendered to CIA custody and immediately subjected to the CIA's enhanced interrogation techniques from May 16, 2003, to May 18, 2003, and then again from July 18, 2003, to July 29, 2003. On June 30, 2003, bin Attash stated that al-Kuwaiti was admired among the men. On July 27, 2003, bin Attash corroborated intelligence reporting that al-Kuwaiti played a facilitation role in al-Qa'ida and that al-Kuwaiti departed Karachi to get married. In January 2004, bin Attash stated that al-Kuwaiti was not close to UBL and not involved in al-Qa'ida operations, and that al-Kuwaiti was settling down with his wife in the summer of 2003. In August 2005, bin Attash stated that Abu Ahmad al-Kuwaiti was not a courier, that he had never heard of Abu Ahmad transporting letters for UBL, and that Abu Ahmad was instead focused on family after he married in 2002. In August 2006, bin Attash reiterated that al-Kuwaiti was not a courier, but rather focused on family life. 4) Ammar al-Baluchi was arrested with Khallad bin Attash in a unilateral operation by Pakistani authorities resulting from criminal leads on April 29, 2003. Upon his arrest, Ammar al-Baluchi was cooperative and provided information on a number of topics while in foreign government custody, including information on Abu Ahmad al-Kuwaiti that the CIA disseminated prior to al-Baluchi being transferred to CIA custody on May ██, 2003. After Ammar al-Baluchi was transferred to CIA custody, the CIA subjected Ammar al-Baluchi to the CIA's enhanced interrogation techniques from May 17, 2003, to May 20, 2003. On May 19, 2003, al-Baluchi stated he fabricated information while being subjected to the CIA's enhanced interrogation techniques the previous day, but in response to questioning, stated that he believed UBL was on the Pakistan/Afghanistan border and that a brother of al-Kuwaiti was to take over courier duties for UBL. In June 2003, al-Baluchi stated that there were rumors that al-Kuwaiti was a courier. In January 2004, al-Baluchi retracted previous reporting, stating that al-Kuwaiti was never a courier and would not have direct contact with UBL or Ayman al-Zawahiri because "unlike someone like Abu Faraj, [al-Kuwaiti] was too young and didn't have much experience or credentials to be in that position." In May 2004, al-Baluchi stated that al-Kuwaiti may have worked for Abu Faraj al-Libi. 5) Abu Faraj al-Libi was captured in Pakistan on May 2, 2005. On May ██, 2005, Abu Faraj al-Libi was rendered to CIA custody. Abu Faraj al-Libi was subjected to the CIA's enhanced interrogation techniques from May 28, 2005, to June 2, 2005, and again from June 17, 2005, to June 28, 2005. It was not until July 12, 2005, that CIA Headquarters sent a set of "Tier Three Requirements Regarding Abu Ahmad Al-Kuwaiti" to the detention site holding Abu Faraj al-Libi. Prior to this, interrogators had focused their questioning of Abu Faraj on operational plans, as well as information on senior al-Qa'ida leadership, primarily Hamza Rab'ia and Abu Musab al-Zarqawi. On July 13, 2005, Abu Faraj al-Libi denied knowledge of Abu Ahmad al-Kuwaiti, or any of his aliases. On July 15, 2005, CIA Headquarters noted they did not believe Abu Faraj was being truthful and requested CIA debriefers confront Abu Faraj again regarding his relationship with al-Kuwaiti. CIA records indicate that CIA debriefers did not respond to this request. On August 12, 2005, having received no response to its previous request, CIA Headquarters again asked Abu Faraj's debriefers to readdress the issue of Abu Ahmad al-Kuwaiti. CIA analysts noted that they "[found Faraj's] denials of even recognizing his name difficult to believe," and suggested that "one possible reason why [Faraj] lied about not recognizing Abu Ahmad's name" is [an attempt] to protect him – leading us to request that base readdress this issue with [Faraj] on a priority basis." Two days later, on August 14, 2005, after being questioned again about Abu Ahmad al-Kuwaiti, Abu Faraj al-Libi "swore to God" that he did not know al-Kuwaiti, or anybody who went by any of his aliases, insisting he would never forget anybody who worked for him. Abu Faraj did suggest, however, that an "Ahmad al-Pakistani" had worked with Marwan al-Jabbur to care for families in the Lahore, Pakistan, area, but said he (Abu Faraj) had no relationship with this al-Pakistani. On August 17, 2005, CIA Headquarters requested that debriefers reengage certain detainees on the role of Abu Ahmad al-Kuwaiti. In response, KSM and Khallad bin Attash claimed that al-Kuwaiti was not a courier and that they had never heard of Abu Ahmad transporting letters for UBL. KSM and Khallad bin Attash claimed that al-Kuwaiti was focused on family after he married in 2002. However, Ammar al-Baluchi indicated that al-Kuwaiti worked for Abu Faraj al-Libi in 2002. A September 1, 2005,

(TS//██████████//NF) At the May 4, 2011, briefing, a Senator asked, "of the people that you talked about as detainees that were interrogated, which of those were *waterboarded* and *did they provide unique intelligence* in order to make this whole mission possible?"[2191] CIA Director Panetta responded:

> "I want to be able to get back to you with specifics, but right now we think there were about *12 detainees that were interviewed,*[2192] *and about three of them were probably subject to the waterboarding process.*[2193] Now what came from those interviews, how important was it, I really do want to stress the fact that we had a lot of streams of intelligence here that kind of tipped us off there, but we had imagery, we had assets on the ground, we had information that came from a number of directions in order to piece this together. *But clearly the tipoff*[2194] *on the couriers came from those interviews.*"[2195]

(TS//██████████//NF) As previously detailed, the "tipoff" on Abu Ahmad al-Kuwaiti in 2002 did not come from the interrogation of CIA detainees and was obtained prior to any CIA detainee reporting. The CIA was already targeting Abu Ahmad al-Kuwaiti and collecting intelligence on at least one phone number and an email address associated with al-Kuwaiti in 2002.[2196] No CIA detainee provided information on Abu Ahmad al-Kuwaiti in 2002, and prior to receiving any information from CIA detainees, the CIA possessed a body of intelligence reporting linking Abu Ahmad al-Kuwaiti to KSM and UBL and to operational targeting of the United States, as well as reporting that Abu Ahmad al-Kuwaiti was "one of a few close

---

CIA report states that Abu Faraj al-Libi identified an "Abu 'Abd al Khaliq Jan," as his "go-between with Bin Ladin since mid-2003," but there was no other CIA reporting to support this assertion. In May 2007, a CIA targeting study concluded that the reporting from KSM and Abu Faraj al-Libi was "not credible," and "their attempts to downplay Abu Ahmad's importance or deny knowledge of Abu Ahmad are likely part of an effort to withhold information on UBL or his close associates." A September 28, 2007, CIA report concluded that "Abu Faraj was probably the last detainee to maintain contact with UBL—possibly through Abu Ahmad," but noted that "Abu Faraj vehemently denied any knowledge of Abu Ahmad." *See* intelligence chronology in Volume II for additional details.

[2191] Italics added.
[2192] Italics added. For a listing of the 12 detainees, *see* CIA's six-page chart entitled, "Detainee Reporting on Abu Ahmad al-Kuwaiti," which lists 12 detainees, all of whom are listed as being in "CIA Custody" (DTS #2011-2004).
[2193] Italics added. CIA records indicate that none of the three CIA detainees known to have been subjected by the CIA to the waterboard interrogation technique provided unique intelligence on Abu Ahmad al-Kuwaiti. To the contrary, there is significant evidence that two of the three detainees—Abu Zubaydah and KSM—failed to provide accurate information likely known to them about Abu Ahmad al-Kuwaiti and/or fabricated information to protect al-Kuwaiti. The third CIA detainee known to have been subjected to the CIA's waterboard interrogation technique, 'Abd al-Rahim al-Nashiri, provided no information on Abu Ahmad al-Kuwaiti. *See* intelligence chronology in Volume II for additional information.
[2194] Italics added. The CIA's June 2013 Response states: "CIA has never represented that information acquired through its interrogations of detainees was either the first or the only information that we had on Abu Ahmad."
[2195] Italics added. CIA testimony from CIA Director Panetta, and transcript of the Senate Select Committee on Intelligence and the Senate Armed Services Committee, May 4, 2011 (DTS #2011-2049).
[2196] CIA record ("Call Details Incoming and Outgoing") relating to calling activity for ██████ phone number #██████: ALEC ██████ (240057Z AUG 02).

associates of Usama bin Ladin"[2197] and "traveled frequently" to "meet with Usama bin Ladin."[2198]

(TS//██████████//NF) The day after the classified briefing, on May 5, 2011, the CIA provided the Committee with a six-page chart entitled, "Detainee Reporting on Abu Ahmad al-Kuwaiti," which accompanied a one-page document compiled by the CIA's CTC, entitled "Background Detainee Information on Abu Ahmad al-Kuwaiti."[2199] In total, the CIA chart identifies 25 "mid-value and high-value detainees" who "discussed Abu Ahmad al-Kuwaiti's long-time membership in al-Qa'ida and his historic role as courier for Usama Bin Ladin." The 25 detainees are divided into two categories. The chart prominently lists 12 detainees—all identified as having been in CIA custody—"who linked Abu Ahmad to Bin Ladin," which the CIA labeled as the most important, "Tier 1" information. The document states that nine of the 12 (9/12: 75 percent) CIA detainees providing "Tier 1" information were subjected to the CIA's enhanced interrogation techniques, and that of those nine detainees, two (2/9: 20 percent) were subjected to the CIA's waterboard interrogation technique. The chart then includes a list of 13 detainees "who provided general information on Abu Ahmad," labeled as "Tier 2" information. The CIA document states that four of the 13 (4/13: 30 percent) "Tier 2" detainees were in CIA custody and that all four (4/4: 100 percent) "CIA detainees" were subjected to the CIA's enhanced interrogation techniques.[2200]

(TS//██████████//NF) On October 3, 2012, the CIA provided the Committee with a document entitled, "Lessons for the Hunt for Bin Ladin," completed in September 2012 by the

[2197] *See* intelligence chronology in Volume II, including CIA record ("Call Details Incoming and Outgoing") relating to calling activity for ████ phone number #████; ALEC ████ (240057Z AUG 02); [REDACTED] 65902 (080950Z AUG 02); ALEC ████ (092204Z AUG 02); ████████ dated 17 September 2001; [REDACTED] 60077 (09/17/2001); DIRECTOR ████ (221240Z AUG 02); and DIRECTOR ████ (251833Z JUN 02).

[2198] *See* intelligence chronology in Volume II, including DIRECTOR ████ (251833Z JUN 02). As described above, Riyadh the Facilitator was eventually rendered into the CIA's Detention and Interrogation Program in January 2004, but CIA records indicate he was not subjected to the CIA's enhanced interrogation techniques. The referenced information was provided in June 2002, while Riyadh the Facilitator was not in U.S. custody, but in the custody of a foreign government.

[2199] Senator McCain and other members requested information on the use of the CIA's enhanced interrogation techniques in the UBL operation at the previous day's hearing and the CIA committed to provide additional information to the members. Senator McCain: "I'm also interested in this whole issue of the 'enhanced interrogation,' what role it played. Those who want to justify torture seem to have grabbed hold of this as some justification for our gross violation of the Geneva Conventions to which we are signatory. I'd be very interested in having that issue clarified. I think it's really important." *See* transcript of the Senate Select Committee on Intelligence and the Senate Armed Services Committee briefing on May 4, 2011 (DTS #2011-2049).

[2200] *See* CIA letter to the Senate Select Committee on Intelligence dated May 5, 2011, which includes a document entitled, "Background Detainee Information on Abu Ahmad al-Kuwaiti," with an accompanying six-page chart entitled, "Detainee Reporting on Abu Ahmad al-Kuwaiti" (DTS #2011-2004). *See also* a similar, but less detailed CIA document entitled, "Detainee Reporting on Abu Ahmad al-Kuwaiti's Historic Links to Usama Bin Laden." The CIA's September 2012 "Lessons from the Hunt for Bin Ladin," compiled by the CIA's Center for the Study of Intelligence (*See* DTS #2012-3826), appears to utilize the same inaccurate information, stating: "In sum, 25 detainees provided information on Abu Ahmad al-Kuwaiti, his al-Qa'ida membership, and his historic role as a courier for Bin Ladin. Nine of the 25 were held by foreign governments. Of the 16 held in CIA custody, all but three had given information *after* being subjected to enhanced interrogation techniques (EITs), although of the 13 only two (KSM and Abu Zubaydah) had been waterboarded" (italics added). As described, the information in this CIA "lessons" report is inaccurate.

CIA's Center for the Study of Intelligence. The CIA Lessons Learned document states, "[i]n sum, 25 detainees provided information on Abu Ahmad al-Kuwaiti, his al-Qa'ida membership, and his historic role as a courier for Bin Ladin." The CIA document then states that 16 of the 25 detainees who reported on Abu Ahmad al-Kuwaiti were in CIA custody, and that "[o]f the 16 held in CIA custody, all but three [13] had given information *after* being subjected to enhanced interrogation techniques (EITs)," before noting that "only two (KSM and Abu Zubaydah) had been waterboarded." [2201]

(~~TS//~~ ██████████████ ~~//NF~~) A review of CIA records found that these CIA documents contained inaccurate information and omitted important and material facts.

- *The May 5, 2011, CIA chart represents that all 12 detainees (12/12: 100 percent) providing "Tier 1" intelligence—information that "linked Abu Ahmad to Bin Ladin"[2202]—were detainees in CIA custody.* A review of CIA records found that the CIA document omitted the fact that five of the 12 listed detainees (5/12: 41 percent) provided intelligence on Abu Ahmad al-Kuwaiti *prior* to entering CIA custody. [2203] In addition, other detainees—not in CIA custody—provided information that "linked Abu Ahmad to Bin Ladin," but were not included in the CIA list. For example, the first detainee-related information identified in CIA records indicating a close relationship between UBL and Abu Ahmad al-Kuwaiti was acquired in July 2002, from a detainee in the custody of a foreign government, Abu Zubair al-Ha'ili (Zubair). According to CIA records, Zubair provided a detailed physical description of Abu Ahmad al-Kuwaiti, information on Abu Ahmad's family, his close connection to KSM, and that "Ahmad al-Kuwaiti: was a one of a few close associates of Usama bin Ladin."[2204] This information would be used to question other detainees, but was omitted in the CIA's "Detainee Reporting on Abu Ahmed al-Kuwaiti" chart.

- *The May 5, 2011, CIA chart also states that nine of the 12 (9/12: 75 percent) "CIA detainees" providing "Tier 1" intelligence were subjected to the CIA's enhanced interrogation techniques.* A review of CIA records found that of the nine detainees the CIA identified as having been subjected to the CIA's enhanced interrogation techniques and providing "Tier 1" information on links between Abu Ahmad al-Kuwaiti and UBL, five of the 9 (5/9: 55 percent) provided information on Abu Ahmad al-Kuwaiti *prior* to being

---

[2201] Italics added. "Lessons from the Hunt for Bin Ladin," dated September 2012, compiled by the CIA's Center for the Study of Intelligence, and provided on October 3, 2012 (DTS #2012-3826).

[2202] The CIA document identified "Tier 1" intelligence as information that "linked Abu Ahmad to Bin Ladin," but inaccurately included CIA detainees under the "Tier 1" detainee reporting list who did not provide information linking "Abu Ahmad to Bin Ladin." For example, the CIA identified Abu Zubaydah and KSM as providing "Tier 1" intelligence that "linked Abu Ahmad to Bin Ladin," despite both detainees denying any significant connection between al-Kuwaiti and UBL.

[2203] Riyadh the Facilitator (information on June 25, 2002 [prior to CIA custody]; CIA custody January █, 2004), Ammar al-Baluchi (information on May 6, 2003 [prior to CIA custody]; CIA custody May █, 2003), Ahmed Ghailani (information on August 1, 2004 [prior to CIA custody]; CIA custody September █, 2004), Sharif al-Masri (information on September 16, 2004 [prior to CIA custody]; CIA custody September █, 2004), and Muhammad Rahim (information on July 2, 2007 [prior to CIA custody]; CIA custody July █, 2007). There are reports that a sixth detainee, Hassan Ghul, also provided extensive information on Abu Ahmad al-Kuwaiti prior to being transferred to CIA custody. *See* intelligence chronology in Volume II for additional information.

[2204] DIRECTOR ██████ (221240Z AUG 02)

subjected to the CIA's enhanced interrogation techniques.[2205] This information was omitted from the CIA document. Of the remaining four detainees who did not provide information on Abu Ahmad al-Kuwaiti until *after* being subjected to the CIA's enhanced interrogation techniques, three were not substantially questioned on any topic prior to the CIA's use of enhanced interrogation techniques.[2206] All three provided information the CIA assessed to be fabricated and intentionally misleading.[2207] The fourth, Abu Zubaydah, who was detained on March 28, 2002, and subjected to the CIA's enhanced interrogation techniques in August 2002, to include the waterboard technique, did not provide information on Abu Ahmad al-Kuwaiti until August 25, 2005, intelligence that was described by CIA officers at the time as "speculative."[2208] These relevant details were omitted from the CIA documents.[2209]

- *The May 5, 2011, CIA chart also states that of the 13 detainees "who provided general information on Abu Ahmad," labeled as "Tier 2" information, four of the 13 (4/13: 30 percent) detainees were in CIA custody and that all four (4/4: 100 percent) were subjected to the CIA's enhanced interrogation techniques.*[2210] A review of CIA records found the CIA document omitted that two of the four (2/4: 50 percent) "CIA detainees" who were described as subjected to the CIA's enhanced interrogation techniques provided intelligence on Abu Ahmad al-Kuwaiti *prior* to entering CIA custody, and therefore *prior* to being subjected to the CIA's enhanced interrogation techniques.[2211] Finally, there were additional detainees in

---

[2205] Ammar al-Baluchi, Hassan Ghul, Ahmad Ghailani, Sharif al-Masri, and Muhammad Rahim.

[2206] Khalid Shaykh Mohammad, Khalid bin Attash, and Abu Faraj al-Libi.

[2207] Khalid Shaykh Mohammad, Abu Faraj al-Libi, and Khalid bin Attash. *See* intelligence chronology in Volume II and CIA testimony from May 4, 2011. CIA officer: "...with the capture of Abu Faraj al-Libi and Khalid Shaykh Mohammed, these are key bin Ladin facilitators, gatekeepers if you will, and their description of Abu Ahmed, the sharp contrast between that and the earlier detainees. Abu Faraj denies even knowing him, a completely uncredible position for him to take but one that he has stuck with to this day. KSM initially downplays any role Abu Ahmed might play, and by the time he leaves our program claims that he married in 2002, retired and really was playing no role." CIA records indicate Khallad bin Attash also downplayed the role of Abu Ahmad al-Kuwaiti, stating several times that Abu Ahmad was focused on family and was not close to UBL, and that he had never heard of Abu Ahmad al-Kuwaiti serving as a courier for UBL.

[2208] DIRECTOR ████ (8/25/2005). On July 7, 2003, and April 27, 2004, Abu Zubaydah was asked about "Abu Ahmed al-Kuwaiti" and denied knowing the name.

[2209] *See* CIA letter to the Senate Select Committee on Intelligence dated May 5, 2011, which includes a document entitled, "Background Detainee Information on Abu Ahmad al-Kuwaiti," with an accompanying six-page chart entitled, "Detainee Reporting on Abu Ahmad al-Kuwaiti" (DTS #2011-2004). *See also* a similar, but less detailed CIA document entitled, "Detainee Reporting on Abu Ahmad al-Kuwaiti's Historic Links to Usama Bin Laden." *See* intelligence chronology in Volume II for additional details.

[2210] *See* CIA letter to the Senate Select Committee on Intelligence dated May 5, 2011, which includes a document entitled, "Background Detainee Information on Abu Ahmad al-Kuwaiti," with an accompanying six-page chart entitled, "Detainee Reporting on Abu Ahmad al-Kuwaiti" (DTS #2011-2004). *See also* a similar, but less detailed CIA document entitled, "Detainee Reporting on Abu Ahmad al-Kuwaiti's Historic Links to Usama Bin Laden." The CIA's September 2012 "Lessons from the Hunt for Bin Ladin," compiled by the CIA's Center for the Study of Intelligence (DTS #2012-3826), appears to utilize the same inaccurate information, stating: "In sum, 25 detainees provided information on Abu Ahmad al-Kuwaiti, his al-Qa'ida membership, and his historic role as a courier for Bin Ladin. Nine of the 25 were held by foreign governments. Of the 16 held in CIA custody, all but three had given information *after* being subjected to enhanced interrogation techniques (EITs)..." (italics added). As described, the information in this CIA "Lessons Learned" report is inaccurate.

[2211] Ridha al-Najjar/al-Tunisi, who was detained in May 2002, first provided intelligence on al-Kuwaiti on June 4/5 2002, and was subsequently transferred to CIA custody on June ██, 2002; and subjected to the CIA's enhanced

foreign government custody "who provided general information on Abu Ahmad" that were not included in the list of 13 detainees. For example, in January 2002, the CIA received reporting from a detainee in the custody of a foreign government who provided a physical description of a Kuwaiti named Abu Ahmad who attended a terrorist training camp.[2212]

- *The October 3, 2012, "Lessons for the Hunt for Bin Ladin" document states that "[i]n sum, 25 detainees provided information on Abu Ahmad al-Kuwaiti, his al-Qa'ida membership, and his historic role as a courier for Bin Ladin."* This is incorrect. As described, additional detainees—not in CIA custody—provided information on Abu Ahmad al-Kuwaiti, including 2002 reporting that al-Kuwaiti "was one of a few close associates of Usama bin Ladin."[2213]

- *The October 3, 2012, "Lessons for the Hunt for Bin Ladin" document also states that 16 of the 25 (16/25: 65 percent) detainees who reported on Abu Ahmad al-Kuwaiti were in CIA custody.* This is incorrect. At least seven of the 16 detainees (7/16: 45 percent) that the CIA listed as detainees in CIA custody provided reporting on Abu Ahmad al-Kuwaiti prior to being transferred to CIA custody.[2214]

- *The October 3, 2012, "Lessons for the Hunt for Bin Ladin" document also states that "[o]f the 16 held in CIA custody, all but three [13] had given information after being subjected to enhanced interrogation techniques (EITs)."*[2215] This is incorrect. Seven of the 13 detainees that the CIA listed as having been subjected to the CIA's enhanced interrogation techniques provided information on Abu Ahmad al-Kuwaiti *prior* to being subjected to the CIA's enhanced interrogation techniques.[2216] Of the remaining six detainees who did not provide information on Abu Ahmad al-Kuwaiti until *after* being subjected to the CIA's enhanced interrogation techniques, five were not substantially questioned on any topic prior to the CIA's use of enhanced interrogation techniques.[2217] (Of the five detainees, three provided information the CIA assessed to be fabricated and intentionally misleading.[2218] The

---

interrogation techniques in October 2002. Hambali, who was detained on August 11, 2003, first provided information on al-Kuwaiti on August 13, 2003. Later, Hambali was rendered to CIA custody on August ██, 2003.
[2212] *See* intelligence chronology in Volume II, including ██████ 63211 (30 JAN 2002).
[2213] DIRECTOR ██████ (221240Z AUG 02)
[2214] *See* intelligence chronology in Volume II, including reporting from Riyadh the Facilitator, Ammar al-Baluchi, Ahmad Ghailani, Sharif al-Masri, Muhammad Rahim, Ridha al-Najjar/al-Tunisi, and Hambali. As detailed, a former CIA officer stated publicly that Hassan Ghul provided reporting on Abu Ahmad al-Kuwaiti prior to being transferred to CIA custody.
[2215] "Lessons from the Hunt for Bin Ladin," dated September 2012, compiled by the CIA's Center for the Study of Intelligence, and provided on October 3, 2012 (DTS #2012-3826).
[2216] *See* intelligence chronology in Volume II, including reporting from Ammar al-Baluchi, Ahmad Ghailani, Sharif al-Masri, Muhammad Rahim, Ridha al-Najjar/al-Tunisi, Hambali, and Hassan Ghul.
[2217] Khalid Shaykh Mohammad, Khalid bin Attash, Abu Yasir al-Jaza'iri, Samir al-Barq, and Abu Faraj al-Libi.
[2218] Khalid Shaykh Mohammad, Abu Faraj al-Libi, and Khalid bin Attash. *See* intelligence chronology in Volume II and CIA testimony from May 4, 2011. CIA officer: "...with the capture of Abu Faraj al-Libi and Khalid Shaykh Mohammed, these are key bin Ladin facilitators, gatekeepers if you will, and their description of Abu Ahmed, the sharp contrast between that and the earlier detainees. Abu Faraj denies even knowing him, a completely uncredible position for him to take but one that he has stuck with to this day. KSM initially downplays any role Abu Ahmed might play, and by the time he leaves our program claims that he married in 2002, retired and really was playing no role." CIA records indicate Khallad bin Attash also downplayed the role of Abu Ahmad al-Kuwaiti, stating several

remaining two provided limited, non-unique, corroborative reporting.[2219]) The sixth, Abu Zubaydah, who was detained on March 28, 2002, and subjected to the CIA's enhanced interrogation techniques in August 2002, did not provide information on Abu Ahmad al-Kuwaiti until August 25, 2005, intelligence that, as noted, was described by CIA officers at the time as "speculative."[2220]

- *The October 3, 2012, "Lessons for the Hunt for Bin Ladin" document also states that "only two [detainees] (KSM and Abu Zubaydah) had been waterboarded. Even so, KSM gave false information about Abu Ahmad...."[2221] The CIA's May 5, 2011, Chart, "Reporting on Abu Ahmad al-Kuwaiti," states that Abu Zubaydah and KSM provided "Tier 1" intelligence that "linked Abu Ahmad to Bin Ladin."* CIA records indicate that both detainees denied any significant connection between al-Kuwaiti and UBL. CIA records further indicate that Abu Zubaydah and KSM, who were both subjected to the CIA's waterboard interrogation technique, withheld information on Abu Ahmad al-Kuwaiti:

  o Abu Zubaydah: "Abu Ahmad K." and a phone number associated with Abu Ahmad al-Kuwaiti was found on page 8 of a 27-page address book captured with Abu Zubaydah on March 28, 2002. In July 2003, Abu Zubaydah stated that he was not familiar with the name Abu Ahmad al-Kuwaiti, or the description provided to him by CIA officers. In April 2004, Abu Zubaydah again stated that he did not recognize the name "Abu Ahmad al-Kuwaiti."[2222] According to a CIA cable, in August 2005, Abu Zubaydah provided information on "an individual whose name he did not know, but who might be identifiable with Abu Ahmad al-Kuwaiti, aka Abu Ahmad al-Pakistani." According to the cable, Abu Zubaydah speculated that this individual knew UBL and al-Zawahiri, but did not think their relationship would be close. Days later a CIA cable elaborated that Abu Zubaydah had speculated on a family of brothers from Karachi that may have included Abu Ahmad.[2223]

---

times that Abu Ahmad was focused on family and was not close to UBL, and that he had never heard of Abu Ahmad al-Kuwaiti serving as a courier for UBL.

[2219] Abu Yasir al-Jaza'iri provided corroborative information in July 2003 that Abu Ahmad al-Kuwaiti was associated with KSM, was best known in Karachi, and appeared to be Pakistani. (*See* DIRECTOR ██████ (111632Z JUL 03).) Samir al-Barq provided information in September 2003 that al-Kuwaiti had provided al-Barq with $1000 to obtain a house in Karachi that al-Qa'ida could use for a biological weapons lab. (*See* ██████ 47409 (191324Z NOV 03), as well as the detainee review of Samir al-Barq in Volume III that details al-Barq's various statements on al-Qa'ida's ambition to establish a biological weapons program.) Neither of these reports is cited in CIA records as providing unique or new information. In October 2003, both detainees denied having any information on the use of Abbottabad as a safe haven for al-Qa'ida. *See* ██████ 10172 (160821Z OCT 03); ██████ 48444 (240942Z OCT 03).

[2220] DIRECTOR ██████ (8/25/2005). On July 7, 2003, and April 27, 2004, Abu Zubaydah was asked about "Abu Ahmed al-Kuwaiti" and denied knowing the name.

[2221] "Lessons from the Hunt for Bin Ladin," dated September 2012, compiled by the CIA's Center for the Study of Intelligence, and provided on October 3, 2012 (DTS #2012-3826).

[2222] In addition to "Abu Ahmad K." being included in Abu Zubaydah's address book, there was additional reporting indicating that Abu Zubaydah had some knowledge of Abu Ahmad al-Kuwaiti. For example, on October 12, 2004, another CIA detainee explained how he met al-Kuwaiti at a guesthouse that was operated by Ibn Shaykh al-Libi and Abu Zubaydah in 1997. *See* intelligence chronology in Volume II.

[2223] *See* DIRECTOR ██████ (252024Z AUG 05) and the intelligence chronology in Volume II.

○ KSM: When KSM was captured on March 1, 2003, an email address associated with Abu Ahmad al-Kuwaiti was found on a laptop believed to be used by KSM. As detailed in this review, KSM first acknowledged Abu Ahmad al-Kuwaiti in May 2003, after being confronted with reporting on Abu Ahmad al-Kuwaiti from a detainee who was not in CIA custody. KSM provided various reports on Abu Ahmad that the CIA described as "pithy." In August 2005, KSM claimed that al-Kuwaiti was not a courier, and that he had never heard of Abu Ahmad transporting letters for UBL. In May 2007, the CIA reported that the denials of KSM and another detainee, combined with conflicting reporting from other detainees, added to the CIA's belief that Abu Ahmad al-Kuwaiti was a significant figure.[2224]

(TS// ████████████ //NF) The CIA detainee who provided the most accurate "Tier 1" information linking Abu Ahmad al-Kuwaiti to UBL, Hassan Ghul, provided the information prior to being subjected to the CIA's enhanced interrogation techniques.[2225] Hassan Ghul was captured on January █, 2004, by foreign authorities in the Iraqi Kurdistan Region.[2226] Ghul was reportedly first interrogated by ███████, then transferred to U.S. military custody and questioned, and then rendered to CIA custody at DETENTION SITE COBALT on January █, 2004.[2227] From January █, 2004, to January █, 2004, Hassan Ghul was questioned by the CIA at DETENTION SITE COBALT. During this period the CIA disseminated 21 intelligence reports based on Ghul's reporting.[2228] A CIA officer told the CIA Office of Inspector General

---

[2224] See intelligence chronology in Volume II, including ALEC ██████ (102238Z MAR 03); HEADQUARTERS ██████ (███████ JAN 04); ██████ 29986 (171741Z AUG 05); ██████ 5594 (201039Z MAY 07).

[2225] As the dissemination of 21 intelligence reports suggests, information in CIA records indicates Hassan Ghul was cooperative with CIA personnel prior to being subjected to the CIA's enhanced interrogation techniques. In an interview with the CIA Office of Inspector General, a CIA officer familiar with Ghul stated, "He sang like a tweetie bird. He opened up right away and was cooperative from the outset." (See December 2, 2004, interview with [REDACTED], Chief, DO, CTC UBL Department, ████████████.) The CIA's September 2012 "Lessons from the Hunt for Bin Ladin," compiled by the CIA's Center for the Study of Intelligence (DTS #2012-3826), states that: "Ghul's tantalizing lead began a systematic but low profile effort to target and further identify Abu Ahmad." On April 16, 2013, the Council on Foreign Relations hosted a forum in relation to the screening of the film, "Manhunt." The forum included former CIA officer Nada Bakos, who states in the film that Hassan Ghul provided the critical information on Abu Ahmed al-Kuwaiti to Kurdish officials prior to entering CIA custody. When asked about the interrogation techniques used by the Kurds, Bakos stated: "...honestly, Hassan Ghul...when he was being debriefed by the Kurdish government, he literally was sitting there having tea. He was in a safe house. He wasn't locked up in a cell. He wasn't handcuffed to anything. He was—he was having a free flowing conversation. And there's—you know, there's articles in Kurdish papers about sort of their interpretation of the story and how forthcoming he was." See www.cfr.org/counterterrorism/film-screening-manhunt/p30560. When asked by the Committee to comment on this narrative, the CIA wrote on October 25, 2013: "We have not identified any information in our holdings suggesting that Hassan Gul first provided information on Abu Ahmad while in ██████ [foreign] custody." See DTS #2013-3152.

[2226] ██████ 21753 ████████████████

[2227] ██████ 21815 ████████████ ; ████████ 21753 ██████ ;
HEADQUARTERS ██████ JAN 04); ████████ 1642 ██████ JAN 04); DIRECTOR ██████ JAN 04)

[2228] For details on the reports, see ████████████ 54194 ████ JAN 04);
1644 ████ JAN 04), later released as HEADQUARTERS ████ JAN 04);
██████ 1645 ████ JAN 04), later released as HEADQUARTERS ████ JAN 04);
██████ 1646 ████ JAN 04), later released as HEADQUARTERS ████ JAN 04);
██████ 1647 ████ JAN 04), later released as HEADQUARTERS ████ JAN 04); 04); ████ CIA ████ FEB 04); ████████ 1650 ████ JAN 04);

that Hassan Ghul "opened up right away and was cooperative from the outset."[2229] During the January █, 2004, to January █, 2004, sessions, Ghul was questioned on the location of UBL. According to a cable, Ghul speculated that "UBL was likely living in Peshawar area," and that "it was well known that [UBL] was always with Abu Ahmed [al-Kuwaiti]."[2230] Ghul described Abu Ahmad al-Kuwaiti as UBL's "closest assistant"[2231] and listed him as one of three individuals likely to be with UBL.[2232] Ghul further speculated that:

> "UBL's security apparatus would be minimal, and that the group likely lived in a House with a family somewhere in Pakistan. Ghul commented that after UBL's bodyguard entourage was apprehended entering Pakistan following the fall of Afghanistan, UBL likely has maintained a small security signature of circa one or two persons. Ghul speculated that Abu Ahmed likely handled all of UBL's needs, including moving messages out to Abu Faraj [al-Libi]...."[2233]

(TS// ████████ //NF) The next day, January █, 2004, Hassan Ghul was transferred to the CIA's DETENTION SITE BLACK.[2234] Upon arrival, Ghul was "shaved and barbered, stripped, and placed in the standing position against the wall" with "his hands above his head" for forty minutes.[2235] The CIA interrogators at the detention site immediately requested permission to use the CIA's enhanced interrogation techniques against Ghul, writing that, during the forty minutes, Ghul did not provide any new information, did not show the fear that was typical of other recent captures, and "was somewhat arrogant and self important." The CIA interrogators wrote that they "judged" that Ghul "has the expectation that in U.S. hands, his treatment will not be severe."[2236] The request to CIA Headquarters to use the CIA's enhanced interrogation techniques further stated:

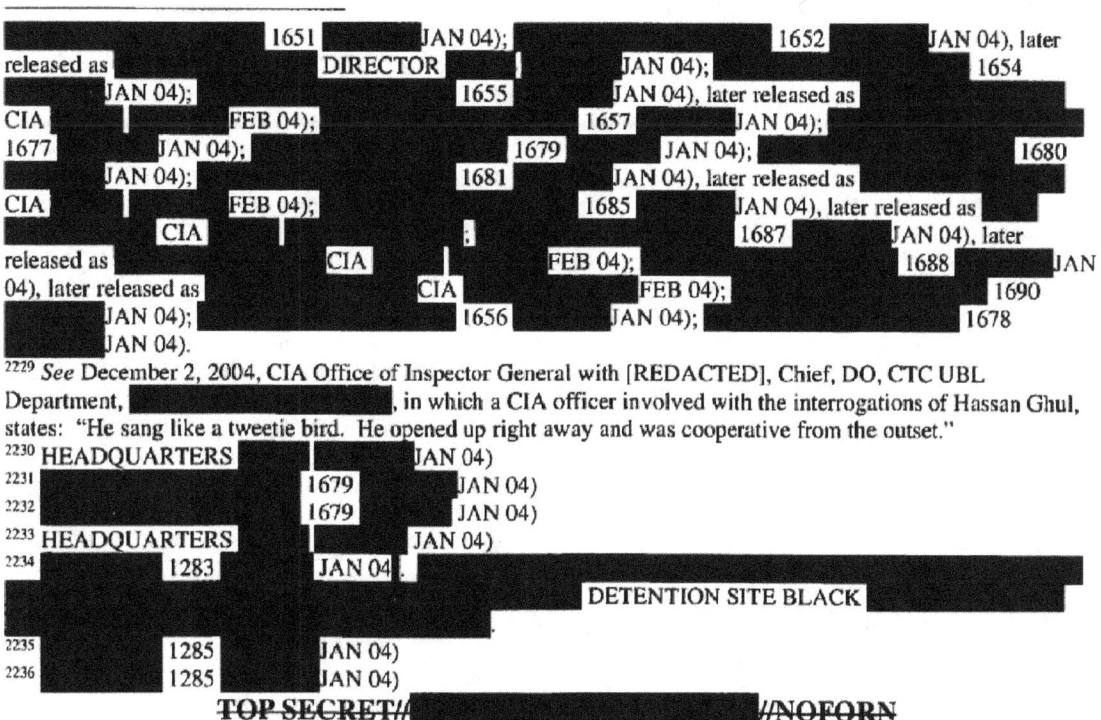

1651 █ JAN 04); █ 1652 █ JAN 04), later released as █ DIRECTOR █ JAN 04); █ 1654 █ JAN 04); █ 1655 █ JAN 04), later released as █ CIA █ FEB 04); █ 1657 █ JAN 04); █ 1677 █ JAN 04); █ 1679 █ JAN 04); █ 1680 █ JAN 04); █ 1681 █ JAN 04), later released as █ CIA █ FEB 04); █ 1685 █ JAN 04), later released as █ CIA █ ; █ 1687 █ JAN 04), later released as █ CIA █ FEB 04); █ 1688 █ JAN 04), later released as 04), later released as █ CIA █ FEB 04); █ 1690 █ JAN 04); █ 1656 █ JAN 04); █ 1678 █ JAN 04).

[2229] See December 2, 2004, CIA Office of Inspector General with [REDACTED], Chief, DO, CTC UBL Department, ████████████ , in which a CIA officer involved with the interrogations of Hassan Ghul, states: "He sang like a tweetie bird. He opened up right away and was cooperative from the outset."
[2230] HEADQUARTERS ████ JAN 04)
[2231] ████ 1679 ████ JAN 04)
[2232] ████ 1679 ████ JAN 04)
[2233] HEADQUARTERS ████ JAN 04)
[2234] ████ 1283 ████ JAN 04 █. ████████████ DETENTION SITE BLACK ████
[2235] ████ 1285 ████ JAN 04)
[2236] ████ 1285 ████ JAN 04)

"The interrogation team believes, based on [Hassan Ghul's] reaction to the initial contact, that his al-Qa'ida briefings and his earlier experiences with U.S. military interrogators have convinced him there are limits to the physical contact interrogators can have with him. The interrogation team believes the approval and employment of enhanced measures should sufficiently shift [Hassan Ghul's] paradigm of what he expects to happen. The lack of these increasd [sic] measures may limit the team's capability to collect critical and reliable information in a timely manner."[2237]

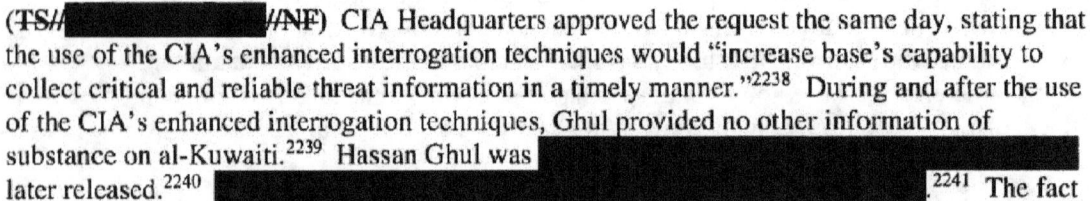

(TS// ██████████ //NF) CIA Headquarters approved the request the same day, stating that the use of the CIA's enhanced interrogation techniques would "increase base's capability to collect critical and reliable threat information in a timely manner."[2238] During and after the use of the CIA's enhanced interrogation techniques, Ghul provided no other information of substance on al-Kuwaiti.[2239] Hassan Ghul was ██████████████████████████ later released.[2240] ████████████████████████████████.[2241] The fact

---

[2237] ████████ 1285 ████████ JAN 04)

[2238] HEADQUARTERS ████████ (████ JAN 04)

[2239] *See* intelligence chronology in Volume II. The CIA's June 2013 Response states that "[a]fter undergoing enhanced interrogation techniques," Hassan Ghul provided information that became "more concrete and less speculative, it also corroborated information from Ammar that Khalid Shaykh Muhammad (KSM) was lying when he claimed Abu Ahmad left al-Qa'ida in 2002." The assertion in the CIA's June 2013 Response that information acquired from Hassan Ghul "[a]fter undergoing enhanced interrogation techniques" "corroborated information from Ammar that Khalid Shaykh Muhammad (KSM) was lying when he claimed Abu Ahmad left al-Qa'ida in 2002" is incorrect. First, the referenced information from Hassan Ghul was acquired prior to the use of the CIA's enhanced interrogation techniques. A CIA cable, HEADQUARTERS ████ (████ JAN 04), explains that based on Hassan Ghul's comments that it was "well known" that UBL was always with al-Kuwaiti (acquired prior to the use of the CIA's enhanced interrogation techniques), CIA Headquarters asked interrogators to reengage KSM on the relationship between al-Kuwaiti and UBL, noting the "serious disconnect" between Hassan Ghul's comments and KSM's "pithy" description of Abu Ahmad al-Kuwaiti. The cable notes that KSM had made "no reference to a link between Abu Ahmed and al-Qa'ida's two top leaders, nor has he hinted at all that Abu Ahmed was involved in the facilitation of Zawahiri in/around Peshawar in February 2003," and that KSM "has some explaining to do about Abu Ahmed and his support to UBL and Zawahiri." Second, as the intelligence chronology in Volume II details, there was a significant body of intelligence well before Hassan Ghul's pre-enhanced interrogation techniques reporting in January 2004 indicating that KSM was providing inaccurate information on Abu Ahmad al-Kuwaiti. *See* detailed information in Volume II intelligence chronology. Third, as detailed in CIA-provided documents (DTS #2011-2004), the CIA described Hassan Ghul's reporting as "speculat[ive]" both during and after the use of the CIA's enhanced interrogation techniques. Finally, as noted earlier, the CIA's June 2013 Response ignores or minimizes a large body of intelligence reporting in CIA records—and documented in the Committee Study—that was acquired from sources and methods unrelated to the use of the CIA's enhanced interrogation techniques. Nonetheless, the CIA's June 2013 Response asserts: "It is impossible to know in hindsight whether we could have obtained from Ammar, Gul, and others the same information that helped us find Bin Ladin *without using enhanced techniques*, or whether we eventually would have acquired other intelligence that allowed us to successfully pursue the Abu Ahmad lead or some other lead without the information we acquired from detainees in CIA custody" (italics added). As detailed in this summary, the most accurate intelligence from a detainee on Abu Ahmad al-Kuwaiti was acquired prior to the use of the CIA's enhanced interrogation techniques, and CIA detainees subjected to the CIA's enhanced interrogation techniques provided inaccurate and fabricated information on al-Kuwaiti. *See* detailed information in the Volume II intelligence chronology.

[2240] ████ 2441 ████████ ; HEADQUARTERS ████████ ████████ ; ████████ 1635 ████████████████ ; ████████ 1712 ████ ; HEADQUARTERS ████████ ; ████ 1775 ████ ; 173426 ████████

[2241] *See* Committee Notification from the CIA dated ████████ (DTS #2012-3802).

that Hassan Ghul provided the detailed information linking Abu Ahmad al-Kuwaiti to UBL prior to the use of the CIA's enhanced interrogation techniques was omitted from CIA documents and testimony.[2242]

(TS// ███████ //NF) While CIA documents and testimony highlighted reporting that the CIA claimed was obtained from CIA detainees—and in some cases from CIA detainees subjected to the CIA's enhanced interrogation techniques—the CIA internally noted that reporting from CIA detainees—specifically CIA detainees subjected to the CIA's enhanced interrogation techniques—was insufficient, fabricated, and/or unreliable.

(TS// ███████ //NF) A September 1, 2005, CIA report on the search for UBL states:

> "Bin Ladin Couriers: Low-level couriers who wittingly or unwittingly facilitate communications between Bin Ladin and his gatekeepers remain largely invisible to us until a detainee reveals them.[2243] Even then, *detainees provide few actionable leads, and we have to consider the possibility that they are creating fictitious characters to distract us or to absolve themselves of direct knowledge about Bin Ladin.* We nonetheless continue the hunt for Abu Ahmed al-Kuwaiti—an alleged courier between Bin Ladin and KSM—and Abu 'Abd al Khaliq Jan, who[m] Abu Faraj identified as his go-between with Bin Ladin since mid-2003, in order to get one step closer to Bin Ladin."[2244]

(TS// ███████ //NF) A May 20, 2007, CIA "targeting study" for Abu Ahmad al-Kuwaiti states:

> "Khalid Shaykh Muhammad (KSM) *described Abu Ahmad as a relatively minor figure and Abu Faraj al-Libi denied all knowledge of Abu Ahmad. Station assesses that KSM and Abu Faraj's reporting is not credible* on this topic, and their attempts to downplay Abu Ahmad's importance or deny knowledge of Abu Ahmad are likely part of an effort to withhold information on UBL or his close associates. These denials, combined with reporting from *other detainees*[2245] indicating that Abu Ahmad worked closely with KSM and Abu Faraj, add to our belief that Abu Ahmad is an HVT courier or facilitator."[2246]

[2242] *See* CIA letter to the Senate Select Committee on Intelligence dated May 5, 2011, which includes a document entitled, "Background Detainee Information on Abu Ahmad al-Kuwaiti," with an accompanying six-page chart entitled, "Detainee Reporting on Abu Ahmad al-Kuwaiti" (DTS #2011-2004). *See also* a similar, but less detailed CIA document entitled, "Detainee Reporting on Abu Ahmad al-Kuwaiti's Historic Links to Usama Bin Laden."
[2243] Significant information was acquired on Abu Ahmad al-Kuwaiti independent of CIA detainees. *See* intelligence chronology in Volume II.
[2244] Italics added. CIA analysis entitled, "Overcoming Challenges To Capturing Usama Bin Ladin, 1 September 2005." CIA records indicate that Abu Faraj al-Libi fabricated information relating to "'Abd al Khaliq Jan."
[2245] Italics added. As detailed, the reporting that Abu Ahmad al-Kuwaiti "worked closely with KSM" and was "one of a few close associates of Usama bin Ladin," who "traveled frequently" to "meet with Usama bin Ladin," was acquired in 2002, from sources unrelated to the CIA's Detention and Interrogation Program.
[2246] Italics added. ███████████ 5594 (201039Z MAY 07). Reporting from CIA detainees Ammar al-Baluchi and Khallad bin Attash—both subjected to the CIA's enhanced interrogation techniques—included similar inaccurate

(TS//██████████████//NF) Additional CIA documents contrasted the lack of intelligence obtained from CIA detainees subjected to the CIA's enhanced interrogation techniques with the value of intelligence obtained from other sources. A November 23, 2007, CIA intelligence product, "Al-Qa'ida Watch," with the title, "Probable Identification of Suspected Bin Ladin Facilitator Abu Ahmad al-Kuwaiti," details how a:

> "review of 2002 debriefings of a [foreign government] detainee who claimed to have traveled in 2000 from Kuwait to Afghanistan with an 'Ahmad al-Kuwaiti' provided the breakthrough leading to the likely identification of Habib al-Rahman as Abu Ahmad. The [foreign government] subsequently informed [the CIA] that Habib al-Rahman currently is living in Pakistan, probably in the greater Peshawar area—according to our analysis of a body of reporting."[2247]

(TS//██████████████//NF) This CIA intelligence product highlighted how reporting from Abu Faraj al-Libi, who was subjected to the CIA's enhanced interrogation techniques and denied knowing Abu Ahmad, differed from that of Hassan Ghul, who—prior to the application of the CIA's enhanced interrogation techniques—stated that "Bin Ladin was always with Abu Ahmad," and that Abu Ahmad had delivered a message to senior al-Qa'ida leaders in late 2003, "probably through Abu Faraj." The document further states that KSM "has consistently maintained that Abu Ahmad 'retired' from al-Qa'ida work in 2002." The CIA document states that the CIA will be working with ██████████████ and the ██████ government, as well as utilizing a database

---

information. Khallad bin Attash was arrested with Ammar al-Baluchi in a unilateral operation by Pakistani authorities resulting from criminal leads on April 29, 2003. On May ██, 2003, bin Attash was rendered to CIA custody and immediately subjected to the CIA's enhanced interrogation techniques from May 16, 2003, to May 18, 2003, and then again from July 18, 2003, to July 29, 2003. On June 30, 2003, bin Attash stated that al-Kuwaiti was admired among the men. On July 27, 2003, bin Attash corroborated intelligence reporting that al-Kuwaiti played a facilitation role in al-Qa'ida and that al-Kuwaiti departed Karachi to get married. In January 2004, bin Attash stated that al-Kuwaiti was not close to UBL and not involved in al-Qa'ida operations, and that al-Kuwaiti was settling down with his wife in the summer of 2003. In August 2005, bin Attash stated that Abu Ahmad al-Kuwaiti was not a courier, that he had never heard of Abu Ahmad transporting letters for UBL, and that Abu Ahmad was instead focused on family after he married in 2002. In August 2006, bin Attash reiterated that al-Kuwaiti was not a courier, but rather focused on family life. Ammar al-Baluchi was arrested with Khallad bin Attash in a unilateral operation by Pakistani authorities resulting from criminal leads on April 29, 2003. Upon his arrest in Pakistan, Ammar al-Baluchi was cooperative and provided information on a number of topics to foreign government interrogators, including information on Abu Ahmad al-Kuwaiti that the CIA disseminated prior to al-Baluchi being transferred to CIA custody on May ██, 2003. After Ammar al-Baluchi was transferred to CIA custody, the CIA subjected Ammar al-Baluchi to the CIA's enhanced interrogation techniques from May 17, 2003, to May 20, 2003. On May 19, 2003, al-Baluchi admitted to fabricating information while being subjected to the CIA's enhanced interrogation techniques the previous day, and in response to questioning, stated that he believed UBL was on the Pakistan/Afghanistan border and that a brother of al-Kuwaiti was to take over courier duties for UBL. In June 2003, al-Baluchi stated that there were rumors that al-Kuwaiti was a courier. In early 2004, al-Baluchi acknowledged that al-Kuwaiti may have worked for Abu Faraj al-Libi, but stated that al-Kuwaiti was never a courier and would not have direct contact with UBL. *See* intelligence chronology in Volume II and detainee reviews of Khallad bin Attash and Ammar al-Baluchi for additional information.

[2247] *See* CIA CTC "Al-Qa'ida Watch," dated November 23, 2007.

of ███████████ to follow-up on an individual traveling within Pakistan with a similar name and date of birth.[2248]

(TS// ███████████ //NF) CIA cable records from early 2008 highlight how the discovery and exploitation of phone numbers associated with al-Kuwaiti ████ had been critical in collecting intelligence and locating the target,[2249] and state:

> "...*debriefings of the senior most detainees who were involved in caring for bin Ladin have produced little locational information*, and it is the final nugget that detainees hold on to in debriefings (over threat info and even Zawahiri LOCINT) given their loyalty to the al-Qa'ida leader. We assess that Abu Ahmad would likely be in the same category as Khalid Shaykh Muhammad and Abu Faraj al-Libi, so we advocate building as much of a targeting picture of where and when Habib/Abu Ahmad travels to flesh out current leads to bin Ladin."[2250]

(TS// ███████████ //NF) On May 1, 2008, a CIA Headquarters cable entitled, "targeting efforts against suspected UBL facilitator Abu Ahmad al-Kuwaiti," documents that the CIA had a number of collection platforms established to collect intelligence on Abu Ahmad al-Kuwaiti in order to locate UBL. The cable closes by stating:

> "although we want to refrain from addressing endgame strategies, HQS judges that detaining Habib should be a last resort, since we have had no/no success in eliciting actionable intelligence on bin Ladin's location from any detainees."[2251]

(TS// ███████████ //NF) While the aforementioned CIA assessments highlight the unreliability of reporting from senior al-Qa'ida leaders in CIA custody, specifically "that KSM and Abu Faraj's reporting" was assessed to be "not credible"—and that their denials "add[ed] to [the CIA's] belief that Abu Ahmad is an HVT courier or facilitator"[2252]—the CIA assessments also highlight that "reporting from other detainees indicating that Abu Ahmad worked closely with KSM and Abu Faraj" was useful.[2253] As documented, the initial detainee-related information linking Abu Ahmad to UBL and KSM did not come from CIA detainees, but from detainees who were not in CIA custody.[2254]

[2248] *See* CIA CTC "Al-Qa'ida Watch," dated November 23, 2007.
[2249] ████ 3808 (211420Z JAN 08); HEADQUARTERS ████ (232217Z JAN 08); ████ 9044 (240740Z JAN 08); ████ 5568 (081633Z FEB 08)
[2250] Italics added. ████ 9044 (240740Z JAN 08).
[2251] HEADQUARTERS ████ (011334Z MAY 08)
[2252] ████ 5594 (201039Z MAY 07)
[2253] ████ 5594 (201039Z MAY 07)
[2254] *See* information in Volume II intelligence chronology for additional details.

IV. Overview of CIA Representations to the Media While the Program Was Classified

A. The CIA Provides Information on the Still-Classified Detention and Interrogation Program to Journalists Who then Publish Classified Information; CIA Does Not File Crimes Reports in Connection with the Stories

(TS// ██████████████ //NF) In seeking to shape press reporting on the CIA's Detention and Interrogation Program, CIA officers and the CIA's Office of Public Affairs (OPA) provided unattributed background information on the program to journalists for books, articles, and broadcasts, including when the existence of the CIA's Detention and Interrogation Program was still classified.[2255] When the journalists to whom the CIA had provided background information published classified information, the CIA did not, as a matter of policy, submit crimes reports. For example, as described in internal emails, the CIA's ██████████████████████ ██████████████████████████ never opened an investigation related to Ronald Kessler's book *The CIA at War*, despite the inclusion of classified information, because "the book contained no first time disclosures," and because "OPA provided assistance with the book."[2256] Senior Deputy General Counsel John Rizzo wrote that the CIA made the determination because the CIA's cooperation with Kessler had been "blessed" by the CIA director.[2257] In another example, CIA officers and the House Permanent Select Committee on Intelligence raised concerns that an article by Douglas Jehl in the *New York Times* contained significant classified information.[2258] ██████████ CTC Legal wrote in an email that "part of this article was based on 'background' provided by OPA. That, essentially, negates any use in making an unauthorized disclosure [report]."[2259]

(TS// ██████████████ //NF) Both the Kessler book and the Jehl article included inaccurate claims about the effectiveness of CIA interrogations, much of it consistent with the inaccurate information being provided by the CIA to policymakers at the time. For example, Kessler's book stated that the FBI arrest of Iyman Faris was "[b]ased on information from the CIA's

---

[2255] On October 28, 2013, the CIA informed the Committee that "CIA policy is to conduct background briefings using unclassified or declassified information" (DTS #2013-3152).
[2256] Email from: ██████████████; to: [REDACTED], ██████████████, [REDACTED], [REDACTED]; cc: ██████████; subject: CIA at War; date: January 20, 2004, at 11:13 AM; email from: ██████████████; to: ██████████; cc: [REDACTED], [REDACTED], ██████████████, [REDACTED]; subject: Re: CIA at War; date: January 21, 2004, at 02:11 PM; email from: ██████████████; to Scott W. Muller, John A. Rizzo, ██████████ ██████████; cc: ██████████████; subject: Re: CIA at War; date: January 21, 2004, at 02:27 PM.
[2257] Email from: John A. Rizzo; to: ██████████████; cc: ██████████████, Scott W. Muller, ██████████████, [REDACTED]; subject: Re: CIA at War; date: January 22, 2004, at 09:28 AM.
[2258] "Rule Change Lets C.I.A. Freely Send Suspects Abroad to Jails," by Douglas Jehl and David Johnston, *The New York Times*, March 6, 2005; email from: ██████████████; to: ██████████; cc: ██████████████, ██████████████; subject: Question on 06 March New York Times revelations; date: April 22, 2005, at 01:38 PM; email from: ██████████; to: ██████████; cc: ██████████████, ██████████████, ██████████; subject: Re: Question on 06 March New York Times revelations; date: April 28, 2005, at 8:12:46 AM.
[2259] Email from: ██████████████; to: ██████████████; cc: ██████████████, ██████████████, ██████████; subject: Re: Question on 06 March New York Times revelations; date: April 28, 2005, at 8:25:23 AM.

interrogation of [KSM]," and that the arrest of Khallad bin Attash was the "result" of CIA interrogations of KSM.[2260] The Jehl article stated that a "secret program to transfer suspected terrorists to foreign countries for interrogation has been carried out by the Central Intelligence Agency... according to current and former government officials." The article stated that a "senior United States official" had "provid[ed] a detailed description of the program," and quoted the official as claiming that "[t]he intelligence obtained by those rendered, detained and interrogated ha[d] disrupted terrorist operations." The senior official added, "[i]t has saved lives in the United States and abroad, and it has resulted in the capture of other terrorists."[2261]

B. Senior CIA Officials Discuss Need to "Put Out Our Story" to Shape Public and Congressional Opinion Prior to the Full Committee Being Briefed

(TS// ███████████ //NF) In early April 2005, ███████████ , chief of ALEC Station, asked CTC officers to compile information on the success of the CIA's Detention and Interrogation Program in preparation for interviews of CIA officers by Tom Brokaw of NBC News.[2262] As ███████ remarked in a Sametime communication with Deputy CTC Director Philip Mudd, during World War II, the Pentagon had an Office of War Information (OWI), whereas the CIA's predecessor, the Office of Strategic Services (OSS), did not. ███████ then noted that "we need an OWI, at least every now and then...."[2263] According to Mudd, concerns within the CIA about defending the CIA's Detention and Interrogation Program in the press were misplaced:[2264]

> "maybe people should know we're trying to sell their program. if they complain, they should know that we're trying to protect our capability to continue. we're not just out there to brag... they don't realize that we have few options here. we either get out and sell, or we get hammered, which has implications beyond the media. congress reads it, cuts our authorities, messes

---

[2260] *The CIA at War*, Ronald Kessler, St. Martin's Press, New York, 2003. As detailed elsewhere, Iyman Faris was already under investigation and Majid Khan, who was then in foreign government custody, had discussed Faris, prior to any mention of Faris by KSM. Likewise, the capture of Khallad bin Attash in April 2003 was unrelated to the reporting from KSM or any other CIA detainee. Kessler's book also stated that Abu Zubaydah "soon began singing to the FBI and CIA about other planned plots," and that "intercepts and information developed months earlier after the arrest of Ramzi Binalshibh... allowed the CIA to trace [KSM]." (*See* Ronald Kessler, *The CIA at War*, St. Martin's Press, New York, 2003.) As detailed elsewhere, Abu Zubaydah did not provide intelligence on al-Qa'ida "planned plots," and KSM's capture was unrelated to information provided by Ramzi bin Al-Shibh. Finally, Kessler's book stated that KSM "told the CIA about a range of planned attacks – on U.S. convoys in Afghanistan, nightclubs in Dubai, targets in Turkey, and an Israeli embassy in the Middle East. Within a few months the transcripts of his interrogations were four feet high." These statements were incongruent with CIA records.
[2261] "Rule Change Lets C.I.A. Freely Send Suspects Abroad," by Douglas Jehl and David Johnston, *The New York Times*, March 6, 2005.
[2262] Email from: ███████ , to: [REDACTED], ███████ , ███████ , [REDACTED], [REDACTED], [REDACTED], ███████ [REDACTED], ███████ , [REDACTED], ███████ , [REDACTED], [REDACTED]; cc: ███████ , ███████ ; subject: FOR IMMEDIATE COORDINATION: Summary of impact of detainee program; date: April 13, 2005, at 5:21:37 PM.
[2263] Sametime communication, between John P. Mudd and ███████ , April 13, 2005, from 19:23:50 to 19:56:05.
[2264] As detailed in this summary, this exchange occurred the day before an anticipated Committee vote on a proposed Committee investigation of the CIA's Detention and Interrogation Program.

up our budget. we need to make sure the impression of what we do is positive… we must be more aggressive out there. we either put out our story or we get eaten. there is no middle ground."[2265]

(TS// ███████████ //NF) Mudd counseled not to "advertise" the discussions between CIA personnel and the media with the CIA "workforce," because "they'd misread it."[2266] After ███████ promised to keep the media outreach "real close hold," Mudd wrote:

"most of them [CIA personnel] do not know that when the w post/ny times quotes 'senior intel official,' it's us… authorized and directed by opa."[2267]

(TS// ███████████ //NF) ███████ sent a draft compilation of plot disruptions to ██████ ██ CTC Legal to determine whether the release of the information would pose any "legal problems."[2268] According to CIA attorneys, information on Issa al-Britani posed no problems because it was sourced to the 9/11 Commission. They also determined that information about Iyman Faris and Sajid Badat that was sourced to press stories posed no legal problems because Faris had already pled guilty and Badat was not being prosecuted in the United States.[2269] On April 15, 2005, a CIA officer expressed concerns in an email to several CIA attorneys about the CIA releasing classified information to the media. There are no CIA records indicating a response to the CIA officer's email.[2270]

(TS// ███████████ //NF) That day, April 15, 2005, the National Security Council Principals Committee discussed a public campaign for the CIA's Detention and Interrogation Program. After the meeting, ALEC Station personnel informed ███████ CTC Legal that scheduled interviews with NBC News of Director Porter Goss and Deputy CTC Director Philip Mudd

---

[2265] Sametime communication, between John P. Mudd and ███████████, April 13, 2005, from 19:23:50 to 19:56:05.

[2266] Sametime communication, between John P. Mudd and ███████████, April 13, 2005, from 19:23:50 to 19:56:05.

[2267] Sametime communication, between John P. Mudd and ███████████, April 13, 2005, from 19:23:50 to 19:56:05.

[2268] Email from: ███████████, Chief of Operations, ALEC Station; to: ███████, ███████, [REDACTED], [REDACTED], [REDACTED], ███████, ███████, [REDACTED], [REDACTED], ███████████ [REDACTED], [REDACTED], ███████████; cc: ███████; subject: Brokaw interview: Take one; date: April 13, 2005, at 6:46:59 PM; email from: ███████; to: ███████; cc: [REDACTED], [REDACTED], ███████, [REDACTED], ███████ [REDACTED], ███████ [REDACTED], [REDACTED], ███████, ███████ [REDACTED], ███████; subject: Re: Brokaw interview: Take one; date: April 13, 2005, at 6:50:28 PM; email from: ███████; to: ███████, [REDACTED], ███████; cc: John A. Rizzo, ███████; subject: Re: Brokaw interview: Take one; date: April 13, 2005, 7:24:50 PM.

[2269] Email from: ███████; to: ███████; cc: [REDACTED], ███████, [REDACTED], John A. Rizzo, ███████; subject: Re: Brokaw interview: Take one; date: April 14, 2005, at 9:22:32 AM.

[2270] Email from: ███████; to: ███████; cc: [REDACTED], ███████, [REDACTED], ███████; subject: Re: Brokaw interview: Take one; date: April 14, 2005, at 8:08:00 AM.

should not proceed so that "we don't get a head [sic] of ourselves...."[2271] On June 24, 2005, however, *Dateline NBC* aired a program that included on-the-record quotes from Goss and Mudd, as well as quotes from "top American intelligence officials."[2272] The program and *Dateline NBC's* associated online articles included classified information about the capture and interrogation of CIA detainees and quoted "senior U.S. intelligence analysts" stating that intelligence obtained from CIA interrogations "approaches or surpasses any other intelligence on the subject of al-Qaida and the construction of the network."[2273] The *Dateline NBC* articles stated that "Al-Qaida leaders suddenly found themselves bundled onto a CIA Gulfstream V or Boeing 737 jet headed for long months of interrogation," and indicated that Abu Zubaydah, KSM, Ramzi bin al-Shibh, and Abu Faraj al-Libi were "picked up and bundled off to interrogation centers." The articles also stated that the capture of bin al-Shibh led to the captures of KSM and Khallad bin Attash.[2274] This information was inaccurate.[2275] There are no CIA records to indicate that there was any investigation or crimes report submitted in connection with the *Dateline NBC* program and its associated reporting.

C. CIA Attorneys Caution that Classified Information Provided to the Media Should Not Be Attributed to the CIA

(TS// ███████ //NF) After the April 15, 2005, National Security Council Principals Committee meeting, the CIA drafted an extensive document describing the CIA's Detention and Interrogation Program for an anticipated media campaign. CIA attorneys, discussing aspects of the campaign involving off-the-record disclosures, cautioned against attributing the information to the CIA itself. One senior attorney stated that the proposed press briefing was "minimally acceptable, but only if not attributed to a CIA official." The CIA attorney continued: "This should be attributed to an 'official knowledgeable' about the program (or some similar obfuscation), but should not be attributed to a CIA or intelligence official." Referring to CIA efforts to deny Freedom of Information Act (FOIA) requests for previously acknowledged

---

[2271] Email from: ███████; to: ███████; subject: Brokaw interview: Take one; date: April 15, 2005, at 1:00:59 PM. The CIA's June 2013 Response states that "[w]ith regard to information related to covert action, authorization [to disclose information to the media] rests with the White House." CIA records made available to the Committee, however, do not indicate White House approval for the subsequent media disclosures. In the summer of 2013, the Committee requested the CIA provide any such records should they exist. No records were identified by the CIA.

[2272] *See* "The Long War; World View of War on Terror," *Dateline NBC*, June 24, 2005. In April 2005, Mudd stated that the program would likely be aired in June. *See* email from: John P. Mudd; to: ███████, subject: Re: Brokaw interview: Take one; date: April 18, 2005, at 08:31 AM.

[2273] "The frightening evolution of al-Qaida; Decentralization has led to deadly staying power," *Dateline NBC*, June 24, 2005.

[2274] "The frightening evolution of al-Qaida; Decentralization has led to deadly staying power," *Dateline NBC*, June 24, 2005; "Al-Qaida finds safe haven in Iran," *Dateline NBC*, June 24, 2005. Notwithstanding this content, the CIA's June 2013 Response states that "[a] review of the NBC broadcast, cited by the *Study*, shows that it contained no public disclosures of classified CIA information; indeed, *the RDI program was not discussed*" (emphasis in the original). In addition to the information described above included in the online articles associated with the broadcast, the broadcast itself described the role of a CIA asset in the capture of KSM and the capture of Abu Faraj al-Libi in "joint US/Pakistani actions" ("The Long War; World View of War on Terror," *Dateline NBC*, June 24, 2005).

[2275] As described elsewhere in this summary and in more detail in the full Committee Study, the captures of KSM and Khallad bin Attash were unrelated to the capture and interrogation of Ramzi bin al-Shibh.

information, the attorney noted that, "[o]ur Glomar figleaf is getting pretty thin."[2276] Another CIA attorney noted that the draft "makes the [legal] declaration I just wrote about the secrecy of the interrogation program a work of fiction...."[2277] ██████████ CTC Legal urged that CIA leadership needed to "confront the inconsistency" between CIA court declarations "about how critical it is to keep this information secret" and the CIA "planning to reveal darn near the entire program."[2278]

D. The CIA Engages with Journalists and Conveys an Inaccurate Account of the Interrogation of Abu Zubaydah

(TS// ██████████████ //NF) In late 2005, the CIA decided to cooperate again with Douglas Jehl of the *New York Times*, despite his intention to publish information about the program. A CIA officer wrote about Jehl's proposed article, which was largely about the CIA's detention and interrogation of Abu Zubaydah, "[t]his is not necessarily an unflattering story."[2279] Jehl, who provided the CIA with a detailed outline of his proposed story, informed the CIA that he would emphasize that the CIA's enhanced interrogation techniques worked, that they were approved through an inter-agency process, and that the CIA went to great lengths to ensure that the interrogation program was authorized by the White House and the Department of Justice.[2280] CIA records indicate that the CIA decided not to dissuade Jehl from describing the CIA's enhanced interrogation techniques because, as ██████████ CTC Legal ██████████ noted, "[t]he EITs have already been out there."[2281] The CIA's chief of ALEC Station, ██████████, who wondered whether cooperation with Jehl would be "undercutting our complaint

---

[2276] Email from: ██████████; to: ██████████; cc: [REDACTED], ██████████, ██████████, ██████████; bcc: ██████████; subject: Re: Interrogation Program--Going Public Draft Talking Points--Comments Due to ████ me by COB TODAY. Thanks.; date: April 20, 2005, at 5:58:47 PM.

[2277] *See* email from: ██████████; to: ██████████; cc: [REDACTED], ██████████, [REDACTED]; subject: Re: Interrogation Program--Going Public Draft Talking Points--Comments Due to ████ me by COB TODAY. Thanks.; date: April 21, 2005, at 07:24 AM. ██████████ was referring to the assault case against David Passaro. The Committee Study does not include an analysis of the accuracy of declarations to U.S. courts by senior CIA officials.

[2278] Email from: ██████████; to: ██████████; cc: ██████████, ██████████, ██████████, [REDACTED], ██████████, [REDACTED]; subject: Re: Interrogation Program--Going Public Draft Talking Points--Comments Due to ████ me by COB TODAY. Thanks.; date: April 25, 2005, at 11:41:07 AM.

[2279] Email from: ██████████; to: ██████████, John A. Rizzo, ██████████, ██████████, [REDACTED], Robert L. Grenier; subject: Doug Jehl – Comprehensive Story on the Capture of Abu Zubaydah and Conception of EITs; date: December 15, 2005, at 02:04 PM.

[2280] Email from: ██████████; to: ██████████, John A. Rizzo, ██████████, ██████████, [REDACTED], Robert L. Grenier; subject: Doug Jehl – Comprehensive Story on the Capture of Abu Zubaydah and Conception of EITs; date: December 15, 2005, at 02:04 PM.

[2281] Email from: ██████████; to: [REDACTED], [REDACTED], [REDACTED], ██████████; cc: [REDACTED], [REDACTED], ██████████; subject: Doug Jehl - Comprehensive Story on the Capture of Abu Zubaydah and Conception of EITs; date: December 15, 2005, at 02:10 PM. Another CIA officer added "I don't like so much talk about EIT's, but that particular horse has long left the barn...." *See* email from: ██████████; to: ██████████; cc: [REDACTED], [REDACTED], [REDACTED], [REDACTED], ██████████, [REDACTED], ██████████; subject: Re: Doug Jehl - Comprehensive Story on the Capture of Abu Zubaydah and Conception of EITs; date: December 15, 2005, at 03:03 PM.

against those leakers," nonetheless suggested informing Jehl of other examples of CIA "detainee exploitation success."[2282]

(TS// ███████████ //NF) While the *New York Times* did not publish Jehl's story, on September 7, 2006, the day after President Bush publicly acknowledged the program, David Johnston of the *New York Times* called the CIA's OPA with a proposed news story about the interrogation of Abu Zubaydah. In an email with the subject line, "We Can't Let This Go Unanswered," the CIA's director of public affairs in OPA, Mark Mansfield, described Johnston's proposed narrative as "bullshit" and biased toward the FBI, adding that "we need to push back."[2283] While it is unclear if Mansfield responded to Johnston's proposed story, Mansfield later wrote in an email that there was "[n]o need to worry."[2284] On September 10, 2006, the *New York Times* published an article by Johnston, entitled, "At a Secret Interrogation, Dispute Flared Over Tactics," that described "sharply contrasting accounts" of the interrogation of Abu Zubaydah. The article cited officials "more closely allied with law enforcement," who stated that Abu Zubaydah "cooperated with F.B.I. interviewers," as well as officials "closely tied to intelligence agencies," who stated that Abu Zubaydah "was lying, and things were going nowhere," and that "[i]t was clear that he had information about an imminent attack and time was of the essence." The article included the frequent CIA representation that, after the use of "tougher tactics," Abu Zubaydah "soon began to provide information on key Al Qaeda operators to help us find and capture those responsible for the 9/11 attacks."[2285] This characterization of Abu Zubaydah's interrogation is incongruent with CIA interrogation records.[2286] CTC stated that the article resulted in questions to the CIA from the country ███████████ ██████████, and assessed that "[d]isclosures of this nature could adversely [have an] impact on future joint CT operations with... ███████ partners."[2287] There are no indications that the CIA filed a crimes report in connection with the article.[2288]

(TS// ███████████ //NF) In early 2007, the CIA cooperated with Ronald Kessler again on another book. According to CIA records, the purpose of the cooperation was to "push back" on Kessler's proposed accounts of intelligence related to the attacks of September 11, 2001, and the

---

[2282] Email from: ███████████; to: [REDACTED]; cc: ███████████, ███████████, ███████████, ███████████, ███████████, ███████████; subject: Re: Doug Jehl - Comprehensive Story on the Capture of Abu Zubaydah and Conception of EITs; date: December 15, 2005, at 8:50:36 PM.
[2283] Email from: Mark Mansfield; to: ███████████, ███████████; cc: ███████████, Paul J. Gimigliano, ███████████; subject: We Can't Let This Go Unanswered; date: September 7, 2006, at 01:12 PM.
[2284] Email from: Mark Mansfield; to: ███████████; cc: ███████████, [REDACTED], ███████████, ███████████, ███████████, ███████████; subject: Re: Immediate re Abu Zubaydah - Re: Fw: We Can't Let This Go Unanswered; date: September 7, 2006, at 3:14:53 PM.
[2285] "At a Secret Interrogation, Dispute Flared Over Tactics," *New York Times*, David Johnston, September 10, 2006.
[2286] *See* Abu Zubaydah detainee review in Volume III and sections on CIA claims related to the "Capture of Ramzi bin al-Shibh" in this summary and Volume II.
[2287] CY 2005 & CY 2006 CTC Media Leaks; September 21, 2006. The document described "the more serious CTC media leaks that occurred in CY 2005 and 2006."
[2288] Senior Deputy General Counsel John Rizzo urged that his colleagues determine whether OPA cooperated with the article "[b]efore we get DOJ or FBI too cranked up on this." *See* email from: John A. Rizzo; to: ███████████; cc: [REDACTED], ███████████, [REDACTED], [REDACTED], ███████████, [REDACTED], ███████████; subject: Re: Fw: Request for Crimes Reports on NYT and Time Magazine Leaks on Interrogation Activities [REDACTED]; date: September 12, 2006, at 5:52:10 PM.

interrogation of Abu Zubaydah,[2289] which a CIA officer noted "give undue credit to the FBI for CIA accomplishments."[2290] After another CIA officer drafted information for passage to Kessler,[2291] ██████████ CTC Legal, ██████████, wrote, "[o]f course being the lawyer, I would recommend not telling Kessler anything." ██████████ then wrote that if, "for policy reasons," the CIA decided to cooperate with the author, there was certain information that should not be disclosed. ██████████ then suggested that "if we are going to do this," the CIA could provide information to Kessler that would "undercut the FBI agents," who ██████████ stated had "leaked that they would have gotten everything anyway" from Abu Zubaydah. [2292]

(TS// ██████████ //NF) After Kessler provided a draft of his book to the CIA and met with CIA officers, the CIA's director of public affairs, Mark Mansfield, described what he viewed as the problems in Kessler's narrative. According to Mansfield, Kessler was "vastly overstating the FBI's role in thwarting terrorism and, frankly, giving other USG agencies—including CIA— short shrift." Moreover, "[t]he draft also didn't reflect the enormously valuable intelligence the USG gleaned from CIA's interrogation program" and "had unnamed FBI officers questioning our methods and claiming their own way of eliciting information is much more effective." According to Mansfield, the CIA "made some headway" in its meeting with Kessler and that, as a result of the CIA's intervention, his book would be "more balanced than it would have been."[2293]

(TS// ██████████ //NF) Later, in an email to Mansfield, Kessler provided the "substantive changes" he had made to his draft following his meeting with CIA officials. The changes included the statement that Abu Zubaydah was subjected to "coercive interrogation techniques" after he "stopped cooperating." Kessler's revised text further stated that "the CIA could point to a string of successes and dozens of plots that were rolled up because of coercive interrogation techniques." The statements in the revised text on the "successes" attributable to the CIA's enhanced interrogation techniques were similar to CIA representations to policymakers and were incongruent with CIA records.[2294]

[2289] Sametime communication between ██████████ and ██████████, 28/Feb/07 09:51:10 to 19:00:42.
[2290] Email from: ██████████; to: ██████████; cc: ██████████; subject: Fact Check on Ron Kessler draft; date: March 13, 2007, at 05:59 PM.
[2291] Email from: ██████████; to: ██████████; cc: ██████████, ██████████, ██████████, ██████████, ██████████; subject: Re: Fact Check on Ron Kessler draft; date: March 14, 2007, at 6:03:45 PM.
[2292] Email from: ██████████; to: ██████████; cc: ██████████, ██████████, ██████████, ██████████, ██████████; subject: Re: Fact Check on Ron Kessler draft; date: March 15, 2007, at 7:07:52 AM .
[2293] Email from: Mark Mansfield; to: Michael V. Hayden, ██████████, Stephen R. Kappes, Michael J. Morell, ██████████, Jose Rodriguez, ██████████; bcc: ██████████; subject: Session with Author Ron Kessler; date: March 15, 2007, at 6:54:33 PM.
[2294] Kessler's changes repeated the representation made in the president's September 6, 2006, speech, which was based on CIA information and vetted by the CIA, that Abu Zubaydah and Ramzi bin al-Shibh "provided information that would help in the planning and execution of the operation that captured Khalid Sheikh Mohammed." With regard to the Second Wave plotting, Kessler stated that "[i]f it had not been for coercive interrogation techniques used on Abu Zubaydah, CIA officials suggest, the second wave of attacks might have occurred and KSM could be free and planning more attacks." As detailed in this summary, and in greater detail in Volumes II and III, the thwarting of the Second Wave plotting and the capture of KSM were unrelated to reporting from Abu Zubaydah. Kessler's changes also included statements about the training and expertise of CIA interrogators, the Department of

(~~TS//~~ ██████ ~~//NF~~) Kessler's "substantive changes" made after his meeting with CIA officials included the statement that many members of Congress and members of the media "have made careers for themselves by belittling and undercutting the efforts of the heroic men and women who are trying to protect us." Kessler's revised text contended that, "[w]ithout winning the war being waged by the media against our own government, we are going to lose the war on terror because the tools that are needed will be taken away by a Congress swayed by a misinformed public and by other countries unwilling to cooperate with the CIA or FBI because they fear mindless exposure by the press." Finally, Kessler's changes, made after his meeting with CIA officers, included the statement that "[t]oo many Americans are intent on demonizing those who are trying to protect us."[2295]

Justice review of the CIA's interrogation techniques, and congressional oversight of the CIA's Detention and Interrogation Program. For example, Kessler wrote, "[b]efore confronting a terrorist, each interrogator was given 250 hours of specialized training." This statement is incongruent with the history of the CIA program. Email from: Ronald Kessler; to: Mark Mansfield; subject: follow-up; date: March 16, 2007, at 10:52:05.

[2295] Email from: Ronald Kessler; to: Mark Mansfield; subject: follow-up; date: March 16, 2007, at 10:52:05.

V. Review of CIA Representations to the Department of Justice

A. August 1, 2002, OLC Memorandum Relies on Inaccurate Information Regarding Abu Zubaydah

(TS// ███████████ //NF) The Office of Legal Counsel (OLC) in the Department of Justice wrote several legal memoranda and letters on the legality of the CIA's Detention and Interrogation Program between 2002 and 2007. The OLC requested, and relied on, information provided by the CIA to conduct the legal analysis included in these memoranda and letters. Much of the information the CIA provided to the OLC was inaccurate in material respects.

(TS// ███████████ //NF) On August 1, 2002, the OLC issued a memorandum advising that the use of the CIA's enhanced interrogation techniques against Abu Zubaydah would not violate prohibitions against torture found in Section 2340A of Title 18 of the United States Code.[2296] The techniques were: (1) attention grasp, (2) walling, (3) facial hold, (4) facial slap (insult slap), (5) cramped confinement, (6) wall standing, (7) stress positions, (8) sleep deprivation, (9) insects placed in a confinement box, and (10) the waterboard. The memorandum relied on CIA representations about Abu Zubaydah's status in al-Qa'ida, his role in al-Qa'ida plots, his expertise in interrogation resistance training, and his withholding of information on pending terrorist attacks.[2297] The OLC memorandum included the following statement about OLC's reliance on information provided by the CIA:

> "Our advice is based upon the following facts, which you have provided to us. We also understand that you do not have any facts in your possession contrary to the facts outlined here, and this opinion is limited to these facts. If these facts were to change, this advice would not necessarily apply."[2298]

[2296] Memorandum for John Rizzo, Acting General Counsel, Central Intelligence Agency, from Jay Bybee, Assistant Attorney General, Office of Legal Counsel, August 1, 2002, Interrogation of al Qaeda Operative (DTS #2009-1810, Tab 1). Also on August 1, 2002, OLC issued an unclassified, but non-public, opinion, from Deputy Assistant Attorney General John Yoo to White House Counsel Alberto Gonzales analyzing whether certain interrogation methods violate 18 U.S.C. §§ 2340-2340A.

[2297] Memorandum for John Rizzo, Acting General Counsel, Central Intelligence Agency, from Jay Bybee, Assistant Attorney General, Office of Legal Counsel, August 1, 2002, Interrogation of al Qaeda Operative (DTS #2009-1810, Tab 1).

[2298] Memorandum for John Rizzo, Acting General Counsel, Central Intelligence Agency, from Jay Bybee, Assistant Attorney General, Office of Legal Counsel, August 1, 2002, Interrogation of al Qaeda Operative (DTS #2009-1810, Tab 1). During a 2008 hearing of the Senate Select Committee on Intelligence, then-Acting Assistant Attorney General Steven Bradbury stressed that the OLC's opinions relied on factual representations made by the CIA. As Bradbury testified, "all of our advice addressing the CIA's specific interrogation methods has made clear that OLC's legal conclusions were contingent on a number of express conditions, limitations and safeguards adopted by the CIA and designed to ensure that the program would be administered by trained professionals with strict oversight and controls, and that none of the interrogation practices would go beyond the bounds of the law." When asked whether information could be elicited from detainees using techniques authorized by the Army Field Manual, Bradbury responded, "I will have to defer, because on those kinds of questions in terms of the effectiveness and the information obtained I have to rely on the professional judgment of the folks involved at the agency, and General [Michael] Hayden I think has spoken to this issue before this Committee." (*See* transcript of hearing of the Senate Select Committee on Intelligence, June 10, 2008 (DTS #2008-2698).) General Hayden's representations to the Committee are described elsewhere in this summary and in greater detail in Volume II.

(TS// ██████████ //NF) The facts provided by the CIA, and relied on by the OLC to support its legal analysis, were cited in the August 1, 2002, memorandum, and many were repeated in subsequent OLC memoranda on the CIA's enhanced interrogation techniques. Much of the information provided by the CIA to the OLC was unsupported by CIA records. Examples include:

- *Abu Zubaydah's Status in Al-Qa'ida:* The OLC memorandum repeated the CIA's representation that Abu Zubaydah was the "third or fourth man" in al-Qa'ida.[2299] This CIA assessment was based on single-source reporting that was recanted prior to the August 1, 2002, OLC legal memorandum. This retraction was provided to several senior CIA officers, including ███████ CTC Legal, to whom the information was emailed on July 10, 2002, three weeks prior to the issuance of the August 1, 2002, OLC memorandum.[2300] The CIA later concluded that Abu Zubaydah was not a member of al-Qa'ida.[2301]

- *Abu Zubaydah's Role in Al-Qa'ida Plots:* The OLC memorandum repeated the CIA's representation that Abu Zubaydah "has been involved in every major terrorist operation carried out by al Qaeda,"[2302] and that Abu Zubaydah "was one of the planners of the September 11 attacks."[2303] CIA records do not support these claims.

- *Abu Zubaydah's Expertise in Interrogation Resistance Training:* The OLC memorandum repeated the CIA's representation that Abu Zubaydah was "well-versed" in resistance to interrogation techniques, and that "it is believed Zubaydah wrote al Qaeda's manual on resistance techniques."[2304] A review of CIA records found no information to support these claims. To the contrary, Abu Zubaydah later stated that it was his belief that all

---

[2299] Memorandum for John Rizzo, Acting General Counsel, Central Intelligence Agency, from Jay Bybee, Assistant Attorney General, Office of Legal Counsel, August 1, 2002, Interrogation of al Qaeda Operative (DTS #2009-1810, Tab 1).

[2300] Email from: ████████████; to: ███████████ with multiple cc's; subject: AZ information; date: July 10, 2002, at 1:18:52 PM. This claim was included in subsequent OLC memoranda. *See* Memorandum for John A. Rizzo, Senior Deputy General Counsel, Central Intelligence Agency, from Steven G. Bradbury, Principal Deputy Assistant Attorney General, Office of Legal Counsel, May 30, 2005, Re: Application of United States Obligations Under Article 16 of the Convention Against Torture to Certain Techniques that May be Used in the Interrogation of High Value Al Qaeda Detainees (DTS #2009-1810, Tab 11).

[2301] CIA Intelligence Assessment, August 16, 2006, "Countering Misconceptions About Training Camps in Afghanistan, 1990-2001."

[2302] Memorandum for John Rizzo, Acting General Counsel, Central Intelligence Agency, from Jay Bybee, Assistant Attorney General, Office of Legal Counsel, August 1, 2002, Interrogation of al Qaeda Operative (DTS #2009-1810, Tab 1). This claim was included in subsequent OLC memoranda. *See* Memorandum for John A. Rizzo, Senior Deputy General Counsel, Central Intelligence Agency, from Steven G. Bradbury, Principal Deputy Assistant Attorney General, Office of Legal Counsel, May 30, 2005, Re: Application of United States Obligations Under Article 16 of the Convention Against Torture to Certain Techniques that May be Used in the Interrogation of High Value Al Qaeda Detainees (DTS #2009-1810, Tab 11).

[2303] Memorandum for John Rizzo, Acting General Counsel, Central Intelligence Agency, from Jay Bybee, Assistant Attorney General, Office of Legal Counsel, August 1, 2002, Interrogation of al Qaeda Operative (DTS #2009-1810, Tab 1).

[2304] Memorandum for John Rizzo, Acting General Counsel, Central Intelligence Agency, from Jay Bybee, Assistant Attorney General, Office of Legal Counsel, August 1, 2002, Interrogation of al Qaeda Operative (DTS #2009-1810, Tab 1).

individuals provide information in detention, and that captured individuals should "expect that the organization will make adjustments to protect people and plans when someone with knowledge is captured."[2305]

- *Abu Zubaydah's Withholding of Information on Pending Terrorist Attacks:* The OLC memorandum repeated CIA representations stating that "the interrogation team is certain" Abu Zubaydah was withholding information related to planned attacks against the United States, either within the U.S. homeland or abroad.[2306] CIA records do not support this claim. Abu Zubaydah's interrogation team was not "certain" that Abu Zubaydah was withholding "critical threat information." To the contrary, the interrogation team wrote to CIA Headquarters: "[o]ur assumption is the objective of this operation [the interrogation of Abu Zubaydah] is to achieve a high degree of confidence that [Abu Zubaydah] is not holding back actionable information concerning threats to the United States beyond that which [Abu Zubaydah] has already provided."[2307]

   B. The CIA Interprets the August 1, 2002, Memorandum to Apply to Other Detainees, Despite Language of the Memorandum; Interrogations of Abu Zubaydah and Other Detainees Diverge from the CIA's Representations to the OLC

(TS// ███████████ //NF) The CIA broadly interpreted the August 1, 2002, OLC memorandum to allow for greater operational latitude. For example, the memorandum stated that the legal advice was specific to the interrogation of Abu Zubaydah and the specific CIA representations about Abu Zubaydah; however, the CIA applied its enhanced interrogation techniques to numerous other CIA detainees without seeking additional formal legal advice from the OLC. As detailed elsewhere, the other detainees subjected to the CIA's enhanced interrogation techniques varied significantly in terms of their assessed role in terrorist activities and the information they were believed to possess. CIA records indicate that it was not until July 29, 2003, almost a year later, that the attorney general stated that the legal principles of the August 1, 2002, memorandum could be applied to other CIA detainees.[2308]

(TS// ███████████ //NF) The August 1, 2002, OLC memorandum also included an analysis of each of the CIA's proposed enhanced interrogation techniques with a description of how the

---

[2305] ████ 10496 (162014Z FEB 03)

[2306] Memorandum for John Rizzo, Acting General Counsel, Central Intelligence Agency, from Jay Bybee, Assistant Attorney General, Office of Legal Counsel, August 1, 2002, Interrogation of al Qaeda Operative (DTS #2009-1810, Tab 1).

[2307] [REDACTED] 73208 (231043Z JUL 02); email from: ███████████ ; to: [REDACTED], [REDACTED], ███████████ , subject: Addendum from [DETENTION SITE GREEN], [REDACTED] 73208 (231043Z JUL 02); July 23, 2004, at 07:56:49 PM. *See also* email from: [REDACTED]; to: [REDACTED]; subject: Re: [SWIGERT and DUNBAR]; date: August 8, 21, 2002, at 10:21 PM.

[2308] Letter from Assistant Attorney General Jack L. Goldsmith III to Director Tenet, June 18, 2004 (DTS #2004-2710). In an August 2003 interview with the OIG, ████ CTC Legal, ███████████ , stated that "every detainee interrogated is different in that they are outside the opinion because the opinion was written for Zubaydah." The context for ███████████ 's statement was the legality of the waterboarding of KSM. *See* interview of ████ ███████████ , by [REDACTED], [REDACTED], and [REDACTED], Office of the Inspector General, August 20, 2003.

CIA stated the techniques would be applied.[2309] However, in the interrogations of Abu Zubaydah and subsequent CIA detainees, the CIA applied the techniques in a manner that a Department of Justice attorney concluded "was quite different from the [description] presented in 2002."[2310] As reported by the CIA's inspector general, the CIA used the waterboarding technique against Abu Zubaydah, and later against KSM, in a manner inconsistent with CIA representations to the OLC, as well as the OLC's description of the technique in the August 1, 2002, memorandum. In addition, the CIA assured the OLC that it would be "unlikely" that CIA detainees subjected to sleep deprivation would experience hallucinations, and that if they did, medical personnel would intervene.[2311] However, multiple CIA detainees subjected to prolonged sleep deprivation experienced hallucinations, and CIA interrogation teams did not always discontinue sleep deprivation after the detainees had experienced hallucinations.[2312] The CIA further represented to the OLC that Abu Zubaydah's recovery from his wound would not be impeded by the use of the CIA's enhanced interrogation techniques.[2313] However, prior to the OLC memorandum, DETENTION SITE GREEN personnel stated, and CIA Headquarters had confirmed, that the interrogation process would take precedence over preventing Abu Zubaydah's wound from becoming infected.[2314] Other CIA detainees were also subjected to the CIA's enhanced interrogation techniques, notwithstanding concerns that the interrogation techniques could exacerbate their injuries.[2315] The CIA also repeatedly used interrogation techniques beyond those provided to the OLC for review, including water dousing, nudity, abdominal slaps, and dietary manipulation.[2316]

(TS// ████████ //NF) At the July 29, 2003, meeting of select National Security Council principals, Attorney General John Ashcroft expressed the view that "while appropriate caution should be exercised in the number of times the waterboard was administered, the repetitions

---

[2309] Memorandum for John Rizzo, Acting General Counsel, Central Intelligence Agency, from Jay Bybee, Assistant Attorney General, Office of Legal Counsel, August 1, 2002, Interrogation of al Qaeda Operative (DTS #2009-1810, Tab 1).

[2310] Department of Justice Office of Professional Responsibility; Report, Investigation into the Office of Legal Counsel's Memoranda Concerning Issues Relating to the Central Intelligence Agency's Use of 'Enhanced Interrogation Techniques' on Suspected Terrorists, July 29, 2009, pp. 140-41 (DTS #2010-1058).

[2311] Memorandum for John Rizzo, Acting General Counsel, Central Intelligence Agency, from Jay Bybee, Assistant Attorney General, Office of Legal Counsel, August 1, 2002, Interrogation of al Qaeda Operative (DTS #2009-1810, Tab 1).

[2312] ████████ 1396 ████████; ████ 1299 (████ JAN 04); ████████ 1308 (████ JAN 04); ████ 1312 (████ JAN 04); ████ 1530 (████ 04)

[2313] Memorandum for John Rizzo, Acting General Counsel, Central Intelligence Agency, from Jay Bybee, Assistant Attorney General, Office of Legal Counsel, August 1, 2002, Interrogation of al Qaeda Operative (DTS #2009-1810, Tab 1).

[2314] ████████ 10536 (151006Z JUL 02); ALEC ████ (182321Z JUL 02). After the use of the CIA's enhanced interrogation techniques on Abu Zubaydah, ████████ reported that "[d]uring the most aggressive portions of [Abu Zubaydah's] interrogation, the combination of a lack of hygiene, sub-optimal nutrition, inadvertent trauma to the wound secondary to some of the stress positions utilized at that stage and the removal of formal, obvious medical care to further isolate the subject had an overall additive effect on the deterioration of the wound." See ████████ 10679 (250932Z AUG 02).

[2315] See Volume III, including detainee reviews of Abu Hazim and Abd al-Karim.

[2316] As described later, the CIA sought OLC approval for these techniques on July 30, 2004, almost two years after the August 1, 2002, memorandum. See letter from ████████ CTC Legal ████████ to Acting Assistant Attorney General Levin, July 30, 2004 (DTS #2009-1809).

described do not contravene the principles underlying DOJ's August 2002 opinion."[2317] Records do not indicate that the attorney general opined on the manner (as opposed to the frequency) with which the waterboard was implemented, or on interrogation techniques not included in the August 2002 opinion. The differences between the CIA's enhanced interrogation techniques, as described by the CIA to the OLC in 2002, and the actual use of the techniques as described in the CIA Inspector General May 2004 Special Review, prompted concerns at the Department of Justice. On May 27, 2004, Assistant Attorney General Jack Goldsmith sent a letter to the CIA general counsel stating that the Special Review "raises the possibility that, at least in some instances and particularly early in the program, the actual practice may not have been congruent with all of these assumptions and limitations." In particular, Goldsmith's letter highlighted the statement in the Special Review that the use of the waterboard in SERE training was "so different from subsequent Agency usage as to make it almost irrelevant."[2318]

    C. Following Suspension of the Use of the CIA's Enhanced Interrogation Techniques, the CIA Obtains Approval from the OLC for the Interrogation of Three Individual Detainees

(TS// ███████████ //NF) The May 2004 CIA Inspector General Special Review recommended that the CIA's general counsel submit in writing a request for the Department of Justice to provide the CIA with a "formal, written legal opinion, revalidating and modifying, as appropriate, the guidance provided" in the August 1, 2002, memorandum. It also recommended that, in the absence of such a written opinion, the DCI should direct that the CIA's enhanced interrogation techniques "be implemented only within the parameters that were mutually understood by the Agency and DoJ on 1 August 2002."[2319] After receiving the Special Review, Assistant Attorney General Jack Goldsmith informed the CIA that the OLC had never formally opined on whether the CIA's enhanced interrogation techniques would meet constitutional standards.[2320] On May 24, 2004, DCI Tenet, Deputy Director John McLaughlin, General Counsel Scott Muller, and others met to discuss the Department of Justice's comments, after which DCI Tenet directed that the use of the CIA's enhanced interrogation techniques, as well as the use of the CIA's "standard" techniques, be suspended.[2321] On June 4, 2004, DCI Tenet

---

[2317] Letter from Assistant Attorney General Jack L. Goldsmith, III to Director George Tenet, June 18, 2004 (DTS #2004-2710). As described above, the CIA's presentation to the NSC principals undercounted the frequency with which KSM and Abu Zubaydah were subjected to the waterboard.

[2318] Letter from Assistant Attorney General Goldsmith to CIA General Counsel Scott Muller, May 27, 2004.

[2319] CIA Office of Inspector General, Special Review – Counterterrorism Detention and Interrogation Program, (2003-7123-IG), May 2004.

[2320] May 25, 2004, Talking Points for DCI Telephone Conversation with Attorney General: DOJ's Legal Opinion Re: CIA's Counterterrorist Program (CT) Interrogation. This position was confirmed in a June 10, 2004, letter (Letter from Assistant Attorney General Jack L. Goldsmith III, to Scott Muller, General Counsel, Central Intelligence Agency, June 10, 2004).

[2321] May 24, 2004, Memorandum for the Record from ███████████, ████ Legal Group, DCI Counterterrorism Center, Subject: Memorandum of Meeting with the DCI Regarding DOJ's Statement that DOJ has Rendered No Legal Opinion on Whether the CIA's Use of Enhanced Interrogation Techniques would meet Constitutional Standards; email from: ██████████, C/RDG; to: [REDACTED]; cc: Jose Rodriguez, [REDACTED], █████ ████, [REDACTED], [REDACTED], ███████████; subject: Interim Guidance for Standard and Enhanced Interrogations; date: May 25, 2004.

issued a formal memorandum suspending the use of the techniques, pending policy and legal review.[2322]

(TS// ███████████ //NF) As described in this summary, on July 2, 2004, Attorney General Ashcroft and Deputy Attorney General James Comey attended a meeting of select National Security Council principals, the topic of which was the proposed CIA interrogation of Janat Gul.[2323] According to CIA records, the attorney general stated that the use of the CIA's enhanced interrogation techniques against Gul would be consistent with U.S. law and treaty obligations, although Ashcroft made an exception for the waterboard, which he stated required further review, "primarily because of the view that the technique had been employed in a different fashion than that which DOJ initially approved."[2324] On July 20, 2004, Ashcroft, along with Patrick Philbin and Daniel Levin from the Department of Justice, attended a National Security Council Principals Committee meeting at which Ashcroft stated that the use of the CIA's enhanced interrogation techniques described in the August 1, 2002, OLC memorandum, with the exception of the waterboard, would not violate U.S. statutes, the U.S. Constitution, or U.S. treaty obligations. The attorney general was then "directed" to prepare a written opinion addressing the constitutional issues, and the CIA was directed to provide further information to the Department of Justice with regard to the waterboard.[2325] On July 22, 2004, Attorney General Ashcroft sent a letter to Acting DCI John McLaughlin stating that nine interrogation techniques (those addressed in the August 1, 2002, memorandum, with the exception of the waterboard) did not violate the U.S. Constitution or any statute or U.S. treaty obligations, in the context of the CIA interrogation of Janat Gul.[2326]

(TS// ███████████ //NF) On July 30, 2004, anticipating the interrogation of Janat Gul, the CIA provided the OLC for the first time a description of dietary manipulation, nudity, water dousing, the abdominal slap, standing sleep deprivation, and the use of diapers, all of which the CIA described as a "supplement" to the interrogation techniques outlined in the August 1, 2002, memorandum.[2327] The CIA's descriptions of the interrogation techniques were incongruent with how the CIA had applied the techniques in practice. The CIA description of a minimum caloric intake was incongruent with the history of the program, as no minimum caloric intake existed prior to May 2004 and the March 2003 draft OMS guidelines allowed for food to be withheld for

---

[2322] June 4, 2004, Memorandum for Deputy Director for Operations from Director of Central Intelligence Re: Suspension of Use of Interrogation Techniques. On June 2, 2004, George Tenet informed the President that he intended to resign from his position on July 11, 2004. The White House announced the resignation on June 3, 2004.
[2323] Janat Gul's interrogation is detailed in Volume III and more briefly in this summary.
[2324] Letter from Assistant Attorney General Ashcroft to General Counsel Muller, July 7, 2004 (DTS #2009-1810, Tab 3); July 2, 2004, CIA Memorandum re Meeting with National Security Advisor Rice in the White House Situation Room, Friday 2 July Re: Interrogations and Detainee Janat Gul; July 6, 2004, Memorandum from Condoleezza Rice, Assistant to the President for National Security Affairs, to George Tenet, Director of Central Intelligence, Re: Janat Gul.
[2325] July 29, 2004, Memorandum for the Record from CIA General Counsel Scott Muller Re: Principals Meeting relating to Janat Gul on 20 July 2004.
[2326] The one-paragraph letter did not provide legal analysis or substantive discussion of the interrogation techniques. (See letter from Attorney General John Ashcroft to Acting DCI John McLaughlin, July 22, 2004 (DTS #2009-1810, Tab 4).)
[2327] Letter from ███████ CTC Legal ███████████ to Acting Assistant Attorney General Daniel Levin, July 30, 2004 (DTS #2009-1809).

one to two days.[2328] The CIA represented to the OLC that nude detainees were "not wantonly exposed to other detainees or detention facility staff," even though nude detainees at the CIA's DETENTION SITE COBALT were "kept in a central area outside the interrogation room" and were "walked around" by guards as a form of humiliation.[2329] The CIA's description of water dousing made no mention of cold water immersion, which was used on CIA detainees and taught in CIA interrogator training.[2330] The CIA representation describing a two-hour limit for the shackling of detainees' hands above their heads is incongruent with records of CIA detainees whose hands were shackled above their heads for extended periods, as well as the draft March 2003 OMS guidelines permitting such shackling for up to four hours.[2331] The CIA further represented to the OLC that the use of diapers was "for sanitation and hygiene purposes," whereas CIA records indicate that in some cases, a central "purpose" of diapers was "[t]o cause humiliation" and "to induce a sense of helplessness."[2332]

(TS// ██████████ //NF) On August 13, 2004, CIA attorneys, medical officers, and other personnel met with Department of Justice attorneys to discuss some of the techniques for which the CIA was seeking approval, in particular sleep deprivation, water dousing, and the waterboard. When asked about the possibility that detainees subjected to standing sleep deprivation could suffer from edema, OMS doctors informed the Department of Justice attorneys that it was not a problem as the CIA would "adjust shackles or [the] method of applying the technique as necessary to prevent edema, as well as any chafing or over-tightness from the shackles." With regard to water dousing, CIA officers represented that "water is at normal temperature; CIA makes no effort to 'cool' the water before applying it." With respect to the waterboard, CIA officers indicated that "each application could not last more than 40 seconds

---

[2328] OMS GUIDELINES ON MEDICAL AND PSYCHOLOGICAL SUPPORT TO DETAINEE RENDITION, INTERROGATION, AND DETENTION, May 17, 2004, OMS Guidelines on Medical and Psychological Support to Detainee Interrogations, First Draft, March 7, 2003. The evolution of OMS Guidelines is described in Volume III of the Committee Study.

[2329] Interview Report, 2003-7123-IG, Review of Interrogations for Counterterrorism Purposes, ██████████, April 14, 2003.

[2330] Email from: [REDACTED] (██████████████); to: ██████████; subject: Memo; date: March 15, 2004. See detainee reviews of Abu Hudhaifa and Muhammad Umar 'Abd al-Rahman aka Asadallah.

[2331] OMS Guidelines on Medical and Psychological Support to Detainee Interrogations, "First Draft," March 7, 2003; ██████████ 28246 ██████████; Interview Report, 2003-7123-IG, Review of Interrogations for Counterterrorism Purposes, ██████, April 5, 2003; Interview Report, 2003-7123-IG, Review of Interrogations for Counterterrorism Purposes, ██████, April 30, 2003; Memorandum for [REDACTED] from [REDACTED] ██████████, November █, 2002, Subject: Legal Analysis of [REDACTED] Personnel Participating in Interrogation at the CIA Detention Facility in ██████████████ "[DETENTION SITE COBALT]"). For example, Ridha al-Najjar was reported to have undergone "hanging," described as "handcuffing one or both of his wrists to an overhead horizontal bar" for 22 hours each day for two consecutive days. See Memorandum for [REDACTED], November █, 2002, Subject: Legal Analysis of [REDACTED] Personnel Participating in Interrogation at the CIA Detention Facility in ██████████ ██████ (aka "[DETENTION SITE COBALT]". See also ██████ 10171 (101527Z JAN 03), indicating that Abd al-Rahim al-Nashiri "remained in the standing position, with hands tied overhead, overnight."

[2332] ██████████ interview of ██████████ [CIA OFFICER 1], December 19, 2002; CIA Interrogation Program Draft Course Materials, March 11, 2003, pg. 28; CTC/RDG Interrogation Program, December 15, 2003, pg. 10. DIRECTOR ██████ (251609Z JUL 02). See also "Standard Interrogation Techniques," attachment to email from: ██████████; to: Scott W. Muller, John Rizzo, [REDACTED], ██████████; subject: revised interrogation discussion; date: July 19, 2004.

(and usually only lasted about 20 seconds)."[2333] As detailed in the full Committee Study, each of these representations was incongruent with the operational history of the CIA program.

(TS// ███████████ //NF) On August 25, 2004, the CIA's Associate General Counsel ███████ sent a letter to the OLC stating that Janat Gul, who had been rendered to CIA custody on July ██, 2004, had been subjected to the attention grasp, walling, facial hold, facial slap, wall standing, stress positions, and sleep deprivation. The letter further stated that CIA interrogators "assess Gul not to be cooperating, and to be using a sophisticated counterinterrogation strategy," and that the further use of the same enhanced interrogation techniques would be "unlikely to move Gul to cooperate absent concurrent use" of dietary manipulation, nudity, water dousing, and the abdominal slap. The letter referenced the reporting from a CIA source,[2334] stating: "CIA understands that before his capture, Gul had been working to facilitate a direct meeting between the ████ CIA ████ source reporting on the pre-election threat and Abu Faraj [al-Libi] himself."[2335]

(TS// ███████████ //NF) The following day, August 26, 2004, Acting Assistant Attorney General Daniel Levin informed CIA Acting General Counsel John Rizzo that the use of the four additional interrogation techniques did not violate any U.S. statutes, the U.S. Constitution, or U.S. treaty obligations. Levin's advice relied on the CIA's representations about Gul, including that "there are no medical and psychological contraindications to the use of these techniques as you plan to employ them on Gul."[2336] At the time, CIA records indicated: (1) that standing sleep deprivation had already caused significant swelling in Gul's legs; (2) that standing sleep deprivation continued despite Gul's visual and auditory hallucinations and that Gul was "not oriented to time or place";[2337] (3) that CIA interrogators on-site did not believe that "escalation to enhanced pressures will increase [Gul's] ability to produce timely accurate locational and threat

---

[2333] August 11, 2004, Letter from [REDACTED], Assistant General Counsel, to Dan Levin, Acting Assistant Attorney General, Office of Legal Counsel; August 27, 2004, Memorandum for the Record from [REDACTED] Re: Meeting with Department of Justice Attorneys on 13 August, 2004, Regarding Specific Interrogation Techniques, Including the Waterboard.

[2334] As described in this summary, and in more detail in the Committee Study, the source later admitted to fabricating information related to the "pre-election" threat.

[2335] Letter from ███████████, Associate General Counsel, CIA, to Dan Levin, Acting Assistant Attorney General, August 25, 2004 (DTS #2009-1809). For Gul's rendition, see ████████ 1512 (████████ 04). According to an August 16, 2004, cable, a CIA interrogator did "not believe that escalation to enhanced measures will increase [Gul's] ability to produce timely accurate locational and threat information." (See ████████ 1567 ███████████ 04).) On August 19, 2004, a cable from DETENTION SITE BLACK noted that the interrogation team "does not believe [Gul] is withholding imminent threat information." See ████████ 1574 (████████ 04).

[2336] Letter to John Rizzo, Acting General Counsel, CIA; from Daniel Levin, Acting Assistant Attorney General, August 26, 2004 (DTS #2009-1810, Tab 6). In May 2005, the OLC again accepted the CIA's representations that a psychological assessment found that Gul was "alert and oriented and his concentration and attention were appropriate," that Gul's "thought processes were clear and logical; there was no evidence of a thought disorder, delusions, or hallucinations," and that there "were not significant signs of depression anxiety or other mental disturbance." See memorandum for John A. Rizzo, Senior Deputy General Counsel, Central Intelligence Agency, from Steven G. Bradbury, Principal Deputy Assistant Attorney General, Office of Legal Counsel, May 10, 2005, Re: Application of 18 U.S.C. Sections 2340-2340A to Certain Techniques That May be Used in the Interrogation of a High Value al Qaeda Detainee (DTS #2009-1810, Tab 9).

[2337] ████████ 1530 (081633Z AUG 04); ████████ 1541 (101228Z AUG 04)

information";[2338] and (4) that CIA interrogators did not believe that Gul was "withholding imminent threat information."[2339]

(~~TS//~~ ██████████ ~~//NF~~) Levin's August 26, 2004, letter to Rizzo was based on the premise that "[w]e understand that [Janat] Gul is a high-value al Qaeda operative who is believed to possess information concerning an imminent terrorist threat to the United States."[2340] Levin's understanding was based on the CIA's representation that "Gul had been working to facilitate a direct meeting between the ██████ CIA ██████ source reporting on the pre-election threat and Abu Faraj [al-Libi]."[2341] This information later proved to be inaccurate. As detailed elsewhere in this summary, the threat of a terrorist attack to precede the November 2004 U.S. election was found to be based on a CIA source whose information was questioned by senior CTC officials at the time.[2342] The same CIA source admitted to fabricating the information after a ██████ in ██ October 2004.[2343] In November 2004, after the use of the CIA's enhanced interrogation techniques on Janat Gul, CIA's chief of Base at DETENTION SITE BLACK, where Janat Gul was interrogated, wrote that "describing [Gul] as 'highest ranking' gives him a stature which is undeserved, overblown and misleading." The chief of Base added that "[s]tating that [Gul] had 'long standing access to senior leaders in al-Qa'ida' is simply wrong."[2344] In December 2004, CIA officers concluded that Janat Gul was "not the link to senior AQ leaders that [CIA Headquarters] said he was/is,"[2345] and in April 2005 CIA officers wrote that "[t]here simply is no 'smoking gun' that we can refer to that would justify our continued holding of [Janat Gul]."[2346]

(~~TS//~~ ██████████ ~~//NF~~) By April 2005, as the OLC neared completion of a new memorandum analyzing the legality of the CIA's enhanced interrogation techniques, the OLC sought information from the CIA on "what [the CIA] got from Janat Gul, was it valuable, [and] did it help anything...." The CIA did not immediately respond to this request, and the CIA's Associate General Counsel ██████████ noted that DOJ personnel had "taken to calling [him] daily" for additional information.[2347] Subsequently, on April 15, 2005, the CIA informed

---

[2338] ██████ 1567 (161730Z AUG 04)
[2339] ██████ 1574 (191346Z AUG 04)
[2340] Letter to John Rizzo, Acting General Counsel, CIA; from Daniel Levin, Acting Assistant Attorney General, August 26, 2004 (DTS #2009-1810, Tab 6).
[2341] Letter from ██████████, Associate General Counsel, CIA, to Dan Levin, Acting Assistant Attorney General, August 25, 2004 (DTS #2009-1809).
[2342] Email from: ██████; to: ██████, ██████, [REDACTED], ██████, ██████; subject: could AQ be testing [ASSET Y] and [Source Name REDACTED]?; date: March ██, 2004, at 06:55 AM; email from: ██████; to ██████; cc: ██████, ██████, [REDACTED], ██████; subject: Re: could AQ be testing [ASSET Y] and [Source Name REDACTED]?; date: March ██, 2004, at 7:52:32 AM. The fabricated source reporting is described elsewhere in this summary.
[2343] ██████ 1411 (██████ 04)
[2344] Email from: [REDACTED]; to: ██████, ██████, ██████; subject: re ALEC ██████; November 10, 2004.
[2345] CIA "Comments on Detainees," December 19, 2004, Notes from a CD from [DETENTION SITE BLACK].
[2346] Email from: [REDACTED] (COB DETENTION SITE BLACK); to: ██████; cc: ██████, ██████; subject: re ██████; date: April 30, 2005.
[2347] Email from: ██████; to: ██████, ██████, ██████, and [REDACTED]; subject: questions from OLC for Art 16 opinion; date: April 12, 2005; email from: ██████;

the OLC that "during most of Gul's debriefings, he has sought to minimize his knowledge of extremist activities and has provided largely non-incriminating information about his involvement in their networks."[2348] On May 10, 2005, the OLC issued a memorandum that stated, "[y]ou informed us that the CIA believed Gul had information about al Qaeda's plans to launch an attack within the United States… [o]ur conclusions depend on these assessments." The OLC referenced ██████'s August 25, 2004, letter on Gul and the pre-election threat.[2349] In a May 30, 2005, memorandum, the OLC referred to Janat Gul as "representative of the high value detainees on whom enhanced techniques have been, or might be used," and wrote that "the CIA believed [that Janat Gul] had actionable intelligence concerning the pre-election threat to the United States."[2350] In the same memorandum, the OLC conveyed a new CIA representation describing the effectiveness of the CIA's enhanced interrogation techniques on Janat Gul, which stated:

> "Gul has provided information that has helped the CIA with validating one of its key assets reporting on the pre-election threat."[2351]

(TS// ███████████████ //NF) There are no indications in the memorandum that the CIA informed the OLC that it had concluded that Gul had no information about the pre-election threat, which was the basis on which the OLC had approved the use of the CIA's enhanced interrogation techniques against Gul in the first place, or that CIA officers had determined that Gul was "not the man we thought he was." In September 2004, the OLC advised the CIA that the use of the CIA's enhanced interrogation techniques against Ahmed Khalfan Ghailani and Sharif al-Masri was also legal, based on the CIA representations that the two detainees were al-Qa'ida operatives involved in the "operational planning" of the pre-election plot against the United States.[2352] This CIA assessment was based on the same fabrications from the same CIA

---

to: ███████████, ███████, ███████████, ███████████, and [REDACTED]; subject: Re: questions from OLC for Art 16 opinion; date: April 14, 2005.

[2348] April 15, 2005, fax to DOJ Command Center, for ███████████, Office of Legal Counsel, U.S. Department of Justice, from ███████, ██████ Legal Group, DCI Counterterrorist Center, re: Janat Gul.

[2349] Memorandum for John A. Rizzo, Senior Deputy General Counsel, Central Intelligence Agency, from Steven G. Bradbury, Principal Deputy Assistant Attorney General, Office of Legal Counsel, May 10, 2005, Re: Application of 18 U.S.C. Sections 2340-2340A to Certain Techniques That May be Used in the Interrogation of a High Value al Qaeda Detainee.

[2350] Memorandum for John A. Rizzo, Senior Deputy General Counsel, Central Intelligence Agency, from Steven G. Bradbury, Principal Deputy Assistant Attorney General, Office of Legal Counsel, May 30, 2005, Re: Application of United States Obligations Under Article 16 of the Convention Against Torture to Certain Techniques that May be Used in the Interrogation of High Value Al Qaeda Detainees (DTS #2009-1810, Tab 11).

[2351] Memorandum for John A. Rizzo, Senior Deputy General Counsel, Central Intelligence Agency, from Steven G. Bradbury, Principal Deputy Assistant Attorney General, Office of Legal Counsel, May 30, 2005, Re: Application of United States Obligations Under Article 16 of the Convention Against Torture to Certain Techniques that May be Used in the Interrogation of High Value Al Qaeda Detainees (DTS #2009-1810, Tab 11), citing *Janat Gul Memo* pp. 1-2. *See* April 15, 2005, fax to DOJ Command Center, for ███████████, Office of Legal Counsel, U.S. Department of Justice, from ███████████, ██████ Legal Group, DCI Counterterrorist Center, re: Janat Gul.

[2352] Letter to John A. Rizzo, Acting General Counsel, CIA; from Daniel Levin, September 6, 2004 (DTS #2009-1810, Tab 7); Letter to John A. Rizzo, Acting General Counsel, CIA; from Daniel Levin, September 20, 2004 (DTS #2009-1810, Tab 8).

source.[2353] Like Janat Gul, Ghailani and al-Masri were subjected to extended sleep deprivation and experienced hallucinations.[2354]

    D. May 2005 OLC Memoranda Rely on Inaccurate Representations from the CIA Regarding the Interrogation Process, the CIA's Enhanced Interrogation Techniques, and the Effectiveness of the Techniques

(TS// ██████████ //NF) On May 4, 2005, Acting Assistant Attorney General Steven Bradbury faxed to CIA Associate General Counsel ██████████ a set of questions related to the CIA's enhanced interrogation techniques, in which Bradbury referenced medical journal articles. The following day, ██████ sent a letter to Bradbury stating that the CIA's responses had been composed by the CIA's Office of Medical Services (OMS). The CIA response stated that any lowering of the threshold of pain caused by sleep deprivation was "not germane" to the program, because studies had only identified differences in sensitivity to heat, cold, and pressure, and the CIA's enhanced interrogation techniques "do not involve application of heat, cold, pressure, any sharp objects (or indeed any objects at all)."[2355] With regard to the effect of sleep deprivation on the experience of water dousing, the CIA response stated that "at the temperatures of water we have recommended for the program the likelihood of induction of pain by water dousing is very low under any circumstances, and not a phenomenon we have seen in detainees subject to this technique."[2356] In response to Bradbury's query as to when edema or shackling would become painful as a result of standing sleep deprivation, the CIA responded, "[w]e have not observed this phenomenon in the interrogations performed to date, and have no reason to believe on theoretical grounds that edema or shackling would be more painful," provided the shackles are maintained with "appropriate slack" and "interrogators follow medical officers' recommendation to end standing sleep deprivation and use an alternate technique when the medical officer judges that edema is significant in any way." The CIA response added that the medical officers' recommendations "are always followed," and that "[d]etainees have not complained about pain from edema." Much of this information was inaccurate.[2357]

[2353] ██████ 1411 (████████ 04)

[2354] [REDACTED] 3221 ███████████ ; [REDACTED] 3242 (██████ 04)

[2355] Letter from ██████, Associate General Counsel, CIA, to Steve Bradbury, Acting Assistant Attorney General, Office of Legal Counsel, May 4, 2005. Multiple interrogation plans for CIA detainees called for "uncomfortably" cool temperatures along with sleep deprivation. See ██████ 10361 ██████ ; ██████████ 1758 ██████ ; ██████ 10654 (030904Z MAR 03).

[2356] Letter from ██████, Associate General Counsel, CIA, to Steve Bradbury, Acting Assistant Attorney General, Office of Legal Counsel, May 4, 2005. The CIA had subjected detainees to cold water baths during periods of sleep deprivation. As a CIA psychologist noted, "I heard [Abu Hudhaifa] gasp out loud several times as he was placed in the tub." (See email from: [REDACTED]; to: [REDACTED]; subject: Memo; date: March 15, 2004.) The inspector general later reported that, as a result of being bathed in ice water, Abu Hudhaifa was "shivering" and interrogators were concerned about his body temperature dropping (2005-8085-IG, at 12). See also ██████ ██████ 42025 ██████ .

[2357] Letter from ██████, Associate General Counsel, CIA, to Steve Bradbury, Acting Assistant Attorney General, Office of Legal Counsel, May 4, 2005. Numerous detainees subjected to standing sleep deprivation suffered from edema. (See ██████████ 34098 ██████ ; ██████ (12502 (011309Z AUG 03); ██████████ 40847 (251619Z JUN 03); ██████ 1246 (171946Z AUG 03); ██████ 10492 (161529Z FEB 03); ██████ 10429 (101215Z FEB 03); ██████ 10909 (201918Z MAR 03); ██████ 42206 (191513Z JUL 03).) Detainees sometimes complained of pain and swelling

(TS// ███████ //NF) Bradbury further inquired whether it was "possible to tell reliably (e.g. from outward physical signs like grimaces) whether a detainee is experiencing severe pain." The CIA responded that "all pain is subjective, not objective,"[2358] adding:

> "Medical officers can monitor for evidence of condition or injury that most people would consider painful, and can observe the individual for outward displays and expressions associated with the experience of pain. Medical officer [sic] can and do ask the subject, after the interrogation session has concluded, if he is in pain, and have and do provide analgesics, such as Tylenol and Aleve, to detainees who report headache and other discomforts during their interrogations. We reiterate, that an interrogation session would be stopped if, in the judgment of the interrogators or medical personnel, medical attention was required."[2359]

(TS// ███████ //NF) As described elsewhere, multiple CIA detainees were subjected to the CIA's enhanced interrogation techniques despite their medical conditions.[2360]

(TS// ███████ //NF) Bradbury's fax also inquired whether monitoring and safeguards "will effectively avoid severe physical pain or suffering for detainees," which was a formulation of the statutory definition of torture under consideration. Despite concerns from OMS that its assessments could be used to support a legal review of the CIA's enhanced interrogation techniques,[2361] the CIA's response stated:

---

in their lower extremities. (*See*, for example, ███████ 2615 (201528Z AUG 07); ███████ 2619 (211349Z AUG 07); ███████ 2620 (221303Z AUG 07); ███████ 2623 (231234Z AUG 07); ███████ 2629 (251637Z AUG 07); ███████ 2642 (271341Z AUG 07); ███████ 2643 (271856Z AUG 07).) As noted, standing sleep deprivation was not always discontinued with the onset of edema.

[2358] Letter from ███████, Associate General Counsel, CIA, to Steve Bradbury, Acting Assistant Attorney General, Office of Legal Counsel, May 4, 2005.

[2359] Letter from ███████, Associate General Counsel, CIA, to Steve Bradbury, Acting Assistant Attorney General, Office of Legal Counsel, May 4, 2005.

[2360] *See*, for example, ███████ 10536 (151006Z JULY 02); ALEC ███████ (182321Z JUL 02); ███████ 10647 (201331Z AUG 02); ███████ 10618 (121448Z AUG 02); ███████ 10679 (250932Z AUG 02); DIRECTOR ███████ MAY 03); ███████ 37754 ███████; 38161 (131326Z MAY 03); DIRECTOR ███████ MAY 03); DIRECTOR ███████ MAY 03); ███████ 34098 ███████; ███████ 34294 ███████; ███████ 34310 ███████. *See also* detainee reports and reviews in Volume III.

[2361] On April 11, 2005, after reviewing a draft OLC opinion, OMS personnel wrote a memorandum for ███████ that stated, "[s]imply put, OMS is not in the business of saying what is acceptable in causing discomfort to other human beings, and will not take on that burden.... OMS did not review or vet these techniques prior to their introduction, but rather came into this program with the understanding of your office and DOJ that they were already determined as legal, permitted and safe. We see this current iteration [of the OLC memorandum] as a reversal of that sequence, and a relocation of those decisions to OMS. If this is the case, that OMS has now the responsibility for determining a procedure's legality through its determination of safety, then we will need to review all procedures in that light given this new responsibility." *See* email from: ███████; to ███████; cc: [REDACTED], ███████, ███████, ███████, ███████, ███████; subject: 8 April Draft Opinion from DOJ – OMS Concerns; date: April 11, 2005, at 10:12 AM.

"[i]t is OMS's view that based on our limited experience and the extensive experience of the military with these techniques, the program in place has effectively avoided severe physical pain and suffering, and should continue to do so. Application of the thirteen techniques[2362] has not to date resulted in any severe or permanent physical injury (or any injury other than transient bruising), and we do not expect this to change."[2363]

(TS// ████████████ //NF) In May 2005, Principal Deputy Assistant Attorney General Steven Bradbury signed three memoranda that relied on information provided by the CIA that was inconsistent with CIA's operational records. On May 10, 2005, Bradbury signed two memoranda analyzing the statutory prohibition on torture with regard to the CIA's enhanced interrogation techniques and to the use of the interrogation techniques in combination.[2364] On May 30, 2005, Bradbury signed another memorandum examining U.S. obligations under the Convention Against Torture.[2365] The memoranda approved 13 techniques: (1) dietary manipulation, (2) nudity, (3) attention grasp, (4) walling, (5) facial hold, (6) facial slap or insult slap, (7) abdominal slap, (8) cramped confinement, (9) wall standing, (10) stress positions, (11) water dousing, (12) sleep deprivation (more than 48 hours), and (13) the waterboard. The three memoranda relied on numerous CIA representations that, as detailed elsewhere, were incongruent with CIA records, including: (1) the CIA's enhanced interrogation techniques would be used only when the interrogation team "considers them necessary because a detainee is withholding important, actionable intelligence or there is insufficient time to try other techniques," (2) the use of the techniques "is discontinued if the detainee is judged to be consistently providing accurate intelligence or if he is no longer believed to have actionable intelligence," (3) the "use of the techniques usually ends after just a few days when the detainee begins participating," (4) the interrogation techniques "would not be used on a detainee not reasonably thought to possess important, actionable intelligence that could not be obtained otherwise," and (5) the interrogation process begins with "an open, non-threatening approach" to discern if the CIA detainee would be cooperative.[2366]

[2362] The OLC was, at the time, analyzing the legality of 13 techniques, including the 10 techniques outlined in the OLC's August 1, 2002, memorandum, and additional techniques for which the CIA sought OLC approval in 2004.

[2363] Letter from ████████████, Associate General Counsel, CIA, to Steve Bradbury, Acting Assistant Attorney General, Office of Legal Counsel, May 4, 2005.

[2364] Memorandum for John A. Rizzo, Senior Deputy General Counsel, Central Intelligence Agency, from Steven G. Bradbury, Principal Deputy Assistant Attorney General, Office of Legal Counsel, May 10, 2005, Re: Application of 18 U.S.C. Sections 2340-2340A to Certain Techniques That May be Used in the Interrogation of a High Value al Qaeda Detainee (DTS #2009-1810, Tab 9); Memorandum for John A. Rizzo, Senior Deputy General Counsel, Central Intelligence Agency, from Steven G. Bradbury, Principal Deputy Assistant Attorney General, Office of Legal Counsel, May 10, 2005, Re: Application of 18 U.S.C. Sections 2340-2340A to the Combined Use of Certain Techniques in the Interrogation of High Value al Qaeda Detainees (DTS #2009-1810, Tab 10).

[2365] Memorandum for John A. Rizzo, Senior Deputy General Counsel, Central Intelligence Agency, from Steven G. Bradbury, Principal Deputy Assistant Attorney General, Office of Legal Counsel, May 30, 2005, Re: Application of United States Obligations Under Article 16 of the Convention Against Torture to Certain Techniques that May be Used in the Interrogation of High Value Al Qaeda Detainees (DTS #2009-1810, Tab 11).

[2366] All of these assertions were inaccurate. See Volume III for examples of CIA detainees being immediately subjected to the CIA's enhanced interrogation techniques, including ████████████ 34491 (051400Z MAR 03). See also Volume III for details on other interrogations in 2003, when at least six detainees that year were stripped and shackled, nude, in the standing stress position for sleep deprivation or subjected to other enhanced interrogation techniques prior to being questioned. They included Asadullah (DIRECTOR ████ (████ FEB

(TS// ███████ //NF) The OLC memoranda also relied on CIA representations regarding specific interrogation techniques that were incongruent with the operational history of the program. For example, the CIA informed the OLC that it maintained a 75 degree minimum room temperature for nude detainees as "a matter of policy," with a minimum of 68 degrees in the case of technical problems. This information was inconsistent with CIA practice both before and after the CIA's representations to the OLC.[2367] The OLC relied on the CIA representation that standing sleep deprivation would be discontinued in the case of significant swelling of the lower extremities (edema), whereas in practice the technique was repeatedly not stopped when edema occurred.[2368] The OLC also repeated CIA representations that constant light was necessary for security, even though the CIA had subjected detainees to constant darkness.[2369] Additional CIA representations accepted by the OLC—and found to be inconsistent with CIA practice —related to: (1) the exposure of nude detainees to other detainees and detention facility staff,[2370] (2) the use of water dousing—specifically the inaccurate representation that the technique did not involve immersion, (3) the use of shackles in standing sleep deprivation, (4) the likelihood of hallucinations during sleep deprivation, (5) the responsibility of medical personnel to intervene when standing sleep deprivation results in hallucinations, and (6) the purpose and the use of diapers on CIA detainees.[2371]

(TS// ███████ //NF) The OLC repeated the CIA's representations that "the effect of the waterboard is to induce a sensation of drowning," that "the detainee experiences this sensation even if he is aware that he is not actually drowning," and that "as far as can be determined, [Abu

---

03)); Abu Yasir al-Jaza'iri ████████ 35558 (████ MAR 03)); Suleiman Abdullah ████ 35787 (████ MAR 03)); ████ 36023 (████ APR 03)); Abu Hudhaifa (████████ 38576 ████ MAY 03)); Hambali ████ 1241 ████ ; and Majid Khan (████ 46471 (241242Z MAY 03), ████ 39077 (271719Z MAY 03)).

[2367] Letter from ████ CTC Legal ████ to Acting Assistant Attorney General Levin, December 30, 2004 (DTS #2009-1809). *See*, for example, ████ 31118 ████ ; ████ 31429 (161303Z DEC 02); ████ 10006 (070902Z DEC 02); [REDACTED] 33962 (211724Z FEB 03); ████ 34031 (231242Z FEB 03); ████ 34575 ████ ; ████ 34354 ████ MAR 03); DIRECTOR ████ MAR 03). Email to: ████ ; from: [REDACTED]; subject: Medical Evaulation/Update ████ (047); date: March █, 2004. Email to: ████ ; from: [REDACTED]; subject: Medical Evaluation/Update ████ (047); date: March 8, 2004. Email to: ████ ; from: [REDACTED]; subject: Medical Evaluation/Update ████ (047); date: March 9, 2004. ████ 2347 (300624Z MAY 05); ████ 1797 (021612Z DEC 05).

[2368] *See*, for example, ████ 10909 (201918Z MAR 03); ████ 2622 (230851Z AUG 07).

[2369] According to a CIA cable, cells at DETENTION SITE COBALT were "blacked out at all times using curtains plus painted exterior windows. And double doors. The lights are never turned on." (*See* ████ ████ 28246 ████ .) Upon finding Ramzi bin al-Shibh "cowering in the corner, shivering" when the light in his cell burned out, interrogators decided to use darkness as an interrogation technique. He was then placed in sleep deprivation "standing, shackled feet and hands, with hands over his head, naked, in total darkness." *See* ████ 10521 (191750Z FEB 03); ████ 10525 (200840Z FEB 03).

[2370] ████ interview of ████ [CIA OFFICER 1], December 19, 2002. CIA Interrogation Program Draft Course Materials, March 11, 2003, p. 28. CTC/RDG Interrogation Program, December 15, 2003. DIRECTOR ████ (251609Z JUL 02). *See also* "Standard Interrogation Techniques," attachment to email from: ████ ; to: Scott W. Muller, John Rizzo, [REDACTED], ████ ; subject: revised interrogation discussion; date: July 19, 2004.

[2371] Letter from ████ CTC Legal ████ to Acting Assistant Attorney General Levin, December 30, 2004 (DTS #2009-1809).

Zubaydah and KSM] did not experience physical pain or, in the professional judgment of doctors, is there any medical reason to believe they would have done so." The OLC further accepted that physical sensations associated with waterboarding, such as choking, "end when the application ends."[2372] This information is incongruent with CIA records. According to CIA records, Abu Zubaydah's waterboarding sessions "resulted in immediate fluid intake and involuntary leg, chest and arm spasms" and "hysterical pleas."[2373] A medical officer who oversaw the interrogation of KSM stated that the waterboard technique had evolved beyond the "sensation of drowning" to what he described as a "series of near drownings."[2374] Physical reactions to waterboarding did not necessarily end when the application of water was discontinued, as both Abu Zubaydah and KSM vomited after being subjected to the waterboard.[2375] Further, as previously described, during at least one waterboard session, Abu Zubaydah "became completely unresponsive, with bubbles rising through his open, full mouth." He remained unresponsive after the waterboard was rotated upwards. Upon medical intervention, he regained consciousness and expelled "copious amounts of liquid."[2376] The CIA also relayed information to the OLC on the frequency with which the waterboard could be used that was incongruent with past operational practice.[2377]

(TS//██████████//NF) The May 10, 2005, memorandum analyzing the individual use of the CIA's enhanced interrogation techniques accepted the CIA's representations that CIA interrogators are trained for "approximately four weeks," and that "all personnel directly engaged in the interrogation of persons detained... have been appropriately screened (from the

---

[2372] Memorandum for John A. Rizzo, Senior Deputy General Counsel, Central Intelligence Agency, from Steven G. Bradbury, Principal Deputy Assistant Attorney General, Office of Legal Counsel, May 10, 2005, Re: Application of 18 U.S.C. Sections 2340-2340A to Certain Techniques That May be Used in the Interrogation of a High Value al Qaeda Detainee (DTS #2009-1810, Tab 9); Memorandum for John A. Rizzo, Senior Deputy General Counsel, Central Intelligence Agency, from Steven G. Bradbury, Principal Deputy Assistant Attorney General, Office of Legal Counsel, May 10, 2005, Re: Application of 18 U.S.C. Sections 2340-2340A to the Combined Use of Certain Techniques in the Interrogation of High Value al Qaeda Detainees (DTS #2009-1810, Tab 10); Memorandum for John A. Rizzo, Senior Deputy General Counsel, Central Intelligence Agency, from Steven G. Bradbury, Principal Deputy Assistant Attorney General, Office of Legal Counsel, May 30, 2005, Re: Application of United States Obligations Under Article 16 of the Convention Against Torture to Certain Techniques that May be Used in the Interrogation of High Value Al Qaeda Detainees (DTS #2009-1810, Tab 11).
[2373] ██████ 10643 ██████ AUG 02); ██████ 10644 (201235Z AUG 02)
[2374] See email from: ██████; to: ██████; cc: ██████; subject: More; date: April 10, 2003, at 5:59: 27 PM.
[2375] ██████ 10644 (201235Z AUG 02); email from: [REDACTED]; to: ██████ and [REDACTED]; subject: Re: So it begins; date: August 4, 2002, at 09:45:09 AM; ██████ 10803 (131929Z MAR 03).
[2376] See Abu Zubaydah and KSM detainee reviews in Volume III, including ██████ 10803 (131929Z MAR 03). See email from: ██████, OMS; to: ██████ and [REDACTED]; subject: Re: Departure; date: March 6, 2003, at 7:11:59 PM; email from: ██████, OMS; to [REDACTED] and [REDACTED]; subject: Re: Acceptable lower ambient temperatures; date: March 7, 2003, at 8:22 PM; email from: ██████, OMS; to: [REDACTED] and [REDACTED]; subject: Re: Talking Points for review and comment; date: August 13, 2004, at 10:22 AM; email from: ██████; to: [REDACTED], [REDACTED], [REDACTED], [REDACTED], and [REDACTED]; subject: Re: Discussion with Dan Levin- AZ; date: October 26, 2004, at 6:09 PM.
[2377] Letter from ██████ CTC Legal ██████ to Acting Assistant Attorney General Dan Levin, August 19, 2004 (DTS# 2009-1809). The OLC, having been informed by the CIA that 40 seconds was the maximum length of a single waterboard application, noted that "you have informed us that this maximum has rarely been reached." This is inaccurate. KSM was subjected to 40-second exposures at least 19 times.

medical, psychological and security standpoints)."[2378] The CIA representations about training and screening were incongruent with the operational history of the CIA program. CIA records indicate that CIA officers and contractors who conducted CIA interrogations in 2002 did not undergo any interrogation training. The first interrogator training course did not begin until November 12, 2002, by which time at least 25 detainees had been taken into CIA custody.[2379] Numerous CIA interrogators and other CIA personnel associated with the program had either suspected or documented personal and professional problems that raised questions about their judgment and CIA employment. This group of officers included individuals who, among other issues, had engaged in inappropriate detainee interrogations, had workplace anger management issues, and had reportedly admitted to sexual assault.[2380]

[2378] Memorandum for John A. Rizzo, Senior Deputy General Counsel, Central Intelligence Agency, from Steven G. Bradbury, Principal Deputy Assistant Attorney General, Office of Legal Counsel, May 10, 2005, Re: Application of 18 U.S.C. Sections 2340-2340A to Certain Techniques That May be Used in the Interrogation of a High Value al Qaeda Detainee (DTS #2009-1810, Tab 9). As described in this summary, when ██████ CTC Legal, ██████ ██████, insisted that CTC Legal vet and review the background of CIA personnel involved in the CIA's interrogations, he directly linked this review to the legality of the CIA's enhanced interrogation techniques. ██████ wrote: "we will be forced to DISapprove [sic] the participation of specific personnel in the use of enhanced techniques unless we have ourselves vetted them and are satisfied with their qualifications and suitability for what are clearly unusual measures that are lawful only when practiced correctly by personnel whose records clearly demonstrate their suitability for that role." The chief of CTC, Jose Rodriguez, objected to this proposal. *See* email from: ██████, CTC/LGL; to: [REDACTED]; cc: Jose Rodriguez, [REDACTED], [REDACTED], ██████; subject: EYES ONLY; date: November ██, 2002, at 03:13:01 PM; email from: Jose Rodriguez; to: ██████, CTC/LGL; cc: [REDACTED], [REDACTED], [REDACTED], [REDACTED], ██████; subject: EYES ONLY; date: November ██, 2002, at 04:27 PM.

[2379] The training to conduct the CIA's enhanced interrogation techniques required only approximately 65 hours of classroom and operational instruction. December 4, 2002, Training Report, High Value Target Interrogation and Exploitation (HVTIE) Training Seminar 12-18 Nov 02, (pilot running).

[2380] Among other abuses, ██████ had engaged in "Russian Roulette" with a detainee. (*See* Memorandum for Chief, Staff and Operations Branch from [REDACTED], ██████, April 3, 1980, Subject: ██████; 1984, Memorandum for Inspector General from [REDACTED], Inspector, via Deputy Inspector General, re ██████, IG-██84.) ██████ [CIA OFFICER 2], who threatened 'Abd al-Rahim al-Nashiri with a gun and a power drill, ██████. He was sent home short of tour twice—once for ██████ and again, a few months before interrogating al-Nashiri, for engaging in

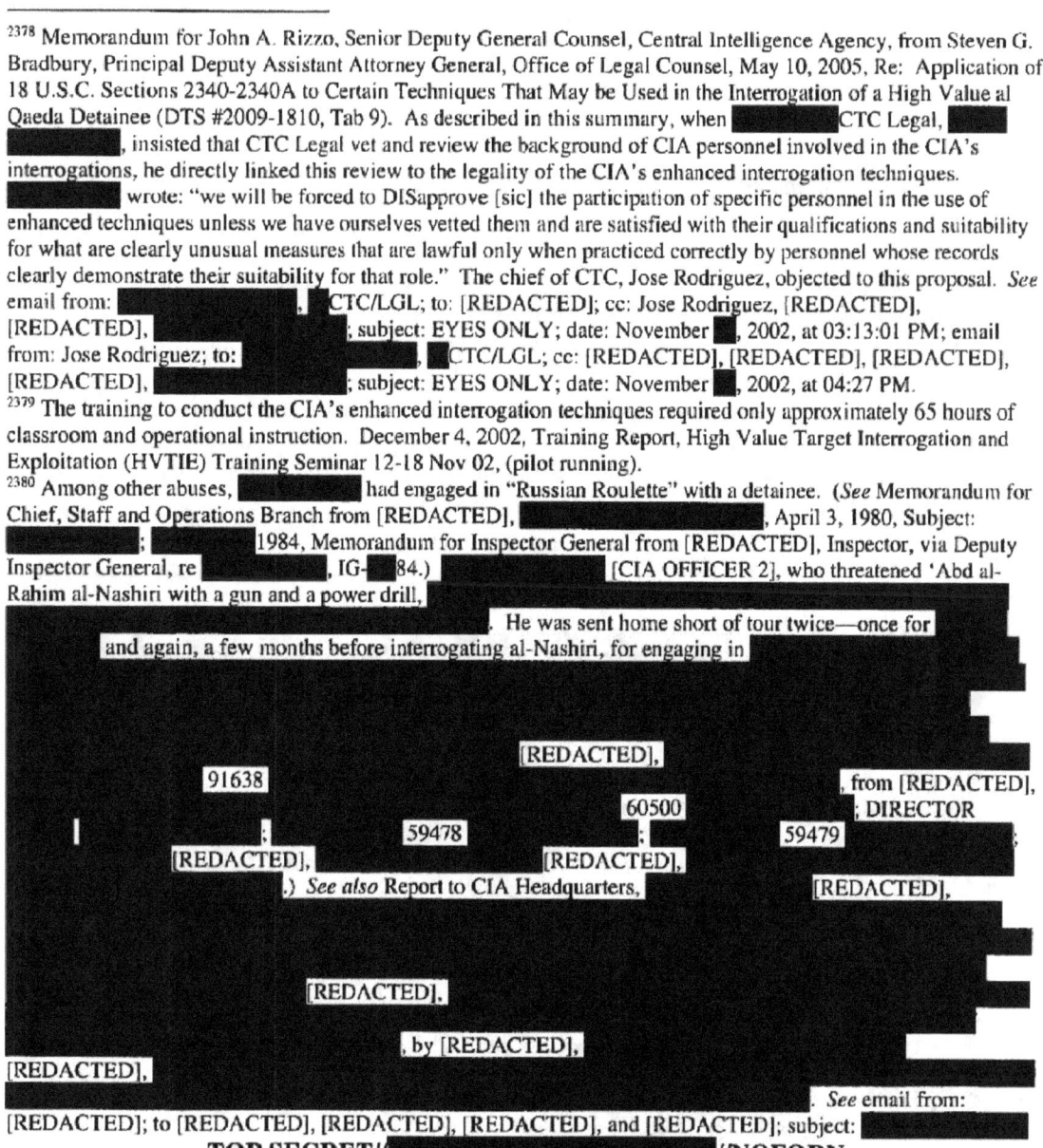

[REDACTED], 91638 ██████ [REDACTED], , from [REDACTED], 60500 ; DIRECTOR ; 59478 ; 59479 ; [REDACTED], [REDACTED], .) *See also* Report to CIA Headquarters, [REDACTED],

[REDACTED],

, by [REDACTED],

[REDACTED],

. *See* email from: [REDACTED]; to [REDACTED], [REDACTED], [REDACTED], and [REDACTED]; subject: ██████

(TS/ ██████████ //NF) Finally, the OLC accepted a definition of "High Value Detainee" conveyed by the CIA[2381] that limited the use of the CIA's enhanced interrogation techniques to "senior member[s]" of al-Qa'ida or an associated terrorist group who have "knowledge of imminent terrorist threats" or "direct involvement in planning and preparing" terrorist actions. However, at the time of the OLC opinion, the CIA had used its enhanced interrogation techniques on CIA detainees who were found neither to have knowledge of imminent threats nor to have been directly involved in planning or preparing terrorist actions. Some were not senior al-Qa'ida members,[2382] or even members of al-Qa'ida.[2383] Others were never suspected of having information on, or a role in, terrorist plotting and were suspected only of having information on the location of UBL or other al-Qa'ida figures,[2384] or were simply believed to have been present at a suspected al-Qa'ida guesthouse.[2385] A year later, ██████ CTC Legal wrote to Acting Assistant Attorney General Steven Bradbury suggesting a new standard that more closely reflected actual practice by allowing for the CIA detention and interrogation of detainees to be based on the belief that the detainee had information that could assist in locating senior al-Qa'ida leadership.[2386] The OLC modified the standard in a memorandum dated July 20, 2007.[2387] By then, the last CIA detainee, Muhammad Rahim, had already entered CIA custody.[2388]

(TS/ ██████████ //NF) The May 30, 2005, OLC memorandum analyzing U.S. obligations under the Convention Against Torture relied heavily on CIA representations about the intelligence obtained from the program. Many of these representations were provided in a March 2, 2005, CIA memorandum known as the "Effectiveness Memo," in which the CIA advised that the CIA program "works and the techniques are effective in producing foreign intelligence." The "Effectiveness Memo" stated that "[w]e assess we would not have succeeded in overcoming the resistance of Khalid Shaykh Muhammad (KSM), Abu Zubaydah, and other equally resistant high-value terrorist detainees without applying, in a careful, professional and

---

██████████████████████ [REDACTED], ████████████████

[REDACTED], ████████. For more information, see Volume III.

[2381] Fax to Acting Assistant Attorney General Levin from ██████████, January 4, 2005 (DTS #2009-1809).

[2382] See detainee reviews for Suleiman Abdullah and Janat Gul in Volume III for additional information.

[2383] See detainee review for Rafiq bin Bashir bin Halul Al-Hami in Volume III for additional information.

[2384] See detainee review for Ridha Ahmad al-Najjar in Volume III for additional information.

[2385] See detainee reviews for Tawfiq Nasir Awad al-Bihani and Arsala Khan in Volume III for additional information.

[2386] Letter from ████ CTC Legal ████████ to Acting Assistant Attorney General Bradbury, May 23, 2006 (DTS #2009-1809).

[2387] Memorandum for John A. Rizzo, Acting General Counsel, Central Intelligence Agency, from Steven G. Bradbury, Principal Deputy Assistant Attorney General, Office of Legal Counsel, July 20, 2007, Re: Application of the War Crimes Act, the Detainee Treatment Act, and Common Article 3 of the Geneva Conventions to Certain Techniques that May Be Used by the CIA in the Interrogation of High Value al Qaeda Detainees (DTS #2009-1810, Tab 14).

[2388] ████████ 6439 (██████████); ██████████ 7516 (██████████). Muhammad Rahim entered CIA custody on July ██, 2007.

safe manner, the full range of interrogation techniques."[2389] The CIA "Effectiveness Memo" further stated that "[p]rior to the use of enhanced techniques against skilled resistors [sic] like KSM and Abu Zubaydah—the two most prolific intelligence producers in our control—CIA acquired little threat information or significant actionable intelligence information." As described in this summary, the key information provided by Abu Zubaydah that the CIA attributed to the CIA's enhanced interrogation techniques was provided prior to the use of the CIA's enhanced interrogation techniques. KSM was subjected to CIA's enhanced interrogation techniques within minutes of his questioning, and thus had no opportunity to divulge information prior to their use. As described elsewhere, CIA personnel concluded the waterboard was not an effective interrogation technique against KSM.[2390]

(TS// ███████ //NF) Under a section entitled, "Results," the CIA "Effectiveness Memo" represented that the "CIA's use of DOJ-approved enhanced interrogation techniques, as part of a comprehensive interrogation approach, has enabled CIA to disrupt terrorist plots, capture additional terrorists, and collect a high volume of critical intelligence on al-Qa'ida." It then listed 11 examples of "critical intelligence" acquired "*after* applying enhanced interrogation techniques":[2391] the "Karachi Plot," the "Heathrow Plot," the "Second Wave," the "Guraba Cell," "Issa al-Hindi," "Abu Talha al-Pakistani," "Hambali's Capture," "Jafaar al-Tayyar," the "Dirty Bomb Plot," the "Shoe Bomber," and intelligence obtained on "Shkai, Pakistan." These representations of "effectiveness" were almost entirely inaccurate and mirrored other inaccurate information provided to the White House, Congress, and the CIA inspector general.[2392] In addition, on April 15, 2005, the CIA provided the OLC with an eight-page document entitled, "Briefing Notes on the Value of Detainee Reporting." The CIA "Briefing Notes" document repeats many of the same CIA representations in the "Effectiveness Memo," but added additional inaccurate information related to the capture of Iyman Faris.[2393]

(TS// ███████ //NF) The OLC's May 30, 2005, memorandum relied on the CIA's inaccurate representations in the "Effectiveness Memo" and the "Briefing Notes" document in determining that the CIA's enhanced interrogation techniques did not violate the Fifth Amendment's prohibition on executive conduct that "shocks the conscience," indicating that this analysis was a "highly context-specific and fact-dependent question." The OLC also linked its

---

[2389] CIA Memorandum for Steve Bradbury at the Department of Justice, dated March 2, 2005, from ██████ , ████ Legal Group, DCI Counterterrorist Center, subject "Effectiveness of the CIA Counterterrorist Interrogation Techniques."

[2390] Interview of ██████ , by [REDACTED] and [REDACTED], Office of the Inspector General, May 15, 2003; Interview of ██████ , by [REDACTED] and [REDACTED], Office of the Inspector General, October 22, 2003; ██████ 11715 (201047Z MAY 03); Sametime Communication, ██████ and ██ ██████ , 15/Aug/06, 10:28:38 to 10:58:00; Interview of ██████ , by [REDACTED] and [REDACTED], Office of the Inspector General, April 3, 2003; Sametime Communication, ██████ and [REDACTED], 02/May/05, 14:51:48 to 15:17:39; Interview of ██████ , by [REDACTED], [REDACTED], and [REDACTED], Office of the Inspector General, August 20, 2003.

[2391] Emphasis in the original.

[2392] *See* list of 20 CIA representations included in this summary and additional details in Volume II. Representations regarding Abu Talha al-Pakistani, which were less frequent, are also described this summary and in greater detail in Volumes II and III.

[2393] April 15, 2005, 10:47AM, fax to DOJ Command Center for ██████ , Office of Legal Counsel, U.S. Department of Justice, from ██████ , ████ Legal Group, DCI Counterterrorist Center. Cover note: "██ , Answers to some of your questions," with attachment entitled "Briefing Notes on the Value of Detainee Reporting."

analysis of whether the use of the CIA's enhanced interrogation techniques was "constitutionally arbitrary" to the representation by the CIA that its interrogation program produced "substantial quantities of otherwise unavailable actionable intelligence."[2394] The CIA's representations to the OLC that it obtained "otherwise unavailable actionable intelligence" from the use of the CIA's enhanced interrogation techniques were inaccurate.[2395]

(TS// ~~███████~~ //NF) The OLC memorandum repeated specific inaccurate CIA representations, including that the waterboard was used against Abu Zubaydah and KSM "only after it became clear that standard interrogation techniques were not working"; that the information related to the "Guraba Cell" in Karachi was "otherwise unavailable actionable intelligence"; that Janat Gul was a "high value detainee"; and that information provided by Hassan Ghul regarding the al-Qa'ida presence in Shkai, Pakistan, was attributable to the CIA's enhanced interrogation techniques.[2396] Citing CIA information, the OLC memorandum also stated that Abu Zubaydah was al-Qa'ida's "third or fourth highest ranking member" and had been involved "in every major terrorist operation carried out by al Qaeda," and that "again, once enhanced techniques were employed," Abu Zubaydah "provided significant information on two operatives... who planned to build and detonate a 'dirty bomb' in the Washington DC area." The OLC repeated additional inaccurate information from the CIA related to KSM's reporting, including representations about the "Second Wave" plotting, the Heathrow Airport plotting, and the captures of Hambali, Iyman Faris, and Sajid Badat.[2397] The OLC relied on CIA representations that the use of the CIA's enhanced interrogation techniques against 'Abd al-Rahim al-Nashiri produced "notable results as early as the first day," despite al-Nashiri providing reporting on the same topics prior to entering CIA custody. The OLC also repeated inaccurate CIA representations about statements reportedly made by Abu Zubaydah and KSM.[2398]

[2394] Memorandum for John A. Rizzo, Senior Deputy General Counsel, Central Intelligence Agency, from Steven G. Bradbury, Principal Deputy Assistant Attorney General, Office of Legal Counsel, May 30, 2005, Re: Application of United States Obligations Under Article 16 of the Convention Against Torture to Certain Techniques that May be Used in the Interrogation of High Value Al Qaeda Detainees.

[2395] *See* specific CIA examples of the "Results" of using the "CIA's use of DOJ-approved enhanced interrogation techniques" in March 2, 2005, Memorandum for Steve Bradbury from ~~███████~~, ~~██~~ Legal Group, DCI Counterterrorist Center, "Effectiveness of the CIA Counterterrorist Interrogation Techniques." The specific representations in the "Briefing Notes" document were similar to those in the CIA's "Effectiveness Memo" and included references to detainee reporting on Jose Padilla, Hambali, Dhiren Barot, Sajid Badat, Iyman Faris, Jaffar al-Tayyar, the Heathrow Airport plotting, and the Karachi plotting.

[2396] For example, as detailed elsewhere in this review, Hassan Gul provided detailed information on al-Qa'ida's presence in Shkai, Pakistan, prior to the use of the CIA's enhanced interrogation techniques.

[2397] Memorandum for John A. Rizzo, Senior Deputy General Counsel, Central Intelligence Agency, from Steven G. Bradbury, Principal Deputy Assistant Attorney General, Office of Legal Counsel, May 30, 2005, Re: Application of United States Obligations Under Article 16 of the Convention Against Torture to Certain Techniques that May be Used in the Interrogation of High Value Al Qaeda Detainees.

[2398] The OLC memorandum stated that "[b]oth KSM and Zubaydah had 'expressed their belief that the general US population was 'weak,' lacked resilience, and would be unable to 'do what was necessary' to prevent the terrorists from succeeding in their goals.'" As described elsewhere in this summary, and in more detail in the full Committee Study, CIA records indicate that KSM and Abu Zubaydah did not make these statements. The memorandum also repeated CIA representations about KSM's comment, "Soon, you will know," and Abu Zubaydah's reported statements about being "permitted by Allah" to provide information. As described in this summary, these representations are not supported by CIA records.

(TS//█████████//NF) Finally, the May 30, 2005, OLC memorandum referenced the CIA Inspector General May 2004 Special Review, stating: "we understand that interrogations have led to specific, actionable intelligence as well as a general increase in the amount of intelligence regarding al Qaeda and its affiliates."[2399] The OLC memorandum cited pages in the Special Review that included inaccurate information provided by CIA personnel to the CIA's OIG, including representations related to Jose Padilla and Binyam Muhammad, Hambali and the "Al-Qa'ida cell in Karachi," the Parachas, Iyman Faris, Saleh al-Marri, Majid Khan, the Heathrow Airport plotting, and other "plots."[2400]

E. After Passage of the Detainee Treatment Act, OLC Issues Opinion on CIA Conditions of Confinement, Withdraws Draft Opinion on the CIA's Enhanced Interrogation Techniques After the U.S. Supreme Court Case of *Hamdan v. Rumsfeld*

(TS//█████████//NF) On December 19, 2005, anticipating the passage of the Detainee Treatment Act, Acting CIA General Counsel John Rizzo requested that the OLC review whether the CIA's enhanced interrogation techniques, as well as the conditions of confinement at CIA detention facilities, would violate the Detainee Treatment Act.[2401] In April 2006, attorneys at OLC completed initial drafts of two legal memoranda addressing these questions.[2402] In June 2006, however, the U.S. Supreme Court case of *Hamdan v. Rumsfeld* prompted the OLC to withdraw its draft memorandum on the impact of the Detainee Treatment Act on the CIA's enhanced interrogation techniques. As ████████ CTC Legal explained, the OLC would prepare "a written opinion 'if we want'… but strongly implied we shouldn't seek it."[2403] As described in a July 2009 report of the Department of Justice Office of Professional Responsibility, the Administration determined that, after the *Hamdan* decision, it would need new legislation to support the continued use of the CIA's enhanced interrogation techniques.[2404]

(TS//█████████//NF) Even as it withdrew its draft opinion on the CIA's enhanced interrogation techniques, the OLC continued to analyze whether the CIA's conditions of confinement violated the Detainee Treatment Act. To support this analysis, the CIA asserted to the OLC that loud music and white noise, constant light, and 24-hour shackling were all for

---

[2399] Memorandum for John A. Rizzo, Senior Deputy General Counsel, Central Intelligence Agency, from Steven G. Bradbury, Principal Deputy Assistant Attorney General, Office of Legal Counsel, May 30, 2005, Re: Application of United States Obligations Under Article 16 of the Convention Against Torture to Certain Techniques that May be Used in the Interrogation of High Value Al Qaeda Detainees.

[2400] Memorandum for John A. Rizzo, Senior Deputy General Counsel, Central Intelligence Agency, from Steven G. Bradbury, Principal Deputy Assistant Attorney General, Office of Legal Counsel, May 30, 2005, Re: Application of United States Obligations Under Article 16 of the Convention Against Torture to Certain Techniques that May be Used in the Interrogation of High Value Al Qaeda Detainees, pp. 10-11, citing IG Special Review, pp. 85-91.

[2401] The Detainee Treatment Act passed on December 30, 2005. Letter from Senior Deputy General Counsel John Rizzo to Acting Assistant Attorney General Bradbury, December 19, 2005 (DTS #2009-1809).

[2402] April 19, 2006, Fax from ████████, ████ Legal Group, CIA Counterterrorism Center to DOJ Command Center for Steve Bradbury (DTS #2009-1809).

[2403] Email from: ████████; to: [REDACTED]; cc: ████████, John Rizzo; subject: FW: Summary of *Hamdan* Decision; date: June 30, 2006, at 4:44 PM.

[2404] Department of Justice Office of Professional Responsibility; Report, Investigation into the Office of Legal Counsel's Memoranda Concerning Issues Relating to the Central Intelligence Agency's Use of 'Enhanced Interrogation Techniques' on Suspected Terrorists, July 29, 2009 (DTS #2010-1058).

security purposes, that shaving was for security and hygiene purposes and was conducted only upon intake and not as a "punitive step," that detainees were not exposed to an "extended period" of white noise, and that CIA detainees had access to a wide array of amenities.[2405] This information is incongruent with CIA records. Detainees were routinely shaved, sometimes as an aid to interrogation; detainees who were "participating at an acceptable level" were permitted to grow their hair and beards.[2406] The CIA had used music at decibels exceeding the representations to the OLC. The CIA had also used specific music to signal to a detainee that another interrogation was about to begin.[2407] Numerous CIA detainees were subjected to the extended use of white noise.[2408] The CIA further inaccurately represented that "[m]edical personnel will advise ending sleep deprivation in the event the detainee appears to be experiencing hallucinations, transient or not."[2409] In a May 18, 2006, letter, ██████CTC Legal, ██████████, wrote to the Department of Justice that "some of these conditions provide the additional benefit of setting a detention atmosphere conducive to continued intelligence collection from the detainee." While the letter referred generally to "constant light in the cells, use of white noise, use of shackles, hooding, and shaving/barbering," it described an intelligence collection purpose only for shaving, which "allows interrogators a clear view of the terrorist-detainee's facial clues."[2410]

(TS//██████████//NF) On August 31, 2006, the OLC finalized two legal analyses on the conditions of confinement at CIA detention sites. The first was a memorandum that evaluated whether six detention conditions in the CIA's detention program were consistent with the Detainee Treatment Act.[2411] The second, provided in the form of a letter, concluded that those same six conditions did not violate the requirements of Common Article 3 of the Geneva

---

[2405] Letter from Senior Deputy General Counsel John Rizzo to Acting Assistant Attorney General Bradbury, December 19, 2005 (DTS #2009-1809). January 25, 2006, Letter to Steve Bradbury, Acting Assistant Attorney General, Office of Legal Counsel, Department of Justice, from ██████████, ██████CTC Legal, CIA (DTS #1809-2009).

[2406] See, for example, ██████████████ 31369 (151028Z DEC 02); ██████ 10361 ██████████████, HEADQUARTERS ██████ (151955Z SEP 05); HEADQUARTERS ██████ (212005Z JUN 05); HEADQUARTERS ██████ (202036Z JUN 05).

[2407] As one example, CIA records indicate that in the CIA interrogation of Ramzi bin al-Shibh, the "the Blues Brothers rendition of 'Rawhide' [was] played." CIA records state that bin al-Shibh's reaction to hearing the song was evidence of his conditioning, as bin al-Shibh "knows when he hears the music where he is going and what is going to happen." (See ██████ 10602 (262020Z FEB 03); ██████ 10591 (252002Z FEB 03); [REDACTED] 1889 (091823Z MAR 03); [REDACTED] 1924 (151729Z MAR 04); ██████ 10361 ██████████.) "Loud noise" was also used to "prevent concentrating, planning, and derailing of the exploitation/interrogation process with interrogation countermeasures (resistance)." See, for example, detainee reviews detailing the detention and interrogations of Lillie and Hambali in Volume III.

[2408] See, for example, ██████ 2505 (272059Z JUN 05). The amenities described by the CIA to the OLC were not available to detainees during earlier iterations of the program.

[2409] April 23, 2006, Fax from ██████████, ██████ Legal Group, CIA Counterterrorism Center to DOJ Command Center for Steve Bradbury (DTS #2009-1809).

[2410] May 18, 2006, Letter to Steven G. Bradbury, Acting Assistant Attorney General, Office of Legal Counsel, from ██████████, ██████CTC Legal, CIA, re: Request for Information on Security Measures (DTS # 2009-1809).

[2411] Memorandum for John Rizzo, Acting General Counsel, Central Intelligence Agency, from Steven G. Bradbury, Acting Assistant Attorney General, Office of Legal Counsel, August 31, 2006, Re: Application of the Detainee Treatment Act to Conditions of Confinement at Central Intelligence Agency Detention Facilities (DTS #2009-1810, Tab 13).

Conventions.[2412] The OLC relied on the CIA's representations related to conditions of confinement for its analysis.[2413] The OLC wrote that "underlying our analysis of all these methods [conditions of confinement] is our understanding that the CIA provides regular and thorough medical and psychological care to the detainees in its custody."[2414] As detailed in this summary, the lack of emergency medical care for CIA detainees was a significant challenge for the CIA.[2415]

(TS// ██████████ //NF) The August 31, 2006, OLC memorandum applying the terms of the Detainee Treatment Act to the conditions of confinement at CIA detention facilities stated that "over the history of the program, the CIA has detained a total of 96 individuals." This was based on a representation made by ██████████ CTC Legal on April 23, 2006.[2416] As of the date of the OLC memorandum, the CIA had detained at least 118 individuals. The OLC memorandum also stated that "we understand that, once the CIA assesses that a detainee no longer possesses significant intelligence value, the CIA seeks to move the detainee into alternative detention arrangements." CIA records indicate that detainees had remained in CIA custody long after the CIA had determined that they no longer possessed significant intelligence. Finally, the OLC memorandum repeated a number of earlier inaccurate CIA representations on the effectiveness of the program, citing both the CIA's "Effectiveness Memo" and its own May 30, 2005, memorandum. Notably, the August 31, 2006, OLC memorandum repeated the same inaccurate representation, which first appeared in an August 2002 OLC memorandum, that Abu Zubaydah was al-Qa'ida's "third or fourth highest ranking member" and had been involved "in every major terrorist operation carried out by al Qaeda." As described, CIA records as early as 2002 did not support these representations, and two weeks prior to the issuance of the August 2006 memorandum, the CIA had published an intelligence assessment stating that Abu Zubaydah had been rejected by al-Qa'ida and explaining how the CIA had come to "miscast Abu Zubaydah as a 'senior al-Qa'ida lieutenant.'"[2417]

[2412] Letter for John Rizzo, Acting General Counsel, Central Intelligence Agency, from Steven G. Bradbury, Acting Assistant Attorney General, Office of Legal Counsel, August 31, 2006 (DTS #2009-1810, Tab 12).

[2413] The OLC did not apply the Detainee Treatment Act or Common Article 3 to the use of shaving or other conditions of confinement in terms of their use as an interrogation technique. The OLC stated that while "the primary purpose of the conditions of confinement we consider here is to maintain the security of the CIA's detention facilities… [m]any of these conditions may also ease the obtaining of crucial intelligence information from the detainees." Nonetheless, the OLC concluded that "the security rationale alone is sufficient to justify each of the conditions of confinement in question." *See* memorandum for John Rizzo, Acting General Counsel, Central Intelligence Agency, from Steven G. Bradbury, Acting Assistant Attorney General, Office of Legal Counsel, August 31, 2006, Re: Application of the detainee Treatment Act to Conditions of Confinement at Central Intelligence Agency Detention Facilities (DTS #2009-1810, Tab 13).

[2414] Memorandum for John Rizzo, Acting General Counsel, Central Intelligence Agency, from Steven G. Bradbury, Acting Assistant Attorney General, Office of Legal Counsel, August 31, 2006, Re: Application of the Detainee Treatment Act to Conditions of Confinement at Central Intelligence Agency Detention Facilities (DTS #2009-1810 Tab 13).

[2415] For additional detailed information, *see* Volume I and Volume III.

[2416] April 23, 2006, Fax to DOJ Command Center for Steve Bradbury, Office of Legal Counsel, from ██████████, ████ Legal Group, CIA Counterterrorism Center.

[2417] CIA Intelligence Assessment, August 16, 2006, "Countering Misconceptions About Training Camps in Afghanistan, 1990-2001." For additional details, *see* the Abu Zubaydah detainee review in Volume III.

F. July 2007 OLC Memorandum Relies on Inaccurate CIA Representations Regarding CIA Interrogations and the Effectiveness of the CIA's Enhanced Interrogation Techniques; CIA Misrepresents Congressional Views to the Department of Justice

(U) On July 20, 2007, the OLC issued a memorandum applying the War Crimes Act, the Detainee Treatment Act, and Common Article 3 of the Geneva Conventions to the CIA's enhanced interrogation techniques. The memorandum noted that, while the *Hamdan* decision "was contrary to the President's prior determination that Common Article 3 does not apply to an armed conflict across national boundaries with an international terrorist organization such as al Qaeda," this challenge to the CIA program was resolved by the Military Commissions Act, which "left responsibility for interpreting the meaning and application of Common Article 3, except for the grave breaches defined in the amended War Crimes Act, to the President."[2418]

(TS// ███████████ //NF) The OLC memorandum determined that six proposed interrogation techniques were legal: dietary manipulation, extended sleep deprivation, the facial hold, the attention grasp, the abdominal slap, and the insult (or facial) slap. The memorandum accepted the CIA's representation that, over the life of the program, the CIA had detained 98 individuals, of whom 30 had been subjected to the CIA's enhanced interrogation techniques.[2419] At the time of the OLC memorandum the CIA had detained at least 119 individuals, of whom at least 38 had been subjected to the CIA's enhanced interrogation techniques.[2420] The inaccurate statistics provided by the CIA to the OLC were used to support OLC's conclusion that the program was "proportionate to the government interest involved," as required by the "shocks the conscience" test. The OLC also noted that "careful screening procedures are in place to ensure that enhanced techniques will be used only in the interrogations of agents or members of al Qaeda or its affiliates who are reasonably believed to possess critical intelligence that can be used to prevent future terrorist attacks against the United States and its interests."[2421] In practice, numerous individuals had been detained by the CIA and subjected to the CIA's enhanced interrogation

---

[2418] Memorandum for John A. Rizzo, Acting General Counsel, Central Intelligence Agency, from Steven G. Bradbury, Principal Deputy Assistant Attorney General, Office of Legal Counsel, July 20, 2007, Re: Application of the War Crimes Act, the Detainee Treatment Act, and Common Article 3 of the Geneva Conventions to Certain Techniques that May Be Used by the CIA in the Interrogation of High Value al Qaeda Detainees (DTS #2009-1810, Tab 14).

[2419] Memorandum for John A. Rizzo, Acting General Counsel, Central Intelligence Agency, from Steven G. Bradbury, Principal Deputy Assistant Attorney General, Office of Legal Counsel, July 20, 2007, Re: Application of the War Crimes Act, the Detainee Treatment Act, and Common Article 3 of the Geneva Conventions to Certain Techniques that May be Used by the CIA in the Interrogation of High Value Al Qaeda Detainees (DTS #2009-1810, Tab 14).

[2420] Although all 119 known CIA detainees had entered CIA custody by July 20, 2007, Muhammad Rahim, the last detainee, had not yet been subjected to the CIA's enhanced interrogation techniques by the time of the OLC memorandum. Muhammad Rahim was rendered to CIA custody on July █, 2007. (*See* ███████ 6439 (███████); ███████ 7516 (███████).) Interrogators began using the CIA's enhanced interrogation techniques on Rahim on July 21, 2007; the day after the OLC Memorandum was issued. *See* ███████ 2467 (211341Z JUL 07).

[2421] Memorandum for John A. Rizzo, Acting General Counsel, Central Intelligence Agency, from Steven G. Bradbury, Principal Deputy Assistant Attorney General, Office of Legal Counsel, July 20, 2007, Re: Application of the War Crimes Act, the Detainee Treatment Act, and Common Article 3 of the Geneva Conventions to Certain Techniques that May be Used by the CIA in the Interrogation of High Value Al Qaeda Detainees (DTS #2009-1810, Tab 14).

techniques, despite doubts and questions surrounding their knowledge of terrorist threats and the location of senior al-Qa'ida leadership. Examples include, among others: Asadullah,[2422] Mustafa al-Hawsawi,[2423] Abu Hudhaifa,[2424] Arsala Khan,[2425] ABU TALHA AL-MAGREBI and ABU BAHAR AL-TURKI,[2426] Janat Gul,[2427] Ahmed Ghailani,[2428] Sharif al-Masri,[2429] and Sayyid Ibrahim.[2430]

[2422] Interrogators had asked CIA Headquarters for the assessments supporting the decision to subject Asadullah to the CIA's enhanced interrogation techniques, noting that "it would be of enormous help to the interrogator to know what is concrete fact and what is good analysis." (*See* ███████ 33963 ███████ ; *see also* ███████ 34098 ███████ ; ███████ 34812 ███████ .) In response, ALEC Station acknowledged that "[t]o be sure, our case that Asadullah should have a good sense of bin Ladin's location is circumstantial." (*See* ALEC ███████ .) The following day, interrogators commented that "it may be that he simply does not know the [locational information on AQ leaders]." *See* ███████ 34310 ███████ .

[2423] Following al-Hawsawi's first interrogation session, Chief of Interrogations ███████ asked CIA Headquarters for information on what al-Hawsawi actually "knows," saying: "he does not appear to the [sic] be a person that is a financial mastermind. However, we lack facts with which to confront [al-Hawsawi]. What we need at this point is substantive information vice supposition." *See* ███████ 34757 (101742Z MAR 03).

[2424] Although CIA records include no requests or approval cables, Abu Hudhaifa was subjected to ice water baths and 66 hours of standing sleep deprivation. He was released because the CIA discovered he was likely not the person he was believed to be. *See* WASHINGTON DC ███████ ; ███████ 51303 ███████ .

[2425] CIA Headquarters initially resisted approving Arsala Khan's capture because of a lack of information confirming that he was a "continuing threat." (*See* ███████ 169986 ███████ , email from: ███████ ; to: ███████ , and [REDACTED]; subject: Denial of Approval to Capture Arsala Khan; date: ███████). Despite doubts that Arsala Khan was the individual sought by the CIA, interrogators subjected him to the CIA's enhanced interrogation techniques "to make a better assessment regarding [his] willingness to start talking, or assess if our subject is, in fact the man we are looking for." *See* ███████ 1373 ███████ .

[2426] The true names of these detainees have been replaced with the capitalized pseudonyms AL-MAGREBI and AL-TURKI. At the time the two detainees were rendered to CIA custody, the CIA was aware that they were then working for a foreign partner government. (*See* ALEC ███ [REDACTED]; [REDACTED] 43773 [REDACTED].) They were subjected to sleep deprivation and dietary manipulation until the CIA confirmed that the detainees had been trying to contact the CIA for weeks to inform the CIA of what they believed were pending al-Qa'ida terrorist attacks. (*See* ███████ 2227 [REDACTED]; ███████ 2233 [REDACTED]; ███████ 2185 [REDACTED]; HEADQUARTERS ███████ [REDACTED]; ███████ 2232 [REDACTED].) After the CIA had determined that AL-MAGREBI and AL-TURKI should not be in CIA custody, the two detainees were held for ███████ additional months before they were released. *See* [REDACTED] 2025 [REDACTED].

[2427] The case of Janat Gul is described above in the context of OLC advice in 2004 and afterwards. As Gul's interrogators noted, "Team does not believe [Gul] is withholding imminent threat information, however team will continue to press [Gul] for that during each session." *See* ███████ 1574 (███████ 04).

[2428] The CIA's assessment of Ghailani's knowledge of terrorist threats was speculative. As one official noted, "[a]lthough Ghailani's role in operational planning is unclear, his respected role in al-Qa'ida and presence in Shkai as recently as October 2003 may have provided him some knowledge about ongoing attack planning against the United States homeland, and the operatives involved." *See* email from: ███████ , CTC/UBLD ███████ (formerly ALEC ███████); to: [REDACTED], [REDACTED], [REDACTED], [REDACTED]; subject: derog information for ODDO on Talha, Ghailani, Hamza Rabi'a and Abu Faraj; date: August 10, 2004.

[2429] As noted above, the credibility of the source implicating Sharif al-Masri, Janat Gul, and Ghailani's connections to a pre-election plot was questioned by CIA officials prior to the application of the CIA's enhanced interrogation techniques against them. The source was later determined to have fabricated the information.

[2430] Five days after interrogators began using enhanced interrogation techniques against Sayyid Ibrahim, interrogators cabled CIA Headquarters requesting information that would "definitively link [Ibrahim] to nefarious

(TS// ████████ //NF) The July 20, 2007, OLC memorandum also stated that the CIA's enhanced interrogation techniques "are not the first option for CIA interrogators confronted even with a high value detainee."[2431] As described in this summary, numerous CIA detainees were subjected to the CIA's enhanced or "standard" interrogation techniques on their first day of CIA custody,[2432] while other detainees provided significant information prior to the use of the CIA's enhanced interrogation techniques. The OLC memorandum also accepted the CIA representation that "[t]he CIA generally does not ask questions during the administration of the techniques to which the CIA does not already know the answers," that the CIA "asks for already known information" during the administration of the CIA's enhanced interrogation techniques, and that when CIA personnel believe a detainee will cooperate, "the CIA would discontinue use of the techniques and debrief the detainee regarding matters on which the CIA is not definitely informed." As the memorandum concluded, "[t]his approach highlights the intended psychological effects of the techniques and reduces the ability of the detainee to provide false information solely as a means to discontinue their application."[2433] This description of the program was inaccurate. As described in this summary, and in more detail in the full Committee Study, CIA interrogators always questioned detainees during the application of the CIA's enhanced interrogation techniques seeking new information to which the CIA did not have answers, and numerous detainees fabricated information while being subjected to the interrogation techniques.

(TS// ████████ //NF) The July 20, 2007, OLC memorandum repeated CIA representations that "many, if not all, of those 30 detainees" who had been subjected to CIA's enhanced interrogation techniques received counterinterrogation training, and that "al Qaeda operatives believe that they are morally permitted to reveal information once they have reached a certain limit of discomfort."[2434] Neither of these representations is supported by CIA records.

---

activity or knowledge by [Ibrahim] of known nefarious activities of al-Qa'ida members, if this is possible." (*See* ████████ 1324 ████████ FEB 04).) Without receiving a response, they continued to subject Ibrahim to the CIA's enhanced interrogation techniques. CIA Headquarters, which rejected an assessment from two debriefers that Ibrahim was, "at best… a low-level facilitator," would later indicate that it was "uncertain" he would meet the requirements for U.S. military or ████ detention. *See* HEADQUARTERS ████ ████ ; HEADQUARTERS ████ ████ .

[2431] The OLC further stated that "enhanced techniques would be used only as less harsh techniques fail or as interrogators run out of time in the face of an imminent threat, so that it would be unlikely that a detainee would be subjected to more duress than is reasonably necessary to elicit the information sought." *See* Memorandum for John A. Rizzo, Acting General Counsel, Central Intelligence Agency, from Steven G. Bradbury, Principal Deputy Assistant Attorney General, Office of Legal Counsel, July 20, 2007, Re: Application of the War Crimes Act, the Detainee Treatment Act, and Common Article 3 of the Geneva Conventions to Certain Techniques that May be Used by the CIA in the Interrogation of High Value Al Qaeda Detainees (DTS #2009-1810, Tab 14).

[2432] *See* Volume III for additional details.

[2433] Memorandum for John A. Rizzo, Acting General Counsel, Central Intelligence Agency, from Steven G. Bradbury, Principal Deputy Assistant Attorney General, Office of Legal Counsel, July 20, 2007, Re: Application of the War Crimes Act, the Detainee Treatment Act, and Common Article 3 of the Geneva Conventions to Certain Techniques that May be Used by the CIA in the Interrogation of High Value Al Qaeda Detainees (DTS #2009-1810, Tab 14).

[2434] Memorandum for John A. Rizzo, Acting General Counsel, Central Intelligence Agency, from Steven G. Bradbury, Principal Deputy Assistant Attorney General, Office of Legal Counsel, July 20, 2007, Re: Application of the War Crimes Act, the Detainee Treatment Act, and Common Article 3 of the Geneva Conventions to Certain

(TS// ███████████ //NF) The memorandum also repeated CIA representations that interrogators were "highly trained in carrying out the techniques," and "psychologically screened to minimize the risk that an interrogator might misuse any technique." These presumptions were central to the OLC's determination that the limitations on interrogations contained in the Army Field Manual were not "dispositive evidence" that the CIA's interrogation program fell outside "traditional executive behavior and contemporary practice," an analysis required as part of the substantive due process inquiry. Specifically, the OLC distinguished U.S. military interrogations from the CIA program by stating that the CIA program "will be administered only by trained and experienced interrogators who in turn will apply the techniques only to a subset of high value detainees."[2435] As described in this summary, and in greater detail in the full Committee Study, the CIA's representations to the OLC were incongruent with the history of the CIA's Detention and Interrogation Program with regard to the training, screening, and experience of interrogators, and the detainees against whom the CIA used its enhanced interrogation techniques.

(TS// ███████████ //NF) The July 2007 OLC memorandum based its legal analysis related to the six interrogation techniques under consideration on CIA representations that were incongruent with the operational history of the program. In reviewing whether standing sleep deprivation was consistent with the War Crimes Act, the OLC noted that its understanding that the technique would be discontinued "should any hallucinations or significant declines in cognitive functioning be observed" was "crucial to our analysis." The memorandum repeated CIA representations that diapers employed during standing sleep deprivation "are used solely for sanitary and health reasons and not to humiliate the detainee," and that, more generally, "[t]he techniques are not intended to humiliate or to degrade."[2436] The OLC's understanding, which, as described, was not consistent with the operational history of the CIA program, was part of its analysis related to the prohibition on "outrages upon personal dignity" under Common Article 3.

(TS// ███████████ //NF) As in the May 30, 2005 OLC memorandum, the July 20, 2007, OLC memorandum conducted an analysis of the "shocks the conscience" test under the Fifth Amendment of the U.S. Constitution, emphasizing the fact-specific nature of the analysis. Citing both the CIA's March 2005 "Effectiveness Memo" and the president's September 6, 2006, speech describing the interrogation program, the July 2007 OLC memorandum repeated the CIA assertion that the CIA's enhanced interrogation techniques produced "otherwise unavailable intelligence." It also repeated CIA representations related to KSM's reporting on the "Second Wave" plotting and Abu Zubaydah's reporting on Jose Padilla, both of which were

---

Techniques that May be Used by the CIA in the Interrogation of High Value Al Qaeda Detainees (DTS #2009-1810, Tab 14).

[2435] Memorandum for John A. Rizzo, Acting General Counsel, Central Intelligence Agency, from Steven G. Bradbury, Principal Deputy Assistant Attorney General, Office of Legal Counsel, July 20, 2007, Re: Application of the War Crimes Act, the Detainee Treatment Act, and Common Article 3 of the Geneva Conventions to Certain Techniques that May be Used by the CIA in the Interrogation of High Value Al Qaeda Detainees (DTS #2009-1810, Tab 14).

[2436] Memorandum for John A. Rizzo, Acting General Counsel, Central Intelligence Agency, from Steven G. Bradbury, Principal Deputy Assistant Attorney General, Office of Legal Counsel, July 20, 2007, Re: Application of the War Crimes Act, the Detainee Treatment Act, and Common Article 3 of the Geneva Conventions to Certain Techniques that May be Used by the CIA in the Interrogation of High Value Al Qaeda Detainees (DTS #2009-1810, Tab 14).

inaccurate.[2437] The OLC memorandum also stated that the use of the CIA's enhanced interrogation techniques had "revealed plots to blow up the Brooklyn Bridge and to release mass biological agents in our Nation's largest cities."[2438]

(TS// ██████████████ //NF) Finally, the July 20, 2007, OLC memorandum asserted—based on CIA representations—that members of Congress supported the CIA interrogation program, and that, by subsequently voting for the Military Commissions Act, those members effectively endorsed an interpretation of the Act that would be consistent with the continued use of the CIA's enhanced interrogation techniques. This interpretation of congressional intent also supported the OLC's constitutional analysis, which stated that there could be "little doubt" that the Act "reflected an endorsement" from Congress that the CIA program "was consistent with contemporary practice, and therefore did not shock the conscience."[2439] Specifically, the OLC memorandum noted that according to CIA representations, prior to the passage of the Military Commissions Act, "several Members of Congress, including the full memberships of the House and Senate Intelligence Committees and Senator McCain, were briefed by General Michael Hayden, director of the CIA, on the six techniques," and that "in those classified and private conversations, none of the Members expressed the view that the CIA interrogation program should be stopped, or that the techniques at issue were inappropriate."[2440] This representation was inaccurate. For example, according to CIA records, during a briefing on September 11, 2006, Senator John McCain informed the CIA that he believed the CIA's enhanced interrogation techniques, including sleep deprivation and the waterboard, were "torture."[2441] On September

---

[2437] Memorandum for John A. Rizzo, Acting General Counsel, Central Intelligence Agency, from Steven G. Bradbury, Principal Deputy Assistant Attorney General, Office of Legal Counsel, July 20, 2007, Re: Application of the War Crimes Act, the Detainee Treatment Act, and Common Article 3 of the Geneva Conventions to Certain Techniques that May be Used by the CIA in the Interrogation of High Value Al Qaeda Detainees (DTS #2009-1810, Tab 14).

[2438] This is a reference to the CIA's representation that KSM, "as a result of EITs," provided critical and unique reporting on Iyman Faris and Majid Khan. As described briefly in this summary, and in greater detail in the full Committee Study, Iyman Faris was already under investigation, and Majid Khan was already in custody, before KSM mentioned them. Khan himself revealed a discussion about poisoning reservoirs prior to his rendition to CIA custody. (See ALEC ████ (210015Z MAR 03).) When Faris, who was likewise not in CIA custody, discussed a plot against the Brooklyn Bridge, the former chief of CTC's Bin Ladin Unit described it as "half-baked," and "more of a nuisance [sic] than a threat." See WHDC ████ (242226Z MAR 03) and email from: ██████████████ ; to: ████████████ , ███████████ , ████████████████ , [REDACTED]; subject: attacks in conus; date: March 25, 2003, at 6:19:18 AM).

[2439] Memorandum for John A. Rizzo, Acting General Counsel, Central Intelligence Agency, from Steven G. Bradbury, Principal Deputy Assistant Attorney General, Office of Legal Counsel, July 20, 2007, Re: Application of the War Crimes Act, the Detainee Treatment Act, and Common Article 3 of the Geneva Conventions to Certain Techniques that May be Used by the CIA in the Interrogation of High Value Al Qaeda Detainees (DTS #2009-1810, Tab 14).

[2440] Memorandum for John A. Rizzo, Acting General Counsel, Central Intelligence Agency, from Steven G. Bradbury, Principal Deputy Assistant Attorney General, Office of Legal Counsel, July 20, 2007, Re: Application of the War Crimes Act, the Detainee Treatment Act, and Common Article 3 of the Geneva Conventions to Certain Techniques that May be Used by the CIA in the Interrogation of High Value Al Qaeda Detainees (DTS #2009-1810, Tab 14).

[2441] Email from: ███████████ ; to ███████████ ; cc: ██████████ , [REDACTED], [REDACTED], [REDACTED], [REDACTED], ████████████ ; [REDACTED], [REDACTED], [REDACTED], [REDACTED], [REDACTED], [REDACTED], [REDACTED]; subject: Briefing for Senator John S. McCain (R-AZ); date: September 11, 2006, at 5:51 PM ("[Senator McCain] asked if I thought 'sleep deprivation' was torture. I responded that I did not and he then added that he had talked with a Marine Colonel friend of his and the Colonel had indicated

27, 2006, Senator Dianne Feinstein, a member of the Senate Select Committee on Intelligence, wrote a letter to CIA Director Hayden stating that she was "unable to understand why the CIA needs to maintain this program."[2442] On September 6, 2006, when the CIA provided its first and only briefing to the full Committee on the CIA program prior to the vote on the Military Commissions Act, Committee staff access was limited to the two Committee staff directors.[2443] In May 2007, shortly after the CIA allowed additional Committee staff to be briefed on the program, other members of the Committee prepared and provided letters to Director Hayden. On May 1, 2007, Senator Russ Feingold wrote that "I cannot support the program on moral, legal or national security grounds."[2444] On May 11, 2007, Senators Chuck Hagel, Dianne Feinstein, and Ron Wyden wrote a letter expressing their long-standing concerns with the program and their "deep discomfort with the use of EITs."[2445]

---

it was and he believed his friend."). In another exchange, the officer who briefed Senator McCain was asked about the Senator's position. CIA officer ███████████ : "so, is the senator on board?..." CIA officer ███████████ : "not totally." ███████ : "if he's moved in our direction at all, you are a miracle worker... was it painful?" ███████ : "Very much so." ███████ : "is the issue the EITs still?" ███████ : "Yep." (*See* Sametime communication between ███████████ and ███████████, 11/Sep/06, 15:47:27 to 18:43:29.) The OLC specifically cited statements from Senator McCain that the Military Commissions Act "will allow the CIA to continue interrogating prisoners within the boundaries established in the bill." Memorandum for John A. Rizzo, Acting General Counsel, Central Intelligence Agency, from Steven G. Bradbury, Principal Deputy Assistant Attorney General, Office of Legal Counsel, July 20, 2007, Re: Application of the War Crimes Act, the Detainee Treatment Act, and Common Article 3 of the Geneva Conventions to Certain Techniques that May be Used by the CIA in the Interrogation of High Value Al Qaeda Detainees (DTS #2009-1810, Tab 14). The OLC did not mention that McCain had specifically objected to the use of sleep deprivation.

[2442] Letter from Senator Dianne Feinstein to Director Hayden, September 27, 2006 (DTS #2006-3717).

[2443] Transcript of hearing of the Senate Select Committee on Intelligence, September 6, 2006 (DTS #2007-1336).

[2444] Letter from Senator Russ Feingold to Director Hayden, May 1, 2007 (DTS #2007-1858).

[2445] Letter from Senators Chuck Hagel, Dianne Feinstein and Ron Wyden, May 11, 2007 (DTS #2007-2102).

VI. Review of CIA Representations to the Congress

A. After Memorandum of Notification, the CIA Disavows Torture and Assures the Committee Will Be Notified of Every Individual Detained by the CIA

(TS// ████████ //NF) Following the September 11, 2001, terrorist attacks and the signing of the September 17, 2001, Memorandum of Notification (MON), the Senate Select Committee on Intelligence ("the Committee") held a series of hearings and briefings on CIA covert actions, including the new authority to detain terrorists. At a November 13, 2001, briefing for Committee staff, ███████ CTC Legal, ████████████, described the CIA's new detention authorities as "terrifying" and expressed the CIA's intent to "find a cadre of people who know how to run prisons, because we don't."[2446] Deputy Director of Operations (DDO) James Pavitt assured the Committee that it would be informed of each individual who entered CIA custody. Pavitt disavowed the use of torture against detainees while stating that the boundaries on the use of interrogation techniques were uncertain—specifically in the case of having to identify the location of a hidden nuclear weapon.[2447]

(TS// ████████ //NF) In meetings with the CIA in February 2002, the month before the capture and detention of Abu Zubaydah, Committee staff expressed concern about the lack of any legal review of the CIA's new detention authorities. ████████ noted that the discussion with Committee staff was "the only peer review" the CIA lawyers had engaged in with regard to the MON authorities, and that the discussion helped refine the CIA's understanding of what MON-authorized activity was in fact legally permissible and appropriate.[2448]

B. The CIA Notifies Committee of the Detention of Abu Zubaydah, but Makes No Reference to Coercive Interrogation Techniques; the CIA Briefs Chairman and Vice Chairman After the Use of the CIA's Enhanced Interrogation Techniques; the CIA Discusses Strategy to Avoid the Chairman's Request for More Information

(TS// ████████ //NF) On April 18, 2002, the CIA informed the Committee that it "has no current plans to develop a detention facility."[2449] At the time of this representation, the CIA had already established a CIA detention site in Country █ and detained Abu Zubaydah there. On April 24, 2002, the CIA notified the Committee about the capture of Abu Zubaydah with the understanding that the location of Abu Zubaydah's detention was among the "red lines" not to be divulged to the Committee.[2450] The notification and subsequent information provided to the

---

[2446] Transcript of Senate Select Committee on Intelligence staff briefing, November 13, 2001 (DTS #2002-0629).
[2447] "We're not going to engage in torture. But, that said, how do I deal with somebody I know may know right now that there is a nuclear weapon somewhere in the United States that is going to be detonated tomorrow, and I've got the guy who I know built it and hid it? I don't know the answer to that." (*See* transcript of Senate Select Committee on Intelligence MON briefing, November 7, 2001 (DTS #2002-0611); *see also* transcript of Senate Select Committee on Intelligence staff briefing, December 11, 2001 (DTS #2002-0615).
[2448] Email from: ████████, SSCI Staff; to: ███ Cleared SSCI staff; subject: Meeting yesterday with CIA lawyers on ████████; date: February 26, 2002 (DTS #2002-0925).
[2449] CIA responses to Questions for the Record (hearing, March 6, 2002), April 18, 2002 (DTS #2002-1800).
[2450] Email from: ████████; to: ████████; subject: Issues for SSCI and HPSCI biweekly update on CT; date: April 9, 2002; Transcript of "Update on War on Terrorism," April 24, 2002 (DTS #2002-1993). Committee notifications of the capture of 'Abd al-Rahim al-Nashiri likewise omitted reference to his location and the use of the

Committee included representations that Abu Zubaydah was a "member of Bin Ladin's inner circle" and a "key al-Qa'ida lieutenant."[2451] These representations were inaccurate. Briefings to the Committee in the spring of 2002 emphasized the expertise of FBI and CIA interrogators engaged in the Abu Zubaydah interrogations and provided no indication that coercive techniques were being used or considered, or that there was significant disagreement between the CIA and the FBI on proposed interrogation approaches.[2452] In early August 2002, after the Department of Justice determined that the use of the CIA's enhanced interrogation techniques on Abu Zubaydah would be legal, the CIA considered briefing the Committee on the CIA's interrogation techniques, but did not.[2453]

(TS// ███████████ //NF) In early September 2002, the CIA briefed the House Permanent Select Committee on Intelligence (HPSCI) leadership about the CIA's enhanced interrogation techniques. Two days after, the CIA's ██████ CTC Legal, ███████████, excised from a draft memorandum memorializing the briefing indications that the HPSCI leadership questioned the legality of the program by deleting the sentence: "HPSCI attendees also questioned the legality of these techniques if other countries would use them."[2454] After ██████████ blind-copied Jose Rodriguez on the email in which he transmitted the changes to the memorandum, Rodriguez responded to ████████'s email with: "short and sweet."[2455] The first briefing for Senate Select Committee on Intelligence Chairman Bob Graham and Vice Chairman Richard Shelby—and their staff directors—occurred on September 27, 2002, nearly two months after the CIA first began subjecting Abu Zubaydah to the CIA's enhanced interrogation techniques. The only record of the briefing is a one-paragraph CIA memorandum stating that the briefing occurred.[2456] The Committee does not have its own records of this briefing.

(TS// ███████████ //NF) Shortly thereafter, in late 2002, Chairman Graham sought to expand Committee oversight of the CIA's Detention and Interrogation Program, including by having Committee staff visit CIA interrogation sites and interview CIA interrogators.[2457] The CIA rejected this request. An internal CIA email from ██████ CTC Legal ███████████

CIA's enhanced interrogation techniques. (*See* Congressional Notification, November 20, 2002 (DTS #2002-4910).) On November █, 2002, the CIA notified the Committee of the death of Gul Rahman at a "detention facility in [Country ██████] operated by the [Country █ government] and funded by CIA." This description, as well as subsequent representations to the Committee, understated the role of the CIA in managing DETENTION SITE COBALT. *See* Congressional Notification, November █, 2002 (DTS #2002-5015); Responses to ██████ Counterterrorism Questions for the Record, Question 3 (DTS #2002-5059).

[2451] Congressional Notification, April 15, 2002 (DTS #2002-1710); CIA responses to Questions for the Record (hearing, March 6, 2002), April 18, 2002 (DTS #2002-1800).

[2452] Transcript of "Update on War on Terrorism," April 24, 2002 (DTS #2002-1993).

[2453] Email from: John Moseman; to: Stanley Moskowitz, et al.; subject: Abu Zubaydah Interrogation; date: August 3, 2002, at 11:34:13 AM.

[2454] Email from: ███████████; to: ██████████; bcc: Jose Rodriguez; subject: Re: immediate coord; date: September 6, 2002. *See also* ALEC ██████ (101607Z SEP 02).

[2455] Email from: Jose Rodriguez; to: ██████████; subject: Re: immediate coord; date: September 6, 2002, at 2:52 PM.

[2456] DIRECTOR ██████ (252018Z OCT02)

[2457] Email from: Stanley Moskowitz; to: John Moseman, Scott Muller, James Pavitt; subject: Graham request for oversight into interrogation; date: December 4, 2002, at 05:58:06 PM; Stanley Moskowitz, Memorandum for the Record, February 4, 2003, "Subject: Sensitive Notification." *See also* email from: Scott W. Muller; to: John A. Rizzo; cc: [REDACTED]; date: December 19, 2002.

indicated that the full Committee would not be told about "the nature and scope of the interrogation process," and that even the chairman and vice chairman would not be told in which country or "region" the CIA had established its detention facilities.[2458] Other emails describe efforts by the CIA to identify a "strategy" for limiting the CIA's responses to Chairman Graham's requests for more information on the CIA's Detention and Interrogation Program, specifically seeking a way to "get off the hook on the cheap."[2459] The CIA eventually chose to delay its next update for the Committee leadership on the CIA's program until after Graham had left the Committee.[2460] At the same time, the CIA rejected a request for the Committee staff to be "read-in" and provided with a briefing on the CIA program.[2461]

> C. No Detailed Records Exist of CIA Briefings of Committee Leadership; the CIA Declines to Answer Questions from Committee Members or Provide Requested Materials

(TS// █████████ //NF) On February 4, 2003, the CIA briefed the new chairman, Senator Pat Roberts, and the two staff directors. Vice Chairman John D. Rockefeller IV was not present. The only record of the briefing, a two-page CIA memorandum, states that CIA officers:

> "described in great detail the importance of the information provided by [Abu] Zubayda[h] and ['Abd al-Rahim al-] Nashiri, both of whom had information of on-going terrorist operations, information that might well have saved American lives, the difficulty of getting that information from them, and the importance of the enhanced techniques in getting that information."[2462]

As described in this summary, and in greater detail in the full Committee Study, Abu Zubaydah and al-Nashiri did not provide actionable intelligence on ongoing plotting, and provided significant reporting prior to the use of the CIA's enhanced interrogation techniques. The CIA declined to provide information pursuant to a request from Chairman Roberts on the location of the CIA's detention site. Finally, the CIA memorandum states that Chairman Roberts "gave his assent" to the destruction of interrogation videotapes; however, this account in the CIA

[2458] Email from: █████████; to: █████████ and █████████; subject: Sensitive Matters for the SSCI Quarterly CA Briefing; date: November 19, 2002. This email included the text of the CIA cables documenting the September 4, 2002, briefing to HPSCI leadership. *See* ALEC ████ (101607Z SEP 02), and the September 27, 2002, briefing to SSCI leadership, DIRECTOR ████ (252018Z OCT02).

[2459] Email from: Stanley Moskowitz; to: John Moseman, Scott Mueller, James Pavitt; subject: Graham request for oversight into interrogation; date: December 4, 2002, at 05:58:06 PM; email from: Stanley Moskowitz; to: John H. Moseman; cc: Scott Muller and James Pavitt; subject: [attached document] Re: Graham request on interrogations; date: December 9, 2002, at 05:46:11 PM.

[2460] Memorandum of December 26, 2002; FOR: Director of Central Intelligence; FROM: Scott W. Muller, General Counsel; SUBJECT: Disposition of Videotapes.

[2461] Memorandum to: Stanley Moskowitz; from: Steven A. Cash; subject: Briefing: Interrogation and Debriefing of individuals in custody related to counterterrorism operations, January 2, 2003 (DTS #2003-0266); Lotus Notes dated January 2 – January 3, between OCA, ODDO, CTC personnel; email correspondences between [REDACTED], [REDACTED], █████████; subject: "SSCI's Request for Staff Briefing on Terrorism Interrogation/Debriefing Techniques."

[2462] Moskowitz Memorandum for the Record, February 4, 2003, "Subject: Sensitive Notification."

memorandum was later disputed by Chairman Roberts.[2463] The Committee has no independent record of this briefing.

(TS// ███████████ //NF) Throughout 2003, the CIA refused to answer questions from Committee members and staff about the CIA interrogations of KSM and other CIA detainees.[2464] The CIA produced talking points for a September 4, 2003, briefing on the CIA interrogation program exclusively for Committee leadership; however, there are no contemporaneous records of the briefing taking place. The CIA talking points include information about the use of the CIA's enhanced interrogation techniques, their effectiveness, and various abuses that occurred in the program.[2465] Many of the CIA representations in the talking points were inaccurate.[2466] The CIA continued to withhold from the Committee, including its leadership, any information on the location of the CIA's detention facilities. On more than one occasion the CIA directed CIA personnel at Guantanamo Bay, Cuba, not to brief a visiting Committee member about the CIA detention facility there, including during a July 2005 visit by Chairman Roberts.[2467]

(TS// ███████████ //NF) In 2004, the Committee conducted two hearings on the CIA's role in interrogating U.S. military detainees at Abu Ghraib prison in Iraq. CIA witnesses stressed that the CIA was more limited in its interrogation authorities than the Department of Defense, but declined to respond to Committee questions about the interrogation of KSM or press reports on CIA detention facilities.[2468] During the first briefing, on May 12, 2004, Committee members requested Department of Justice memoranda addressing the legality of CIA interrogations.

[2463] Moskowitz Memorandum for the Record, February 4, 2003, "Subject: Sensitive Notification." For information on Senator Roberts's objections, *see* "Destroying C.I.A. Tapes Wasn't Opposed, Memos Say," by Scott Shane, *The New York Times*, dated February 22, 2010.

[2464] Transcript of CIA briefing for the Senate Select Committee on Intelligence, March 5, 2003 (DTS #2003-1156); Transcript of "Intelligence Update," April 30, 2003 (DTS #2003-2174); Transcript of Senate Select Committee on Intelligence briefing, September 3, 2003 (DTS #2004-0288); email from: ███████████; to: [REDACTED]; subject: Re: EYES ONLY Re: Question Regarding Interrogations from SSCI Member Briefing on KSM Capture; date: March 17, 2003.

[2465] CIA Interrogation Program: DDO Talking Points, 04 September 2003.

[2466] For example, the talking points included inaccurate data on the waterboarding of Abu Zubaydah and KSM; stated that two unauthorized techniques were used with a detainee, whereas 'Abd al-Rahim al-Nashiri was subjected to numerous unauthorized techniques; and inaccurately stated that the offending officers were removed from the site. The talking points also stated that the use of the CIA's enhanced interrogation techniques "has produced significant results," and that the "[i]nformation acquired has saved countless lives...." *See* CIA Interrogation Program: DDO Talking Points, 04 September 2003.

[2467] Because the Committee was not informed of the CIA detention site at Guantanamo Bay, Cuba, no member of the Committee was aware that the U.S. Supreme Court decision to grant certiorari in the case of *Rasul v. Bush*, which related to the *habeas corpus* rights of detainees at Guantanamo Bay, resulted in the transfer of CIA detainees from the CIA detention facility at Guantanamo Bay to other CIA detention facilities. *See* HEADQUARTERS ███████████, subject "RESTRICTED ACCESS TO [DETENTION SITE COBALT] AND [DETENTION SITE ORANGE]"; email from: ███████████; to ███████████; cc: Jose Rodriguez, [REDACTED], ███████████, [REDACTED], ███████████, [REDACTED], [REDACTED]; subject: guidance to ███ gitmo; date: May 14, 2004; forwarding final cable: HEADQUARTERS ███ (141502Z MAY 04), subject "Possible Brief to US Senator"; email from: Stanley Moskowitz; to: [REDACTED]; cc: [REDACTED]; subject: Re: guidance to ███ gitmo; date: May 14, 2004; CIA responses to Questions for the Record, March 13, 2008 (DTS #2008-1310); "CODEL Roberts to Miami/Guantanamo, 7-8 July 2005," dated 5 July, ███ 902860.

[2468] Transcript of hearing, May 12, 2004 (DTS #2004-2332); Transcript of hearing, September 13, 2004 (DTS #2005-0750).

Despite repeated subsequent requests, limited access to the memoranda was not granted until four years later, in June 2008, by which time the CIA was no longer detaining individuals.[2469]

(TS//████████████//NF) While the CIA continued to brief the Committee leadership on aspects of the CIA's Detention and Interrogation Program, there are no transcripts of these briefings. One briefing, on July 15, 2004, discussed the detention of Janat Gul.[2470] An email from ████████████CTC Legal stated that the "only reason" the chairman and vice chairman were informed of the detention of Janat Gul was that the notification could serve as "the vehicle for briefing the committees on our need for renewed legal and policy support" for the CIA's Detention and Interrogation Program.[2471] At the July 2004 briefing, the minority staff director requested full Committee briefings and expanded Committee oversight, including visits to CIA detention sites and interviews with interrogators—efforts that had been sought by former Chairman Graham years earlier. This request was denied.[2472]

D. Vice Chairman Rockefeller Seeks Committee Investigation

(TS//████████████//NF) On February 3, 2005, Vice Chairman Rockefeller began a formal effort to conduct a comprehensive Committee investigation of the CIA's detention, interrogation and rendition activities, including a review of the legality and effectiveness of CIA interrogations.[2473] On March 3, 2005, a CIA official wrote that Vice Chairman Rockefeller was "convinced that we're hiding stuff from him" and that the CIA had planned a detailed briefing to "shut Rockefeller up."[2474] The only Committee records of this briefing, which took place on March 7, 2005, are handwritten notes written by Vice Chairman Rockefeller and the minority staff director.[2475] Shortly after this briefing, the vice chairman reiterated his call for a broad Committee investigation of the CIA's Detention and Interrogation Program, which he and the ranking member of the HPSCI, Jane Harman, described in a letter to Vice President Cheney.[2476] There is no Committee record of a response to the letter.

[2469] Transcript of Senate Select Committee on Intelligence hearing, May 12, 2004 (DTS #2004-2332). Muhammad Rahim, the CIA's last detainee, was transferred to U.S. military custody on March 13, 2008. *See* ██████ 3445 ████████████; ██████ 9754 ████████████; ██████ 8405 ████████████; ██████ 8408

[2470] Handwritten notes of SSCI Minority Staff Director Andrew Johnson (DTS #2009-2077); CIA notes (DTS #2009-2024, pp. 92-95); CIA notes (DTS #2009-2024, pp. 110-121).

[2471] Email from: ████████████, to: [REDACTED]; subject: Re: Priority: congressional notification on Janat Gul; date: July 29, 2004.

[2472] Handwritten notes of SSCI Minority Staff Director Andrew Johnson (DTS #2009-2077); CIA notes (DTS #2009-2024, pp. 92-95); CIA notes (DTS #2009-2024, pp. 110-121).

[2473] February 3, 2005, letter from Senator Rockefeller to Senator Roberts on "the Committee's upcoming agenda," (letter incorrectly dated February 3, 2004).

[2474] Sametime message discussion between ████████████ and [REDACTED], March 3, 2005.

[2475] The notes indicate that CIA briefers provided inaccurate information. For example, the notes indicate that "[w]e screen carefully _all_ people who might have contact with detainees" (emphasis in the Vice Chairman's notes) and that "positive incentives" are used prior to "coercive measures." In a reference to the waterboard, the notes state, the detainee "thinks he's drowning, even though they are breathing." *See* handwritten notes of then-Committee Minority Staff Director Andrew Johnson (DTS #2009-2077, Image 1) and handwritten notes of Senator Rockefeller.

[2476] Letter to Senator Roberts from minority SSCI members, March 10, 2005 (DTS #2005-1126); Letter to Vice President Cheney from Vice Chairman Rockefeller and Representative Harman, March 11, 2005; Letter from Senator Rockefeller, March 11, 2005.

(~~TS//~~████████████~~//NF~~) On April 13, 2005, the day before an anticipated Committee vote on the vice chairman's proposed investigation of the CIA program, the chief of ALEC Station, ██████████, and the deputy chief of CTC, Philip Mudd, discussed a press strategy to shape public and congressional views of the program. As previously detailed, Mudd wrote:

> "we either get out and sell, or we get hammered, which has implications beyond the media. congress reads it, cuts our authorities, messes up our budget. we need to make sure the impression of what we do is positive."[2477]

(~~TS//~~████████████~~//NF~~) The next day, CIA Inspector General John Helgerson briefed several members of the Committee on limited aspects of the CIA's Detention and Interrogation Program. According to Helgerson, Chairman Roberts' "motive was to have a presentation that made clear that CIA IG is looking at all appropriate detention and interrogation issues, as (he told me privately beforehand) the Committee will be voting today on whether to launch their own inquiry." Helgerson added that "Roberts said 'I know how that vote is going to come out, but I want the minority to go away knowing this is in good hands.'"[2478] The proposed investigation was not approved by the Committee. The Committee nonetheless subsequently approved legislation requiring CIA reports on renditions and plans for the disposition of high-value CIA detainees, as well as requesting expanded Committee staff access to the program beyond the Committee staff directors.[2479] In addition, Vice Chairman Rockefeller requested full Committee access to over 100 documents related to the May 2004 Inspector General Special Review.[2480] On January 5, 2006, after multiple rounds of negotiations with the CIA for the documents, the chief of staff to Director of National Intelligence John Negroponte wrote a letter rejecting the request. The letter had been prepared by the former ████ CTC Legal, ██████, ██████████, who was by then serving as a CIA detailee in the Office of the Director of National Intelligence.[2481]

[2477] Sametime communication, between John P. Mudd and ██████████████, April 13, 2005, from 19:23:50 to 19:56:05.

[2478] *See* email from: CIA Inspector General John Helgerson; to: ██████████████; subject: this afternoon's briefing; date: April 13, 2005. There is no Committee transcript of the briefing. CIA records state that the briefing covered "updates on the half dozen key abuse cases," ghost detainees, and renditions. The notes do not reference the CIA's enhanced interrogation techniques. In response to a question from Vice Chairman Rockefeller, Helgerson explained that the CIA was "preparing a comprehensive briefing" on detention and interrogation activities for the Committee.

[2479] Compartmented Classified Annex to Report No. S. 109-142, Intelligence Authorization Act for Fiscal Year 2006, as Reported by the Select Committee on Intelligence (DTS #2005-4028).

[2480] *See* Letter from John A. Rizzo to John Rockefeller, August 16, 2005 (DTS #2005-3522). The DNI, pursuant to the advice of former ████ CTC Legal, ██████████████, supported the CIA's proposed limitations on Committee access to the documents (email from: ██████████; to: Michael Leiter; cc: David Shedd, ██████████ and others; subject: Review of Documents Requested by Senator Rockefeller; date: December 16, 2005; Letter from David Shedd to Andy Johnson, January 5, 2006 (DTS #2006-0373)).

[2481] Letter from David Shedd to Andy Johnson, January 5, 2006 (DTS #2006-0373); email from: ██████ ██████████; to: Michael Leiter; cc: David Shedd, ██████████ and others; subject: Review of Documents Requested by Senator Rockefeller; date: December 16, 2005.

E. In Response to Detainee Treatment Act, the CIA Briefs Senators Not on the Committee; Proposal from Senator Levin for an Independent Commission Prompts Renewed Calls Within the CIA to Destroy Interrogation Videotapes

(TS// ███████████ //NF) In October and November 2005, after the Senate passed its version of the Detainee Treatment Act, the CIA, directed by the Office of the Vice President, briefed specific Republican senators, who were not on the Select Committee on Intelligence, on the CIA's Detention and Interrogation Program. (The full membership of the Committee had not yet been briefed on the CIA interrogation program.)[2482] The briefings, which were intended to influence conference negotiations,[2483] were provided to Senator McCain;[2484] Senators Ted Stevens and Thad Cochran, the chairmen of the Appropriations Committee and Defense Appropriations Subcommittee;[2485] Majority Leader Bill Frist;[2486] and Senator John Cornyn (CIA records state that Cornyn was not briefed on the CIA's specific interrogation techniques).[2487] Meanwhile, a proposal from Senator Carl Levin to establish an independent commission to investigate U.S. detention policies and allegations of detainee abuse resulted in concern at the CIA that such a commission would lead to the discovery of videotapes documenting CIA interrogations. That concern prompted renewed interest at the CIA to destroy the videotapes.[2488]

[2482] According to an email from John Rizzo, the subject of one such meeting was "how the current version of McCain potentially undercuts our legal position." (*See* email from: John A. Rizzo; to: ███████, ████, ██; cc: [REDACTED], [REDACTED], ████████, [REDACTED], [REDACTED], [REDACTED], [REDACTED], [REDACTED]; subject: IMMEDIATE HEADS UP: VP Meeting with Appropriations Committee Leadership Tomorrow re McCain Amendment; date: October 17, 2005, at 10:49:39 AM; email from: John Rizzo; to: ████████; cc: [REDACTED], [REDACTED], [REDACTED], [REDACTED], [REDACTED], [REDACTED], [REDACTED], ██████████, [REDACTED], [REDACTED], [REDACTED], [REDACTED]; subject: Re: IMMEDIATE: Re: Sen. Frist req for briefing on impact of McCain Amendment; date: October 31, 2005, at 10:53:16 AM.

[2483] Email from: John A. Rizzo; to: ████████, ████████; cc: [REDACTED], [REDACTED], ████, ████, [REDACTED], [REDACTED], [REDACTED], [REDACTED], [REDACTED]; subject: IMMEDIATE HEADS UP: VP Meeting with Appropriations Committee Leadership Tomorrow re McCain Amendment; date: October 17, 2005, at 10:49:39 AM.

[2484] Email from: John Rizzo; to: ████████; cc: [REDACTED], [REDACTED], [REDACTED], [REDACTED], [REDACTED], [REDACTED], [REDACTED], ██████████, [REDACTED], [REDACTED], [REDACTED], [REDACTED], ████████, [REDACTED], [REDACTED]; subject: Re: IMMEDIATE: Re: Sen. Frist req for briefing on impact of McCain Amendment; date: October 31, 2005, at 10:53:16 AM; ████ Talking Points for OVP Sponsored Meeting with Sen McCain; Impact of McCain Amendment on Legal Basis for CTC's HVD Detention and Interrogation Program, 20 October 2005.

[2485] Email from: John Rizzo; to: ████████; cc: [REDACTED], [REDACTED], [REDACTED], [REDACTED], [REDACTED], [REDACTED], [REDACTED], ██████████, [REDACTED], [REDACTED], [REDACTED], [REDACTED], ████████, [REDACTED], [REDACTED]; subject: Re: IMMEDIATE: Re: Sen. Frist req for briefing on impact of McCain Amendment; date: October 31, 2005, at 10:53:16 AM.

[2486] Email from: John Rizzo; to: ████████; cc: [REDACTED], [REDACTED], [REDACTED], [REDACTED], [REDACTED], [REDACTED], [REDACTED], ██████████, [REDACTED], [REDACTED], [REDACTED], [REDACTED], ████████, [REDACTED], [REDACTED]; subject: Re: IMMEDIATE: Re: Sen. Frist req for briefing on impact of McCain Amendment; date: October 31, 2005, at 10:53:16 AM; email from: John A. Rizzo; to: David R. Shedd; cc: [REDACTED]; subject: Re: BRIEF READOUT: 31 OCT FRIST BRIEFING; date: November 1, 2005, at 2:53:40 PM.

[2487] Email from: John A. Rizzo; to: [REDACTED]; cc: ████████, [REDACTED], [REDACTED], ████; [REDACTED]; subject: Re: Senator Cornyn; date: November 30, 2005, at 12:50:11 PM.

[2488] On October 31, 2005, John Rizzo wrote an email stating that "Sen. Levin's legislative proposal for a 9/11-type outside Commission to be established on detainees seems to be gaining some traction, which obviously would serve

Senator Levin's amendment to establish the commission failed on November 8, 2005.[2489] The CIA destroyed the CIA interrogation videotapes the following day.[2490]

F. CIA Director Goss Seeks Committee Support for the Program After the Detainee Treatment Act; CIA Declines to Answer Questions for the Record

(TS// ██████████ //NF) In March 2006, three months after passage of the Detainee Treatment Act, the CIA provided a briefing for five Committee staffers that included limited information on the interrogation process, as well as the effectiveness of the CIA interrogation program.[2491] The briefings did not include information on the CIA's enhanced interrogation techniques or the location of CIA detention sites.[2492] A week later, on March 15, 2006, CIA Director Porter Goss briefed the full Committee on CIA detention matters, but did not provide the locations of the CIA's detention facilities, or a list or briefing on the CIA's enhanced

---

to surface the tapes' existence." Rizzo then added that "I think I need to be the skunk at the party again and see if the Director is willing to let us try one more time to get the right people downtown on board with the notion of our [sic] destroying the tapes." ██████████, a senior CIA attorney who had viewed the videotapes, responded, "You are correct. The sooner we resolve this the better." ██████████ CTC Legal, ██████████, also agreed that "[a]pproaching the DCIA is a good idea," adding, "[c]ommissions tend to make very broad document production demands, which might call for these videotapes that should have been destroyed in the normal course of business 2 years ago." *See* email from: John A. Rizzo; to: ██████████; [REDACTED], [REDACTED], ██████████, [REDACTED], [REDACTED]; subject: Re: principals want PR plan to publicly roll the CTC program in some fashion; date: October 31, 2005, at 10:37 AM; email from: ██████████; to John A. Rizzo; cc: [REDACTED], [REDACTED], [REDACTED], ██████████; subject: Re: principals want PR plan to publicly roll the CTC program in some fashion; date: October 31, 2005, at 12:32 PM; email from: ██████████; to: John A. Rizzo; cc: [REDACTED], [REDACTED], ██████████, [REDACTED], [REDACTED]; subject: Re: principals want PR plan to publicly roll the CTC program in some fashion; date: October 31, 2005, at 11:45 AM. *See also* interview of ██████████, by [REDACTED] and [REDACTED], Office of the Inspector General, June 17, 2003.

[2489] *See* Senate Roll Call Vote #00309, November 8, 2005, 5:37pm, on Amendment #2430.

[2490] [REDACTED] 27089 (090627Z NOV 05)

[2491] A review of the Committee record of this briefing indicates much of the information provided by the CIA was inaccurate. For example, according to the Committee's Memorandum for the Record, CIA briefers stated "the plan divorces questioning from coercive measures." CIA records indicate, however, that questioning and the use of the CIA's enhanced interrogation techniques were combined in practice. According to Committee records, CIA officials stated that Khalid al-Masri had and maintained connections to al-Qa'ida, and that he was released "when the CIA reached a point in debriefings that required [foreign government] assistance," which was not forthcoming. The CIA Inspector General would later determine that when CIA officers questioned al-Masri, "they quickly concluded that he was not a terrorist," and that there was "insufficient basis to render and detain al-Masri." CIA officers referenced the captures of Hambali, Sajid Badat, Jose Padilla, and Iyman Faris, as well as the disruption of the West Coast/Second Wave plotting, the Heathrow Airport plotting, and the Karachi plotting. As detailed in this summary, the CIA consistently provided inaccurate representations regarding the plotting and the capture of the referenced individuals. CIA briefers also compared the program to U.S. military custody, stating that "the CIA can bring far more resources – debriefers, analysts, psychologists, etc. – per detainee than is possible at large scale facilities such as Guantanamo Bay, Cuba." As described, the chief of Base at DETENTION SITE BLACK complained of "problem, underperforming" and "totally inexperienced" debriefers almost a year prior to this briefing. As further described, an inspector general audit completed three months after the briefing described the lack of debriefers at CIA detention facilities as "an ongoing problem." (Senate Select Committee on Intelligence, Memorandum for the Record, "CIA Briefing on Detention Program," March 8, 2006 (DTS #2006-1182).)

[2492] Senate Select Committee on Intelligence, Memorandum for the Record, "CIA Briefing on Detention Program," March 8, 2006 (DTS #2006-1182).

interrogation techniques.[2493] At this hearing Director Goss explained to the Committee that "we cannot do it by ourselves," and that "[w]e need to have the support of our oversight committee."[2494] Goss then described challenges to the CIA's Detention and Interrogation Program as a result of the Detainee Treatment Act, as well as strained relations with countries hosting CIA detention sites after significant press revelations.[2495] Director Goss described the program as follows:

> "This program has brought us incredible information. It's a program that could continue to bring us incredible information. It's a program that could continue to operate in a very professional way. It's a program that I think if you saw how it's operated you would agree that you would be proud that it's done right and well, with proper safeguards."[2496]

(TS// ███████████ //NF) Contrasting the CIA program to the abuse of prisoners in U.S. military detention at the Abu Ghraib prison in Iraq, Director Goss stated that the CIA program:

> "is a professionally-operated program that we operate uniquely.... We are not talking military, and I'm not talking about anything that a contractor might have done... in a prison somewhere or beat somebody or hit somebody with a stick or something. That's not what this is about."[2497]

(TS// ███████████ //NF) Addressing CIA interrogations, Director Goss testified that "we only bring in certain selected people that we think can give us intelligence information, and we treat them in certain specific ways" such that "they basically become psychologically disadvantaged to their interrogator." Explaining that the key to a successful interrogation was "getting a better psychological profile and knowing what makes someone tick," Director Goss stated, "just the simplest thing will work, a family photograph or something." Goss then represented that the CIA's interrogation program is "not a brutality. It's more of an art or a science that is refined."[2498]

[2493] By the time of the briefing, press disclosures had resulted in widespread public discussion about some of the CIA's reported enhanced interrogation techniques, including the waterboard. Goss was thus asked by a member of the Committee whether the CIA had undertaken a "technique by technique" analysis of the effectiveness of the program. Goss responded that the problem with such an analysis is that the techniques were used "in combination." Asked by the member for a comparison of "waterboarding versus sleep deprivation," Goss responded that "waterboarding is not used in conjunction with anything else." As detailed elsewhere, this testimony was inaccurate. Goss then referred to sleep deprivation, dietary manipulation, and "environment control" as "alleged techniques." See transcript of Senate Select Committee on Intelligence briefing, March 15, 2006 (DTS #2006-1308).

[2494] Director Goss stated: "I've had to seriously consider whether passage of the McCain amendment was a congressional disapproval of the CIA use of EITs. I don't think it was, and I don't think that was the message you sent me. But I have to at least get that assurance, that that's not what you were saying to me." See transcript of Senate Select Committee on Intelligence briefing, March 15, 2006 (DTS #2006-1308).

[2495] Transcript of Senate Select Committee on Intelligence briefing, March 15, 2006 (DTS #2006-1308).

[2496] Transcript of Senate Select Committee on Intelligence briefing, March 15, 2006 (DTS #2006-1308).

[2497] Transcript of Senate Select Committee on Intelligence briefing, March 15, 2006 (DTS #2006-1308).

[2498] Transcript of Senate Select Committee on Intelligence briefing, March 15, 2006 (DTS #2006-1308).

(TS// ███████████ //NF) After the hearing, the Committee submitted official Questions for the Record related to the history, legality, and the effectiveness of the CIA's Detention and Interrogation Program. The CIA did not respond.[2499]

(TS// ███████████ //NF) In May 2006, the Committee approved legislation requiring the CIA to provide reports on the CIA's detention facilities (including their locations), the CIA's interrogation techniques, the impact of the Detainee Treatment Act on the CIA program, CIA renditions, and the CIA's plans for the disposition of its detainees. The legislation also called for full Committee access to the CIA May 2004 Inspector General Special Review, as well as expanded member and Committee staff access to information on the CIA's Detention and Interrogation Program.[2500] In July 2006, the new CIA director, General Michael Hayden, provided a briefing for the chairman and vice chairman in which he described the Detainee Treatment Act as a "safehaven" that potentially permitted the CIA to use its enhanced interrogation techniques.[2501]

G. Full Committee First Briefed on the CIA's Interrogation Program Hours Before It Is Publicly Acknowledged on September 6, 2006

(TS// ███████████ //NF) On September 6, 2006, President Bush publicly acknowledged the CIA program and the transfer of 14 CIA detainees to U.S. military custody at Guantanamo Bay, Cuba. Hours prior to the announcement, CIA Director Hayden provided the first briefing on the CIA's "enhanced interrogation" program for all members of the Committee, although the CIA limited staff attendance to the Committee's two staff directors.[2502] Due to the impending public acknowledgment of the program, the briefing was abbreviated. At the briefing, the CIA's enhanced interrogation techniques were listed, but not described. Director Hayden stated that the techniques were developed at the Department of Defense SERE school and were "used against American service personnel during their training." He testified that "once [a detainee] gets into the situation of sustained cooperation," debriefings are "not significantly different than what you and I are doing right now." Hayden sought "legislative assistance" in interpreting Common Article 3, stated that he had not asked for an opinion from the Department of Justice, and represented that he had been informed informally that seven interrogation techniques "are viewed by the Department of Justice to be consistent with the requirements of the Detainee Treatment Act."[2503] Director Hayden declined to identify the locations of the CIA's detention facilities to the members and stated that he personally had recommended not expanding

---

[2499] Letter from Vice Chairman Rockefeller to Director Goss, containing Questions for the Record, May 10, 2006 (DTS #2006-1949); Letter from Chairman Roberts to Director Goss, May 4, 2006 (DTS #2006-1876).

[2500] Classified Annex to Report No. S. 109-259, the Intelligence Authorization Act for Fiscal Year 2007 (DTS #2006-2208). Compartmented annex (DTS #2006-2209).

[2501] Hayden stated that *Hamdan v. Rumsfeld* had effectively prohibited the use of the CIA's enhanced interrogation techniques. He then described an "action" that would define Common Article 3 according to the Detainee Treatment Act, which was in turn "anchored" in the Convention Against Torture to "which the Senate express[ed] reservation." As described, two months later, the President sought Congressional approval of the Military Commissions Act. Based on handwritten notes by the Committee minority staff director.

[2502] Transcript of Senate Select Committee on Intelligence briefing, September 6, 2006 (DTS #2007-1336).

[2503] As described above, the CIA had sought the Department of Justice's opinion on the application of the Detainee Treatment Act to the CIA's enhanced interrogation techniques. The draft memorandum was withdrawn after the U.S. Supreme Court case in *Hamdan v. Rumsfeld*.

Committee staff access beyond the two staff directors already briefed on the CIA's Detention and Interrogation Program.[2504]

(~~TS//~~ ████████ ~~//NF~~) There were no other Committee briefings or hearings on the CIA's Detention and Interrogation Program prior to the Senate's September 28, 2006, vote on the Military Commissions Act. As described, the Department of Justice later concluded that the CIA's enhanced interrogation techniques were consistent with the Military Commissions Act in part because, according to the CIA, "none of the Members [briefed on the CIA program] expressed the view that the CIA interrogation program should be stopped, or that the techniques at issue were inappropriate."[2505] However, prior to the vote, Senator McCain—who had been briefed on the CIA program—told CIA officials that he could not support the program and that sleep deprivation, one of the interrogation techniques still included in the program, as well as waterboarding, were torture.[2506] Members of the Committee also expressed their views in classified letters to the CIA. Senator Dianne Feinstein informed the CIA that Hayden's testimony on the CIA program was "extraordinarily problematic" and that she was "unable to understand why the CIA needs to maintain this program."[2507] In May 2007, shortly after additional Committee staff gained access to the program, Senator Russ Feingold expressed his opposition to the program, while Senators Feinstein, Ron Wyden, and Chuck Hagel described their concerns about the CIA program and their "deep discomfort" with the use of the CIA's enhanced interrogation techniques.[2508]

(~~TS//~~ ████████ ~~//NF~~) On November 16, 2006, CIA Director Hayden briefed the Committee.[2509] The briefing included inaccurate information, including on the CIA's use of dietary manipulation and nudity, as well as the effects of sleep deprivation.[2510] Before speaking

---

[2504] Transcript of Senate Select Committee on Intelligence briefing, September 6, 2006 (DTS #2007-1336). The transcript includes the following exchange: Senator Feingold: "...you make it tougher on me and the members of the Committee by the decision to not allow staff access to a briefing like this. Was it your recommendation to deny staff access to this hearing?" CIA Director Hayden: "It was."

[2505] Memorandum for John A. Rizzo, Acting General Counsel, Central Intelligence Agency, from Steven G. Bradbury, Principal Deputy Assistant Attorney General, Office of Legal Counsel, July 20, 2007, Re: Application of the War Crimes Act, the Detainee Treatment Act, and Common Article 3 of the Geneva Conventions to Certain Techniques that May be Used by the CIA in the Interrogation of High Value Al Qaeda Detainees (DTS #2009-1810, Tab 14).

[2506] Email from: ████████; to ████████; cc: ████████, [REDACTED], [REDACTED], [REDACTED], [REDACTED], ████████; [REDACTED], [REDACTED], [REDACTED], [REDACTED], [REDACTED], [REDACTED], [REDACTED]; subject: Briefing for Senator John S. McCain (R-AZ); date: September 11, 2006, at 5:51 PM.

[2507] Letter from Senator Feinstein to Director Hayden, September 27, 2006 (DTS #2006-3717).

[2508] Letter from Senator Feingold to Director Hayden, May 1, 2007 (DTS #2007-1858); Letter from Senators Feinstein, Wyden and Hagel to Director Hayden, May 11, 2007 (DTS #2007-2102).

[2509] As in the September 6, 2006, briefing, only two staff members were permitted to attend.

[2510] Director Hayden testified that detainees were never provided fewer than 1,000 calories a day. This is inaccurate. There were no calorie requirements until May 2004, and draft OMS guidelines from March 2003 indicated that "[b]rief periods in which food is withheld (1-2 days), as an adjunct to interrogations are acceptable." (See OMS GUIDELINES ON MEDICAL AND PSYCHOLOGICAL SUPPORT TO DETAINEE RENDITION, INTERROGATION, AND DETENTION, May 17, 2004; OMS Guidelines on Medical and Psychological Support to Detainee Interrogations, First Draft, March 7, 2003.) Director Hayden testified that detainees were "not paraded [nude] in front of anyone," whereas a CIA interrogator told the inspector general that nude detainees were "kept in a center area outside the interrogation room," and were "'walked around' by guards." (See Interview Report, ████

about the CIA's enhanced interrogation techniques, however, Director Hayden asked to brief the Committee on the recent capture of the CIA's newest detainee, Abdul Hadi al-Iraqi, who was not subjected to the CIA's enhanced interrogation techniques. Vice Chairman Rockefeller and two other members of the Committee expressed frustration at the briefing that Director Hayden's description of Hadi al-Iraqi's capture was preventing what was expected to be an in-depth discussion of the CIA's enhanced interrogation techniques.[2511]

(TS// ████████ //NF) On February 14, 2007, during a hearing on CIA renditions, Director Hayden provided inaccurate information to the Committee, to include inaccurate information on the number of detainees held by the CIA. ███████████, the deputy chief of the ████████ Department in CTC and the previous deputy chief of ALEC Station, provided examples of information obtained from the CIA Detention and Interrogation Program.[2512] After providing the examples, ████████ closed her testimony with the statement that "[t]here's no question, in my mind, that having that detainee information has saved hundreds, conservatively speaking, of American lives."[2513]

(TS// ████████ //NF) On March 15, 2007, in a speech to a gathering of ambassadors to the United States from the countries of the European Union, Director Hayden stated that congressional support for the CIA's Detention and Interrogation Program assured the continuity of the program:

> "I mentioned earlier that it would be unwise to assume that there will be a dramatic change in the American approach to the war on terror in 2009. CIA got the legislation it needed to continue this program in the Military Commissions Act passed by our Congress last fall. And let me remind you that every member of our intelligence committees, House and Senate, Republican and Democrat, is now fully briefed on the detention and interrogation program. This is not CIA's program. This is not the President's program. This is America's program."[2514]

████████, April 14, 2003.) ████████ testified that standing sleep deprivation is discontinued when swelling or "any abnormality" appears. This was inaccurate. For example, KSM's standing sleep deprivation continued, notwithstanding pedal edema and abrasions on his ankles, shins and wrists, as well as the back of his head. (*See* ████████ 10916 (210845Z MAR 03); ████████ 10909 (201918Z MAR 03).) Director Hayden testified that "mental conditions that would be of normal concern do not present themselves until a person has experienced more than 100 hours of sleep deprivation," however at least three detainees experienced hallucinations after being subjected to fewer than 96 hours of sleep deprivation. See ████████ 1393 (201006Z OCT 03); ████████ 48122 ████████; ████████ 1299 (████████ JAN 04); ████████ 1312 (████████ JAN 04); ████████ 1530 (████████ 04); ████████ 3221 ████████; ████████ 3241 (████████ 04).

[2511] Transcript of Senate Select Committee on Intelligence hearing, November 16, 2006 (DTS #2007-1422).
[2512] This testimony included inaccurate information. For example, ████████ testified that KSM "identified sleeper cells inside the U.S., [and] the information allowed the FBI to identify that and take action." She further testified that KSM "identified the second wave of attacks against the U.S. that were planned after 9/11," that Abu Zubaydah "really pointed us towards [KSM] and how to find him," and that Abu Zubaydah "led us to Ramzi bin al-Shibh." *See* transcript of Senate Select Committee on Intelligence hearing, February 14, 2007 (DTS #2007-1337). Additional information on the testimony is included in the full Committee Study.
[2513] Transcript of Senate Select Committee on Intelligence hearing, February 14, 2007 (DTS #2007-1337).
[2514] DIRECTOR ████ (152227Z MAR 07)

H. The CIA Provides Additional Information to the Full Committee and Staff, Much of It Inaccurate; Intelligence Authorization Act Passes Limiting CIA Interrogations to Techniques Authorized by the Army Field Manual

(TS// ████████ //NF) On April 12, 2007, CIA Director Hayden testified at a lengthy hearing that was attended by all but one committee member, and for the first time, the CIA allowed most of the Committee's staff to attend. The members stated that the Committee was still seeking access to CIA documents and information on the CIA's Detention and Interrogation Program, including Department of Justice memoranda and the location of the CIA's detention facilities.[2515] Director Hayden's Statement for the Record included extensive inaccurate information with regard to Abu Zubaydah, CIA interrogators, abuses identified by the ICRC, and the effectiveness of the CIA's enhanced interrogation techniques.[2516] Director Hayden's Statement for the Record also listed five examples of captures and four examples of plots "thwarted" purportedly resulting from information acquired from CIA detainees, all of which included significant inaccurate information.[2517] Director Hayden's Statement for the Record further included the following representation with regard to the effects of legislation that would limit interrogations to techniques authorized by the Army Field Manual:

> "The CIA program has proven to be effective... should our techniques be limited to the [Army] field manual, we are left with very little offense and are relegated to rely primarily on defense. Without the approval of EITs... we have severely restricted our attempts to obtain timely information from HVDs who possess information that will help us save lives and disrupt operations. Limiting our interrogation tools to those detailed in the [Army] field manual

---

[2515] Senate Select Committee on Intelligence, Transcript of hearing, April 12, 2007 (DTS #2007-3158).

[2516] For example, the Statement for the Record claimed that Abu Zubaydah was "an up-and-coming lieutenant of Usama Bin Ladin (UBL) who had intimate knowledge of al-Qa'ida's current operations, personnel and plans." It also stated that "[a]fter the use of these techniques, Abu Zubaydah became one of our most important sources of intelligence on al-Qa'ida, and he himself has stated that he would not have been responsive or told us all he did had he not gone through these techniques." The Statement claimed that CIA interrogators were "carefully chosen and screened for demonstrated professional judgment and maturity," and that "they must complete more than 250 hours of specialized training before they are allowed to come face-to-face with a terrorist." Claims made in the Statement refuting the abuses identified by the ICRC were repeated by Director Hayden during the hearing, and are described in an appendix to this summary. The Statement for the Record also included inaccurate information about past congressional oversight, claiming that "[a]s CIA's efforts to implement [new interrogation] authorities got underway in 2002, the majority and minority leaders of the Senate, the speaker and the minority leader of the House, and the chairs and ranking members of the intelligence committees were fully briefed on the interrogation program." See Witness Statement for the Senate Select Committee on Intelligence from CIA Director Hayden, for April 12, 2007, hearing (DTS #2007-1563).

[2517] The Statement for the Record included claims of effectiveness similar to those made in other contexts by the CIA, related to the captures of Hambali (on which Director Hayden elaborated during the hearing), Issa al-Hindi ("KSM also provided the first lead to an operative known as 'Issa al-Hindi'"), Sajid Badat ("[l]eads provided by KSM in November 2003 led directly to the arrest of [Badat]"), Jose Padilla ("Abu Zubaydah provided information leading to the identification of alleged al-Qa'ida operative Jose Padilla"), and Iyman Faris ("[s]oon after his arrest, KSM described an Ohio-based truck driver whom the FBI identified as Iyman Faris, already under suspicion for his contacts with al-Qa'ida operative Majid Khan"). The statement also described the "thwarting" and "disrupting" of the "West Coast Airliner Plot" (aka, the Second Wave plotting), the "Heathrow Airport plot," the "Karachi plots," and "Plots in the Saudi Peninsula." See Witness Statement for the Senate Select Committee on Intelligence from CIA Director Hayden, for April 12, 2007, hearing (DTS #2007-1563).

will increase the probability that a determined, resilient HVD will be able to withhold critical, time-sensitive, actionable intelligence that could prevent an imminent, catastrophic attack."[2518]

(TS// ████████████ //NF) At the April 12, 2007, hearing, Director Hayden verbally provided extensive inaccurate information on, among other topics: (1) the interrogation of Abu Zubaydah, (2) the application of Department of Defense survival school practices to the program, (3) detainees' counterinterrogation training, (4) the backgrounds of CIA interrogators, (5) the role of other members of the interrogation teams, (6) the number of CIA detainees and their intelligence production, (7) the role of CIA detainee reporting in the captures of terrorist suspects, (8) the interrogation process, (9) the use of detainee reporting, (10) the purported relationship between Islam and the need to use the CIA's enhanced interrogation techniques, (11) threats against detainees' families, (12) the punching and kicking of detainees, (13) detainee hygiene, (14) denial of medical care, (15) dietary manipulation, (16) the use of waterboarding and its effectiveness, and (17) the injury and death of detainees. In addition, the chief of CTC's ████████ ████████ Department provided inaccurate information on the CIA's use of stress positions, while Acting General Counsel John Rizzo provided inaccurate information on the legal reasons for establishing CIA detention facilities overseas.[2519] A detailed comparison of Director Hayden's testimony and information in CIA records related to the program is included in an appendix to this summary.

(TS// ████████████ //NF) In responses to official Committee Questions for the Record, the CIA provided inaccurate information related to detainees transferred from U.S. military to CIA custody.[2520] The Committee also requested a timeline connecting intelligence reporting obtained from CIA detainees to the use of the CIA's enhanced interrogation techniques. The CIA declined to provide such a timeline, writing that "[t]he value of each intelligence report stands alone, whether it is collected before, during, immediately after or significantly after the use of [the CIA's enhanced interrogation techniques]."[2521]

[2518] Witness Statement for the Senate Select Committee on Intelligence from CIA Director Hayden, for April 12, 2007, hearing (DTS #2007-1563).

[2519] Senate Select Committee on Intelligence, Transcript of hearing, April 12, 2007 (DTS #2007-3158).

[2520] The Committee had asked for specifics related to the assertion in Director Hayden's written statement that the CIA program was effective in gaining intelligence after detainees successfully resisted interrogation under U.S. military detention. The CIA's response referenced only one detainee, Abu Ja'far al-Iraqi, stating that he was "unwilling to become fully cooperative given the limitations of the U.S. military's interrogation and detention regulations." The CIA's response to Committee questions then asserted that "[i]t was not until Abu Jaf'ar was subjected to EITS that he provided detailed information [about] his personal meetings with Abu Mus'ab al-Zarqawi and Zarqawi's advisors," and that "[i]n addition, Abu Jaf'ar provided information on al-Qa'ida in Iraq (AQI) finances, travel, and associated facilitation activities." The provided information was inaccurate. CIA records indicate that, while still in U.S. military custody, Abu Ja'far described multiple meetings with al-Zarqawi, other members of al-Qa'ida in Iraq, and individuals who were to serve as al-Zarqawi's connection to senior al-Qa'ida leadership. Abu Ja'far also provided insights into al-Zarqawi's beliefs and plans. *See* ████████ 32732 (████ OCT 05); ████████ 32707 (████ OCT 05); ████████ 32726 (████ OCT 05); ████████ 32810 (████ OCT 05); ████████ 32944 (████ OCT 05).

[2521] CIA Response to Senate Select Committee on Intelligence Questions for the Record, June 18, 2007 (DTS #2007-2564).

(TS// ███████████ //NF) In May 2007, the Committee voted to approve the Fiscal Year 2008 Intelligence Authorization bill, which required reporting on CIA compliance with the Detainee Treatment Act and Military Commissions Act. In September 2007, John Rizzo withdrew his nomination to be CIA general counsel amid Committee concerns related to his role in the CIA's Detention and Interrogation Program. On August 2, 2007, the Committee conducted a hearing that addressed the interrogation of Muhammad Rahim, who would be the CIA's last detainee, as well as the president's new Executive Order, which interpreted the Geneva Conventions in a manner to allow the CIA to use its enhanced interrogation techniques against Muhammad Rahim. At that hearing, the CIA's director of CTC, ███████████████, provided inaccurate information to the Committee on several issues, including how the CIA conducts interrogations.[2522] Members again requested access to the Department of Justice memoranda related to the CIA program, but were denied this access.[2523]

(TS// ███████████ //NF) On December 5, 2007, the conference committee considering the Fiscal Year 2008 Intelligence Authorization bill voted to restrict the CIA's interrogation techniques to those authorized by the Army Field Manual. Opponents of the provision referenced Director Hayden's testimony on the effectiveness of the CIA's enhanced interrogation techniques in acquiring critical information.[2524] On December 6, 2007, the *New York Times* revealed that the CIA had destroyed videotapes of CIA interrogations in 2005.[2525] The CIA claimed that the Committee had been told about the destruction of the videotapes at a hearing in November 2006.[2526] A review of the Committee's transcript of its November 16, 2006, hearing found that the CIA's claim of notification was inaccurate. In fact, CIA witnesses testified at the hearing that the CIA did not videotape interrogations, while making no mention of past videotaping or the destruction of videotapes.[2527]

[2522] For example, the director of CTC, ███████████████, testified that detainees "are given ample opportunity to provide the information without the use of EITs" (Senate Select Committee on Intelligence, Transcript of hearing, August 2, 2007 (DTS #2007-3641). As detailed in this Study, numerous detainees were subjected to the CIA's enhanced interrogation techniques immediately upon being questioned.

[2523] Senate Select Committee on Intelligence, Transcript of hearing, August 2, 2007 (DTS #2007-3641).

[2524] Transcript, Committee of Conference on the Intelligence Authorization Act for Fiscal Year 2008, December 5, 2007 (DTS #2009-1279).

[2525] "C.I.A. Destroyed Tapes of Interrogations," *The New York Times*, December 6, 2007 (published in the December 7, 2007, edition of the newspaper).

[2526] Press Release, entitled, "Chairman Rockefeller Says Intel Committee Has Begun Investigation Into CIA Detainee Tapes; Senator Expresses Concern that CIA Continues to Withhold Key Information," Office of Senator Rockefeller, December 7, 2007.

[2527] Transcript of Senate Select Committee on Intelligence hearing, November 16, 2006 (DTS #2007-1422). The CIA's June 2013 Response states only that "[w]e acknowledge that DCIA did not volunteer past information on CIA's process of videotaping the interrogation sessions or of the destruction of the tapes...." The Committee review found that in testimony to the Committee in November 2006, CIA witnesses responded to questions about videotaping in terms of current practice, while avoiding any reference to past practice. This was similar to what was conveyed in June 2003, to David Addington of the Office of the Vice President, by CIA General Counsel Scott Muller. In June 2003, the CIA's General Counsel Scott Muller traveled to Guantanamo Bay, Cuba, with White House Counsel Alberto Gonzales, the Vice President's counsel David Addington, Department of Defense General Counsel Jim Haynes, Patrick Philbin from the Department of Justice, and NSC Legal Advisor John Bellinger. According to CIA records, during the trip, White House officials asked CIA General Counsel Muller about the CIA Inspector General's concerns regarding the waterboard technique and whether the CIA videotaped interrogations, as David Addington had heard tapes existed of the CIA's interrogations of Abu Zubaydah. In an email to CIA colleagues providing details on the trip, Muller wrote: "(David Addington, by the way, asked me if were [sic]

(TS// ███████████ //NF) At the CIA briefing to the Committee on December 11, 2007, Director Hayden testified about: (1) the information provided to the White House regarding the videotapes, (2) what the tapes revealed, (3) what was not on the tapes, (4) the reasons for their destruction, (5) the legal basis for the use of the waterboard, and (6) the effectiveness of the CIA's waterboard interrogation technique. Much of this testimony was inaccurate or incomplete. Director Hayden also testified that what was on the destroyed videotapes was documented in CIA cables, and that the cables were "a more than adequate representation of the tapes." Director Hayden committed the CIA to providing the Committee with access to the cables.[2528]

(TS// ███████████ //NF) On February 5, 2008, after the House of Representatives passed the conference report limiting CIA interrogations to techniques authorized by the Army Field Manual, Director Hayden testified in an open Committee hearing against the provision. Director Hayden also stated, inaccurately, that over the life of the CIA program, the CIA had detained fewer than 100 people.[2529] On February 13, 2008, the Senate passed the conference report.[2530]

I. President Vetoes Legislation Based on Effectiveness Claims Provided by the CIA; CIA Declines to Answer Committee Questions for the Record About the CIA Interrogation Program

(TS// ███████████ //NF) On March 8, 2008, President Bush vetoed the Intelligence Authorization bill. President Bush explained his decision to veto the bill in a radio broadcast that repeated CIA representations that the CIA interrogation program produced "critical intelligence" that prevented specific terrorist plots. As described in this summary, and in greater detail in Volume II, the statement reflected inaccurate information provided by the CIA to the president and other policymakers in CIA briefings.[2531] Three days later, the House of Representatives

---

taping interrogations and said he had heard that there were tapes of the Zubaydah interrogations. I told him that tapes were not being made)." *See* email from: Scott Muller; to: John Rizzo, ███████████, and ████ ████; subject: Report from Gitmo trip (Not proofread as usual); date: June █, 2003, at 5:47 PM.

[2528] Senate Select Committee on Intelligence, Transcript of hearing, December 11, 2007 (DTS #2007-4904). In the spring of 2008, after the Committee agreed on a bipartisan basis to continue investigating the destruction of the interrogation tapes, Chairman Rockefeller and Vice Chairman Bond pressed the CIA to provide the operational cables promised by Director Hayden. *See* April 21, 2008, letter from Chairman Rockefeller and Vice Chairman Bond, to Director Hayden (DTS #2008-1798). *See also* May 8, 2008, letter from Chairman Rockefeller and Vice Chairman Bond, to Director Hayden (DTS #2008-2030).

[2529] Senate Select Committee on Intelligence, Transcript of hearing, February 5, 2008 (DTS #2008-1140).

[2530] U.S. Senate vote to adopt the conference report on February 13, 2008, 4:31 PM. H.R. 2082 (Intelligence Authorization Act for Fiscal Year 2008).

[2531] The President's veto message to the House of Representatives stated that "[t]he CIA's ability to conduct a separate and specialized interrogation program for terrorists who possess the most critical information in the war on terror has helped the United States prevent a number of attacks, including plots to fly passenger airplanes into the Library Tower in Los Angeles and into Heathrow Airport or buildings in downtown London" (Message to the House of Representatives, President George W. Bush, March 8, 2008). The president also explained his veto in his weekly radio address, in which he referenced the "Library Tower," also known as the "Second Wave" plot, and the Heathrow Airport plot, while representing that the CIA program "helped us stop a plot to strike a U.S. Marine camp in Djibouti, a planned attack on the U.S. consulate in Karachi...." (*See* President's Radio Address, President George W. Bush, March 8, 2008). As detailed, CIA representations regarding the role of the CIA's enhanced interrogation techniques with regard to the Second Wave, Heathrow Airport, Djibouti, and Karachi plots were inaccurate.

failed to override the veto.[2532] On May 22, 2008, the CIA informed the Committee that the vetoed legislation "has had no impact on CIA policies concerning the use of EITs."[2533] As noted, CIA Director Goss had previously testified to the Committee that "we cannot do it by ourselves," and that "[w]e need to have the support of our oversight committee."[2534] As further noted, the OLC's 2007 memorandum applying the Military Commissions Act to the CIA's enhanced interrogation techniques relied on the CIA's representation that "none of the Members expressed the view that the CIA interrogation program should be stopped, or that the techniques at issue were inappropriate."[2535]

(TS// ████████████ //NF) In June 2008, the CIA provided information to the Committee in response to a reporting requirement in the Fiscal Year 2008 Intelligence Authorization Act. The CIA response stated that all of the CIA's interrogation techniques "were evaluated under the applicable U.S. law during the time of their use and were found by the Department of Justice to comply with those legal requirements." This was inaccurate. Diapers, nudity, dietary manipulation, and water dousing were used extensively by the CIA prior to any Department of Justice review. As detailed in the full Committee Study, the response included additional information that was incongruent with the history of the program.[2536]

(TS// ████████████ //NF) On June 10, 2008, the Committee held a hearing on the Department of Justice memoranda relating to the CIA's Detention and Interrogation Program, to which the Committee had recently been provided limited access.[2537] At the hearing, ████████ CTC Legal provided inaccurate information on several topics, including the use of sleep

---

[2532] U.S. House of Representatives Roll Call Vote 117 of the 110th Congress, Second Session, March 11, 2008, 7:01 PM.

[2533] CIA Responses to Questions for the Record from the 6 March 2008 SSCI Covert Action Hearing, May 22, 2008 (DTS #2008-2234).

[2534] Transcript of Senate Select Committee on Intelligence briefing, March 15, 2006 (DTS #2006-1308).

[2535] Memorandum for John A. Rizzo, Acting General Counsel, Central Intelligence Agency, from Steven G. Bradbury, Principal Deputy Assistant Attorney General, Office of Legal Counsel, July 20, 2007, Re: Application of the War Crimes Act, the Detainee Treatment Act, and Common Article 3 of the Geneva Conventions to Certain Techniques that May be Used by the CIA in the Interrogation of High Value Al Qaeda Detainees (DTS #2009-1810, Tab 14).

[2536] The CIA response stated that during sleep deprivation, the detainee is "typically... handcuffed in front of his body," and "will not be permitted to hang from [the handcuffs]," despite the practice of detainees being subjected to the technique with their hands above their heads, and reports of detainees hanging from their wrists at DETENTION SITE COBALT. The response stated that "adult diapers and shorts [are] for sanitary purposes," and that "caloric intake will always be at least 1,000 kcal/day," although CIA records indicate that the purpose of the diapers in several cases was humiliation and there were no caloric requirements until May 2004. The response stated that "[n]o sexual abuse or threats of sexual abuse are permitted," despite an insinuation that a family member of a detainee would be sexually abused. The response stated that "[t]he detainee may not be intentionally exposed to detention facility staff," even though detainees at DETENTION SITE COBALT were walked around nude by guards. The response stated that during water dousing, water "cannot enter the detainee's nose, mouth, or eyes," but did not acknowledge detainees being immersed in water. Finally, the CIA response described limitations on the use of the waterboard that were exceeded in the case of KSM. (*See* Response to Congressionally Directed Actions cited in the Compartmented Annex to Report 110-75, June 16, 2008 (DTS #2008-2663).) This response was provided notwithstanding the presidential veto of this legislation on March 8, 2008.

[2537] The Committee had been provided four copies of the memoranda for a limited time. *See* Senate Select Committee on Intelligence, Transcript of hearing, June 10, 2008 (DTS #2008-2698).

deprivation and its effects.[2538] Acting Assistant Attorney General Steven Bradbury also testified, noting that the Department of Justice deferred to the CIA with regard to the effectiveness of the CIA interrogation program.[2539] The Committee then submitted official Questions for the Record on the CIA's enhanced interrogation techniques and on the effectiveness of the program, including how the CIA assessed the effectiveness of its interrogation techniques for purposes of representations to the Department of Justice.[2540] The CIA prepared responses that included an acknowledgment that ██████████ CTC Legal, ██████████, had provided inaccurate information with regard to the "effectiveness" of the CIA's enhanced interrogation techniques.[2541] The prepared responses were never provided to the Committee. Instead, on October 17, 2008, the CIA informed the Committee that it would not respond to the Committee's Questions for the Record and that instead, the CIA was "available to provide additional briefings on this issue to Members as necessary."[2542] In separate letters to Director Hayden, Chairman Rockefeller and Senator Feinstein referred to this refusal to respond to official Committee questions as "unprecedented and... simply unacceptable,"[2543] and "appalling."[2544]

[2538] ██████████ CTC Legal repeated the representation that during sleep deprivation, detainees' hands were shackled "about chin to chest level," and stated that "[i]f there is any indication, such as the legs begin to swell, or things of that nature, that may terminate the sleep deprivation." ██████████ CTC Legal also stated, inaccurately, that "we cannot begin to implement any of the measures, absent first attempting to get information from the individual in an up front and non-coercive way." He added, also inaccurately, that "if the individual cooperates and begins to talk to you, you never go into the interrogation program."

[2539] Senate Select Committee on Intelligence, Senate Select Committee on Intelligence, Transcript of hearing, June 10, 2008 (DTS #2008-2698).

[2540] Questions for the Record submitted to CIA Director Michael Hayden, September 8, 2008, with a request for a response by October 10, 2008 (DTS #2008-3522).

[2541] *See* CIA document prepared in response to "Questions for the Record" submitted by the Senate Select Committee on Intelligence on September 8, 2008. The Committee had inquired why information provided by Abu Zubaydah about Jose Padilla was included in the CIA's "Effectiveness Memo" for the Department of Justice, given that Abu Zubaydah provided the information to FBI Special Agents prior to being subjected to the CIA's enhanced interrogation techniques. The CIA response, prepared but never sent to the Committee, stated that the CTC attorney who prepared the CIA "Effectiveness Memo," ██████████, "simply inadvertently reported this wrong." The unsent CIA response added that "Abu Zubaydah provided information on Jose Padilla while being interrogated by the FBI," and cited a specific CIA cable, ████████ 10991. In contrast to the CIA's unsent response to Committee questions in 2008, the CIA's June 2013 Response states: "[t]he Study also claims Abu Zubaydah had already provided [Jose Padilla's] 'Dirty Bomb' plot information to FBI interrogators prior to undergoing CIA interrogation, but this is based on an undocumented FBI internal communication and an FBI officer's recollection to the Senate Judiciary Committee seven years later." The CIA's June 2013 Response also represents that "[w]hile we have considerable information from FBI debriefings of Abu Zubaydah, we have no record that FBI debriefers acquired information about such an al-Qa'ida threat." As detailed in this summary, this is inaccurate. The CIA's June 2013 Response further states that "CIA correctly represented Abu Zubaydah's description of Jose Padilla as an example of information provided after an individual had been subjected to enhanced interrogation techniques." The CIA's unsent response to Committee questions in 2008 acknowledged that "[d]uring the initial timeframe Abu Zubaydah (AZ) was waterboarded the interrogation team believed that AZ was compliant and was not withholding actionable threat information," but ALEC Station "had additional information they felt linked AZ with more planned attacks," and that "[a]s a result, the interrogation team was instructed to continue with the waterboarding based on ALEC Station's belief." Finally, the unsent responses acknowledged that notwithstanding CIA representations to the Department of Justice regarding amenities available to CIA detainees, "[t]he amenities of today evolved over the first year and a half of the program," and that Abu Zubaydah was not initially provided those amenities.

[2542] CIA Letter to Chairman John D. Rockefeller, IV, October 17, 2008 (DTS #2008-4131).

[2543] Letter from Chairman John D. Rockefeller, IV to CIA Director Michael Hayden, October 29, 2008 (DTS #2008-4217).

[2544] Letter from Senator Feinstein to CIA Director Michael Hayden, October 30, 2008 (DTS #2008-4235).

VII. CIA Destruction of Interrogation Videotapes Leads to Committee Investigation; Committee Votes 14-1 for Expansive Terms of Reference to Study the CIA's Detention and Interrogation Program

(TS// ███████████ //NF) The Committee's scrutiny of the CIA's Detention and Interrogation Program continued through the remainder of 2008 and into the 111th Congress, in 2009. On February 11, 2009, the Committee held a business meeting at which Committee staff presented a memorandum on the content of the CIA operational cables detailing the interrogations of Abu Zubaydah and 'Abd al-Rahim al-Nashiri in 2002.[2545] CIA Director Hayden had allowed a small number of Committee staff to review the cables at CIA Headquarters, and as noted, had testified that the cables provided "a more than adequate representation" of what was on the destroyed CIA interrogation videotapes.[2546] The chairman stated that the Committee staff memorandum represented "the most comprehensive statement on the treatment of these two detainees, from the conditions of their detention and the nature of their interrogations to the intelligence produced and the thoughts of CIA officers and contractors in the field and Headquarters."[2547] After the staff presentation, the vice chairman expressed his support for an expanded Committee investigation, stating, "we need to compare what was briefed to us by the Agency with what we find out, and we need to determine whether it was within the guidelines of the OLC, the MON, and the guidelines published by the Agency."[2548] Other members of the Committee added their support for an expanded investigation, with one member stating, "these are extraordinarily serious matters and we ought to get to the bottom of it... to look at how it came to be that these techniques were used, what the legal underpinnings of these techniques were all about, and finally what these techniques meant in terms of effectiveness."[2549]

(TS// ███████████ //NF) The Committee held two subsequent business meetings to consider and debate the terms of the Committee's proposed expanded review of the CIA's Detention and Interrogation Program. The first, on February 24, 2009, began with bipartisan support for a draft Terms of Reference.[2550] The Committee met again on March 5, 2009, to consider a revised Terms of Reference, which was approved by a vote of 14-1.[2551]

(TS// ███████████ //NF) On December 13, 2012, after a review of more than six million pages of records, the Committee approved a 6,300-page Study of the CIA's Detention and

---

[2545] *See* Committee business meeting records and transcript from February 11, 2009 (DTS #2009-1420).

[2546] Senate Select Committee on Intelligence, Transcript of hearing, December 11, 2007 (DTS #2007-4904). In the spring of 2008, after the Committee agreed on a bipartisan basis to continue investigating the destruction of the interrogation tapes, Chairman Rockefeller and Vice Chairman Bond pressed the CIA to provide the operational cables promised by Director Hayden. *See* letter from Chairman Rockefeller and Vice Chairman Bond, to Director Hayden, April 21, 2008 (DTS #2008-1798); letter from Chairman Rockefeller and Vice Chairman Bond, to Director Hayden, May 8, 2008 (DTS #2008-2030).

[2547] Senate Select Committee on Intelligence, Transcript, business meeting, February 11, 2009 (DTS #2009-1420)

[2548] Senate Select Committee on Intelligence, Transcript, business meeting, February 11, 2009 (DTS #2009-1420)

[2549] Senator Ron Wyden (D-OR). Senate Select Committee on Intelligence, Transcript, business meeting, February 11, 2009 (DTS #2009-1420).

[2550] Transcript, business meeting, February 24, 2009 (DTS #2009-1913)

[2551] Transcript, business meeting, March 5, 2009 (DTS #2009-1916)

Interrogation Program.[2552] On April 3, 2014, by a bipartisan vote of 11-3, the Committee agreed to send the revised findings and conclusions, and an updated Executive Summary of the Committee Study to the president for declassification and public release.

[2552] After the receipt of the CIA's June 27, 2013, Response to the Committee Study of the CIA's Detention and Interrogation Program, and subsequent meetings between the CIA and the Committee in the summer of 2013, the full Committee Study was updated. The final Committee Study of the CIA's Detention and Interrogation Program exceeds 6,700 pages and includes approximately 38,000 footnotes.

VIII.   Appendix 1: Terms of Reference

Terms of Reference
Senate Select Committee on Intelligence Study of the
Central Intelligence Agency's Detention and Interrogation Program

Adopted March 5, 2009

The Senate Select Committee on Intelligence's study of the Central Intelligence Agency's (CIA) detention and interrogation program consists of these terms of reference:

- A review of how the CIA created, operated, and maintained its detention and interrogation program, including a review of the locations of the facilities and any arrangements and agreements made by the CIA or other Intelligence Community officials with foreign entities in connection with the program.

- A review of Intelligence Community documents and records, including CIA operational cables, relating to the detention and interrogation of CIA detainees.

- A review of the CIA's assessments that particular detainees possessed relevant information and how the assessments were made.

- An evaluation of the information acquired from the detainees including the periods during which enhanced interrogation techniques (EITs) were administered.

- An evaluation of whether information provided to the Committee by the Intelligence Community adequately and accurately described the CIA's detention and interrogation program as it was carried out in practice, including conditions of detention, such as personal hygiene and medical needs, and their effect on the EITs as applied.

- An evaluation of the information provided by the CIA to the Department of Justice Office of Legal Counsel (OLC), including whether it accurately and adequately described:

    a. the implementation, effectiveness and expected effects of EITs;

    b. the value of information obtained through the use of EITs; and

    c. the threat environment at the time the EITs were being used or contemplated for use on CIA detainees.

- An evaluation of whether the CIA's detention and interrogation program complied with:

    a. the authorizations in any relevant Presidential Findings and Memoranda of Notification;

    b. all relevant policy and legal guidance provided by the CIA; and

    c. the opinions issued by the OLC in relation to the use of EITs.

- A review of the information provided by the CIA or other Intelligence Community officials involved in the program about the CIA detention and interrogation program, including the location of facilities and approved interrogation techniques, to U.S. officials with national security responsibilities.

The Committee will use those tools of oversight necessary to complete a thorough review including, but not limited to, document reviews and requests, interviews, testimony at closed and open hearings, as appropriate, and preparation of findings and recommendations.

IX. Appendix 2: CIA Detainees from 2002 – 2008

#	CIA Detainees	Date of Custody	Days in CIA Custody	
1	**Abu Zubaydah**	███ 2002	1,59█	~~TS~~ ████ ~~NF~~
2	Zakariya	██ 2002	36█	
3	Jamal Eldin Boudraa	██ 2002	62█	
4	Abbar al-Hawari, aka Abu Sufiyan	██ 2002	36█	
5	Hassan Muhammad Abu Bakr Qa'id	██ 2002	51█	**KEY**
6	**Ridha Ahmad Najar, aka Najjar**	██ 2002	69█	
7	Ayub Marshid Ali Salih	████ 2002	4█	**Bold Text:** Detainees in bold text were subjected to the CIA's enhanced interrogation techniques.
8	Bashir Nasir Ali al-Marwalah	████ 2002	4█	
9	Ha'il Aziz Ahmad al-Mithali	████ 2002	4█	*Italics Text:* Detainees in italics have not been previously acknowledged by the CIA to the SSCI.
10	Hassan bin Attash	████ 2002	59█	
11	Musab Umar Ali al-Mudwani	████ 2002	4█	#: Detainee number on main detainee spreadsheet; based on date of CIA custody. Number is based on a designation made by the Committee, not the CIA.
12	Said Saleh Said, aka Said Salih Said	████ 2002	4█	
13	Shawqi Awad	████ 2002	4█	
14	*Umar Faruq, aka Abu al-Faruq al-Kuwaiti*	████ 2002	41█	Note on Redaction: The last digit of days in CIA custody is redacted.
15	Abd al-Salam al-Hilah	████ 2002	59█	
16	*Karim, aka Asat Sar Jan*	████ 2002	6█	
17	*Akbar Zakaria, aka Zakaria Zeineddin*	█████ 2002	5█	
18	***Rafiq bin Bashir bin Halal al-Hami***	████ 2002	5█	
19	***Tawfiq Nasir Awad al Bihani***	████ 2002	5█	
20	**Lutfi al-Arabi al-Gharisi**	████ 2002	38█	
21	*Dr. Hikmat Nafi Shaukat*	████ 2002	7█	
22	*Yaqub al-Baluchi aka Abu Talha*	████ 2002	8█	
23	Abd al-Rahim Ghulam Rabbani	█████ 2002	54█	SOURCE INFORMATION
24	**Gul Rahman**	█████ 2002	1█	CIA Fax to SSCI Committee Staff, entitled, "15 June Request for Excel Spreadsheet," June 17, 2009. DTS #2009-2529.
25	**Ghulam Rabbani aka Abu Badr**	█████ 2002	54█	
26	**Abd al-Rahim al-Nashiri**	██████ 2002	1,37█	
27	*Haji Ghalgi*	█████ 2002	18█	CIA detainee charts provided to the Committee on April 27, 2007. Document in Committee Records entitled, "Briefing Charts provided to committee members from CIA Director Michael Hayden at the closed Hearing on April 12, 2007, concerning EITs used with CIA detainees, and a list of techniques." DTS #2007-1594.
28	*Nazar Ali*	█████ 2002	3█	
29	*Juma Gul*	█████ 2002	8█	
30	*Wafti bin Ali aka Abdallah*	█████ 2002	8█	
31	*Adel*	█████ 2002	6█	
32	*Qari Mohib Ur Rehman*	█████ 2002	6█	
33	*Shah Wali Khan*	████ 2002	2█	CIA operational cables and other records produced for the Committee's Study of the CIA's Detention and Interrogation Program.
34	*Hayatullah Haqqani*	█████ 2002	8█	
35	Bisher al-Rawi	█████ 2002	█	
36	Jamil el-Banna, aka Abu Anas	█████ 2002	█	

#	CIA Detainees	Date of Custody	Days in CIA Custody	
37	**Ghairat Bahir**	██2002	51	
38	Pacha Wazir	██2002	33	~~TS~~ ██████ ~~NF~~
39	Muhammad Amein al-Bakri	██2003	49	
40	Abdullah Midhat Mursi	██2003	11	
41	**Ramzi bin al-Shibh**	██2003	128	
42	Ibn Shaykh al-Libi	██2003	114	
43	**Muhammad Umar 'Abd al-Rahman, aka Asadallah**	██2003	15	**KEY**
44	*Abu Khalid*	██2003	2	**Bold Text:** Detainees in bold text were subjected to the CIA's enhanced interrogation techniques.
45	**Khalid Shaykh Mohammad**	██2003	126	
46	**Mustafa Ahmad al-Hawsawi**	██2003	126	*Italics Text:* Detainees in italics have not been previously acknowledged by the CIA to the SSCI.
47	**Abu Yasir al-Jaza'iri**	██2003	124	
48	**Suleiman Abdullah**	██2003	43	
49	Hamid Aich	██2003	4	**#:** Detainee number on main detainee spreadsheet; based on date of CIA custody. Number is based on a designation made by the SSCI, not the CIA.
50	Sayed Habib	██2003	49	
51	**Abu Hazim, aka Abu Hazim al-Libi**	██2003	72	
52	**Al-Shara'iya, aka Abd al-Karim**	██2003	48	
53	Muhammad Khan (son of Suhbat)	██2003	38	
54	*Ibrahim Haqqani*	██2003		
55	**Ammar al-Baluchi**	██2003	118	
56	**Khallad bin Attash**	██2003	118	
57	**Laid Ben Dohman Saidi, aka Abu Hudhaifa**	██2003	46	
58	**Majid Khan**	██2003	118	
59	Mohammad Dinshah	██2003	26	**SOURCE INFORMATION**
60	Muhammad Jafar Jamal al-Qahtani	██2003	34	
61	Abu Nasim al-Tunisi	██2003	32	CIA Fax to SSCI Committee Staff, entitled, "15 June Request for Excel Spreadsheet," June 17, 2009. DTS #2009-2529.
62	**Mohd Farik bin Amin, aka Abu Zubair**	██2003	115	
63	Zarmein	██2003	19	
64	Hiwa Abdul Rahman Rashul	██2003	11	CIA detainee charts provided to the Committee on April 27, 2007. Document in Committee Records entitled, "Briefing Charts provided to committee members from CIA Director Michael Hayden at the closed Hearing on April 12, 2007, concerning EIT's used with CIA detainees, and a list of techniques." DTS #2007-1594.
65	Adel Abu Redwan Ben Hamlili	██2003	30	
66	Shaistah Habibullah Khan	██2003	21	
67	**Samr Hilmi Abdul Latif al-Barq**	██2003	8	
68	Ali Jan	██, 2003	34	
69	Muhammad Khan (son of Amir)	██2003	1	
70	Modin Nik Muhammad	██2003	20	CIA operational cables and other records produced for the Committee's Study of the CIA's Detention and Interrogation Program.
71	Abdullah Ashami	██2003	27	
72	**Bashir bin Lap, aka Lillie**	██2003	110	
73	**Riduan bin Isomuddin, aka Hambali**	██2003	128	

#	CIA Detainees	Date of Custody	Days in CIA Custody	
74	Sanad 'Ali Yislam al-Kazimi	███ 2003	26█	**TS** ███ **NF**
75	Salah Nasir Salim Ali, aka Muhsin	███ 2003	59█	
76	Abd Qudra Allah Mala Azrat al-Hadi	███ 2003	8█	
77	Bismullah	███ 2003	█	
78	Sa'id Allam	███ 2003	8█	
79	Sa'ida Gul	███ 2003	8█	
80	Shah Khan Wali	███ 2003	8█	**KEY**
81	Yahya, aka Rugollah	███ 2003	8█	**Bold Text:** Detainees in bold text were subjected to the CIA's enhanced interrogation techniques.
82	Zakariya 'abd al-Rauf	███ 2003	8█	
83	Zamarai Nur Muhammad Juma Khan	███ 2003	8█	*Italics Text*: Detainees in italics have not been previously acknowledged by the CIA to the SSCI.
84	*Abdullah Salim al-Qahtani*	███ 2003	3█	
85	*Awwad Sabhan al-Shammari*	███ 2003	3█	#: Detainee number on main detainee spreadsheet; based on date of CIA custody. Number is based on a designation made by the SSCI, not the CIA.
86	Noor Jalal	███ 2003	23█	
87	**Majid Bin Muhammad Bin Sulayman Khayll, aka Arsala Khan**	███ 2003	5█	
88	*Aso Hawleri*	███ 2003	2█	
89	Mohd al-Shomaila	███ 2003	54█	
90	Ali Saeed Awadh	███ 2003	17█	
91	**Adnan al-Libi**	███ 2003	23█	
92	Muhammad Abdullah Saleh	███ 2004	48█	
93	Riyadh the Facilitator	███ 2004	12█	
94	Abu Abdallah al-Zulaytini	███ 2004	21█	
95	Binyam Ahmed Mohamed	███ 2004	11█	
96	Firas al-Yemeni	███ 2004	95█	
98	Khalid 'Abd al-Razzaq al-Masri	███ 2004	12█	**SOURCE INFORMATION**
97	**Hassan Ghul**	███ 2004	94█	CIA Fax to SSCI Committee Staff, entitled, "15 June Request for Excel Spreadsheet," June 17, 2009. DTS #2009-2529.
99	**Muhammad Qurban Sayyid Ibrahim**	███ 2004	26█	
100	Saud Memon	███ 2004	74█	
101	*Gul Rahman (2)*	███ 2004	3█	CIA detainee charts provided to the Committee on April 27, 2007. Document in Committee Records entitled, "Briefing Charts provided to committee members from CIA Director Michael Hayden at the closed Hearing on April 12, 2007, concerning EITs used with CIA detainees, and a list of techniques." DTS #2007-1594.
102	Hassan Ahmed Guleed	███ 2004	90█	
103	Abu 'Abdallah	███ 2004	87█	
104	**ABU BAHAR AL-TURKI**	[REDACTED] 2004	Approximately 13█	
105	**ABU TALHA AL-MAGREBI**	[REDACTED] 2004	Approximately 13█	
106	Abd al-Bari al-Filistini	███ 2004	77█	CIA operational cables and other records produced for the Committee's Study of the CIA's Detention and Interrogation Program.
107	Ayyub al-Libi	███ 2004	30█	
108	Marwan al-Jabbur	███ 2004	77█	
109	Qattal al-Uzbeki	███ 2004	80█	

#	CIA Detainees	Date of Custody	Days in CIA Custody	
110	Janat Gul	███ 2004	92█	**TS** ███████ **NF**
111	Ahmed Khalfan Ghailani	███ 2004	73█	**KEY**
112	Sharif al-Masri	███ 2004	81█	
113	Abdi Rashid Samatar	███ 2004	65█	**Bold Text**: Detainees in bold text were subjected to the CIA's enhanced interrogation techniques.
114	**Abu Faraj al-Libi**	██ 2005	46█	
115	Abu Munthir al-Magrebi	█ 2005	46█	*Italics Text*: Detainees in italics have not been previously acknowledged by the CIA to the SSCI.
116	Ibrahim Jan	██████	31█	
117	Abu Ja'far al-Iraqi	████ 2005	28█	#: Detainee number on main detainee spreadsheet; based on date of CIA custody.
118	Abd al-Hadi al-Iraqi	███ 2006	17█	Number is based on a designation made by the SSCI, not the CIA.
119	Muhammad Rahim	██ 2007	24█	

Sources: CIA Fax to SSCI Committee Staff, entitled, "15 June Request for Excel Spreadsheet," June 17, 2009 (DTS #2009-2529); CIA detainee charts provided to the Committee on April 27, 2007; document in Committee records entitled, "Briefing Charts provided to committee Members from CIA Director Michael Hayden at the closed Hearing on April 12, 2007, concerning EITs used with CIA detainees, and a list of techniques" (DTS #2007-1594, hearing transcript at DTS# 2007-3158); and CIA operational cables and other records produced for the Committee's Study of the CIA's Detention and Interrogation Program.

** Gul Rahman, listed as detainee 24, was the subject of a notification to the Senate Select Committee on Intelligence following his death at DETENTION SITE COBALT; however, he has not appeared on lists of CIA detainees provided to Committee.

X. Appendix 3: Example of Inaccurate CIA Testimony to the Committee- April 12, 2007

*Testimony of Michael V. Hayden, Director, Central Intelligence Agency
to the Senate Select Committee on Intelligence, April 12, 2007*[2553]

CIA Testimony	Sampling of Information in CIA Records
The Interrogation of Abu Zubaydah	
DIRECTOR HAYDEN: "Now in June, after about four months of interrogation, Abu Zubaydah *reached a point where he refused to cooperate and he shut down.* He would not talk at all to the FBI interrogators and although he was still talking to CIA interrogators *no significant progress was being made in learning anything of intelligence value.* He was, to our eye, employing classic resistance to interrogation techniques and employing them quite effectively. And it was clear to us that we were unlikely to be able to overcome those techniques without some significant intervention."	Abu Zubaydah was rendered to CIA custody on March ██, 2002. The CIA representation that Abu Zubaydah stopped cooperating with debriefers who were using traditional interrogation techniques is not supported by CIA records. In early June 2002, Abu Zubaydah's interrogators recommended that Abu Zubaydah spend several weeks in isolation from interrogation while the interrogation team members traveled ████ "as a means of keeping [Abu Zubaydah] off-balance and to allow the team needed time off for a break and to attend to personal matters ████," as well as to discuss "the endgame" for Abu Zubaydah ████ with officers from CIA Headquarters. As a result, Abu Zubaydah spent much of June 2002 and all of July 2002, 47 days in total, in isolation. When CIA officers next interrogated Abu Zubaydah, they immediately used the CIA's enhanced interrogation techniques, including the waterboard. Prior to the 47 day isolation period, Abu Zubaydah provided information on al-Qa'ida activities, plans, capabilities, and relationships, in addition to information

---

[2553] Transcript at DTS #2007-3158. The CIA's June 2013 Response states: "We disagree with the *Study's* conclusion that the Agency actively impeded Congressional oversight of the CIA Detention and Interrogation Program. ...As discussed in our response to Conclusion 9, we also disagree with the assessment that the information CIA provided on the effectiveness of the program was largely inaccurate. Finally, we have reviewed DCIA Hayden's testimony before SSCI on 12 April, 2007 and do not find, as the *Study* claims, that he misrepresented virtually all aspects of the program, although a few aspects were in error....The testimony contained some inaccuracies, and the Agency should have done better in preparing the Director, particularly concerning events that occurred prior to his tenure. However, there is no evidence that there was any intent on the part of the Agency or Director Hayden to misrepresent material facts." The CIA's June 2013 Response states that the CIA has "identified a number of broad lessons learned" and includes eight recommendations. The CIA's only recommendation related to Congress was: "Recommendation 8: Improve recordkeeping for interactions with Congress. Direct the Director of the Office of Congressional Affairs (OCA) and the Chief Information Officer to develop a concrete plan to improve recordkeeping on CIA's interactions with Congress. OCA's records going forward should reflect each interaction with Congress and the content of that interaction. OCA should work with the oversight committees to develop better access to transcripts of CIA testimony and briefings. This plan should be completed within 90 days of the arrival of a new Director of OCA."

| | on its leadership structure, including personalities, decision-making processes, training, and tactics. Abu Zubaydah provided this type of information prior to, during, and after the utilization of the CIA's enhanced interrogation techniques.[2554]

Abu Zubaydah's inability to provide information on the next attack in the United States and operatives in the United States was the basis for CIA representations that Abu Zubaydah was "uncooperative," and for the CIA's determination that Abu Zubaydah required the use of the CIA's enhanced interrogation techniques to become "compliant" and reveal the information the CIA believed he was withholding. At no point during or after the use of the CIA's enhanced interrogation techniques did Abu Zubaydah provide the information sought.[2555] |
|---|---|
| DIRECTOR HAYDEN: "This really began in the spring of 2002 with the capture of Abu Zubaydah. At that time we deployed a psychologist who had been under contract to CIA [Dr. SWIGERT], to provide real-time recommendations to help us *overcome what seemed to be Abu Zubaydah's very strong resistance to interrogation...* We also made arrangements for [Dr. DUNBAR]. [Dr. DUNBAR] was the ███ psychologist for the Department of Defense's SERE program, DOD's Survival, Escape, Recovery and Evasion program, the program of training we put our troops, particularly our airmen, through so that they can withstand a hostile environment." | The CIA testimony that SWIGERT was deployed to "overcome what seemed to be Abu Zubaydah's very strong resistance to interrogation" is not supported by internal CIA records. Rather, CIA records indicate that CIA CTC officers anticipated Abu Zubaydah would resist providing information and contracted with SWIGERT prior to any meaningful assessment of Abu Zubaydah and his level of cooperation.

• On April 1, 2002, at a meeting on the interrogation of Abu Zubaydah, ███ CTC Legal ███ ███ recommended that SWIGERT—who was working under contract in the CIA's OTS—be brought in to "provide real-time recommendations to overcome Abu Zubaydah's resistance to interrogation." (Abu Zubaydah had been in CIA custody for ███.) That evening, SWIGERT, and the CIA OTS officer who had recommended SWIGERT to ███, prepared a cable with suggestions for the interrogation of Abu Zubaydah. SWIGERT had monitored the U.S. Air Force's Survival, Evasion, Resistance, and Escape (SERE) training. SWIGERT, who had never conducted an actual interrogation, encouraged the CIA |

[2554] See intelligence reporting charts in Abu Zubaydah detainee review in Volume III, as well as a CIA paper entitled, "Abu Zubaydah," dated March 2005. Similar information was included in, "Abu Zubaydah Bio," a CIA document "Prepared on 9 August 2006."

[2555] See Abu Zubaydah detainee review in Volume III.

to focus on developing "learned helplessness" in CIA detainees.[2556]

- Following the suggestion of ███████ CTC Legal, CTC contracted with SWIGERT to assist in the interrogation of Abu Zubaydah.

- As described in the Abu Zubaydah detainee review in Volume III, almost immediately after Abu Zubaydah's transfer to CIA custody on March █, 2002, Abu Zubaydah's medical condition deteriorated and Abu Zubaydah was transferred to the intensive care unit of a ███████████ hospital in Country █. During this time, FBI personnel continued to collect significant intelligence from Abu Zubaydah. According to an FBI report, during the period when Abu Zubaydah was still "connected to the intubator" at the hospital and unable to speak, he "indicated that he was willing to answer questions of the interviewers via writing in Arabic." While in the intensive care unit of the hospital, Abu Zubaydah first discussed "Mukhtar" (KSM) and identified a photograph of KSM.

- When Abu Zubaydah was discharged from the ████████ hospital and returned to the CIA's DETENTION SITE GREEN on April 15, 2002, he was kept naked, sleep deprived, and in a cell with bright lights with white noise or loud music playing. The FBI personnel objected to the coercive aspects of Abu Zubaydah's interrogation at this time, as they believed they were making substantial progress building rapport with Abu Zubaydah and developing intelligence without these measures. (During their questioning of Abu Zubaydah, the FBI officers provided a towel for Abu Zubaydah to cover himself and continued to use rapport building techniques with the detainee.[2557])

[2556] See Volume I, including ███████ 178955 (012236Z APR 02); April 1, 2002 email from [REDACTED] to [REDACTED], re: Please coord on cable attached; and email from [REDACTED] to [REDACTED], cc: ████████, April 1, 2002, re: POC for [SWIGERT]– consultant who drafted Al-Qa'ida resistance to interrogation backgrounder (noting that CTC/LGL would contact SWIGERT).
[2557] See Abu Zubaydah detainee review in Volume III.

DIRECTOR HAYDEN: "We wanted [SWIGERT's and DUNBAR's] ideas about what approaches might be useful to get information from people like Abu Zubaydah and *other uncooperative al-Qa'ida detainees that we judged were withholding time-sensitive, perishable intelligence.* Keep in mind, as a backdrop for all of this, this wasn't interrogating a snuffy that's picked up on the battlefield. The *requirement to be in the CIA detention program is knowledge of [an] attack against the United States or its interests or knowledge about the location of Usama bin Ladin or Ayman al-Zawahiri.*"	The representation that the "requirement to be in the CIA detention program is knowledge of [an] attack against the United States or its interests or knowledge about the location of Usama bin Ladin or Ayman al-Zawahiri" is inconsistent with how the CIA's Detention and Interrogation Program operated from its inception.[2558] As detailed elsewhere, numerous individuals had been detained and subjected to the CIA's enhanced interrogation techniques, despite doubts and questions surrounding their knowledge of terrorist threats and the location of senior al-Qa'ida leadership.
DIRECTOR HAYDEN: "We began in 2002, in the spring of 2002. We had one very high value detainee, Abu Zubaydah. *We knew he knew a lot. He would not talk.* We were going nowhere with him. The decision was made, we've got to do something. We've got to have an intervention here. What is it we can do?"	The representation that Abu Zubaydah "would not talk" is incongruent with CIA interrogation records. The CIA representation that the CIA "knew [Abu Zubaydah] knew a lot" reflected an inaccurate assessment of Abu Zubaydah from 2002, prior to his capture, and did not represent the CIA's assessment of Abu Zubaydah as of the April 2007 testimony. • Prior to Abu Zubaydah's capture, the CIA had intelligence stating that Abu Zubaydah was the "third or fourth" highest ranking al-Qa'ida leader. This information was based on single-source reporting that was retracted in July 2002—prior to Abu Zubaydah being subjected to the CIA's enhanced interrogation techniques. Other intelligence in CIA databases indicated that Abu Zubaydah was not a senior member of al-Qa'ida, but assisted al-Qa'ida members in acquiring false passports and other travel documents. Still other reporting indicated that, while Abu Zubaydah served as an administrator at terrorist training camps, he was not the central figure at these camps.

[2558] *See* Volume I for additional details.

- After Abu Zubaydah was subjected to the CIA's enhanced interrogation techniques in August 2002, the chief of Base at DETENTION SITE GREEN wrote: "I do not believe that AZ was as wired with al-Qa'ida as we believed him to be prior to his capture."[2559]

- In August 2006, the CIA published an assessment that concluded that "misconceptions" about Afghanistan training camps with which Abu Zubaydah was associated had resulted in reporting that "miscast Abu Zubaydah as a 'senior al-Qa'ida lieutenant.'" The assessment concluded that "al-Qa'ida rejected Abu Zubaydah's request in 1993 to join the group."[2560]

CIA representations that interrogators "were going nowhere with [Abu Zubaydah]" prior to the use of the CIA's enhanced interrogation techniques are also incongruent with CIA records.

- Prior the use of the CIA's enhanced interrogation techniques, Abu Zubaydah provided information on al-Qa'ida activities, plans, capabilities, relationships, leadership structure, personalities, decision-making processes, training, and tactics. Abu Zubaydah provided this type of information prior to, during, and after the utilization of the CIA's enhanced interrogation techniques.

- A quantitative review of Abu Zubaydah's disseminated intelligence reporting indicates that more intelligence reports were disseminated from Abu Zubaydah's first two months of interrogation—prior to the use of the CIA's enhanced interrogation techniques—than were derived during the two-month period during and after the use of the CIA's enhanced interrogation techniques.[2561]

[2559] Email from: [REDACTED] (outgoing Chief of Base at DETENTION SITE GREEN): to: [REDACTED] subject: "Assessment to Date" of AZ; date: 10/06/2002, at 05:36:46 AM.
[2560] CIA Intelligence Assessment, August 16, 2006, "Countering Misconceptions About Training Camps in Afghanistan, 1990-2001."
[2561] *See* Abu Zubaydah detainee review in Volume III, including monthly intelligence reporting charts.

CIA's Enhanced Interrogation Techniques and the SERE School	
DIRECTOR HAYDEN: "After lengthy discussion, [Dr. SWIGERT] suggested that we might use the interrogation approaches that had been, for years, safely used at the DOD survival school -- in other words, the interrogation techniques that we were training our airmen to resist. Those techniques have been used for about 50 years, with no significant injuries." VICE CHAIRMAN BOND: "And the techniques you are using are boiled down, is it true, from the SERE school?" DIRECTOR HAYDEN: "All of them are techniques that have been used in the SERE school, that's right, Senator."	The CIA consistently represented that the CIA's enhanced interrogation techniques were the same as the techniques used in the U.S. Department of Defense SERE school. However, CIA interrogation records indicate there were significant differences in how the techniques were used against CIA detainees. For example, a letter from the assistant attorney general to the CIA general counsel highlighted the statement in the Inspector General Special Review that the use of the waterboard in SERE training was "so different from subsequent Agency usage as to make it almost irrelevant."[2562] Prior to the use of the CIA's enhanced interrogation techniques against Abu Zubaydah, the chief of Base at the detention site identified differences between how the SERE techniques were applied in training, and how they would be applied to Abu Zubaydah: "while the techniques described in Headquarters meetings and below are administered to student volunteers in the U.S. in a harmless way, with no measurable impact on the psyche of the volunteer, we do not believe we can assure the same here for a man forced through these processes and who will be made to believe this is the future course of the remainder of his life... personnel will make every effort possible to insure [sic] that subject is not permanently physically or mental harmed but we should not say at the outset of this process that there is no risk."[2563]
Department of Justice Approval	
DIRECTOR HAYDEN: "This list of recommended techniques then went to the Department of Justice for their opinion regarding whether or not the	As described in this summary, the August 1, 2002, Department of Justice OLC memorandum relied on inaccurate information provided by the CIA concerning Abu Zubaydah's position in al-Qa'ida and the interrogation team's assessment of whether Abu Zubaydah

---

[2562] Letter from Assistant Attorney General Goldsmith to CIA General Counsel Scott Muller, May 27, 2004. For more information on the SERE program, *see* the Senate Armed Services Committee Inquiry into the Treatment of Detainees in U.S. Custody, December 2008. *See also* statement of Senator Carl Levin relating to the inquiry, December 11, 2008: "In SERE school, our troops who are at risk of capture are exposed in a controlled environment with great protections and caution – to techniques adapted from abusive tactics used against American soldiers by enemies such as the Communist Chinese during the Korean War. SERE training techniques include stress positions, forced nudity, use of fear, sleep deprivation and, until recently, the Navy SERE school used the waterboard. These techniques were designed to give our students a taste of what they might be subjected to if captured by a ruthless, lawless enemy so that they would be better prepared to resist. The techniques were never intended to be used against detainees in U.S. custody."

[2563] [REDACTED] 73208 (231043Z JUL 02)

techniques were lawful. DOJ returned a legal opinion that the 13 techniques were lawful, didn't constitute torture, and hence could be employed for CIA interrogations."[2564]	was withholding information about planned terrorist attacks. The OLC memorandum, which stated that it was based on CIA-provided facts and would not apply if facts were to change, was also specific to Abu Zubaydah. The CIA nonetheless used the OLC memorandum as the legal basis for applying its enhanced interrogation techniques against other CIA detainees.[2565]
	*Resistance Training*
VICE CHAIRMAN BOND: "How far down the line [does al-Qa'ida] train [its] operatives for interrogation resistance?" DIRECTOR HAYDEN: "I'm getting a nod from the experts,[2566] Senator, that it's rather broadly-based." VICE CHAIRMAN BOND: "So even if you captured the al-Qa'ida facilitator, probably the army field manual stuff are things that he's already been trained on and he knows that he doesn't have to talk." DIRECTOR HAYDEN: "We would expect that, yes, Senator."	A review of CIA records on this topic identified no records to indicate that al-Qa'ida had conducted "broadly-based" interrogation resistance training. The CIA repeatedly represented that Abu Zubaydah "wrote al Qaeda's manual on resistance techniques."[2567] This representation is also not supported by CIA records. When asked about interrogation resistance training, Abu Zubaydah stated: "… both Khaldan camp and Faruq [terrorist training] camp at least periodically included instruction in how to manage captivity. He explained that in one instance, Khaldan had an Egyptian who had collected and studied information from a variety of sources (including manuals and people who had been in 'different armies'). This Egyptian 'talked to the brothers about being strong' and 'not talking.' Abu Zubaydah's response to this

---

[2564] The August 1, 2002, OLC memorandum addressed 10 interrogation techniques. The May 10, 2005, OLC memorandum addressed 13 techniques.

[2565] "Our advice is based upon the following facts, which you have provided to us. We also understand that you do not have any facts in your possession contrary to the facts outlined here, and this opinion is limited to these facts. If these facts were to change, this advice would not necessarily apply." (*See* Memorandum for John Rizzo, Acting General Counsel, Central Intelligence Agency, from Jay Bybee, Assistant Attorney General, Office of Legal Counsel, August 1, 2002, Interrogation of al Qaeda Operative (DTS #2009-1810, Tab 1).) CIA records indicate that it was not until July 29, 2003, that the Attorney General stated that the legal principles of the August 1, 2002, memorandum could be applied to other CIA detainees. (*See* June 18, 2004, letter from Assistant Attorney General Jack L. Goldsmith III to Director Tenet (DTS #2004-2710).) In a subsequent interview with the OIG, however, ███████ CTC Legal, ███████████, stated that "every detainee interrogated is different in that they are outside the opinion because the opinion was written for Zubaydah." The context for ███████'s statement was the legality of the waterboarding of KSM. *See* Interview of ███████████, by [REDACTED], [REDACTED], and [REDACTED], Office of the Inspector General, August 20, 2003.

[2566] Other CIA attendees at the hearing included John Rizzo, ███████ and ███████. ███████, former ███ CTC Legal, attended for the ODNI.

[2567] Memorandum for John Rizzo, Acting General Counsel, Central Intelligence Agency, from Jay Bybee, Assistant Attorney General, Office of Legal Counsel, August 1, 2002, Interrogation of al Qaeda Operative (DTS #2009-1810, Tab 1).

	was to take him aside—out of the view of the brothers—and explain to him that it was more important to have a 'super plan--not expect a superman.'"[2568] Abu Zubaydah explained that he informed trainees at the training camp that "'no brother' should be expected to hold out for an extended time," and that captured individuals will provide information in detention. For that reason, the captured individuals, he explained, should "expect that the organization will make adjustments to protect people and plans when someone with knowledge is captured."[2569]
CIA Interrogators, U.S. Military Interrogators, and the Army Field Manual	
DIRECTOR HAYDEN: "All those involved in the questioning of detainees have been *carefully chosen and carefully screened.*[2570] The average age of our officers interrogating detainees is 43. Once they are selected, they must complete more than 250 hours of specialized training for this program before they are allowed to come face-to-face with a	This CIA testimony is incongruent with internal CIA records and the operational history of the program. • On November █, 2002, after the completion of the first formal interrogation training class, ███████ CTC Legal, ████████████, asked CTC attorney ████████ to "[m]ake it known that from now on, CTC/LGL must vet all personnel who are enrolled in, observing or teaching – or otherwise associated with – the class."[2572] The chief of CTC, Jose Rodriguez, objected to this approach, stating: "I do not think that CTC/LGL should or would want to get

---

[2568] ████ 10496 (162014Z FEB 03). On July 25, 2002, a CIA Headquarters cable stated that Abu Zubaydah was the "author of a seminal al-Qa'ida manual on resistance to interrogation techniques." (*See* DIRECTOR ████ (251609Z JUL 02)). As a result of an ACLU lawsuit, in April 2010, the CIA released a document stating that Abu Zubaydah was the "author of a seminal al-Qa'ida manual on resistance to interrogation techniques." (*See* ACLU release entitled, "CIA Interrogation of AZ Released 04-15-10.") No CIA records could be identified to support this CIA assessment.

[2569] ████ 10496 (162014Z FEB 03)

[2570] The CIA's June 2013 Response states that "[w]e concede that prior to promulgation of DCI guidance on interrogation in January 2003 and the establishment of interrogator training courses in November of the same year, not every CIA employee who debriefed detainees had been thoroughly screened or had received formal training. After that time, however – the period with which DCIA Hayden, who came to the Agency in 2005, was most familiar – the statement is accurate." CIA records indicate that the first interrogator training course was established in November 2002. General Hayden became the CIA Director on May 30, 2006. After this time two CIA detainees entered CIA custody, one of whom was subjected to the CIA's enhanced interrogation techniques.

[2572] Email from: ██████████, /CTC/LGL; to: [REDACTED]; cc: Jose Rodriguez, [REDACTED], [REDACTED]. ██████████; subject: EYES ONLY; date: November █, 2002, at 03:13:01 PM. As described above, Gul Rahman likely froze to death at DETENTION SITE COBALT sometime in the morning of November █, 2002. ██████████'s email, however, appears to have been drafted before the guards had found Gul Rahman's body and before that death was reported to CIA Headquarters. *See* [REDACTED] 30211 ██████████, describing the guards observing Gul Rahman alive in the morning of November █, 2002. Gul Rahman's death appeared in cable traffic at least ████ after ████████'s email. No records could be identified to provide the impetus for ████████'s email.

terrorist. And we require additional field work under the direct supervision of an experienced officer before a new interrogator can direct an interrogation."

DIRECTOR HAYDEN: "The Army field manual was also written to guide the conduct of a much larger, much younger force that trains primarily to detain large numbers of enemy prisoners of war. That's not what the CIA program is."

DIRECTOR HAYDEN: "[The Army Field Manual has] got to be done by hundreds and hundreds of teenagers in battlefield tactical situations."
SENATOR JOHN WARNER: "Without the benefit of a tenth of the training of your professionals."
DIRECTOR HAYDEN: "Exactly."[2571]

into the business of vetting participants, observers, instructors or others that are involved in this program. It is simply not your job. Your job is to tell all what are the acceptable legal standards for conducting interrogations per the authorities obtained from Justice and agreed upon by the White House."[2573] Contrary to CIA Director Hayden's comments and Statement for the Record that "[a]ll those involved in the questioning of detainees are carefully chosen and screened for demonstrated professional judgment and maturity," CIA records suggest that the vetting sought by ████████ did not take place. The Committee reviewed CIA records related to several CIA officers and contractors involved in the CIA's Detention and Interrogation Program, most of whom conducted interrogations. The Committee identified a number of personnel whose backgrounds include notable derogatory information calling into question their eligibility for employment, their access to classified information, and their participation in CIA interrogation activities. In nearly all cases, the derogatory information was known to the CIA prior to the assignment of the CIA officers to the Detention and Interrogation Program. This group of officers included individuals who, among other issues, had engaged in inappropriate detainee interrogations, had workplace anger management issues, and had reportedly admitted to sexual assault.[2574]

- Director Hayden's testimony on the required hours of training for CIA interrogators is inconsistent with the early operational history of the program. Records indicate that CIA officers and contractors who conducted CIA interrogations in 2002 did not undergo any interrogation training. The first interrogator training course, held in November 2002, required approximately 65 hours of classroom and operational

[2571] In addition, ████████, Former Chief, ████████████████, CTC, testified: "First off, we have thirteen interrogators and, of that thirteen, eleven are contract employees of ours, and they've all been through the screening process, they've all been through our vetting process, and they are certainly more than qualified. They are probably some of the most mature and professional people you will have in this business."
[2573] Email from: Jose Rodriguez; to: ████████, CTC/LGL; cc: [REDACTED], [REDACTED], [REDACTED], [REDACTED], ████████; subject: EYES ONLY; date: November █, 2002, at 04:27 PM.
[2574] For additional detailed information, see Volume III.

	instruction.[2575] The initial training was designed and conducted by ███████, who had been sanctioned for using abusive interrogation techniques in the 1980s, and ███████, who had never been trained in, or conducted interrogations. In April 2003, ███████ [CIA OFFICER 1] was certified as an interrogator after only a week of classroom training.[2576] In 2003, interrogator certification required only two weeks of classroom training (a maximum of 80 hours) and 20 additional hours of operational training and/or actual interrogations.[2577]

Other Members of the Interrogation Team	
DIRECTOR HAYDEN: "All interrogation sessions in which one of these lawful procedures is authorized for use has to be *observed by nonparticipants* to ensure the procedures are applied appropriately and safely. *Any observer can call 'knock it off' at any time.* They are authorized to terminate an interrogation immediately should they believe anything unauthorized is occurring." SENATOR SNOWE: "So you also mentioned that there are non-participants who are observing the interrogation process. Who are these non-participants?"	This testimony is incongruent with CIA records, for example: • During the interrogation of Abu Zubaydah, CIA personnel at DETENTION SITE GREEN objected to the continued use of the CIA's enhanced interrogation techniques against Abu Zubaydah, stating that it was "highly unlikely" Abu Zubaydah possessed the threat information CIA Headquarters was seeking.[2578] When the interrogation team made this assessment, they stated that the pressures being applied to Abu Zubaydah approached "the legal limit."[2579] CIA Headquarters directed the interrogation team to continue to use the CIA's enhanced interrogation techniques and instructed the team to refrain from using "speculative language as to the legality of given activities" in CIA cables.[2580]

[2575] December 4, 2002 Training Report, High Value Target Interrogation and Exploitation (HVTIE) Training Seminar 12-18 Nov 02, (pilot running).

[2576] DIRECTOR ███████ APR 03)

[2577] Interrogator Selection, Training, Qualification, and Certification Process; approximately January 29-February 4, 2003.

[2578] *See* ███████ 10604 (091624Z AUG 02) and ███████ 10607 (100335Z AUG 02). In an email, the former SERE psychologists on contract with the CIA, who largely devised the CIA enhanced interrogation techniques, wrote that Abu Zubaydah stated he was "ready to talk" the first day after they used the CIA's techniques. Speaking specifically of the waterboard technique, they wrote, "As for our buddy; he capitulated the first time. We chose to expose him over and over until we had a high degree of confidence he wouldn't hold back. He said he was ready to talk during the first exposure." *See* email from: [REDACTED]; subject: "Re: [SWIGERT and DUNBAR]"; date: August 21, 2002, at 10:21 PM.

[2579] ███████ 10607 (100335Z AUG 02)

[2580] Email from: Jose Rodriguez; to: [REDACTED]; subject: "[DETENTION SITE GREEN]," with attachment of an earlier email from: [REDACTED]; to: [REDACTED]; date: August 12, 2002. *See also* the section on Abu Zubaydah's interrogation in this summary and the Abu Zubaydah detainee review in Volume III.

DIRECTOR HAYDEN: "They could be other interrogators, medical personnel, chief of base, debriefers, analysts."

SENATOR SNOWE: "Do they ever raise concerns during this process, during these interrogations?"

DIRECTOR HAYDEN: "Everybody watching has – every individual has an absolute right to stop the procedure just by saying 'stop.'"

SENATOR SNOWE: "Did it happen? It's never happened?"

DIRECTOR HAYDEN: "No, we're not aware. I'm sorry. John [Rizzo] and [████████] point out it's just not the ability to stop it; it is an obligation to stop it if they believe something is happening that is unauthorized."

- During the KSM interrogation sessions, the CIA chief of Base directed that the medical officer at the detention site not directly contact CIA Headquarters via the CIA's classified internal email system, to avoid establishing "grounds for further legal action." Instead, the chief of Base stated that any information on KSM's interrogations would be first reviewed by the chief of Base before being released to CIA Headquarters.[2581] Prior to KSM's third waterboard session of March 13, 2003, the on-site medical officer raised concerns that the session would exceed the limits of draft OMS guidelines for the waterboard.[2582] The waterboard session was conducted after an approval email from a CTC attorney at CIA Headquarters.[2583] The medical officer would later write that "[t]hings are slowly evolving form [sic] [medical officers] being viewed as the institutional conscience and the limiting factor to the ones who are dedicated to maximizing the benefit in a safe manner and keeping everyone's butt out of trouble."[2584]

- As was the case with several other CIA detainees, 'Abd al-Rahim al-Nashiri was repeatedly subjected to the CIA's enhanced interrogation techniques at the direction of CIA Headquarters, despite opposition from CIA interrogators.[2585]

- The CIA Inspector General Special Review states that CIA "psychologists objected to the use of on-site

---

[2581] Email from: [REDACTED]; to: ████████; cc: ████████; subject: Re: MEDICAL SITREP 3/10; date: March 11, 2003, at 8:10:39 AM.

[2582] Email from: [REDACTED]; to: ████████; cc: ████████, ████████, Jose Rodriguez; subject: re: Eyes Only – Legal and Political Quand[]ry; date: March 13, 2003, at 11:28:06 AM.

[2583] Email from: ████████; to: [REDACTED]; cc: Jose Rodriguez, ████████, ████████, ████████, ████████; subject: EYES ONLY – Use of Water Board; date: March 13, 2003, at 08:28 AM.

[2584] Email from: [REDACTED]; to: ████████; cc: ████████; subject: Re: State cable; date: March 13, 2003, at 1:43:17 PM. The previous day, the medical officer had written that "I am going the extra mile to try to handle this in a non confrontational manner." See email from: [REDACTED]; to: ████████; cc: ████████; subject: Re: MEDICAL SITREP 3/10; date: March 12, 2003, at 5:17:07 AM.

[2585] See, for example, the report of investigation of the Inspector General: "By mid-2002, Headquarters and [DETENTION SITE BLUE] were at odds regarding [DETENTION SITE BLUE]'s assessment on Al-Nashiri and how to proceed with his interrogation or debriefing. On several occasions throughout December 2002, [DETENTION SITE BLUE] reported via cables and secure telephone calls that Al-Nashiri was not actively resisting and was responding to questions directly. Headquarters disagreed with [DETENTION SITE BLUE]'s assessment because Headquarters analysts thought Al-Nashiri was withholding imminent threat information." See Report of Investigation, Office of the Inspector General, Unauthorized Interrogation Techniques at [DETENTION SITE BLUE] (2003-7123-IG), 29 October 2003, p. 18 (DTS #2003-4897).

	psychologists as interrogators and raised conflict of interest and ethical concerns." According to the Special Review, this was "based on a concern that the on-site psychologists who were administering the [CIA's enhanced interrogation techniques] participated in the evaluations, assessing the effectiveness and impact of the [CIA's enhanced interrogation techniques] on the detainees."[2586] In January 2003, CIA Headquarters required that at least one other psychologist be present who was not physically participating in the administration of the CIA's enhanced interrogation techniques. According to ██ ███████ OMS, however, the problem still existed because "psychologist/interrogators continue to perform both functions."[2587]
SENATOR SNOWE: "Did any CIA personnel express reservations about being engaged in the interrogation or these techniques that were used?" DIRECTOR HAYDEN: "I'm not aware of any. These guys are more experienced. No."	This statement is incongruent with CIA records. For example, from August 4, 2002, through August 23, 2002, the CIA subjected Abu Zubaydah to its enhanced interrogation techniques on a near 24-hour-per-day basis. The non-stop use of the CIA's enhanced interrogation techniques was disturbing to CIA personnel at DETENTION SITE GREEN. These CIA personnel objected to the continued use of the CIA's enhanced interrogation techniques against Abu Zubaydah, but were instructed by CIA Headquarters to continue using the techniques. The interrogation using the CIA's enhanced techniques continued more than two weeks after CIA personnel on site questioned the legality "of escalating or even maintaining the pressure" on Abu Zubaydah. CIA records include the following reactions of CIA personnel expressing "reservations about being engaged in the interrogations" and the use of the techniques: • August 5, 2002: "want to caution [medical officer] that this is almost certainly not a place he's ever been before in his medical career... It is visually and psychologically very uncomfortable."[2588]

[2586] Special Review, Office of the Inspector General, Counterterrorism Detention and Interrogation Activities (September 2001 – October 2003) (2003-7123-IG), 7 May 2004, p. 35 (DTS #2004-2710).
[2587] Special Review, Office of the Inspector General, Counterterrorism Detention and Interrogation Activities (September 2001 – October 2003) (2003-7123-IG), 7 May 2004, p. 40 (DTS #2004-2710).
[2588] Email from: [REDACTED]; to: ███████████, [REDACTED]; subject: Re: Monday; date: August 5, 2002, at 05:35AM.

- August 8, 2002: "Today's first session... had a profound effect on all staff members present... it seems the collective opinion that we should not go much further... everyone seems strong for now but if the group has to continue... we cannot guarantee how much longer."[2589]

- August 8, 2002: "Several on the team profoundly affected... some to the point of tears and choking up."[2590]

- August 9, 2002: "two, perhaps three [personnel] likely to elect transfer" away from the detention site if the decision is made to continue with the enhanced interrogation techniques.[2591]

- August 11, 2002: Viewing the pressures on Abu Zubaydah on video "has produced strong feelings of futility (and legality) of escalating or even maintaining the pressure." With respect to viewing the interrogation tapes, "prepare for something not seen previously."[2592]

The chief of CTC, Jose Rodriguez—via email—instructed the CIA interrogation team to not use "speculative language as to the legality of given activities" in CIA cable traffic.[2593] Shortly thereafter, circa December 2002, the CIA general counsel had a "real concern" about the lack of details in cables of what was taking place at CIA detention sites, noting that "cable traffic reporting was becoming thinner," and that "the agency cannot monitor the situation if it is not documented in cable traffic."[2594] The CIA's chief of interrogations—who provided training to CIA interrogators—expressed his view that there was

---

[2589] Email from: [REDACTED]; to: [REDACTED], ███████████, [REDACTED]; subject: Update; date: August 8, 2002, at 06:50 AM.
[2590] Email from: [REDACTED]; to: [REDACTED], ███████████, [REDACTED]; subject: Update; date: August 8, 2002, at 06:50 AM.
[2591] Email from: [REDACTED]; to: [REDACTED], [REDACTED]; subject: Re: 9 August Update; date: August 9, 2002, at 10:44 PM.
[2592] Email from: [REDACTED]; to: ███████████, [REDACTED]; subject: Greetings; date: August 11, 2002, at 09:45AM.
[2593] Email from: Jose Rodriguez; to: [REDACTED]; subject: [DETENTION SITE GREEN]; date: August 12, 2002.
[2594] Interview Report, 2003-7123-IG, Review of Interrogations for Counterterrorism Purposes, Scott W. Muller, September 5, 2003.

	"excess information" in the Abu Zubaydah interrogation cables.[2595]
Reporting Abuses	
DIRECTOR HAYDEN: "Any *deviations from approved procedures and practices that are seen are to be immediately reported and immediate corrective action taken*, including referring to the CIA Office of Inspector General and to the Department of Justice, as appropriate."	This testimony is not supported by CIA records, for example: • Multiple individuals involved in the interrogation of CIA detainee 'Abd al-Rahim al-Nashiri failed to report inappropriate activity. With regard to the unauthorized use of a handgun and power drill to threaten al-Nashiri, one CIA interrogator stated he did not report the incidents because he believed they fell below the reporting threshold for the CIA's enhanced interrogation techniques, while noting he did not receive guidance on reporting requirements. The chief of Base stated he did not report the incidents because he assumed the interrogator had CIA Headquarters' approval and because two senior CIA officials had instructed him to scale back on reporting from the detention site to CIA Headquarters. The inappropriate activity was discovered during a chance exchange between recently arrived CIA Headquarters officials and security officers.[2596] • There were significant quantitative and qualitative differences between the waterboarding of KSM, as applied, and the description of the technique provided to the Department of Justice. Neither CIA interrogators nor CIA attorneys reported these deviations to the inspector general or the Department of Justice at the time. • Additionally, CIA records indicate that at least 17 detainees were subjected to CIA enhanced interrogation techniques for which they were not approved.[2597]
Detainee Statistics	

[2595] Interview Report, 2003-7123-IG, Review of Interrogations for Counterterrorism Purposes, ~~████████~~. April 7, 2003.

[2596] Report of Investigation, Office of the Inspector General, Unauthorized Interrogation Techniques at [DETENTION SITE BLUE] (2003-7123-IG), 29 October 2003, p. 24 (DTS #2003-4897).

[2597] *See* Volume III for details.

DIRECTOR HAYDEN: "What you have there is a matrix. On the lefthand side of the matrix are the names of the *30 individuals in the CIA program who have had any EITs used against them*. Mr. Chairman and Vice Chairman and Members, you've heard me say this before. In the history of the program, *we've had 97 detainees*. Thirty of the detainees have had EITs used against them."	This testimony is inaccurate. At the time of this testimony, there had been least 118 CIA detainees. CIA records indicate at least 38 of the detainees had been subjected to the CIA's enhanced interrogation techniques.[2598]
Legal Basis for CIA Detention and Interrogation	
DIRECTOR HAYDEN: "The Army field manual is designed for the folks at Guantanamo to interrogate a rifleman that was in the employ of Gulbuddin Hekmatyar. That guy never gets into our program. The *ticket into*	This testimony is incongruent with CIA detention and interrogation records. For example, numerous individuals had been detained and subjected to the CIA's enhanced interrogation techniques, despite doubts and questions surrounding their knowledge of terrorist threats and the location of senior al-Qa'ida leadership. They include Asadullah,[2599] Mustafa al-Hawsawi,[2600] Abu Hudhaifa,[2601]

[2598] *See* Volume III for details. As discussed in this summary and in greater detail in the full Committee Study, on January 5, 2009, a CIA officer informed Director Hayden that additional CIA detainees beyond the 98 CIA detainees previously briefed to Congress had been identified. A CIA chart indicated there were "13 New Finds," additional individuals who had been detained by the CIA, and that the new true number of CIA detainees was now at least 112. After the briefing with Director Hayden, the CIA officer sent a record of this interaction via email only to himself, which stated: "I briefed the additional CIA detainees that could be included in RDI numbers. DCIA instructed me to keep the detainee number at 98 -- pick whatever date i needed to make that happen but the number is 98." (*See* email from: [REDACTED]; to [REDACTED]; subject: Meeting with DCIA; date: January 5, 2009, at 10:50 PM.) Shortly thereafter, the final draft of prepared remarks by Director Hayden to President-elect Obama's national security team state: "There have been 98 detainees in the history of the CIA program."

[2599] Interrogators had asked CIA Headquarters for the assessments supporting the decision to subject Asadullah to the CIA's enhanced interrogation techniques, noting that "it would be of enormous help to the interrogator to know what is concrete fact and what is good analysis." (*See* ████████ 33963 ████ 34098 ████; ████████ 34812 ████.) In response, ALEC Station acknowledged that "[t]o be sure, our case that Asadullah should have a good sense of bin Ladin's location is circumstantial." (*See* ALEC ████████.) The following day, interrogators commented that "it may be that he simply does not know the [locational information on AQ leaders]." *See* ████████ 34310 ████.

[2600] Following al-Hawsawi's first interrogation session, Chief of Interrogations ████████ asked CIA Headquarters for information on what al-Hawsawi actually "knows," saying "he does not appear to the [sic] be a person that is a financial mastermind. However, we lack facts with which to confront [al-Hawsawi]. What we need at this point is substantive information vice supposition." *See* ████████ 34757 (101742Z MAR 03).

[2601] Although CIA records include no requests or approval cables for the use of the CIA's enhanced interrogation techniques, Abu Hudhaifa was subjected to ice water baths and 66 hours of standing sleep deprivation. He was released because the CIA discovered he was likely not the person he was believed to be. *See* WASHINGTON DC ████████; ████ 51303 ████

this program is knowledge of threat to the homeland or the interests of the United States or knowledge of location of 1 or 2."	Arsala Khan,[2602] ABU TALHA AL-MAGREBI[2603] and ABU BAHAR AL-TURKI,[2604] Janat Gul,[2605] Ahmed Ghailani,[2606] Sharif al-Masri,[2607] and Sayyid Ibrahim.[2608] The CIA represented to the OLC that the CIA would only use its enhanced interrogation techniques against detainees who had knowledge of imminent threats or direct involvement in planning and preparing of terrorist actions. Not until July 20, 2007, more than three months after this testimony, did the OLC approve the use of the CIA's enhanced interrogation techniques against detainees based

[2602] CIA Headquarters initially resisted approving Arsala Khan's capture because of a lack of information confirming that he was a "continuing threat." (*See* [REDACTED] 169986 [REDACTED]; email from: [REDACTED]; to: [REDACTED], and [REDACTED]; subject: Denial of Approval to Capture Arsala Khan; date: [REDACTED].) Despite doubts that Arsala Khan was the individual sought by the CIA, interrogators subjected him to the CIA's enhanced interrogation techniques "to make a better assessment regarding [his] willingness to start talking, or assess if our subject is, in fact the man we are looking for." *See* [REDACTED] 1373 [REDACTED]

[2603] Authorization to use the CIA's enhanced interrogation techniques against ABU TALHA AL-MAGREBI was sought in order to "identify inconsistencies in [ABU BAHAR AL-TURKI's] story." *See* [REDACTED] 2186 [REDACTED]

[2604] The true names of these detainees have been replaced with the capitalized pseudonyms AL-MAGREBI and AL-TURKI. At the time the two detainees were rendered to CIA custody, the CIA was aware that they were then working for a foreign partner government. They were subjected to sleep deprivation and dietary manipulation until the CIA confirmed that the detainees had been trying to contact the CIA for weeks to inform the CIA of what they believed were pending al-Qa'ida terrorist attacks. After the CIA had determined that AL-MAGREBI and AL-TURKI should not be in CIA custody, the two detainees were held for [REDACTED] additional months before they were released.

[2605] Janat Gul's CIA interrogators wrote: "Team does not believe [Gul] is withholding imminent threat information, however team will continue to press [Gul] for that during each session." (*See* [REDACTED] 1574 ([REDACTED] 04).) The interrogation of Janat Gul is described in this summary and detailed in Volume III.

[2606] The CIA's assessment of Ghailani's knowledge of terrorist threats was speculative. As one CIA official noted, "[a]lthough Ghailani's role in operational planning is unclear, his respected role in al-Qa'ida and presence in Shkai as recently as October 2003 may have provided him some knowledge about ongoing attack planning against the United States homeland, and the operatives involved." *See* email from: [REDACTED], CTC/UBLD [REDACTED] (formerly ALEC [REDACTED]); to: [REDACTED], [REDACTED], [REDACTED], [REDACTED]; subject: derog information for ODDO on Talha, Ghailani, Hamza Rabi'a and Abu Faraj; date: August 10, 2004.

[2607] As noted above, the credibility of the source implicating Sharif al-Masri, Janat Gul, and Ghailani's connection to a pre-election plot was questioned by CIA officials prior to the application of the CIA's enhanced interrogation techniques against the detainees. The source was later determined to have fabricated the information.

[2608] Five days after interrogators began using the CIA's enhanced interrogation techniques against Sayyid Ibrahim, interrogators cabled CIA Headquarters requesting information that would "definitively link [Ibrahim] to nefarious activity or knowledge by [Ibrahim] of known nefarious activities of al-Qa'ida members, if this is possible." (*See* ([REDACTED] 1324 [REDACTED] FEB 04).) Without receiving a response, they continued using the CIA's enhanced interrogation techniques against Ibrahim. CIA Headquarters, which rejected an assessment from two CIA debriefers that Ibrahim was, "at best... a low-level facilitator," would later indicate that it was "uncertain" he would meet the requirements for U.S. military or foreign government detention. (*See* HEADQUARTERS [REDACTED]; HEADQUARTERS [REDACTED].) Other detainees, Abd al-Karim and Abu Hazim, were subjected to the CIA's enhanced interrogation techniques "in an attempt to more rapidly assess [their] knowledge of pending attacks, operational planning, and whereabouts of UBL." *See* [REDACTED] 36843 [REDACTED]; [REDACTED] 36908 [REDACTED].

	on their suspected knowledge of the locations of UBL or Ayman al-Zawahiri.[2609] Prior to July 20, 2007, in the case of at least six CIA detainees, the use of the CIA's enhanced interrogation techniques was nonetheless predicated on the assessment that the detainees possessed "locational information" on senior HVTs, to include UBL or Ayman al-Zawahiri.[2610]
Intelligence Reporting from Overall Detainee Population	
DIRECTOR HAYDEN: "Since we began this in the summer of 2002, the 97 detainees have helped us by their testimony create 8,000 intelligence reports." SENATOR SNOWE: "Of the 8,000 intelligence reports that were provided, as you said, by 30 of the detainees –" DIRECTOR HAYDEN: "By all 97, ma'am."[2611]	CIA representations suggesting that every CIA detainee provided intelligence reporting are not supported by CIA records. A detailed reporting chart is provided in Volume II. CIA reporting records indicate that 34 percent of all CIA detainees produced no intelligence reports, and nearly 70 percent produced fewer than 15 intelligence reports. Of the 39 detainees who were, according to CIA records, subjected to the CIA's enhanced interrogation techniques, nearly 20 percent produced no intelligence reports, while 40 percent produced fewer than 15 intelligence reports.

[2609] The OLC defined a High-Value Detainee as "a detainee who, until time of capture, we have reason to believe: (1) is a senior member of al-Qai'da or an al-Qai'da associated terrorist group (Jemaah Islamiyyah, Eqyptian [sic] Islamic Jihad, al-Zarqawi Group, etc.); (2) has knowledge of imminent terrorist threats against the USA, its military forces, its citizens and organizations, or its allies; or that has/had direct involvement in planning and preparing terrorist actions against the USA or its allies, or assisting the al-Qai'da leadership in planning and preparing such terrorist actions; and (3) if released, constitutes a clear and continuing threat to the USA or its allies" (Memorandum for John A. Rizzo, Senior Deputy General Counsel, Central Intelligence Agency, from Steven G. Bradbury, Principal Deputy Assistant Attorney General, Office of Legal Counsel, May 10, 2005, Re: Application of 18 U.S.C. Sections 2340-2340A to Certain Techniques That May Be Used in the Interrogation of a High Value al Qaeda Detainee (DTS #2009-1810, Tab 9); Memorandum for John A. Rizzo, Senior Deputy General Counsel, Central Intelligence Agency, from Steven G. Bradbury, Principal Deputy Assistant Attorney General, Office of Legal Counsel, May 30, 2005, Re: Application of United States Obligations Under Article 16 of the Convention Against Torture to Certain Techniques that May be Used in the Interrogation of High Value Al Qaeda Detainees (DTS #2009-1810, Tab 11)). Memorandum for John A. Rizzo, Acting General Counsel, Central Intelligence Agency, from Steven G. Bradbury, Principal Deputy Assistant Attorney General, Office of Legal Counsel, July 20, 2007, Re: Application of the War Crimes Act, the Detainee Treatment Act, and Common Article 3 of the Geneva Conventions to Certain Techniques that May Be Used by the CIA in the Interrogation of High Value al Qaeda Detainees (DTS #2009-1810, Tab 14) ("The CIA informs us that it currently views possession of information regarding the location of Osama bin Laden or Ayman al-Zawahiri as warranting application of enhanced techniques, if other conditions are met.")

[2610] Ridha Ahmad al-Najjar (███ 11542 ███; ALEC ██████ ; Ghairat Bahir ███ 31118 ██████ ; 'Umar 'Abd al-Rahman aka Asadullah (CIA ███ ███ 40471 ███ 10673 ███ ; DIRECTOR ███ 10673 ███ ; ███ 10732 ███ ; Adnan al-Libi ███ 1478 ███ ; ███ 1758 ███ ; Majid Bin Muhammad Bin Sulayman Khayil aka Arsala Khan ███ 1370 ███ ; Sayyid Ibrahim (███ 1294 ███ .

[2611] Similar representations had been made by Director Hayden on September 6, 2006. Senator Bayh: "I was impressed by your statement about how effective the [CIA's enhanced interrogation] techniques have been in eliciting important information to the country, at one point up to 50 percent of our information about al-Qa'ida. I think you said 9000 different intelligence reports?" Director Hayden: "Over 8000, sir." Senator Bayh: "And yet

CIA Detainee Reporting and Captures of Terrorists	
DIRECTOR HAYDEN: "Detainee reporting has played a role in nearly every capture of key al-Qa'ida members and associates since 2002."	The CIA consistently represented that the interrogation of CIA detainees using the CIA's enhanced interrogation techniques resulted in critical and otherwise unavailable intelligence that led to the capture of specific terrorists, to include, among others: KSM, Majid Khan, Ramzi bin al-Shibh, Iyman Faris, Saleh al-Marri, Ammar al-Baluchi, Khallad bin Attash, Sajid Badat, and Dhiren Barot.[2612] These representations were inaccurate.
The CIA's Detention and Interrogation Program Led to the Capture of Hambali and the Karachi "Cell"	
DIRECTOR HAYDEN: "March 2003, KSM gives us information about an al-Qa'ida operative, Majid Khan... KSM was aware that Majid had been recently captured. KSM, *possibly believing that Khan was talking*, admitted to having tasked Majid with delivering $50,000 to some of Hambali's operatives in December 2002... So now we go to [Majid] Khan and we tell him, hey, your uncle just told us about the money. *He acknowledged that he delivered the money to an operative named Zubair. He provided Zubair's physical description and phone number. Based on that* ██ *captured Zubair in June.*"	The chronology provided in this testimony, which is consistent with other CIA representations, is inaccurate. Prior to KSM's capture, in early January 2003, coverage of a known al-Qa'ida email account uncovered communications between the account and a former Baltimore, Maryland, resident, Majid Khan. The communications indicated that Majid Khan traveled to Bangkok for terrorist support activities and was in contact there with a "Zubair."[2613] By this time, the CIA had significant intelligence indicating that a "Zubair" played a central supporting role in Jemaah Islamiyah (JI), was affiliated with al-Qa'ida figures like KSM, had expertise in ████████████ in Southeast Asia, and was suspected of playing a role in Hambali's October 12, 2002, Bali bombings.[2614] On March 6, 2003, the day after Majid Khan was captured (the capture was unrelated to CIA detainee reporting), and while being questioned by foreign government interrogators using rapport-building techniques, Majid Khan described how he traveled to Bangkok and provided $50,000 USD to Zubair at the behest of al-Qa'ida.[2615] Majid Khan's physical description

---

this has come from, I guess, only thirty individuals." Director Hayden: "No, sir, 96, all 96" (Senate Select Committee on Intelligence, Briefing by the Director, Central Intelligence Agency, on the Central Intelligence Agency Detention, Interrogation and Rendition Program, September 6, 2006 (DTS #2007-1336)).

[2612] *See*, for example, ██████████, Memorandum for the Record; subject: Meeting with Deputy Chief, Counterterrorist Center ALEC Station; date: 17 July 2003; Memorandum for: Inspector General; from: James Pavitt, Deputy Director for Operations; subject: re (S) Comments to Draft IG Special Review, "Counterterrorism Detention and Interrogation Program" (2003-7123-IG); date: February 27, 2004; attachment: February 24, 2004, Memorandum re Successes of CIA's Counterterrorism Detention and Interrogation Activities; CIA briefing slides entitled, "*CIA Interrogation Program,*" dated July 29, 2003, presented to senior White House officials; Hearing of the Senate Select Committee on Intelligence, February 14, 2007 (DTS #2007-1337). For additional details, *see* Volume II.

[2613] ALEC ██████ (170117Z JAN 03)

[2614] *See* intelligence chronology in Volume II.

[2615] A cable describing the foreign government interrogation of Majid Khan stated, "[a foreign government officer] talked quietly to [Majid Khan] alone for about ten minutes before the interview began and was able to establish an

	of Zubair matched previous intelligence reporting already collected on Zubair.[2616]
	When confronted with this information, KSM confirmed the reporting, but denied knowing Zubair.[2617]
	By May 2003, the CIA learned that a source the CIA had been developing, [REDACTED], received a call from a phone number associated with Zubair. When the source was contacted by the CIA, he described a Malaysian man [REDACTED][2618] [REDACTED] later, the source alerted the CIA that Zubair would be [REDACTED]. Acting on this information, Thai authorities, [REDACTED], captured Zubair on June 8, 2003.
DIRECTOR HAYDEN: *"Zubair enters the program.* During debriefing, Zubair reveals he worked directly for Hambali. He provides information on [REDACTED] Hambali and a company [REDACTED]."*	This testimony is incongruent with CIA records. Prior to entering the CIA's Detention and Interrogation Program, while still in foreign government custody, Zubair was questioned about his efforts to obtain fraudulent documents, as well as his phone contact with [REDACTED] [Business Q].[2619] Zubair admitted to seeking illegal [REDACTED] documents on behalf of Hambali, as well as using [REDACTED] [Business Q].[2620] CIA detention records do not state what immediate investigative steps the CIA or Thai authorities took with regard to [REDACTED] [Business Q], although signals intelligence had indicated that Zubair had been in frequent contact with the company.[2621] After being rendered to CIA custody, Zubair was immediately subjected to the CIA's enhanced

excellent level of rapport." (*See* [REDACTED] 13678 (070724Z MAR 03).) Records indicate that this information was also disseminated in FBI channels. *See* ALEC [REDACTED].

[2616] *See* intelligence chronology in Volume II.

[2617] [REDACTED] 13678 (070724Z MAR 03), disseminated as [REDACTED]; [REDACTED] 10865 (171648Z MAR 03), disseminated as [REDACTED]; [REDACTED] 10866 (171832Z MAR 03). Prior to Majid Khan's reporting in foreign government custody, the CIA was aware from sources outside of the CIA detainee program that KSM had used couriers to transfer money to Hambali. Even while being questioned about such transfers, however, KSM made no mention of Majid Khan. *See* DIRECTOR [REDACTED] (251938Z SEP 02); ALEC [REDACTED] (072345Z MAR 03); [REDACTED] 10755 (111455Z MAR 03), disseminated as [REDACTED]

[2618] [REDACTED] 84783 [REDACTED]; [REDACTED] 84837 [REDACTED]

[2619] [REDACTED] 84854 [REDACTED]; [REDACTED] 84876 [REDACTED]; [REDACTED] 87617 [REDACTED]

[REDACTED]; [REDACTED] 84908 [REDACTED]

[2620] [REDACTED] 84908 [REDACTED]

[2621] [REDACTED] 84908 [REDACTED]

	interrogation techniques.[2622] After days of being questioned about other matters, Zubair was asked about his efforts to obtain ███ documents for Hambali, at which point he again acknowledged using ████████ ████████ [Business Q] ████████ .[2623] When Thai authorities approached "a contact" at ██████████ [Business Q], they were provided ████████ [2624]
DIRECTOR HAYDEN: "Working with [an entity of a foreign government], we used that information to capture another Hambali lieutenant, a fellow named Lillie -- who is also on your list [of CIA detainees] -- who provided the location of Hambali. And that location information led us to his capture."	In an operation that included surveillance of ██████ [Business Q], Hambali associate Amer was arrested on August 11, 2003.[2625] Amer was immediately cooperative and assisted in the arrest of Lillie hours later at approximately 6:00 PM.[2626] During his arrest, Lillie was found to have a key fob in his possession imprinted with an address of an apartment building in Ayutthaya, Thailand. In response to questioning, "within minutes of capture," Lillie admitted that the address on the key fob was the address where Hambali was located. Less than four hours later, Hambali was captured at the address found on the key fob.[2627] According to the chief of the CTC's Southeast Asia Branch: "[The CIA] stumbled onto Hambali. We stumbled onto the [source]... picking up the phone and calling his case officer to say there's ████████ ...we really stumbled over it. It wasn't police work, it

[2622] ██████████ 40568 ██████████
[2623] ██ 84876 ██ ; ██ 84908 ████
40915 ██ ; ██ 41017 ██ .

██████████████████████████████████
██████████████████████████████████
██████████████████████ In response to this
information, ████ wrote, "Wow..this is just great... you guys are soooo closing in on Hmabali [sic]."
See email from: ████ ; to: ████ , and others; subject: "wohoo---hilite for EA team
pls....aliases for Hambali"; date: June ██ , 2003, at 9:51:30 AM.
[2624] ██ 86449 ██████
[2625] ██ 87409 ██ ; ██ 87617 ██████
[2626] ██ 87414 ██ ; ██ 87617 ██████

██████████████████████████████████
██████████████████████████████████
[2627] Lillie provide this information immediately and prior to entering CIA custody. *See* ████ 9515 ████
██ ; ██ 87617 ██ ; ██ 87414 ██ ;
██ , "Hambali Capture."

	wasn't good targeting, it was we stumbled over it and it yielded up Hambali."[2628]
KSM, Hambali, and the Karachi "Cell" (the al-Ghuraba Group)	
DIRECTOR HAYDEN: "Bringing this story full circle, 'Abdul al-Hadi then identifies a cell of JI operatives whom Hambali had sent to Karachi for another al-Qa'ida operation. We take this information from Abdul Hadi to his brother, Hambali. Hambali then admits that he was grooming members of the cell for a U.S. operation, at the guidance of KSM -- remember, this is where this started -- and we're almost certain these were the guys trying to implement KSM's plot to fly hijacked planes into the tallest buildings on the west coast of the United States."	CIA Director Hayden's reference to "the guys trying to implement KSM's plot to fly hijacked planes into the tallest buildings on the west coast of the United States," is a reference to the al-Ghuraba student group and KSM's "Second Wave" plotting detailed in this summary and in greater detail in Volume II.[2629]

A review of CIA records found that contrary to CIA representations, Hambali's brother, 'Abdul al-Hadi, aka Gunawan, who was in foreign government custody, did not identify a "cell of JI operatives whom Hambali had sent to Karachi for another al-Qa'ida operation." He identified "a group of Malaysian and Indonesian students in Karachi" who were witting of his affiliation with Jemaah Islamiyah.[2630] CIA officers on site recalled other intelligence reporting indicating that KSM planned to use Malaysians in the "next wave of attacks," connected it to Gunawan's statements about Malaysian students, and reported that Gunawan had just identified "a group of 16 individuals, most all of whom are Malaysians."[2631] Records indicate that it was this initial analysis that led the CIA to consider the group a KSM "cell" for the "next wave of attacks."

While Hambali was being subjected to the CIA's enhanced interrogation techniques, he was confronted about KSM's efforts to find pilots, as well as information on the al-Ghuraba group—which the CIA assessed was a KSM "cell." Hambali told his CIA interrogators "that some of the members of [the al-Ghuraba group] were destined to work for al-Qa'ida if everything had gone |

[2628] CIA Oral History Program Documenting Hambali capture, interview of [REDACTED], interviewed by [REDACTED], on November 28, 2005.

[2629] [REDACTED] 45915 (141431Z SEP 03). *See also* February 27, 2004, Memorandum for CIA Inspector General from James L. Pavitt, CIA Deputy Director for Operations, entitled "Comments to Draft IG Special Review, "Counterterrorism Detention and Interrogation Program," which contains a February 24, 2004, attachment entitled, "Successes of CIA's Counterterrorism Detention and Interrogation Activities"; CIA Intelligence Product entitled, "Jemaah Islamiya: Counterterrorism Scrutiny Limiting Extremist Agenda in Pakistan," dated April 18, 2008; KSM and Hambali reporting from October 2003 in Volumes II and III.

[2630] ████████ 15359

[2631] ████████ 15359

according to plan," and that "KSM told him to provide as many pilots as he could."[2632]

Months later, on November 30, 2003, after three weeks of being questioned by a debriefer "almost entirely in Bahasa Indonesia," Hambali admitted to fabricating information during the period he was being subjected to the CIA's enhanced interrogation techniques. According to Hambali, he fabricated these claims "in an attempt to reduce the pressure on himself" and "to give an account that was consistent with what [Hambali] assessed the questioners wanted to hear."[2633] A November 30, 2003, cable noted that CIA personnel "assesse[d] [Hambali]'s admission of previous fabrication to be credible." Hambali then consistently described "the al-Ghuraba organization" as a "development camp for potential future JI operatives and leadership, vice a JI cell or an orchestrated attempt by JI to initiate JI operations outside of Southeast Asia." This description was consistent and corroborative of other intelligence reporting.[2634]

A wide body of intelligence reporting indicates that, contrary to CIA representations, the al-Ghuraba group was not "tasked" with, or witting, of any aspect of the "Second Wave" plotting.[2635]

While KSM's reporting varied, KSM stated "he did not yet view the group as an operational pool from which to draft operatives."[2636] An October 27, 2006, CIA cable stated that "all of the members of the JI al-Ghuraba cell have been released,"[2637] while an April 18, 2008, CIA intelligence report referencing the al-Ghuraba group

---

[2632] See the intelligence chronology in Volume II, including [REDACTED] 45953 (151241Z SEP 03) [REDACTED] 1323 (161749Z SEP 03).

[2633] ████ 1142 (301055Z NOV 03)

[2634] See intelligence chronology in Volume II. Although NSA signals intelligence was not provided for this Study, an April 2008 CIA intelligence report on the Jemaah Islamiya noted that the al-Ghuraba group "consisted of the sons of JI leaders, many of whom completed basic militant training in Afghanistan and Pakistan while enrolled at Islamic universities in Karachi," and that this assessment was based on "signals intelligence and other reporting." See CIA Intelligence Product entitled, "Jemaah Islamiya: Counterterrorism Scrutiny Limiting Extremist Agenda in Pakistan," dated April 18, 2008.

[2635] See intelligence chronology in Volume II.

[2636] ████████ 10223 (221317Z OCT 03); ████████████

[2637] WASHINGTON DC ████ (272113Z OCT 06)

	makes no reference to the group serving as potential operatives for KSM's "Second Wave" plotting.[2638]
The Interrogation Process	
DIRECTOR HAYDEN: "As before, with these seven [enhanced interrogation techniques] we use the least coercive measures to create cooperation at a predictable, reliable, sustainable level. They are used to create a state of cooperation. Once the state of cooperation is created, we simply productively debrief the detainee. On average, we get to that state of cooperation in a period measured by about one to two weeks." "When we're asking him questions during that period of increased stress, when we're being more rather than less coercive, *we are generally asking him questions for which we know the answers.* Otherwise, how do we know we have moved him from a spirit of defiance into a spirit of cooperation? And only after we have moved him into this second stage do we then begin to ask him things we really think he knows but we don't."	This testimony is incongruent with CIA records. As is detailed throughout the Committee Study, CIA detainees were frequently subjected to the CIA's enhanced interrogation techniques immediately after being rendered to CIA custody.[2639] CIA interrogators asked open-ended questions of CIA detainees, to which the CIA did not know the answers, while subjecting detainees to the CIA's enhanced interrogation techniques. This approach began with Abu Zubaydah, whose interrogation focused on him being told to provide "the one thing you don't want me to know,"[2640] and remained a central feature of the program. Numerous CIA detainees were determined never to have reached a "state of cooperation." Several detainees, when subjected to the CIA's enhanced interrogation techniques, transitioned to normal debriefing, and were then subjected to one or more additional periods of being subjected to the techniques.[2641]

[2638] CIA Intelligence Product entitled, "Jemaah Islamiya: Counterterrorism Scrutiny Limiting Extremist Agenda in Pakistan," dated April 18, 2008.

[2639] Numerous detainees were stripped and shackled, nude, in the standing stress position for sleep deprivation or subjected to other enhanced interrogation techniques prior to being questioned by an interrogator. *See* for example KSM ███ 34491 (051400Z MAR 03); Asadullah (DIRECTOR ███ (███ FEB 03)); Abu Yasir al-Jaza'iri ███████ 35558 (███ MAR 03)); Suleiman Abdullah (███ 35787 (███ MAR 03); ███ 36023 (███ APR 03)); Abu Hudhaifa ███ 38576 (███ MAY 03)); Hambali ███ 1241 ███ ; and Majid Khan (███ 46471 (241242Z MAY 03); ███ 39077 (271719Z MAY 03).

[2640] ███ 10016 (120509Z APR 02); ███ 10594 (061558Z AUG 02)

[2641] *See* detainee reviews in Volume III for additional information.

Use of Detainee Reporting	
DIRECTOR HAYDEN: "Nothing that we get from the program, however, is used in isolation. It's a data point that then has to be rubbed up against all the other data points we have available to us."	The CIA regularly disseminated intelligence reports based on uncorroborated statements from CIA detainees. The reports, some of which included fabricated or otherwise inaccurate information, required extensive FBI investigations.[2642] For example, the CIA disseminated information that KSM had sent Abu Issa al-Britani to Montana to recruit African-American Muslim converts.[2643] In June 2003, KSM stated he fabricated the information because he was "under 'enhanced measures' when he made these claims and simply told his interrogators what he thought they wanted to hear."[2644] Other KSM fabrications led the CIA to capture and detain suspected terrorists who were later found to be innocent.[2645]
The Religious Foundation for Cooperation	
DIRECTOR HAYDEN: "This proposed program you have in front of you has been informed by our experience and it has been informed by the comments of our	The CIA made a similar representation to the Department of Justice in the context of Abu Zubaydah.[2647] CIA records do not indicate that CIA detainees described a religious basis for cooperating in association with the CIA's enhanced interrogation techniques.[2648]

[2642] For example, on May 15 and May 16, 2003, the FBI hosted a conference on KSM and investigations resulting from KSM's reporting. The agenda included al-Qa'ida recruitment efforts in the U.S., a topic on which KSM had provided significant fabricated information. (*See* Memorandum from: [REDACTED]; for: ████████████. [REDACTED], ████████, ████████, ████████, [REDACTED], [REDACTED], ████ [REDACTED], [REDACTED], ████████, [REDACTED], ████████, [REDACTED], [REDACTED], [REDACTED], [REDACTED], [REDACTED], ████, ████, [REDACTED], [REDACTED], [REDACTED], [REDACTED], [REDACTED], [REDACTED], ████, [REDACTED], [REDACTED]; date: 8 May 2003.) *See also* Email from: [REDACTED]; to: ████████ ████████; cc: ████████, ████████; subject: Thanks from FBI; date: May 17, 2003, at 7:25:15 PM; ████ 12095 (222049Z JUN 03); ████ 12558 (041938Z AUG 03); ████ 31148 (171919Z DEC 05); ████ 31147 (171919Z DEC 05), disseminated as ████████.

[2643] ████ 10942 (221610Z MAR 03), disseminated as ████████; ████ 10948 (222101Z MAR 03), disseminated as ████████.

[2644] ████ 12095 (222049Z JUN 03)

[2645] The CIA captured and detained two individuals whom KSM had identified as the protectors of his children. KSM later described his reporting as "all lies." *See* ████████ 34569 (061722Z MAR 03); ████ 1281 (130801Z JUN 04).

[2647] The CIA has referred only to Abu Zubaydah in the context of this representation. *See* Memorandum for John A. Rizzo, Senior Deputy General Counsel, Central Intelligence Agency, from Steven G. Bradbury, Principal Deputy Assistant Attorney General, Office of Legal Counsel, May 30, 2005, Re: Application of United States Obligations Under Article 16 of the Convention Against Torture to Certain Techniques that May be Used in the Interrogation of High Value Al Qaeda Detainees. The OLC document states: "As Zubaydah himself explained with respect to enhanced techniques, 'brothers who are captured and interrogated are permitted by Allah to provide information when they believe they have 'reached the limit of their ability to withhold it' in the fact of psychological and physical hardships."

[2648] While there are no records of CIA detainees making these statements, the Deputy Chief of ALEC Station, ████████████, told the Inspector General on July 17, 2003, that the "best information [the CIA] received on how to handle the [CIA] detainees came from a walk-in [a source ████████████ to volunteer information to the CIA] after the arrest of Abu Zubaydah. He told us we were

detainees. It's built on the particular psychological profile of the people we have and expect to get -- al-Qa'ida operatives. Perceiving themselves true believers in a religious war, detainees believe they are morally bound to resist until Allah has sent them a burden too great for them to withstand. At that point -- and that point varies by detainee -- their cooperation in their own heart and soul becomes blameless and they enter into this cooperative relationship with our debriefers."
DIRECTOR HAYDEN:
"Number one, we use the enhanced interrogation techniques at the beginning of this process, and it varies how long it takes, but I gave you a week or two as the normal window in which we actually helped this religious zealot to get over his own personality and put himself in a spirit of cooperation."

VICE CHAIRMAN BOND:
"Once you get past that time period, once you have convinced them that Allah gives them the green light, that's when you get the 8,000 intelligence reports."

The CIA has referred only to Abu Zubaydah in the context of this representation. As detailed, Abu Zubaydah referenced religion in the context of his cooperation prior to being subjected to the CIA's enhanced interrogation techniques. On May 14, 2002, more than two months before Abu Zubaydah began his August 2002 enhanced interrogation period, Abu Zubaydah told interrogators that "if he possessed any more information on future threats, then he would provide this information to us to help himself, claiming that 'the sharia' gives him permission to do so in his current situation."[2649] Abu Zubaydah also made a similar statement to his interrogators approximately a week later—again, prior to the use of the CIA's enhanced interrogation techniques—stating that he had "prayed his 'Istikharah' (seeking God's guidance) and was now willing to tell what he really knew," and "that he had received guidance from God" to cooperate to "prevent his captured brothers from having a difficult time."[2650] Further, Abu Zubaydah maintained that he always intended to provide information and never believed he could withhold information from interrogators.[2651] In February 2003, he told a CIA psychologist that he believed every captured "brother" would talk in detention, and that these "brothers should be able to expect that the organization will make adjustments to protect people and plans when someone with knowledge is captured."[2652] Abu Zubaydah stated he conveyed this perspective to trainees at a terrorist training camp.[2653]

---

underestimating Al-Qa'ida. The detainees were happy to be arrested by the U.S. because they got a big show trial. When they were turned over to [foreign governments], they were treated badly so they talked. Allah apparently allows you to talk if you feel threatened. The [CIA] detainees never counted on being detained by us outside the U.S. and being subjected to methods they never dreamed of." *See* ██████████, Memorandum for the Record; subject: Meeting with Deputy Chief, Counterterrorist Center ALEC Station; date: 17 July 2003.

[2649] ██████ 10262 (151138Z MAR 02)
[2650] ██████ 10262 (151138Z MAR 02)
[2651] ██████ 10496 (162014Z FEB 03)
[2652] ██████ 10496 (162014Z FEB 03)
[2653] ██████ 10496 (162014Z FEB 03)

DIRECTOR HAYDEN: "That's correct, Senator, when we get the subject into this zone of cooperation. I think, as you know, in two-thirds of the instances we don't need to use any of the techniques to get the individual into the zone of cooperation." SENATOR NELSON: "How do you suspect that al-Qa'ida operatives are training in order to counter your techniques?" DIRECTOR HAYDEN: "You recall the policy on which this is based, that we're going to give him a burden that Allah says is too great for you to bear, so they can put the burden down."[2646]	
Threats Related to Sodomy, Arrest of Family	
DIRECTOR HAYDEN: "Many assertions [in the ICRC report] regarding physical or threatened abuse egregious and are simply not true. On their face, they aren't even credible. Threats of acts of sodomy, the	This testimony is incongruent with CIA interrogation records. • As documented in the May 2004 Inspector General Special Review and other CIA records, interrogators threatened 'Abd al-Rahim al-Nashiri, KSM, and Abu Zubaydah with harm to their families.[2654]

[2646] In addition, CIA officer ███████████ testified at the April 12, 2007, Committee hearing: "I spoke with Zubaydah. I was at one of these facilities for several months and I spent around 18 hours a day with Abu Zubaydah. At the conclusion of my time, as I was leaving the facility, he spoke with me, and he said there is something I need you to understand – to go back to the question that came earlier about walling and a collar. He looked at the plywood wall in the cell and said I want to thank you for that. I've had a lot of time to sit and reflect, and I understand why that's there. That's there so I don't get hurt. In terms of the totality of the experience, his advice was I may have been the first person, but you need to continue to do this because I need to be able to live with who I am and I will continue to be the religious believing person I am, but you had to get me to the point where I could have absolution from my god to cooperate and deal with your questions. So he thanked us for bringing him to that point, beyond which he knew his religious beliefs absolved him from cooperating with us." There are no CIA records to support this testimony.

[2654] According to the Inspector General Special Review, a debriefer threatened al-Nashiri by saying "[w]e could get your mother in here," and, "[w]e can bring your family in here." In addition, one of KSM's interrogators told the inspector general that the psychologist/interrogators told KSM that, if anything happens in the United States, "[w]e're going to kill your children." (*See* Special Review, pp. 42-43; interview of ███████████, by [REDACTED] and [REDACTED], Office of the Inspector General, 30 April 2003; interview of ███████████, by [REDACTED] and [REDACTED], Office of the Inspector General, 22 October 2003; ███████████ 10757 (111505Z MAR 03).) According to a CIA cable, a case officer "used [Abu Zubaydah's] 'family card' to apply more psychological pressure on [Abu Zubaydah]." The cable stated that the case officer "advised [Abu Zubaydah] that even if [Abu Zubaydah] did not care about himself...[Abu Zubaydah] should at least care about his family and keep

arrest and rape of family members, the intentional infection of HIV or any other diseases have never been and would never be authorized. There are no instances in which such threats or abuses took place."	• Rectal exams were standard operating procedure for security purposes. A June 2002 cable noted that Abu Zubaydah was mildly "tense," "likely an anticipatory reaction given his recent unexpected rectal exam" the previous day.[2655] • At least five detainees were subjected to rectal rehydration or rectal feeding. There is at least one record of Abu Zubaydah receiving "rectal fluid resuscitation" for "partially refusing liquids."[2656] According to CIA records, Majid Khan was "very hostile" to rectal feeding and removed the rectal tube as soon as he was allowed to.[2657] KSM was subjected to rectal rehydration without a determination of medical need, a procedure that KSM interrogator and chief of interrogations, ██████, would later characterize as illustrative of the interrogator's "total control over the detainee."[2658] Marwan al-Jabbur was subjected to what was originally referred to in a cable as an "enema," but was later acknowledged to be rectal rehydration.[2659] Both al-Nashiri[2660] and Majid Khan were subjected to rectal feeding.[2661]

in mind their welfare; the insinuation being [that] something might happen to them." *See* ██████ 10095 (220713Z APR 02)

[2655] ██████ 10507 ██████. CIA leadership, including CIA General Counsel Scott Muller and DDO James Pavitt, were also alerted to allegations that rectal exams were conducted with "excessive force" on two detainees at DETENTION SITE COBALT. *See* email from [REDACTED]; to [REDACTED]; cc: ██████, ██████, [REDACTED]; subject: ACTIONS from the GC Update this Morning, date: ██████ 12:15 PM; Email from ██████; to: [REDACTED]; cc: ██████, [REDACTED], [REDACTED], [REDACTED], subject: ACTIONS from the GC Update this Morning; date: ██████ 1:23:31 PM; Email from ██████; to: [REDACTED]; cc: ██████, [REDACTED]; subject: Re: ACTIONS from the GC Update this Morning REQUEST FOR STATUS UPDATE; date: ██████, at 10:47:32 AM. ██████ 3223 ██████; HEADQUARTERS ██████ ██████

[2656] ██████ 10070 ██████

[2657] [REDACTED] 3868 (291534Z DEC 04); [REDACTED] 3868 (291534Z DEC 04). *See also* HEADQUARTERS ██████ (302114Z NOV 04).

[2658] ██████ 34491 (051400Z MAR 03); Interview of ██████, by [REDACTED] and [REDACTED], Office of the Inspector General, 27 March 2003. ██████, ██████ the Office of Medical Services (OMS), described the rectal rehydration of KSM as helping to "clear a person's head" and effective in getting KSM to talk.

[2659] *See* ██████ 2563 ██████; email from: ██████; to: ██████, [REDACTED], [REDACTED], [REDACTED], [REDACTED]; subject: Re: TASKING – Fw: ██████; date: March 30, 2007; DTS #2007-1502.

[2660] As described in the context of the rectal feeding of al-Nashiri, Ensure was infused into al-Nashiri "in a forward-facing position (Trendlenberg) with head lower than torso." *See* ██████ 1203 (231709Z MAY 04).

[2661] According to CIA records, Majid Khan's "lunch tray," consisting of hummus, pasta with sauce, nuts, and raisins was "pureed" and rectally infused. *See* ██████ 3240 (231839Z SEP 04).

	• Three detainees, Ramzi bin al-Shibh, Khallad bin Attash and Adnan al-Libi, were threatened with rectal rehydration.[2662]

Punches and Kicks	
DIRECTOR HAYDEN: "Punches and kicks are not authorized and have never been employed."[2663]	This testimony is incongruent with CIA records. Interviews conducted for two CIA internal reviews related to Gul Rahman's death provided details on CIA interrogations at the CIA's DETENTION SITE COBALT. In an interview report, CIA contractor DUNBAR described the "hard" or "rough" takedown used at DETENTION SITE COBALT. According to the interview report of DUNBAR, "there were approximately five CIA officers from the renditions team… they opened the door of Rahman's cell and rushed in screaming and yelling for him to 'get down.' They dragged him outside, cut off his clothes and secured him with Mylar tape. They covered his head with a hood and ran him up and down a long corridor adjacent to his cell. They slapped him and punched him several times. [DUNBAR] stated that although it was obvious they were not trying to hit him as hard as they could, a couple of times the punches were forceful. As they ran him along the corridor, a couple of times he fell and they dragged him through the dirt (the floor outside of the cells is dirt). Rahman did acquire a number of abrasions on his face, legs, and hands, but nothing that required medical attention. (This may account for the abrasions found on Rahman's body after his death. Rahman had a number of surface abrasions on his shoulders, pelvis, arms, legs, and face.)"[2664] The use of the "hard" or "rough" takedown, as used on Gul Rahman, was described by the CIA officer in charge of the CIA's DETENTION SITE COBALT as "employed often in interrogations at [DETENTION SITE COBALT] as 'part of the atmospherics.'"[2665]

[2662] *See* Volume III for additional information.

[2663] The CIA's June 2013 Response states, "DCIA Hayden stated that 'punches' and 'kicks' were not authorized techniques and had never been employed and that CIA officers never threatened a detainee or his family." The CIA's June 2013 Response adds: "Part of that assertion was an error. The DCIA would have been better served if the Agency had framed a response for him that discussed CIA's policy prohibiting such conduct, and how the Agency moved to address unsanctioned behavior which had occurred (including punches and kicks) and implement clear guidelines."

[2664] Memorandum for Deputy Director of Operations, from ███████████, January 28, 2003, Subject: Death Investigation – Gul RAHMAN, pp. 21-22.

[2665] CIA Inspector General report, "Report of Investigation, Death of a Detainee ██████████," (2003-7402-IG), April 27, 2005, at 38.

Hygiene	
DIRECTOR HAYDEN: "Detainees have never been denied the means -- at a minimum, they've always had a bucket -- to dispose of their human waste."	This testimony is incongruent with CIA records. CIA detainees, particularly those subjected to standing sleep deprivation, were routinely placed in diapers. Waste buckets were not always available. In the interrogation of Abu Hazim, a waste bucket was removed from his cell for punishment. According to a CIA cable, Abu Hazim "requested a bucket in which he could relieve himself, but was told all rewards must be earned."[2666]

Medical Personnel and Medical Care	
DIRECTOR HAYDEN: "The medical section of the ICRC report concludes that the association of CIA medical officers with the interrogation program is 'contrary to international standards of medical ethics.' That is just wrong. The role of CIA medical officers in the detainee program is and always has been and always will be to ensure the safety and the well-being of the detainee. The placement of medical officers during the interrogation techniques represents an extra measure of caution. Our medical officers do not recommend the employment or continuation of any procedures or techniques."	CIA records detail how throughout the program, CIA medical personnel cleared detainees for the use of the CIA's enhanced interrogation techniques and played a central role in deciding whether to continue, adjust, or alter the use of the techniques against detainees. For example: • Prior to the initiation of the CIA's enhanced interrogation techniques against Abu Zubaydah, CIA Headquarters, with medical personnel participation, stated that the "interrogation process takes precedence over preventative medical procedures."[2667] • Abu Ja'far al-Iraqi was provided medication for swelling in his legs to allow for continued standing sleep deprivation.[2668]

[2666] ███████████████ 37493 ████████

[2667] ALEC ████ (182321Z JUL 02). According to the CIA attorney who reviewed the videotapes of the interrogation of Abu Zubaydah, "the person he assumed was a medical officer was dressed completely in black from head to toe, and was indistinguishable from other [interrogation] team members." *See* June 18, 2003, Interview Report of [REDACTED], Office of General Counsel Assistant General Counsel.

[2668] Abu Ja'far al-Iraqi was subjected to nudity, dietary manipulation, insult slaps, abdominal slaps, attention grasps, facial holds, walling, stress positions, and water dousing with 44 degree Fahrenheit water for 18 minutes. He was shackled in the standing position for 54 hours as part of sleep deprivation, and experienced swelling in his lower legs requiring blood thinner and spiral ace bandages. He was moved to a sitting position, and his sleep deprivation was extended to 78 hours. After the swelling subsided, he was provided with more blood thinner and was returned to the standing position. The sleep deprivation was extended to 102 hours. After four hours of sleep, Abu Ja'far al-Iraqi was subjected to an additional 52 hours of sleep deprivation, after which CIA Headquarters informed interrogators that eight hours of sleep was the minimum. In addition to the swelling, Abu Ja'far al-Iraqi also experienced an edema on his head due to walling, abrasions on his neck, and blisters on his ankles from shackles. *See* ████ 1810 (████ DEC 05); ████ 1813 (████ DEC 05); ████ 1819 (████ DEC 05); ████ 1847 (████ DEC 05); ████ 1848 (████ DEC 05); HEADQUARTERS ████ (████ DEC 05). *See* additional information on Abu Ja'far al-Iraqi in Volume III.

DIRECTOR HAYDEN: "The allegation in the report that a CIA medical officer threatened a detainee, stating that medical care was conditional on cooperation is blatantly false. Health care has always been administered based upon detainee needs. It's neither policy nor practice to link medical care to any other aspect of the detainee program." SENATOR HATCH: "Has there been any use of any kind of drug or withholding of any kind of drug or medication?" DIRECTOR HAYDEN: "No, absolutely not."	This testimony is incongruent with CIA records. For example, as CIA interrogators prepared for the August 2002 "enhanced interrogation" phase of Abu Zubaydah's interrogation, the CIA's DETENTION SITE GREEN noted, and CIA Headquarters confirmed, that the interrogation process would take precedence over preventing Abu Zubaydah's wounds from becoming infected.[2669] DETENTION SITE GREEN personnel also stated that delaying a medical session for 72 hours after the start of the new phase of interrogation would convey to Abu Zubaydah that his level of medical care was contingent upon his cooperation.[2670] On August 10, 2002, the medical officer at DETENTION SITE GREEN stated that, under the model of medical intervention that the detention site was following during the most aggressive interrogation phase, Abu Zubaydah's medical status was likely to deteriorate to an "unacceptable level" over the next two weeks.[2671] On August 25, 2002, the Base stated that the "combination of a lack of hygiene, sub-optimal nutrition, inadvertent trauma to the wound secondary to some of the stress techniques utilized at that stage, and the removal of formal obvious medical care to further isolate the subject had an overall additive effect on the deterioration of the wound."[2672] Abu Zubaydah lost his left eye while in CIA custody. In October 2002, DETENTION SITE GREEN recommended that the vision in his right eye be tested, noting that "[w]e have a lot riding upon his ability to see, read and write." DETENTION SITE GREEN stressed that "this request is driven by our intelligence needs vice humanitarian concern for AZ."[2673] CIA detainees Abu Hazim and Abd al-Karim each broke a foot while trying to escape capture and were placed in casts; Abd al-Karim's medical evaluation upon entry into CIA custody included a recommendation that he not be subjected to "extended standing for a couple of weeks,"

2669 ████████ 10536 (151006Z JULY 02); ALEC ████ (182321Z JUL 02)
2670 ████████ 10536 (151006Z JULY 02)
2671 ████ 10607 (100335Z AUG 02)
2672 ████ 10647 (201331Z AUG 02); ████████ 10618 (121448Z AUG 02); ████████ 10679 (250932Z AUG 02)
2673 ████████ 11026 (070729Z OCT 02)

which was then extended to three months.[2674] A cable describing the CIA enhanced interrogation techniques to be used on the two detainees stated that the interrogator would "forego cramped confinement, stress positions, walling, and vertical shackling (due to [the detainees'] injury)."[2675] Abd al-Karim was nonetheless subjected to two 45-minute sessions of cramped confinement,[2676] repeated walling, and a stress position that involved placing his "head on [the] wall, bent at waist, shuffled backwards to a safe, yet uncomfortable position."[2677] As part of sleep deprivation, he was also "walked for 15 minutes every half-hour through the night and into the morning."[2678] A few days later, a cable stated that, even given the best prognosis, Abd al-Karim would have arthritis and limitation of motion for the rest of his life.[2679] Meanwhile, Abu Hazim was subjected to repeated walling.[2680]

Subsequently, and despite the aforementioned recommendation related to Abd al-Karim and a recommendation from a regional medical officer that Abu Hazim avoid any weight-bearing activities for five weeks,[2681] interrogators sought and received approval to use standing sleep deprivation on al-Karim and Abu Hazim.[2682]

Abu Hazim underwent 52 hours of standing sleep deprivation,[2683] and Abd al-Karim underwent an unspecified period of standing sleep deprivation.[2684]

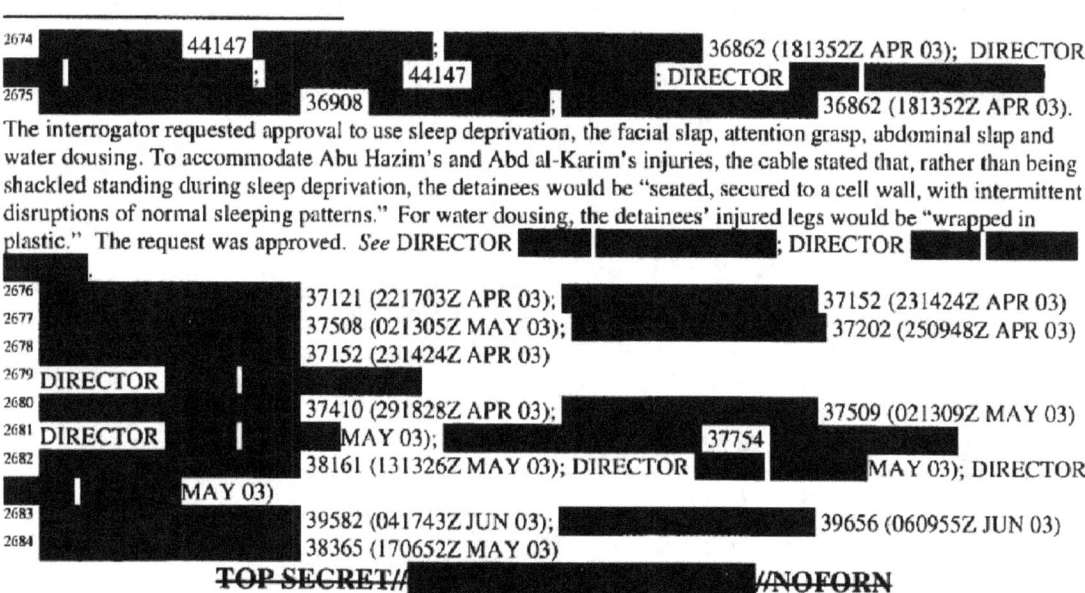

[2674] ████ 44147 ████████; ████████ 36862 (181352Z APR 03); DIRECTOR ██████ ; ████ 44147 ████ ; DIRECTOR ████████████

[2675] ████████ 36908 ████ ; ████████ 36862 (181352Z APR 03). The interrogator requested approval to use sleep deprivation, the facial slap, attention grasp, abdominal slap and water dousing. To accommodate Abu Hazim's and Abd al-Karim's injuries, the cable stated that, rather than being shackled standing during sleep deprivation, the detainees would be "seated, secured to a cell wall, with intermittent disruptions of normal sleeping patterns." For water dousing, the detainees' injured legs would be "wrapped in plastic." The request was approved. See DIRECTOR ████ ████████ ; DIRECTOR ████ ████

[2676] ████████ 37121 (221703Z APR 03); ████████ 37152 (231424Z APR 03)
[2677] ████████ 37508 (021305Z MAY 03); ████ 37202 (250948Z APR 03)
[2678] ████████ 37152 (231424Z APR 03)
[2679] DIRECTOR ████ ████
[2680] ████████ 37410 (291828Z APR 03); ████ 37509 (021309Z MAY 03)
[2681] DIRECTOR ████ ████ MAY 03); ████████ 37754 ████
[2682] ████████ 38161 (131326Z MAY 03); DIRECTOR ████ MAY 03); DIRECTOR ████ MAY 03)
[2683] ████████ 39582 (041743Z JUN 03); ████████ 39656 (060955Z JUN 03)
[2684] ████████ 38365 (170652Z MAY 03)

	Interrogators left Asadullah, a detainee with a sprained ankle, in the standing sleep deprivation position. When Asadullah was subsequently placed in a stress position on his knees, he complained of discomfort and asked to sit. He was told he could not sit unless he answered questions truthfully.[2685] Due to a lack of adequate medical care at CIA detention sites and the unwillingness of host governments to make hospital facilities available, CIA detainees had care delayed for serious medical issues. See, for example, the detainee reviews for Janat Gul, Hassan Guleed, Mustafa al-Hawsawi, Ramzi bin al-Shibh, and Firas al-Yemeni in Volume III.
Dietary Manipulation	
DIRECTOR HAYDEN: "And, in the section [of the ICRC report] on medical care, the report omits key contextual facts. For example, Abu Zubaydah's statement that he was given only Ensure and water for two to three weeks fails to mention the fact that *he was on a liquid diet [was] quite appropriate because he was recovering from abdominal surgery at the time.*"	This testimony is inaccurate. CIA records detail how Abu Zubaydah was fed solid food shortly after being discharged from the hospital in April 2002.[2686] In August 2002, as part of the CIA's enhanced interrogation techniques, Abu Zubaydah was placed on a liquid diet of Ensure and water as both an interrogation technique, and as a means of limiting vomiting during waterboarding.[2687] In planning for the interrogation of subsequent detainees, the CIA determined that it would use a "liquid diet."[2688] At least 30 CIA detainees were fed only a liquid diet of Ensure and water for interrogation purposes.[2689]
Waterboarding and Its Effectiveness	
SENATOR HATCH: "So this is not tipping the board and putting his head underneath the water." DIRECTOR HAYDEN: "No. It's slightly inclined, cloth,	This testimony is incongruent with CIA interrogation records. As described in the Study, the waterboarding of KSM involved interrogators using their hands to maintain a one-inch deep "pool" of water over KSM's nose and mouth in an effort to make it impossible for KSM to ingest all the water being poured on him.[2690] According to the

---

[2685] Asadullah was also placed in a "small isolation box" for 30 minutes, without authorization and without discussion of how the technique would affect his ankle. *See* ██████ 34098 ██████; ██████ 34294 ██████; ██████ 34310 ██████

[2686] In May 2002, ██████ stated that variety was introduced into Abu Zubaydah's diet; in addition to his daily intake of two cups of kidney beans, one cup of rice, Ensure, and juice, Abu Zubaydah was given a piece of fried chicken, Coke, and several cups of hot tea. *See* ██████ 10327 (240624Z MAY 02).

[2687] Email from: [REDACTED]; to: ██████ and [REDACTED]; date: August 4, 2002, at 09:45:09AM.

[2688] ██████ 10961 (260650Z SEP 02)

[2689] *See* detainee reviews in Volume III.

[2690] Email from: [REDACTED]; to: ██████; cc: ██████; subject: Re: Sitrep as of AM 3/15; date: March 15, 2003, at 3:52:54 AM; Interview of ██████, by [REDACTED] and

pouring of water under the rules I just laid out, Senator."	attending medical officer, the technique became a "series of near drownings."[2691]
DIRECTOR HAYDEN: "[W]aterboarding *cannot take place any more than five days out of a total of 30 days.* There *cannot be more than two sessions per day.* A session is described as being strapped to the board. No session can last longer than two hours. In any session, *there can be no more than six pourings of the water greater than ten seconds in duration.* Under *no circumstances can any detainee be under the pouring of the water a total of more than twelve minutes in any 24-hour period,* and one pouring cannot exceed, one application cannot exceed 40 seconds."	This testimony is incongruent with CIA interrogation records. For example, KSM was waterboarded on nine separate days over a two-week period. On March 13, 2003, KSM was subjected to three waterboard sessions in one day. Over March 12-13, 2003, he was subjected to five waterboard sessions in 25 hours. During that same period, he was subjected to the pouring of water for more than twelve minutes during a 24-hour period.[2692] In regard to the description of "pouring," a CIA record related to Abu Zubaydah states that: "Each iteration of the watering cycle consisted of four broad steps: 1) demands for information interspersed with the application of the water just short of blocking his airway 2) escalation of the amount of water applied until it blocked his airway and he started to have involuntary spasms 3) raising the water-board to clear subject's airway 4) lowering of the water-board and return to demands for information."[2693]
SENATOR NELSON: "On KSM, was it waterboarding that you were able to get the information from him?" DIRECTOR HAYDEN: "Yes, sir, *it was.*" SENATOR NELSON: "Although it took you a long time to break him?"	This testimony is incongruent with CIA interrogation records. CIA personnel—including members of KSM's interrogation team—believed that the waterboard interrogation technique was ineffective on KSM.[2694] The on-site medical officer told the inspector general that, after three or four days, it became apparent that the waterboard was ineffective, and that KSM "hated it but knew he could manage."[2695] KSM interrogator ██████████ told the

---

[REDACTED], Office of the Inspector General, May 15, 2003. *See also* interview of ██████████, by [REDACTED] and [REDACTED], Office of the Inspector General, May 15, 2003.

[2691] Email from: ██████████; to: ██████████; cc: ██████████; subject: More; date: April 10, 2003, at 5:59: 27 PM.

[2692] ██████████ 10800 (131909Z MAR 03); ██████████ 10801 (131918Z MAR 03); ██████████ 10802 (131921Z MAR 03); ██████████ 10803 (131929Z MAR 03)

[2693] CIA record entitled, "Aggressive Interrogation Phase Synopsis," Abu Zubaydah, August 2002.

[2694] Similarly, participants in the interrogation of Abu Zubaydah wrote that Abu Zubaydah "probably reached the point of cooperation even prior to the August institution of 'enhanced' measures –a development missed because of the narrow focus of the questioning. In any event there was no evidence that the waterboard produced time-perishable information which otherwise would have been unobtainable." *See* CIA Summary and Reflections of ██████████ Medical Services on OMS participation in the RDI program, at 41.

[2695] Interview of ██████████, by [REDACTED] and [REDACTED], Office of the Inspector General, May 15, 2003.

DIRECTOR HAYDEN: "He had nine separate days in which waterboarding took place. He also was subject[ed] to sleep deprivation and I believe his deprivation was the longest of any detainee's, at one stretch, and I think that may be what Senator Hatch was referring to by that 180 number. That's the number of hours at one stretch."	inspector general that KSM had "beat the system,"[2696] and assessed two months after the discontinuation of the waterboard that KSM responded to "creature comforts and sense of importance" and not to "confrontational" approaches.[2697] KSM debriefer and Deputy Chief of ALEC Station ████████████ told the inspector general that KSM "figured out a way to deal with [the waterboard]."[2698] ████████ CTC Legal, ██████████, told the inspector general that the waterboard "was of limited use on KSM."[2699] CIA records indicate that KSM was subjected to the waterboard interrogation technique at least 183 times.
	Injuries and Deaths
DIRECTOR HAYDEN: "The most serious injury that I'm aware of – and I'll ask the experts to add any color they want, Senator – is bruising as a result of shackling."	This testimony is incongruent with CIA interrogation records. CIA records indicate that CIA detainees suffered physical injuries beyond bruising from shackling, as well as psychological problems: • During a waterboard session, Abu Zubaydah "became completely unresponsive, with bubbles rising through his open, full mouth." He remained unresponsive after the waterboard was rotated upwards and only regained consciousness after receiving a "xyphoid thrust."[2700] • Multiple CIA detainees subjected to prolonged sleep deprivation experienced hallucinations, and CIA interrogation teams did not always discontinue sleep deprivation after the detainees had experienced hallucinations.[2701]

[2696] Interview of ████████, by [REDACTED] and [REDACTED], Office of the Inspector General, October 22, 2003.

[2697] ████████ 11715 (201047Z MAY 03). In August 2006, ████████ wrote in a Sametime communication that KSM and Abu Zubaydah "held back" despite the use of the CIA's enhanced interrogation techniques, but added "I'm ostracized whenever I suggest those two did not tell us everything." *See* Sametime Communication, ████████ ████████ and ████████, 15/Aug/06, 10:28:38 to 10:58:00.

[2698] Interview of ████████, by [REDACTED] and [REDACTED], Office of the Inspector General, April 3, 2003. ████████ also wrote in a 2005 Sametime communication that "we broke KSM... using the Majid Khan stuff... and the emails." *See* Sametime Communication, ████████ and [REDACTED], 02/May/05, 14:51:48 to 15:17:39.

[2699] Interview of ████████, by [REDACTED], [REDACTED], and [REDACTED], Office of the Inspector General, August 20, 2003.

[2700] Email from: ████████, OMS; to: [REDACTED] and [REDACTED], subject: Re: Acceptable lower ambient temperatures; date: March 7, 2003; email from: ████████, OMS; to: [REDACTED] and [REDACTED]; subject: Re: Talking Points for review and comment; date: August 13, 2004; email from ████████; to: [REDACTED], [REDACTED], [REDACTED], [REDACTED], and [REDACTED]; subject: Re: Discussion with Dan Levin – AZ; date: October 26, 2004.

[2701] ████████ 1396 ████; ████ 1299 (██████ JAN 04); ████████ 1308 (████ JAN 04); ████ 1312 (██████ JAN 04); ████ 1530 (████ 04)

	• Some detainees exhibited significant bruising and swelling unrelated to shackling. For example, a medical officer noted that, in addition to the swelling of his ankles and wrists, Ramzi bin al-Shibh had a bruise on his brow.[2702]
	• During the application of the CIA's enhanced interrogation techniques, KSM was described as "[t]ired and sore," with abrasions on his ankles, shins, and wrists, as well as on the back of his head.[2703] He also suffered from pedal edema[2704] resulting from extended standing.[2705]
	• At the CIA's DETENTION SITE COBALT, CIA interrogators used "rough takedowns," described as taking a naked detainee outside of his cell, placing a hood over his head, and dragging him up and down a long corridor while slapping and punching him. Gul Rahman, after his death, was found to have surface abrasions on his shoulders, pelvis, arms, legs, and face.[2706]
SENATOR LEVIN: "Did anybody die?" DIRECTOR HAYDEN: "No." SENATOR LEVIN: "Not one person?" DIRECTOR HAYDEN: "No one. The Committee is aware that there was an individual who died in CIA custody prior to the initiation of this program." SENATOR LEVIN: "Prior to the initiation of what?" DIRECTOR HAYDEN: "This program. In fact, the discipline of this program is a product of or	This testimony is incongruent with CIA records. • Gul Rahman died in CIA custody at the CIA's DETENTION SITE COBALT after being rendered there on November █, 2002. At the time, DETENTION SITE COBALT was described as a place where the CIA could detain suspected terrorists for the purposes of "intense interrogations" by CIA officers.[2707] DDO James Pavitt told the inspector general that "there were some who say that [DETENTION SITE COBALT] is not a CIA facility, but that is 'bullshit.'"[2708] • CIA records reveal that Gul Rahman was subjected to what the CIA chief of interrogations described as

---

[2702] ████████ 10429 (101215Z FEB 03)
[2703] ████████ 10916 (210845Z MAR 03)
[2704] Swelling of the feet.
[2705] ████████ 10909 (201918Z MAR 03)
[2706] Memorandum for Deputy Director of Operations, from ████████████, January 28, 2003, Subject: Death Investigation – Gul RAHMAN, pp. 21-22. *See* Volume III for additional injuries resulting from CIA interrogations.
[2707] ALEC ████████ ████████
[2708] August 21, 2003, Interview Report of James Pavitt, (pursuant to 2003-7123-IG), Deputy Director of Operations.

result of the undisciplined activity that took place earlier."	"coercive techniques without authorization."[2709] At ALEC Station's request, CIA contractor Hammond DUNBAR conducted an assessment of Gul Rahman to determine which CIA enhanced interrogation techniques should be used on him.[2710] While the CIA's enhanced interrogation techniques were never authorized, DUNBAR interrogated Rahman, once employing the "insult slap" enhanced interrogation technique without CIA Headquarters approval.[2711] On November ██, 2002, Gul Rahman was shackled to the wall of his cell in a short chain position,[2712] which required him to sit on the bare concrete.[2713] Rahman was wearing a sweatshirt, but was nude from the waist down. On November ██, 2002, the guards at DETENTION SITE COBALT found Gul Rahman's dead body.[2714] Although a CIA employee tried to perform CPR, Gul Rahman remained unresponsive and was declared dead.[2715] An autopsy report by the CIA found that the cause of Gul Rahman's death was "undetermined," but that the clinical impression of the medical officer who conducted the autopsy was that the cause of death was hypothermia.[2716]
DIRECTOR HAYDEN: "[Gul Rahman] was not part of this program, but I understand it was in CIA custody."	
	Stress Positions	
SENATOR LEVIN: [Reading a SSCI staff document, "Summary Notes of the February 14, 2007 ICRC Report"] "Prolonged stress standing position, naked, armed chained above the head [?]	This testimony is inaccurate. There are multiple descriptions of CIA detainees being forced to stand with their arms shackled above their heads for extended periods of time at the CIA's DETENTION SITE COBALT.[2717] In one example, a U.S. military legal

---

[2709] ██████████ 29520 ██████████ ; email dated November █, 2002, from CIA interrogator ██████████, to CTC/LGL Officer ██████████ with the subject line, "Another example of field interrogation using coercive techniques without authorization."

[2710] ██████████ 29909 ██████████ ; ALEC ██████████

[2711] Report of Investigation, Death of a Detainee ██████████ (2003-7402-IG), 27 April 2005, p. 23 (DTS #2005-1957).

[2712] In the short chain position, a detainee's hands and feet are shackled together by a short chain.

[2713] [REDACTED] 29520 ██████████

[2714] January 27, 2003, Memorandum from [REDACTED], Chief, Counterintelligence Evaluation Branch, Counterespionage Group Counterintelligence Center, to Deputy Director for Operations, Subject: Death Investigation – Gul Rahman.

[2715] January 27, 2003, Memorandum from [REDACTED], Chief, Counterintelligence Evaluation Branch, Counterespionage Group Counterintelligence Center, to Deputy Director for Operations, Subject: Death Investigation – Gul Rahman. The circumstances surrounding Gul Rahman's death are described in detail in both reports prepared by the Counterintelligence Center and a 2005 report prepared by the Inspector General. *See* April 27, 2005, CIA Inspector General, Report of Investigation, Death of a Detainee ██████████ (DTS #2005-1957).

[2716] FINAL AUTOPSY FINDINGS, by [REDACTED], MD, CASE #: OMS A-01-02.

[2717] ██████████ 28246 ██████████ ; Interview Report, 2003-7123-IG, Review of Interrogations for Counterterrorism Purposes, ██████████, April 5, 2003; Interview Report, 2003-7123-IG,

DIRECTOR HAYDEN: "Not above the head. Stress positions are part of the EITs, and nakedness were part of the EITs, Senator."	advisor observed the technique known as "hanging," involving handcuffing one or both wrists to an overhead horizontal bar. The legal advisor noted that one detainee was apparently left hanging for 22 hours each day for two consecutive days to "break" his resistance.[2718]
	CIA records indicate that multiple detainees were shackled with their hands above their heads at other CIA detention sites. For example, *see* detainee reviews in Volume III, to include 'Abd al-Rahim al-Nashiri,[2719] Hassan Ghul,[2720] and KSM.[2721] According to CIA cables, Abu Zubaydah was handcuffed "high on the bars."[2722]
	Draft OMS guidelines on interrogations, noted that detainees could be shackled with their arms above their heads for "roughly two hours without great concern," and that the arms could be elevated for between two and four hours if the detainee was monitored for "excessive distress."[2723]
Legal Reasons for Overseas Detention	
SENATOR WHITEHOUSE: "Has there been any consideration at any point within the Agency that the purpose in locating facilities overseas is either to avoid liability under American statutes or to avoid the ability of any court to claim jurisdiction because they would not know where these took place? Is there an element of	Mr. Rizzo's testimony is incongruent with CIA records. After the capture of Abu Zubaydah, ████ CTC Legal, ████████████, prepared a PowerPoint presentation laying out the "pros" and "cons" of six detention options. The pros for detention in Country █, where Abu Zubaydah would be rendered, included "[n]o issues of possible U.S. [court] jurisdiction." The cons for a CIA facility in the United States included "[c]an't foreclose ability of U.S. [courts] considering Habeas Corpus petition."[2724]

Review of Interrogations for Counterterrorism Purposes, ████████████, April 30, 2003; Memorandum for [REDACTED] from [REDACTED] ████████████ November █ 2002, Subject: Legal Analysis of [REDACTED] Personnel Participating in Interrogation at the CIA Detention Facility in ████████████ (aka "[DETENTION SITE COBALT]").

[2718] Memorandum for [REDACTED] from [REDACTED] ████████████ November █ 2002, Subject: Legal Analysis of [REDACTED] Personnel Participating in Interrogation at the CIA Detention Facility in ████████████ (aka "[DETENTION SITE COBALT]").

[2719] Email from: [DETENTION SITE BLUE] COB ████████████; to: ████████████; subject: EYES ONLY - [████████] ONLY -- MEMO FOR ADDO/DDO; date: January 22, 2003.

[2720] ████████ 1285 ████████

[2721] ████████████ 34491 (051400Z MAR 03); ████████ 10654 (030904Z MAR 03); ████████ 10752 (102320Z MAR 03)

[2722] ████████ 10487 (181656Z JUN 02); ████████ 10393 (020543Z JUN 02)

[2723] OMS GUIDELINES ON MEDICAL AND PSYCHOLOGICAL SUPPORT TO DETAINEE INTERROGATIONS, "First Draft," March 7, 2003.

[2724] PowerPoint presentation, Options of Incarcerating Abu Zubaydah, March 27, 2002.

providing legal defense to the participants in these applications?" MR. RIZZO: "Well, certainly not the first."	In late 2003 and early 2004, the U.S. Supreme Court's decision to accept certiorari in the case of *Rasul v. Bush* prompted a decision by the CIA, in coordination with the Department of Justice, to transfer five CIA detainees held at Guantanamo to other CIA detention facilities.[2725]

[2725] Email from: Scott W. Muller; to: ████████████, [REDACTED]; cc: [REDACTED]; subject: Detainees in Gitmo; date: January ██ 2004; email from Scott W. Muller; to: [REDACTED]; subject: DCI Meeting with Rice; date: January ██ 2004; email from: Scott Muller; to: James Pavitt, ████████████; cc: George Tenet, John McLaughlin, [REDACTED], [REDACTED], ████████████, [REDACTED], ████████████; subject: CIA Detainees at GITMO; date: February ██ 2004.

Senate Select Committee on Intelligence

Committee Study of the Central Intelligence Agency's Detention and Interrogation Program

Additional Views

SENATOR UDALL ADDITIONAL VIEWS

SEN. UDALL ADDITIONAL VIEWS TO THE EXECUTIVE SUMMARY OF THE COMMITTEE STUDY ON THE CIA'S DETENTION AND INTERROGATION PROGRAM
June 9, 2014

This summary of the Study of the CIA's Detention and Interrogation Program is over five years in the making and highlights the key facts and findings in the much more comprehensive, nearly 6700-page report that the Senate Select Committee on Intelligence voted to initiate in 2009. This Study has been rightly called one of the most significant examples of oversight in the history of the U.S. Senate. It is based on a documentary review of more than 6 million pages of CIA and other records, and raises critical questions about intelligence operations and oversight, many of which remain highly relevant today.

The Committee's Study details the numerous flaws in the CIA's Detention and Interrogation Program. Among them: It was allowed to be shaped and conducted by individuals who didn't understand what they were doing and who had a financial stake in representing the program as effective. It was run by personnel with insufficient training. It was managed incompetently by senior CIA personnel. The "enhanced interrogation techniques" were far more brutal than anyone understood. Perhaps most importantly, these techniques did not work. Nonetheless, the program was sold to the White House, the Department of Justice, the Congress, and the media as a necessary program that provided unique information that "saved lives."

The significance of the Committee Study lies in the words written in its pages. But the history of the Study itself is also an important story that needs to be told.

Chairman Feinstein, who has shouldered the greatest responsibility and deserves the greatest credit for seeing this project to completion, and former Chairman Rockefeller, who served as the Committee's ranking member and then Chairman during the time when the CIA was conducting its program, are best able to speak to the earliest days of the Study and the events that led the Committee to undertake this enormous task. And after five years of courageous leadership in pushing this Study forward, navigating partisan rancor and CIA obstacles, Chairman Feinstein can certainly speak most authoritatively to all the twist and turns on the road to the Study's release.

But as a newer member of the Committee, I also have a perspective to share. And I believe that the history of the CIA's program isn't complete without a full telling of the events that came after the program ended, to include this Committee's efforts – and mine – to complete and declassify the Study of the CIA's Detention and Interrogation Program.

As a new member on the Committee in 2011, I was briefed on the origins and status of the Study and began reading early drafts and discussing the way forward with Committee colleagues. I had always believed that the CIA's program – with its "enhanced interrogation techniques," renditions, and black sites – was a stain on our country's recent past. But I was deeply disturbed to learn specifics about the flaws in the program, the misrepresentations, the brutality. During this time, I also learned about the dedicated Committee staff who were working every day and late into the nights at the CIA-leased off-site facility, where they sifted through millions of CIA records, and in our Committee spaces in the Senate, where they continued to write the thousands of pages that would become the first comprehensive review of the CIA's program.

By late 2012, the Study was largely complete. In December 2012, I supported the Chairman and other Committee colleagues in voting to approve the Study, which we then provided to the White House and Executive Branch agencies for "review and comment." The CIA took over six months to produce its comments on the Study, during which time I and other Committee members repeatedly requested that CIA personnel meet with Committee staff to discuss the report. The CIA declined all requests to meet with its oversight committee on this matter.

In January 2013, President Obama nominated John Brennan to serve as the next CIA director. I hoped that as a career CIA officer, Brennan would understand the opportunity before him to lead the Agency in correcting the false record that the Committee's Study uncovered and instituting the necessary reforms to restore the CIA's reputation for integrity and analytical rigor. During his nomination hearing, I stressed to Mr. Brennan that this Study isn't just about the past. Acknowledging the flaws of this program is essential for the CIA's long-term institutional integrity – as well as for the legitimacy of ongoing sensitive programs. The findings of this Study directly relate to how other CIA programs are managed today. The CIA cannot be its best unless it faces the serious and grievous mistakes of this program – to include the false representations made to policymakers and others – to ensure these mistakes never happen again.

I also expressed my belief to Mr. Brennan that the government has an obligation to the American people to face its mistakes transparently, help the public understand the nature of those mistakes, and correct them. I asked him whether he believes the CIA has a responsibility to correct any inaccurate information that was provided to the previous White House, the Department of Justice, Congress, and the public regarding the CIA's Detention and Interrogation Program. Mr. Brennan said yes.

Mr. Brennan has yet to make any corrections to the public record. Instead, the CIA engaged in efforts to obstruct and undermine the Committee's oversight efforts. In spring 2013, as the CIA prepared its comments on the Study, we heard through the public statements of unnamed current intelligence officials and named former officials – those who have a clear stake in preserving the myth of the program's value – that the CIA was highly critical of the Committee's report, believing it to be "political" and "biased."

In May 2013, still awaiting the CIA's promised response to the Committee Study, I wrote to President Obama, underlining the importance of correcting the public record if it was determined that inaccurate information had been conveyed to the American people by the U.S. government and urging a swift response from the CIA to the Committee Study. I received no reply.

On June 27, 2013, the CIA finally submitted its 122-page formal response to the Committee, though it was not the correction of the record that many of us hoped it would be. Instead, a CIA spokesman said that although the Agency "agrees with a number of the study's findings," the Study contained "significant errors." A White House spokeswoman noted "factual questions" about the Study. But the CIA only identified one factual error in its response – and it was one that had no impact on the report and was quickly corrected. More worrisome, the CIA continued to cling to false narratives about the effectiveness of the program in its written response – only admitting to the factual errors in its own response in meetings with Committee staff. The Committee requested that the CIA resubmit a written response reflecting corrections to the errors that the CIA acknowledged in meetings, but the CIA submitted no revised response. As such, the last document the CIA submitted to the Committee on this program continues to be riddled with factual errors and misstatements.

In July 2013, as a member of the Senate Armed Services Committee, I attended the nomination hearing of Stephen Preston – then CIA General Counsel – to be General Counsel at the Department of Defense. His answers to questions regarding his role in and support of the CIA's June 27, 2013, response concerned me enough that I asked him to answer additional questions for the hearing record. His answers to my additional questions contrasted with statements provided by the CIA in its response to the Committee Study, admitting that the CIA's efforts "fell well short" of current standards for providing information to its oversight committees, as is required by law; that CIA briefings to the Committee included "inaccurate information"; that the CIA's efforts had again fallen "well short of our current practices when it comes to providing information relevant to [the Justice Department's Office of Legal Counsel]'s legal analysis"; and that by reviewing the CIA's records, it would be possible to determine whether information provided after the use of brutal interrogation techniques had already been obtained from other sources, something the CIA continued to officially claim was "unknowable."

But Stephen Preston wasn't the only CIA official to disagree with the standard CIA narrative on its detention and interrogation program. As I discovered in late 2013, an internal CIA review of the program initiated under former Director Panetta corroborates some of the significant findings of the Study and acknowledges significant errors made during the course of the CIA's program – but this internal review conflicts with the CIA's own official response provided to the Committee, which denies or minimizes those same errors.

As Chairman Feinstein so eloquently outlined in her floor speech on March 11, 2014, drafts of the so-called Panetta review had been provided to Committee staff years before – apparently unknowingly or mistakenly by the CIA. When the disparity between its conclusions and the CIA's June 27, 2013, response to the Committee became clear, Committee staff grew concerned that the CIA was knowingly providing inaccurate information to the Committee in the present day – which would be a serious offense and a deeply troubling matter for this Committee, the Congress, the White House, and our country. To preserve evidence of this potential offense, Committee staff securely transported a printed portion of the draft Panetta review from the CIA-leased facility to the Committee's secure offices in the Senate.

At the December 2013 nomination hearing of Caroline Krass – who was slated to replace Preston as the CIA's top lawyer – I asked Ms. Krass to ensure that a final copy of this review would be made available to the Committee, since it raised fundamental questions about why a review the CIA conducted internally years ago – and never provided to the Committee – is so different from the CIA's formal written response and from the many public statements of unnamed and former CIA officials. Chairman Feinstein had made the same request in an earlier letter. Although the Committee had a draft of the review already in its possession, I believed then – as I do now – that it was important to make public the existence of this internal document and its conclusions and to obtain a final version.

In early January 2014, I wrote a letter to President Obama reiterating my request that the final draft of the Panetta review be provided to the Committee. The CIA needed to reconcile the fact that it agreed with the Committee behind closed doors with its continued CIA criticisms of the Study in public. But instead of coming clean, the Agency chose to double down on its denials.

In early March 2014, I wrote another letter to President Obama, restating my interest in the final Panetta review. In that letter, I also alluded to "unprecedented action" that the CIA had recently taken against the Committee, calling it "incredibly troubling for the Committee's oversight responsibilities and for our democracy." As news reports made clear on March 4, 2014, and Chairman Feinstein explained further in her March 11, 2014, speech, that action was the CIA's unauthorized search of the Committee's computers at the off-site facility – a search conducted out of concern that Committee staff already had access to the Panetta review, a document they were fully cleared to see. More troubling, despite admitting to the

Committee that the CIA conducted the search, Director Brennan publicly referred to "spurious allegations about CIA actions that are wholly unsupported by the facts."

The CIA never asked the Committee whether or how it had access to the review conducted under Director Panetta. Instead, without notifying the Committee, the CIA searched the Committee computers that the agency had agreed were off limits, and in the process, the CIA may have violated multiple provisions of the Constitution (including both the Speech and Debate Clause and the Fourth Amendment) as well as federal criminal statutes and Executive Order 12333. Director Brennan declined to respond to further questions about the CIA's actions to the Committee, and instead, the CIA's acting general counsel – who was involved in the 2005 decision to destroy the CIA's interrogation videotapes – filed a crimes report with the Department of Justice about the Committee staff's actions to preserve the Panetta review documents. The CIA's Inspector General also referred the CIA search to the Department of Justice, and the Senate Sergeant at Arms continues to conduct a forensic review of the Committee's computers.

The matter of the Panetta Review remains unresolved, but serves to emphasize the fact that the CIA is unwilling or unable to submit itself to honest and transparent oversight by the Congress. The agency not only hasn't learned from its mistakes of the past, but continues to perpetuate them.

Meanwhile, even as the threat of criminal prosecution and inquiry persisted, Committee staff continued to work at the direction of the Members in preparing the Committee Study for declassification and release. After months spent incorporating comments from the CIA's June 27, 2013, response – to ensure that the CIA's views on the Study's findings were represented – Committee staff completed a revised Committee Study that grew from 6,300 pages to nearly 6,700 pages. On April 3, 2014, in a bipartisan 11 – 3 vote, the Committee moved to submit for declassification the nearly 500-page Executive Summary and 20 findings and conclusions of the Committee Study on the CIA's Detention and Interrogation Program.

This was a proud day for the Committee – for the Chairman who led this vital effort, for other members who worked alongside her, and for Committee staff, who put their lives on hold for years while completing this seminal work. This was also a proud day for the American people – who deserve to understand this dark chapter in our history and why it is still relevant today.

The American people also deserve to read as much of this history as possible. That is why the Chairman and I and many of our colleagues called repeatedly for the fullest possible declassification of the Executive Summary and the Study's findings and conclusions, with only redactions as necessary for real national security concerns, not to avoid embarrassment. The American people deserve a proper and accurate accounting of the history, management, operation, and effectiveness of this program – and they have the right to know what the government has done on their behalf. It is my hope that we can soon release not just the Executive Summary, but the entire 6,700 pages of the Committee's Study, for the American people.

SENATOR HEINRICH ADDITIONAL VIEWS

Additional Views of Senator Martin Heinrich

In January 2009, President Obama signed Executive Order 13491, limiting interrogations by any American personnel to the guidelines in the Army Field Manual, and reinforcing the commitment that prisoners in U.S. custody are entitled to rights under the Geneva Conventions. This officially ended a dark period in American history that, in reality, had already effectively collapsed under the weight of poor policy decisions, ineffectiveness, bad management, and public disclosures.

I came to this Committee believing that the press accounts and books I read had adequately prepared me for what took place in this program. I was wrong.

Compounding this is the fact that my ignorance was not unique: the CIA deliberately kept the vast majority of the Senate and House Intelligence Committees in the dark until the day the president revealed the detention and interrogation program to the world in 2006 – four years after it began.

Even then, misrepresentations to the Committee about the effectiveness of the CIA's detention and interrogation program continued, in large part because the CIA had never performed any comprehensive review of the effectiveness of the program or the actions of its officers. Myths of the "effectiveness" of torture have been repeated in the press, perpetrating the fable that this was a necessary program that "saved lives." My hope is this meticulously detailed, near 7,000-page Committee study finally puts those lies to rest.

Those who were responsible for the CIA's detention and interrogation program will continue to exploit public ignorance of what took place in the program to argue that the study is one-sided or biased, or that it lacks important details or context. In the course of their efforts, they will misrepresent what is or is not in the study, while selectively picking through the executive summary in an effort to support their arguments.

However, the full study contains far more information and detail than could ever be captured in an executive summary. That is why I firmly believe the release of the executive summary should not be the last step in this process, but the first. It is my hope that someday soon there will be a public release of the full Committee study. If this deplorable chapter is to truly be closed and relegated to history, the full study should be declassified and released. The president has that authority, and I hope he will exercise it.

This study represents years of hard work by Members and staff who faced a number of obstacles in completing the work: the CIA taking years to dump millions of unsorted documents in a massive database while resisting requests for additional information; the executive branch withholding thousands of pages of documents from the Committee; and current and former officials anonymously misrepresenting the contents and the findings of the study in the press. The list could go on. The fact that this study was finished is a testament to the dedication of Chairmen Rockefeller and Feinstein in deciding that oversight is worth it, regardless of how long it takes.

This is an objective and fact-based study. It is a fair study. And it is the only comprehensive study conducted of this program and the CIA's treatment of its detainees in the aftermath of the September 11 attacks.

The reality is that the president's signature on Executive Order 13491 is only valid until the next national crisis emerges and moves a well-meaning, but misguided president to rescind the order. It is worth remembering that years before this detention and interrogation program even began, the CIA had sworn off the harsh interrogations of its past; but in the wake of the terrorist attacks against the United States, it repeated those mistakes by once again engaging in brutal interrogations that undermined our nation's credibility on the issue of human rights, produced information of uneven – and often questionable – value, and wasted millions of taxpayer dollars.

This study should serve as a warning to those who would make similar choices in the future: torture doesn't work. It is therefore my hope that Members of Congress will read this study and join me in the conclusion that we must never let this happen again. We need to shut the door on abusive interrogations completely through legislative action that leaves no loopholes, and no room for interpretation.

SENATOR
KING
ADDITIONAL
VIEWS

Additional Views of Senator King

(U) I joined the Senate Select Committee on Intelligence in January 2013, approximately four years after President Obama issued an Executive Order to end the detention and interrogation program of the Central Intelligence Agency (CIA). As such, I was not involved in the inception and initial stages of the committee's review of the program. After carefully reading this study's lengthy executive summary, the CIA's response, and other relevant documents, it is clear to me that some detainees were subjected to techniques that constituted torture. Such brutality is unacceptable, and the misconduct on the part of some of the individuals involved in the use of enhanced interrogation techniques, which is documented in the study, is inexplicable. Based upon this review, it appears to me that the enhanced interrogation techniques were not effective in producing the type of unique and reliable information claimed by the agency's leadership, and should never again be employed by our government.

(U) In the course of conducting vigorous oversight with respect to this program, it is also important to bear in mind several points. First, in the wake of the September 2001 attacks, our government was inundated with endless leads to track down. There was genuine fear and uncertainty about follow-on strikes, which may explain, but not excuse, the actions that are the subject of this study. Second, we live in a dangerous world with all-to-real enemies and I believe firmly that intelligence is our nation's first line of defense against terrorism. As such, the CIA and other intelligence agencies are vital to keeping us safe and the disturbing nature of the study's findings should not be used to undermine our overall intelligence enterprise. Lastly, it should be understood that those responsible for the mismanagement and misconduct associated with the detention and interrogation program are not representative of the many dedicated professionals serving our nation, often in anonymity, at the CIA. Having met with many CIA officers, I have great respect for their intellect, dedication, courage, and sacrifice.

(U) Despite the unquestionable professionalism of the vast majority of CIA personnel, the study demonstrates that the detention and interrogation program was mismanaged, that some within the leadership of the CIA actively impeded congressional oversight, and that agency officials misrepresented the program's effectiveness.

(S) The study finds that CIA headquarters failed to keep accurate records on those it detained and placed individuals with limited experience in senior detention and interrogation roles. Even after a detainee died of hypothermia at a detention facility in November 2002, many of these practices continued without adequate oversight. In its response to the study, the CIA states that delegating management of this particular facility to a junior officer "was not a prudent managerial decision given the risks inherent in the program."[1] It is difficult to imagine a greater understatement of what occurred. More accurately, in the words of one of the CIA's senior interrogators, the program was "a train wreak [sic] waiting to happen."[2]

---

[1] Central Intelligence Agency's Response to the SSCI's Study of the CIA's Detention and Interrogation Program, June 27, 2013. Response to Conclusion 15, p. 42.
[2] SSCI Study of the CIA's Detention and Interrogation Program, April 3, 2014, Executive Summary, p. 68.

SENATOR ROCKEFELLER ADDITIONAL VIEWS

(U) Of the many examples of impeding congressional oversight documented in the study, none is more striking than the decision by CIA leaders to destroy videotapes of CIA interrogations out of a concern that Congress might discover evidence of misconduct and brutality. There is no excuse for this decision and those involved should no longer be associated with the CIA or the United States government.

(S) Most significantly, the study finds that the CIA's justification for the use of enhanced interrogation techniques rested on inaccurate claims of their effectiveness. In its official response to the study, the CIA contradicts many of its previous claims of unqualified effectiveness by arguing that it is now "unknowable" whether the same information could have been acquired without the use of enhanced interrogation techniques and further contends that its past assertions were "sincerely believed but inherently speculative."[3] Yet in the long and unfortunate history of this program, no one in the CIA's leadership expressed such an equivocal view of the techniques' effectiveness. What was once certain is now "unknowable;" this migration of rationales underlines for me the magnitude of the prior misrepresentations.

(S) I have to assume that in many cases the representations of effectiveness were believed by the individuals who made them. However, the CIA also admits in its response that it never attempted to develop a "more sustained, systematic, and independent means by which to evaluate the effectiveness of the approaches used with detainees."[4] It states further that its reviews of the program's effectiveness were "heavily reliant on the views of the practitioners" – including the contract psychologists who designed and executed the techniques.[5]

(U) If such a sustained, systematic, and independent evaluation was impractical, as the CIA now claims, then it follows that the CIA's assertions about the effectiveness of such techniques were largely guesswork. In the end, policymakers based their decisions about a program so at variance with our past practices and values on anecdotal information, rather than on a verifiable process. This, in my opinion, is among the seminal failings of the program and the CIA's leadership during this period.

(U) Finally, I am deeply disturbed by the implications of the study for the committee's ability to discharge its oversight responsibility. The core of the oversight function rests in large part upon the interaction of our committee with representatives of the various intelligence agencies, most particularly the CIA. Because it appears from the study that the committee was continuously misled as to virtually all aspects of this program, it naturally raises the extremely troubling question as to whether we can trust the representations of the agency in connection with difficult or sensitive issues in the future. If our principal oversight approach is based on frank and open communication with the CIA's leadership, and we cannot fully rely upon the answers we receive, then the entire oversight function is compromised.

---

[3] Central Intelligence Agency's Response to the SSCI's Study of the CIA's Detention and Interrogation Program, June 27, 2013, Response to Conclusion 9, p. 23.

[4] Central Intelligence Agency's Response to the SSCI's Study of the CIA's Detention and Interrogation Program, June 27, 2013, Response to Conclusion 10, p. 24.

[5] Central Intelligence Agency's Response to the SSCI's Study of the CIA's Detention and Interrogation Program, June 27, 2013, Response to Conclusion 10, p. 25.

(U) As a committee, we should discuss this matter to determine if additional steps may be necessary to ensure that we are getting accurate information. I believe that our solemn responsibility to provide vigilant legislative oversight over the intelligence activities of the United States requires serious consideration of this problem.

(U) I agree with my colleagues in the minority who note that the Department of Justice's decision to begin a criminal investigation in 2009 prevented the committee from conducting most interviews and required the study to rely mainly on documents provided by the CIA. I am also disappointed that the study could not utilize the expertise of the minority through a joint review, as has been the committee's practice. While I believe the study is accurate, this is a fundamental lesson that will inform my approach to the committee's work in the years ahead.

(U) In conclusion, upon joining the committee in 2013 I endeavored to undertake a thorough review of the study, the CIA's response, and other relevant documentation. I also discussed this matter with Democrats and Republicans on the committee, the staff members involved in writing the study and the minority staff, the CIA personnel who drafted the agency's response, a former senior military interrogator, current CIA officers bravely serving our nation in harm's way, a former top FBI official, and numerous Maine people – including human rights experts and leaders of the religious community.

(U) Based upon this review, I voted to approve declassification of the study because I believe our nation's reputation as a beacon of openness, democratic values, human rights, and adherence to the rule of law is at stake. Our credibility – and ultimately our influence – in the world is dependent upon this reputation, and it is our obligation to admit when we fail to meet America's high standards. I believe we can protect intelligence sources and methods and still declassify a significant portion of the study to accomplish this goal.

(U) As then Secretary of State Colin Powell said in 2004, following the scandals at Abu Ghraib prison,

> "Watch America. Watch how we deal with this. Watch how America will do the right thing. Watch what a nation of values and character, a nation that believes in justice, does to right this kind of wrong. Watch how a nation such as ours will not tolerate such actions."[6]

(U) In the last analysis, America's real power is based upon our values and how we put those values into practice. As with any individual – or great nation – we will occasionally stumble, but when we do, we acknowledge our failings – as we have in this case – and move on, true to ourselves and to the better angels of our nature.

ANGUS S. KING

---

[6] Powell, Colin. "Commencement Address." Wake Forest University. 17 May 2004.

SENATOR COLLINS ADDITIONAL VIEWS

Additional Views of Senator Collins

(U) The use of torture is deplorable and is completely contrary to our values as Americans. For as long as I have served in the Senate, I have cast votes in opposition to torture and inhuman treatment of detainees. I cosponsored and voted in favor of Senator John McCain's Detainee Treatment Act of 2005, which banned "cruel, inhuman, and degrading" treatment of any prisoner in the custody of any U.S. government agency, and I supported the Military Commissions Act of 2006, which bolstered the Detainee Treatment Act's prohibition on abusive interrogations.

(U) The Senate Select Committee on Intelligence (SSCI) *Review of the Central Intelligence Agency's (CIA's) Detention and Interrogation Program* devotes much of its report to supporting its judgment that enhanced interrogation techniques (EITs) were ineffective in acquiring intelligence. While I agree with the Central Intelligence Agency's (CIA's) current position that it is "unknowable" whether or not its "enhanced interrogation techniques" elicited significant intelligence that would not otherwise have been obtained, the fact remains that torture is wrong. The Convention against Torture and Other Cruel, Inhuman, or Degrading Treatment or Punishment, which the United States ratified in 1994, is clear: "No exceptional circumstances whatsoever, whether a state of war or a threat of war, internal political instability or any other public emergency, may be invoked as a justification of torture."

(U) The method by which the SSCI report was produced was unfortunate, to say the least, and will cause many to question its findings. In my years of service on the traditionally bipartisan Homeland Security and Governmental Affairs Committee (HSGAC), the Senate's chief oversight committee, the congressional reports I have coauthored have almost always been the result of collaborative, bipartisan investigations. Indeed, even a subject as controversial as the treatment of detainees can lead to the production of a strong bipartisan report, as demonstrated by the Senate Armed Services Committee's *Inquiry into the Treatment of Detainees in U.S. Custody* drafted by Chairman Carl Levin and Ranking Member John McCain and approved by voice vote in November 2008. When I joined the Senate Select Committee on Intelligence in January 2013, I was disappointed to learn that the Committee's investigation into the CIA's Rendition, Detention, and Interrogation (RDI) program had not been conducted in a similarly bipartisan manner.

(U) Since joining the Committee, I have sought to compensate for this missed opportunity and have encouraged greater dialogue among the CIA and the majority and minority Committee staff members, and extensive conversations have indeed occurred. Following the delivery of the CIA's feedback to the Committee's report in June 2013, I asked that we hold a hearing prior to a vote to declassify this report that would have included CIA witnesses. Such a hearing would have permitted a robust and much-needed debate about the claims made in the report compared to the rebuttals in the Agency's formal response. Unfortunately, this hearing did not occur.

(U) In the absence of a formal Committee hearing, I was briefed directly by veteran, career CIA analysts who provided feedback on the report's factual accuracy and analytic quality. Two Senators from both sides of the aisle joined me in this worthwhile briefing.

(U) I also sought to improve the report by recommending revisions and greater precision in the Review's Findings & Conclusions, and I appreciate Chairman Feinstein incorporating some of my edits.

(U) In addition to the partisan nature of the staff investigation, the report has significant intrinsic limitations because it did not involve direct interviews of CIA officials, contract personnel, or other Executive branch personnel. John Rizzo, one of the chief architects of the program, has stated publicly that he would have been happy to be interviewed, and he said a number of his colleagues would have as well. The absence of interviews significantly eroded the bipartisan cooperation that existed when the SSCI Review began and calls into question some of the report's analysis.

(U) The lack of interviews violated the Committee's bipartisan Terms of Reference that were approved by an overwhelming 14-1 vote in March 2009. The Terms of Reference describe the purpose, scope, and methodology of the Review, and they include the following statement: "The Committee will use the tools of oversight necessary to complete a thorough review including, but not limited to, document reviews and requests, interviews, testimony at closed and open hearings, as appropriate, and preparation of findings and recommendations." Yet, there were no interviews, no hearings, and no recommendations. By comparison, the SASC's 2008 *Inquiry into the Treatment of Detainees in U.S. Custody* included 70 interviews, written responses from more than 200 individuals in response to written questions, two hearings, and at least two subpoenas.

(U) Documents never tell the full story and lack context. As the former Chairman or Ranking Member of the Senate's chief investigative committee for ten years, I found that interviews were always key sources of information for every investigation our Homeland Security Committee conducted. In the 2012 HSGAC investigation into the attacks in Benghazi, for example, we discovered one of our most alarming findings in a discussion with the Commander of U.S. Africa Command, General Carter Ham. We learned that he was unaware of the presence of CIA officers in Benghazi, despite the fact that his Command had responsibility to prepare for the evacuation of U.S. government personnel.

(U) The bipartisan Terms of Reference also called for the production of policy recommendations, but not one is included in the Review's Findings & Conclusions or its Executive Summary. Ironically, it was the CIA, rather than the Committee, that first developed recommendations to address the mismanagement, misconduct, and flawed performance that characterized too much of the CIA's Detention & Interrogation program. I have identified several recommendations that should be implemented as soon as possible.

(U) Despite these significant flaws, the report's findings lead me to conclude that some detainees were subject to techniques that constituted torture. This inhumane and brutal treatment never should have occurred.

(TS/ ██████████ /NF) The Review also raises serious concerns about the CIA's management of this program. I particularly agree with its conclusions that the CIA was not prepared to conduct the RDI program, that the CIA failed to conduct a comprehensive evaluation of the effectiveness of the use of EITs, that the CIA rarely held officers accountable for misconduct and mismanagement related to the RDI program, and that the CIA allowed a conflict of interest to exist among contractors responsible for too much of the RDI program. Is there any function that could be more inherently governmental than the questioning of high-level al Qaeda detainees in CIA custody? Yet, the CIA relied heavily on contractors for its RDI program and even had contractors evaluate the program.

(U) The Review's most significant finding deals with the ineffectiveness of EITs in collecting valuable intelligence. As a Senator who strongly opposes torture, I would have welcomed a well-documented finding that reached this judgment. Unfortunately, the evidence cited does not sustain the Review's categorical judgment that EITs were ineffective at acquiring valuable intelligence.

(U) For example, the Review concedes that some detainees were subject to EITs so soon after their capture that it is impossible to determine whether the information they provided could have been obtained through non-coercive debriefing methods. Here the report gets it right: there is no way to know what information these particular detainees would have provided without the use of EITs because the detainees were not afforded that opportunity for very long. Yet, the report draws a different and much more definitive conclusion: EITs were categorically ineffective at acquiring valuable intelligence.

(TS/~~███████████~~/NF) It is also striking to me that two highly experienced public servants who are both widely respected for their integrity and impartiality, examined the program at two different times, independently of each other, and they both rendered the same verdict regarding the effectiveness of EITs. In 2011, former CIA Director Leon Panetta, and in 2005, a well-regarded ~~███████████████████████~~ both took the position that we simply can never know for sure if the information obtained from detainees who were subjected to EITs would have been obtained through other non-coercive means.

(TS/~~███████████~~/NF) A letter from then-Secretary of Defense Leon Panetta to Senator John McCain sums up his conclusion on the effectiveness of EITs with respect to the Osama bin Laden raid: "Some of the detainees who provided useful information about the facilitator/courier's role had been subjected to enhanced interrogation techniques. Whether those techniques were the 'only timely and effective way' to obtain such information is a matter of debate and cannot be established definitively." According to the Review's own Executive Summary, ~~██████~~ said the following about the effectiveness of the CIA's enhanced interrogation techniques: "here enters the epistemological problem. We can never know whether or not this intelligence could have been extracted though alternative procedures."

(U) It bears repeating that torture need not be ineffective to be wrong. The United States correctly answered the question of whether torture should be prohibited when our nation ratified the Convention against Torture in 1994. The prohibition against torture in both U.S. law and international law is not based on an evaluation of its efficacy at eliciting information. Rather, the prohibition was put in place because torture is immoral and contrary to our values.

(U) There are three findings about the RDI program that warrant attention because they provide important perspective and context about the CIA program.

(U) First, even as the mistreatment of detainees was occurring, senior CIA officials repeatedly sought legal approval from the Department of Justice (DOJ) in an effort to make sure each the EITs employed by CIA officers did not constitute torture. For example, the CIA suspended the program and/or sought legal approval prior to conducting EITs on Abu Zabaydah and several times afterwards: in 2004 after a new attorney in DOJ's Office of Legal Counsel (OLC), Jack Goldsmith, said the Department had never formally opined on whether EITs met constitutional standards, in 2005 when another attorney in OLC assessed OLC had not provided a substantive ruling on whether certain EITs violated portions of the Convention Against Torture, after passage of the Detainee Treatment Act of 2005, and after the Supreme Court's decision in *Hamdan v. Rumsfeld* and the passage of the Military Commissions Act of 2006.

(U) Second, the problems of the detention program were frequently whole-of-government failures, not just CIA's alone. Legal opinions issued by OLC are almost never withdrawn, especially by the same Administration that issued them. Yet, that is exactly what happened in this case. Why was the original legal analysis by the Department of Justice so inadequate regarding such an important issue? CIA should not have made definitive claims about the effectiveness of EITs, but independent of the material facts represented by CIA, the withdrawal of the original August 1, 2002, OLC classified legal analysis demonstrated that it was too flawed and lacked the legal rigor necessary to serve as the basis for a controversial and questionable program.

(TS/ ██████████ NF) Third, the Review's Findings & Conclusions understate the degree to which the U.S. Government failed to focus on an end game for CIA detainees in the program by not moving them to military installations, even as the CIA repeatedly sought to move the detainees out of its custody in 2005 after many had ceased producing valuable intelligence.

(U) In the absence of recommendations in the SSCI's report, I believe four actions should be taken to prevent the terrible mistakes in the CIA's RDI program from ever happening again.

(1) *Outlaw waterboarding of detainees once and for all.* President Obama implemented this policy when he took office by signing Executive Order 13491, which requires all government agencies, not just the Department of Defense, to adhere to the techniques in the Army Field Manual 2-22.3. Codifying this prohibition would make this restriction even more explicit than the Detainee Treatment Act of 2005. I voted in favor of the Fiscal Year 2008 Intelligence Authorization Act in February 2008, which would have restricted the interrogation techniques employed by CIA personnel to only those covered in the Army Field Manual. Unfortunately, this legislation was vetoed on March 8, 2008.

(2) *Reduce the number of programs now shared exclusively with the Gang of Eight, which consists of the Chairman and Vice Chairman of the intelligence committees and the leadership of both chambers of Congress, so more member of the oversight*

committees have access to significant information. Congress was informed about the RDI program to the bare minimum required by the National Security Act and no further. Most members of the intelligence committees, not to mention the rest of Congress, officially learned about the program on the same day President Bush announced it to the world in September 2006. In this case, adherence to the letter of the law rather than the spirit of the law resulted in insufficient oversight. As former CIA attorney John Rizzo has said:

> The decision in 2002 to limit congressional knowledge of the EITs to the Gang of 8 and to stick to that position for four long years—as the prevailing political winds were increasingly howling in the other direction—was foolish and feckless...For our part, we in the CIA leadership should have insisted at the outset that all members of the intelligence committees be apprised of all the gory details all along the way, on the record, in closed congressional proceedings.

(3) *Strengthen the review process at the Department of Justice (DOJ) Office of Legal Counsel (OLC) for legal opinions concerning sensitive intelligence activities.* The Intelligence Community (IC) requires and deserves to have confidence that OLC can produce valid, durable legal analysis upon which it can rely. At the same time, the IC needs to inform OLC if material facts related to sensitive programs that have previously been reviewed have changed.

(4) *Improve CIA controls in the management of covert action.* The unauthorized use of EITs beyond those approved by DOJ OLC, along with the many shortcomings in CIA's management of the RDI program, require CIA to implement greater and more detailed controls regarding sensitive programs.

(U) My vote to declassify this report does not signal my endorsement of all of its conclusions or its methodology. I do believe, however, that the Executive Summary, and Additional and Minority Views, and the CIA's rebuttal should be made public with appropriate redactions so the American public can reach their own conclusions about the conduct of this program. In my judgment, the "enhanced interrogation techniques" led, in some instances, to inhumane and brutal treatment of certain individuals held by the United States government.

Senator John D. Rockefeller IV – Additional Views

The Senate Intelligence Committee's entire Study on the CIA's Detention and Interrogation Program is the most in-depth and substantive oversight initiative that the Committee has ever undertaken, and it presents extremely valuable insights into crucial oversight questions and problems that need to be addressed at the CIA.

Moreover, this Study exemplifies why this Committee was created in the first place - following the findings of the Church Committee nearly 40 years ago - and I commend Chairman Feinstein for shepherding this landmark initiative to this point.

It is my hope and expectation that beyond the initial release of the Executive Summary and Findings and Conclusions, the entire 6,800 page Study will eventually be made public with the appropriate redactions. Those public findings will be critical to fully learning the necessary lessons from this dark episode in our nation's history, and to ensuring that this never happens again.

It has been a long, hard fight to get to this point. Especially in the early years of the CIA's Detention and Interrogation Program, it was a struggle for the Committee to get the most basic information – or any information at all – about the program.

The Committee's Study of the Detention and Interrogation Program is not just the story of the brutal and ill-conceived program itself. This Study is also the story of the breakdown in our system of governance that allowed the country to deviate, in such a significant way, from our core principles.

One of the profound ways that breakdown happened was through the active subversion of meaningful congressional oversight – a theme mirrored in the Bush Administration's warrantless wiretapping program during the same period.

As a matter of my own history with this issue, I first learned about some aspects of the CIA's Detention and Interrogation Program in 2003, when I became Vice Chair of the Committee. At that point, and for years after, the CIA refused to provide me with additional information I requested about the program or share information regarding the program with the full Committee. The briefings I received provided little or no insight into the CIA's program. Questions or follow up requests were rejected, and at times I was not allowed to consult with my counsel or other members from my staff.

It was clear that the briefings were not meant to answer my questions, but were intended only to provide cover for the Administration and the CIA. It was infuriating to realize that I was part of a box checking exercise the Bush Administration planned to use – and later did use – so they could disingenuously claim that they had "fully briefed Congress."

In the years that followed, I fought – and lost – many battles to obtain credible information about the Detention and Interrogation Program. As Vice Chair I tried to launch a comprehensive investigation into the program, but that effort was blocked. Later, in 2005, when I fought for access to over 100 specific documents cited in the Inspector General report, the CIA refused to cooperate.

The first time the full Senate Intelligence Committee was given any information about the CIA's Detention and Interrogation Program was September 2006. This was years after the program's inception, and the same day President Bush informed the public of the program's existence.

The following year, when I became Chairman, the new Vice Chairman, Kit Bond, agreed with me to push for significant additional access to the program – including Senators' access to our staff's counsel on these matters. We finally prevailed and got this access, which enabled us to have much needed hearings on the program, and we did. As Chairman, I made sure we scrutinized it from every angle. However, the challenge of getting accurate information from the CIA persisted.

In the same time period, I also sent two Committee staffers to begin reviewing cables at the CIA regarding the agency's interrogations of Abu Zubaydah and al-Nashiri. I firmly believed we had to review those cables, which are now the only source of important historical information on this topic because the CIA destroyed its videotapes of the interrogation sessions. The CIA did this against the explicit direction of the White House and the Director of National Intelligence.

The investigation I began in 2007 grew under Chairman Feinstein's dedication and tremendous leadership into a full study of the CIA's Detention and Interrogation Program. The more the Committee dug, the more it found, and the results we uncovered are both shocking and deeply troubling.

First, the Detention and Interrogation Program was conceived by people who were ignorant of the topic and made it up on the fly based on the untested theories of contractors who had never met a terrorist or conducted a real-world interrogation of any type.

Second, it was executed by personnel with insufficient linguistic and interrogation training, and little if any real-world experience.

Third, it was managed incompetently by senior officials who paid little or no attention to crucial details, and it was rife with troubling personal and financial conflicts of interest among the small group of CIA officials and contractors who promoted and defended it.

Fourth, it was physically severe, far more so than any of us outside the CIA ever knew.

Finally, its results were unclear at best, but it was presented to the White House, the Department of Justice, the Congress, and the media as a silver bullet that was indispensable to "saving lives." In fact, it did not provide the intelligence it was supposed to provide, or that CIA officials argued it provided. To be perfectly clear, these harsh techniques were not approved by anyone – ever – for the low-bar standard of learning "useful information" from detainees. These techniques were approved because Bush Administration lawyers and officials were told, and believed, that these coercive interrogations were absolutely necessary to elicit intelligence that was unavailable by any other collection method and would save American lives. That was simply not the case.

Nevertheless, for all of the misinformation, incompetence, and brutality in the CIA's program, the Committee's Study is not, and must not be, simply a backward looking condemnation of past mistakes. The Study presents a tremendous opportunity to develop forward looking lessons that must be central to all future intelligence activities.

The CIA developed the Detention and Interrogation Program in a time of great fear, anxiety and unprecedented crisis; but it is at these times of crisis when we need sound judgment, excellence, and professionalism from the CIA the most. When mistakes are made, they call for self-reflection and scrutiny. For that process to begin, we first have to make sure there is an accurate public record of what happened. The public release of the Executive Summary and Findings and Conclusions is a tremendous and consequential step toward that goal.

For some I expect there will be a natural temptation to reject, cast doubt on, or rationalize parts of the Study that are disturbing or embarrassing. Indeed the CIA program's dramatic divergence from the standards that we hold ourselves to is hard to reconcile. However, we must fight that shortsighted temptation to wish away the gravity of what this Study has found.

How we deal with this opportunity to learn, and improve, will reflect on the maturity of our democracy. As a country, we are strong enough to bear the weight of our mistakes, and as an institution, so is the CIA. We must confront this dark period in our recent history with honesty and critical introspection. We must draw lessons, and we must apply those lessons as we move forward. Although it may be uncomfortable at times, ultimately we will grow stronger, and we will ensure that this never happens again.

SENATOR
WYDEN
ADDITIONAL
VIEWS

ADDITIONAL VIEWS OF SENATOR WYDEN

Having served in Congress for nearly thirty-five years, and having served on the Intelligence Committee for over thirteen, I can easily say that this report is among the most detailed and comprehensive that I have ever seen. In addition, the investigation that produced it has been one of the most thorough and diligent that Congress has conducted during my tenure. I am proud to have been able to support it, and I would like to thank the extremely dedicated and talented staff who worked incredibly hard to produce it in the face of significant obstacles. Also, I commend Chairman Feinstein, and her predecessor Senator Rockefeller, for their leadership on the issue of interrogations.

However, I would be remiss if I let this opportunity go by without adding some brief additional thoughts that go beyond the scope of this report and touch on broader issues of secrecy and transparency. In my view certain aspects of the disturbing history surrounding coercive interrogations highlight broader problems faced by those who lead intelligence agencies, and those who oversee them.

In particular, I have long been concerned about the problems posed by government officials' reliance on what is effectively secret law. As I have said before, when laws are secretly interpreted behind closed doors by a small number of government officials, without public scrutiny or debate, it dramatically increases the likelihood of government agencies taking actions that the American public would not support.

Most Americans expect their government to gather information about genuine threats to national security and public safety, and they recognize that this information can sometimes be gathered more effectively when some details about how it is collected remain secret. But Americans also expect government agencies to operate at all times within the boundaries of publicly understood law. Americans in the 21st century don't expect their military and intelligence agencies to publish every single detail of their operations any more than they expected George Washington to publish his strategy for the Battle of Yorktown. But Americans absolutely expect that the law itself will not be secret – and as voters they have a need and a right to understand what government officials think the law actually means, so that they can decide whether particular laws need to be changed and ratify or reject decisions that their elected officials make on their behalf.

It is clear that a central problem with the CIA's secret detention and interrogation program was that it relied on secret interpretations of the law that went well beyond both the law's plain meaning and the public's understanding of what the law permitted. And this problem was unfortunately not confined to the CIA. During the same time period, the NSA relied on secret legal interpretations from the Department of Justice (and, later, the Foreign Intelligence Surveillance Court) as the basis for a massive expansion of its domestic surveillance activities. Both history and common sense made it clear that these secret interpretations of the law would not stay secret forever, and the predictable result was a robust public backlash and an erosion of confidence in US intelligence agencies and in government more generally.

Another serious problem that can be seen in both the CIA interrogation case and the NSA surveillance case is the way that reliance on a secret body of law helped spawn a culture of misinformation, in which senior government officials repeatedly made inaccurate and misleading statements to the public and the press regarding intelligence agencies' authorities and activities. In addition to misleading the public about how the law was being interpreted, these statements often inaccurately characterized the effectiveness of these controversial programs – much of what CIA officials said about the effectiveness of coercive interrogations was simply untrue.

Beyond the problem of secret law, it is also clear that excessive secrecy within the government contributed to a troubling lack of oversight. This lack of oversight meant that bad decisions were not corrected, and shocking mistakes were often allowed to proliferate and be repeated. While some individual members of Congress and the executive branch pushed hard for more oversight of CIA interrogation activities, the argument that information about these programs needed to be kept tightly guarded even within the government was allowed to prevail.

This is an argument that has been frequently been made when oversight bodies in Congress and the executive branch have attempted to learn more about potentially controversial secret programs. Intelligence officials will naturally tend to argue that it is necessary to limit access to information about sensitive intelligence collection methods to keep those methods from being publicly disclosed. If this imperative is not balanced against the need for informed and vigilant oversight of intelligence activities, then effective oversight can be stymied by excessive secrecy, leaving these agencies much more likely to make serious errors and repeat them.

In the case of the CIA interrogation program, of course, the fact that this impulse toward secrecy was allowed to outweigh the need for robust, well-informed oversight is particularly egregious because CIA officials were at times providing information to the press (including information that was often inaccurate and misleading) at the same time that congressional requests for information were being stonewalled. It is an unfortunate fact that intelligence agencies' legitimate mandate for secrecy has often been used to hide programs and activities from people who might criticize them.

Fortunately, the solution to these problems is straightforward, even if it isn't easy. Members of Congress and the executive branch must continually push for the information that they need to do their jobs, and intelligence officials must avoid taking actions that obstruct this important oversight. And everyone involved must remember that there is ultimately no substitute for oversight from the public itself, which is why all government agencies – even intelligence agencies – should constantly be pressed to make as much information available to the public as possible. Finally, everyone who values the legitimacy of our democratic institutions must remember that the government's understanding of laws, treaties and the Constitution shouldn't just be public when government officials find it convenient. This information should be public all the time, and every American should be able to find out what their government thinks the law means.

The vast majority of the men and women who work at America's intelligence agencies are overwhelmingly dedicated professionals who make enormous sacrifices to help keep our country safe and free, and they should be able to do their jobs secure in the knowledge that they have the confidence of the American people. By remembering these principles and working hard to adhere to them, I believe that those of us who are lucky enough to serve in government can ensure the protection of both American security and American values, and give these men and women the confidence that they deserve.

RON WYDEN

www.ingramcontent.com/pod-product-compliance
Lightning Source LLC
Chambersburg PA
CBHW080323290526
45793CB00006B/1192